WE'LL TAKE A CUP OF KINDNESS YET

WE'LL TAKE A CUP OF KINDNESS YET

Memoir & Manifesto

John Throne
International Socialist

Published by

THE DRUMKEEN PRESS
11 Limavady Road,
Waterside. L'Derry. BT47 6 JU
Northern Ireland.
Email: loughfinn@aol.com
Read our blog at: weknowwhatsup.blogspot.com
On Facebook at: http://www.facebook.com/FactsForWorkingPeople

© John Throne, 2018

ISBN 978-0-9553552-3-3

The moral right of the author has been asserted.

FRONT COVER IMAGE The Grianán of Aileach ringfort (c.6th century), Inishowen, County Donegal
BACK COVER PAINTING The Sower, oil on canvas by Jean-François Millet, 1865
The Walters Art Museum, Baltimore, Maryland

For information and reviews of The Donegal Woman, visit www://thedonegalwoman.com

Set in 11.5 on 13 point Quadraat
by SUSAN WAINE

PRINTED IN IRELAND

CONTENTS

THE THING IS THIS

HE TIME AND PLACE of our birth, the circumstances and experiences of our childhood and lives, the interaction between all of these, combine to make us who we are. Marks, scars, physical and mental, positive and negative, are left upon us. To ignore this reality is to live in a state of confusion and lack of understanding.

My mother brought me into the world on 18 April 1944 in a small farmhouse up a lane outside the village of Lifford, County Donegal, in the Republic of Ireland. On my every birthday I think of her and her pain as she laboured to give me life. I owe her my existence. I am forever in her debt.

My family were small farmers and Protestants. My uncle was the 'man of the house', after my father died young. My uncle was also the District Master of the Orange order in East Donegal. I was taught to believe in the Protestant religion and the Orange Order, taught that the way things were could not be changed, that the smart thing to do was to knuckle down and accept the world as it was. But something happened along the way of my conservative, capitalist, sectarian upbringing. I became an atheist and international socialist. In this book I try to explain how this happened and how it was positive for my life.

I describe my experiences and the evolution of my ideas in an effort to contribute to the new movements of struggle internationally. Tens of millions of working people and youth are on the move worldwide. The movements which brought down the Stalinist regimes in the former Soviet Union, the Arab Spring, the millions who are on the streets of the cities of the world fighting the euphemistically named 'austerity', that vicious offensive of world capitalism against working people and against the environment and life on earth. Tens of thousands of people in Ireland, the country of my birth, have taken to the streets and the voting booths to change life for the better. They have done this by fighting the so-called 'austerity' but also by supporting same-sex marriage and as part of this and other actions, the dictatorial, pro-capitalist, anti-woman, religious hierarchies have been forced onto the defensive. A new generation and large sections of the older generations are changing themselves, Ireland, and the world for the better. I am filled with joy.

There is also the rising of the women of the world against their extra oppression. From the women's marches and women's political action against the predator-in-chief Trump and the Trumpism in the USA; to the women in the USA fighting to have control over their own bodies; fighting against state violence, racism, sexism, violence and inequality; against environmental destruction and poverty; to the women in India fighting the brutal rape culture and the poverty; to the women who rose against the Mubarak dictatorship in Egypt; to the Kurdish women fighting ISIS arms in hand in the Middle East; to the Polish women who rose and defeated the extreme right wing government's attempt to ban their right to choose; to the women in Russia leading the fight for decent housing and for democratic rights; to the women rising against their sweatshop conditions and the violence against them in South East Asia and Latin America and Africa; to the indigenous women in Latin America fighting the multi-national corporations to defend the environment, to the women in Europe fighting the so-called 'austerity', there is the rising of women. And we have yet to hear the voice of the hundreds of millions of women of the new Chinese working class. 50% of the world's factory workers today are women. A new era is unfolding. In this new era women will be in the front ranks.

As this process of change and struggle unfolds many of its participants are looking at their lives in a different way. People who would never before have thought of taking to the streets and confronting capitalism and its state forces are now doing so. We see this, for example in the battle against charging people for water in the famously wet country of Ireland and the attacks on living standards in general in Ireland and internationally. New forces are taking action. I personally have found it inspiring to be present at meetings and actions of working people where they are organising to defeat the attacks on their living standards and in the process exchanging ideas on the source of these attacks and what they have to do to defeat them. Working people talking about the International Monetary Fund, the World Bank, a new world is opening. Working people are more conscious than ever before that capitalism is sick. This experience of struggle and the ideas rising out of it leads its participants to seek, consciously or unconsciously, for ways to make struggle a more central feature of their lives. To these activists and fighters I try in this book to explain how I came to, and have managed to maintain, my life of struggle against the existing system, against the powers that be, against capitalism. I hope my story will be helpful to those in struggle.

I have written one other book – *The Donegal Woman*. It is based on the life of my grandmother, a Donegal woman born on a small farm in the Eastern foothills of the Donegal mountains. I wrote it as a tribute to my grandmother, as a way to give her a voice. It became a best seller. It did so for a number of reasons. It was published at a time when the heretofore mostly hidden epidemic of sex abuse by the Irish Catholic hierarchy had forced its way to the surface. The women of Ireland wanted this talked about, wanted the abusers and their institutions to be held accountable. They were no longer prepared to be silent. Even though my grandmother was not a Catholic and not abused by a priest, *The Donegal Woman* was part of this demand by women to have their special abuse acknowledged and those responsible to be held accountable. *The Donegal Woman* told the story of my grandmother, who was physically, sexually and economically abused. But it also told the story of a woman who was not broken by this oppression and the system from which it sprang. It explained how her struggle to survive and to bring up her children gave her strength and an increased understanding of her world. It is not a story of defeat. It is a story of struggle and gains made against adversity. I never met my grandmother. She died before I was born. My mother told me her story shortly before her own death. I consider my grandmother and my mother to have been heroines. I consider them to have the strength and the spirit of the women who are rising today throughout the world.

It was easier to write *The Donegal Woman* than it has been to write this book. That is because this book is about my own personal and political life. It is more difficult to assess my actions and their relationship to events. Am I too easy on myself concerning the decisions I have made in my life? Am I too hard? All I can do is try to honestly tell my story. To attempt to identify the mistakes I consider I have made and those I consider I have not made. Do I get the balance right? I do not know. I leave it to you the reader to decide. But I can say this: As I come towards the end of my days I do not regret how I have tried to live my life. I cannot say like Edith Piaf sings that I have no regrets but I can say I do not regret how I have tried to live my life. This is because I did not make the biggest mistake of all. That is the mistake of giving up the struggle to understand the world and to change it for the better. As part of this approach I adopted a set of simple principles in my early twenties, and I have stuck with these ever since. They are: to try to understand the world and my place in it; and as I do so anything I see that I think is wrong try to organise and fight against it; and as I do so anything I see that I think is right try to organise and fight for it. By following these basic simple principles I have had and continue to have a very good life.

My life has also been given direction, and hence made fulfilling, because I have been lucky enough to be able to get a glimpse of the big picture, that is to become conscious of how the world works and my place within it. In particular I have come to see that I do not exist in isolation. I live in and am part of a system. I have come to see that my life unfolds as part of a system and so I have been able to have a better and more balanced view of my life. The understanding that I lived in a system came to me one day as I dug a drain in one of my uncle's fields in Donegal. I stopped, spade in hand.

This understanding came together there in my brain as I dug the dark brown Donegal soil, as I sank the sharp edged spade down into through the green grass, as I made a dam with the soil along the edge of the stream that was overflowing, as I watched the long beaked seagulls following me to jab at the upturned soil for worms, it came to me that what I was doing, that what and who I was could not be seen in isolation. It was not me and the spade. It was me and the spade and the soil, the grass, the over-flowing stream, the sea gulls, the economic realities that made that field and the need to have that field drained so it could grow crops. We, all of us and all of the comings and goings and all of the life and non-life that made the scene of which I was part were part of a system. The workers in some far off land who dug the iron ore, the workers in some far off foundry who shaped the iron ore into the spade were also part of the system of which I was part. This, I realised, was the way I would have to look at the world, at my world, at my life. It was the only way I could have any chance of understanding the world or of finding my place in the world. I would later make more progress and see that not only did I live in a system but that I lived in a particular system, the capitalist system, and a capitalist system that was at the end of its days, that was in an advanced stage of decay. I would come to see that I had to be against that capitalist world, that capitalist system, if I was to be at one with my own personal world.

As an international socialist organiser I would later explain this reality to many people. One of them would once say to me: 'Thanks be for revolutionaries. I used to think I was the problem but now I see that I am okay, it is the world that is the problem, that is wrong.' Seeing that it was the system that was wrong, that it was capitalism that was wrong, that she herself was alright helped this person. It helped me and it will help all who come to see this reality.

I came to appreciate that to try and understand ourselves as separate from the system in which we lived would be like trying to be motionless in a constantly moving ocean. I came to understand that if this capitalist system was allowed to continue, it would, through climate change, nuclear war, pollution, drought, flooding, poverty and starvation, destroy life on earth as we know it. If it was not over-thrown in the decades ahead, capitalism would wipe out the human species. Already an estimated 50% of all species are in the process of being destroyed. (Centre for Biological Diversity) I came to see that this was the system, the reality, I lived in and that I could not isolate myself from this system, that I had to try and change it or accept that I would perish within it or with it.

I also came to understand that if capitalism was not ended the children of today would have no future. Fighting to end capitalism is the responsibility of all humans. In particular it is the responsibility of all parents. The concept of parental responsibility has to be expanded. It is not sufficient to feed and clothe our children. It is not sufficient to help them get over the flu, to comfort and put a band aid on them when they fall and cut their knee. This is not sufficient. We have to also fight to prevent them from being wiped out when, as will be the case if capitalism continues to exist, life on earth as we know it will be destroyed. Protecting our children, ensuring a future for them and in fact for the human species, means organising against the capitalist system. This is part of parental and human responsibility. If parents and all people are not fighting to end capitalism we are not fulfilling our responsibilities as parents or as members of the human species.

My struggle to end capitalism and to build a new world motivated me to evolve from conservative, religious, sectarian ideas, from being lost and adrift in the world, to becoming a conscious active fighter to change the world for the better. It allowed me to come to understand the need for an international, democratic, socialist, sustainable society under the collective ownership, guidance, control and management of working people, that is a society under the ownership, guidance, control and management of the collective brain of the working class. I believe in this future and work for this future. It is my reason for living. I have not been bought. I have not been broken. I consider this an achievement.

My struggle to end capitalism has also motivated me to try and understand the new advances in science and technology that are exploding around us, the Internet, social media, having the equivalent of just about all of the libraries and much of the knowledge of the world at our finger tips, the ability to communicate as never before. In 1995 less than 1% of the world's population was connected to the Internet. Today, close to half the world's population are connected. A dramatic qualitative change has taken place in communications and the spreading of ideas and knowledge.

As this increasingly happens and as more people see that capitalism is going into deeper crisis and is destroying life on earth, people's loyalty to the system is weakened and more of the secrets of capitalism are leaked and spread and made available to the people of the world. Capitalism has to use the new technology. But the more it does so, given the damage it as a system is doing to life on earth, given that it is increasingly seen as destroying life on earth as we know it, the more its system leaks like a sinking, rotting, wooden barge. Its battle to stay afloat and in control is described by some as 'technological imperialism', that is, the struggle by the international capitalist class to see to it that all advances in new technology are used exclusively for its benefit, for its rent, interest, profit, power and control. And to hell with the working people of the world and to hell with the health of the planet.

Capitalism's rule depends on its ability to dominate and control the consciousness of the working class. That is to convince the working class that capitalism is the only system and that the working class cannot create an alternative system. This means that the struggle against capitalism is the struggle for the consciousness of the working class. The ability of capitalism to dominate and control the consciousness of the working class is being weakened daily on several fronts. It increasingly demonstrates that it is destroying the planet through climate change. It increasingly demonstrates that it is unable to feed clothe, house, educate, keep healthy the people of the planet. It increasingly threatens nuclear war. One study shows that a nuclear war between India and Pakistan, never mind one between the major nuclear powers, would kill one billion people and lead to a ten year winter on the planet. Along with being weakened by the increasing awareness of these realities the new communications systems, the social media, make it possible to reveal capitalism's secrets, to expose its nightmarish, cruel, vicious, reality as never before.

However, realising that capitalism is rotten, exposing capitalism's secrets is not enough. A sense of history is necessary. It is necessary to base ourselves on history. As was recently said in relation to the threat presented by the present US President's lack of knowledge of history – 'History is no joke.' That is if we do not understand history we do not know where we are and the possibilities, positive and negative, for the future.

Humanity developed from primitive hunting and gathering societies, to slavery, to feudalism to capitalism. History demonstrates that when a society comes to a point where it can no longer make progress then it, as is the case with capitalism today, reaches a fork in the road. And two options exist for humanity.

If there is a class or force that can break out of the death grip of the old, outdated, rotting system and take society forward, then new societies can emerge which are more progressive, materially and culturally.

If on the other hand there is no class or force that can overthrow the old system and build a new more progressive society and take the human species forward then the old system collapses. See the remnants of such collapses in the pyramids and remnants of huge cities and burial tombs scattered across the earth in the deserts jungles and oceans, and in our own Newgrange. Airborne laser scanners have recently found multiple huge cities between 900 and 1400 years old in the Cambodian jungles. These had elaborate water systems and urban planning. These were part of the Kymer empire which was the largest empire on earth in the 12th century. That empire, that society collapsed. So will the capitalist society of today. This is the lesson of these collapsed societies. Capitalist society will also collapse, it is collapsing.

So the question facing the human species today is this: Is there a class or force in the world at this time which can step up and end capitalism and take society forward? The answer to this is an emphatic 'yes'. This force is the working class. The working class today is greater in number than ever before. It is a majority in just about every sizeable country on the planet. Think alone of the new gigantic working class that has been created by the development of industry in China. And many other countries of South East Asia, and Latin and Central America and Africa and elsewhere. At the same time, new technology makes more possible than ever the bringing together of the collective power, the collective labour, the collective brain of the world's working class and for this collective power and labour and this collective brain to become the decisive force on the planet.

In the past when the working class tried to challenge capitalism and build its own world, it established workers' councils. Examples of these are the Paris Commune of 1871, the worker' councils in the Russian revolutions of 1905 and 1917, the workers' council in the Limerick workers' uprising of 1919, the workers' committees in the French general strike of 1968 and many others. The working class has the capability to and will again and again challenge capitalism and in doing so it will organise its workers' councils, its workers' committees. It will seek to draw in the support of the rural poor, who have shown their tendency to establish peasants' councils, and unify these in an international unified network which can have available to it all the knowledge of the resources of the world and the needs of the world. Through this international unified network the working class has the power to put together a democratic socialist plan which can organise production to utilise the available resources on the planet, to meet the existing needs of all people on the planet and do so in a sustainable way.

Such an international network of workers' councils, workers' committees, drawing into its orbit the peasants' councils would constitute the collective brain of the working class. This collective brain of the working class and all working people would be a gigantic, unified, organic entity that would be continually thinking, discussing and exchanging ideas and knowledge, and continually making democratic decisions, continually fine-tuning and adjusting its world economy and related to this the life of the human species. This, the collective brain of the working class, the collective power of the working class, is the new force that can take society forward and give a future to life on earth. Given the explosion of new technology and communications, and the increased, diverse and international reach of the working class, the working class can come together and develop and utilise its collective brain as never before. If there is to be a future for life on earth as we know it, if there is to be a future for humanity, it will be on this basis and this basis only.

This alternative of workers' councils and workers' committees and peasants' councils is not some dream of the author of this book. Already mentioned are the examples of workers' councils and workers' committees given above. In 1968 the French working class carried out the largest general strike in an economically advanced industrial country in history. As it did so it occupied its workplaces universities and schools. It elected committees which for a brief period ran these workplaces, universities and schools. Here is part of the statement of the 'Council for the Maintaining of the Occupations', the body coordinating the general strike and occupations. The statement reads: 'The Workers' Councils are manifestly the only solution, since all other forms of revolutionary struggle have ended in the opposite of what they wanted'. Paris May 31st. 1968. The 1968 French general strike and occupations and this statement by the 'Council for the Maintaining of the Occupations' shows the possibility for the future, shows the way in which the working class will act to try to change the world, will try to build a new world which will be run by and for the working people of the world and which will seek to protect life on earth.

The working class is stronger today in numbers, more international and more diverse than ever before. Women are in the paid workforce as never before. The working class is stronger relative to all other classes, to the capitalist class and the middle classes than ever before. It is like a huge chisel with enormous weight, heft, and potential power. But it has a terrible weakness. It has no cutting edge. It is blunt. This is so because its leadership, that is the leadership of the trade unions and mass traditional workers' parties such as the social democratic parties, such as the Stalinist parties, the latter now mainly collapsed but where they do still exist they too, as is the case with all the leaderships of all the mass workers' organisations, support capitalism. The result is that these leaderships prevent the working class from seeing how to end capitalism, prevent the working class from ending the rule of the capitalist class and taking control of society into its own hands. These leaderships will be responsible if capitalism continues to exist and in doing so destroys life on earth as we know it.

The task of all who want to change the world for the better, to prevent capitalism from destroying life on earth as we know it, is to remove these pro-capitalist leaderships. And to do so in whatever way is necessary and effective. Think how again and again our struggles have been undermined and sabotaged by the leaderships of the existing mass organisations, the social democratic parties, the labour parties, the trade unions, or been defeated because these leaderships were not prepared to fight to end capitalism. The task is to build a new international leadership in the working class, a new international organisation of hundreds of millions dedicated to ending capitalism, and a new leadership prepared to do so if necessary in the most ruthless manner. This is the task that surpasses all others. Yes this is no small task, it is no small challenge. But it is the only way in which life on earth can be preserved. People have to get their heads around the central importance of this task and adjust their lives to fight to achieve this task.

There are today people who see their role as to expose the dirty secrets of the capitalist world. They do this mostly by social media. The role these people play in exposing capitalism's dirty secrets makes it more difficult for capitalism to dominate the consciousness of the working class. Think of the Panama Papers, the Paradise Papers. But these people have a fatal weakness. They do not recognise the role of the working class as the progressive force in history at this time. In fact they do not even recognise the existence of the working class. They therefore have no alternative to the capitalist system. Exposing capitalism's secrets is not enough. The alternative that the working class can provide must be understood and explained and fought for. The delusions of these people can be seen in a statement by Assange, the founder of Wikileaks. He stated: 'Wikileaks is designed to make capitalism more free and ethical'. Capitalism as a system addicted to profit which is the unpaid labour of the working class can never be free or ethical. Working people will not give up part of their labour unless forced do so, therefore capitalist society cannot be free. And a system that is based on unpaid labour can never be ethical.

There are also people like the world-acclaimed physicist Stephen Hawking who see the crisis facing human society and the planet and who do suggest an alternative. Hawking suggests that for the human species to have a future it will have to migrate to another planet. Such a migration is totally unrealistic, is impossible. But not only that how could a system which is destroying life on earth and has to flee to another planet to escape from the destruction it itself had caused, build anything but a rotten system on any other planet, do anything but destroy that other planet also. The human species moving to another planet is totally unrealistic and will never happen.

What the people who confine themselves to exposing capitalism's dirty secrets and people like Hawking who understands the crisis facing capitalism and human society have in common is that they do not base themselves on historical materialism, that is, on how there have been different systems in the past, each being overthrown by another, or collapsing, as they were no longer able to take society forward. These people do not recognise that capitalism is in its death agony, but much more importantly they do not recognise the existence of the working class and that in this period of history it is the working class that can end capitalism and build a new world. This is a fundamental and fatal weakness. It leaves these people with no alternative to the unfolding catastrophe of capitalism.

The international socialist revolutionary Leon Trotsky explained things in this way. He explained that the world was ripe for capitalism to be ended and socialism to be established, and that the working class was capable of carrying out these tasks and building a new world. He stated: 'All talk to the effect that historical conditions have not yet "ripened" for socialism is the product of ignorance or conscious deception. The objective prerequisites for the proletarian revolution have not only "ripened": they have begun to get somewhat rotten. Without a socialist revolution, in the next historical period, a catastrophe threatens the whole culture of humanity. The turn is now to the working class, i.e. chiefly to its revolutionary vanguard. The historical crisis of humanity is reduced to the crisis of the revolutionary leadership.' Leon Trotsky, The Transitional Programme, 1938.

This is a correct summing up of the situation of humanity today. History is dominated by the crisis of capitalism which will, through climate change, nuclear war, pollution, drought, flooding etc., destroy life on earth as we know it. Just like the old societies disappeared, sank under the seas, were grown over by the jungles, were covered by the deserts, present society, life on earth as we know it, if capitalism lasts, will also be destroyed. This time the destruction will surpass anything that was ever seen before. Climate change and nuclear war both threaten. Human society and life on earth as we know it is threatened with extinction. The brutal truth is that if life on earth as we know it is to be preserved and developed, capitalism has to be overthrown. This is what Trotsky meant by 'the crisis of humanity' when he wrote back in 1938. And what Trotsky meant when he wrote that the 'crisis of humanity is reduced to the crisis of the revolutionary leadership' was that it was only the working class internationally which had the power to end capitalism and build a new world, but that it was prevented from doing so by its pro capitalist leadership. And therefore this pro capitalist leadership had to be removed and replaced by a new international revolutionary socialist leadership of the working class. The central task facing the human species is the building of such a leadership.

Because of my struggle against capitalism, and because I have an alternative to this rotten system for which I struggle, that is international democratic socialism, and because I have never given up struggling for this alternative, I have been able to ward off nihilism, cynicism, defeatism, pessimism, despair and psychological crisis. I have managed to maintain my integrity, my fighting spirit, my laughter and my appreciation of beautiful things. I, like all people, need to fight for an alternative to the present decaying system of capitalism, need to struggle for an alternative world, if we are to maintain our health, physical and mental and live life as close as possible to our full potential.

Having and struggling for such an alternative has made my life good. When I see the rivers and seas and mountains, when I see the flowers and plants and the great variation of species, I am uplifted and filled with joy. When I see the sea otter, the black crow, the big panda, the great silverback, the elephant, the leaping salmon, the Connemara pony, the little sparrow, the fat breasted robin, the little Chihuahua, I am filled with awe. When I see the art of Van Gogh, read the literature of Joyce, hear the music of Beethoven, listen to the voice of Billie Holliday, I am enriched and nurtured and inspired. When I see the kindness and humanity and solidarity that comes alive in people in struggle even though they live in a system which seeks to destroy that kindness and humanity and solidarity, I am filled with hope. My spirit soars.

I have travelled on all five continents of the world and lived for prolonged periods in some of its cities. Derry, Dublin, London, New York and Chicago. I hope to live more years yet. I wish to meet with and struggle in solidarity with more of the people of the world who are trying to change things for the better. I wish to be inspired and educated by them. I wish to share my experiences with them, share my own years of revolutionary struggle with them, to fight together with them against the filth of the present capitalist system, against the criminal, obscene, capitalist class that runs that system, against the threat to life on earth which that system and that class represents. I dedicate this book to all who seek to take a similar road.

A final word on this book. I have divided it into six parts. Some parts will be more familiar to my readers than others. Parts four and five will be less easy to relate to for all but those who have tried to build a revolutionary organisation. Part three is no walk in the park either. But please do not be put off by the less familiar parts. Please also if necessary be prepared to consider that this book does not necessarily have to be read in order. If you find it better to read a few parts and then skip a part and then come back to the skipped part or parts later then consider this. I am sure parts one and two and six will be easily accessible to all my readers. These parts deal more with my own personal experiences. As I have learnt and I am sure we have all learnt, nothing is fixed and rigid in our world. Nothing proceeds in a straight line. This book need not be read from front cover to back cover in a straight line either. This book is not all heavy political discourse as some of this foreword might suggest. Consider the title of Chapter one, Part one – 'Digging a Hole for a Short Legged Bull'. I would ask my readers to also remember that this is as my front cover explains: 'A Memoir and a Manifesto'. I try to integrate my family my personal and political lives as a way of helping us see how our personal world can be, I would suggest has to be, linked to trying to change the world, that is to being a revolutionary. Thank you again all who read my book. I hope it will be of use.

John Throne.
International Socialist, 2018

PART 1

AGAINST THE GRAIN

CHAPTER 1

DIGGING A HOLE FOR A SHORT-LEGGED BULL

L IFFORD IS THE COUNTY TOWN of Donegal, the most north-westerly county in Ireland. To this day it has the County Council offices. In the past it held the old jail and courthouse. In previous times of British rule the jail and courthouse were used to try, sentence, hang or deport anybody who challenged that rule. Built into the walls of our family's barn were a number of long square stones with holes in them. These were from the cell windows of the old jail. The holes were for the bars. I did not know how or why my family had these jail sills. I would later wonder whether it had to do with their political views and did they want to be associated with the jail and British rule. I would later give these sills to a museum of Irish heritage. In those, my youthful days, I imagined the prisoners looking out between the bars. For some reason, even then my sympathies were with the prisoners.

Lifford sits on the west bank of the River Finn which rises in the Donegal mountains in the Republic of Ireland, which is ruled from Dublin. At Lifford, the River Mourne, which flows down from the Sperrin Mountains in Northern Ireland, which is ruled from London, flows into and merges with the Finn. When they come together they form the River Foyle and flow north through the City of Derry, into Lough Foyle, and on into the Atlantic Ocean. When they become the Foyle it is impossible to tell what water is from what source. Unfortunately the peoples of the area do not always mingle so well.

All these rivers are tidal. The Finn is tidal up past Lifford and up past what was my family's small farm. I would watch and wonder at the waters as they came and went. In my mind's eye I could see the tides rise and fall in all the rivers and on all the shores of all the lands of the world. There were little streams which flowed down from the hills behind our house, crossed under the main road, and on down into the River Finn. On my way home from school I would stop at these, dam them up, then sweep the dam away and watch the water rush on again to join the waters in the river below. I imagined myself doing the same thing someday, going out on to the waters of the world. I was lucky to have the beauty of the rivers and hills and the green grass and the meadows.

My family's house sat looking east on the side of the hill of Killandaragh which sloped down to the River Finn. To go to school I cycled down the lane and turned north along the west bank of the Finn which at that point formed the border between Southern Ireland and Northern Ireland. I then crossed east over the River Foyle at Lifford bridge and up along the north bank of the Mourne, up over the 'camel's hump' and into Strabane, the neighbouring town to Lifford. This took me from Lifford in County Donegal in the mainly Catholic Republic of Ireland, into Strabane in County Tyrone in the mainly Protestant North of Ireland. It was no wonder I was always thinking of different countries, religions, rivers and oceans. Three tidal rivers and two sectarian states every school day on my old rusted green bicycle with the bent frame. I was a 'world' traveller from the word go. Just as I was lucky to live in the beautiful surroundings of rivers and hills I was lucky also to live in that complex border land. It provoked me to think of things political and historical and religious and the relationship between all of these.

My family's small farm was thirty-five acres in size. It was big enough to keep our heads above water but not big enough to keep at bay the fear that someday the whole entity might sink. My mother was always talking about the workhouse and afraid we might end up there. We had no electricity and no indoor plumbing when I was young. The toilet was an outhouse with a bucket and torn up squares of newspaper hanging on a nail. Its contents were dumped by hand in the midden with the waste of the farm animals. We always had good food to eat but we were not well off financially.

I was close to my father until his early death in 1956. He was only in his fifties. I was twelve. My father looked after the livestock and did general work on the farm. He also bought and sold cattle at the fairs. Only men went to these fairs. The farm animals and products the women reared and bred such as hens and ducks and geese and turkeys and eggs were either consumed by the family or sold at the farmyard or to local shops. On occasion my mother would tie a turkey to the rack on the back of her bike and cycle off to sell it to a neighbour.

My father liked the odd drink on the fair days. My mother was always trying to get him to give it up. For a while, in her desperation she kept me from school and sent me with him to the fairs with instructions to me to keep him out of the pubs. This did not work. I was only a child and he was my father. Instead he took me into the pubs, set me up at the counter on a tall stool, filled me with orange juice and himself with whiskey, and had the back and forward with everybody.

My father would on occasion try to give up the drink. He once sought help from the family Bible, an old hard-backed copy which was kept unused in a cabinet in the parlour. I remember that night very clearly. After coming home drunk from a fair my father gathered the family around him. He then took this Bible and held it in his out-stretched up-turned hand in front of himself and all of us and swore he would never drink again. I was impressed, even frightened, by the solemnity of this ceremony. But in a month or two he came home drunk again and my father and the whole Bible and God thing took a knock.

The fairs and the pubs were theatre. There were many colourful characters. It was not just about selling or buying an animal. It was how it was done. Some of the most flamboyant of the dealers would shout at each other, would run away from each other pretending the price was so outrageous that they were insulted by the whole thing, they would rip their coats open, they would pull off their caps and tear their hair. Then others standing round would go after them and drag them back to shout and deal again and increase or decrease the offered or asked for price. The onlookers were not just onlookers, they were also part of the theatre. They would at times grab the hands of the buyer and seller and place them one on top of the other, then holding the hands together they would spit on their own hand and with a loud slap smack down on the hands of the buyer and seller, the idea being that by this blow the deal would be sealed. Then there was the luckspenny. If the buyer and seller were close in price but neither wanted to yield totally they would resort to arguing over the luckspenny, how much it should be. This would be a small sum that the seller would give back to the buyer 'for luck'. It lubricated the deal. The whole process involved a lot of impromptu and original dialogue and drama. At my first fairs I thought the dealers were going to fight. My father was good at this theatre.

When my mother sent me to the fairs with my father this allowed me to travel. Raphoe, Stranorlar, Convoy, Donegal Town, these would be names of some of the small towns that would forever live in my memory along with my father, the cattle buying and selling. My favourite fair was Donegal Town. We went there on the small Donegal Railway. In the cold mornings I could take off my shoes and hold my sock covered feet against the hot pipes in the carriage as we travelled up through the beauty of Barnesmore Gap. We would cycle or walk to the other fairs which were closer. I did not think of it then but I suppose my father was proud of me, of having a son he could take with him and show off. My mother later told me that when she had her children before me and they were all girls my father would hardly speak to her for weeks. That was the Ireland of the time.

Going to those fair days with my father allowed me to get to know him better, to see and hear him with his cattle dealing and his storytelling and his interaction with others. He always had some yarn. No sooner would he enter a pub than people would gather round to hear his latest. My father was one of the leaders of the Orange order in east Donegal. He was also treasurer of the Lifford Orange lodge. In spite of this he drank mostly in the Catholic pubs where there were more people and was more life. Unfortunately in some of these there were Catholics who would at first pretend to be friendly with my father but when he would get drunk they would let their sectarianism come out. On one occasion two such people beat him up and left him bleeding. I was traumatised watching this. It was not right. It was at that moment that sectarianism became part of my understanding and at that moment also that I realised that I hated it.

It was the first time I saw the harsh violence of sectarianism. I had heard it being continually talked about in my home and when I was amongst exclusively Protestant gatherings. Heard the talk of 'our kind' of 'their kind', of 'one of our own'. I knew that I did not like this talk. I wanted to believe that everybody was the same, that everybody was equal. But this talk of 'our kind' and the 'other kind' of 'our sort' and the 'other sort', these various ways of dividing people up along religious lines was not something I liked. I also imagined, and was to find out later that I was correct, that a similar kind of talk went on in Catholic gatherings.

When he went to the fairs my father carried a bamboo stick with a leather strap. With this strap he would hang the stick on his wrist when he was making or receiving payment for a deal. He also wore a white loose scarf tied in a knot and hanging down the front of his neck and chest. I could see my mother look at him as he went off. He was a tall, broad-shouldered man. He wore his hair combed straight back in the old Celtic style, not that he knew it was the old Celtic style. If he had he would probably not have worn it that way. My father was good looking and had style. My mother liked how he looked.

My mother and father had five children between them. Four girls, my sisters, all older than me. I was the youngest and the only boy. My two sisters above me in age were identical twins. They were known as the 'Twin Thrones'. They were hard to tell apart. A neighbour solved this problem when, if he saw one of them alone, he would say: 'Hello Angela, are you Mary?', or 'Hello Mary, are you Angela?' My oldest sister was called Kathleen and the one between her and the twins was called Margaret. All 'Protestant', all 'English' Names.

My father bought and sold only one breed of cattle – Aberdeen Angus. These were small black animals, with short legs, sturdy bodies and broad foreheads. He always kept one of them as a bull. Local farmers would bring their cows to have them 'serviced'. The bull would often be too short in the leg for the taller cows. When this was so my father would say: 'John go and get the spade.' Coming back I would dig a hole about one foot square and one foot deep. The hind legs of the taller cow would then be backed into this and the bull would be able to mount and enter her and my father would say: 'Job done', and laugh like he had pulled a fast one on the bull. As if the bull was not happy for the sex. My father was glad for the money the bull earned. He also liked the chat with the farmers who brought their cows.

I could see by the way my father acted with the Aberdeen Angus cattle that there was more than money and socialising involved. He not only looked at the Aberdeen Angus cattle, he felt their haunches and their foreheads and their ears, he turned his head to the one side and the other and examined them, moved in close and peered at them, on occasion he would brush their hair this way or that. He made up to them. He seemed to go into a sort of inward trance within himself as he did this at times. I could see that the cattle filled some deeper need within him.

It would be later in my life that I would understand what had been going on. My father never had access to art in the way that this is understood. But like everybody, no matter how deep the thirst for art is buried, no matter how damaged, no matter how battered, no matter how broken, the thirst for art exists in the human species, and in other species too. Once, in later days, I was in Mexico City. There was a group of huge stones set together in formation on the sidewalk. They were placed in relation to each other so that they were a sculpture. I did not know what they touched in me, what I recognised in them, but it was something. Then a Mexican family came along. They were peasants in the white peasant garb. I watched them. They were not talking to each other. They were silent in the big city just walking slowly, the man in front, one after the other. Then they saw the large stone formation. Without a word to each other as one they stopped, perfectly still, their mouths quietly breathing, intent. They stood for moments and looked at the art. They never said a word to each other. I watched them absorb that formation of stones. I watched it absorb something from them. It struck something deep within them, something in their life and experience which they recognised, something which enriched them. It held them there on that sidewalk both physically and mentally. It was their art. They might not have been able to articulate this, but they had stopped silent and looked. There was a reason for this. Everyone has a thirst, a hunger for art. To one degree or another everybody has their art or struggles to have their art or is damaged by not having their art. I would learn more on this later in my life.

My father's hunger for art was unconscious but it existed. It was partially satiated by the wee Aberdeen Angus cattle. It was by looking at them, by touching them, by observing the look in their eye as they looked in his eye, that he tried for his art. I caught him once sitting on a rock in the wee field behind the barn with his hand out and he scratching and stroking the head of a small Aberdeen Angus calf. It was the most peaceful and wonderful moment in which I had ever 'caught' him. He jumped up embarrassed. What a society. It made my father ashamed of his son seeing him in one of his most beautiful moments, relating in gentleness with another living creature he so liked.

As my father entered his forties and fifties his health deteriorated. The last fair we attended together was Stranorlar. He was not well. He bought eighteen Aberdeen Angus cattle that day. As he did so we stored them one after another in a yard which was used by many other dealers. We had to be able to differentiate his cattle from all the rest. My father's style was not confined to his bamboo stick and his scarf. He also carried a set of narrow pointed scissors in a leather case in his inside pocket. As he bought each animal he made a horizontal cut in the hair across the back of its right haunch. This too was part of his art. The leather-cased scissors and the hair-styled right haunch of the Aberdeen Angus.

That night in Stranorlar, the combination of his failing health and the drink left my father unable to go to the yard to get the cattle. He had hired a man with a cattle lorry to take them home. This man had a torch and with his help I was able to go through the dung-filled yard, select the Aberdeen Angus with the cut hair mark on their right haunch and one by one load them up onto the lorry. They did not want to go. As we put each one up the rest tried to escape. But we eventually managed to get them loaded. We then drove over to the pub where my father was drinking. I went in to get him. The driver sat outside with the engine of his lorry running.

I told my father we had the cattle loaded and were ready to go. He spoke loudly so the whole pub could hear. 'Tell that Tommy boy to switch off that machine of his and come in here and have a drink. He is only wasting petrol. And sure the night is only started.' I did not think the driver would come in but I went out and gave him the message. He answered gruffly that he was not coming in. He said he had another load after ours and had to be getting on. I went in and told my father. He was not pleased. He announced loudly to the pub. 'Look at that, sure your man will not shut off that lorry of his and come for a drink. He just wants to get home. Sure there is no craic in him at all.' And grumbling to the rest of the pub and himself we left. I was glad he did not stay. That way there would be no trouble.

'Come on now Tommy, help me up here into the cab,' my father said to the driver. Loaded up and with me in the middle between him and the driver we headed off in the direction of home. With Tommy double declutching and myself trying to keep my legs out of the way of the gear stick, my father began to talk to the driver. 'Tommy tell me now. Why are you not in the Order? Sure you are one of our own. If you were in the Order sure you would get more work. We look after our own.' My father was talking about the Orange Order. 'I want to be able to take every man's work Bobby.' My father's name was Robert but he was always referred to as Bobby. My father answered: 'Tommy you are looking at it the wrong way. If you join the Order then you will be sure to get all your own kind's work.' The conversation drifted off as my father had the drink in him and Tommy did not want to argue. Doing so could damage his business prospects.

My father's health continued to deteriorate rapidly. He became exhausted and disorientated. His skin turned dark. The local doctor had no idea what was wrong and in his ignorance and stupidity and arrogance sent my father for electric shock treatment. He obviously thought that by tying him down and shooting electric currents into his brain that the brain cells might come together in a different and better order. It was like the story about the monkey and the unlimited supply of pencils and paper. Give it enough of both and a long enough period of time and it would create a work of genius. The whole thing was garbage and barbaric. I grew to hate this doctor. I later found out that my father had hypothyroidism and Addison's disease. I would inherit these illnesses and almost die from them myself in my middle age.

One day I was playing at a stream on my way home from school. The previous night my father had lost consciousness. I felt guilty and thought that I should go home to help milk the cows. I got on my bicycle. When I arrived home there were two cars in the yard behind the house. We had no car. I went inside and up to my father's bedroom. He was lying on his back in the bed. Two doctors were arguing over which of them had the right to treat him. My uncle Willie who lived in the house with us and who was my father's brother, was also in the room, and was explaining that he had called in a second opinion. I had heard him say he was going to do this the night before because my father was getting worse and also because my uncle did not trust the regular doctor who was a Catholic. He had said maybe the Catholic doctor was not that interested in curing an Orangeman. My uncle had heard that this doctor was reputed to have said something to that effect.

I slipped around the squabbling doctors and went over and looked down at my father who was lying on his back on the bed. He was unconscious and breathing heavily with longer and longer gaps between each breath. Then his mouth opened and his tongue protruded up and out and a rattle came from his throat. I waited for him to take another breath. But he did not. I waited some more. But still he did not. Then I realised: I had just watched my father breathe for the last time. I had just watched him die. I wondered how it could happen, that a person could just stop like that, that their whole system could give up life like that. The doctors were so busy arguing over who was going to get paid for treating my father they did not notice he had died. It was 1956, my father was fifty-seven, I was twelve.

I turned away from my father's deathbed and slipped past the arguing adults and down the stairs and out of the house. My four sisters and mother and aunt were in the parlour, as it was called, with the wife of the second opinion doctor. I did not want to see any of them. I went outside, my two dogs joined me and I headed up the lane behind the house. After walking for fifteen minutes I climbed over the hedge into the wood with its ancient oak and beech and fir trees and its mountain ash under growth. There were tracks with which I was familiar and along which I often played. I went to the tall fir tree where I regularly lay to think about things. My two dogs joined me for heat, the wee ratter lying on my chest and the sheepdog up against my side.

I lay and thought about my father. I thought of the day the previous year I had spent with him in Portrush. We had sat together watching the divers at the blue pool. The sun was shining on the rocks and it was warm. My father liked this as his illnesses left him cold. I thought about the days we had spent in the fairs together, the times in the pubs where he told his yarns. These times would never come again. I wished I could cry. I did not know why I could not cry. In later years I would look back and realise how much I missed with my father dying. He was a man of laughter. He was a social man. I would later grow to have these qualities. Maybe we could have had them together. But we never did. I would never know how this affected me.

I had looked up to and admired my father. But I had also very much disliked and been saddened by his drinking and when my mother and he would argue about this. My mother would say that he would drink us out of house and home and that he was killing himself with that auld drink. That if it was not for the 'weans', us children, she would leave him and go back and get a job in one of the big houses she had worked in. She said she was well thought of in those places and could easily get a job. These arguments would make me very upset. Sometimes I would go out of the house and lie in the hay barn with my two dogs. So it was us children that were keeping my father and mother together and my mother so unhappy. Sometimes I wished that my mother and my father would separate. Sometimes I would be so distraught that for a moment or two I would wish that one of them would die. But none of these things happened so I just screwed my pain down deep and held on to it. Maybe this was why I did not cry. Maybe my emotions were too constricted. They could not release themselves. Maybe also while I was sad that my father was dead, at the same time a bit of me thought that now there would be no more of the arguments. I would lie with my two dogs in the barn and think of these things.

After some time in the wood I felt guilty because I was not helping back at home so I got up and headed back towards the house. As I jumped down from where the wood ran along the lane I landed beside two ladies who lived in a small cottage further up the hill and who were walking to the village. They were an unconventional couple for that time. Both were married but both had thrown their husbands out of their homes and marriages and lives. They owned the cinema and dancehall in the village. It was unusual for women to have these prominent businesses, in fact any businesses, in those times. When there was any trouble in their dance hall or cinema they acted as their own bouncers. They were independent tough ladies. Most people looked down upon them. I did not. I admired their toughness and independence.

'John, John how is your father today? Is he improving?' I was still young and had no diplomatic skills and did not know how to answer this question except to be brutally direct. 'He is dead.' My blunt answer was followed with a few seconds silence. Then: 'Dead, Bobby is dead? It cannot be. Aw glory be to God. It cannot be. Sure God would not take him. Sure your mother needs him. Sure you need him, sure you are only a wean.' Both ladies broke out into keening and crying.

I did not know how to respond. They were saying that God had taken my father, that is killed him. They were obviously very upset that my father was dead, but then at the same time they were saying glory be to the God they said had taken him, had killed him. I could not make head nor tail of it. I walked on down the lane and left them to their lamenting. They did not make any sense to me. This God I kept hearing about took another knock.

Down at the house the yard was filling with cars and people. I went into the byre where some neighbours were sitting on wooden stools milking the cows. I went to help but a family friend stopped me and ordered me to go into the house and be with the rest of the family. I was glad not to have to help with the milking but at the same time I felt guilty. My mother was sitting crying in the kitchen surrounded and supported by my sisters and aunt. My uncle stood to the side. My mother spoke first: 'John your poor father, where were you? We were worried about you.' I did not answer.

My uncle spoke. 'John this is terrible about Bobby. We cannot believe it. But we have to see that while we do not understand it that it is all part of God's plan. And we can never understand nor can we question God's plan.' My uncle had to get his God off the hook. This sounded like what the two ladies had said. The tragedy of my father's death had to be given some bigger meaning if it was to be accepted. It was all part of God's plan. And glory be to God. Even at that early age I could not accept that. This God was not coming out of things too well.

My uncle continued: 'And another thing, and John you can be sure of this too. I have always been told that I have broad shoulders. Well they will bear all the extra burden that will be on them now with Bobby gone.' My uncle was a good man. He was reassuring us all that he was there for us.

As I stood listening to my uncle talking I noticed that neither he nor I were crying. My mother and aunt and sisters were all in tears, but my uncle and I were not. I wondered more about my own not crying. Maybe it was more than what I thought. Maybe it was something wrong with us males, why could we not cry? Were we in some way disabled, damaged?

My father was waked for three days and three nights. The house was full nonstop. Everybody, relatives, neighbours, friends, just about everybody who came brought something: sandwiches, cakes, cigarettes. Teapots and kettles were borrowed from neighbours. Everybody was fed and watered. There were so many people this had to be done in shifts. There was no alcohol as people knew my mother did not want it and this was respected. The men who drank did so furtively outside from flat half bottles of whiskey they kept concealed in their inside coat pockets. Sure you could not wake Bobby without a wee drop was the sentiment.

During part of this waking period I was sent to the home of some neighbours who owned a small hotel. The idea was to distract me from the sorrow of my father's death. Two young men lived there. They were in their early twenties and talked to me about their hunting and fishing and rugby playing and kept me entertained. But I felt guilty that I was not at home with the rest of my family. I was separated from them at this important time of grieving. It was one of the first cracks in my relations with the rest of my family. Such cracks would grow and multiply in the years ahead.

My father's funeral was the biggest that ever went down the Lifford Road. Protestants and Catholics, Orangemen and non-Orangemen, people who knew my father from the cattle dealing and fairs, people who knew him from his drinking in the pubs, neighbours, relatives, they were all there. A funeral such as this was a great social and bonding event in rural Ireland at that time. Old friends and acquaintances were seen, enemies were tolerated and even sometimes shook hands and made up, news and gossip was exchanged, business possibilities were considered. My father's death was the catalyst for all this. I was impressed.

But I was also confused. Why were no women walking behind the coffin from our house to the graveyard? My mother and aunt and sisters had all stayed behind looking down the lane as the cortege had moved off. Yet there was I, younger than any of them, walking with the men. The women cried, the men did not cry, the men walked, the women did not walk, what was this men and women thing all about anyway? I would struggle to understand this for many decades to come. But it was there at my father's funeral that I first saw the inequality between men and women and from this I would later come to see the importance of standing against the unequal treatment of women.

As the funeral neared the village I saw a man standing up ahead on the side of the road. When the hearse came close he snapped his heels, stood to attention and saluted. Looking rigidly ahead he held this stance until the hearse had passed. He was a neighbour and Catholic who had been in the Free State Army. He was saluting and standing to attention as a sign of respect for my father. I liked what he did. But I had been taught to believe he was the enemy. Now the confusion over the men/women thing was added to with confusion over the Protestant/Catholic thing, the nationalist/unionist thing.

My father was buried in Lifford graveyard. It was very old. Its once vertical gravestones had sunk in the soft earth and come to lean to one side or the other. It also had large rectangular horizontal gravestones with dates and names carved on them that were by then mostly unreadable. These lay flat on side and end stones. It had old gnarled yew trees and ivy. A fighter from the 1798 rebellion against British rule was buried there. The graveyard had character and history.

Close family friends had dug my father's grave. It was a deep hole. I found it threatening. I did not want my father to go into it. What if he was not dead? He would never be able to get out of the coffin or out of the grave. But nobody else seemed worried about this so I put it out of my mind.

The coffin was lowered down and a soft cloth pad laid on top of it to dull the sound of the clay and stones when the grave was being filled. Then a strange ritual took place. Rows of men lined up, marched past the grave, took small silk bows from their lapels and dropped these on top of my father's coffin. They were members of the Royal Black Preceptory, the Protestant organisation of which my father was a leading member. This was a ritual of that organisation and the way its members showed respect for its dead.

After this was over and the preacher had said his words my uncle took me by the hand and led me to the edge of the grave. We stood and looked in. Then he led me back. We watched while groups of men, all Protestants, stepped forward and took the shovels from the mound of soil and began to cover my father's coffin. In the Ireland of that time it was the tradition that people's coffins were covered by people of 'their own kind'. And also only by men. The men who covered my father's coffin did so carefully, gravely and with reverence. I could see they thought it was an honour. I was again impressed. When they were finished with their shovelling they placed the side and end stones back around the grave and slid the large flat stone into its place on top of these. The carvings on this stone were of our family going back up to at least 200 years but the weather and the elements had made them mainly unreadable. I could see that the men covering the coffin and replacing the stones felt important and with a place by these actions.

My uncle had a friend who had a car. He drove us both back up to the house. The women had been preparing and the eating and tea drinking started again. This feeding of the mourners by the women along with their weeping was their main contribution to the burial ritual. The men marched, the men carried the coffin and dug the grave, the women fed the mourners and wept.

Slowly people began to drift away. Eventually it was evening and there was nobody left but the family and two close women relatives who had come to stay for a day or two. My mother turned to me and told me to go up to bed. I did so, climbing the stairs slowly and with sadness. I lay down on the feather mattress and covered myself with the sheet and blankets. The room had no heating. But on the feather mattress and under the cotton sheets and the feather filled cover I was warm and alive. But my father was lying cold and dead in the graveyard. I felt sad and alone. I fell asleep. I was exhausted with the events of the last days.

PORTINURE – ON THE FINN'S WEST BANK

M Y FAMILY'S FARM was in the townland of Portinure, one mile south of the village of Lifford. The fields ran in a narrow strip from the River Finn up to the top of the hill of Killandaragh. I wondered how that came to be, how things were before there was that strip, who measured out that strip, who had occupied that land before my family came there. I had heard talk of the old clans who owned the land collectively. I was later able to find out that my family had lived there for at least 200 years but before that I did not know. I wanted to believe our place was called Portinure because there had once been a port on the river at that point. Later when I had my DNA tested I found out I was 29% Scandinavian. Maybe the Vikings had come up at high tide. Seeing as half the Viking warriors were on occasion women, maybe some distant great-, great-, great-, great-grandmother was a Viking and stayed. I could see her with her shield and flashing sword. I wanted to believe this too. Our family name was neither Irish nor Scottish and we could have been there a lot longer than 200 years so this could have been so.

After the death of my father eight people lived at Portinure: my mother, my uncle, my aunt – my uncle's wife, my four sisters and myself. My mother was by far and away the dominant person in the household. She rose before dawn and worked to after dusk. She helped with the farm animals, made the bread, the butter, the jam and did the cooking. On Mondays she hand-washed the clothes of the entire household in a large oblong shaped zinc tub. She was a small woman and when she was finished this washing she would be bent to the one side with exhaustion and her hands would be white and slack skinned. One of the fingers on her left hand was bent from where she broke it when she was breaking sticks for the fire and it had not set right. To me it was a symbol of her hard life.

My mother did not legally own the farm so she did not dominate in that way. She was the central figure in the household through the amount of work she did, through her intelligence, through the strength of her personality and from being the mother of us five children. From the combination of these qualities and roles came the power of her voice and her authority. We all felt guilty and inadequate when we compared ourselves to how hard she worked and what she meant to the family. And if we did not she was not shy to point this out to us. She had no choice but to do so to make sure we played our part in keeping the place together. There was not much to spare in Portinure.

Before marrying my father my mother worked as a servant in the homes of rich Protestant farmers and merchants. On one occasion she worked in the home of a liberal capitalist family in the City of Derry. She acquired new skills and knowledge in that urban, culturally more advanced household, new ways of cooking, new ways of baking, new ways of furnishing the house. She had been well thought of by all her employers. This was shown by the pieces of mahogany furniture and silverware they gave her when she married. These were on display in the parlour of our home. They were a source of great pride to my mother. To her they represented how this class valued her. They also helped her confront her sense of social inferiority, that in some way she and her family were not good enough. An idea which this class and its system had put in her head in the first place.

But the furniture and the silverware were not all this class gave my mother, put in the head of my mother, during her time in their big houses. She also received their ideology, that the rich had the right to be rich and to rule, that this was natural, that those who had wealth deserved to have it and those who were poor were so because it was their own fault. She also received the idea that nothing could be done to change things. That the way things were, was the way they were meant to be. The smart thing was to knuckle down and accept this. My mother was a conservative.

But things were not without contradiction. My mother was an intelligent, strong woman with a good heart. She also had a personal experience outside those big houses. She remembered the poverty and difficult life of her own mother and family. As a result she tended to feel sympathy for poor people, Protestant or Catholic, whom she knew individually. This would on occasion bring her into conflict with the ideas she had been taught by the class of people she worked for in the big houses.

However, while she felt sympathy for poor people, Protestant or Catholic, whom she knew individually, my mother did not feel sympathy for the Catholic people as a whole, even though they as a people tended to be worse off than the Protestant people. To do so would have been too threatening to the system that existed and to the little bit of advantage my mother and our family had from being Protestant in that system.

We lived just over the border in East Donegal in the Republic of Ireland. We were less than a half hour bicycle ride from Protestant-dominated Northern Ireland. My mother and the family, as with most of the Protestants who lived in this part of Donegal, looked to the Protestant system which ran Northern Ireland, and from which they could gain some small benefits, some crumbs. By associating with the Protestant Orange network around the border and across the border in the North, they could get permits to work there even though they lived in the South. These work permits were supposedly only for people with special skills, but my uncle, through his position in the Orange Order, was able to get my sisters and many Protestants such work permits. Restricting work permits was one way the Northern Protestant state kept the numbers of Catholics less than the numbers of Protestants and kept control of the state.

Catholics in the South could not get work permits to work in the North in the way my Protestant sisters could. Young Catholic men from the South would tend to overcome this by marrying young Catholic women from the North and so were able to move into and live and work in the North and have access to the better benefits and opportunities there. Protestants and Catholics had different ways of skinning cats.

My mother was a kind woman and this expressed itself in spite of her being trapped in the sectarian world. An example of this was her friendship with a neighbouring Catholic man called Arty who on occasion worked around Portinure. My mother respected him for his hard work and honesty. He was very religious, going to chapel every Sunday without fail. After my father died my mother loaned him my father's bicycle, an Orangeman's bicycle, so he did not have to walk to his Catholic church. I noticed that she would always go out and speak to him when he collected the bicycle. I asked her what was going on. She said he had no money for the collection. She put it this way: 'You could not have a man going to his place of worship with nothing to put in the plate.'

I did not know what to make of it. My mother, a Protestant, part of an Orange Order family, was giving money to a Catholic man to put in the plate of the Catholic Church. I concluded that at times my mother's good heart would overcome the sectarian views she had been taught by her employers and their system. Knowing and respecting Arty my mother chose to ignore the fact that he was Catholic and that the money, her money, her Protestant money, was going to the Catholic Church. Rather it was going to Arty. But this was not the whole of it. My mother was more intelligent than that. She had to deal with the sectarian issue more thoroughly. So she reset the entire interaction by framing it as that you could not have a man going to his place of worship with nothing to put in the plate. It was made into 'a place of worship', made into a 'plate'. It was no longer the Catholic Church and money to the Catholic Church. By doing this my mother made the entire transaction fit into her world view. My mother was not so slow.

My mother also helped Arty in another way. He had laboured on the building sites in London for twenty years. Naturally enough he did not want to pay taxes. So to get out of doing so, and in spite of being unmarried he claimed he had a wife and children back home in Ireland. For this he regularly needed letters from his 'wife' and the names and birthdays of all his 'children'. My mother would make up these non-existent people and write him letters from them and post them to him. I can still see her sitting at the big kitchen table by the light of the oil lamp making sure she got the names and birthdays right. There it was again. Helping out a Catholic. And even more of a contradiction in this case – helping a Catholic man swindle the Protestant British Crown out of taxes. When I later lived in London I wondered was I was walking past a government building where my mother's letters for Arty lay in some dusty file. I would have liked to have seen them. They would have brought me back to the nights of my childhood with my mother in the kitchen and her writing Arty's letters by the oil lamp, back to memories of a more innocent and less painful time.

Arty, this illiterate labourer directly affected my own life. I first saw him when he had just returned after his twenty uninterrupted years of labouring in London. He had come to see my mother and was standing in our kitchen with his back to the fire heating himself. He was dressed in a double breasted suit and shirt and tie and polished shoes. He was a handsome man and very proud of how good he looked with his coming home outfit. He explained that he had bought them in Petticoat Lane Market. I looked at him with his wide lapels and the tie with the big Windsor knot. I had never seen anything like the style of it before. Under my breath I said to myself: I have to get out of here and get a suit like that, get to Petticoat Lane Market, get to London. Arty's outfit, coming into our home, like the streams and rivers that flowed away from our home, brought the wider world into my world and made me think more about getting out into that wider world.

But Arty's stylish clothes did not last long. He went to work labouring, sometimes at Portinure, and sometimes for other farmers. His stylish clothes which I had first seen him wearing were the only set of clothes he had so he wore them when digging drains, cleaning out byres, whatever work he was at. He had no reserves of money to buy work clothes. When he was in England he had sent all his spare money home to his father and brothers. They told him they were using it for the farm and to keep up the place. Instead they were spending it on themselves, drinking it. As they did so they laughed and scorned him for being so naïve as to believe what they told him, that they were using it to fix up the farm yard and invest in the land. They swindled him. This was cruel. Very soon his stylish clothes were ruined. I looked at him with sorrow.

Arty had a brother called Huey. On occasion he also worked around Portinure. Every now and then Huey would go on the 'tear', that is 'The Drink', for weeks. Before he would have exorcised his demons he would run out of money and would come to my mother for a loan. She would say: 'Sit down there Huey. You will kill yourself with that auld drink. I will make you something to eat to sober you up.' At that Huey would jump up and shout: 'You will do no such thing. It has taken me six weeks to get this drunk and now you want to sober me up.' The result was always the same; she made him a cooked meal with some of her famous home baked wheaten bread, he ate it, and then she loaned him some money. When he went off the 'tear' he would come back, sit down and again my mother would make him a cooked meal. My mother and he would talk about this and that. Then before he left he would say: 'How much do I owe you Mrs Throne?' My mother would tell him. He never questioned did he owe her anything or the amount. He just handed over what she said. There was total trust between this Catholic man and Protestant woman. I would watch in silence. According to the society in which I lived this was not what was supposed to happen between a Protestant and a Catholic.

Huey was a man of great humour, with a tongue for words, some that belonged to everybody and some entirely his own. I would later wish that Joyce had known him. He would also get up to all kinds of escapades. He once told my mother and I that recently he had got very drunk in Harte's bar in Lifford. And that after the pub shut he had to walk home. On the way home from the village there was a sharp corner. He claimed he was so drunk that he could not get round that corner in the normal way. He tried and tried but no good. He would keep going back on himself. Eventually the only way he made it was by turning and reversing round it. My mother as was usual when she was feeding somebody was leaning up against the kitchen wall by the stove with her hand up grasping the mantelpiece. I watched her as she laughed and laughed at Huey's tale of having to back, to reverse round the corner. It was a pleasure to see her laugh. Her life made her laughing rare.

My mother had regular contact with another group of Catholic men whom she knew individually. These were the postmen. They were all Catholics as we lived in a sectarian Catholic state. It was a mirror image of the North only there it was the Protestants who got the public sector jobs.

The postmen came every morning on their bicycles to deliver the mail. Even if they did not have mail they came to Portinure anyway to get their tea and bread and jam, to have their morning break on their delivery run. They would bring my mother the gossip of the day. When she got older and I had left home they would fill her coal bucket and bring it in for her. There was hospitality, kindness, solidarity, a tendency against religious sectarianism, my mother's good bread and jam, and maybe later even an unspoken support for my mother because of my political activities, all mixed up in why they chose my mother's Protestant house for their morning break and why they helped her with her coal bucket. When she died many years later and was buried from my sister's house in Derry some of these postmen travelled there for her funeral. When I saw them there I was shocked to realise that for the past decades, they had been seeing my mother more regularly than I.

My mother's friendship with Catholics was overwhelmingly with Catholic working class people. Business people and farmers of both religions were inevitably in competition with each other in their struggle for profits and economic advantage. Because of the religious divide in Ireland this competition had a particularly nasty edge to it. In later years while settling up my family's affairs I was swindled out of money by two Catholic businessmen. Their motivation for swindling me was greed but their justification for swindling me was that I was 'not one of their own', that is, not a Catholic. It was these sort of realities that saw my mother with her good heart and her own class background having friendships with mainly working class Catholics not Catholic business people.

But there were other elements in my mother's outlook towards Catholics. Later when I lived in the USA I learnt that there was this idea of 'good' African Americans and 'bad' African Americans. The 'good' ones were those who did not talk of the racist injustice of the past and present and did not demand that this be faced up to and ended. The 'bad' ones were those who insisted on speaking of this racist past and present and demanded it be faced up to and ended. Just like there were 'good' African Americans and 'bad' African Americans in the USA, in the sectarian world of Protestant Ireland there were 'good' Catholics and 'bad' Catholics. The 'good' ones did not speak of the sectarian injustice they suffered, the 'bad' ones did. The 'bad' ones were referred to as being 'bitter'. My Mother thought there were 'good' Catholics and 'bad' Catholics.

During this time when I was growing up the travelling people still came around selling their tins. It was before plastic arrived and wiped out their market. My mother would sometimes buy one and sometimes not. But whether she bought one or not she always made the travelling man something to eat. She would say that you could not let anybody leave your house with their mouth open, that is empty, without giving them something to eat. Her own family's experience of poverty was still very powerful in her. I would watch the travelling man as he sat on the outside window ledge and drank his tea and ate his bread and jam. While she fed him, unlike other working men like Arty, Huey and the postmen, she did not invite him into the house to eat. Unlike these others he ate outside. There were the classes within the classes. As I watched him eat I wondered about why my mother made this class difference. I also wondered where the travelling man slept at night. I did not like this travelling man being treated worse than Arty and Huey and the postmen, I did not like this discrimination.

My mother's early life had been very difficult. Her father, my grandfather, was a man of hardened emotions. He had to fight to stay afloat after the early death of his wife, my mother's mother, my grandmother, and to carry out what he saw as the responsibilities of his job as the land agent for the local landowner. To collect the rents and keep the landowner's tenants 'in line' demanded a 'firm hand'. Her father thought that he had to control my mother's mother and all his children also with a 'firm hand'. My mother said of him: 'Father was not good to mother.' This was a serious criticism coming from my mother who very seldom said anything negative about any relative. My mother's own mother had died young after having given birth to five children and after having being sexually and physically abused by a farmer to whom she worked as a labourer in the hiring fair system. I was to write of my grandmother's life later in my book *The Donegal Woman*.

My mother was intelligent and strong and could read and write. But other than the natural world around her she did not get a chance to have access to the more beautiful creations in life, to great literature and art, to the flowers on the stems of our world. She never read a book. She said she had no time. She never saw a great work of art. At night when she finished her normal day's work in the house and around the farmyard she would knit sweaters which she would sell to supplement the family budget. She was always busy. She would say: 'A woman's work is never done.'

But in spite of all this, like my father with his unconscious struggle for art which was reflected in his Aberdeen Angus cattle, my mother too, struggled unconsciously for art. There was some of this in her sweater knitting. But it was in her butter making that it really fought to be out. When she made the butter she shaped it into rectangular shapes with her wooden butter pats.

These pats, like little rectangular-shaped table tennis bats, had carved designs on them. She used these to make the rectangular butter slabs her own, making her marks and shapes and diagrams on them. They did not hang in a gallery, even better they sat on our kitchen table and hung in my mother's thoughts and feelings, in the thoughts and feelings, conscious and unconscious of all of us. No matter how busy she was she made these patterns on the butter. Along with the butter making my mother was famous for her baking. She was at this non-stop except for Sundays. Her bread was renowned in the neighbourhood. On her large rectangular shaped loaves she would always make a cut long ways across the middle and cross ways from side to side in the middle. When the scone was baked these came out as grooves which gave the loaf the look of a piece of art. When she died and was buried one of the wreaths laid on her grave was in the shape of a loaf.

Along with her butter making and bread baking my mother would wash and iron the clothes of the entire household. She would do so until they were perfect. The linen tablecloths and the white shirts, not a stain or mark on them, her own and all our clothes ironed with that heavy iron until there was not a wrinkle in them. All of this was her art. Later in life I would mourn for her when I realised that she did not have the time or the opportunity to know and enjoy the history and the great finer aspects of the arts. What would she have thought if she had some days off and the time and the money to spend a few days in Paris and walk in the Louvre, to let the great art seep into her. My mother's favourite flower was the daffodil. This too was part of her struggle for art. Wherever I went for the rest of my life I would, when they were in season and available, pick a bunch of daffodils in her memory and put these in a vase wherever I happened to be.

When I was around ten years old my mother and I were in Strabane. Some weeks earlier I had heard a soldier in a military band play a trumpet at our family's church. Its power and clarity moved me very much. I wanted to make that sound. There was a trumpet for sale in a shop window. I said to my mother: 'I would like that.' She peered through the glass at the price tag and said: 'I am sorry, I could not afford to buy you that. We do not have the money.' We walked on. Many years later when she was ill and I was visiting her she pulled herself up on her sick bed and said to me: 'I am sorry I was not able to buy you that trumpet.' I shrank into myself in shame and self-hatred and guilt for having ever asked for it. She had been thinking about not being able to buy me that trumpet all her life. How I detested the cruelty and ignorance of my youth. How I detested the suffering and pain caused to my mother by the poverty and the system that created that poverty.

I underestimated my mother in many ways and on many occasions. Once she spoke to me about myself, and the rest of her children. She said: 'I am sorry I could not have had another son. If I had it would have taken a lot of the weight off you.' She was thinking that if I had had a brother that the pressure on me to live up to the family's expectations and the role they hoped I would play could have been shared out, could have been diluted.

I am ashamed that I did not fully appreciate my mother. She was a kind, insightful, strong and intelligent woman. She had a very good heart. But she had the misfortune to always be under assault by a brutal system.

Throughout the rest of my life I would always regret that we did not agree more and that I was not able to make her life more bearable and even happy. She did everything she could for me. She worked to make me see what she thought was the best for me. And I would go on to turn it all down, to reject it all. This was a terrible cruelty. I apologise to my mother and her memory. I also recognise that it was not only damaging to my mother but it was also damaging to me. And in my early days I did not know the half of it. I only came to understand the full extent of her pain and suffering and the damage done to both of us by our conflicts as I grew older and became more mature. Again and again I broke my mother's heart and again and again twisted my own in agony.

My Uncle Willie, as he was called, was my father's brother. He was the 'man' of the house. He was so because the house and farm were in his name and because he was the oldest male. However in reality, in many ways he came second in authority after my mother. In most households he would have been the central dominant person. But he and his wife my Aunt Martha were childless and this along with the very strong qualities of my mother and her being the mother of the only children in the house left this not always so. He did not know how to handle the reality that my mother was the source of the children who, as he thought, were the future of the place. Not being the father of the children weakened him in the household. However this did not mean that he did not concern himself with the day to day goings on of the place, did not mean that he was not central to decisions especially in relation to the farm and its workings, crops, animals and the rest.

My uncle was always worried that the farm would fail, that we would go broke. He shared my mother's view that the only way we would keep the place afloat was if we worked our fingers to the bone. Before my father's death he and my father worked together on the farm. My uncle was the oldest. By custom he was in line for ownership of the farm and my father would have had to move away, get a job. But it never came up. My uncle shared the farm with his brother and all of us and that was that. There never was any mention never mind any conflict over this. This was exceptional given the emphasis on property in rural Ireland at the time. My uncle put human decency and solidarity with the rest of the family before property. And we were not even his children. He was a good man. I was positively influenced by this good quality of his. I compared him to the many other small property owners of both religions who would have pulled out their own teeth with a pair of pliers for a bit of a swampy field. In his own way and without thinking he was doing so my uncle helped me see that there were things more important than fighting to own property.

My uncle was the 'District Grandmaster of the Orange Order in East

Donegal'. This was a central part of his life. He recruited and lectured new members and built this organisation. When I was young I was taken to the Orange Order's 'big days', as they were called. The main one was the 12th of July, or as it was called, 'The Twelfth'. The Orange organisations would come together in a central location, play their pipes and flutes and drums and march and listen to speeches from their leaders including my uncle. My uncle was a committed Orangeman. He did not swear. His only expletive if it could be called that was 'rottenwell'. He never had more than one drink and then only once a year on the 'The Twelfth'.

My uncle was also the leader of the local Lifford Orange Lodge. Its members and families would meet on the morning of the Twelfth at the Orange Hall in the village. Before they would leave to get on their bus to go to the central gathering point my uncle would give a speech in the hall. 'We are going out today on this solemn occasion to celebrate our religion. We must act properly. We must see to it that there is no drunkenness and that we all conduct ourselves. Do not let ourselves or our religion down.' At this all would look at each other and solemnly shake their heads in agreement, including my father.

The Lodge formed up outside the hall, assembled behind its pipe band and marched along the village street over the bridge into Northern Ireland where it boarded its bus. It could have got the bus to come to the hall but it wanted to assert, even flaunt, its right to march on the streets of the Catholic village in Catholic Southern Ireland. It was usually an orderly colourful procession. The skirl of the pipes, the kilt-wearing band members, the banner flying in the breeze, all added to the event.

Later in the day it would return after meeting with other lodges and hearing the speeches and of course having a few, maybe more than a few, drinks. The lodge and the band were different on their return than when they had left. The drink had had its effect. There was an increased assertiveness to the music, an increased swagger to the marching. My father, along with a friend of his, always carried the large banner. This was a long tapestry with painted scenes on both sides suspended between two poles. Between the big days it was stored in the 'banner boxes' in our house. The scenes on the banner were of military victories of Protestant forces over Catholic forces. Images of loving your neighbour as yourself were not painted on these Christian banners.

My father would always have more than some drink in him on the way home from the big days. His head shaking agreement with my uncle's speech of the morning when my uncle had called for no drinking or drunkenness was forgotten. My uncle would be enraged at his own brother defying him on the drink. Under the influence of the drink, the banner my father and his friend were carrying would sway and threaten to overcome the efforts of him and his friend to keep it aloft. But if they were in danger of losing control other lodge members would rush forward and help. Laughing and shouting encouragement at each other they would keep it flying. My father would shout across to his friend on the other pole: 'Howl her up there Davy. She'll not get away from us. We have her.' It was like their fight against the wind and gravity and their own being somewhat drunk was a fight against the alien religious forces that according to the Orange ideology were out there lurking.

The Orange Order was a Protestant organisation. It claimed it did not look down on Catholics but this was not the case. Its marches and demonstrations were to proclaim Protestant superiority and its hundreds of lodges and halls organised its membership in a way that allowed it to control the state of Northern Ireland under the supervision of and on behalf of the London government. The North was a 'Protestant state for a Protestant people', as one Protestant politician put it, and the Orange Order was the instrument which made this a reality on the ground.

But just as with my father and mother, my uncle had a good heart. And he also had a common experience with his small farmer neighbours, Catholic and Protestant. This regularly brought his thinking and actions into conflict with the ideology of the Orange Order. On one occasion a Catholic neighbour's cow fell in the river. Its death would have been a big loss to this family. The man's son rushed to Portinure for help. My uncle grabbed one of the horses and I grabbed a rope and we ran back with the young man. My uncle tied one end of the rope to the horse's harness while I, being the only swimmer, jumped into the river, put the other end down under the cow's belly, brought it up again on the other side, and threw it back up on the bank where my uncle tied it again to the horse's harness. The horse pulled, the men pulled, I shouted and beat the cow on the back end and in a panic it made a lunge and out it came. We had saved the Catholic's cow.

My mother and aunt had rushed after my uncle and me. They had brought a bucket of warm mash for the cow so she would not die of the foundering from her time in the cold river. They also brought a can of hot tea and sandwiches for us men. The cow greedily ate down the mash, every now and then shaking herself and sending the water flying in all directions. The rest of us drank our tea and ate our sandwiches and talked and laughed together proud and excited at having worked together collectively and successively.

I enjoyed the excitement and challenge of saving the cow. I enjoyed the solidarity as we worked together. I enjoyed the camaraderie between us Catholics and Protestants as we stood around and ate our sandwiches and drank our tea and talked and laughed together. But I could not stop thinking that if Catholics were so bad why had we saved the Catholic's cow? Why had we not let the Catholic's cow drown? Letting it die would have been the logic of the sectarian outlook of society. My questioning of the whole religious sectarian thing increased.

I could see that there were contradictions in it all. That again and again the good hearts of my uncle and my mother and others in our family would get over the sectarianism. Also that on occasions the common interests such as saving a neighbour's cow would overcome the sectarianism because all small farmers could see the importance of this and how they would need help if they were ever in the same situation. I could see that. But I was also to increasingly see that the powers that were, the governments in London, Dublin and Belfast, representing minorities as they did, the minorities being the rich and property-owning classes, and hierarchies of the churches Protestant and Catholic alike, also supporting and representing the capitalist system of the rich minorities, all needed to divide the majority, that is the non-rich. The rich were a tiny minority, to rule they had to divide the majority. So a powerful sectarian-based structure was held in place by the top elite minorities to this end and people like my family and neighbours in spite of their best instincts and common interests were again and again trapped in this system.

My uncle was the horseman on the farm and along with his leading role in the Orange Order his life revolved around his horses and the work he did with these. Every drill and swathe had to be straight. The horses' coats and manes had to be perfectly cut, the hooves perfectly shod. Their harness had to be perfectly oiled. Every night before he went to bed he went out to their stables and patted down their beds of straw and talked to them and groomed them. My uncle felt for those horses. Through them he expressed a large part of himself. They were his therapy, but they were also more than that. The horses with their perfectly groomed and cut coats and their shod hooves, their polished harness, the straight drills and swathes he produced by working with the horses, all were part of my uncle's struggle for his art. My uncle's horses were to him like my father's Aberdeen Angus cattle were to my father. My uncle's art was very much with straight lines and always to be neat and clean and ordered. This flowed from his religious and political beliefs and position in society. This was the way he wanted society to be so it was the way he strove for his 'art' to be. There was no wild disorder, no mad inspirational flights of exaltation in my uncle's politics or his art. This was a pity. This damaged my uncle's art.

My Aunt Martha was married to my uncle. She was also my mother's biological sister. My father and uncle had married two sisters. My uncle and aunt were childless. They were very kind to us children treating us as their own. At times the pressure of my mother's life would get too much for her, our misbehaviour would not help, and she could get angry with us. My Aunt Martha would on such occasions intervene and say: 'aw sure be easy on them they are only weans.' My mother would turn on her and tell her we were her weans and keep out of it. I would feel terrible for my aunt when this would happen. I would rather my aunt would have not defended us.

My aunt was the last woman to come to live at Portinure. She was therefore at the bottom of the seniority list. She had to do the worst jobs such as emptying the outdoor toilet bucket. I thought this was wrong that instead it should be shared out. But I was too young and immature and lacking in confidence to say this. After all that was the way things were done.

I felt sorry for my aunt because of her position in the household, but in the wider world she was married to the District Master of the Orange Order of East Donegal. At events of this organisation my uncle would be sitting at the top table and my aunt would be by his side dressed neatly in her tweed suit. She had good taste. When my uncle would go out to dance my aunt would be dancing with him. I was glad for her, glad that she had some recognition and prominence even if it was not completely in her own right but as my uncle's, the master's, wife.

My Aunt Martha also had her struggle for her art. She had a small patch of a garden in which she grew vegetables to supplement the family's diet. But she did not leave it there. As well as keeping this garden neat and productive by growing vegetables she grew patches of small flowers. When these were in bloom she would bring them into the house and put them on the table in a vase. Her favourites were not the strong clean lined stems of the daffodils of my mother, hers were small fragile multi coloured flowers, in particular the Sweet Pea. I was many years older before I realised that my aunt's Sweet Pea flowers were part of her struggle for her art.

My four sisters also lived in Portinure for some years after my father died. Being older than me and I being a boy, while we got on together there was not much interaction between us. I was drawn to my father when he was alive and then to my uncle after my father's death. We were also treated differently in that I was spoiled. My sisters were expected to help in the house. I was never expected to help in the house. Yet at special times when a lot was going on such as harvest time and spring planting time my sisters were expected to help in the fields.

My oldest sister was Kathleen. Like all my sisters she was very intelligent. She went to the local technical school and learnt office skills and got a job in the office of a Protestant-owned mill across the border in the North of Ireland. The head teacher in her school would later say that she was the most intelligent student he ever had. She developed a relationship with a local man whom my uncle would get a job as a policeman across the border in Strabane. He was not an attractive person and being a policeman and the way he got that job accentuated his negative qualities, his insecurity, his lack of confidence and from these his tendency to bully my sister. My mother ordered my sister to break off the relationship. But my sister was stubborn. She eventually married this man and moved out. I was still young at that stage and supported my sister. My mother turned out to be right and I turned out to be wrong. This man physically abused my sister. I could not see any struggle for art in my sister.

The man in her life could have helped her in this. He played the bagpipes. You would have thought that having music in his life would have nurtured his better qualities and that of my sister's also. But it did not. It was a political question. The divide and rule politics of the system dominated the music. He played the pipes in the Orange band. This was associated with keeping the Catholics down. This was the main reason he played the bagpipes, to keep the Protestants up and the Catholics down. The result was he and my sister, who went to all his bagpipe gatherings, rather than being uplifted and cultured and enriched by the music were brutalised by the music. It is hard to become cultured and enriched by music or any form of art, if the main purpose of that music or art is to put others down. In such circumstances the art tends to get pushed aside, the spirit becomes hardened. I was to see this later when I lived in Chicago when the racist Chicago cops strutted with their pipe band.

Decades later my sister Kathleen died. I had not seen her for many years. My political views and activities by that time were well known. The result was that her family banned me from attending her funeral. That sectarianism that divide and rule was nasty.

My second oldest sister was Margaret. She was a mean-spirited person and a snob. She looked down on those she considered beneath her. Her snobbery was cultivated by the fact that she worked in the office of a Protestant lawyer and knew the secrets of his clients. This added to her feeling of superiority. She shared these secrets with my mother and in this way my mother learnt not only gossip, but a better understanding of how the world worked. This was positive for my mother but negative for my sister. It gave her a feeling that she could trade this information for favouritism from our mother and allow her to lord it over the rest of us. When in later years it became clear this was not the case, that my mother had principles, and would not be bought by information from a lawyer's office, my sister became very bitter towards our mother. Like with my sister Kathleen I could see no desire for any art within her. She was too bitterly ambitious and narrow and snobbish for the wonder of art. A kind and gentle man wanted to marry her but she turned him down because she thought he 'was not good enough for her'. He was a lucky man she turned him down. She married a man as unpleasant as herself, one who tried to overcome his own inadequacy and insecurity and inferiority, as well as to try and make himself feel important, by continually telling lies to stir up conflict in our family.

When my sister Margaret would die many years later I had the same experience as I had with my older sister Kathleen. This person and his family banned me from attending her funeral. The main reason was their hatred of my political views but of course banning me made this person feel that he was important, that he had power.

My sisters, Mary and Angela, came next above me. They were identical twins. They wore the same clothes, slept in the same bed and cycled together to the same school. They were good to me. At an early age I developed tooth decay. My family did not have the money to pay for a dentist. My twin sisters were working in two different shops in Strabane as shop assistants at the time and put their money together and paid. I owe them for still having my own teeth. My twin sisters' struggle for art as far as I could see was confined to how they dressed.

My twin sisters would go on to marry two brothers as my mother and aunt had married two brothers. Mary would become deputy mayor of the City of Derry for the Protestant Unionist party. My mother would have been very proud of her daughter being deputy mayor of the city where she had worked as a servant. Mary was a good person and we were later to become good friends. She likes people and in spite of being the deputy mayor of Derry for a period and a city councillor numerous times over, there is not a hint of snobbery in her being. Mary is married to Ernie. He and I, and also my sister and I, have very different political views in relation to British imperialism. We came to an unspoken agreement not to talk about such politics. In this way we maintained our friendship.

My mother developed Alzheimer's and lived the last years of her life with Mary and Ernie and their three daughters. Mary's family, Mary herself, Ernie her husband, their three daughters helped my mother more than I. I am ashamed of this. I can still see Mary and Ernie with their arms round my mother helping her up their stairs when she was in the last years of her life. I owe them and their family a great debt.

Before they moved to live in Derry, Mary and Ernie owned a small hotel in the village of Claudy. The IRA blew up the village, killing and wounding friends of Mary and Ernie and injuring Mary herself. She was to have fragments of metal and pain in her leg for the rest of her life. Mary went on to be the spokesperson demanding answers to this bombing. As well as this Ernie's younger brother was shot dead by the IRA on a building site where he was working as an electrician. These events were part of the sectarian rmilitary offensive of this organisation.

As mentioned, I would later write a book based on the life of our grandmother. It was not in line with conventional Unionist and Protestant views, yet Mary helped me promote it with the greatest enthusiasm. She did so explaining away what were for her, the difficult parts, by saying that I saw them as being true and that you had to tell what you saw as the truth. My sister got this belief in telling what she saw as the truth from our mother.

Mary eventually ended up living with her husband and her three daughters in the City of Derry. This and her political activity brought her into the urban world. This was very beneficial and in the years to come would help her adopt and advocate progressive views on gay rights and on women's right to choose. Advocating these views widened the gap between her and our other sisters.

Mary's twin sister Angela took a more twisted route. She married a man who was unable to grow out of his hill farmer roots in rural Tyrone, unable to break free from his obsession with money and property. This damaged Angela. She was already confused by, and jealous of, Mary's success in her chosen fields, and especially her being deputy mayor of Derry and a well-known public figure. In her resentment Angela deliberately and determinedly and in a consciously hurtful way estranged herself from Mary, her own twin sister. Her spite went so far as to deny Mary a copy of a photo of them when they were still children at school, sitting at their school desk drinking their bottles of free school milk together. Angela's antagonism to Mary caused a lot of pain to Mary and also damaged Angela's own family and herself. It was not excusable. Angela could not break free from her competition with Mary a competition was that was based on jealousy.

My sisters had basically the same upbringing, the same parents, lived until their marriages in the same place, yet turned out differently. There seems to have been a number of reasons for this. A combination of the men they married, the professions of these men, the qualities or lack of qualities of these men plus the economic and social conditions and the locations in which they lived. Related to this was their attitude to marriage.

All my sisters believed that once married they should stay married. So in spite of the very negative personal qualities of the husbands of Kathleen, Margaret and Angela they twisted and damaged themselves to fit into their husbands' worlds and either accede to their demands or find ways to live with these demands. They did not consider divorcing their husbands. As they all after marriage lived in the North of Ireland divorce was then an option to them unlike if they had lived in the South where it was illegal. But my three sisters, Kathleen, Margaret and Angela never considered this and so were damaged by their relationship with their men.

Mary's experience was different. Her world was broader than my other sisters. Mary helped run the hotel which was owned by her and her husband and so was a more confident and balanced person. Running their hotel brought Mary and her husband Ernie into contact with a wider strata of people than any of my other sisters. Moving to live in the City of Derry for which she was deputy mayor and on numerous occasions a city councillor and brought Mary into a more urban and more modern world. This brought more modern views and ways of living into Mary's life. While Mary's views on politics and religion remained conservative and very different from mine, her views on issues such as women's rights and gay rights were progressive. Mary's personal trajectory was shaped in a more positive way by her own qualities, and also by her social and economic and family environment.

CHAPTER 3

MY MALE PRIVILEGES

I WAS THE YOUNGEST in Portinure and the only male child. There is no getting away from the fact that there is male privilege. Anybody who wants to understand the world and tries to ignore this will fail. My gender and also my place in the family as the youngest child made me doubly privileged over my sisters. Doors were opened to me that were not opened to them. We did not start from an even playing field. This was unjust. Even at a very early age I could see this special treatment and did not like it but I did not know what to do about it.

However being privileged did not mean my mother did not discipline and punish me. She believed that punishment was part of growing up, of preparing me for the harsh world out there. She believed if she did not punish me the world would punish me even harder. The way she saw it was that she was only getting me into shape for the life ahead. When I was younger she would, as she called it, 'take the sally rod' to me. She would send me to the hedge to get a stick from a sally bush. It had to be flexible enough to hurt me but not break any bones. Going to the hedge and maybe having to go back a couple of times to get a stick with the right flexibility was almost as bad as the beating. On occasions I would bring too thick a stick hoping she would be afraid to do me damage and so would not punish me, but she was too crafty for me and always sent me back for one that was the proper thickness. Then she would give me a real doing for trying to be too smart. My mother was a character.

I would cry out in pain when my mother would hit me on the bare legs with the sally rod. When I did she would shout: 'Crying out is it. I will give you something to cry out about. Here take that. This will put an end to your crying. There will be no more of that. Here, is it more you want. This will stop your crying.' I could not make head nor tail of it. It was she who was beating me and making me cry out. Then she was beating me more to make me stop crying out.

Many years later I saw Richard Pryor, the African American comedian, describe how his grandmother whipped him and shouted at him in exactly the same way. My mother's goings on around the beating also made me think of the women who lamented my father's death, blamed God for killing him and then said glory be to God. I think my mother felt I needed to be punished so she did what she saw as her duty and beat me, but this hurt her, especially when I cried out, so then she tried to stop the hurt she herself was causing to me, and also to herself, by beating me more to keep me quiet. The whole thing was a madness.

When I got bigger and my mother stopped beating me with the sally rod she stepped up her use of the rod of guilt. 'After all I have done for you and this is what I get. I wish God would reach down and take me now. Your father would turn in his grave if he knew how you were treating me.' The rod of guilt was worse than the sally rod. However in spite of the sally rod and the guilt rod I still got preferential treatment relative to my sisters.

Part of this was being enrolled in the Boy Scouts in Strabane. My sisters were not enrolled in the Girl Guides. The Boy Scouts were Protestant and met in the Protestant scout hall. But all did not go according to the segregation indoctrination plan of the sectarian divide and rule society. Events intervened. A bank manager from England came to town. He was a Catholic. His son, also a Catholic, was allowed to join the Protestant scouts. None of the Catholic boys in Strabane were allowed to join. I was not stupid. The local Catholics were not English and few of their families had money. I was seeing that money, nationality, class and religion were all mixed up even if I did not know how.

I was made the leader of the main patrol in the scout troop. I was thirteen. We were entered for an all-Northern Ireland weekend scouting competition. This involved camping out for a weekend and competing against other troops. We came second in all of the North. This was a very good achievement from a troop from a small town. But I was not happy. I felt there was discrimination and that we should have come first. I sensed a hesitancy on behalf of the Scoutmasters, even the Strabane Scoutmasters, in their praise. I thought that maybe it was because at the camp I had got into a fight and beaten up a member of another scout patrol and got Strabane a bad name. Or maybe it was because I was not of the right class. Maybe they would have preferred it if I had been from the urban small business class like themselves with their clean finger nails not the rural small farmer class. This experience made me more wary about the ideas I was being taught and the experiences that I was having.

The scout troop organised a trip to London. Again as part of my special privileges as the male and youngest child, my family, especially my mother, gathered the money together somehow and I was allowed to go. The reasoning was that it was a consolation for the death of my father. But my sisters had lost their father too and none of them were consoled with a trip to London. Once again my sisters were being discriminated against. I could see this and the seeds of my opposition to discrimination in any form, gender, religion, race, age, sexual orientation or whatever, were further cultivated.

We sailed from Belfast to Liverpool. For the first time I was at sea. It was not rough, just a rolling swell. But it was still the sea. I exulted. My muscles expanded and contracted as I struggled to stay on my feet against the rise and fall of the boat. My mind and thinking expanded also. I could not get enough of it all. I spent the night's crossing on the bow looking ahead and feeling the power as the waters rolled in from the east and challenged the boat's drive for Liverpool. I looked down at the black waters. Man, I thought, this was good.

But while excited by being at sea I was looking forward to London. I was not disappointed by that great city. Its giant buildings overwhelmed me. The Thames with its non-stop water traffic pulled me like a magnet. The streets and parks full of people of all colours and shapes and sizes rushing everywhere excited me. I could not get enough of it. I began to think that maybe I was a city person, not a country person, that rural Ireland and its small villages were not for me. My visit also made me realise that in London people did not seem to want to know whether I was a Catholic or a Protestant, it seemed that nobody cared. This was the first time I thought seriously that there were people who did not care what religion a person was. Maybe not only was I not a country person but maybe I was not a religion person either.

Even though I would later come to dislike them one of the two highlights of my trip to London was the zoo. We walked past cage after cage of what were to me strange animals. Then we rounded a corner and there it was: the great silverback. I could not take my eyes off it as it sat with its back against the wall of its cage glowering at us. Even imprisoned it had more dignity than all of us put together. I could not move. I stayed while the rest of the troop moved on. The Scoutmaster came back and told me to come. I said that I wanted to stay with the great silverback and he could get me on the way back. He asked me why I wanted to stay. I said because 'He is like me.' The Scoutmaster scoffed: 'He is not like you or like me. We have souls.' This made no sense to me. I did not know what a soul was. I could not see it, I could not touch it, I could not hold it in my hand. I felt more attachment to the silverback than to the Scoutmaster. I felt the Scoutmaster was a bully and an idiot. I felt the silverback was like me because of his shape but much more so because of the intelligent way he observed and interacted with his surroundings and especially ourselves.

A keeper came and threw some tomatoes into his cage. The silverback reached down and picked one of them up. He peeled off the skin with his teeth and spat it out. Just like I did with an apple. Then he began to eat the skinned tomato. All the time he was watching us watching him and not moving. I did not say anymore to the Scoutmaster. But I knew he was of ignorance. In the Sunday school at home they talked about us humans and compared us to all the other species, they talked about God and heaven and hell and us being different because we had a soul. They sneered at people who did not believe this. They spoke of some man called Darwin and how he thought that we were descended from monkeys. They sneered at his stupidity. But there in front of me was the silverback. I realised then and there and for certain. I was not with the Scoutmaster nor the Sunday school. I was with this Darwin man. Or as I would learn to put it later, I believed in evolution.

Back in Lifford the word got around: 'Throne believes we come from monkeys.' It was a topic of conversation and mockery for weeks. Then one day a man stopped me. He was known in the village as having 'hands for anything', that is being a very skilled worker. He handed me a brown paper bag. 'This is for you,' he said, and without waiting for an answer he moved on. It was like he did not want to be seen handing me the package, like there was something explosive and dangerous in the package, like it was an underground transaction. Which in a way it was. The bag contained a hard-back copy of Darwin's Origin of the Species. I was not able to read that book for many years but later I did and it has stayed on my bookshelves all my life. I thank the man with hands for everything.

The other highlight of my trip to London was my adventure to the camp of the Girl Guide troop. Our scout troop was sharing a field in Mill Hill East with other scout and guide troops. I was physically bigger than most of the other scouts and some of the girls were returning my looks. I asked a particularly good looking one which tent she was in. As we leaned close and she told me I smelled her long blond perfumed middle class hair. I was excited.

That night when the others in my tent were asleep I slipped out and down to the girl's tent. I crawled under the tent wall. The girl was waiting for me. We did not speak just began to kiss and feel each other. She was in her pyjamas. I felt her body through the thin material. I had only kissed one girl before. It was back home on a Sunday school excursion to Portrush. We went there by train. There were two tunnels on the way and no lights in the train. On the way back from the last excursion I had reached over in the dark tunnel, took the young girl opposite by the arms, raised her up and kissed her on the mouth. It was a kiss of youth. Our lips closed and pressed tightly together. When we came out of the tunnel there was no regret, only pride and defiance in both our eyes. I was proud of the girl and of myself.

This young girl in London was more experienced. She did not hold her lips together. She took the initiative and we kissed with our lips wet and apart and our tongues intermingling and slipping in and out of each other's mouths. I was extremely aroused. We felt each other's bodies. Our passion lifted us up out of the everyday ordinariness of our daily lives. Our breaths came faster and faster.

Then it began to rain, the drops beating on the tent roof, and with them a voice calling. 'Quick, quick, that is the guide mistress. She is coming to see if we are alright. You have to go.' Angry and frustrated and cursing I slipped out under the tent wall and ran bent over up the field. On the way I stopped to shelter under a tree. I turned and looked around. I could see down over the great vast city lights of London. Earlier, the majestic silverback, now the girl's body, my own desire, and sexuality, and with these the great city of London, I was entering a new period in my life. And I knew that my life would be different. I had the audacity to come down and be with one of the Guides. None of the rest of the Scouts did so. I had recognised the importance of the great silverback. None of the rest of the Scouts had done so. My life and I would be different.

At this time I was attending a primary school in a big square grey block building on the Derry road in Strabane. Why did so many of the houses of the richer Protestants, the Protestant clergymen, the Protestant schools in the North and even in the South close to the border seem to be big square stone buildings? Was it siege architecture? Only Protestant boys attended this school. The various churches, especially the Catholic Church, but all churches in the North, believed in segregated education. They all wanted to brainwash the children of their members and it was easier to do this if they could keep them separate. This fuelled sectarianism. All the churches would have blood on their hands in the sectarian conflict that lay ahead.

I learnt to read and write at this primary school. This was important. To make us learn and to enforce discipline the teachers punished us by hitting us with canes and straps. They split the canes and cut the straps down the middle so they would hurt more effectively, have a higher rate of productivity. I came to dislike these teachers and their beatings. But I also learnt to take pain and not show it. This and the reading and writing would prove to be useful to me.

The school brought in a temporary teacher with a cravat and a double barrelled name. I wondered was there a connection between his double barrelled name and the split straps and canes? He spoke in a loud braying voice to show he was superior and should not be amongst us lower class lot. He enjoyed beating us and throwing the chalk duster at us. One day he said that we all had to study harder or we would end up as dustmen. A fellow student spoke up. 'What is wrong with being a dustman? Dustmen are needed.' I knew this young man, his father was a dustman and a drinking partner of my father.

The teacher was taken aback by my fellow student's words. Then he recovered himself. 'Well I suppose you are right. But do not let it be you who is the dustman. Let it be somebody else.' I supported the student. He was right and the teacher was wrong. In the years to come I would see that student, then a grown man, sitting with his head bent forward drinking in the Catholic pubs. I tried to draw him into the struggles in which I was to become involved but could never manage it. I especially wanted to involve him as I was indebted to him for what he taught me that day when he had spoken up and I thought maybe I could do something for him in return.

This school was not just a Protestant only school but it was also a boys' only school. So for the first years of my education I was separated not only from Catholics but also from girls. This was damaging. For a time it hindered my ability to interact with Catholics and to relate spontaneously with girls of my own age.

All students had to leave the primary school when they were eleven. Those from the North could do an exam and if they passed, this allowed them to go on to a secondary school, known as a Grammar School, in the North for free. I could not do this exam as I was from the South of Ireland. But in spite of this my family decided to send me to the Grammar School in Strabane even though they had to pay. I could have gone to the secondary school in Lifford, but I would have had to learn Irish. My uncle refused to agree to this. I always regretted not learning a second language. Knowing two languages makes it easier to learn a third and a fourth and so on. This was another example of where the siege mentality of the Protestant population and the sectarian nature of the system damaged the Protestant population and myself.

Sending me to the Grammar School was more discrimination against my sisters. There was never any talk about them being paid for and going to a Grammar School. My family said that as well as the Irish the other reason I was being sent to the Grammar School in Strabane was because I was smart. I did not believe this. My sisters were smart too but they were being sent to technical schools not Grammar Schools. These prepared them for office and shop jobs. I was being prepared for other and more varied options.

The fees for this grammar school were not small. My mother paid them by extra work. She bought day old chicks and reared and sold them. She and my aunt knit extra sweaters and sold these. They reared extra turkeys at Christmas time and sold these. I helped with these tasks but not willingly. I hated working in the hen dung and worried would I smell the next day when I went to school, would some of the girls I was looking at know I was working with hens? At the same time I was ashamed at having these thoughts when my mother and aunt were working so hard to pay my school fees.

The pressure built up on me. I had to work around the farmyard before and after I went and came from school. I had to help my mother and aunt with the tasks we did to earn the fees. I had to listen to my mother when she would get angry with me for not studying harder. The worst thing was she was right. I found that by listening in class I could always come very near to the top of my class. So I did not bother to do much studying. My mother suspected this and naturally it made her angry. Her anger in turn made me angry and guilty at the same time.

In spite of being given the privilege of being sent to that Grammar School I did not retain much of what I learnt. But there was one exception. A temporary art teacher put up a print on the wall. I liked the art teacher and was always looking at her body and trying to see down her cleavage. She was a city person and modern in her dress. But while I liked the teacher and her low neckline I did not like the print. It was Van Gogh's Noon Rest, two peasants, a man and a woman lying resting and at peace on a pile of straw in a field. I disliked the print. But I could not stop looking at it. It would not leave me alone. I can see it to this day. When my appreciation of art developed I would go on to admire Van Gogh above all other painters. I would come to believe that Van Gogh was the man, the greatest of all painters. I read his book, Dear Theo. It contained letters to his brother. They made me understand that life, if it was to be worthwhile, was a struggle and also made me realise how little I knew about art, ideas, and the relationship between nature and life and struggle and ideas and art.

But at that stage of my development and with my lack of artistic appreciation all Van Gogh's print did was keep catching my eye and annoying me, at times making me angry and in spite of her low neck line resent the art teacher for putting it up, and even at times going as far as to make me feel the print was attacking me. I did not understand that my reaction to the print represented a great achievement for Van Gogh and his art. Holding the eye and engaging the mind of a youthful rural ignoramus like me was no mean feat. I did not understand that what was happening was that the print, Van Gogh's shapes and strokes of powerful colour, the topics of his paintings, his portrayal of the peasants at peace, were fighting with me, fighting to unleash my potential ability to see the world in all its mad, wonderful, conflicting glory, fighting to free me from seeing things in their literal conventional bourgeois 'reality', fighting to free me to be free, fighting to allow me to see the 'truth' that was greater than the 'truth'.

But maybe there even was more to it than this. Something more directly related to myself. In Van Gogh's letters to his brother he referred to himself as a 'peasant painter'. He spoke of immersing himself in the lives of the peasantry and also the workers whom he painted. At that time I was struggling to escape from the world of my peasant family, maybe Van Gogh's print was confusing me at that time in this struggle. Maybe his embrace of the peasant life hampered my struggle to be free of the peasant life. Maybe his embrace of the positive, rich side of peasant life was an obstacle to me at that time in my life, in that phase of my life and struggle. Maybe his embrace of these things just seemed to be holding me back at that time. I wanted to escape from peasant life. Van Gogh was embracing peasant life or rather one aspect of peasant life. Maybe because I did not understand that Van Gogh was embracing, not peasant life, but rather the positive authentic aspects of peasant life, as a way of rejecting what was phony and superficial in bourgeois life and art, was what was confusing me, was what was alienating me from his print. Maybe I thought he was pushing me back towards peasant life rather than that he was embracing the positive in peasant life in order to liberate himself and us all artistically and liberate me from the negative aspects of peasant life and at the same time defend me from the negative aspects of bourgeois and petit bourgeois life. Whatever it was there was something going on as I could not get that print out of mind.

I wish I knew the name of the art teacher who put up that Van Gogh print. I would like to thank her. I thought of her many years later when I visited Van Gogh's museum in Amsterdam. When I saw Van Gogh's Self Portrait in the gallery in Paris, saw his Starry Night. I stood in front of Van Gogh's self-portrayal and wept. Seeing the Van Gogh print in the art class at the Grammar School in Strabane, seeing the great silverback in the zoo in London, slipping under the wall of the young girl's tent and kissing and touching her and being kissed and touched by her in return, these were all part of my special privileges as the male child. Having these special privileges was not right, not fair to my sisters. But they made me a more complete person and not only that, they strengthened me in my opposition to discrimination and in my determination to fight discrimination in whatever form I met it for the rest of my life. These experiences and these understandings were all part of my male privileges.

CHAPTER 4

DIVIDE AND RULE AND THE SIEGE MENTALITY

IT WAS NOT ONLY MY FAMILY and neighbours and fellow school students who influenced me when I was growing up. There was the wider society with which I interacted. To live in Ireland at that time was to live in a country dominated by a combination of British colonialism and British imperialism and their Protestant unionist allies and the Roman Catholic hierarchy. Colonialism was a system where the major world powers militarily invaded, robbed and plundered and directly ruled the weaker countries and regions of the planet. Imperialism developed out of and in some cases existed simultaneously with, colonialism. Imperialism was a system which, while still using the colonial methods of direct military invasion and rule and outright plundering where it suited it, and could get away with it, also used the capital it accumulated to invest in and buy up the rest of the world and plunder it in this way. It also used its capital to buy up the labour power of the world. Britain was originally a major colonial power and then for the latter part of the 19th century and into the 20th century, the number one colonial imperialist power on the planet.

Ireland had the misfortune to exist cheek by jowl with this monster. British colonialism and British imperialism both plundered Ireland. They cut down its great oak forests and carted them off, they extracted and robbed its agricultural product, they seized the land from the local clans and privatised it. They created and forcibly put in place what was known as the Anglo Irish landlord class. This class helped run the country on behalf of British colonialism and British imperialism. British colonialism and British imperialism forcibly imported and installed the Scottish peasantry, the Ulster Scots, into Ulster in what was known as the Plantation of Ulster. Its aim was to create a loyal population in Ireland, to create a secure foothold for itself in part of Ireland and as part of this lay the basis for divide and rule. Part of this process was seizing the land of the mainly Catholic peasantry and giving it either to the planted mainly Protestant Scots Irish peasantry in the north east or to the Anglo Irish landlord class partly in the north east and also throughout the whole island. The planting of the mainly Protestant Scottish peasantry as a secure foothold for British rule was successful. In spite of the odd occasion such as the 1798 rising led by Henry Joy McCracken, a Protestant and whose forces were mainly Protestant, the divide and rule policy of the British ruling class has continued its hold to this day.

The Anglo Irish landlord class was a vital instrument of rule for British colonialism and British imperialism. They had their houses and land holdings and servants spread across the country. They produced the forces for the legal and political apparatus through which British colonialism and imperialism ruled. They helped recruit forces for the lower ranks of the state apparatus, the police and local militias. This is not to say that every member of this Anglo Irish landlord class was totally in the pocket of British colonialism and British imperialism. There were exceptions, people like Wolfe Tone, Parnell, there were also writers and poets in this class like Yeats, who opposed the butchery of British rule. But in the main this Anglo Irish landlord class was overwhelmingly an agent of British colonialism and British imperialism.

Part of British colonial and imperialist rule over Ireland was the most extreme repression of the mainly Catholic Irish poor as they sought to eat and live. Millions were slaughtered or starved to death. 'To hell or to Connaught' was one of the slogans of British colonialism and British imperialism towards the Irish poor, that is be killed or to be ethnically cleansed from the better land in the east to the rock-strewn, impoverished land in the western province of Connaught. At the same time millions more were shipped abroad, in the death ships to North America and the Caribbean. The repression and slaughter was so great that Ireland was the only country in the world which had less people at the end of the 1800s than it had at the beginning.

The failure of the potato crop in the mid-1800s is blamed for this fall in population. But this is not correct. What happened was British colonialism and British imperialism enforced mass starvation and genocide on the Irish people. During the years of the failure of the potato crop, which was the main staple food of the peasantry, Ireland was producing and exporting enough food, grain, meat etc. to feed its population many times over. But

British colonialism and British imperialism used its military power to seize and export this food, to pay the rent to the Anglo Irish landlord class and also to starve and break the Irish poor.

I once spoke to a very old man and asked him had he ever known anybody who had experienced the Irish starvation. He said he had not but that he had known a man whose grandfather had done so. This man's grandfather had told him that he had walked from Strabane to Derry at the time of the starvation. This was a distance of fourteen miles, and on the way this man had passed sixteen dead bodies on the side of the road, all had died of starvation. This old man told me that many aspects of life, many sayings came from the time of the starvation. There was the saying that somebody was so tight-fisted they would follow a crow a mile to see if it would drop the spud it was holding in its beak. The experience of the starvation could and never should be expected to leave the psychology of the Irish people. As part of my struggle to understand and explain history I would never use the term the 'Irish famine'. To me there was no famine, there was the starvation imposed on the Irish peasantry by British colonialism and British imperialism. There was the genocide of the Irish peasantry imposed by British colonialism and British imperialism.

Along with British colonialism and British imperialism and its Protestant Unionist elites in the north-eastern Scots Irish population, the other major force in Irish society at that time was the Catholic hierarchy. While British colonialism and British imperialism militarily forced the Irish peasantry to hand over their produce to pay their rent to the Anglo Irish landlords, the Catholic hierarchy used their pulpits to the same end. They preached to the Irish Catholic poor that it would be a sin not to pay their rents. The Catholic hierarchy wanted to maintain the stability of the system in which they had some power and from which they drew benefits. The poor could only pay their rent by allowing their non-potato food crops to be seized and taken out of the country. This was what happened. This was the reason for the deaths of millions in the great starvation, not the failure of the potato crop. It was not a famine. It was deliberate mass starvation. The military repression of British colonialism and British imperialism, and the use of their pulpits by the Catholic hierarchy combined were what imposed this genocide on the Irish people. It was a class system that existed in Ireland. The British ruling class sat on top of the pyramid. The Catholic hierarchy helped this British rule. It was also guilty.

The other force, if it could be called a force in Ireland at that time, was the Irish capitalist class. In the south and west this was virtually non-existent and without political or economic power. At best it was a smattering of small producers with no market of any significance. In the North there would later develop a Protestant industrial capitalist class based mainly around engineering and shipbuilding. This class would be an appendage of British capitalism. In reality there was no independent Irish capitalist class of any significance, at the time of the starvation of the genocide.

The situation in Ireland at that time was similar to what exists in many countries of the world today. The populations of today's super exploited countries are ruled over and plundered by colonialism and imperialism. Their populations are starving. Meanwhile their wealth, foodstuffs, minerals, oil, gas etc. are seized and shipped out. Enough wealth is being wasted or seized from these super exploited countries to provide for the entire population of the world. Inevitably, this extreme exploitation, this starvation and repression leads to revolt. This is why Irish history and the history of all the super exploited countries is a history of rebellion and revolt and war.

The British colonial and imperialist classes, the classes which controlled Ireland had the same problem as that of all ruling classes in all countries. They and their stooges and agents were only a small minority, a very small proportion, of the population. The vast majority of the people were the Irish Catholic poor. And these Irish Catholic poor hated the British ruling class which had taken their land in the north east or had made them pay exorbitant rents all over Ireland. And which had brought them repression, starvation and genocide. Anywhere a small minority tries to rule a majority the small minority has the problem of being a minority. And in every case this small minority tries to deal with this problem the same way. That is it seeks to divide the majority amongst themselves – Divide and Rule. The British ruling class became experts at this strategy. They developed it first in Ireland and then took it with them to every corner of the globe they sought to rule. The idea was simple, keep the exploited majority class fighting amongst themselves and they would not be able to unite to fight the exploiting minority class. In Ireland the division that was used was mainly religious – Protestant versus Catholic. Churchill, the British right wing politician and war criminal, explained it bluntly when he explained that when the Irish rise up 'play the Orange card'. In other words turn Protestant against Catholic. It was that conscious and blatant.

In other parts of the world divide and rule was based on many factors. On the person's nationality, the colour of a person's skin, the tribal affiliation, the language they spoke, the shape of their countenance, their religion or different versions of their religion, their gender, whatever difference could be identified was sought out and cultivated by colonialism and imperialism. These systems have the main and overwhelming responsibility for the internecine conflicts, the civil wars, which exist in the world to this day. They deliberately sought out differences and cultivated them.

Divide and rule in Ireland was along two main fault lines. The best known and most recognised, was religious, Catholic versus Protestant. But there was another major fault line – gender. The male was turned against the female. The biological differences were used to put the female into second place and to justify their super exploitation. Colonialism, imperialism, the major organised religions, all practiced discrimination against women, and cultivated division along gender lines, that is keeping control through the special oppression of women and especially the female worker and part of this was using women as cheap or unpaid labour. The colonial and imperialist forces, the Irish elites both economic and religious, the Irish churches and institutions whether Protestant or Catholic, all used gender as a basis for divide and rule and filling their pockets and collection plates. Think about it, where did the money come from to build all those churches that exist in Ireland. The full-time organisers for the churches, the priests and clerics and nuns and clergymen and women, etc. did not go out and work and earn it. And on top of that somebody had to pay for the food, housing and clothing of the churches full time organizers while they were doing their preaching blackmailing and bullying.

Faced with rebellion after rebellion by the Irish poor, British colonialism and British imperialism ever sought a more solid basis for their divide and rule strategy. One major step they took in this regard was the Plantation of Ulster in the early 1600s. This transported Protestant Scottish peasants to the north-east of Ireland, to six of the nine counties of what was the province of Ulster where it 'planted' them. The mainly indigent Catholic peasants were driven off their land and it was given to these mainly Protestant peasants. Or they were driven on to the less productive land. In this way the country's population was more decisively divided between Protestant and Catholic. Divide and rule was given a more solid material base in the very soil itself. Given a more secure foothold.

My family was Protestant. We lived in County Donegal, the most north-western county in Ireland. It would become part of the Republic of Ireland, or Southern Ireland, after the division of the country which arose from the War of Independence in the early 1920s. Southern Ireland declared itself in its constitution to be, and it was, a Catholic state. The Catholic hierarchy dominated education and health and dictated social, political and personal life. Divorce and contraception were illegal. The southern political parties and politicians literally bowed the knee to the Catholic hierarchy. The Catholic hierarchy, like British colonialism and British imperialism also used divide and rule to keep their power.

When Ireland was divided after the War of Independence in the early 1920s, six of the nine counties of Ulster remained under the control of British imperialism, of London. This small political entity had a majority Protestant population. Like the South of Ireland was a Catholic state the

North of Ireland was a Protestant state. Its economy, its state apparatus, its politics were controlled by the Protestant Orange Order machine under the supervision of London. The Catholic minority was a discriminated against minority in a Protestant state.

There were four provinces in Ireland. Ulster, the most north-easterly had nine counties. However to establish a secure northern Protestant state such a state could not be based on the nine counties of Ulster. This would have included too many Catholics in the new state. So the three counties of Donegal, Monaghan and Cavan, which were part of the Province of Ulster, and which had large Catholic populations, were excluded. Our family lived in east Donegal right up against what was to be the border with the North. Our fields ran down to the River Finn, which at that point was the border with the Protestant North. The result was that my family and the rest of the Protestant population in East Donegal were excluded from the new Northern Protestant state. The Donegal Protestants were bitter about this but their fear of being acted against by the Catholic majority in the Southern state was so great that they maintained their loyalty to Britain and they went along. Also while excluded from the Northern state their proximity to it resulted in these Protestants still looking to ally themselves with and to get support from the Protestant population over the border in Northern Ireland, and to get some crumbs from the table of the Northern state which was still under British rule.

Maybe my ancestors were not part of this Northern Protestant Scots Irish stock which was planted in the north-east of Ireland. Neither our name nor DNA were Scottish. But this was no longer relevant. The British ruling class, which ruled all of Ireland at the time of the plantation had established their rule in such a way as to create a northern Protestant population which in the main had the better land and marginal privileges in that area. This Protestant population saw itself as being dependent upon British colonialism and British imperialism for support against the Catholic population on whose land they had been 'planted', and they therefore tended to be loyal to London, hence to be 'Loyalists'. My Protestant family had this outlook. After the division of Ireland into two states in the early 1920s and them being left in the Catholic South this view was reinforced. They more than ever saw themselves as surrounded by a majority Catholic population in a southern Catholic sectarian state and living under a state of siege not only in that new state but in Ireland as a whole. My family, like the Protestant population as a whole North and South, had a siege mentality, and like all people who have a siege mentality, they were damaged.

There were differences within the Protestant population in Ireland as a whole and also in the South. After the War of Independence and the establishment of the Republic of Ireland in the southern twenty-six counties, there remained a Protestant population throughout the Republic. This was mainly in the north west but there were pockets of Protestants scattered throughout the new southern state also. This population in turn had differences within it. There were the better off sections some in the countryside and some in the cities, owners of shops and somewhat larger farms. They were a minority of the Protestants and they mainly lived away from the border. They tended to keep their heads down. They could see no way to impose themselves as part of the ruling elite again. However the majority of the Protestants in the South were less well-off farmers and unskilled workers who lived close to the border with the North and they thought they could get some support from the northern Protestant state and so tended to raise their head to some extent and to express their Protestantism and loyalism to a greater degree.

There was not a sectarian divide in the South comparable to the sectarian divide in the North where the state was built on this foundation, but it still existed because of the harsh Catholic hierarchy domination. The main reason for the difference between North and South was that the Protestant minority in the South was a much smaller proportion of the population and as a result not a threat to the state. The ruling Catholic state knew this and tolerated the Protestant minority and the small number of Orange lodges. The elite of the Protestant minority knew this. They paid lip service to being loyal to Britain but they did not march and parade. They looked after number one and encouraged people like my uncle and the less well-off Protestants around the border to march and parade.

My family were part of these poor Protestant farmers on the border. This reality and the mentality that came from this was central to my family's world. Its effect could not be exaggerated. While its seeds were deliberately and consciously sown and cultivated by British colonialism and British imperialism it also had its roots in the fear, conscious or unconscious, that the land on which the Scots Irish had been planted, which had been forcibly taken from the Catholic peasantry would be taken back, that the marginal privileges some of the Protestant population had been given would be taken away, that the people who had been displaced would rise up. Living with this defensive mentality meant that every new idea and development was treated with suspicion. Nothing was examined on its own merits, but instead looked at to see if it threatened to break the siege, if it might pull down the walls of the fortress. My family had this outlook. Fear of everything new extended into every area of their lives. They tried to instil this in me. I came to resent, then hate, this way of thinking. It threatened to cut me off from all that was new, exciting and progressive in the world.

I tried to tackle this way of looking at things with my mother when I visited her in later years. I took with me a video of a play of the short story by the Irish writer James Joyce – The Dead. Many believe it the best short story ever written. I put it in the video player and sat down with my mother to watch it. I thought she would relate to it because it was about a dinner party in an upper class house and she liked to see the old furnishings and mannered ways. My mother herself had been a servant in such houses. The video was not five minutes playing until my mother turned to me and said: 'Do you think they would be Protestants or Catholics?' This was a brutal example of how the great things in life were cut off from the Protestant population by the siege mentality and religious sectarianism. I did not think whether the diners were Protestant or Catholic, I was interested in where at one point one of the diners got up and left the dinner saying she was going to hear the socialist James Connolly speak at a meeting. This was totally missed by my mother. It was not her fault. It was the result of the all-pervasive propaganda machine of British colonialism and imperialism.

The siege mentality way of looking at things was accompanied by the idea of Protestant superiority. I was continually told that Catholics could not be trusted, they were lazy, they were dirty, and on and on. This indoctrination originated with British colonialism and British imperialism and their divide and rule strategy and it was fed to the Protestant population by the Protestant organisations such as the Protestant political parties, the Orange Order with their hundreds of lodges, and the Protestant churches. The British ruling class controlled these organisations and saw to it that they pumped out this divisive poison. The Protestant population had to be kept, not only in fear and under threat, and in a state of siege, but also believing they were superior. On occasion this divide and rule policy would break down such as in the 1798 rebellion led by the Protestant Henry Joy McCracken, the 1932 unemployed movement in Belfast, when Protestants and Catholics united and rebelled, but these movements were put down by state violence and control through the divide and rule policy was re-established. When I was told that the Catholic population could not be trusted I thought well what could be expected after all that had been done to them by British colonialism and imperialism over the centuries.

Many years later I would visit the USA. In that country I saw that the majority of European Americans, like the majority of Protestants in Northern Ireland, also had a siege mentality. They were indoctrinated by the European American ruling class into thinking they had to at all times keep their guard up against the Native Americans whose land had been stolen; against the African Americans, who for the three hundred years of slavery were paid no wages; against the Hispanic population who were the low paid workers, and in some cases whose land had also been stolen; and the males were told they had to stand against the less well paid, or in many cases, unpaid, female workers.

Of course part of the labour of the European American working class was also stolen. But the propaganda machine of US capitalism was powerful and along with this its economy produced a sufficient surplus, which combined with the looted wealth from its foreign invasions and occupations allowed it to make some concessions to sections of the European American working class. This tended to prevent the majority of the European American working class from seeing reality. The workers' leaders encouraged this low class consciousness and state of siege by their refusal to organise and lead a united working class movement. So like the Protestants of Northern Ireland, the majority of European Americans also lived in a state of siege. They too tended to fear all that was new, all that was spontaneous, anything that might break down the walls of the fortress.

As part of this siege mentality European America, like the Protestant population in Northern Ireland, feared their own mental and bodily spontaneities and rhythms. Every spontaneous impulse and instinct, every spontaneous movement, every spontaneous thought or half thought, all had to be filtered first before it was expressed. All this had to be done to make sure the fortress walls would not be broken. One result of this was that in the main, the music and dance and art of European America was constrained and tended to lack genuine organic spontaneous life. In dance and music the hips and breasts were not to move. The bum in particular was not to shake. The women's rear end was especially dangerous as it could attract the economically, socially, politically, racially and religiously indiscriminate penis and this could pair the 'wrong' woman with the 'wrong' man and throw the whole system of property and power and control and racism and divide and rule out of whack.

But in the 1960s in the USA the African American people broke out of their imprisonment, stormed into the European American world and cracked the whole siege wide open. They took to the streets in the African American revolt and brought with them their explosion of revolution with their dance, art and music, the jazz, the rock and roll and the blues. African Americans had just about nothing to defend in America. They did not have to be always rigid and proper, they did not have to censor their ideas, keep their asses and bodies rigid and unmoving to maintain the system. They had little at stake in the system. So they were not afraid of the new and the life and the spontaneous, they could shake their asses and breasts and bodies and create new sounds and calls and rhythms. As they rebelled they transformed the music and dance of the world. Including my world. They also shook up the Irish dance with its sexually oppressed rigidity. 'Riverdance' would later explode across the world. It was no accident that its original leading proponent was from Chicago where he had been influenced by the African American tap dancers and culture.

In these years of the 1950s and '60s in the Catholic dance halls of Northern Ireland and even some of the Protestant dance halls some asses also began to shake. In one large dance hall the owners tried to stand against the stream and hired staff to try and force the dancers to restrain themselves. One of the asses that began to shake in the North of Ireland was mine. The siege mentality was cracking. I was with it all the way. My world was looking in a different direction. Hammer in hand to bring down the fortress wall, shaking ass to break the siege, I was part of this new movement.

I backed away from the music and rhythms of the Protestant world. While I was attracted to the skirl of the pipes and their wildness, I was repelled by their right wing political ideas and their rigid marching military style straight lines, their being used to express Protestant dominance and division. The right wing, militaristic, sectarian ideas which dominated the Protestant pipe bands put me off the pipes. Even later when there was an effort to have Protestant and Catholic bands play together it just could not make it. The sectarianism was stronger than the music.

The divide and rule strategy of the British ruling class was most damaging to the Catholic population. It drove millions of them from their land. It excluded them from many positions in the economy. For a time it made their religion illegal. The Catholic population suffered much worse under British rule and the divide and rule strategy than the Protestant population. This was the case even though for a time the Presbyterian population also suffered discrimination.

Another factor which led to this was the role of the Catholic Church hierarchy, the other major power in Ireland at that time along with British colonialism and British imperialism. The Catholic Church was originally the church of feudalism. But when capitalism became the dominant system on the world stage the Catholic Church adapted and became the main church of capitalism. As such its hierarchy had enormous power and also had its own interests worldwide. And in Ireland, as elsewhere, these interests of the undemocratic all male hierarchy did not always coincide with the interests of the members of the church.

This hierarchy indoctrinated its membership into believing that unless it followed its repressive rules it would burn in hell forever. It used this ideological terrorism and its apparatus of full-time organisers, its nuns, priests, bishops, cardinals, popes, its property, to drive home this threat. Then it offered an escape route. This was to join and support the Catholic Church, go to its confessions, pay it money and do what it was told. This blackmail, this terrorism, was the way it kept control over its 'flock', the way it kept hundreds of millions of people in its organisation. It then used this organisation, these hundreds of millions, today over one billion, to seek to achieve its objectives.

One of these objectives in Ireland at that time was to use its position there to reconvert the English ruling class and society back to Catholicism. To this end the Catholic Church played a dishonest opportunist game with its base in Ireland. At the time of the 1916 uprising in Dublin against British rule, to maintain its efforts to influence the British elites, the Catholic hierarchy in the Vatican praised the 'zeal' with which the Catholic hierarchy in Ireland had supported the suppression of the uprising. Later, after the murder of the 1916 leaders had swung a large proportion of the Catholic population against British rule and in support of the War of Independence, the Catholic Church changed its tune, paid lip service to Irish independence and made a deal with the new Irish twenty-six county state. In return for supporting this new state it got control over much of its workings and was able to have it declared a Catholic state.

The Catholic hierarchy never put its resources behind the struggle to end British rule. It wanted to remain attached to the British imperialist power to have a better chance of re-converting it back to Catholicism. The Catholic population was manipulated and its interests sacrificed to this end and to the overall ends of the power and wealth of the Catholic hierarchy and machine. The most influential powers in Ireland, British colonialism and British imperialism, and the Roman Catholic Church hierarchy, all exploited and repressed and divided the population and one result of this was the Protestant people remaining in their state of siege.

While divide and rule most definitely damaged the Catholic people more than the Protestant people, it also damaged the Protestant people and especially the Protestant working class. It prevented them from seeing that their own economic and class interests were separate from the Protestant employers' interests, and again and again cut across the Protestant working class uniting with the Catholic working class and fighting for working class interests both Protestant and Catholic.

In return for giving marginal privileges in jobs and housing to a section of the Protestant workers, the employers got a more docile workforce, one trained in the ideas of the siege and to stick with their boss and not speak out. 'Stick with your own kind', I was told again and again. This of course meant your own religion, not your own class. And this way of looking at things benefited and was used by all employers, Protestant and Catholic. It lowered all workers' class consciousness and weakened working class unity and so hurt the wages and conditions of all workers, Protestant and Catholic, and increased the profits of all employers, Protestant and Catholic.

My family got some marginal privileges from being Protestants. My mother and her sisters got jobs as servants in the big houses of the Protestant landed gentry and capitalist class. My mother's brother, my uncle, got a job in a management position in a local woollen mill. My sisters would later get jobs in Protestant businesses. But these marginal privileges did not make up for the damage that was done by the siege mentality which so much blocked access to the progressive ideas in life. And also to class consciousness.

As I entered my early teens I found the 'Protestant' way of looking at things harder and harder to accept. It got to the point where I had had enough. The first outright breach, believe it or not, took place in a clothes shop in Strabane. I was fifteen. It was over a new suit. Up to that time my mother controlled the money and so determined what I wore. Under the influence of the siege mentality Protestant males tended to cling longer to the old fashions and colours such as tweeds and suits with the wide trouser bottoms of the time. New styles threatened the siege. I hated the old styles.

The Protestant shop owner knew our family was Protestant and that we were small farmers. He brought down the usual tweed suits with their wide trouser bottoms. I'd had enough. I cracked and spoke out. 'I want a black suit with tight trousers.' My mother was astounded. 'You cannot have that. That is what them corner boys wear. You will shame us altogether.' Corner boys was the term used to refer to young men, mostly Catholic, who could not get jobs and would spend much of their day standing on the street corners. Imagine the effect on people who cannot get a job and stand with empty pockets day after day on a street corner. Imagine the effect on their family and social and personal lives.

My mother tried to get me to back down on the suit. The shop owner, after first helping her, then went silent. I would soon be paying for my own clothes and I suppose he did not want to risk losing my future business. He left my mother out on a limb. I was seeing the cowardice of the small business class. After some time and seeing that I was not going to budge my mother said: 'Well I suppose there is no point in getting him something he will not wear. What have you got in what he is talking about?' The shop owner brought out a number of black suits with tight trousers. So, I thought, he had clothes for Protestants and clothes for Catholics. Even his stock was sectarian. I walked out of the shop with my black suit and tight trousers. With these I looked like a modern person and in the Northern Ireland of that time, like a Catholic. It was a blow to the siege mentality.

Probably prompted by this rebellion of mine over the suit, steps were taken to try and bring me further into the world of Protestantism and the Orange Order. These steps were meant to give me a wider view of my family's world and how I could benefit from playing a role in, being part of that world. I was the nephew of the master of the Orange Order in East Donegal. I should be groomed for a lower level or middle level role in the system. My sisters were not promoted in this way. There were no Grand Mistresses of Orange Orders. Eventually they were to develop women's

Orange Orders but these were mainly confined to making tea and sandwiches for the males. No steps were taken to groom my sisters for leading roles. My sister Mary was one of the few women to play a leading role in Protestant politics in later years. She did so because of her intelligence and will and extreme diplomacy and by allowing the men to overall still be in charge.

The Orange Order lodge in Lifford needed a new banner. My uncle organised a member with a car, made a list of better-off Protestants and set off to ask them for donations. I was taken along as part of my grooming. Most of the people my uncle approached were big farmers or merchants and all had money. They tended to live in the large square rectory type houses in the countryside and had servants. I had never been in such places before.

The owner of the first house greeted my uncle: 'Hello Willie. How are you? Is this Bobby's young fella? He is big for his age.' Always the phony flattery, the soft soap, the lubrication for the exploitation. He ordered his servant: 'Here Victoria, get these men a cup of tea.' He spoke to his servant like she was not wanting to give us tea and he had to intervene to get her to act on our behalf. I thought my mother had probably been ordered about like this and I did not like it. I looked round at the soft-cushioned armchairs and the carpets. The floor in the main room, the kitchen, in our house was of rough stone flags chiselled out of a quarry up on top of the hill. You could not take your shoes off and the dogs would not lie on it because it was so cold. But this man had carpets. How come? Weren't we all Protestants, weren't we all the 'one kind'.

'Well what can I do for you Willie?' My uncle replied: 'Well the Lodge needs a new banner and we are trying to see if we can raise the funds. I am wondering if you could see your way to make a donation.' 'Of course, of course Willie, you know you do not have to ask twice.' And with that he pulled a chequebook out of his pocket, wrote a cheque and handed it over to my uncle. I had never seen a chequebook before. We did not even have a bank account. I was also surprised to see how easily the man had handed over the money. It was only years later I realised that I had been watching a member of a better off and more conscious class handing over funds to an organisation that defended his class interests. He was not making a donation he was making an investment.

The rich merchant farmer, he owned a wholesale business as well as his big farm, then went on: 'Willie, have you seen what is going on in America? Them black boys are trying to get up, civil rights and that. They had better watch out over there. If them black boys get up they will never get them put down again. But it is not only that. If them boys get up some of these boys here might want to get up too.' As he said this he jerked his thumb back over his shoulder.

'And it might not be only the other kind. Some of our own boys might get ideas above their station too. That is what is so important about your organisation Willie. It teaches the Protestant workingman his place. That they are better sticking with their own kind. We will look after them. If they started to think about getting up, if they started to get ideas that they could do things for themselves it could be bad.'

This Protestant employer was not only giving my uncle a cheque, he was telling him what he and his organisation should say to the Protestant working class, he was giving my uncle the 'line' along with the cheque. I also got the impression he was talking to me, giving me the line too, grooming me too. This angered me.

By this time we had the electricity and the radio and I had heard on the news about the US civil rights movement. I agreed with what the black people were demanding – equal rights and to stop being beaten and killed. It was only fair. Yet here was this man saying that he was against this. And on top of that telling my uncle he should be against it too. But not only that, he was telling my uncle how important it was for the Orange Order to tell this to the Protestant workers. He was telling my uncle how important his organisation, the Orange Order, was in keeping the Protestant workers in their place and thinking in a sectarian way.

His words were like bombs going off in my head. That was the finish of the Orange Order for me. I did not agree with what I was hearing. The Scoutmaster had failed to convince me that he was right and Darwin was wrong. Now this rich farmer merchant employer was failing to convince me that racism and the suppression of black people in the US was right. And closer to home he was failing to convince me that sectarianism and the Orange Order were right. And if what he had said was not enough, this rich farmer and merchant and employer was not even a member of the Orange Order himself. In fact just about none of the better off farmers and merchants we visited for donations were active members of the Orange Order. They lived in their big houses on their big farms with their mainly Protestant workers and servants, gave the Orange Order money and told it what to think. But they left it to the poorer Protestants like my uncle to do the dirty work, the grunt organising work. I was becoming more alienated from the views of the Protestantism and Orangism of my family by the day. I rejected the divide and rule and the siege mentality. I looked at these rich Protestant farmers in their big square houses, with their carpets, in their tweeds, with their low paid servants, and seethed.

One thing struck me out of the whole thing about the siege mentality and the word siege. Part of the history that was used to cultivate sectarianism amongst sections of the Protestant population was the glorification of the Siege of Derry of 1688/1689. This was when Protestant forces successfully defended the city against Catholic forces. The forces that rule the North go to great lengths to celebrate the Siege of Derry. On the 12th of August every year there is a Protestant parade in the city to celebrate how the city had held out. This is the only way the word siege exists amongst the Protestant ideology, the Protestant consciousness. When much more central to the situation and interests of the Protestant working class is another siege entirely. That is the siege mentality which flows from the sectarian divide and rule policies of British colonialism and British imperialism and which is used to keep the Protestant working class down. The last thing the powers that are in the North and Britain want is any talk about the siege mentality and how it helps them continue to rule and exploit. It would be better for the Protestant working class and the working class as a whole if there was less talk of the Siege of Derry and talk more of the siege mentality, its origins, and the damage it does.

CHAPTER 5

CONFLICTS AND CALLUSES

I T WAS A BEAUTIFUL spring morning. The sun was shining and the dew was on the grass. I was standing in the kitchen looking down over the fields to the river. Its waters glinted in the sun. I was 16 years old. It was 1960. The beauty and peace of the scene contrasted with the harshness of my thoughts. I had made a decision. I had enough of working before and after school, of feeling guilty for not studying harder, of having my mother and aunt work so hard to pay my school fees. I had had enough of the school teaching me reading, writing and arithmetic but not teaching me about life.

I braced myself and turned to my mother who was putting the duck eggs on the stove to boil for breakfast. 'Mother, I am leaving school. I am going to come home and work on the farm.' My mother was shocked and very strongly opposed. She wanted me to stay at school, get qualifications for some sort of white-collar job and keep the farm as well. She thought her previous job as a servant and my father's as a small farmer did not have what she considered enough respect. She wanted 'better' for me. A white collar 'respectable' job and keep the farm. How badly I was to let her down.

'John, John, you have to think long and hard about this. If you leave school you will not be able to go back. You should stay on and finish and get a good job and we can keep the farm too. Sure that teacher he said to me at the last prize day that if you stayed at school you could have what he called an honours degree on any subject you wanted.'

That night we talked it over with my uncle and aunt and sisters. All said I should stay at school. But I argued my case and eventually there was no great resistance to my determination to leave. There was no tradition of higher level education in our family. And there was also the money of it.

Things were not easy on that front. If I left there would be no more fees to pay and not only that, I would be another pair of hands on the farm. So reluctantly it was agreed. I would leave in June. As this decision was taken neither my family nor I had any idea how different things would turn out from what was envisaged there in our kitchen that night.

But my mother did not totally concede. She insisted that I go to an agricultural school for a year to prepare me for work on the farm. She was doing her best to get me 'an education'. This was, naturally enough, a Protestant agricultural school. It was in the Southern county of Tipperary. I did an examination and got a grant. I learnt little at that school about farming. Half of every day was spent working on the school's farm and not getting paid. The other half was spent listening to lectures.

Many of these lectures were on religion. The school openly said its priority was teaching religion not agriculture. After a few of these lectures I began to speak up. On one occasion the headmaster and preacher who was in charge of the school asked the assembled student body why we thought people believed in God. For a time nobody answered. Then I raised my hand. He called on me. I said it was because people were afraid of going to hell. This was so obvious to me. What other reason could there be? This preacher went into a loud scornful outburst of laughter meant to humiliate and intimidate me. Afraid of going to hell, of course not, people believed in God because they loved God. I said nothing but was even more convinced that preachers and people who believed in God were not too prepared to honestly discuss.

The school organised a day trip to Dublin. It was the first time I was in that city. I was impressed by how busy it was and how the men and women were so fashionably dressed. I had no idea then that I would spend years in that city and how much a role it would play in my life. Before we left to go back to the school on Saturday night I saw that the Sunday papers were on sale. The Sunday papers on sale on Saturday night! I was shocked. This made me think that things were not always as they seemed or as they were made out to be. It was worth the day trip to Dublin for that alone.

I began to play rugby at that school. And it was there I got my first concussion. I was taken to the local hospital. I could not remember who I was, where I was, what had happened. It was frightening. While in the hospital a nun came round and sprayed me with so-called 'holy water'. By that time I was recovering. After a few minutes she rushed back and apologised and explained that she did not know I was not a Catholic and hoped I was not offended. I said nothing as I felt I had nothing to say. It never occurred to me to feel offended. I felt that I could only be offended if I believed that the so-called holy water meant something. To me it was just water. And she had not sprayed enough on me to wet me.

My injury meant that I had to leave that school early and return home. I began work on my uncle's farm. Initially I settled in okay. Every morning I would get up and get out the buckets and the wooden stool and help milk the cows. Then I would clean out their dung and wheel it to the midden in the wheelbarrow. Then depending on the time of year I would help with the planting of the spuds, the making of the hay, the cutting of the oats and wheat and round again to the planting of the spuds. In between times I would be cutting hedges, digging drains, repairing barns and byres, the daily maintenance of the farm.

But while I was settling in I was not content. It is true I would get small interludes of peace. These came when I was working alone. Digging a drain, cutting a hedge, working near the flow of water, the smell of a cut branch, the occasional moment when I would lie down and rest and look at the sky. My two dogs would go with me everywhere. On cold days they would look up at me in reproach for having them out in that weather. They would pull my coat down from the hedge and lie on it. I felt guilty for keeping them out in the cold. But they wanted above all to stay with me. My relationship with my dogs was in a way closer than my relationship with my family. They did not try to shape my views, they did not ask for any commitment. I was able to be at one with them. Sometimes they would look up into my eyes and their expression made clear they wanted to be able to talk to me. At such times I would yearn to be able to talk to them. I also thought that from their expression the only reason they could not talk was physical not intellectual. They had thoughts. It was just that they could not express them in precise sounds.

When I would be working out in the fields away from the house my mother or aunt would bring me out my afternoon tea and bread. The tea would be in a small tin container with a wire handle. I would sit on a rock or in the hedge and eat. My dogs would sit with me with their ears up hoping for some food. I would always give them bits of my jam filled sandwich. These too were moments of peace.

However my mind was never fully on my work. It was always drifting or thinking of something else. My hands may have been digging a drain with a spade, or cutting a hedge with a billhook or cutting rushes with a scythe but at just about all times my mind would be fumbling to try and see who and what I was, where I was in the world, how the world worked. Gradually and unstoppably the dominant theme in my thoughts became the struggle to understand the world, to understand my place and role in that world. I did not know.

On one occasion I was weeding a field of turnips. My legs were protected with sacks which were tied on them with cords. I crawled up and down between the drills. It was slow work. I had to select the weeds from the turnip plants and pull out the weeds. For the one and only time I became totally absorbed in what I was doing. I forgot about the world and how it worked, I forgot about not knowing who I was relative to the rest of the world, I forgot about not knowing my place or role in the world. For a few moments I was not searching and uneasy. For a few minutes I was completely at peace. Then I suddenly became aware that I was at peace. When I did so I pulled myself up with a jerk. I did not want this peace. This was the road to me ending up with the peace of a dulled mind, of a passivity of spirit and intellect. It was the peace of a slow death. It was a bovine peace. It was chewing the mental and spiritual cud. I did not want that..

I wondered about this. I did not look down on people who were content with the soil and the land and working with these, being absorbed by these. A bit of me wished I could be content to live this way. But I was not. I did not know why. I worried that if I became content crawling with sack-protected legs up and down turnip drills with my mind empty except for what it took to select the weeds from the turnip plants I would never find a more fulfilling and challenging role in the world. I had nothing against turnips and weeds and having my legs protected by sacks, nothing against this work. I had nothing against people who did this work. If I had been content with this it would have been one thing. But I was not. I hungered for something different. I needed to know my place in the world. So I broke my crawling, turnip weeding peace. I drove myself back into my usual state, searching, wondering, scratching, unhappy, without contentment, without peace in the world. I crushed the peace of allowing myself to be part of the turnip drills of rural Donegal. I felt better. Such peace was dangerous. I welcomed back my troubled mind.

Our farm had a four-year rotation. A different crop was planted in each field every four years. There were no artificial fertilisers or pesticides. The animal's manure was the fertiliser. I did not know it then but I was eating organic food. I did not know there was such a thing as organic food. However the corporations soon penetrated our world and with them their poisonous chemicals. The old people complained. 'Them spuds are not like before. They used to be balls of flour. Now look at them.' I thought these old people were just against any change. I scoffed at them. It took me years to realise that on this they were right. There were many things where change, the capitalist driven change, was not for the better.

My uncle continued to work the land with the horses. But he was getting old and would not be able to walk up and down the steep fields much longer. For a time he tried to resist getting a tractor. He correctly said that they were bad for the land as their weight prevented the soil from breathing. But he could not stop the mechanisation of the country and the farm. Tractors were more productive than horses if you left out the long term negative effects on the soil and that they used diesel and lubricating oil which damaged the environment. Tractors meant less hard work for the farmer. Capitalism equalled tractors, equalled 'progress'. The farm horses and the men who could work them were melting away.

Our farm had to get a tractor for another reason: myself. My uncle and mother and aunt knew that I would not continue to work on the farm with horses. Anyway I did not know how to work with horses. There would have to be a tractor. The largest Protestant-owned garage in the county was contacted. Buying from 'your own kind', from your own religion, was part of sectarianism's economic base.

The owner of the garage himself showed up. This was unusual. It would normally have been one of his sales people. He was given tea in the parlour. That was also unusual. He started with the flattery. How my uncle had such a good place. How he had heard so much about him, how he was the best horse man in the county, how he was sorry he had never met him before. I was not fooled. He could have met him before if he wished. Flattery was one of the weapons the upper classes used to control and exploit those they saw as the lower classes. I felt humiliated for my uncle. A tractor was bought. It was well maintained with a re-conditioned engine. The garage owner was making sure my uncle got a good machine. It would be bad for his business to sell my uncle, a leader of the Orange Order, a heap of scrap. I would later meet this garage owner on the street in Letterkenny and he would ask me into a hotel where he bought me lunch. He was trying to consolidate his position with me whom he saw as a possible future influential Orange Order leader. He misjudged the situation.

The decision to get the tractor seemed simple enough to me. But I was leaving something out. My uncle's horses would have to go. And those horses were a central part of his life, his therapy and his art. They knew his every touch on the reins, his every instruction. They knew every click of his tongue, every order of his voice, his every nuance and tone. A great organic and powerful, and yes emotional, and yes affectionate system of communication had been built up over the years between the horses and my uncle as he had turned them at the ends of the fields, steered them in their straight furrows and swathes, guided them as they pulled the carts up the steep lanes, shoed their hooves, clipped their coats, brushed their manes, polished their harness.

Two horse dealers came and bought my uncle's three horses. These dealers were humped over with the craft which came with their profession. They put their own rope halters on my uncle's horses and led them away. All that was left to my uncle were the horses' harnesses and empty stalls. It was terrible. To this day I can see their tails and hind ends swaying as they disappeared down round the corner of the lane. They put up no resistance.

They had no idea they had just seen my uncle for the last time, that they had just heard the sound of his voice for the last time, that they had just felt the stroke of his hand for the last time. My uncle on the other hand knew he would never see them again and he knew what lay ahead.

His horses were going to France to be killed in a slaughter house. His relationship with them was about to be destroyed forever with a violent blow to the head. Jack, Nell and Bob, would soon no longer exist. As the extent of the destruction that lay ahead penetrated my imagination I was overwhelmed. What had taken years to build up between intelligent beings, my uncle and his horses, the communication and affection between them, was going to be shattered, destroyed, blown apart in a few seconds in a dirty, blood-stained slaughter house in another land. I closed my eyes to try and avert my thoughts from the shattered skulls, the broken bones, the spurting blood, the horses' howls of pain and terror as they were destroyed. They would not even be destroyed together. One would inevitably be first. The others would see. The others would hear. The others would know. For the first time I began to realise what was happening and for what I was partly responsible. I tried to close down my imagination.

I could not stop thinking what was going through my uncle's head. His horses which had been so much part of him, were gone for good. We had sent them off to be killed. And not only was he going to miss them for themselves and his relationship with them but what was he going to do with the skills he had developed to work and communicate with them? These skills were now useless. Not only was the pain of loss engulfing him but an enormous vacuum had opened in his life. And this was partly because of me, to keep me there at home on the farm.

As I stood there looking at my uncle with the image of the disappearing and soon to be murdered horses in my mind I felt I would be crushed by my role in this tragedy, in this pain. There could no longer be any doubt about it. I would have to stay and work with the tractor on the farm now. The decisive reason my uncle had sacrificed his horses, was to keep me at home and working on the farm. I would have to keep my end of the bargain. There was no other thing for it. At least that was what I thought at the time.

But the more I considered what was going on the more I could see that under the present system of things the killing of the horses was inevitable. I did not know how to work with them. I and the farm had to enter the modern world with its tractors. It was a brutal insoluble reality, it was cruel in the extreme in its contradiction. The only alternative would have been for me to have learnt to work the horses, to have set myself back into the old world, watched as the new world moved ahead. In the process I would inevitably have been forced to even more resist the modern world. I would have become an eccentric ploughman in dirty clothes, dirty hair, a toothless grin, mean, laughing in a mirthless bitter cackling laugh, while the world went ahead on its tractors' capitalist wheels. Only a different world could have averted the tragedy and at that time I knew of no different world.

I could not talk to my uncle about the loss of his horses so the gap between us widened. If only we could have sat down and talked about how much it had hurt him to get rid of them and wept together. But to do so would have been to talk to each other about our emotions, our pain, our feelings. I did not know, my uncle did not know, how to do this. To do so was thought to be a sign of weakness and was not done. The men did not share their pain and feelings in our house, the men did not weep in our house. The pain of the horses' going went unarticulated, unshared. Thoughts in our minds could not become words. The gap between my uncle and I widened. That was not good.

I handled the trauma in my usual way. I closed my mind to what had happened. I stunted and cauterised my emotions and feelings. I tried to blot out all thought of the hurt to my uncle. I averted my eyes from the places in the fields and lanes where he had turned his horses. The pain and guilt was too great. I dealt with the pain in the same way that I dealt with the pain that came from my struggles with my mother and my family over our different views. I again stunted and cauterised my emotions and feelings. In doing so I was damaging and hardening myself psychologically and emotionally. I was also increasingly, if only half consciously, being forced towards the realisation that farming and Lifford were not for me.

But the fullness of that understanding was in the future. In the meantime I tried my best to settle into my work on the farm. The physical part was not bad. I was big, six foot tall and strong. I could carry the 112 pound sacks of corn up the thirteen steps to my uncle's barn, I could carry and load the fifty-six pound bags of potatoes onto the tractor and trailer, I could cut the corn and the rushes with the scythe. No, the problem was I was with my uncle and mother and aunt most of every day and so the differences in our ideas and approach to things became more obvious and acute and painful. I was not prepared to keep my mouth shut and go along. I considered that to do so would have been an insult and a disrespect to my family and to myself.

The amount of the work I did on my uncle's farm was not a problem. I was not lazy. But there was conflict over the quality of the work. My uncle wanted it done perfectly, every drill straight as an arrow, every furrow and swathe the same. He felt humiliated when people would go past on the main road and think that he was responsible for the crooked drills and furrows and swathes. When he had worked the fields with his horses he had been proud when the passers-by had seen the quality. His ploughed fields were his art exhibitions. And there was no impressionism in my uncle's art exhibitions, all had to be straight and complete and of a part. I did not care whether the drills were crooked or not, my argument was that as long as the ploughed field was brown at the end that was okay. He would get angry at this, but as he could not drive the tractor there was nothing he could do. I was too young and immature and unthinking to recognise the validity of my uncle's grievance at the time. Why should a person not want to be proud of their work? But the problem was my uncle wanted me to do the work his way, to create the art he created with his work. This was impossible because I had a different head and different thoughts.

Another point of conflict in our relationship was how we dealt with the economics of the farm. The animals and the produce were bought and sold by negotiating. Or as I increasingly thought of it by lying, the seller saying the product was worth more and the buyer saying it was worth less. I had seen this before with my father in the fairs and had not disliked it. This was because of the theatrical aspect and the drama of the fairs and also because I was younger. But my uncle was not good at this. Maybe it was that, like me, he was not into the 'lying'. I came to hate the dishonesty of the dealing. I remember the field I was standing in, it was called the Toberdoney, I remember the colour of the cow my uncle and the buyer were lying about, it was a roan with long horns, when I realised that I did not want to have anything to do with this way of making a living, this lying, as I increasingly saw it. Under my breath I said to myself: 'I do not want this way.' I did not realise at the time that 'this way' was the inevitable workings of rural capitalism at that time.

My uncle tried to pass on the buying and selling to me. I saw the reality. I tried to set a price and that was that and no negotiation, no lying. But this was a complete failure as nobody believed that a price was set and that was that. They just thought that I was trying another way of negotiating. Trying harder to bluff. Usually when I would not budge the prospective buyer would just walk away. There was no other way to buy and sell our animals and produce under the existing system other than 'lying'. My uncle and I were trapped in that system, that rural capitalism. I was being unfair both to him and to myself.

While these issues would continually surface, my conflict with my family was even more general and fundamental and also more political. My uncle and mother and aunt were conservatives. They believed that the system that existed was the best that could be under the circumstances, that it would only cause trouble to try and change it. They believed that the way to live was to find your place in the existing status quo. This meant in my family's case, the East Donegal Protestant status quo, it meant to keep in with the Protestant powers that be, and get what you could that way. Had they not made progress in the world with this approach? Why should it not work for me also? Change was not possible so knuckle down and accept what was what. This was their view. I could not do this. I believed the world could be changed for the better. I did not know how or to what but I believed it could and for some reason I could not give up this belief.

This difference led to continual disagreement and argument. I did not know a fraction of what I was talking about. At the same time my family were very convinced of their ideas. In their opinion they had the evidence to back them up. The farm was no longer in debt. It was true that we still had no bank account or surplus but the way my family looked at it was that we were getting by and even making progress. This was in spite of every year it being a struggle to make ends meet, in spite of our financial difficulties keeping my uncle and mother and aunt continuously in a state of worry and regular talk of the threat of the workhouse, in spite of all this leaving little room for joy in our home. In spite of all this they still thought that the advantage of sticking with the Protestant powers that be and their system was an open and shut case. I did not. But I had no alternative.

My conflict was most intense with my mother. I was her only son and she was not going to let me go without the most ferocious fight. In this she used all her intelligence and will. She was a very strong woman. But she must be given the greatest credit for how she acted in this struggle. One thing she never did. After my uncle died and my mother came to legally own the family farm she never once used her ownership of the farm to try and force me to adopt her ideas. Not only that, she kept trying to sign the farm over to me without any conditions. I resisted as I knew if I accepted there would be the danger that along with ownership of the farm I would take on the thinking of the small farmer. My mother was a very principled woman, an outstanding woman.

But this did not mean we did not have many disagreements. And she was a fighter. And her pressure was hard to take. She had brought me into the world and raised me. I owed her a lot. I had to harden myself against her attempts to get me to accept her ideas. I further stunted and cauterised my feelings and emotions in order to do so. This was the only way I could endure the hurt I was causing her and the rest of my family and myself. Dealing with my emotions and feelings in this way damaged me as a human being. I was preventing many of the positive emotions from developing within myself or between myself and my family. I could not afford to let positive emotions develop. I was increasingly emotionally brutalised and hardened. But I saw it as the inevitable price I had to pay to fight for my own ideas, as the necessary way I had to act to defend myself from the pressure of my family's ideas and the ideas of the Orange Order and Protestantism and the general conservatism of holy Catholic and Protestant Ireland.

It was around this time, I was around 18 to 19, that I decided not to have children. I felt if I had children I would be under more pressure to fit in. I felt that to have children would demand that I open myself up to others and caring for others and specifically for any children I might have and the mother of any children I might have. I felt this would soften me psychologically and emotionally. I felt that having a child, holding a child, being the father to a child would demand a warm and caring approach from me both to the mother of any children I might have and to the children. I felt that to have children would make it harder for me to resist the pressures and the ideas of my family and the Protestant milieu and ideology and conservative views of society in general.

Not fitting into my family's views was an important element to this decision. To have had children would have made us more a 'family', made me more a part of a 'family'. It would have been harder to keep all the pressures at bay, all the emotions in check, emotions which could threaten to make me agree with my family's views or at least keep quiet about my opposition to their views. I did not fully understand this at that time. It was more an instinct. But it was not without a foundation. Fighting the ideas of my family and my Protestant background, fighting to understand the world and my place in it, fighting to find an alternative to the present world, all these fights brought me up against many alternative ideas. My family's ideas were most powerful and close to me. If I had had children the family would have been strengthened and the fight against my family's ideas would have been harder. If my family and I had had the same ideas it would have been different, easier. But we did not. So I sacrificed having children to the struggle for ideas. Looking back on it I think I had little choice if I was to conduct that struggle with the determination that was necessary to find my place in the world.

However it was not without cost. It was many years later before I realised what I had denied myself, the enormity of this sacrifice, the great cost. I was walking in Dublin. I was with two friends and we were passing Liberty Hall, the trade union headquarters. My friends had their two and a half year old little red-headed daughter with them. She was an intelligent and charming and beautiful child. To cross the road I took her small hand in mine. I felt like I would melt into gentleness and caring as I held the tiny hand and as I looked down at the little curly red head. I pushed these feelings back inside and down and into myself. Did how I felt in that moment not confirm me in my belief that I had to resist having children and a family if I was to resist the pressure of the ideas that threatened me.

Later on in my life I would get together with my permanent companion Bonnie. She had a little grandson. He, with his long, wild hair, was full of intelligence, inquisitiveness, laughter, mischief and wilfulness. I called him Wee Boy. It suited him so it stuck. We would play together. He was a character. Our relationship was life enhancing. I gave up a lot by not having children for what I understood were the demands of the struggle to understand the world, for my role in the world, for what I would come to think of later as the demands of the revolution. But I think I had no choice and so therefore made the right decision. That does not mean it was without pain and sacrifice. I would in the future have a vasectomy to be sure I did not have a child.

Central to my decision not to have children was that I did not know who I was, what I believed. I thought that this being the case what could I tell the children, how could I live as an example to the children? I felt that to have children would demand I know my role in the world. It would demand that I knew what my future was to be and be in a position to secure that future. I did not have any of these pieces of knowledge or capacities. So I felt I was in no position to have children. Most parents took the norms of society and imposed these on their children. But I rejected the norms of society for myself. So how could I accept these norms for my children if I had any? So I closed off this option from my life. I never discussed this with anybody, just closed it off. Closed myself off to having children. In doing so I further damaged myself emotionally and psychologically, but also toughened myself emotionally and psychologically.

It was at this time that I considered the word and the concept of 'love'. I felt as a word it was just about useless in the struggle for understanding and for a good life. It meant different things to different people and in different contexts. A person could beat up his or her partner and say it was because he 'loved' her or him and he or she had done something which made him or her mad. A person could abandon an established relationship and the responsibilities that went with this and say it was because he or she 'loved' somebody else.

However living in a world where the word love was thrown about with such abandon it was impossible not to engage with the word. I sought to deal with this by seeking clarification of what was meant in whatever circumstance the word was used, by seeking context whenever the word was used. Was it romantic love that was being talked about. Holding hands and walking by the ocean, gentleness and extreme sensitivity, pushing aside all thought of the real world with all its difficulties. Such romantic love while it could be pleasurable for a time could not last in the face of the reality of life. It was impossible for romantic love to last in the horror of so much of life under capitalism, in the horror of the mass poverty and starvation and slaughter which was the experience of so many in the capitalist world. Or if it was not romantic love what kind of love was being talked about. Was it love such as the relationship between friends, that is solidarity and kindness? Was it the love for an idea or a cause? I saw the use of the word 'love' without clarification and context as of no use.

I would later learn that Joyce said that 'love was wishing good for another'. And that Trotsky would speak of 'love without base calculation'. I felt that these explanations confirmed my view that the word 'love' on its own was of little use. It had to be explained, it had to be given context. The phrase 'I love you' came easily off the tongue, but in so many cases it only confused or even worse covered up the reality, and at times a reality which was the opposite of what was being suggested.

Then there was the God of 'love'. I was supposed to follow the instructions in books such as the Bible because I 'loved' God and he/she 'loved' me. And this supposed God 'loved' me so much that he/she 'created' me with all my problems and contradictions and when these made me act in ways which hurt others, and act incorrectly according to the approved books, then this God who 'loved' me would send me to burn in hell for ever. I concluded that the word 'love' on its own was so imprecise that it was not of use. Instead I thought of what was spoken of as 'love' as treating people with a view to helping myself and them to see the world in a way that gave us all a better chance of having a decent life and having a better understanding of our world. That is I tried to live in a way that would increase the consciousness of myself and all to whom I related, increase all our consciousness. What was generally thought of as love I came to see as acting to others in a way that raised the consciousness of all concerned. That did not lead others and myself to become more cynical, more bitter, more hopeless, rather to increase the hopes and desires of all concerned.

As I matured I would increasingly add kindness and solidarity to the overall combination of ideas, emotions, feelings, psychologies, ways of acting that would determine how I tried to behave in relationships. Kindness was high on the list, to act with kindness. Kindness did not get much coverage in the capitalist culture in which I lived. Kindness led too easily to solidarity, that is helping others. This was not good for capitalism which wanted every person acting for themselves and the devil take the hindmost. In this way the capitalist class could better atomise society, keep control and exploit. Kindness, solidarity, the next thing would be working together as a group and then as a class. Maybe, horror of horrors, even go on to organise trade unions. For this reason capitalism frowned upon kindness.

My mother did not use the word 'love'. She had brought us into the world and did everything she could for us. As she saw it she had done her 'duty'. She did not have to say 'love'. I do not think it ever occurred to her to use the word. I think that like me she did not use it because she understood that it could mean just about anything. It was like the way she hated strangers or people who barely knew each other kissing each other on the cheek or hugging and casually saying 'I love you'. My mother was an honest working woman and needed precision in her life and in her speech. And she had seen the word 'love' come with many cruelties. To my mother she did her 'duty' and looked after us, that was better than 'love'. 'Duty', not 'love' was her word. 'Duty' not 'love' was how she saw her relationship to all of us. With 'duty' the responsibilities could be more concrete, clearly defined and understood. I would later read how Van Gogh sought to see his life in terms of duty.

At this time I knew the pain of my resistance to the pressure of my family to accept their views was leaving me in a dangerous place. Instead of trying to fight for my ideas I could have taken other roads. I could have become cynical about all ideas, a nihilist. This would have left me useless as a human being. Or I could have scoffed and derided my family and their ideas and scorned and hated them personally especially my mother. But I did neither of these. Either would have been unjust to my mother, my family and myself. My mother was a good woman. My family were good people. My mother and family cared for me. My mother had been brought up in poverty in the eastern foothills of the Donegal Mountains, she was offered no alternative. There was no way she could have been reasonably expected to have different ideas from the ones she had and the ones she wanted me to accept. I could not hate her. This would have been a most grave injustice to her and most grave and damaging to all our family.

But there was something else. To have taken this road would not only have been treating my mother and family in a way that would have been entirely unjust to them given their life experience, but it would have been very wrong for me also. To do so, that is to lie to myself about my mother and family and why they held the ideas they did, and to hate them as the way to fight their ideas, would have meant that I would have had to abandon any chance of myself having a life of integrity. It would have been entirely false and unjust and dishonest to blame my family's wrong ideas on their having some flaw within themselves as opposed to being the result of the conditions in which they had been brought up and the influences under which they had lived. That would have been a terrible road for me to take, a staggering price for me to pay. A staggering injustice to my family. To have taken it would have been to build my life upon a lie. To have taken it would have been to destroy myself.

So as I saw it I had no choice. I had to struggle openly and honestly against the ideas of the Protestant and the Catholic and the capitalist conservative world and as part of this against the ideas of my mother and family, all of which I disagreed with. At the same time I had to make sure I did not allow myself to hate my family or disrespect them. I had to try and understand why they believed what they did. I was only able to do this to anything like a full extent when I would be introduced to the ideas of Marxism many years later. That was when I came to understand that social conditions tended to determine social consciousness. In the meantime I hung on instinctively, knowing my mother and uncle and aunt and family were good people and that I was not a bad person and try and not let our disagreements destroy our relationships and lives entirely. But this was not easy and as well as that it was extremely painful to my mother. I was breaking her heart.

My debates with my family were frequently about religion and inevitably about my family's Protestant religion. My fight against religious ideas was made much more difficult by the role of the Catholic Church and the Catholic population. My uncle and mother and aunt would say that the Catholic Church ran the South of Ireland and that the Catholic population did what they were told by the priests. I had no credible answer for this because as far as I could see it was just about true. The fact was the South blatantly declared itself to be a Catholic state and its leaders, like the Labour leader Corish in the South, declared himself a Catholic first and an Irishman second, and as well as this just about every Catholic did obey their unelected, undemocratic, anti-women leaders, the nuns, the priests, the bishops, the cardinals and the popes.

The role of the Catholic Church in the South of Ireland has recently been further exposed by the horrors revealed in their running of laundries worked by women who were treated as slaves, the children's homes and the mass graves in some of these, the stealing and selling of children and child sex and physical abuse. Some of these atrocities were known back then. My relatives would point to these and say: 'See what are we telling you. Look at what they do. And they look after and cover up for their own too, so we need to look after our own.' It was years before I would hear of James Joyce and other Irish writers and revolutionaries from Catholic backgrounds who would stand up to the Catholic hierarchy. I desperately needed them back then. But of course it was precisely because they would have been of use to people like me, have enlightened people like me, that they were banned. I would later rejoice when I would come home and see the quotes from Joyce on bronze plaques in the sidewalks of Dublin. The Catholic hierarchy lost the battle with James Joyce.

To my family I would point to the fact that the North of Ireland was a Protestant state, as the South was a Catholic state and I was opposed to both. But this had no effect on my mother and family. They either refused to acknowledge this or justified it by saying well so what if it is, the South is a Catholic state and look at what would happen if the North were taken over by the South. 'Them priests would run everything and then where would we be?' I had no answer to this either when rights such as access to contraception and divorce were banned in the South by the order of the dictatorial Catholic hierarchy.

My debates with my family on religion evolved to where I questioned the existence of God. For a few months I read a chapter of the Bible every night to see if I could find any answers. Instead I found it to be centuries old nonsense with one part contradicting the other. In one love your neighbour as yourself, in another an eye for an eye. In one the meek would get their reward in heaven, in another the poor would inherit the earth. One, the poor getting the earth, was a revolutionary concept against the powers that be, the other, the meek getting their reward in a non-existent heaven was a counter revolutionary concept, the idea being to be meek, to leave the powers that be in power, just wait, and they would get their reward in heaven. I threw the Bible down. There were no answers in it for me. I also remembered how my father had got the Bible out and swore on it that he would give up drinking and he was back on the whiskey in a month. The Bible, any of its many versions, no longer had any authority or intimidatory power over me.

I would occasionally get into debates with urban middle class Catholic youth who considered themselves smarter than me, more learned and sophisticated and so thought they could taunt me about not believing in a god. They asked me what I would do if there was a god and he or she (with them it was always he) came down to earth. I said I would fight him or her. If he or she was so cruel as to make people and control people and then send them to hell to burn forever if they did not do what he or she told them to do, when he or she had supposedly made them, then I would want no part of him or her. I would never be so cruel as to do what their god was supposed to do. Fuck them and their god, I would deliberately say fuck. This would drive them away in fear. They were not so sophisticated and cocky then.

As it became known I was no longer a supporter of the Orange Order and the Protestant religion this elicited a sectarian response from some Catholics. One of them approached me. Slyly pretending to be my friend and he was just passing on what he had heard he said: 'You know your woman, you know that one who has the wee sweet shop, she is always kissing the altar's rails. Well you know what she said to me. It would be great if we could turn [that is convert to Catholicism] that Throne.' I was a juicy target as my family were so prominent in the Orange Order. Turning me would have been a big coup for the sectarian Catholics. I had as much contempt for these people and their sectarian ways as I had for Protestant sectarianism. It was two sides of the same coin.

While not agreeing on general ideas my mother and uncle and aunt provided me with a powerful and extremely positive example in another area, one which I would follow all my life. They believed in ideas and fought for these ideas. They had principles and fought for these principles. Their ideas and principles were Protestantism, Loyalism, treating people well who treated them well. Their fight for these principles provided me with the example that people should have principles, should have guidelines within which they should live their lives. They did not say this to me explicitly. It was just the way they lived. For them it was just natural. It was never questioned. You had to believe in something. I owe my family a great debt for teaching me this lesson. I will never be able to repay that debt. I would go on to fight to live my life in a principled manner. To believe in something. But it was not uncomplicated.

My mother and uncle and aunt having and fighting for ideas and principles inspired me to have and fight for principles. I compared them favourably to the many people who either hid their beliefs or believed in nothing. However while being inspired by their having ideas and principles and fighting for these the problem was I disagreed vehemently with the content of, and just about all the most important of their ideas and principles. For example that things could never be changed. I had only a bit of a half idea of how things could be changed or to what, but I did believe they could be changed and for the better. Look did I not get a different style of a suit? That was a change, and a change for the better. The siege had cracked if only a little. And then on Catholics being inferior and to be spurned, did they themselves not again and again act to our Catholic neighbours in a helpful and kind manner. I would come into conflict again and again on these issues. So while I was impressed and inspired by my family having principles and fighting for these I did not agree with the actual content of their principles and so we were in continual disagreement.

This struggle with my family was to stand me in good stead in the future. When the revolutionary organisation that I would later join and to which I would give most of my adult life became corrupt, and its leadership expelled and fired me and tried to break me by lying about me and slandering me, and when the majority of its membership walked away, I stayed and fought. I had learnt to stand up for myself and my principles. And I learnt to do so to a great extent through the struggle with my family. I had been psychologically and emotionally toughened in that struggle. This was one of the greatest contributions my family could have given to me. I will be forever in their debt.

As I became clearer on the ideas with which my family and I did not agree, I was also simultaneously groping to find ideas that made sense to me, ideas for which I could fight. Ploughing the fields, milking the cows, cleaning the byres, going about the work in Portinure, this search never left me. The problem was the direction in which I was seeking to clarify my ideas and principles was very different from that of my mother, uncle and aunt. This caused a lot of pain and damage to all of us. I came to look at the effects of this struggle on me in this way.

My class position in society, that is my work on the farm, meant I had to do hard physical labour. Inevitably this caused calluses on my hands. These were hardened knots of flesh caused by the friction between my hands and the tools I had to use to do this labour. They were damage to my hands. But they were also protection for my hands. Given the nature of my work, which flowed from my class position in society, the development of these calluses was inevitable and necessary. That is, overall they were positive. However this was not one sided. There was also a negative side to the calluses. They made my hands less sensitive.

At the same time, and again due to my class position in society and along with this my desire to understand that society and to develop an independent understanding of my role in that society, I had to do hard mental labour. This meant struggling against the ideas of that society and of my family. Inevitably this created friction between myself and my family and society, and this, just as was the case with the friction between my hands and the tools I used for my physical work, caused calluses. These were calluses which developed on my consciousness, psychology and emotions. Like the calluses on my hands they were necessary and inevitable and overall were positive in that they made me tough and this allowed me to fight to understand the world and to resist the right wing ideas. But again like those calluses on my hands there was a negative side to these calluses in that they made my consciousness, my psychology, my emotions less sensitive.

I came to understand that everything came with a price. The calluses on my hands were necessary and protective and made my physical work more possible, but they also made my hands less sensitive. The calluses on my consciousness, my psychology, my emotions were necessary and protective and made me better able to fight for an understanding but they also made my consciousness, my psychology my emotions less sensitive.

This meant that while overall I was more capable of carrying out the essential tasks of my life, the physical labour to earn a living, the mental labour to fight for an understanding, I was less capable of carrying out the more delicate physical tasks of life, or of understanding the more sensitive possibilities of consciousness, of psychological, emotional and also inevitably flowing from this, of artistic life. With my callused and therefore less sensitive hands I was less capable of painting a beautiful work of art, I was less capable of playing the violin. With my less sensitive psychology, consciousness and emotions I was less capable of writing a beautiful verse of poetry. The calluses stood in the way. This was not good. This was not desirable. But it was inevitable and given my class position in society and my struggle for an understanding it was necessary.

As I was coming to understand this I was also coming to see that just because you cannot fulfil your desires, realise your potential, does not mean that you do not miss being able to do so. And even more insidious, just because you do not know you have certain desires, and cannot fulfil these desires, and just because you do not understand what is your potential and that you cannot realise your full potential, this does not mean that you do not miss being able to fulfil those desires, realise that potential. It was decades before I realised how much I missed not being able to paint a beautiful work of art or write a beautiful verse. It was only when I saw and came to be able to go a bit of the way to appreciate Van Gogh in all his power and beauty, kindness and peacefulness, pain and savagery and glory; only when I was able to read and half absorb some of Joyce in all its beauty, complexity, simplicity and power; only when I was able to half appreciate a Beethoven symphony with all its power; only when I was able to be moved by the wonder of the opera; only when I was able to let the blues and jazz enter into my head; only when I was able to half appreciate the beauty of the ballet, that I realised what I could never do. The inevitable and necessary calluses on my hands, the inevitable and necessary calluses on my consciousness, on my psychology, on my emotions stood in my way. There would be times when I would be distraught when I would think about what I could never do.

It was only when I realised the damage that had been done that I came to understand the rage, the anger, the anguish that would at times consume me. These were because of the frustration of not being able to fulfil my desires, realise my potential, express myself to the fullest. I would later read that Engels said that freedom was the recognition of necessity. My calluses were necessities and inevitabilities given my position in society and my struggle for an understanding. I had to recognise this. Only by doing so could I have the maximum freedom that was for me possible. I would never be able to have full freedom. There was no such thing. What was necessary was to recognise what degree of freedom I could have and live with this. This was the best I could do.

I held and examined and turned over in my head this phrase of Engels that freedom was the recognition of necessity. As on other occasions, I would get angry at Marx and Engels. Why did they have to state things in such a complicated manner? Freedom being the recognition of society meant to me recognising what we could do and what we could not do and by doing so we could achieve the greatest degree of balance in our lives, that is we could have the greatest possible freedom in our lives.

Anyway, when I came to understand what Engels was saying, life became more bearable. I accepted the inevitability of the calluses but sought to limit their extent as much as possible. This is what would give me the most freedom, not absolute freedom, there was no such thing, but the maximum degree of freedom that was possible for me given my class position in society and the time in history in which I lived. I concluded that it would be idealistic for me to expect more. I had to recognise necessity.

But in doing so I also realised I would have to be careful. I would have to avoid trying to minimise the calluses too much or I would not be able to do the hard physical and mental labour which was necessary. I would have to recognise and accept the development of the calluses to the extent that this allowed me to do my work and fight for my ideas. Life was not going to be simple. I would have to be clear on my position in class society, I would have to be clear on my priorities, I would have to be clear what was possible in the context of my world, I would have to get the balance right. I would have to understand what was possible for me given my time and class. I would have to continually figure out and fight for and calibrate and recalibrate my own personal balance, my balance in my relating to society overall.

Many years later I would read of Dick Gregory, the African American fighter against racism and injustice and also well-known comedian. I would read that he said: 'The Negro has a callus growing on his soul, and it's getting harder and harder to hurt him there.' He too thought of his struggle and of calluses. Again and again as I grew in years, I was to come to learn from and understand more from the struggle of the African American people.

I am glad to say that I have been able to continue to struggle for this callus balance throughout my life. This is not to say that I have been able to achieve it at all times. But I have been able to keep fighting for it at all times. I think this was the best I could do. This was me recognising necessity. I also think that given where I came from it has not been a bad achievement. I inflicted the least amount of pain on my family and myself that was possible while at the same time carrying out to the maximum the struggle to understand the world, to relate positively to that world, to fight to change that world and to realise my own potential.

Looking back on this now one thing always puzzles me. There was a piano in our small farm house. Where did that come from? I think it came from a wedding present one of my mother's former employers gave her. Most likely one that her rich employers thought was no longer up to what they saw as their standards. No one ever played it. It never occurred to me to try and play it. Or to anybody to have me taught to play it. Of course there was money involved and anyway what would I want to play it for? I had the potatoes to dig and the cows to milk and the corn to cut. And anyway was I not a male? But if I had learnt to play the piano this could have changed my life. Like if I had been able to get the trumpet and learn how to play it. I could have been a classical pianist or maybe a Donegal Fats Domino or maybe a Donegal Louis Armstrong. I could maybe have had a different life. But it was a class question, an economic question, a cultural question, a gender question. The struggle to realise my full potential involved all of these.

My struggle for understanding and my role meant the most severe struggle against the ideas of my mother and my family. I was rejecting all my mother and my family thought was good for me and all she and they worked so hard to accumulate to have to hand over to me. This was a terrible cruelty from me. One from which neither my mother nor my family nor I would ever recover. The terrible pain of it. If only I could have given in and made us all happy. But if I had given in I would have made everybody even more unhappy. We were stuck in this insoluble contradiction of class society and the different ways in which my family and I related to that class society. The insoluble, the no solution, the pain on my mother's and family's lives, this was what was what. But it was not only that, it was also, and this was the positive, this pain hardened, toughened my psychological, emotional and intellectual life. It better prepared me to struggle for revolutionary ideas and a revolutionary organisation.

CHAPTER 6

THE DRINK – TO DROWN
OR NOT TO DROWN THE SORROWS

AS I MADE MY WAY in my world of those times there were many fronts on which I had to fight. One was 'The Drink'. It was everywhere. It needed no further explanation than those two words. Nobody thought when you talked of 'The Drink' you were talking about water. Nobody called it alcohol. Nobody thought 'The Drink' referred to a cup of tea. Everybody knew what was being talked about.

First there was 'The Drink' and my family. My father's drinking, even though limited, was sore on the family's finances, made his illnesses worse and led to conflict between him and my mother. But I was confused. My father only drank on the fair days, and the big days, about once a month or so. He did not spend that much money on the drink. Yet my mother was always on at him about money and the drink. Was there something else other than the money, something my mother was not saying?

My father was an intelligent, humorous and attractive presence of a man. With only a few drinks in him he would retain these qualities, even more so these qualities would be enhanced. There were good times that stood in my memory when he had only a few drinks. When he would come home from the fairs he would always bring some bacon wrapped in paper in his coat pocket. My mother would fry this up with some eggs and serve it to him with her home-made wheaten bread. This was my father's favourite meal. I would be given share of this. My mother and aunt and uncle and sisters would not get any. My mother thought everybody could not afford to eat bacon. The rest of the family had to make do with sitting tortured with the smell of it. I never thought of this at the time, but this was another special privilege I had as the male child. It was another example of my privileged position in the family and discrimination against the rest of the family.

When my father would sit down to eat this meal he would keep the family laughing as he recounted the events of the day. What the Squealer Haughey had said, (named Squealer because of his high pitched voice), when he was trying to buy a cow from Big Man McCrossan for a lesser price (Big Man because of his big stomach); what the last of the Ronson litter, a small man, who suffered from the Small Man Syndrome, always trying to appear more than he was, said when he was trying to sell his young bullocks to the humourless cynical Patterson. What the emaciated Smyth with his long coat flying behind him, shouted as he ran screaming at the top of his voice away from the cattle he was looking to buy. 'That boy, that boy,' Smyth would shout, 'he is trying to put his hand in my pocket and take the few shillings I have, and do it in front of the whole of you.' My father would use the theatre of the fairs as the basis for his storytelling there at our kitchen table.

As my mother's food was served up and my father began to eat he talked less and less and my mother would take over the conversation and get on to him about his drinking and once again get on about how he was going to drink us into the workhouse. My father would go quiet under this criticism. I could see he was ashamed. I was ashamed for him too. He was humiliated and I was humiliated for him too. So was my uncle. He would get up and go out to groom the horses when this happened. He knew my mother was right but he did not want to have to listen to it and see his brother like that and hear my mother get on to him.

Sometimes my father would get very drunk and have to get a ride home. On those occasions if the person knew him they would usually leave him off at the bottom of the lane. This was because my mother would sometimes blame whoever brought him home for getting him drunk. I thought this was unfair to the driver and also my father. He did not need any help to get drunk. He was more than able to do it on his own. When he was expected home we would watch for car lights turning at the bottom of the lane. On one occasion we saw lights turning but when after a while there was no sign of my father my mother sent me down to see what was going on. I found him lying with his feet in the stream and his boots and the bottom of his trouser legs wet. I was able to help him enough so he could grab onto the hedge and get to his feet and together we staggered up the lane. My father was no longer such an attractive personality in such circumstances.

I came to think that my mother's anger at my father for drinking was not only over the issue of money or that it was bad for his health. She also did not like to see him lose his humour, his outgoing personality, his dignity, his poise as he did when he stopped talking as he ate or as he did when he got so drunk he could not make it home and instead fell in the stream. She felt ashamed for him and also for herself when he was found lying in the stream at the bottom of the lane or when he was sitting eating without being able to entertain us with his stories. My father was a better person without the drink and she wanted that better person.

I noticed over time that my father would get drunk quicker than others. When I would grow up and inherit his diseases I realised that this was because these disabilities, hypothyroidism, Addison's disease, weakened his ability to consume alcohol to any significant extent. He would end up in the stream not just because of the drink but also because of his illnesses. At such times he would lose his attractive qualities, the qualities that made me and my mother proud of him at other times. My mother wanted the sober man, the man with the qualities of the man she was proud of, the man she married. It was not only the money.

My different ideas were already causing pain to my mother. I did not want to add more. So I decided to stay away from 'The Drink'. I did not want her to fear that I would end up on the drink. So when I would go into the pubs, the centres of social life, I drank soft drinks. One young man who was always sitting bent over behind a pint of Guinness told me I was lucky. I did not have to spend money on drink, that I was mad enough without it. I took it as a compliment. I thought he was maybe right. And not being into spending money I was pleased for this reason also.

Concern for my mother's feelings was not the main reason I decided not to drink. I looked around and saw that it tended to be the most talented, the potentially most gifted, who were sorest on the drink. There was Huey who could put words together like no other person I knew. There was my friend who was one of the best soccer players around. There was James who had St Vitus Dance and could not control his movements and voice but who had a knowledge of things. There was the man with hands for everything who had given me Darwin's book. They were all sore on the drink. There was something going on.

I did not find it hard to see what. Society was sick. The more talented a person was, the more potential a person had, the more difficult these people found it to express themselves and to realise their potential in this sick society. So their frustration was the greatest. So they needed to sedate themselves more than others. And the road they tended to take in the Ireland of that time was to try and escape into the bottle. The more talented they were the more the society frustrated them, therefore the more they had to drown their sorrows, sorrows caused by living in a society which was rotten, which could not give them a way to live their lives to the fullest. I was not going to do this. I was not going to drown my sorrows, I was going to learn from my sorrows, even to nurture my sorrows, and in this way be strengthened. There were of course those who had already been badly damaged by society and needed to forget this damage. The drink was a way to try and do this also. But this too was a dead end. It was to escape into the bottle. It was simply drowning their sorrows. And you could not drown your sorrows without doing damage to yourself, without drowning at least a part of yourself. Living in a bottle, like living with a siege mentality, was not a good way to live. Drowning what was best in you was not a good way to live.

'The Drink' was of course connected directly to the big picture. British colonialism and British imperialism exploited and repressed the Irish people. It crushed the Catholic population most directly. But it also repressed and twisted the thinking of the Protestant people as it forced them to play their role in the divide and rule strategy. The Roman Catholic hierarchy and ideology also played its repressive part. The leaders of the Protestant churches too. The Irish population both Protestant and Catholic were frustrated and angry about the role the system forced them to play. All were prevented from realising their full potential. This was at the root of why 'The Drink' was so prevalent in Irish society.

I saw myself as part of this process where I was not able to realise my potential, develop my talents and abilities. Nor at that time did I know my role in the world. I was regularly confused and frustrated. I had days when I would be down and days when I would be up. I knew that if I drank, on the days I would be down I would be tempted to take to 'The Drink'. And those down days would not just be any days. They would be the most important days if I was to figure things out. Figuring out was hard work. If I drank I would not do this hard work. If I drank I would try to escape not figure out. I would run away not fight to figure out, not fight to understand. If I drank I would never be able to get out of my confusion and dead end. If I drank I would not be able to escape from the dead hand of rural Ireland. So on behalf both of my mother and the struggle for my own consciousness and a life worth living I decided not to drink. This was another debt I partially owed to my mother and her strong, even hard, approach to life. Her continual criticism of my father for drinking made it impossible for me to ignore what was going on. This, along with observing what was happening to the most talented people around me, helped me in my decision to stay off 'The Drink'. This was far and away a positive decision, but it was not without its complication given its relationship to another area of my life. It affected my ability to figure out the other big issue with which I was confronted at that time: The Sex.

CHAPTER 7

THE SEX – NEVER A CAPPELLA

I WAS IN MY TEENS, healthy and well fed. I had a powerful sex drive. When I got up in the morning I had to do press ups to get my erection to subside before going down to breakfast. Everywhere around me I saw the young girls, the mature women, the curves and movements of their bodies and their limbs. There was no way I could ignore them. I did not want to ignore them. I was crazy about them. In jest I would murmur to myself under my breath. That is not right. That should be all banned. It was not right that a man had to be surrounded by this all the time. It was enough to drive a man crazy. And I would look at all of them, all shapes and sizes. I would laugh silently to myself as I talked under my breath about them being all banned. Yes there would be some chance of that.

I had no idea what to do about these beautiful female bodies, about the long limbs, the round curves, the indented spines, the gentle softness of the hands, the soft cheeks. Ah I would think it was not right. Such beauty, such allure for me, such desire to touch, to put my cheek against the cheek, to hold the warm shape of the female body against mine. I would breathe deep and swear. Goddamn the misery of it, the even the anguish of it, of not being able to be fully part of the sexual world.

If I drank it might have been different. With drink in me I could have maybe pushed the complications and worries to the back of my mind, acted spontaneously, and tried to do what my body wanted. This might have 'solved' things in the short term but it would have made them worse in the longer term. I would have probably made some girl pregnant when I was not capable personally or financially of being a father. So when my sexual drive was at its most powerful, I was not able to find a healthy way to express it. This was not good. A drive that is blocked still exists and finds some other, usually destructive way, to express itself.

There was another way that not drinking affected my sexual world. But this time in a positive way. If I had drank I could have possibly pushed aside what I saw as the injustice in how society looked at sex and women. The male-dominated society encouraged the males to seek to have as much sex as possible. But at the same time this very same society condemned women who had sex outside of marriage. This was hypocritical and unfair to women. It was another case of discrimination against women. The term for a woman who had a lot of sex was always negative, whereas the term for a man who had a lot of sex always portrayed him as some sort of clever fellow. I was aware of this.

Seeing this injustice restrained me in my efforts to have sex. But it did not mean my sexual urge went away. What it did was make me more critical of society, more convinced that there was something wrong with society and that it had to be changed. How women were treated and looked upon was a major factor in making me think there was something wrong with society.

An elderly relative died at this time and left our family her few fields. As these were a distance away they were sold and the proceeds made it possible for the family to buy its first car. My sisters' boyfriends all had cars, neither my uncle or mother or aunt could drive, so I had the use of this car any time I wanted it. This allowed me to travel further afield and meet more people.

The main places young people met were dances. These were mostly segregated between the religions. The Protestant churches and organisations had their dance halls and the Catholic Church had its dance halls. These dances were ways the different churches made money. It was hypocritical the way these anti sex organisations made money out of the sexual attraction of the youth to each other, this sexual attraction which they were always trying to condemn and control and exploit. This religious segregation of the dancing also meant that the various institutions built their bases and partly financed themselves through keeping the religions, keeping people divided. This contributed to the violent years to come. I ignored this segregation and went to both Protestant and Catholic dances. When I went to the Catholic halls I tended to be looked at with hostility by the males. But I did not care. There were good looking women and girls at both Catholic and Protestant dance halls. I was not there for religion and I was not going to be intimidated. There were also the privately owned mega dance halls. These brought the best bands and helped introduce rock 'n' roll to the area. I went to these also.

I met Barbara at one of the small Protestant halls. She was a very good looking tall slender girl. I watched her dancing with her skirt swirling out showing her legs. She said yes when I asked her to dance. I could smell her perfume and feel her soft skin, and the touch of her hair. I was not a bad dancer. We danced the rest of the night. In the slow dances I could feel myself against her and she did not pull back from my aroused body. She let me drive her home.

Barbara's house was in a small row of local authority houses of lower paid Protestant working class families. I switched off the engine and put my arm around her. We kissed and I felt her body. Her small breasts demanded attention, her lips and cheeks and neck also, I tried to put my hand up her skirt but she caught it and said no in a sharp voice. But she did not stop me continuing to kiss her face and lips and neck and feel her breasts. The calculation of this far and no further at this time of our first time being together.

'I have to go in John. My father will be angry if we stay here parked any longer.'

'Okay. But maybe we can go out again.'

We made a date for the next Friday. When I arrived a week later Barbara answered the door. She was looking good. 'You have to come in. My father and mother want to meet you.' That was the last thing I wanted to do. Meet her parents. Sure I had tried to put my hand up their daughter's skirt the week before. They would probably know just by looking at me.

Barbara's father and mother were sitting in two armchairs on each side of an open fire. Her mother was friendly and stood up and shook my hand. The father glowered at me and sat where he was. I knew what he was thinking: what would I be trying to do to his good looking daughter?

Barbara rescued us: 'We have to leave, we are going to the pictures in Strabane. They will be starting soon.' On the way back from the pictures we stopped in a little tree covered lane off the main road which we were to make our own. We kissed and felt each other as before. This time Barbara allowed me to touch her inside her clothes and up her skirt. We were both very aroused. We continued to go out together every weekend.

We either went to the cinema or to a local fish and chip shop which had a good jukebox. I would play the rock 'n' roll records, and we would listen to the African American singers from the US. The other young people in this café were Catholic working class and or unemployed. Most of the young people I had gone to school with at the grammar school were urban middle class and Protestant and got together in their own homes or remained within their Protestant worlds. I was not invited to their homes.

Every time I collected Barbara I had to go in and meet her parents. Her father's attitude to me changed. Barbara told me it was because he was in the Orange Order and had heard my uncle was a leader of that organisation and that I was an only son and my family had a small farm. He had obviously concluded that I was an acceptable potential son-in-law. I said nothing. I did not tell him of the mess in my head and my touching of the smooth skin of his daughter.

I had initially been confused about Barbara and her family. They were Protestants. But Barbara worked in a shirt factory where the workforce was mainly Catholic. I came to know that her father was a low paid unskilled worker and needed the money she earned. I was excited that Barbara worked in a shirt factory. I had never gone out with a factory worker before. I wanted to understand their world better. I related to them as they were workers who were looked down upon by the farmer community like my own family because they seldom had property. And in the case of my family because they were mainly Catholic. Barbara told me there were almost 100 workers in her factory, mostly but not all Catholic. But she also opened my eyes by telling me that they tended to get along as they were working together at similar jobs and getting similar wages and had similar problems.

After a few weeks going out together Barbara and I got seriously aroused. We undressed and for the first time I entered a woman's body. It also appeared that it was the first time that Barbara had sex. I was no sooner inside Barbara's body than I was on the verge of having an organism. I knew I had to stop. I pushed myself back and looked at Barbara, at her face and eyes and mouth. I said: 'Barbara, Barbara.' Speaking to her, saying her name, brought her back to me as a whole person, not just some receptacle for my penis and my sperm. This calmed my urgent desire to have an orgasm. I was no longer just inside her body and physically connecting with her, but I was connecting with her as a person with her voice and thoughts and mind. I was talking to her and our minds were meeting. I was acting in consideration for her and for both of us. It was no longer just our sexes that were meeting. We were not just shutting our eyes and pounding each other. The desire to have an orgasm was diluted in the deepening of this overall more comprehensive communication. I was to learn this and it was to stay with me for the rest of my life: concern for a sexual partner, kindness for a sexual partner, thoughts about the feelings and desires of a sexual partner, these were the essential elements that made for good sex.

At that time Barbara and I were both determined that she would not get pregnant. We had never talked about marriage or any permanent relationship. If she had got pregnant without marriage this would have been a crisis for her with her family, her church and Protestant milieu.

While I shared Barbara's wish that she not get pregnant for the same reasons she did, I had an additional reason. I was increasingly aware that I did not know what I believed, what I wanted to do with my life, what my role in life should be. I increasingly knew that I was not happy working on my uncle's farm. The result of this was that just as I held myself back from any kind of a full relationship with my family I did the same with Barbara. I stunted and cauterised my emotions and feelings once more, this far and no further with my feelings and emotions, as it had been and was with my family in the past, now it was with Barbara. I did this so I could stand against any possible pressure to commit to a permanent relationship, and at the same time not to be pulled into to a religious and world view with which I did not agree. I had to remain personally uncommitted until I understood my place in the world, until I knew what I believed. If Barbara had got pregnant there would have been a lot of pressure on me to settle down on our family's small farm in Donegal and give up any idea of finding some different role, in the world. So together we tried to avoid Barbara getting pregnant. However things were not simple.

After we had been going out for some months Barbara and I were having sex when she said: 'Please, Please, do not stop, come inside me. Do not stop. Come inside me.' Our method of 'contraception' was for me not to have an orgasm inside Barbara. Barbara's words so excited me that I acted irresponsibly and I had an orgasm inside her. Barbara held me very tight afterwards, wrapping her legs around me, and pulling my neck and head down against her. I felt she wanted me to say something new, to make some acknowledgement that something special had happened, that some commitment had been made by me. But I hardened myself, further stunted and cauterised myself, and said nothing.

After we had this unrestrained irresponsible sex I knew I had done something wrong. I had risked getting Barbara pregnant with all the problems this would have meant for both of us but especially for her. We did not play anymore that night as we disentangled from each other. We were silent as we drove home. We continued to go out together but I worried that Barbara might be pregnant. As a result I became quiet and morose on our dates. I was afraid to ask her about her period. But one night I could not put it off anymore. She became angry with me. 'So that is why you have been so quiet. You are worried I am pregnant. I am okay for you to take out and do it to me but you are worried that I might be pregnant and you might be stuck with me.' I did not know what to say. After all she was not far wrong.

We went out a few more times after that. Barbara told me I did not have to worry that she was not pregnant. Then she told me she did not want to go out with me anymore for a while until we would see what would happen. I was both saddened and relieved by this. I liked Barbara and would miss our times together. But I was relieved that I was no longer in what was close to a permanent relationship when I did not know what I was doing with my life.

It was obvious to my family that something had happened when I stopped going out with Barbara. My mother in particular saw this. She waited and took her chance to probe. 'John do you remember what I told you. Any girl you meet you leave her the way you find her. There are plenty of ones out there just looking for a boy like you with a farm coming to them, and no debt on it. And you have no brothers. Then there are them other kind. There is nothing they would like more than to turn you. You need to watch out.' My mother's words shocked me. She knew much more about the world than I. I had never thought of myself as potential prey before. What she said helped me make a bit more sense of things. There was more to it than just me not knowing my role in the world. There was also that I was in a predatory world. In a world where, especially amongst the small farming class, the middle and upper classes, the indoctrination to use sex and marriage to achieve a better economic position was very great.

I had been indoctrinated into thinking that sex outside of marriage was a sin, into thinking that one of my most powerful urges should only be given expression after I got some preacher's permission. To get this I had to give money and gifts to and be a member of some church. I had been indoctrinated to believe that sex outside of marriage was supposedly punishable by burning in hell forever. This was the story. But there was a way out.

The churches could give 'forgiveness'. The Catholic Church did this through its confessional and rituals, the Protestant churches by their preachers' words and rituals. But the racket was the same. Make people feel guilty and afraid that if they exercised one of their most powerful urges, if they had sex, without the sanction of the preachers and the churches, without belonging to the churches and paying money to the churches, they would burn in hell forever.

The more I thought of it the more I could see it was a con trick, a racket. It was like drugs. Hook people on a drug and then monopolise the sale of the drug they were hooked on. Sex was even better than the drugs, the person was born already with a powerful desire for sex, already pretty much hooked, addicted to the drug, to sex, the churches did not have to hook them, to addict them. They just had to manipulate the addiction. This is what they did and the way they did so gave them a lot of money and power. It was a racket and a good one. The way in which the churches, especially the Catholic Church manipulated sex for its own ends of power and wealth was very great. Its full time organisers, priests etc. were not allowed to marry so they would have no children to whom they could pass on any money or property they might have. It would stay with the Church. Then there was the pressure on women to have as many children as possible. Priests visited women who had no children and demanded to know why they were not 'doing their duty'. The numbers had to be kept up, the women had to be kept controlled by having as many children as possible. It was a racket alright, a racket at the root of which was control and wealth. I detested the hypocrisy and cynicism of the leaderships of the religious organisations.

But I did not think I yet had the full story. What about what my mother said about the farm. What was its relationship to sex? When I thought more it was not too hard to figure out. My family had worked hard all their lives to keep their farm and get it out of debt. They did not want some strange woman coming in and squandering that. They wanted a woman who would fit in and accept the ideas and morals and the existing economic realities and her place in those. They wanted a woman who would marry me, accept me as the boss and leave the farm legally in my hands and their hands. They wanted a woman who would not have sex with other men in case another man's child ended up owning their farm.

Even though Barbara's father had no property he and she were caught in this web also. Her father was a worker with little class consciousness, that is did not think of himself as a worker. He hoped to move up in the world not by class struggle, but by keeping in with the bosses and also by his good looking daughter marrying somebody with property. But this would be very unlikely if Barbara was known to have sex with different men. If she did she would not be seen as reliable. So she had to be indoctrinated also. No sex until she had got together with a man, who had property, and to whom she could be married and whose children, and only his children, she would bear.

Her family had no land and no capital. Barbara's indoctrination was aimed at trying to get her and her family some capital by moving up in the world through her good looks, through staying in her church, obeying her church, paying money to her church, abiding by the rules of that church, and by not having sex outside of marriage and as a result having a good chance of getting a man with property to marry her. Of course Barbara's healthy desires kept getting in the way of this. Her healthy body, just like mine, called out for sex while her and her family's social and economic position and her religious indoctrination ordered her not to have sex until she was married. It was a tortured cruel contradiction for Barbara and all women and it was especially so in that non contraception Ireland.

While Barbara's indoctrination was to give her and her family the chance to acquire some capital and to keep the whole system working as the property owning classes and the churches wanted, my indoctrination was to give my family the best chance of holding onto the property and little capital, that is the few fields, they already had and also keep the whole system of economics and politics and power and religion and gender roles working as the property owning classes wanted. Both of us were indoctrinated to act in a way so as to give us a small stake, or the possibility of a small stake, in the system on top of which sat the ruling wealthy, private property owning, sexist ruling class.

Along with my own struggle to find my role in the world, there was a whole system of economics, private property, politics, power, religion and gender depending on people like Barbara and I toeing the line. There was no way either Barbara or I had the slightest understanding of this at the time but that was the reality in which we lived. I would only know the whole machinations of it much later when I would get to know better how the world worked. But just because I did not know how that was the way things were, private property, power, politics, religion, gender roles, sex, and the way they combined together in the class based society in which I lived, did not mean that my life was not enmeshed in and made more difficult by this system. The combination of processes that combined to make up that system and my determination not to fit into that system was what ended the relationship between myself and Barbara. That system, capitalism in backward rural Ireland in the 1960s, and my refusal to fit into that system finished my relationship with Barbara. Once again my refusal, my inability to fit into society, a society which I could not understand but with which I disagreed, damaged my personal and family relations but also and this was the positive side, further hardened and toughened me psychologically and emotionally.

After my relationship with Barbara ended I began to go to the dances in the City of Derry. These had much better music and those in attendance were mainly working class young people from the city who were around my own age. And they were mostly Catholic. And the young women mostly worked in the shirt factories. They were more sophisticated, more urban, more confident, and more outgoing than I. They helped me take a further step out of my rural Protestant world. I enjoyed these young women with their confidence and their more fashionable clothes and their cheek. Our adventures together also helped me take a further step towards a more spontaneously sexual world.

They also helped me better understand their world of the shirt factories and the urban working class. I had got a glimpse of this from Barbara but here in these dance halls just about all the young women worked in the shirt factories. I enjoyed very much how they would get together and laugh and tease each other, I enjoyed the confidence they had. I admired how, on occasion, the odd one would have the audacity to make it clear she wished to get together with me. I developed a relationship with one of these young women who lived in the short narrow street called the Bogside. Driving her home at night from the dance hall I saw the poverty of this part of the city for the first time. It shocked me. I had no idea the role that area and name 'the Bogside' would later play in my life.

The dances I went to in Derry were mainly in the big dance halls with the big bands and the better music. There were some very good dancers at these. I would watch when on occasion one young man would take to the floor and dance with two young women at the one time. It seemed to me the best dancers were from Catholic working class backgrounds. I would later understand that this was because being from this background they were less restrained because they were not pressurised by their position in society to keep a tight grip on themselves, to not 'make a show' of themselves' they could shake their asses. They were not so 'tight assed' as the more upper class Catholic population or the Protestant population.

Not knowing what I was later to understand and feeling guilty after holding myself back with Barbara and hurting her, and not allowing any relationship to develop with anybody else for the same reasons, for a time I considered giving up a personal life and sexual relations entirely. I considered secluding myself. I still had my powerful sex drive but I still did not know what to do with it in a way that was satisfying to myself and to whomever I would be involved. It never occurred to me to masturbate. This was a good thing, the way not drinking was a good thing. Abstaining from both meant that I did not have any release, instead I was forced to keep searching for the answers to the questions and desires I had.

As I thought about my experience with Barbara I tried to draw up some rules for myself in relation to sex. One was to always try and talk about it with any possible partner before we would have sex, to make sure any possible partner wanted to and openly acknowledged they wanted to have sex. Another was to always try and make sure anyone I was having sex with would have pleasure like I was having. Another rule was to always make sure that I took precautions so that my partner would not become pregnant. These were my rules. I tried to keep to them. However I have to say I did not always succeed in doing so. I regretted this very much. Trying to keep to these rules restrained the spontaneity of my sex life. This was mainly because given the repression in society in relation to women having sex outside marriage most women did not want to talk about having sex. They were, in most cases, more prepared to do it than talk about it.

During this time when I was considering giving up sex altogether I heard about a mission in my family's Presbyterian church in Strabane. An American hellfire preacher was visiting for a week. Even though I was well on the way to not believing in any god I decided to go along. Maybe I would hear something of interest, even something that would help. Night after night the preacher went on, unless we gave up our sins, such as going to the cinema, having sex, and unless we gave our lives to Jesus we would burn in hell forever. I was confused on this. How could we burn forever? Sure would we not eventually burn down to an ash until there was nothing left to burn? But I was not into the details of burning fires too much. I was just trying to figure out the confusions of my life, the confusions in my head.

On the last night of the mission the preacher stepped up the pressure.

Presumably he needed a big collection before going back to the US. He repeated the threats. Unless we gave our lives to Jesus then we would all burn in hell for ever. There was no alternative. No more sinning, no more cinema, no more sex outside of marriage. Not that I was having any at the time anyway. But the idea was I had to give up even wanting to have any. The preacher put a lot of emphasis on sex. The irony of course was that the more he ranted about sex the more I wanted to have some sex. But as the burning in hell terrorism of the preacher built I became more afraid of this burning forever. So on the last night when he asked for those who wanted to give their life to Jesus to put up their hands, with the vision of the terrible flames rising up around me, and me burning in hell forever, I am ashamed to say I caved in and raised my hand.

As soon as I did so I felt unclean, stupid, cowardly, ashamed, humiliated, weak. I had no idea what it meant to give my life to Jesus. I had no idea what or who this Jesus was. I did not know any Jesus. Who was this Jesus anyway? I had no idea. I had no idea even if this Jesus was a man or a woman or alive or dead. But there I had given my life to him or her. Whatever that meant. I left the church feeling doltish, like an idiot. Sure was it not the case that I did not even really believe there was a God.

But I was always lucky. A friend told me once that if I fell in the river I would come out with a salmon in each pocket. Maybe he was not so far wrong. Anyway I was lucky that night. I was rescued. And it was the beauty of nature which partly did the job. It was a beautiful summer night. I was seventeen years old. I drove out over Lifford Bridge and south on the Coneyburrow Road towards my home. I stopped the car and got out. The moon was full in a clear sky. The countryside was as bright as day. The three rivers, the Finn, the Mourne, the Foyle, glinted in the moonlight. I was surrounded by beauty. This was not a night, an environment to give my life to Jesus, whatever that meant, it was not a night to succumb to the fear of burning in hell forever, whatever that meant. The humiliation and confusion and despair and cowardice I felt after putting up my hand in the church began to fall away. The beauty of nature reached out to me and lifted me up and rescued me. I felt cleansed and strong and confident again.

But it was not only the beauty of nature that night that rescued me as I looked at the beauty of the moon, the rivers, the hills. I had been at a dance down in Porthall a few weeks earlier. It too was a beautiful night, with a full moon, the dance was in a big marquee down by the river. Towards the end of the night I danced with a young girl. She was slim and extremely attractive. She wore a light cardigan and skirt. I held her in my arms as we danced and I felt her body against mine. I thought of the beauty and soft slender touch of that young woman. The hellfire preacher said there was something wrong with my attraction to this young woman's beauty. That could not be right. That preacher was an idiot and a conman with his threats and collection plates. No more than being attracted to the beauty of the nature of the night was there anything wrong with being attracted to the beauty of this young woman. So there and then I made a decision.

To give my life to Jesus, whatever that meant, would be to give up all that was beautiful in life, and instead live a life of fear and self-denial and constrained existence and ignorance, of the idiocy and fear of burning in hell forever, whatever that meant. I looked again at the moon and the beauty of the moonlit night. I thought again of the young woman in the dancehall in Porthall. I thought again of the young women in the dance halls in Derry when they would get together and laugh and laugh and tease each other. I compared these things of beauty and life to the preacher's grotesque threat of burning in hell forever. Then and there I decided. I would not yield. Then and there I took my life back from Jesus, whoever he or she was. He or she would have to do without it. I needed it for myself.

I would learn that healthy sexual relations did not need the placing of some preachers hand on somebody's head, or the paying of some money into some church's plate, or the bowing down before some figure in intimidating robes, or the signing of a piece of paper. I would learn that wonderful healthy, pleasurable sexual relations were based on the great sexual energy of peoples' bodies and minds merging together with kindness, respect, and mutual caring. Burning in hell forever had nothing to do with it. Financial or commercial or property or religious relations had nothing to do with it. I would later read a study done in multiple countries which asked women what they most wanted in sexual partner. The number one answer by far was kindness. But a full understanding of what was a healthy approach to sex was still in the future. Meanwhile on that front while I was learning, I still had a way to go.

CHAPTER 8

A SCYTHE'S BLADE

ICONTINUED MY WORK on the farm. I took up playing rugby with Strabane, the local team. This would temporarily help rid me of my frustrations and anger at not being able to understand my life and realise my potential to anything like the full extent. With the resulting pent up anger and frustrations I needed some outlet. And the violence of the rugby partially provided this. The violence of the rugby was regulated. It was an alternative to other forms of violence which could have ended me up in jail or other trouble. I would come out of the games feeling spent and exhausted and calm. But this would only last for a day or two until the rage and frustrations and alienation would build again. I was good at the rugby and played for the North West of Ireland on one occasion when I was eighteen.

But I had a problem. I again began to get concussions from injuries on the field. I had these on at least nine different occasions. They were severe. It was shocking not to be able to see objects clearly, not to be able to remember my own name or the names of those around me. No other player on the team had these. I could not find out why it was only me. The club management were mainly employers and they treated me as they treated their workers. When I was concussed, instead of taking me to the hospital they left me standing on the side of the pitch. These concussions would combine with other health issues to give me serious problems when I was older. When I would in later years become a revolutionary socialist, something of which my mother strongly disapproved, she would try to console herself by saying; 'You are not right, it was since you got all those batters in the head.' So much for my socialist ideas.

These years after I left school at sixteen made up a very confusing and frustrating period in my life. Leaving school, trying to work with my family on the farm; trying to deal with our different views; trying to figure out personal sexual relations; and above all trying to figure out my place and role in the world – I did not feel I was making any progress on any front.

I did not have many close friends. One was a young man whose father ran a horse-riding school. He was Catholic. He was very intelligent and very talented at all sports. We would play these different sports together, rugby, soccer, tennis, Gaelic football. He was better than me at all of these except rugby. We would also debate the things we saw going on in the world. He was more conservative than I. I had another friend. He was also Catholic. He was mad about a young Protestant woman whose father was very sectarian. I used to go to her house and collect her and we pretended to her father she was going out with me, 'a good Protestant'. This couple would later marry and he would 'turn' to be a Protestant. I suppose I was a sort of match maker.

It was an overcast and wet day in nineteen sixty four. I was nineteen. I was working in the meadow by the river with Arty. We were cutting rushes to cover the potato pits. As I looked at him swinging the scythe in front of me I thought of the twenty years he had worked in London. I thought about seeing him standing in the house in Portinure in his fashionable clothes when he returned and how this made me want to go and see the world. I thought about my own visit to London. That is where I had seen the great silverback and kissed and touched the girl in the tent. I had learnt new things there. And right then and there it struck me. If I was to learn new things and figure out my role and place in life and in the world I would have to go away again and see more of that world. I would never be able to figure things out stuck in Lifford. How could I understand the world, see my role in the world unless I saw more of the world. This conclusion came to me without warning. But when it came it came.

However then I stopped in my tracks with a bunch of untied rushes in my hands. What about my family? This would be bad. My uncle had sold his horses to keep me at home? I had left school when my mother had wanted me to stay on and get some qualifications. For a second I thought that I could not do it. That it would be too much pain for my family. But I pushed these thoughts aside. I had to do it. I had to go and see what was what and what was my role. I needed to see more of the world and learn who I was and what was my role within that world. Rupturing – stunting – cauterising – the tearing of flesh – the crushing of emotions – the repressing of some of my own most healthy psychological impulses – the inflicting of hurt and more hurt, these were all unavoidable if I was to fight to find my role and my place in the world. But I was going to do it. I had no choice. I readied myself to tell my family and to hurt them. I bared my teeth and clenched my fists.

I thought about how my going would hurt my family but I did not think much about how they would keep the farm going without me. They had when I was at school full time. They could hire somebody else and pay them. This was not a major issue for me. The major issue was how my going would hurt my family. In the end a young male relative of the family came and lived with them and helped. He was a good person and in fact got on with my family better than I did.

As I came to this conclusion that I had to go and see the world I continued tying the bunches of rushes. Arty swung the scythe before me. I saw the hole in the back of his wellington into which the water leaked and which kept his foot permanently wet. He drew back the sharp edged scythe to take another swing and I saw a small frog fall over on its side with the blood leaking from its belly where Arty had accidently cut it. I felt for that frog. It was finished. Life was hard. Life was going to be hard for my family too when I told them my new decision. I wished I could have saved the frog. I wished I could save my family from the cut I was about to inflict upon them when I told them what I was going to do. I wished I did not have to cut my family's belly with the sharp edge of my leaving. But there are things that at times cannot be avoided. Just as the swing of the sharp cutting edge of the scythe ended the wee frog's life in terrible pain, so too would the swing of my own personal scythe cause irreparable pain to my family.

That night everybody in the household was sitting round the big table in the kitchen after having the evening meal. Without any build up I said: 'I am thinking about going away for a while, to see other places. I want to see if everyplace is like here where they all want to know if you are a Catholic or a Protestant, where they all look at you to see if you have any money and how much. I want to see where I fit into it all.' I wanted to say also to see how men and women relate to each other, what this sex and gender thing was all about. But I knew this would be dismissed as ridiculous by my family so I left it out.

My family stared at me in shock. What was I saying? Go away? Sure wasn't the farm here for me, paid off and out of debt? What would I go away for? Sure half the country would give their eye teeth for my situation. And now things were getting even better. Did I not have a car to drive about in? They could not believe what I was saying. None of us knew that this was the beginning of the disintegration of the entire plan and aspiration my family had for themselves and for me. But that is what it was. It was an earthquake in our family relations. Things would never be the same again.

My mother recovered first: 'You cannot leave us John. Sure we are depending on you to take over the place. Sure your uncle got rid of the horses to keep you here. Sure we have done everything we could.' My uncle joined in. 'John some of them places you might have to work in out there might not be as easy for you as here. You are better off here.' The debate went back and forward. But I was insistent. In the end I was surprised how quickly the resistance gave way. It was not because my family did not want me to stay, it was because they saw how determined I was to go. My mother recognised this first. I think she always suspected that one way or another I would never fit in.

She said, 'I do not want you to go. But I should have seen this coming. Whenever we went to the Sunday school picnic every year in Portrush all you ever wanted for a toy was a boat. And you were never away from them streams. You have been wanting to go all these years and I suppose you did not even know it. And then there was that time you went away to Uncle George's without telling us. Just got up one Sunday morning and took off. Left us that note: "Gone to Uncle George's." Maybe that was like a practice. I do not want you to go but I will not stand in your way.' My mother was referring to when I was thirteen and had got up early from bed one Sunday morning, got out my bicycle and without telling anybody quietly left the house and cycled the forty miles to my father's Uncle George's house up past Donegal Town. I got sick out of that adventure from drinking out of a stream by the roadside in Barnesmore Gap.

I did not realise until many years later how that adventure of mine, taking off without telling anybody and cycling to my father's uncle's house must have made my family think that there was something different about me. That they would have to be prepared for shocks from me. It was one thing after another. After leaving school and going to work on the farm I was now changing my mind and leaving the farm and going abroad. After my family's attempt to introduce me into the Orange Order world and to groom me for that world I rejected that world. After being introduced into the religious sectarian world of the churches I rejected that world. After being told that the debt free farm would be mine for the keeping I rejected that also. My family must not have known whether they were coming and going with me. I would increasingly feel sorry for them and for the pain I was inflicting on them.

It was a great tribute to my family how good they were in helping me prepare to leave. They were very kind and intelligent people. They did not want me to go but they helped me to go. They helped me get money for my ticket and to keep me until I found a job when I got there. And this when they thought I might not be coming back. I decided I would go to Canada as it was the easiest country to get into. My family drove me to Belfast in two cars, our own and one belonging to the boyfriend of my sister Mary.

The ship was boarding when we arrived. For the first time in my adult life I hugged my mother. With the cruelty of youth I did not think about what she and my family were going through. They must have been thinking that they might never see me again. There was no flying back and forward for holidays in those days. I went up the gangplank, the boat cast off, drifted out into the channel and we were on our way. I stood at the rail looking back at my mother. She was standing waving a small white lace handkerchief. She must have taken it especially from her chest of drawers to wave me off. It was an Ulster linen handkerchief. Was this not a sign of the richness and depth of feeling and spirit of my mother, her linking, even if unconsciously, my going to the art of the Ulster linen handkerchief. I would come to be attracted to Ulster linen as part of my world of art. Maybe this was because of my mother's small waving Ulster linen handkerchief. Soon she and the handkerchief were out of sight. It was the ending of an era for both of us, the ending of our close relationship as mother and son. I was twenty.

There was another thing I was only to think of later about my mother and that day. My mother had been born and lived most of her life in Donegal. The longest distance she had ever been from Donegal was Belfast. She travelled to there on two occasions. The first time was when my father was in the last months of his life and he went to Belfast to see what was hoped to be a better doctor. This was not successful. My father died a short time later. After the doctor told my father he could not help him, that it was probably all in his head my father was very angry. We left the doctor's office and my father rushed ahead down the street. My mother suggested we stop and get a cup of tea. But my father was so angry and frustrated he ignored this suggestion. My mother spoke to me on a number of occasions of how upset she was by this. Not being able to stop for a cup of tea in a small café in a big city. I was taken to Belfast with my mother and father on that occasion. Part of the male privilege.

The second time my mother was in Belfast was on that day to see me off on my travels. She must have felt that this could also be like a death in the family. Maybe I would never come back. Maybe she would never see me again. But with the thoughtlessness of youth, with my determination to get out there and see the world and learn, I sailed away oblivious. Again the cruelty of youth.

My family drove back home in the two cars. I went below deck to get something to eat. I sat with two men from Belfast who were emigrating to Canada. They had families and they told me they were going to get jobs and bring their families out as they believed that trouble was coming in the North. They mentioned about the right wing sectarian bigot Paisley and his marches against the Irish flag being flown. They were right that trouble was coming. I did not give their views much thought. I was focused on my coming adventures, on arriving in Liverpool, on getting to Canada, on finding out new things and new places. I was focused on finding a new life for myself, on finding a role and place for myself in the world. Little did I know that I would find these back home from where I was leaving, back in the very coming troubles from which the two Belfast men were escaping, back in what I then thought was the backward Ireland from which I was fleeing.

CHAPTER 9

A MINE – A LUMBER CAMP –
NEW YORK CITY

CHANGING BOATS at Liverpool I had a day to spare before boarding the liner to Montreal. I took some of the travelling money I had and bought myself a good quality black genuine leather jacket. It was another step away from rural Protestant Donegal and its tweeds. I was to wear this jacket every day for years to come. I would become known in some circles as 'your man in the black leather jacket'.

The liner for Montreal was enormous compared to the ship on which I had sailed years earlier from Belfast to Liverpool. It had a huge dining room with white table cloths where we were served breakfast, dinner and evening meals. It was a luxury holiday for me. There was no pressure on me to get up and milk the cows. I had never experienced anything like it before.

I spent the week-long voyage in the company of a young Burmese girl. She was beautiful with her black hair and soft brown skin. I was very attracted to her every part. She was perfectly suited to my lips, my fingers and my own skin. We both had to share our cabins with others. We spent many hours in the ship's cinema where we pleasured each other in a gentle but enthusiastic way.

We sailed up the St Lawrence. It was April and the banks of the river were still grey and dirty from the winter's snows. Great chunks of ice floated past in the water as the spring thaw had not completed its work. I was not impressed as I was used to the green of Ireland. But then was this not why I had left Ireland, to see new things and new places? And the grey and dirty banks of the St Lawrence were new things. It was my first conscious realisation that new things were not always beautiful or good things. But then I could only learn so much from the beautiful green of Ireland.

The boat docked and for the first time I was on a new continent. I parted from my Burmese friend who was staying in Montreal. I travelled down to Toronto. My first night there I went into the city centre and into a pub. Sitting drinking my soda water and lime I was approached by a tall man. How are you? I realised by his smile and tone and his hand on my shoulder that he was not just being friendly. I realised he was gay and looking to see what was what. This was the first time I had been approached by a gay man but I knew what was going on. I said sorry but I like women. He laughed. 'Well you won't get many in here. The women don't come into this bar.' Then I realised I had gone into a gay bar. He took me outside and pointed to another bar up the street. Try there and that is what I did. I was proud of myself that I had no animosity to this man for thinking I was gay and trying to get to know me. He was right about the other pub. I met a woman there and she took me home. We had a pleasurable evening.

The post-war economic upswing was still on and jobs were plentiful. At the job centre the man in charge suggested that I should go down to New York City as he knew they were looking for cops. He could set it up. He must have been on the take from the New York City police department. I said I would never be a cop. I would never arrest somebody for doing something I would do myself. He assured me that was not a problem. That in fact I was exactly the kind of person who would be a good cop, somebody who could be flexible about whom I would arrest and whom I would not, bend the rules a bit. Not everybody was the same you know he said. He smiled knowingly to me as he said this. I was insulted by his insinuations.

I found a job in a mine in a small town called Wawa in the wilds of north-west Ontario. I headed there on the train, got a room in a large dormitory for seasonal workers and went to the mine for my instructions and gear. I started the next day. The ore was dug out of the mine at the front and sent back on conveyor belts to big drums called breakers. Inside these were huge iron hammers. These smashed the ore into smaller pieces and from there it was moved on further up to the surface on other conveyor belts. My job was to clean up the spillage around the breakers and belts with a shovel.

I had never worked in such conditions before. The noise was all but unbearable as the breakers did their job. Dirt and dust was everywhere. The only light was a small yellow bulb. I thought of the beauty around our family's farm. I could see the three rivers at home flowing and glinting and merging on their way to the ocean. I remembered the quietness of the countryside and the soft rain falling. I contrasted these memories with my present surroundings. But again this was what I wanted, to see and experience new things and new places. It was this new type of harshness and new environment I needed and wanted. So I learnt to absorb the dirt and noise of the mine. I stopped seeing them as enemies that I had to avoid getting on my skin and in my eyes and ears. Instead I let them come to me, seeing them as agents for learning and change, for growth.

After every shift I would go into the showers with the rest of the workers and wash off the dirt. It was good to get clean again and away from the noise. The shift was made up of men from many lands. This was because it was hard, dirty, dangerous work, work easy to come by for the mainly immigrant workers like myself. These workers usually stayed in the mine for only a temporary period after they arrived in the country and then as soon as they accumulated some savings they moved on to an easier, safer job, a better job. Everybody was known by the country of their origin except for the one Native Canadian man. He was known as Marty. I was known as Irish. My Protestant family at home would not have been happy to hear me being called that. I kept quiet most of time and listened to the chat. I took pleasure in looking forward to each shift being over, more money earned and a time of rest ahead.

After a few weeks Marty approached me. He must have been observing me and noticed something in me. He did not approach any of the other workers. He invited me back to his place to listen to some music. He lived in a small shack on the edge of town. My head being full of stereotypes I expected country and western music. He took his coat off and threw it on the back of a chair and put on a record. 'This is the man. You will like him.' He poured himself a large glass of brandy. He held the bottle up to me and asked: 'Do you want some Irish?' I answered, 'No thanks, I do not drink.' 'Well do not worry about that. If there is any good in you, you will before it is all over.' And he laughed to himself knowingly and, lying back, closed his eyes and sipped his liquor.

The music began. I had never heard anything like it before. It came in great thunderous waves, then it would quiet down to almost nothing, you would have to strain to hear it, then it would rise again to rolling explosive crescendos. I resisted it. It was not familiar to me. In my backwardness I labelled it the big shots' music. It was not my music. I sat and listened and let no expression pass my face. I did not want to offend my host. This was the first time I heard Beethoven's Fifth Symphony. I was to owe Marty for the rest of my life.

After some time my new friend asked me my name. 'John,' I said. Marty responded: 'As you know I am called Marty. I was given a proper tribal name when I was born but they took me away to one of those Christian mission schools and took away my name and just about everything else. They called me Marty instead.'

'That was not right man,' I replied.

'It sure was not. But John you do not have an Irish name. I read the English came and took away the Irish names and gave you all English ones. That is probably why you are called John.'

I was stunned. I had never thought of that before. In a way I was worse off than Marty. At least he knew he did not have his birth and native name.

'Marty, I never thought of that. I wish I knew what my family's Irish name was or if they had an Irish name. I think Sean is the Irish for John, but I do not know what was my family's original Irish birth name. Or if they had an original Irish birth name. It would not have been Throne anyway. That is not an Irish name. Maybe it was something totally different and it was changed.'

There in Marty's shack I realised I did not really know who I was. I was living in Ireland speaking English with an English first name and with a last name that nobody knew where it came from. 'Marty, see the way you are called Marty, can I not call you your native name? Sure it is up to me what I call you.' 'Naw, you only think that. There are more things out there than you and me. It is too late to go back to calling me my native name now. If I did so or we did so it could bring trouble. Calling myself my native name could get me accused of being some sort of radical militant, one of those American Indian Movement ones or something. Marty will have to do.' I shook my head and said nothing. Marty was not only educating me in music but also in the ways of the world.

Some days later Marty invited me round again, this time to eat. We were becoming friends. For the first time I smelled garlic. I did not know what it was. He filled up with brandy as before and sitting down in his big chair we listened to Beethoven and another piece of music by a man called Stravinsky. It was the 'Rite of Spring'. 'Listen to this Irish. He was a great one too.' I sat back and took Marty's advice about how to listen to the music. He had explained to me that the rich kept all that was best to themselves and left us the scraps. But we were outfoxing them and listening to their music. We were not making do with the scraps. Even though when I would later come to hear jazz and soul and other music and see that Marty was not totally correct in his thinking about music in that way at that time his interpretation, his way of looking at it helped me to relax and let the great music into me. I was stealing from the rich. That was good. I liked that. I smiled to myself. But I did not know what I was to learn many years later. I was only enjoying a fraction of that music because my ear was so untrained and insensitive to its complexity and richness.

I did not drink or smoke, only spent on the essentials. With what I saved and what I had left over from when I arrived I soon had enough to take a trip. I decided on New York City. I quit the job, left my gear with Marty, the only person I trusted, and headed off to hitch the 1,000 or so miles to New

York. I thought about that. Marty was the only person I trusted yet he was the most exploited and discriminated against of all the people I knew in Wawa. The two Irish people I knew half well there were open racists and they also hated Catholics. I shook my head and left to hitch to New York City.

But the Canadian drivers must have thought all hitch hikers were serial killers as after two days I had only got three rides. I gave up and took the Greyhound bus. I fell asleep, woke at US customs and immigration, fell asleep and woke up several more times until there it was, the gigantic skyline of New York City.

Manhattan was the island at the centre of New York's five boroughs. It was a forest of skyscrapers where millions of people went up and down and lived and went to work and shopped and strolled and rushed every day. Millions of other people came from the city's other four boroughs every day to work in Manhattan. They travelled by train, bus, every kind of automobile. There were far too many people on far too little space. This and the city's racial mix and commerce and industry gave Manhattan its great energy and diversity. It was like a giant engine where the people and the vehicles and the machines and the products moved like a piston in and out of a cylinder, up and down in a cylinder. I thought about how much concrete and steel, how much human labour, how many sore backs, how many broken limbs, how many chapped knuckles, how many dead workers, had gone to build this city. I had never seen anything like it. I could not get over it.

I booked into a small hotel off Broadway and slept. In the morning I went out and ate in a diner and then went for a walk. People were rushing at me from all directions. I was not used to it. I thought I should meet the eyes of everybody and say hello. It was only polite. That was what we did in Lifford. But of course my New Yorkers did not even notice I was there. I felt I was having a nervous breakdown as I tried in vain to make contact. I stopped and leaned against a wall, gasping for breath and looking up to avoid seeing the hurrying crowds of people. I was having an anxiety attack as I tried to engage and say hello to everybody. I had to stop it. The peasant had to learn how to survive in the big city.

In the evening I asked the man behind the hotel desk where I should go for some night life. He directed me to Greenwich Village. I headed down. I came upon a club that was full of people, and from which music was blaring. I had never heard such music before. It sounded a bit like rock and roll but it was not rock and roll. I went in and sat at the bar and ordered my usual soda water and lime. There was an African American man in the seat beside me. I asked him: 'What kind of music is this?' 'What man? You have never heard the blues? You got to have the blues now and then. Where you from man?' I told him I was from Ireland. 'You must need the blues there too,' he said with a knowing laugh. I listened to the music. 'But you will not get into the blues drinking soda water man. You need a shot to take the edges off. With that and the blues the whole world can just float away.' And he laughed contentedly and knowingly to himself. I shook my head. Blues or no blues I was going to keep away from the drink until I had figured out my place in the world.

What the African American man said sounded like what Marty had said when I told him I did not drink and Marty chuckled to himself and told me not to worry that if there was any good in me I would before it was all over. Did Marty mean before my life was all over? Was this the same with the blues, were the blues like the drink for those times when you were too low and needed to be soothed, or needed to howl at the moon or needed to blot out what you were thinking? What about my father and the drink? Did he have the Donegal small farmer blues? I sat and let this thought and this new music come to me.

The next day riding on the subway and walking the streets I found I was getting used to the sound and the speed of the city and gradually coming to be able to enjoy the tremendous mixture and numbers of people, to be able to look at them without panicking or without feeling I had to make eye contact and speak to every one of them and getting every one of them to speak to me. When I conquered this I was no longer so stressed out. But I was worried.

What was it that I was I conquering? Was I developing the ability to be around a lot of people and not connect with them? But was this good? Was I not cauterising and stunting myself once again, this time not against my family or Barbara or my Protestant milieu, but this time against the millions of New Yorkers, against as I would later think about it, against the masses, against the working class. Was I back to the calluses again, back to the stunting and cauterising again, back to the defensive stance, back to another kind of siege mentality? I concluded I was. But I concluded that as I still did not know my place in the world this was, at least to some extent, inevitable. I would later find that I was right on this, that when I found my class position in society and my revolutionary socialist position in society rather than being in any way alienated from the masses in society I would be integrated into the masses of society.

Each night of the ten days I spent in New York I went to Greenwich Village. One night I went to a different bar where there was different music. I found it even stranger to my uncultured ear. I would later find out it was jazz and the world's greatest jazz musicians were in Greenwich Village at that time. But I found it overwhelming in its intense variety and newness, it seemed to me to be just noise, and so I only went to that jazz bar the one time. I knew there was something important about it but I was not able to get the feel for it. I would later hear of Louis Armstrong, Miles Davis, Billie Holliday, Ella Fitzgerald, if I had only had somebody to explain to me what was going on. I went back to the blues bar.

Every night I was in the blues bar I met the same African American man. The night before I left I was there as usual sitting at the counter with my new found friend when everything went quiet around us and everybody turned to stare at the TV screen. It was filled with images of thousands of black youth fighting the cops on the streets of Watts in Los Angeles. It was the Watts Uprising.

The African American man turned and said to me: 'What do they expect? They fuck us at every turn, give us no jobs, call us animals, send us to fight in Vietnam and they expect us to lie down and take it. Irish, I am happy tonight. The man is getting it. Look at them young ones in Watts. They are giving it to him. The Man deserves all he gets. I am happy I am alive to see this.' As he spoke he wiped tears from his cheeks with the back of his hand. 'You are right,' I said. 'People should be treated equally. They should stop attacking and killing black people.' I thought about that racist farmer merchant at home and hoped he was seeing this and getting alarmed.

My friend and I kept quiet and watched the uprising. There were people of different racial backgrounds in the bar. Some of the European Americans were uncomfortable, frightened, turning away from the TV screen. One of them shouted at the barman: 'Turn that of, we do not want to watch that.' But the African American man and I turned round on our stools and shouted: 'No leave it. We want to see it.' For a few seconds the uprising threatened to spread to the bar, but then the European American backed down, muttering to himself and we went on watching.

The images of the uprising brought tears flowing down my face. I clenched my fists in pride at the young people in the uprising and in frustration that I was not part of it. I was filled with the most powerful energy. This was the way things should be. My family was wrong. I was right. Things could be changed. These black youth and workers were changing things in the streets of Los Angeles in front of my eyes. I celebrated their uprising. I was learning new things and the African American youth and workers of Watts and my African American friend in that bar in New York, and Marty up in Canada were my teachers. I thanked them all in my mind.

As I was heading back to Canada the next day I left the bar early and walked up Broadway towards my hotel. I was still filled with energy and laughter and joy and power from watching the uprising. I wanted to share this, to share myself, with somebody. In front of me were two beautiful looking women in their early twenties. They were talking and laughing and giggling, bending forward and holding their sides. And on occasion they would glance over their shoulder at me. I asked them how they were. They said they were well. I told them that was good. I asked them where they were from. They said they were from Puerto Rico originally. I was very attracted to their dark skin and afro hair styles. I said I was from Ireland.

We came to a subway stop. One of them said she had to get her train there. 'Jenny, Irish here can walk you on up to your stop. Can't you Irish.' I smelled a plot. I liked it. When we got up to my hotel I asked Jenny would she like to come in. She said yes. I was worried when I saw there was a cop talking to the man behind the front desk. But both of them ignored us.

There was no shower in my room, only a small wash hand basin and off the room a small toilet. Jenny went in and used the toilet and after she was finished I did the same. When I came out she was sitting on the bed. I sat down beside her and we kissed. Then she said: 'Wait Irish, I am all sweaty. Let me have a wash.' And without anything more she stood up pulled off her shirt, and her skirt and panties and standing naked began to wash herself. She pushed her sex out over the basin washing herself and looking over her shoulder at me said, 'You do not mind Irish', and laughed.

Mind? Mind? Far from minding I was aroused fit to burst by Jenny's audacity and nakedness and beauty and colour. When she was finished I got the courage to follow her lead and took off my clothes and washed as she had. We then joined each other on the bed. Is it okay I asked her, about the getting pregnant? She said yes do not worry. And being young and full of the energy and drive of our years we pleasured each other for hours.

Jenny taught me new things. She offered all of her body to my lips. This was new to me and I gratefully accepted it and received a pleasure and intimacy I had never before experienced. She took all of my body to her lips. This was also new to me, and this too gave me a pleasure and intimacy I had never before experienced. We pleasured each other and played and laughed together, we did not hide what we were doing from each other, we did not close our eyes tight or grit our teeth, we did not feel guilty about what we were doing, we shared and celebrated and laughed in our pleasure. We thought about the needs and desires of each other. I entered the world of passionate, all-engrossing, civilised sex. Not civilised in the sense of restrained, hypocritical, bourgeois civilisation, but civilised in the sense of thinking about each other and what each other wished for and desired. I had found one of the things I wanted to find when I had left on my travels. The way of sex, in my case the man and the woman, the to and the fro of it all, the laughter of it all. Exhausted, Jenny and I fell asleep for a brief few hours in our sex bed.

When the sun rose Jenny jumped up: 'Irish I have to go. My kids are with my mother and I have to go and get them to school and then get to work. It was good last night. But I have to go. Hey Irish have you got a few dollars. I need something for my kids' lunch.' I gave Jenny twenty dollars and asked her was that okay. She said yes that was good. She dressed and throwing a kiss over her shoulder rushed out the door.

I sat on the bed and thought about what had happened. Had I just paid for sex? I concluded that I had not. That what Jenny and I had together we both wanted to have together and it was only right that as I had more money than her I should share some of it. I knew how some of the backward males at home would see this but I was not them. If I was I would still be stuck in Lifford. What Jenny and I had together was healthy and joyful and clean and guilt-free.

Jenny was a New Yorker, a good looking, urban, working class woman in one of the most sophisticated cities in the world. She was living the best years of her life in the 1960s, the decade of revolution and change, the time of the pill and women having increasing control over their own bodies. She was full of confidence in herself as a woman and a person. She helped give me confidence that I could have a better and different personal and sexual life. She confirmed for me that my struggle to get over the old religious anti-sexual prejudices with which I had been indoctrinated at home was correct. She confirmed for me that it was all lies that women were in some way no good if they had sex outside of marriage. She helped me see how a man and a woman could have wonderful respectful sex full of laughter and joy. This was a big contribution to my life. I added Jenny to Marty and my African American friend in the pub, to the man with hands for everything back home in Lifford, to the great silverback, to my list of teachers.

I thought about the difference between what I had with Barbara and what I had with Jenny. Why was my time with Jenny so carefree and guilt-free? Why did my time with Barbara end so fraught and conflicted? Was I not the same me. Well I was and I was not. I was not because the circumstances were different in New York with myself and with Jenny than they were in rural Ireland with Barbara.

With Barbara the whole weight of backward Irish society pressed down on our shoulders, private property, class, religion, gender, politics. I was the son of a small property owner set to inherit a small farm. This inevitably influenced how we related to each other. Barbara's family and milieu hoped that she would marry me and be part of a property-owning family. My family on the other hand was worried this might happen. They wanted me to marry somebody who already had property and in this way add to the property they themselves had. I went out for a while with a young woman, she was an only child and her family had a three hundred acre farm, my family were very pleased with her. Well my mother was more reserved. Her life had taught her that there were few free lunches. I did not want to get married to anybody, three hundred acres or not, because I did not know my place in the world. But I knew it was not on a small or for that matter a large farm outside Lifford. The personal sexual relations between Barbara and I were carried on within this environment and as a result deformed, fraught, conflicted and with a not good end.

Things were different entirely with Jenny in New York. I was a visitor passing through. She knew I was leaving the next day. There were no complications such as property or family. It would never have occurred to her that I was the possible heir to a small farm in Ireland and if it had what would it have meant to her anyway? It would have been unimaginable to her to leave New York City and go and live in Lifford. It would have been completely outside any concept she would have had of her life. So with this we were able to enjoy ourselves together for a night, without entanglements and property and religion weighing on our shoulders, and with the availability of contraception and so without the risk of Jenny becoming pregnant. We were able to be together without seeing our actions as ways to get our hands on property or advantages or seeing our activities as threats to property and advantages. On top of that we were genuinely physically attracted to each other and able to share laughter and our erotic energy. And along with this there was a kindness in us and so we wanted to share our pleasurable sexuality. There was also my energy after watching the Watts uprising. This combination of factors made what we had possible and exciting and healthy. This was why I could give Jenny twenty dollars without any negative complications. This is why Jenny could take twenty dollars from me without any negative complications.

After washing I went down to eat. The same man was on the desk. 'Hey Irish you had that one in your room last night. You owe me.' I said okay and gave him a ten dollar bill. 'Is that alright?' He said it was. New York, the USA, it was hard to get away from the dollar.

I boarded the bus back to Canada, picked up my things from Marty, said goodbye and thanked him, and headed out west and got a job in a lumber town called Marathon. Logs were floated in off the lake onto elevators, cut into short lengths and shunted along moving belts to the mill where they were processed into paper pulp. I worked at the junction between two sets of belts keeping the junction from becoming blocked. At night I could see the Northern lights. In spite of the noise of the thumping logs going from one belt to another it was better than the mine.

As soon as I got into town I began to look for a girlfriend. It had not occurred to me that I would have any problem. After all Jenny and I had got together easily. And after all back home I was always able to get a girlfriend. But I got a surprise. I could not get a girl to go out with me. I got so frustrated that one night I said to a girl I had asked out in the diner: 'What is wrong? Why will you not go out with me?'

She looked at me and then hesitated as she decided whether or not to tell me. 'I do not go out with boys who work in the mill, who are seasonal workers in the mill, and live in those dormitories. You do not even have a car. I would never hear the end of it if I went out with you.' I was so shocked that I could not answer. It had never occurred to me. So that was it. I was not good enough for her. I was part of the unskilled, temporary, low-paid workforce. It was a class question.

Back home I was the nephew of a man who owned a farm, the presumed inheritor of that farm, a future property owner even if the property was small. I had a car. I lived in a house my family had lived in for at least 200 years. In this town I was a seasonal worker without roots or property. I was a 'nobody'. Or maybe at best I was just a pair of hands. And a pair of hands was not good enough for girls whose families had more than a pair of hands. And in that town all the families who had children and daughters were in management in the lumber mill and so saw themselves as in a higher class than me, that is having more than a pair of hands.

I was in shock after this young woman told me why she would not go out with me. But she had done me a big favour. She helped me see how my class position in society affected my personal life. Back home I had never given that much thought. But now I knew if I had I been a low paid temporary worker with nothing at home it would have been a different story there too. I thought of the young men in the café who could not afford to buy their girlfriends a pea supper when I could afford to buy Barbara a pea supper. The role of class entered into my understanding of my personal life in a real and conscious way for the first time.

As soon as I had earned some money in the lumber town I headed on west. I got a job for a while with a farmer who grew wheat. I spent days sharpening the blades on his combine harvester. I slept in a bunk in his barn and washed in a bucket of water. I was brought into the house to eat. I suppose that was something. But I did not stay long. The wheat farm was isolated. I had no car. All I could do at night was lie in the barn. Not so bad but a bit like my grandmother when she was hired out and had to sleep in a barn. I could not stick the isolation. And I was learning nothing, I already knew how to sharpen blades for cutting wheat. On top of that this farmer was a miserable individual. All he did from morning to night was complain about how broke he was. Not unlike the farmers at home. Soon I had had enough. I quit, got a Greyhound bus and headed on west.

That is where I was, barrelling west on a Greyhound bus, when the Rockies came into view. I stared and stared. I could not believe it. At first I thought it was clouds in the sky they were so high. But no it was the gigantic Rockies. They were spectacular. I took them all in as the bus drove on west, up and up, round and round the curving road, then down and down the curving road, and at last down into British Columbia, and Vancouver. So I thought the British stole this too. Otherwise why could it be called 'British' Columbia? I wondered where the Columbia came from, and I wondered what the native people had called it. Not British Columbia, I was sure of that.

I was not broke when I arrived in British Columbia. I did not want to go to work right away. I asked around where people hung out and was directed to the beach at English Bay. British Columbia! English Bay! British imperialism had no shame. Massacre the native people and rename everything after itself. Like they renamed Marty. I got the bus out to English Bay and swam and lay in the sun. It was the first day in my adult life that I spent lying doing nothing on a beach. It would also be my last.

As I lay there I thought about my travels so far. I was doing good seeing new places, meeting new people, learning new things. I felt no desire to stay in one place and make permanent friends. I wanted to move on and keep seeing more new places and meeting more new people and learning more new things.

CHAPTER 10

TO SEA

WHEN I WAS PLAYING in the streams at home and when I was looking at the tides going in and out at Lifford and Strabane and Portrush I had always dreamed of going to sea. Now here I was at the ocean and the tides were right there. A log came in and out on each wave. It brought me to my senses. I sat up with a start. What was I thinking? I was right by the ocean. I had no ties or commitments. But what was I doing? I was lying on the beach, on dry land. I was shocked at my behaviour. I was a disgrace. I even looked around for a moment thinking would anybody be able to figure out my stupidity. I immediately jumped up, gathered my stuff, caught the bus downtown to the docks and signed on as an ordinary seaman on a Norwegian bulk carrier.

The bulk carrier was the length of a city block. It was loading a cargo of wheat getting ready to head down the west coast of the US and Mexico, through the Panama Canal and across the Atlantic to Gdansk in Poland. It was designed to carry ores and grains and loose cargo. As the most recent to have signed on I was the lowest in seniority and so my cabin was at the bottom of the hull of the ship where the noise of the engine and the propeller was greatest. Sometimes when coming awake I would think the noise was my uncle shouting at me to get up and milk the cows.

We sailed three days after I signed on. The cry went up, all hands on deck. Everybody was necessary to untie from the dock and turn the huge vessel into the channel and out to sea. The officers shouted commands, the engine throbbed, the propeller turned and took the pressure off the thick ropes which tied the ship to the dock fore and aft. The dockers slipped the ropes free, the ship swung out. We were off. I could not wait.

I was on the eight to twelve shift, eight to twelve in the morning and eight to twelve in the evening. On the morning shift I cleaned the toilets and showers and chipped rust of the decks and if the weather was right I painted the rust spots. During the evening shift I spent one hour up on the bow of the ship on watch for the lights of other ships. If I saw one I rang the bell, one for starboard, two for port and three for dead ahead. That was my favourite time, up there in the dark by myself.

Some nights when up front I would hear splashing down in the water. I would lean over the rail to see what was happening. One night the moon was full and I saw it was dolphins. They were riding the shock wave, a surge of water that was pushed in front of the ship. I had to be careful as I kept forgetting to watch out for lights from oncoming ships I was so attracted to these creatures. I wished I could get down there with them and ride on their backs and grasp their fins and hold on. Shouting and laughing we would ride the shock wave together.

I would lean over the ship's rail. Looking down into the dark ocean as it slipped back behind us. Listening to the swish as the huge ship slipped through the water heading south. Gazing at the stars above. Looking down at the playing dolphins. These were beautiful times. And I was alone. Nobody to bother me. Just myself and the sea and the sky and the ship and the dolphins. I would later read and learn Masefield's poem where he wrote of the lonely sea and the sky. That was it.

At the end of each hour I would swap with the other ordinary seaman on my shift and go back to the wheelhouse and steer the ship under the command of the officer. When steering we would keep the needle, which was controlled by the ship's wheel, in line with the selected degree on the compass and in this way keep the ship on course.

On the evening of my second day at sea the storm hit. Great waves and gales rolled in from across the Pacific. In spite of its cargo of wheat, which acted as ballast, the ship was thrown around and battered as if it was a toy. It rolled from side to side, it lifted up at the bow and sank down at the stern, it lifted up at the stern and sank down at the bow. It rolled over from side to side. Its huge steel structure fought for survival against the power of the sea. This was great. I had no idea at the time how many bulk carriers were lost at sea. But it would have made no difference if I had known. For me it was where I wanted to be and what I wanted to be doing. I wanted to be in struggle with the sea.

And it was not only the power of the sea and the storm and the gale, there was also the beauty and drama of it all. The white caps on the waves, the green and grey as they rolled in and broke on the ship and rolled on past to the Oregon coast, the noise as they merged with the gale and the storm, all was buffeted by all, the sea, the ship, the waves, the gale, the storm all merging in a non-stop battle.

But a couple of hours from the end of my shift on the first day of the storm things began to change. I no longer felt so wonderful. My stomach began to demand some less rocky place to rest. My exhilaration at riding the raging power of the sea was replaced by a horrible sickness. I tried to hold myself against the rolling of the ship to give myself a chance to feel better. But this made it worse.

Towards the end of the shift I threw up, all that was in my stomach went over the side. I clung to the rail and vomited. An older seamen came out on deck. As soon as he saw me being sick over the rail he shouted. 'Get away from that rail. A night like this, a big one could come over and that would be the end of you. Get back, be sick wherever you want but not there.' I did not answer him, just went inside and down to my cabin. He was right. I was an idiot.

Hour after hour I spent in the toilet being sick. I became exhausted and fell asleep in my bunk. Then I heard the roar. 'Get up, what do you think it is? A holiday camp?' It was one of the ship's officers. 'Get up. Your shift started an hour ago. Sick or not sick you work on this ship.' And that is what I did. And for the next four days through raging seas and sick stomachs and vomiting I worked my shifts. I thought of my uncle saying that I might not have it so good working at some of the places I would end up.

On the fourth day the storm subsided. I also began to get my sea legs, began to be able to adjust to the roll and pitch of the ship. Now once again the storm, rather than making me sick, made me feel full of power and exhilaration. I rejoiced again as the ship rolled and plunged and leapt and fought in the waves.

Working in the harshness of the mine with its noise and darkness, working in the lumber mill and the tedious nights shifting the logs, now at sea and having come through days of sea sickness and finding my sea legs, being shouted at by the officer and having to take it, having to work whether I was sick or not, I was getting toughened up. This was good. But it was more than that. I was no longer working for a family member, or as an individual as I had at home on my uncle's farm. I was working as part of groupings of workers employed and hired and ordered about by a boss or bosses I did not know. What was happening was that I was being proletarianised, that is I was becoming a member of the working class. I was moving from one class to another. It would affect the rest of my life. I was being made to understand that I could not do what I liked in life. Instead I was the object of great pressures, great forces. I was becoming a worker in a bosses' world. Moving from one class to another was not an easy thing, was not without great tensions. I would come to understand that better later. But that would be for later. I would also understand that my moving from one class to another was essential for my development and to my realising my potential.

When I was not on shift I was either in my cabin or in the mess where the ship's crew members ate and hung out. The ship's carpenter was from the Cape Verde Islands and the bosun was from Spain. They were close friends. They would regularly come up from their own smaller mess. They singled me out and told me their stories and jokes and made me laugh. I had not yet reached the stage in my life where I was a storyteller so I could not respond to their stories with my own. But they enjoyed keeping me going.

One night things got more serious. I asked Verdes, he was always called Verdes, as the Spanish man was called Spanish and I was called Irish: 'Verdes, why do you only hang out with me here?' Both Verdes and Spanish went silent. Then I got the impression that they decided to trust me and answer my question. Their hesitation reminded me of the hesitation of the young woman in Marathon when I asked her why she would not go out with me. Her hesitation came from the tendency in polite society not to speak of class. My friends' hesitation came from the tendency in mixed race society not to speak of race.

It was Verdes who answered. 'Look Irish I am black. And Spanish is not much whiter. There are men on this ship who do not like us for that. It would be easy for them to hit us one and dump us overboard and we would never be seen again. We keep our distance from them. With you it is different, we know you would not do that.' I put my head down. I was ashamed of my ignorance. 'Do not worry about it Irish. The world should not be like that but it is.'

One night only Verdes appeared. He told me why. Spanish had fought in the Spanish Civil War against Franco. I had never heard of Franco or the Spanish Civil War. 'What do you mean?' I asked. 'Sometimes he gets a bit down and he has to be alone. He cannot go home to Spain, they would go after him, that Franco crowd, kill him. The big shots, the Catholic Church, they all backed Franco. Hundreds of thousands were killed. Spanish told me he went round the battlefields in the morning and bayoneted the wounded enemy. They did not shoot them because they did not want to waste bullets. That has an effect on a man.' I sat and thought of Spanish and all the things I did not know.

After a few days we entered the Panama Canal. The green vegetation on both sides was beautiful. I had never seen anything like its lushness. Verdes was the most skilled man on the wheel and was steering the ship through the narrow waterway. The officers recognised his skill and in spite of him being black they had him steer. They did not want to risk any damage to the ship or the canal and the company to lose money. When it was money it did not matter that Verdes' skin was black. The only colour in which they were interested in those circumstances was the green of the dollar. If Verdes' black skin could bring them more green then they were on board with that.

Spanish came and stood beside me where I leaned over the rail as we made our way through the canal. 'Irish the Yanks invaded Columbia and stole a bit of it to make Panama, so they could build this canal for themselves. Panama, Pan American, you see. And to dig it they brought ones in from all over. Nearly 30,000 died digging it. All for the Yanks.' Spanish spit down into the water. I felt the same way.

It was not winter yet but crossing the North Atlantic to Gdansk was brutally cold. I had no winter clothes and at times felt my life was in danger as the wind cut its way through me. But we made it to Gdansk. It was my first visit to what they called a Communist, or as I would later call it, a Stalinist, country. I did not know what to expect.

The street lights and the lights in the windows of the shops and houses were weak and yellow. This at first repelled me. Was it not just a dump? But after a few days I adjusted and then I got to like the weak yellow lights better than the garish aggressive lights of the West, better than Times Square. The Gdansk lights were peaceful and, subtle. I was not being attacked. I was not being over stimulated at every turn.

At nights myself and some shipmates would go ashore to a pub which had music and dancing. The atmosphere was good. The customers sang together. I was astounded to hear them sing 'It's a long way to Tipperary'. How could this be? Then Spanish explained it to me. 'They learnt it from the Irish somewhere during the war. Your fellow country-men must have been homesick.' I became friends with a Polish lady there and she took me home to her apartment which she shared with her children and another family and their children. I would later understand that this two families in the one apartment was a reflection of the failure of the Stalinist regimes to provide for the needs of their populations.

On a day off I visited a Polish graveyard. It reminded me of Lifford where my father was buried. It had similar worn tombstones and trees and ivy. There were a few old men there speaking in Polish. I could only explain by drawing a map with a stick on the ground that I was from Ireland. But in spite of not being able to speak each other's language we seemed to be able to communicate in some way. Maybe there was something in the experience of the Polish and the Irish that was in common and helped. For one thing invasion and occupation by foreign powers was a shared experience.

The ship sailed again, headed for Brazil, up the Amazon river for a load of iron ore. We were crossing the Atlantic empty. A storm hit and with no cargo for ballast we were tossed about like an empty plastic bottle. At times the front three quarters of the giant structure was lifted right out of the water and would come down with a great splat. Some mornings I would come on deck and there would be flying fish all over the place. They would have leapt out of the water at night when the ship was low and ended up on the deck. I felt for them. But there was the power of the sea, the variation, the wildness of the sea, I was mad about it all.

Coming on deck one morning to start my shift I was surprised to see the ocean was brown. Verdes explained. The Amazon was such a big and fast flowing river it brought down so much silt and sand that it discoloured the ocean out to before you could even see land.

As we got closer to shore and into the river and the banks came closer, I could see the vegetation was almost as lush and green as Panama. Our destination was the end of a giant conveyor belt that emerged out of the jungle. We edged in under it and tied up. The holds were opened and the belt started running and one after another the holds were filled with ore. So this was how it worked. The rich countries came to the poor countries and took what they had. The wealth of this poor country was being taken to the rich country. All the poor country got was some money for the ore and all the workers got was the lowest of wages for digging it out. The rest of the wealth from the ore and what would be made out of it went to the corporations in the rich country.

Around the base of the belt were a couple of dozen huts made out of pieces of wood and flattened out soda cans. The families who lived in them were barefoot with shapeless pieces of clothing hanging from their shoulders. The young women offered themselves to the ship's crew for any few dollars they could get. Like the country's ore the young people were also for sale. One beautiful young black girl came on board. She walked up to me. Saying 'dollars' she put her back against the ships rail, closed her eyes, parted her legs and pulled up her rag of a dress. I loved the way she looked, the beautiful colour of her skin and hair, the slim shape of her small round breasts, her long legs the warm v of her sex. I wished I could have gone with her in a way that would not have been buying her like a piece of ore. But this was not possible. So I turned away.

She moved on to another crew member. He was a European American from a southern US state. I had heard him say how he hated African American people. But this did not stop him from taking this young black woman. He grunted and bared his teeth as he thrust aggressively between her legs and drove her again and again against the ship's hard iron rail. She kept her head turned to the one side and upwards and her eyes closed trying to have as little contact with the rapist's face, with the rapist as a person, as possible. Between the conveyor belt and shipping the ore to the USA and watching this racist I had to fight to remind myself that it was the American system that was rotten, that there were good Americans.

When the ship was loaded we set off down river. One effect of the speed of the current was that the riverbed was continually shifting and sand banks were always forming, moving and reforming. Before we reached the ocean we hit a sandbank and stuck fast. There we were, with a ship load of iron ore stuck in the middle of the Amazon, right on the terrible heat of the equator.

For the deckhands like me who were daily chipping rust and painting on the roasting decks this heat was bad. On the second day I could not take it anymore. With another crewmember, a young Australian called Chester Harris with whom I would become friends, we went to the front of the ship, climbed up on the rail and dived down into the river to cool off. My dive took me out from the side of the ship and down deep. I had underestimated the speed of the current. So by the time I surfaced I was going past the gang plank which was hanging down near water level at the stern of the ship.

Chester had not dived but had jumped straight down into the river and so was close to the ship's side. He was also a better swimmer than I. So he made it quicker to the bottom of the gang plank and climbed up on its bottom step. I struggled to avoid being washed away down river. I wondered was I going to drown. Or maybe the piranha fish would eat me. However with a major effort I managed to get closer to the gang plank and Chester caught my wrist and helped me scramble on board. It was close.

When this was going on the ship's captain and officers were leaning over the rail shouting orders at us. The rest of the crew were leaning over the rail and roaring encouragement. Some locals who were on a small canoe trying to sell things sat astounded and disbelieving at the stupidity of anybody who would jump into the river with its lethal current and its killing piranhas. I realised that I was in danger of death as I struggled. But for some reason I felt no panic. Instead I felt that I was observing myself and the whole scene from on high. Along with that the image of my home in Lifford contested for space in my mind. My Australian friend saved my life that day. We would make contact many decades later when I wrote my book The Donegal Woman. Chester by that time had become a well-known artist.

To get the ship free from the sandbank they flew down some so-called expert from New York. He did not even come on board. He just contacted the ship and told the captain to drop anchor. This was done and within two days the river washed the sandbank away and the ship floated free. Sometimes you get free by taking action and sometimes you get free by doing nothing and letting what holds you take action. It was a new concept to me. I did not know at the time but I was being introduced to an element of the dialectic. I would learn more about that later.

We were headed for New Orleans. Before we got there Verdes and Spanish confided in me that they were signing off and I could come with them if I wanted. I then made one of the worst mistakes of my life. I did not accept their invitation. I would have learnt so much from them if I had. It is likely I would have found the alternative that I was looking for much quicker, that I would have learned my role in the world, my place in the world, much sooner than I did.

But I was young and with the stupidity of youth. And also by the time they told me of their plans I had been talking to some of the other younger crew members and we had decided to sign off in New Orleans pool our money, buy a boat and sail around the Caribbean. The fact that none of us knew anything about navigation or sailing a boat never entered our heads. Spanish and Verdes in their wisdom tried to talk me out of it but when they saw I was determined they shook their heads and laughed and told me to be careful.

We did not tell the ship's officers we were signing off until the last minute. We wanted to get our tests and shots for the tropical diseases. This was normal after working in the tropics. On my second day in New Orleans I went to the doctor. I was sitting on a soft seat in the waiting room looking at a glossy magazine noticing nothing that seemed to be unusual. Then I was called and walked down the hallway to the doctor's office. On the way I passed a door into another waiting room. I looked in. There were only African American people in that room. They had no soft seats, only wooden benches, and they had no magazines, glossy or otherwise.

I was in a state of shock when I went into the doctor. So this really existed, this up front segregation and open blatant discrimination. The doctor gave me my shot and talked in a friendly way about where I had been and where I was from. He claimed he was part Irish himself. We were buddies according to him. I was disgusted to hear him and ashamed to think that he could think I would in any way be associated with him.

The pain of the shot was nothing to the shock I had received when I saw his segregated waiting rooms. I was too stunned to ask him why he was discriminating against African American people. I walked up the hall and again looked into the African American waiting room. When I came to the European Americans' waiting room I saw with different eyes. I had seen racism in all its unapologetic reality. For the first time I realised that I was privileged, of a privileged race, me with my soft seated waiting room and glossy magazines. Verdes had told me about the racism, but I only began to understand it there in that doctor's office in New Orleans.

That night Verdes and Spanish took me to Preservation Hall where African American musicians played jazz. I was honoured by their invitation. Looking back I think Spanish and Verdes were in a way trying to groom me like my family had been trying to groom me only they were doing it from the left while my family were doing it from the right. We sat in Preservation Hall and listened to some of the world's greatest jazz musicians. I had heard jazz in one of the pubs in Greenwich Village in New York City but both there and in New Orleans my untrained ear, the remnants of my rigid, narrow-minded, frightened, defensive siege mentality self, prevented me from getting anything like the most out of it. But I knew I was listening to something special. Like in the African American peoples' waiting room at the doctor's clinic these African American world-class musicians were sitting on hard wooden benches. And their hall was a broken down garage. I was thinking a lot of new thoughts about the USA and about race.

Myself and my five other crew members signed off. I said goodbye to Verdes and Spanish and thanked them for all they had taught me. I was halfway into the city from the docks when I realised that I did not know their real names. I wanted to run back and ask them but what difference would it have made. We could not have kept in touch. They lived on the sea. They had no homes. They had no Portinure. I wondered where they would end their lives.

The six of us who were planning to buy a boat and sail the Caribbean rented a double room off Bourbon Street, the centre of the city's night life. All of us stayed in this one room, sneaking in late at night. By day we prowled the city's boatyards looking for a boat. We did not know what we were doing. At night we went to the pubs and clubs. We were soon broke.

On one of these days I did not go boat hunting but went to the library instead. When I had been working in the lumber mill in Canada I had met a young man from Quebec. He said to me one day: 'Well what do you think of Joyce then?' I looked at him. 'Who is Joyce?' 'You know, the Irish writer. Some say he is the greatest writer ever.' I turned away from him in humiliation. I had never heard of Joyce.

I asked the librarian in New Orleans for a book by Joyce. She only had *Finnegans Wake*. I took it from her and went to a table. I tried to read it. I thought I had concussion. That was what it was like. I would understand some words, I would have no understanding of others, yet others would seem familiar and drift in and out of my consciousness and understanding and sub-consciousness giving me some sort of hint of a feeling that I understood something or I should understand something.

I put the book back. I knew as I did there was something important about it and I would return to it. For a second the thought of Van Gogh's print on the wall at school flitted into my head. *Finnegans Wake* seemed like reality yet was not reality, just like Van Gogh's print seemed like reality but was not reality, or was Van Gogh's print and *Finnegans Wake* the real reality? My head struggled to reach up and understand. I felt that the understanding was there somewhere just out of my reach. I was frustrated but I was also spurred to keep on searching to understand both Van Gogh and Joyce.

When I did return to read Joyce many years later I was to understand that Joyce would have been proud if he had heard that a young man from rural

Ireland reading *Finnegans Wake* in a New Orleans library for the first time thought he had concussion. I came to understand that the book was a brilliant and powerful confirmation of Joyce's genius, or as he put it his ability at times to reach states of exaltation. Part of my problem in trying to read it that day was that I tried to force it into my head rather than letting it come to me. And on top of that I was not ready to read that book. In fact I would not live long enough to ever be fully ready, even near partially ready, to read that book. It was too high above me on the cliff face. Years later I would come to understand that Joyce had great time for Van Gogh. He applied the word 'exaltation' to both himself and Van Gogh. Exaltation was a word Van Gogh used in his own struggle for expression. I was not so far wrong in thinking there was some connection between Van Gogh and Joyce.

I looked for other Irish books after I put back *Finnegans Wake*. I saw and read one by a writer called AE titled *The National Being*. I saw and read a book of the poems of Padraig Colum. I saw and read a book of the poems of William Butler Yeats. I worked my way through some of these and on leaving the library I stole these books, took them with me. This only seemed right. They could get more. I needed them. This was irresponsible on my part. On board the ships to come when I was homesick I would read these and memorise some of the poems. *Down by the Sally Gardens* by Yeats I would always remember and sing in the shower. I memorised *The Lake Isle of Innisfree*. There, in African American New Orleans, I became more Irish.

Before I left the New Orleans library I struggled to understand the atmosphere. There was something about it? The large room was full of African American youth. But this was not all. They were studying, intent, silent, reading. I did not know that I was watching part of the African American revolt developing itself. But I did feel that I was in the midst of something serious, something that would change things in the world, something that maybe could change my own world. I knew I wanted to be part of this, to allow it to enter into me and to change me. But I only got a glimpse of what I was seeing, only a brief half glimpse, it would be years before I would fully understand.

VIETNAM

THE ATTEMPT OF MY FRIENDS and I to buy a boat ended when our money ran out. So our little group parted ways and I signed on another ship. With each passing day I regretted more not going with Verdes and Spanish. However the port was very busy and I had many choices of boats on which to sign. When I saw there was one heading for Vietnam I looked no further. I knew that was where I had to go. If I was going to learn more of how things worked it would be there. Two worlds were colliding in that small country in the clash of massive weaponry. I was bound to learn something. I also thought about the African American youth in the library. The African American man in New York had told me a lot of them were being sent to Vietnam. Maybe I could meet some of them there and learn from them too.

This new ship was much smaller and more beat up than the previous one. It seemed that they were using anything that could float. It rolled out across the Gulf of Mexico, through the Panama Canal and west across the Pacific with its cargo of rice. Just like the first ship this one was also Norwegian. Apparently they had a big merchant fleet and not enough people wanting to work on them. Maybe the big fleet came from the experience and skills the country had learnt from the Viking days. Maybe they had learnt some of these skills sailing up the Lough Foyle. Just like the first ship I had been on this one too had its menu of bread, boiled potatoes and boiled fish. Healthy enough but it was not very tasty. I augmented it by buying a big box of apples which the officers let me keep in the ship's cold room.

I was on the eight to twelve shift again. One night after my shift I was walking back from the bow of the ship. The stars were shining from a clear sky. I went into the empty mess and turned on the radio. My breath stopped, my mouth opened, my body went still. I had heard Beethoven and Stravinsky with Marty in his shack in Canada. I had heard the blues with my friend in the pub in Greenwich Village in New York. I had heard the jazz with Verdes and Spanish in Preservation Hall in New Orleans. Now I was hearing something else. I waited in suspense to see if they would give the singer's name and any other information. They did. It was Nancy Wilson, an African American jazz singer from the US. I was immediately a convert. I sat in the mess of the rolling ship, breathing deep, letting the music into me, and letting my world expand.

How come African Americans had created the rock 'n' roll, the jazz, the blues, these great new types of music that touched me and that changed the music of the world? I would later learn that they created them out of their struggle and experience against the nightmare of slavery and racism and their refusal to be broken by these systems. African Americans expressed this refusal to be broken partially through these types of music. To maintain their struggle over the centuries they could not only do so through open armed struggle. They had to also fight in a way that expressed their rebellion and which also made it difficult for the slavers and their system to accuse them of rebelling. In a way that they could rebel but also give them a breathing space. They did this partially through their music. They created these styles of music also because they were not part of the elite in society, this meant they were not constrained in their expression, as they would have been if they felt they had to prop up society. They could create new music.

It was not unlike the Irish and their indirect way of talking. Centuries of repression made the Irish very cautious about expressing themselves directly or clearly. To do so would make it more likely that they would have been arrested, deported, hanged, imprisoned. So we Irish hardly ever gave a straight answer or spoke directly, we also tended to make up words and expressions. These were defensive measures. But we did not want to sound dumb. So we found expressions to cover this reality. It was partly out of this that the Irish oral tradition came, the great Irish writers and poets and songsters. I would later find out that I was much closer to African Americans in regards to speech than I was to Irish Americans who had not come through the same degree of repression of African Americans or to a lesser extent the Irish in Ireland.

The form of this music rebellion of African Americans was like the Irish way of talking, it was indirect, it was subtle, and in some cases it was with totally new sounds. Maybe a bit like Joyce's invented words. There was a terrible pain and suffering and heroism in these African American types of music. I would listen to Nancy Wilson and singers like Nina Simone and Billy Holliday and Lead Belly for the rest of my life. African American people changed the world's music and dance. Back home I would share their music and share Nancy Wilson with my closest friends.

At last Vietnam appeared on the horizon. This was one of the best parts of being at sea, arriving at a new port, tying up, seeing a new country, seeing a new culture, meeting new people. The port was Da Nang, the main US base in South Vietnam for bombing the North. We were bringing rice to a country which had been one of the main rice growing countries in the world but where rice growing had been deliberately destroyed by US imperialism's military invasion as a way to try and control the people and win the war.

We tied up. I looked at the Vietnamese dockers, so physically slight compared with Americans or Irish, dressed in a piece of cloth like a skirt and wearing flip flops made of old tires on their feet. No protective clothing or shoes there. They did not look at us as we threw them the ropes to tie us to the dock. What did they think of us, we these people of a different world who destroyed their rice and then brought them other rice, who destroyed their land and bombed their people? I wanted to say: 'I am against it. I do not support it.' But I could not speak the language and even if I could what would it have meant? They would not have believed me. I should be doing something to oppose the war if I was against the war.

I was on watch the first night so I could not go ashore. But after a few hours' sleep the next day I headed downtown. The main street of Da Nang was filled with shops which had almost everything you could buy in the more economically advanced capitalist countries. There were long lines of US military outside doors down side streets. These were brothels worked by Vietnamese women. There were also crews of women working on the streets fixing potholes. Their boss was always a man and on numerous occasions I saw these men strike the women to make them work harder. The women seemed inured to these blows and this treatment. I was shocked and enraged.

The walking and the stimulation of this new land tired me out. I sat down on a concrete step. 'Hey mister. You got dollars.' It was two young Vietnamese boys about twelve years old. I gave them a dollar. They spoke some English. As I tried to talk to them another man came along and sat with us. He was Japanese. I wondered what he was doing in the country. He was reserved when the young Vietnamese began to talk to him. He seemed more interested in why a white man, a civilian, whom he probably thought was European American, was talking to these youths. The young people tried to befriend him by running down Vietnam. 'Vietnam number 10. Japan and America number 1.' I was humiliated for the two young people but said nothing. I was impressed when the Japanese man spoke up. 'No. Be proud of your own country. Vietnamese people good people.' This quieted the young boys. And it taught me a lesson too. I wondered where this Japanese man was coming from.

I met the two young boys again the next day. They took me to their neighbourhood. They had to buy food for their family. I went with them and decided I would pay. The market was inside a huge hangar type building. When I entered the smell of rotted vegetables and meats almost made me throw up. I compared this to the city's main street and the goods on sale there and the money in the pockets of the US military and the money they spent on the women in the brothels.

Every morning I worked on board the ship. The sun came up over the South China Sea. It was spectacularly beautiful and made me glad to be alive. But the sun was not the only thing that came up over the South China Sea. There were also the B52 bombers that took off from Da Nang airport with their cargoes of death and destruction. They were off to bomb the North. Later in the day they would come back in staggered formation after having dropped their lethal loads. I watched them land and thought of what they had done and my opposition built against the war and the world as it was.

I could not understand all that was swirling around me. But I knew I wanted to stay in Vietnam to try and learn. The US was fighting through its stooge regime in the South and the Stalinist countries through their proxy in the North and the Viet Cong. This was a knockdown, drag out war of world significance. I felt that if I could have a further look at this it would help me better understand things. I hitched a lift out to the American air base, a gigantic city of steel and concrete and canvas. It was dominated by a number of main runways and running off these smaller runways, and off these even smaller runways, at the end of which were parking places for the planes. Beside the planes were large tents where the aircrews lived and slept. Some American companies were making a lot of money out of the war by building the planes, making the uniforms and the tents and the rest.

I went to the administration centre of the base and into the large tent and up to a desk and asked the officer for work. Hearing my accent he spoke to me in what I could recognise was Irish. But how could it be? He explained by boasting to me that he had been brought up by Irish parents in the Bronx, New York City. They were fluent Irish speakers and they had taught him the language. According to him this made us friends. I did not respond to this. I just went on again to ask him for work. I felt hostile to him for being able to speak Irish when I was not. And on top of that being there fighting for American imperialism.

Soon it was clear we were no longer 'friends'. 'There is no work for you here. We get Charlie to do the labouring work you are talking about. We do not have to pay him what we would have to pay you. And besides if he is killed by incoming fire who cares. It will be by his own people. It is only right.' And he dismissed me arrogantly and with a sneer. I was disgusted by his racism and his claim to be Irish.

After two days in the country and in spite of my political ignorance I knew the US could not win their war. They were alienating just about everybody. The women being beaten in the street to make them work harder, the families who had to buy the rotten meat and vegetables, the majority who had to watch the US military eat well while they did not, the women in the brothels with the lines outside, the people who were being bombed by the B52s in the North, the fighters who were being killed in the jungles in the South. There was no way the US could win.

I went ashore with a crewmember from Louisiana. He was a crude character who looked down on anybody he thought was weaker than him and this, in his opinion, was all other races and all women. Walking down the street with me he said: 'Come on let us have a whore to ourselves before we ship out. The place is full of them. Look at that.' And he pointed to the lines outside the brothels. I went with him, my better thinking pushed to the back of my mind by my thoughts of, and my longing for, the smooth soft softness of a woman's skin.

The line moved slowly but eventually we were inside a badly lit shop front. There was a corridor that ran down to the back of the building with doors opening off it. An older Vietnamese woman was shouting: 'Come on boys. Come on boys. Number 1 women here. Number 1 women here. Dollars! Dollars!' Seeing there were two of us together she grasped both our arms and pushed us together into one of the rooms. 'There number one woman. Have her good. But first the dollars, the dollars.' We paid her.

The room was bare except for a thin mattress and a small crate-like box which held a sleeping baby. On the mattress sat a Vietnamese woman who looked to be in her twenties. She had a fixed artificial smile on her face and when we entered she leaned back on her elbows and emaciated body. 'Hey boys, hey boys. Come on. Which first, which first?' My crewmate gave a cruel laugh and stepped forward and said: 'That is me mamosan. I am first.'

The woman lay back on the bed and spread her legs. 'Come on boy. Quick. Me number one.' And she reached down and caught his penis and directed it into her body. She began to push up and down against him and he began to thrust down on her. As they beat at each other the noise wakened the baby in the crate. It began to cry. The woman called to the baby over her shoulder. She spoke in Vietnamese. By her tones she was alternatively threatening and comforting as she tried to keep the baby quiet.

Meanwhile she continued to keep thrusting up against the man and he kept thrusting down on her. And the baby kept crying. But this had no effect on the man as he kept driving at the woman with an arrogant concentrated look on his face. It was like he was trying with his brutal thrusts to find something he had lost inside her. Maybe, I thought, it was his compassion.

The woman could not ignore the baby's crying. She wanted to care for it, to comfort and quiet it. But she had work to do, money to make. She held on to the man with one arm, waved at the baby with the other and shouted at it. Multi-tasking. But the baby kept crying. The man stopped before the baby stopped. He came in the woman and pulled himself out of her, got to his feet buttoned his pants, all the time sneering and grunting with a superior air. He was proud of himself. He had done her good. It seemed like he saw what he had just done as his contribution to the US war effort. I wondered had he made a baby in that woman in those moments and if so what kind of a life it would have.

I stood in shock. I thought about what was being done to this country and the Vietnamese people, about what had just been done to this woman, about the actions of this ignorant aggressor I was with, turned into what he was by those who ran the US and the system which existed there. This ignorant aggressor and those who had sent him there pounding the women on thin, dirty mattresses, making the babies cry in fear, bombing the land and men and women and children in it. I could not do this. I turned and walked out of the room with its dirty mattress, crying child and mother who could see no other way to survive but sell herself to somebody who despised her. I turned and walked away from that small horrific piece of the US war that I had watched in that room.

'Irish, Irish, where are you going? They have your money. You paid them. I know she is no beauty but what do you expect, she is a whore. Come on back and do her.' I did not answer him. I just walked on back out of the building and up the side alley and onto the main street. My head hung in shame as I headed back towards the ship. I had had enough, enough of being seen with him and enough of that room with that poor woman and her child.

I walked out on to the main street and turned towards the docks and my ship and the clean water of the sea. And it was there I came to a realisation. It was there the penny dropped. I was not going to find what I was looking for by travelling. All I was finding was further and further confirmation of what I already knew, that is that the world in which I lived, the system in which I lived, all the systems in the world were rotten. But I was getting nowhere in either finding a way to live in the existing world, getting anywhere in finding an alternative to that world. I was only wasting my time.

My trip to Vietnam, walking down the main street of Da Nang that day was a watershed in my travels. I had seen the big corporations of the western countries robbing the poor countries like where they took the ore from up the Amazon. I had seen where the US bombed Vietnam to steal this wealth and the wealth of south east Asia and to keep control of the region. I had seen the different system in Poland where people seemed resigned to having little rather than nothing, seemed prepared to accept they could never realise their potential. These were good experiences to have. They confirmed me in my belief that all the systems of the world were rotten. But they did not teach me anything new, did not teach me what I needed to learn. They did not solve my problem. They did not show me an alternative to these existing systems. And above all, this is what I needed and why I had come on my travels in the first place.

It was true that I had seen the Watts Uprising on TV in the pub in New York. This had strengthened my belief that things could be changed, that people would fight for change. It was true that in Vietnam I could see the people refuse to be bombed into smithereens by the vastly superior weaponry of the US. It was true that I had met and been inspired by people like Marty and Verdes and Spanish, by their refusal to accept the existing world, but it remained the case that I could see no alternative to the systems that existed, systems which, the more I travelled, the more I saw were rotten.

I had left home to try and find my role in society and to find an alternative system. But in spite of my travels I was no closer to achieving either. So there in Vietnam, on that main street of Da Nang, I made a decision – there was no point in travelling anymore. I was going to go back home again and maybe something would turn up. If I could not find a role in society by travelling, if I could not find an alternative to existing society by travelling and by seeing the horror of Vietnam I was not going to find it by travelling haphazardly any further.

Maybe what I had absorbed on my travels would, after all, help me to see things better when I would go home again. Maybe help me to find my role to find an alternative, even though I had not been able to find either of these when I was at home before. Going home again was the only thing I could think of to do. I wished again I had gone with Verdes and Spanish.

The ship I was on was heading back across the Pacific for another cargo of rice and would turn round and come back again to Vietnam. I could see no point in that. I looked for a ship that was heading for Europe and would allow me to go home again. But not able to find one going direct to Europe I signed on one that was heading for Australia. On the way to Australia that ship made stops in the Philippines, Malaysia and Singapore. I saw these countries and their poverty, heat and humidity.

When I got to the port of Freemantle in Western Australia, I signed off the ship I was on. For a time I worked in a steel yard lifting loads of steel beams onto trucks with a hoist. When I had saved some money I headed out to have a look at the rest of the continent, or as I learnt it was sometimes called, I went on my version of walkabout. The colour of the land was spectacular. In its most arid parts the soil was red and the vegetation so sparse that the red was just about totally dominant. I hitched my way east from Perth across the desert, along the South coast and up the East coast. I did not know there were poisonous snakes and all sorts of wild animals so in between my rides I slept out in an old sleeping bag in the bush at night. It was dangerous. At times there would be stampeding wild horses, there would be the noise of a big kangaroo, the trample of a herd of camels, and of course the slithering snakes, but in my ignorance all I felt was the peace and beauty of the Australian bush at night.

I hitched back west again along the south coast of the continent. I spent a night in a camp of the Aboriginal people. I had got a lift with a racist driver who bought drink and called into the homes of the Aboriginal people, gave them this drink, and exploited them sexually. I left him and hitched on up the coast of Western Australia. I was picked up by the owner of a carnival which travelled from town to town. I worked for him operating his big Ferris wheel for a time. He told me how the native people had been treated very badly and how the white colonists had stolen the land. He, like Marty and Verdes and Spanish and my African American friend in the pub in Manhattan, helped me to better understand the world and the crimes of the upper classes and colonialism and imperialism.

Hitching back down the west coast again towards Perth I worked for a time on a crayfish boat. The night before I quit I pulled up a pot and reached in for a couple of crayfish. In the dark I did not see the small octopus. Hidden in their fleshy body octupuses have a strong sharp beak. This one struck and cut my hand. I grabbed it with my other hand, pulled it from the pot and cut its head off with the jagged edged knife that was kept for this purpose. Since I have gotten older I sometimes think of the pain I inflicted on that octopus. After all it had just been going about its business eating other sea animals. I would console myself by thinking of what it was doing to the other animals. The blood was streaming from my hand. I tore a piece from my shirt, tied it round the wound and thought no more about it.

Quitting the crayfish boat I got a berth on a ship at Freemantle. It was headed across the South coast of Australia and then it would turn around and sail back to Europe. A few days into my voyage on the new ship my hand became badly swollen and the veins in my arm turned blue. I showed it to a ship's officer and he said it was blood poisoning. The octopus I thought. It had got its revenge. Our next port was Adelaide. I was sent to the doctor who immediately sent me to the hospital. I spent a few days lying back and getting treated by the nurses. It was enjoyable. Slowly my poisoning went away. Lying in the hospital bed I felt guilty thinking of the hard work my family and especially my mother would be doing at home.

The ship I was on had sailed before I was discharged from the hospital. The ship's company's local agent brought me a ticket to fly to Sydney to re-join the ship. That was my first time on a plane. I thanked and apologised to the octopus. It was a propeller plane and I was sitting by the window. Sparks kept coming out of the engine and this made me a bit nervous but I consoled myself that the plane had probably made this trip hundreds of times and so on average things should work out. They did. I reached Sydney and got back on board the ship.

We turned round and sailed back across the South coast of Australia calling at Melbourne and Adelaide. In Melbourne I had a day ashore and I struck up a conversation with a young woman outside a small café. 'Are you Irish?' she asked me. 'Yes.' And for the first time I saw somebody's lip literally curl up in contempt. She got up and walked away. 'I don't like the Irish. They are dirty.' I felt like I would explode with rage. Never before had such a thing been said to me. I could not get over the injustice of it. This must be what African American and African people felt every day. This incident reminded me of the woman in Canada who condemned me because I was a low paid seasonal worker. Race and class, divide and rule, destruction of human relations.

We sailed up through the Indian Ocean and into the Red Sea. The war against Britain was raging in Aden. I could hear the gunfire at night. My sympathy was with the rebellion. It was only right people should control their own country. We sailed on through to the Suez Canal. It was very different from the Panama Canal. The Suez was on the flat dry desert with no lush vegetation like Panama.

We tied up and a local man came on board and promised that he would take us ashore to a night club with 'girls from every country in the world' and he would throw in a trip to the Pyramids. A few of us said okay. One of the ships officers had taken a liking to me because he managed the ships soccer team when we were ashore and played other ships' teams and I was a half decent player. He joined us for the trip to the nightclub and the pyramids. It was true the nightclub had women from many countries. But after an hour or so the ship's officer and I demanded to see the pyramids. The guide tried to talk us out of it. It seemed like we were the only people who had ever asked him to fulfil this part of his offer. But we insisted and eventually the guide took us off across the desert in a rickety car.

The moon lit the desert like it was day. The soft brown colour of its sandiness blended with the shrubs and plants and made a beautiful calm surrounding night. Animals scurried out of the way of the lights of the car. Other than the odd big camel I did not know what they were. The air was comfortable on my skin. Not the humid aggressive heat of South East Asia or the Amazon but a dry warmth. It was a night for me.

After some time we came to a hut in the desert. The guide pulled the car over. A piece of sacking hung across the door of the hut. The guide shouted and a small thin man came out. They talked and gestured at us and then the thin man ran round behind the hut. In a few seconds he came back leading a huge camel.

The man had a small stick and with this he gently tapped the back of the camel's legs until it got down on its knees. 'Up, Up.' the guide said to us and pointed to the camel's back. We looked at the owner of the camel and he also gestured to us to get up on the animal's back. We did so, myself in the front and the officer behind holding on to me. And off we went trotting through the desert. I wondered what they would have said in Lifford if I had come trotting on a camel across Lifford Bridge. I smiled there under the moonlit, star-filled desert sky.

It did not take long until the pyramids took shape before us. My breath came quiet and slow. I had never seen their like before. I could not get over how well shaped they were. How their edges reaching up into the sky were so true. What skills the people who planned and made them must have had. But I also thought how many slaves had died to build them, how many of the then rich were buried in them? Seeing the pyramids there that night gave me a greater respect for history, made me think more about history. I also looked at the man who was leading the camel and thought about him and his ancestors and how they had probably been around since the pyramids were built. He, like myself, and all things were part of history.

The ship sailed up to Naples and I signed off. I found the road north and set off to hitch to Rome, Genoa, into France, on into England and Ireland and home. As usual I slept in the hedges and fields in my sleeping bag. One night north of Naples I was left off in the dark in the countryside and climbed over the hedge and lay down. When I awoke in the morning the sun was shining and I was in a hay field. An old lady dressed all in black was turning over the hay with a fork. She paid no attention to me as she went about her work. I thought of my mother. It was a nice way to wake up. I smiled at her and got on the road again.

I found Rome oppressive with its authoritarian buildings and architecture. I could not afford its museums or galleries nor in my backwardness did I have any inclination to visit them. After walking around for a day I found my way out to the road north again. As I got my lifts and made my way the land became more fertile and rich. But I liked the dry poor south better.

I reached Genoa. With its port and sea I was a happy man. I met a wealthy, attractive woman in a restaurant. She was in her thirties. We talked. She was fluent in English. She wanted to know who I was, what I was doing there. She seemed interested that I was a seaman. I had learnt that there were women who saw seamen as fitting into their lives. We would be in port for a few days and then gone. No complications. They could have someone for a few days and then be back to their usual lives.

I spent a few days with this woman in her luxurious home. For the first time I saw marble counter tops and marble floors. In the evenings we would sit on her outside upstairs window porch and look out over the city, the ships and the ocean. It was beautiful and peaceful. Like Marty she played me some of the rich people's music. She explained to me it was Italian opera. I liked it.

After a few days having played and laughed and explored together I felt the urge to move on to get back to Ireland. I could also see my new-found friend was also thinking we had spent enough time together. She took me to a store and bought me a large bag of bread and cheese and a ticket, complete with bunk, on the train for Paris. I did not feel in any way used. It did not occur to me that I should. Later I would wonder if it had been a rich man and a younger poorer woman would it have been different?

In Paris and I was agast. I wondered at the beauty of its buildings and boulevards and the Seine. I looked down over the wall along the river bank and there were two Nordic looking young people, a young woman and a young man. The young woman was topless and posing and the young man was taking her picture. She looked good. Paris! I walked to the Eiffel Tower. I did not go up as I did not like heights.

I thought about staying longer in that staggeringly beautiful city. It was so different from the dark oppressive Rome. I would later learn it was referred to as the city of light. I could see why. I would in my later years with my companion Bonnie visit it many times. But I was in a hurry to get home now that I felt that I was not going to find an alternative way of looking at the world, or an alternative system by travelling any more. So I stayed only three days sleeping in the stations and parks in my sleeping bag. Then I hitched to Calais, took the ferry to Dover and was in England.

My welcome to England was nasty. I lay down in my sleeping bag on the railway station platform to wait for the train to London. The manager came out and called me a bum and ordered me out of his station or he would call the police. I was catching the wrath of the small-minded English middle class, angry because the empire from which it had received some crumbs was disappearing. I was a sign of the disorder that was replacing that empire. And to make it worse was I not also one of the dirty Irish? This, along with what the Australian woman had said about how she hated me because I was one of the dirty Irish, combined to strengthen my hatred of racism, and all kinds of bigotry and discrimination.

CHAPTER 12

HOME AGAIN - DECLASSED

I HAD ENOUGH MONEY to fly to Dublin. As the plane descended towards the city, the sight of the bay and the green fields made me hold my breath. I was home. I had left when I was twenty. Now I was twenty two. The year was 1966. My travels had taken me to five continents and many different countries. They had confirmed me in my belief that the way the world was run was rotten. They had further weakened the prejudices with which I had been brought up. They had taught me about racism and the looting of the poor countries by the rich. They had left me more open to finding an alternative way. This was good.

I had met people who were forward looking in the way they saw things such as Spanish and Verdes and Marty, and some who were backward such as the racist who went with the Vietnamese woman in Da Nang and the woman who curled her lip at me for being a dirty Irish. I was a different, more knowledgeable person. The trajectory of my travels had taken me in the right direction, that is to be more critical of the existing systems in the world. But this was not enough. I still lacked that which I needed most, an understanding of what was to be my role in the world, I still lacked any vision of an alternative world. That was where I was as I hitched from Dublin up to Lifford.

I allowed the Irish accents and the talk of the drivers to welcome me home. It was easy to hitch in Ireland. People liked to talk and liked company. I walked from Strabane with my bag on my shoulder. I took in the rivers and the streams where I used to play. I thought of my father's funeral. I thought of myself and my family whom I was about to meet again. My travels had moved me further from their way of seeing things. This worried me. I stopped and looked over Lifford Bridge, down into the River Foyle. The tide was coming in. I looked at the fisherman in his body waders casting his fly, the peace of him. I did not feel at peace. I was about to meet my family again with this wider gap that was between us. This was not likely to be a recipe for peace.

As I came closer to Portinure I saw a man digging a drain along the side of the road. It was Arty. It was only fitting that he would be the first person I would see on my return. I had been with him when I realised I had to leave. His back was to me and he was bent over the spade. He wore a pair of old wellington boots as usual. All the time I had been away, all the places I had been, and he was still going about in leaky boots and wet feet.

I called: 'Arty, Arty.' He straightened up, saw me, and gave his gurgling welcoming laugh. I had not been greeted like this since I left. 'John. John. It's yourself. Sure man I am more than glad to see you. The ones up at Portinure will be glad to see you too. They did not know you were coming back. Here man put it there.' And he held out his hard callused hand and we shook.

'How are you Arty?' I asked. 'Ah sure I am well you know. And not only that I am getting married.' 'Getting married? That is great Arty.' I had in mind that he had met some kind woman who had seen the goodness in him. 'Who are you getting married to Arty?' Then he told me. I knew her. She was a woman who was well known for exploiting people. I was so stunned I blurted out what I really felt. 'Arty that women will treat you bad. Why are you getting married to her?'

He looked at me and said, 'Sure it is what I have to do John. Sure I have to do right by her.' 'What do you mean? Do you mean that you slept with her?' He nodded his head. 'But Arty that does not mean you have to marry her. And at her age there is no chance she will have a baby. And I bet you this sleeping with her was not your idea, it was hers. Am I not right?' He nodded his head in agreement. 'Arty that woman will use you as cheap labour.' 'John, John I have to do what's right. I should not have done it and that is that.' I shook my head in anger and frustration. My anger at the churches increased. I knew what that woman would do to Arty. The religion was still going about its dirty ways.

Arty believed whatever the Catholic Church told him. He followed its dictates to the letter. Now he had ended up where he was going to be super exploited for the rest of his life. The woman he was marrying was a Protestant. So the Catholic Church could claim it had got a new recruit. For another member and to be able to say it had turned a Protestant, it was prepared to sell out Arty to a miserable life. And this is what happened. Arty died in misery and with only the bits of rags of clothes on his back. I was not feeling so good to be home. I walked on shaking my head, trying to put Arty out of my mind.

I looked at the clear water flowing in the stream he was digging. I tried to let this lift my spirits. I had missed the streams and clear flowing water. But I could not stop thinking of Arty. In a way the reason I liked him was because he believed in and stood for principles, in his case his Catholic principles, but they were the wrong principles, all you had to do to see this was look at where they had landed him. It was important to stand for principles but they had to be the right principles, they had to be principles which stood against exploitation and which corresponded to reality.

I reached the lane and turned up towards Portinure. In the yard behind the house my mother was coming out of the pantry carrying a bucket of milk. My uncle was walking with an armful of straw from the barn. My aunt was feeding the ducks at the duck house. It was as if I had never been away, as if all the countries I had visited did not exist. My mother and uncle and aunt turned and looked at me. 'Hello. I am back.' We all froze in place. As was our tradition nobody embraced each other or showed welcoming emotion. That was not our way. For a minute none of my family said anything. Then my mother spoke. 'It is good you are back John, we need your help about the place.' My uncle and aunt greeted me in a similar way.

I knew they were feeling more than they were expressing. I knew they were glad to see me. But they, just like myself, could not easily express positive feelings. Their lives had been too hard. They had no choice but to conclude that unrelenting work was all that would keep them going. This is the way they thought. And it was this to which they gave priority in their lives. This was the way they contributed to and related to the rest of the family. And it was in this way they saw my return, to help in this unrelenting work. I did not have their excuse of their hard lives for not being able to express my positive emotions. In a way I was worse than them.

But I was still angry. My family was no longer poverty stricken. The children were grown and gone except myself who wanted or needed nothing from them. They could live comfortably on their debt free farm. But they could not break from their work and more work routine and way of thinking. They could not stop worrying that things would go bad and they would end up in the workhouse, and they could not see me without thinking of me as helping with this work and getting me into this way of looking at things.

I knew they saw me as their own and they cared very much for me. But they never asked me a single question about the countries I had been to, the things I had seen, the people I had met, they were determinedly not interested. They did not want any talk of my experiences abroad in case this might normalise these and encourage me to leave again. I had left once and by a miracle I came back. They did not want to take another chance. If I left again I might not come back, and then who would take over the farm. The generations of work to keep it and get it out of debt would be for nothing.

Though I came home from my travels without an alternative, on some things I had stronger opinions than ever. I was even more against the sectarianism of Irish culture both Protestant and Catholic. I was more against mass poverty and war both of which I had got a glimpse when I was away. I was still against the idea that nothing could be changed for the better. I was against the idea that some people were not as good as others. But I could not build a new life on what I was against. I had to know what I was for. My travels had not given me this. In one way I was worse off than before. I was more strongly convinced than ever that the systems which existed were wrong. But that was about it. I was no closer to seeing an alternative system or how one could be created, nor was I any closer to seeing my place, my role in the existing world. I was adrift.

In the meantime I had to make a living. I did some work around my uncle's farm. I linked up with a couple of smugglers and began to smuggle electronic goods, automotive parts, cigarettes and alcohol. We carried these on our backs across an old unused railway bridge over the River Finn. I worked as a bouncer in a dance hall. I contacted two men in Strabane who taught me how to poach fish and we went to work. I provided the capital, the car and the money to buy the nets and boat, they provided the knowledge and together we provided the labour. I made money in all these activities.

For a time I took a job driving and helping a local vet. He drank too much and had a bad heart. He taught me how to horn and castrate animals. This vet was a Protestant so working with him took me into many of the farmyards of the Protestant farmers in the area. These farmers and their tight-fisted approach to money, part of the siege mentality, clutching desperately on to every last penny, strengthened me in my resolve not to give in to my family's pressure to be a farmer on their farm.

This vet's wife harassed him continually. She accused him of always being late leaving for work in the morning, of drinking during the day, of spending too long on each job. He steamed with rage and frustration as she kept on at him but he kept his mouth shut. This man had an award from the British Army for taking the vocal cords out of mules and donkeys in World War II in Asia. The animals carried supplies but they would bray and give away their position to the other side's forces. His wife silenced him just as he had silenced the pack animals. At least he had the drink for an anaesthetic.

One day his wife came to me and attacked Catholics as no good, lazy and dirty. She was expecting agreement. I took this expectation of hers that I would agree with her as an insult. I said I did not agree and that I was against sectarianism. Her face screwed up and went red with rage. She stuck out her chest, threw back her head, turned and stalked off. It was not only what

I had said but that I had dared to contradict her and I being only the hired help.

The next Monday morning I went to work as usual. The vet was nowhere around. Another man was standing sheepishly by the car. The vet's wife came out and said to me in an aggressive tone: 'You do not work here anymore. This man has taken your place. You are paid up. Leave my yard.' It took a while before I realised that I had lost my job for speaking out against sectarianism. Her husband the war hero had hid silent while I was being fired.

Word got around that I knew how to castrate pigs and did it for less than the vets. My surgeon's tools were simple, a couple of razor blades and a jar of hot water with salt in it to disinfect the cuts. I would sit down, hold the pig between my knees on its back, push the testicle out until it bulged, slit the skin and the testicle would then just pop out. It would be hanging by a few veins and cords. I would cut these, pour in some salt water and the operation was over. I never had any deaths or complications. I was a successful pig testicle surgeon.

I did some work with my uncle's tractor and trailer hauling for local contractors and farmers. On one occasion a retired ex-British Army officer who lived locally hired me to cart some soil. There were two other workers. Unlike the ex-British army officer and myself the other two workers were Catholic and also unlike us they were from families with no property. When it came to lunchtime the officer told me to come into the dining room and eat with him and his wife. This left the other two workers eating alone in the kitchen. I was so surprised that I went along. But I was ashamed. It was blatant class and religious discrimination. It was also that I was being asked to eat with the Army officer and his wife so they would have a better opportunity to indoctrinate me into their pro-British, right wing way of thinking.

When we were eating, this ex-British Army officer said to me: 'I want you to keep them boys working. You know them, the other kind, if they get away with it they will only swing the lead. I am counting on you.' Divide and rule to get more work done. I thought about this the rest of the day and into the night. He had assumed that I would be his non-commissioned officer and keep the ranks in this case the Catholic ranks in line. I supposed he had assumed this because my family had the small farm, the bit of property, and I was from a Protestant background. The next day when he asked me to eat with him and his wife in their dining room I said: 'No, it is okay I will eat in the kitchen.' This time it was his turn to be surprised. I sat down and ate with the two workers in the kitchen. I knew I had done the right thing, taken the right side in the class divide.

My various ways of making a living allowed me to integrate more with local people at this time. These were mainly Catholics, mostly the men I fished and smuggled with. There was Lying Pat. His wife was ambitious and when they were young, as Pat told it, and in the height of passion for her, he allowed her to talk him into going into debt and buying a small farm. He explained to me that was the reason he had a husky voice. It had taken him every weekend for over ten years in various bars to pour that farm down his throat and out of his life.

Lying Pat was given this name because he was a very good storyteller. He carried with him a pair of women's reading glasses, the kind that could be bought in a general store without a prescription. He always had the ones with the ornate multi coloured sticking out frames with little stars on them. If he was going to tell a particularly outrageous lie or story he would carefully remove these glasses from his inside pocket, polish them with the lapel of his jacket, carefully put them on and look his listeners intently in the eye. This was by way of a prop to set off his story and to bring in the listener. When people would see him put on the glasses they would rush to gather round.

Lying Pat knew the best pubs in the area and introduced my non-drinking self to them all. On the weekends I went regularly to Harte's Bar in Lifford. It was the best of them. Just about every character in the area went there on Saturday night. Well just about every Catholic character. The bar was not popular with Protestants as its owners had in the past stored up eggs until they were rotten and then organised to have them thrown at the Lifford Orange band and lodge as it marched home from its big day. I was the only non-Catholic I ever knew of who went to that bar.

There was Dennis who was a regular. He had spent time working in Glasgow and it was said had been in one of the gangs there. He had scars on his face. For a time I went out with his niece. When he would get a few drinks he would take me by the lapels and shake me and tell me that if I did not treat his niece right I would pay for it. At such times the bar would become silent, worried there would be a fight but I could only laugh and laugh as I was genuinely amused, and also genuinely impressed, by how protective he was of his niece. After he would shake me a bit, and he would think he had given me enough of a warning, and also, after all, he did not want to be too sore on me as I was his niece's boyfriend and who knows she might be even able to turn me. And not to mention the farm. So Dennis would then try to buy me a drink and with this the whole bar would let out its collective breath. There was going to be no fight, drinks were thrown back, and the chat and laughter would start again, and Dennis the Catholic and John, the who-knows-what, would be best pals again.

Dennis had an interesting relationship with my father when my father was alive. It reflected the complexity of the sectarian divide. Dennis the Catholic was coming back on the boat from Glasgow on one occasion. It was the 11th of July night. There were large numbers of members of the Orange Order, of Protestants on the boat. They were coming to Northern Ireland to take part in the parades. Dennis had beaten up one of these Orangemen. In the course of this he had taken his orange sash from him.

A few weeks later Dennis and my father were drinking together in a pub in Lifford. In the course of this Dennis took the orange sash out of his pocket. 'Here Bobby, I have been keeping this for you. I took it off one of your boys on the boat from Glasgow. I thought you would a better man to have it than that boy.' My father accepted the sash and brought it home, brought home the orange sash that Dennis the Catholic had taken off the Orangeman on the boat. The sectarian divide was not a simple issue. It could come and go, it could express itself differently with different people and with the same people at different times. My father liked Dennis's orange sash. He chuckled to himself about it. He gave no thought to the Orangeman from whom it had been violently taken by Dennis the Catholic.

This Dennis, my father and the sash made me think of my mother, giving Arty my father's bicycle to ride to mass. My mother, the wife of the Protestant Orangeman my father, would, after my father's death loan my father's bicycle to Arty the Catholic to go to mass. She would also give him money to put in the plate. Her human decency and empathy would overcome the sectarianism with which she had been indoctrinated.

Thinking of these things strengthened me in my belief that if it was not for the vicious and conscious divide and rule policies carried out by British colonialism and British imperialism and by the various elites in Ireland Catholic and Protestant, people's good nature and humour would have had a better chance of becoming dominant and the country would have been a better place to live in.

There was another character in Harte's bar, he was called Icebox. Huey, another regular in the bar, had given him this name because he was so short and so extremely thin, just about emaciated, the exact opposite of an icebox. Icebox saw himself as a Republican. This was before the Republican movement became a major force. At the time Icebox was just about the only person in the village who openly and defiantly declared himself to be a Republican. His Republicanism in those days was confined to talking of the past glorious defeats. He would regularly try to convert me, once giving me a small spool of film of The Citizen Army. He would wait for me when I was coming home from school, on a few occasions he invited me into his house, played republican songs, always emphasising the role played in Republicanism by Protestants.

He liked the whiskey. On one occasion, when I was in the pub, he ordered a 'little Baby Powers'. This was his drink. He usually could only afford one or at most two, and as was his habit he let the whiskey sit for a while on the bar counter so he could savour it, look at it. The beautiful amber colour of it, think about the whole history and culture of it and not only of the whiskey, but of Ireland and the entire Irish nation. And tugging at the front of his waistcoat thinking of himself also: Was he not a decent man altogether? A citizen of the great Irish nation? Sure you could not get better. Icebox was a man of dreams. On this particular occasion Icebox went into the toilet to empty himself out in anticipation of the whiskey. A man had to make the proper preparation for a good whiskey. Otherwise half the pleasure of the whole thing could be lost.

When Icebox was gone to the toilet big James Thompson stepped forward and lifted Icebox's whiskey and threw it back, drank it. The bar went silent. What the hell? What would happen when the wee man would come back? Icebox came out of the toilet. He swiggled the waist band of his trousers side to side to be sure they were straight. He tugged down at the front of his waistcoat. He looked around him to make sure the rest of the bar was watching him as he stepped forward to the whiskey. Icebox's whole ritual around drinking the whiskey was a form of performance art. But what the hell? Where was it? There was only an empty glass on the bar counter where his whiskey had been.

Icebox stood and looked and looked while trying to appear not to be looking. Where was his whiskey? The rest of the bar had gone silent. Pretending not to be looking the whole bar held its breath to see what would happen. Icebox could not believe it. He stood up on the foot rail of the bar counter and looked over to see if somebody, as a joke, had put his whiskey behind the counter and replaced it with the empty glass that was there. But no, there was nothing. At this point Icebox lost it.

'Okay. O–f**king–kay. Where is it? Where is my f**king whiskey?' Nobody spoke. The barman said nothing either. Nobody said anything. Everybody was in on the drama. Big James stood silent with an innocent look. The tension built. Icebox repeated his demand. Then Big James could not take it any longer. After all the point was for Icebox to know what had happened. James said: 'Ah f**k you Icebox. I drank your f**king whiskey. Sure a wee shape of a man like you. A whiskey is too much for you', and saying this James threw his head back and broke out in great peals of laughter.

There was no way Icebox was going to stand for this. After all he was the top Republican in town, the only Republican in town. A whole movement's, a whole nation's history, reputation and tradition and culture and honour was at stake. And himself too, he had a reputation to keep up. He went for James. But James was over six foot tall and Icebox was only five foot. He could not reach him. So he climbed on a bar stool and threw himself at James. James was so busy laughing he could not defend himself. The two of them went down in a heap on the floor. The rest of the bar rushed to the two combatants laughing and shouting advice.

'Get him Icebox. A man has no right to take another man's whiskey. There is no way that is right.' 'Easy James. Sure the Icebox has a point. You should not have drunk his wee Powers. Sure leave him alone there now, sure you have 60 pounds on him. Put him up another one and let it go at that.' The conflict was resolved when the barman put up another, larger and free whiskey for Icebox. Icebox accepted this but maintained his self-esteem by pretending to be still trying to get free from the men who were holding him back from attacking James again. He shouted a warning to big James never to do such a thing again or he would pay for it and the bar went back to its normal weekend theatre and laughter.

Icebox would later die and because of his years of claiming to be a Republican, and allowing his house to be used by Republicans on the run from the North when the Troubles started, the local Republican movement, then much bigger, gave him a military funeral complete with gunshots over his grave. Huey was to the fore again. He composed the obituary. It consisted of the idea that if Icebox had known he would have got such a funeral he would have died years before. Huey earned many free drinks on the basis of telling and retelling that story.

Harte's bar was a centre of theatre and humour and drama. It was full of talent. There were people in it who, if they had been given a chance, could have more than held their own against the professional people who dominated in these fields. I had enjoyable nights there. When I would return many years later and visit that bar it was full of slot machines. All the theatre of it was gone. Capitalism!

With the poaching and smuggling and odd jobs and the earnings from doing some work for my uncle I was not short of money. I got myself a caravan and parked it on Lough Swilly with a view of the ocean, the smell of the tides going in and out. It was my place to go and have privacy for my personal life. I bought a small fishing boat and fished on the Swilly. I had a big car to get about in. On the surface things looked pretty good. But under the surface it was different. There was an emptiness in my life. I could not see what was my place and role in the world. This left me with up days and down days. On my down days it would seem there was no point to things. On my up days some positive events in my poaching or smuggling or personal life would have gone well and I would feel good. But then one day I took an important step forward in understanding what was going on.

I was snedding turnips in my uncle's field beside the lane up to Portinure when the thought came to me. I was pulling the turnips out of the ground and cutting of their leaves and cutting the clay from their roots. The thought so excited me that I did not watch what I was doing and instead of cutting the clay off the root of the turnip I buried the snedding hook in the back of my hand. I had the scar for years to come. But it was well worth it.

I had been born into the small farmer class, or as I would later learn it could be called the rural petit bourgeois. Then I had gone on my travels and during that time I moved into a different class – the working class. Working in the mine, the lumber mill, on board ship, I was part of the working class. Since I had returned I had moved out of the working class and made a living partly as self-employed, partly working for my uncle, partly at jobs such as driving for the local vet, partly at criminal activities such as smuggling and poaching, partly as a bouncer at a dance hall. I was no longer part of the working class. I had moved back out of the working class. But I had not moved into any other class. Rather I had a foot in various different classes or sub classes. I moved between different classes and sub classes. Sometimes I had a foot in one class or sub class and at the same time the other foot in another class or sub class. I had become as I was to later think of it, declassed.

When abroad being part of the working class gave me an identity, gave me a working class consciousness. Gave me a confidence in myself. I knew who I was, I knew to which class I belonged. But now back home and making a living in these different ways I was no longer rooted in the working class. I was working yes, but not as part of the collective working class, not as part of a workforce working for a boss as I had been in the mine, in the lumber mill, on the ships. I did not know what class I was in, I did not know because I was not in any class. I was staggering between the rural petit bourgeois class, the criminal class, the self-employed class. I was being declassed. My working class consciousness which I had developed when abroad and which had given me stability was under assault. My working class identity which I had developed when I was abroad was being undermined. This was the source of the problem, the source of my confusions and want, the source of my up and down days.

I applied for a job as a lorry driver in a local flour mill. This would have given me regular hours and regular wages. I would have been a worker again, part of the working class again, part of the workforce in that mill, with a common experience and interest with the rest of the workforce in that mill, working for the private owner and boss of that mill. I was only half conscious what I was doing, that I was trying to get back into the working class again. Trying to get back a working class consciousness and working class identity again. However my effort was not successful. The owner of the mill sat across the desk and looked at me like I was insane. I suppose he wondered how I could be so naive to think that he would let me anywhere near his mill when I had such a reputation as a smuggler, a poacher, and somebody who had no regard for the law. I might even get into stealing from him and get other drivers at it too.

My family could see I was not happy. To them the issue of my being declassed never entered their head. It never crossed their mind that I had been declassed, that I did not know to which class I belonged, in fact did not belong to any one class, and this was the major cause of my discontent.

My family tried to solve things the only way they knew, through work, and specifically getting me to work again on their farm. Most of the fields of the farm were being rented out to others as I did not want to work them and my uncle no longer had horses and could not drive the tractor. My mother put it to me straight: 'John, look there is no point in letting out these fields to them others when we could make more farming them ourselves. We want you to start ploughing and sowing and to get some livestock and settle down right. You are only wasting your time with that poaching and smuggling and anyway it makes us look bad. This place is to be yours. You know that. We have worked hard all our life and got it free from debt, the least you can do is take it on and farm it. There are many who would give their right arm for this place. We will always be here to back you up and to help you. You know that.'

My mother was right from where she stood. My uncle and aunt felt the same as my mother and they were right from where they stood. They were trying to get me back into the class from which I had come and into which they had reared me. They did not see it in these class terms. They saw it as getting me to take on the farm and by so doing integrate back into the family. But this would have meant me going back into the small farmer class. My family were trying to get me to take on and build upon what they had built, the debt-free farm, and be part of the small farmer class. I rejected and fought against this.

My mother and uncle and aunt were very hurt by my rejection of what they saw as integrating back into the family again, my rejection of taking on the farm for which they had worked so hard to put on a sound footing and free from debt, and as they saw it, for me. But I would not accept the taking over and working my family's farm, the farm for which they had worked so hard and which they saw as to be passed on to me. I would not accept the position in their class which they offered me. This was one of the greatest rejections and insults I could give them. I knew that, but I would not give in. This rejection was breaking all our hearts. Not only had I broken from my family's religion and all religion, but now also I was breaking from my family's small farming class or as they saw it, breaking from all their plans and hopes for me. This was a brutal cruelty that my trajectory, that I, was imposing on my family.

It was not that if I took the farm that they would come with it. I believed strongly that they must have their time to live there and to have a living from the income of the farm to which they had contributed all their lives. Anything else would have been totally unacceptable to me. The issue was different. If I took the farm I would be signing on to be a small farmer, signing on to the small farmer's way of looking at the world, signing on to hire workers and to start thinking like a person who hires workers, signing on to be a small farmer who was always worried about money and always talking and grumbling about money, signing on to be part of the small farmer class. I was not going to do that. That would destroy my spirit. I could see around me too many examples of demoralised, damaged spirits who had taken this road. I was not going to be one of them. I refused to yield.

Not being able to find a place for myself in the economic world I thought I would again take a look at, see if I had sorted myself out properly, in the religious world. I had 'taken my life back from Jesus' years before but was this all that there was to it? I had been 'baptised' in my mother's Presbyterian church and had 'communion' in it. 'Baptised'? 'Communion'? The more I thought of these words the more I disliked them and the whole concept of organised religion. 'Baptise' was somebody else, a him, back then it was always a him, giving me a name, usually a name of some mythical Christian figure. 'Communion' was me relating to some Christian leader and him, back then it was always a 'him', talking on my behalf, to some god, and the god was also always a him, and a god in whom I did not believe. It was just garbage. But anyway I decided to see if I could clear up the 'baptise' and the 'communion' business. Make sure that all my religious links were cut. Maybe that would help the confusions and want in me. This was further cutting my links with my family.

I went to see the clergyman at my family's church. He was a small round man with little presence. His wife ushered me in and offered me tea. I thanked her but refused. It was better to be in combat mode from the beginning. 'I want my name taken off the books of the church. I do not believe in it anymore, I do not believe there is a god.' His expression said he did not get many visitors like me. 'Well John, it is not that simple. You were baptised in this church and you had your communion here. These are facts. They cannot be erased. But tell me why do you want to do this?'

'I do not believe in God, a heaven and hell, it is nonsense, and I know I especially do not believe in what organised religion, what the churches do. They divide people along religious lines. I do not agree with this. Look at the schools how they are divided along religious lines. That is not right. Also look at all the poor people round the world. That is not right. But the churches say the poor will always be with us. They accept poverty as inevitable. That is also not right.'

'Well John I agree with you about the poor. We have to do all we can to help them.' I interrupted, 'But do you believe that there will always be poor people.' I found myself falling back on arguments I had heard from Spanish and Verdes on the ship. 'If the rich were not so rich and if things were shared out evenly there could be enough for everybody. But the rich are too powerful and greedy to let this happen. The churches back the rich. These are the reasons why people are poor.'

'Well now John there are many different views on this.' Here we go again I thought, the old lawyer's talk to get out of doing anything to change things. 'John I personally agree with many things you say here about the poor and what could be done. I think there could be a lot more help for them.' I interrupted again. 'Well then if you stand up in church on Sunday and say this, say that the poor could be helped a lot more if it was not for the rich using their power to oppose helping the poor, that the poor need not always be with us, then I will come back and discuss with you again.'

'Oh now John I have my elders to answer to. If I said what you want me to say I would not be here long. I cannot do what you ask.' 'So the poor are to be sacrificed to the opinions of the elders and to your job. This is not right. You see these are the kind of things that convince me that there is no place for me in churches and organised religion and all this god business.'

I rose and left that little man, that little man who gave a speech every Sunday to the members of his Presbyterian church and a speech which no members were allowed to stand up and question or debate. I was satisified with myself for confronting the preacher. I thought it was my responsibility not to bow before preachers who claimed to speak for some god and in this way intimidate people.

I would later have confrontations with organisers, with preachers from the Catholic church. In my civil rights days some years later I tried to rent a hall from the local Catholic preacher for a civil rights meeting. I addressed him as Mister. He demanded I address him as Father. I refused. He was not my father. As a result he refused to rent me the hall. On another occasion some years later I was waiting for a flight at Dublin airport. It was the time of a major event of the Catholic church in Dublin with many of its full time organisers in the city from around the world. It was also the time when the sexual abuse in the Catholic church and the covering up of that abuse by the Catholic hierarchy was being exposed. I saw four of these people, all men, sitting in their long dresses, some black dresses some multi coloured dresses, all meant to make them stand out different from other people and to intimidate. I went up to them.

I said: 'I do not believe you boys have the neck to come to this country. After what is being exposed now about your full time organisers abusing children, about how you have covered up this abuse by your full time organisers'. The four men looked at me in astonishment. They had never been spoken to like this before in holy Catholic Ireland. Then the older one recovered himself and said. 'Go on with you now and god bless you'. I replied: 'I will go on when I like and not before. And keep your so called blessing from god. There is no god. You claim there is and claim to speak for this non existent god. You do so to allow you to keep people down, so you can act as if women are inferior, so you can hoard your wealth in the Vatican bank, so you can justify poverty as being inevitable'. I turned and left them. I did not think it was correct to be respectful to unelected people who claimed to be always right, who thought the rich had the right to rule, who supported capitalism and who thought women were inferior.

I would only understand later that the major churches, the Catholic Church, the Anglican Church or Church of Ireland, the Presbyterian Church, the Lutheran Church, the Mormon Church, all the major churches needed the poor to exist. Their claim to be helping the poor was essential to allow them to get away with having their palatial buildings, their enormous wealth, to allow them to sell the outlandish ideas such as the virgin birth, a person coming alive again after being murdered and floating up into the sky, a creature lurking under the earth with fires stoked and waiting. And also justify the luxury in which their top full time organizers, bishops, arch bishops, cardinals popes etc., lived. How many times was I to hear when I criticised organized religion: Well you may have a point but they help the poor. But all the churches consciously and determinedly prop up the system, capitalism, which is responsible for the poor. I was later also to come to see that what applied to these major churches did not apply to the same extent to the small community churches such as the African American community churches in the USA which were more under the influence of working class African American people.

I called in to see my mother after my conversation with the clergyman in the Presbyterian church in Strabane. It was obvious that I was in thought. She asked me what was going on. I recounted the conversation that I just had with the clergyman and also explained to her again that I did not believe in organised religion and did not believe in God. She rebuked me and called out. 'God save us from what you are thinking and saying. Is there no end to you breaking my heart? God has helped us all our lives and we have a good place here and plenty to eat and a roof over our head and food to eat and we are out of debt. Do not be throwing all that back in his face. And look at the other thing. We will all die and if you do not believe in our God then you will not go to heaven. We will never meet again.'

'Mother I do not believe there is such a place as heaven. And if there is one I can think of lots of relatives and so-called friends with whom I would not want to spend an eternity. Wandering around forever never being able to get them out of my sight. And we have a place that is out of debt because of your hard work and the rest of the family's hard work not any god. No I do not believe there is a heaven. I believe when we die we die and that is that.'

At this my mother began to call out again: 'God save me. God turn my son's head right. Let him see the truth before it is too late. John stop with this. Go back to your church and your God.' Any kind of talk about religion with my mother would turn out like this, her being very hurt and trying to make me change my mind. Her thinking that my lack of belief in a god would mean we would not meet after death, I felt terrible but there was no backing down.

My uncle had been listening to this conversation and intervened. Years earlier he had tried to get me into the Orange Order. While he had long given up on this he was not yet prepared to give up trying to keep me believing in God. 'Your mother is right John. There is no doubt there is a God. He made the world and gave His son to save us all.' I thought these must be the kind of ideas he preached in his lectures when he was building the Orange Order.

'Uncle I do not believe this. Look at what they ask us to believe. That this supposed God's son was born from a virgin birth, nobody would believe such a thing if a young woman told us this today. That this supposed son of God rose from the dead and floated up into heaven. The church leaders treat us like we are idiots. I do not believe these things. To get us to believe this nonsense they dress it up with fancy costumes for their full-time preachers, with big beautiful buildings, with the most beautiful of music and art, all to sell a bunch of infantile lies. I am not fooled.'

My uncle kept quiet and never again tried to convince me there was a God or to go back to the church. I did not know if he did not want to talk to me about virgins anymore or if he was just fed up arguing with me.

My mother had this strong position on God and religion when she talked to me. But I noticed she hardly ever went to church herself. Every Sunday she would stay at home and cook the roast beef dinner for when the rest of the family would return from church. I would later wonder if her experiences with her church and the preachers and her mother being raped and made pregnant and married off by her church left her with some doubts about the churches herself. And while she saw it as her duty to insist I do what she saw as right she was not so committed to the day to day demands of religion herself. But perhaps there was a simpler explanation. Maybe it was also that with all the rest of the household off at church she had the house all to herself for once and she could put her creative talents to work making the Sunday dinner. I would later wonder what my mother would think about during those times of solitude and dinner making. I wished I could have been able to share her thoughts. To be allowed to exchange between us all the deepest thoughts of both our minds.

The situation from my return from my travels had brought more and more conflict between myself and my family. They could not change me and they could not accept me as I was. I could not change them nor could I agree with them. Not a day went by but I felt the guilt of this. I was making my family's lives a misery. And at the same time I was not even doing anything constructive to change the world for the better. I did not know how, I did not know what to do. There seemed to be no way out.

I began to think of ending my life. What was the point of going on? I was only a bother to myself and everyone around me. For months this option drifted in and out of my head. I thought about how it would remove me from the impasse in which I found myself. I could not do what my family wanted or it would destroy my principles and beliefs and integrity. If this happened I would have to get some way to live with this and that would mean the bottle and this would also destroy me and also destroy my family. I seemed stuck in an insoluble contradiction. No matter what way I turned there seemed to be no way out.

It was June 1968, a beautiful summer day. The sun was shining and a small breeze was blowing. I was cutting a hedge with a billhook in one of my uncle's upper fields. I could see down over the rivers. It was a beautiful view. But it was not enough. I felt I had reached the limits of my struggle with my family, with my lack of an alternative, my confusions, my want, my understanding that I did not support the world the way it was while at the same time not being able to figure out any alternative. I felt that I could not go on with hurting my family and myself anymore, go on in this dead end anymore. I decided that in spite of the beautiful day that was in it, the beauty of the hills, the fields, the rivers, the beautiful countryside, my two dogs looking up at me, I was going to end my life.

I stood leaning on the billhook beside some burning hedge cuttings. The smoke gave off a strong, earthy, organic, peaceful smell. It was a smell which I would always associate with rural life in Donegal. It would always be precious to me. But in spite of all that I took off and walked down toward the river. The surface of the Finn was smooth. The tide was going out and the water was brown from the drain off from the mountain lakes and bogs upstream. I had on a pair of heavy work boots and a pair of jeans and a shirt. I climbed up on the bank and sat down. Yes, why not? I could see no other way. End it. That was best. My dogs walked after me as if all was normal.

I got up to throw myself into the flowing waters. But the closer I got to doing so the more stupid it seemed. It would crush my mother and my family altogether. I myself would never have any good relationships with anybody as I would not be around. I would never find my role or place in the world. I would never be able to find out how to change the world for the better never find out an alternative to the present rotten system. Then another idea struck me. I was a good swimmer. Even if I threw myself in I would probably not drown anyway. I would most likely panic and swim to stay afloat. I would not be able to drown myself. And would my dogs not jump in after me? And what would happen to them?

I started to laugh. And the more I thought about it the more and louder I laughed. I was well and truly stuck. I was against the way of the world but I could not find a way to change it. I could not find a way to live in it or an alternative system with which to replace it, and now I realised that I could not even drown myself to get out of it. I lay back on the river bank in the warm sun and continued to laugh. I exhausted myself with my laughter and lay quietly in peace for some time, looking at the sky and smelling the earth and the river and the rushes and the trees, and with my two dogs, the sheep dog as usual lying up against my side and the wee ratter on my chest.

As I lay there by the river bank another thought entered my head. I bared my teeth in defiant anger as it gained strength. What kind of cowardly defeatism was this? I was disgusted with myself. And look could I still not laugh? Did this not show that my spirit was not broken? I needed to pull myself together. And that is what I did. I got to my feet and turned away from the river and from all thoughts of the suicide business forever. I was going to live. Maybe just living and being able to laugh was good enough for the minute and who knew, maybe something would turn up.

Not trying to drown myself told me that I was not serious about killing myself. There were other ways I could have ended my life. I could have cut my wrists. I could have taken poison. But thankfully reality had sunk in. Suicide was the worst of all possible options. It was also the most selfish of options as it would have totally ruined my mother's and uncle's and aunt's lives. It would have been the act of a selfish, cowardly person. From that day on from where I walked with my two dogs away from the bank of the River Finn, suicide was completely and permanently erased from my consciousness as an option.

I looked around. The river, the meadows, the fields were beautiful. The sun glinting on the water, the green grass, the brown hedges, a salmon jumping upstream, I embraced this beauty and life. I turned and began to walk back up towards the upper fields again, to my hedge cutting and the smell of my burning cuttings. I intended to live. I rejoiced. My dogs ran around me, alternatively looking up to see where we were going and sniffing the ground looking for something to chase and to kill and eat.

I passed the entrance to the badger's den. It had been there for years. The badger did not try to drown itself. It did not think about killing itself. It and its family fought tenaciously for life. And it did so with nothing like the weapons and advantages we humans had, I as a human had. The badger had a correct grip on life, a correct view of the reality of its world, of its relationship to its world. It had no doubts. It fought to live. I took a lesson from the badger. Like the badger and its family I was going to fight to live.

PART 2

OPPORTUNITIES MISSED – THE NORTH IMPLODES

CHAPTER 13

MY BEARINGS

I T WAS OCTOBER 1968. I was only half aware of it but as I headed back up to the top hill field and my hedge cutting the world was exploding around me. Millions were on the streets in the US demanding civil rights and opposing US imperialism's war in Vietnam. The Vietnamese people were breaking the US invasion. US soldiers were killing their own officers in protest at being forced to fight. Opposition to all US wars and occupations was rising to new heights. The biggest general strike and movement of workplace occupations in history had just taken place in France. Czechoslovakian and Polish workers and students were opposing the Stalinist dictatorships. Left movements were rising in Central America, Latin America, Africa, South East Asia and Central Asia. And in Ireland itself unemployed, anti-war, housing, women's rights, civil rights movements were on the streets. Regimes and systems were being shaken all around the globe.

These events were being covered on the TV, the radio and the newspapers. There were some statements about them in the local newspapers from the Derry Labour Party, the largest and most left wing branch of the trade union-based Northern Ireland Labour Party (NILP) in the North. This NILP branch stood for working class unity and socialism. I was beginning to think that maybe I would find an alternative after all.

However my family opposed all these struggles and movements. I on the other hand supported them and wanted to participate. My problem was how to do so without a fundamental conflict and break with my family, without hurting them even further than I already had. I was in danger of being politically paralysed by this conflict. But events on 5th October 1968 changed everything.

The US civil rights movement had inspired a civil rights movement in Northern Ireland against the discrimination suffered by the Catholic minority there. A civil rights march was organised in Derry for 5th October 1968. The Northern Ireland police viciously attacked this march. This was recorded by a TV crew and within hours was being watched in millions of homes around the world. These events changed my world. I vowed I would never again let the threat of a conflict with my family stop me from fighting for what I believed.

The next morning, 6th October 1968, I drove to Derry at the crack of dawn. It was Sunday and the roads were deserted. I drove fast. I was on my way to see Cathy Harkin, the secretary of the Derry Labour Party. Cathy lived on Butcher Street in the Catholic enclave inside the city walls. The roadway and sidewalks outside her door were littered with stones, rocks and broken bottles from the previous night's battle with the police. I picked my way through this debris, this symbol that a new era had begun in the North.

Cathy was a smart, strong, combative, working class woman and one of the leaders of the Derry Labour Party. She spoke her mind and fought for her beliefs. She was a dedicated socialist. She also fought for women's equality when the rest of us, even many women activists, hardly thought about this at that time. Cathy was a pioneer, a leader and a fighter. She would die young from cancer. This was a tragedy. I knew Cathy through my friend Dolores who lived in the Bogside, the main Catholic area of the city.

Cathy answered my knock with sleep in her eyes. She must have thought I was mad waking her up at that hour. But what I was feeling had been building in me for years and could not wait. Contrary to my usual politeness I did not even say hello. Instead I said, 'Cathy I have to get involved in this.' These were my exact words. Cathy gave me the date of the next meeting of the Labour Party. I thanked her and let her get back to her bed.

Before I left the sleeping city I drove over through the Fountain, the main Protestant enclave inside the city walls. The contrast was stark. There were no stones or rocks or broken bottles littering the streets and sidewalks. There had been no battle with the police in that area. I looked at the curtained windows and the closed doors and wondered what the people inside were thinking as they lay in their beds or made their breakfast. Did they realise that the events of the night before had changed their lives forever?

I knew they had changed mine. That morning at Cathy's door on Butcher Street, inside the walled City of Derry, under the impact of the events of the day and night before, I found my role in the world, I found my place in the world. I found my bearings. From then on I would be a conscious, active fighter against injustice and to try to change things for the better. During the rest of my life the conclusion I came to that day would remain my guiding principle. This conclusion was: Whenever I saw things that I thought were wrong I would speak out and try to organise against them; whenever I saw things that I thought were right I would speak out and try to organise for them. I would never again be a passive, inert member of society.

It was only then that I realised how and to what extent I had been preparing myself for that moment. I had refused to capitulate to the ideas of my family and my Orange Protestant conservative background. I was toughened by this. I had rejected the Catholic ideology that surrounded me. I had avoided permanent relationships. I had avoided having children. I was able to make a living with odd jobs here and there of one kind or another and this gave me a certain economic freedom. I was ready and able to take my place as an activist in the movement for change. And this is what I did. I threw myself into producing papers and flyers, organising meetings, rallies and marches. I took my first steps to becoming a revolutionary.

Derry was the second largest city in the North and the closest to where I lived. The electoral boundaries were drawn so that if voting took place along religious lines the two-thirds majority Catholic population could only elect one third of the city councillors, while the one third minority Protestant population could elect two-thirds. This was unjust and a recipe for inevitable conflict.

Along with this religious discrimination, there was class discrimination. In local elections only people with property could vote. Those who lived in local, publically-owned housing could not vote. People who owned multiple houses could have up to six votes. In parliamentary elections there was the so-called business vote, which was only for those who owned businesses. These electoral laws affected the Catholic population as almost 90% of commercial property was owned by Protestant business people. But these property-based voting laws also negatively affected the Protestant working class.

Protestants who had no property were also discriminated against relative to Protestants and Catholics who had property. The voting system for the local elections in Derry, and it was these elections which determined who ran the city on a day to day basis, was based on religious discrimination against the Catholics but also on class discrimination against all workers, Protestant and Catholic. This meant that there was potential for a united working class struggle, but this potential was not realised. This opportunity was missed.

An estimated one quarter of a million potential voters were prevented from voting in local elections in Northern Ireland by these property qualifications. It was estimated that 60% of these were Protestant. The civil rights movement ended these property qualifications and won 'one person, one vote' for all, Protestant and Catholic and those of whatever belief in local elections. The Protestant political parties opposed the civil rights movement. Yet it was the civil rights movement that won full voting rights for all workers, including Protestant workers.

At the root of this political system in the North was the drive for wealth, power and control by the British ruling elite, their allies amongst the elite in the North, and all the elites which had wealth and power throughout Britain and Ireland. To keep control in the North, the ruling Protestant elite gave the first chance at jobs and housing and some marginal privileges to Protestants. This was the strategy of divide and rule. It had been put in place by the British ruling class when they first invaded and took over Ireland. This ruling class and this strategy was primarily responsible for all the problems and suffering that was to follow.

All the elites used divide and rule to keep control of their 'flocks'. They all gained money and power out of divide and rule. By dividing the workers, the strength and consciousness and wages of all workers, Protestant and Catholic, were kept lower, and the profits and power of all employers, Protestant and Catholic, were kept higher, and the money kept rolling in to the sectarian collection plates of all the different churches.

I was thinking of these things as I drove back up to Lifford from my visit to Cathy. My uncle was seriously ill in Lifford hospital from the after-effects of a stroke. I braced myself for meeting him and my family. In spite of his stroke he was still conscious. I collected my aunt and took her down to visit him. My aunt and other family members sat by his bed. I did not stay long. This hurt my uncle and all of us. It would have hurt my family a lot more if they had known where I had just been and the commitment I had just made.

I tried not to think about the increased stresses that would now erupt in my family. Instead I attempted to enjoy the beautiful autumn day. Autumn was my favourite season. I walked down from the hospital to the river Foyle which flowed past its gardens. It was beautiful and peaceful. The tide was going out. As I did many times I watched the fly fishermen cast their lines across the water. They wore hip waders and stood against the stream. I would now be standing against the stream of the political and religious views of my family and my Protestant background as never before.

I looked at the falling yellow and brown leaves and thought of my visit to Derry and Cathy and my joining the struggle for civil rights. In spite of the increased tensions I knew would now be in my life, I felt some peace. I had at last found my place in the world. But it was not only peace that I felt. My heart was heavy as I thought of my uncle dying and how the decision to join the civil rights movement and the Derry Labour Party would hurt him and all my family. It was going to be a struggle. I did not want to hurt them further but I could see no other way.

The police violence on 5th October created a mass movement in the

North as tens of thousands who had previously thought nothing could ever be changed took to the streets. This movement was overwhelmingly Catholic. Some Protestant students were involved and a small minority of Protestant workers were somewhat sympathetic. However the overwhelming majority of the Protestant population was opposed. This was because the civil rights movement was portrayed by the Protestant elite and the Northern and British states as threatening to take away the marginal privileges of the Protestants and so for this reason was seen by most of the Protestant population as having to be defeated. The strategy of the siege mentality and divide and rule was being used and was working.

The forces that were pushing this siege mentality and divide and rule propaganda were powerful. They included the British and Northern governments, the Protestant churches and institutions, the Orange Order with its 700 lodges and halls and its people in the leading positions of the police and the civil service and the Protestant-owned businesses in Northern Ireland. The message was driven home, the false claim was made that the civil rights movement was an IRA front which wanted to take away all the privileges and rights of the Protestant people and force them into a united Catholic Ireland. It had to be opposed.

With this propaganda to face, with the privileges and power of the Protestant elite and the marginal privileges of the Protestant working class, it would have been hard to win Protestant workers to the civil rights movement under any conditions. But when the leadership of the civil rights movement fell into the hands of right wing Catholic nationalists and Republicans it was impossible. The take-over of the movement by the right wing nationalists and Republicans happened at a meeting in the City Hall in Derry following the 5th October march. It was attended by over 200 people. There was a large organised contingent of Catholic business people and supporters of the Catholic hierarchy. They came, obviously organised beforehand, and determined to take charge. And they did so. The meeting set up the Citizens' Action Committee (CAC). The events around and following the 5th October march had shocked these elements as it threatened their relationship with the Northern state and their control of the Catholic population. They moved to reassert their control.

I was devastated as I watched these right wing forces take control of the movement. I could not believe the radical groups which had brought the mass movement into being, groups such as the Labour Party, the Labour Party Young Socialists, the Housing Action and Unemployed Action committees, the Republican Clubs etc. were allowing this to happen without a fight. These groups did not know what to do nor could they work together to oppose the Catholic middle class and its Catholic hierarchy organised grouping. The right wing forces of the business people, used to being in charge, and who were helped and advised by the Catholic hierarchy, were much better prepared to seize the leadership and they did so.

As this took place in front of my eyes I could not see how I could get Protestants involved in the movement when it would be run by these right wing Catholics. But one after another of these types spoke and the more radical and left groups allowed themselves to be pushed aside. One of the most prominent leaders of the left, a member of the Derry Labour Party was actually elected onto the leading body of the CAC but he refused to take the position. I could only conclude that the left forces were afraid of taking the leadership, of fighting for the leadership, of the movement they had brought into being.

I realised that the right wing Catholic forces which seized the leadership had no wish to involve the Protestant working class, not only that, but they had no wish to involve the Catholic working class either. They only wanted to get things back in control, back in the hands of their own class, that is the Catholic capitalist and middle class and the Catholic hierarchy and re-establish these groups' previous relatively cosy relationship with the Northern state.

I listened to the meeting and thought about what it would sound like to Protestant workers, the majority of people in the North. The reality of the meeting and the CAC meant there was little in it for them. I thought about myself. If I had not been dedicated to fighting to change things I would have walked away from that meeting. I could never have supported, and never did support, the Catholic middle class nationalists and representatives of the Catholic hierarchy who came and took over the leadership of that meeting and the newly emerging movement. Some may think I am exaggerating the role of the Catholic hierarchy but it is unimaginable to think that this force with all its history, with all its property, all its full-time organisers, all its churches and their members would have stood by and let this new mass movement do its own thing. This was not the way this organisation worked. In every situation worldwide where it had resources it used these resources to attempt to direct events in its own interests.

I could not understand how anybody who stood against repression, who stood against the special oppression of women, who stood for people's rights, economic and democratic, who stood against one country ruling another could be a member of the Catholic church. It was an undemocratic, male-dominated, anti-women organisation. It was the main church of capitalism. I could understand how through tradition, through the con tricks of guilt and burning in hell forever etc., and the confessional then giving a way out, the Catholic hierarchy could indoctrinate and control people. But I believed that people should not join any church or be part of any organised religion.

I came to take the position that people should not belong to the Catholic church or to any organised religion because these were all built on lies and guilt and support for capitalism. I refined this position somewhat by explaining that if people could not resist joining such organisations then they should at the very least build oppositions within these organisations. Oppositions which would fight for democratic debate and discussion, that is not one preacher, always male in the Catholic church, talking to a silent audience which could not speak back. Oppositions that would fight for all positions within the churches to be elected by one person, one vote of the membership. Oppositions which would fight for equality between the sexes, that is in the Catholic and other churches and religions, Muslim, Hindu, etc., women to have the same right as men to be leaders.

Of course this would have been dangerous, especially in the Catholic Church. The Catholic church hierarchy when faced with opposition in its ranks from the Liberation Theology in the 1970s, assisted US imperialism in murdering the leading members of the opposition in its own church. That is assisted US imperialism in murdering its own members. The Liberation Theology wanted the church to be the church for the poor not for the rich. This was not and never will be acceptable to the Catholic hierarchy.

There was a possible alternative to the civil rights movement being taken over by the right wing Catholic forces. This was to build a movement for civil rights for all, including the Protestant working class who were discriminated against in the electoral field, reach out to the Protestant working class by fighting for well-paid secure jobs for everybody, for decent affordable housing for everybody, for living wages for everybody. And for these to be fought for through the 250,000-strong trade union movement which was made up of Protestant and Catholic workers. And to unite all workers for these demands against all bosses, Protestant and Catholic. The Derry Trades Council which brought together the trade unions in the city, which represented the trade unionists in the city, both Protestant and Catholic, and which had the potential to give such a lead, refused to offer this alternative. Instead the right wing Catholic capitalist nationalists and the representatives of the Catholic hierarchy took over. The movement was therefore cut off from any chance of winning the Protestant working class and building a united working class movement.

As that meeting ended I felt very discouraged by the role played by the more radical forces. But I also felt discouraged by my own role. I could have spoken up and put forward a united working class alternative. And even if I could not have influenced the meeting to any extent, such an intervention would have allowed me to explain to Protestant and Catholic workers what I had done and appeal to them to join me in the struggle to build a united working class alternative. But I was too inexperienced to take this action.

The opportunity was missed. I resolved that I would develop myself so that I would be better able to help fight for such an alternative in the future.

After the meeting in Derry I involved myself as quickly and as much as possible in the civil rights movement. This meant disengaging more and more from my old life. I played rugby for Strabane at the time. The next civil rights march coincided with a rugby match. I told the club I would not be playing. 'I am going to a Civil Rights march.'

Club members, Protestant and Catholic alike, tried to convince me to play. The Catholics in the club were mainly middle class and so less touched by the rising civil rights movement at that early stage. There were two players from well-off backgrounds. One was Protestant and one Catholic. Both had attended expensive boarding schools and their families owned farms and businesses. They were the most sexist and sectarian people in the club.

The Protestant approached me first and after trying to flatter me about how good a player I was and how they needed me he went on: 'You must have some good looking woman at those marches that you are going to. That is what it is. Come on you can do her at night.' These were his exact words.

Then the Catholic approached me. I had dated his sister once and he had not spoken to her for months afterwards. Not knowing I knew this he acted like he was my best friend. 'Come on man, we need you. Sure I should be going to that march more than you. I am a Catholic. Come and play instead. You must have a woman there that you are riding. That is what it is. Come and play and you can ride her after.' These were his exact words. I was disgusted with both of them.

Then the club captain and his wife approached me. 'I hear you are going to some march of Fenians. You are a Protestant. What are you doing there?' I responded angrily. 'First of all I am not a Protestant. I do not believe in God. But you are a schoolteacher. And you are supposed to be teaching children to act and think right and here you are attacking people for their religion and for asking for their civil rights.'

His wife then spoke, her face screwed up and red with rage. 'You are a disgrace to your family. Your father and uncle were Orangemen and good Protestants and now you are going to Civil rights marches.' I answered sharply. 'You are right. My father and uncle were Orangemen. Yours were not. Yours were too cowardly, hiding their sectarianism and property behind the backs of people like my father and uncle. I have more respect for my father and uncle. At least they had the courage to take an open stand.'

In spite of the fact that I liked playing rugby I gave it up. I could no longer tolerate the middle class sectarian attitudes. Instead I took up playing soccer and played for Strabane. All the players on the team were from a Catholic background except myself. I was not a bad player. But there was a sectarian element involved in the soccer too. The club captain on one occasion told me that while I was a more than good enough player to be on the team I never would have been invited to join if I had not been involved in the civil rights movement. I knew the club manager and he was a decent and respected person. I tried to get him involved in the civil rights movement but he would always run off shaking the daily tabloid at me and saying, 'I stick to the back pages.' Meaning he only read the sports pages in the paper. He did not read the political pages.

I never experienced anything like the march in Derry which followed the events of 5th October. On November 16th 10,000 to 15,000 people walked across Derry Bridge from the mainly Protestant Waterside to the mainly Catholic City side. The choice of route was to try and make clear that the civil rights movement was not sectarian and stood for unity between Protestants and Catholics. This approach was possible at that time because the right wing Catholic business people, the Catholic hierarchy, the Nationalists and Republicans had not yet had time to completely stamp their Catholic sectarianism on the movement.

Largely forgotten now, this march, in spite of being overwhelmingly Catholic, was of great significance. Not only because of its route and its size, but also because it marched behind the US civil rights anthem, 'We Shall Overcome', not behind any Republican or nationalist song. The African American revolt in the USA was leading us. I wished I could have shared this with the young African American students I had seen in the library in New Orleans. I wished I could have shared it with the African American man I had met in the pub in Grenwish Village in New York City. But I could not so I did all I could, I thanked them under my breath.

While taking part in the march I stood up on a parapet of the bridge and looked over to the City side and back to the Waterside. The bridge was filled from end to end and from sidewalk to sidewalk. It was a sight to see. I would later live and work in other countries and return to visit Ireland and Derry and when I did I would look at the bridge and thank that mass of people who built and participated in that march, who with one voice sang 'We Shall Overcome'. They further opened for me the road to struggle and revolution, saved me from giving up hope and wasting my life.

I marched with Dolores and Cathy and their friends, most of whom were in the Derry Labour Party. After meeting and discussing with Cathy and Dolores a few times, and after seeing that they were the most thoughtful and non-sectarian people in the movement, and that they were socialists and the Derry Labour Party was socialist, I joined the Labour Party and also came to regard myself as a socialist. Dolores and Cathy were central to me coming to regard myself as a socialist. I am indebted to them. We became close friends.

International events also affected the civil rights movement and myself. The 1968 Olympics were on at the time. I was lying on an old armchair by my mother's fireside watching them on her TV. It was 16th October 1968. The medals were being handed out for the 200-metre sprint. Under the inspiration and as part of the rising mass movements worldwide, the two African Americans, Tommie Smyth who had won the gold and John Carlos who had won the bronze and the white Australian, Peter Norman, who had won the silver stepped to the podium. They bowed their heads. Then, in a spectacular action which sent shock waves around the world, and which made me leap to my feet, the two black athletes each raised a clenched fist in a black glove in a defiant salute.

The athletes later explained their actions. Smyth's raised fist represented Black Power. Carlos' raised fist represented unity in black America. Smyth's black scarf stood for black pride. Both athletes wore black socks and no shoes which represented poverty in racist America. They wore strings of beads to represent the lynching of black Americans that was still taking place. And one of them opened his jacket in solidarity with his African American and European American fellow workers back home in New York City. They had only the two black gloves so the Australian Peter Norman who had won the silver medal and who was also on the podium played his part by wearing an Olympic Project for Human Rights badge.

This was the most popular medal ceremony of all time. The sweat forced its way out of my forehead. My fists clenched. My teeth ground in rage and inspiration and excitement. I felt my heart would burst. I wanted to strike the whole racist and dirty power structure of the world. I would never be able to repay my debt to these men. In difficult times I would think of the stand they took and this would inspire me to continue with my own struggle. I can still see them in my mind's eye, standing there straight and tall, the fastest men in the world, defying that racist unjust world.

The top official of those Olympic Games gave the US team an ultimatum. Either they would send Tommy Smyth and John Carlos home or he would send the whole US team home. This same official was in the Olympic management of the 1936 Olympics when the German athletes gave the Nazi salute and he had not a word to say. He was a dirty, cowardly racist.

When Tommy Smyth and John Carlos got home they were driven out of job after job for their stand. Peter Norman was isolated and discriminated against by the Australian Olympic Committee and by many Australians when he returned to his native land. He was not allowed to participate in the lap of honour for Australian Olympic athletes in 2000 and he died in depression and alcoholism. As a sign of their respect for him the two African American athletes, Tommy Smyth and John Carlos from the 1968 medal ceremony and protest, travelled to Australia and carried his coffin at his funeral. They did not forget the role played by Peter Norman. They showed their admiration and gratitude for the role played by Peter Norman.

Looking at these athletes taking their stand at the medal ceremony struck me like a thunder bolt there in my family's small farmhouse in Donegal. I had to talk about it. But my family would only see the athletes as causing trouble and being like them 'Catholic civil rights ones'. Another example of how the siege mentality cut the Protestant workers and Protestants off from so much of what was progressive and inspirational in the world. I jumped in my car and rushed into the pub in Strabane where the youth and the more radical people in the Catholic population tended to drink. It was packed. Pushing the door open I ran in. 'Did you see that? Did you see that? Did you see your men at the Olympics?' I shouted in my excitement. But the response was not immediately what I expected.

Two older men, Catholics, turned and said: 'So what, them coloured boys have nothing to do with us.' I was enraged. I shouted at them: 'What are you talking about? They are fighting for the same as we are. You are only two racist fuckers,' and I rushed to attack them. I wanted to hit somebody. I had to get that built up excitement out of my system some way. The pub went silent. Then two young men stepped between us. They were two of the best athletes and soccer players in the town. 'It is alright Throne. Do not listen to those fuckers. They do not know what they are talking about. Sure those boys getting the medals were great and putting their fists up too, and look at how fit they were as well. The fastest men in the world.' At that the two older men with their racism went silent and in that small pub in Strabane, Tommy Smyth and Peter Norman and John Carlos were celebrated. And I was part of that worldwide celebration and inspiration. I had found my place in the world.

CHAPTER 14

BACKLASH

BUT FINDING MY PLACE in the world, as with all things, came with a price. There was a backlash against my involvement in the civil rights movement. It hit my family hard. A few days after the big march in Derry I visited my mother. She was distraught. She turned to me from where she was baking bread in the kitchen. 'How could you do it? Your father is in his grave. Your poor uncle is at death's door. And there you are out marching with that crowd. When I was in Strabane today that Mrs Stevenson turned her back on me and walked away like I was dirt. And when I asked that Throne man, that cousin of ours, that man who has always come here and been fed, for a lift home, he said he would not give me one, that I would be better suited getting my son under control. John you have to stop this. I cannot take it. I did not do anything to deserve this.' The system was working through my family to try and put me back in line.

My aunt came into the house from where she had been feeding the ducks. She sat down on a chair in the kitchen and held her head in her hands. She wept. 'John your uncle is dying in Lifford hospital. Sure what you are up to will break his heart. For his sake if for nothing else stop it. Sure them other kind are only laughing at you behind your back. They want all for themselves and we would have nothing. They want their priests to rule us. That's what all their talk about civil rights is about. Putting us down.' My political ideas and activities were not easy for any of us.

My family was always well informed about my civil rights involvement. Protestants told them because they wanted to attack me and used my family to do so. They also wanted to hurt my family. But this was not universal. There was the very odd Protestant who supported what I was doing. One

Protestant about my own age told me that he supported what I was doing and wished he had the courage to do the same but his father owned a petrol station and garage and if he did what I did he would be left with nothing. Catholics would also tell my family what I was doing. These in the main wanted to crow about my support for civil rights and get a dig in at my family. This was nasty.

But there were also Catholics who tried to shield my family from what I was doing. The man who had stood to attention at my father's funeral was a postman and lived a field down below my mother's house. On a number of occasions postcards with sectarian threats and dirty accusations against me were sent to my mother's address. This postman risked his job and did not deliver these as he knew they would hurt my mother and aunt. Next time he would see me he would give them to me. He was a good man.

I tried to have as little debate as possible with my family on my civil rights activities as I knew it would come to nothing. But at the same time I would not let my mother and my aunt and uncle and how they felt determine how I acted. I thought of the Catholic people in the civil rights movement and how their families supported them and what they were doing. For me it was different and more difficult. The Protestant population saw me as a traitor. I wished that my family and I were together in the civil rights struggle. I deeply regretted the pain I was causing them but I had to stand up for what I believed and for my principles. It was tragic but my family was paying for what they themselves had taught me, that is, to stand up for what I believed in. The problem was we believed in different things.

My resolve to stand by my new life of struggle was put to the test very quickly and in a way that hurt my family and I very much. Years of smoking had ruined my uncle's lungs and he was getting weaker by the day. Every night I took my aunt to visit him in hospital. When I arrived one night to collect her and bring her home she was standing by his bed. Neither of them saw me arrive. 'Martha, why does John not talk to me? My heart is sore. He leaves you off and goes and we never talk.' I broke out in sweat with my shame. This man who thought of me as his own son was dying, and I was not talking to him. I could not talk to him without the things that were between us coming up. Religion, politics, the land, on everything there was disagreement. Neither of us were prepared to change our views so we were always in conflict. I wanted to talk to him, to say some words of friendship and respect and kindness and thanks to this man who had been there for me all my life. But I could not. I was not yet mature enough to be able to talk with somebody close to me and avoid subjects on which we disagreed.

It was like I was trapped, held back by a giant claw. When people were dying they could be at their most powerful. They could ask for commitments and promises which they would not ask for at other times. I knew I would say no to any request that I go back to believing in God or that I join the Orange Order. Even in the face of my uncle dying in the bed in front of me I knew I would not give in. But I wanted to avoid having to hurt him too directly if I could. So I ended up speaking to him as little as possible. But this hurt him badly too. The situation was insoluble.

Before my uncle became ill he travelled regularly throughout East Donegal giving recruitment lectures in Orange Halls. I drove him to these but never went in as I was not going to join. We hardly spoke a word to each other as we drove to and from these events. This and my not joining the Orange Order hurt him very much and shamed him in front of the members of that, his own organisation, the organization of which he was a leader. Its members must have wondered why I did not come into his lectures. I do not know what explanation he gave them. I knew he wanted me to be part of what he was doing and to be proud of me and me to be proud of him. But it could not be. Ballintra, Laghey, Donegal Town, Stranorlar, Raphoe, St Johnston, Lifford, these were some of the towns in which I sat outside Orange halls in a car on a cold night waiting for my uncle who was recruiting others to the Orange Order.

The night inevitably came when my mother and I got word to go down to the hospital right away. My uncle was worse. My aunt was already there. When we arrived he was dead. I looked at him lying ashen faced in the bed. He had been a good man. He had stepped in after my father died. Then he had come up against the division in society, the ideas and behaviour that flowed from that division, that division that had been created by British colonialism and British imperialism. He came up against me and my ideas and my opposition to that division. This was not his fault. He believed what he had been told to believe.

But neither was it my fault. I believed what I believed and to have abandoned my beliefs would have broken me. I would have had no principles left. I would have been rudderless, without ballast, I would have been crushed on the rocks of the divided sectarian society. If I was to live a life of integrity I had no choice but to stand for my beliefs and this inevitably meant conflict with him and the rest of my family. I wish it could have been otherwise. I wished I had not brought so much hurt and disappointment into his and my family's lives.

As I looked at him lying there dead I thought that maybe he was lucky he died when he did. What would it have been like for him with me active in the civil rights movement? His fellow brethren and friends in the Orange Order would have condemned me and looked down on him and pitied him. As one of the main Orange Order leaders in Donegal it would have been a terrible fate for him, seeing what had been his favourite nephew, whom he had looked on as his son, not only refuse to join and march with the Orange

Order but instead join and march in the civil rights movement. And many in the Catholic population would have laughed at him behind his back. In death he was spared all that.

His wake and funeral were like my father's. The wake lasted three days and three nights. Everybody was fed and watered. The neighbours brought food and cigarettes and help came from all sides. It was a Black funeral also like my father's. The members of that organisation lined up and took the little black silk bows from their lapels and dropped them into the grave. People from all religious backgrounds were there. The size and the ecumenical attendance was a tribute to my uncle's character and the respect he had built over the years. I mourned him in his death. He had been a good man. But while I mourned him and recognised he had been a good man, this did not in any way shake my commitment to my new life of organising against injustice and sectarianism.

I was living in a caravan at Dunree Fort on the Lough Swilly at that time. I had bought the caravan from the husband of Margaret, my sectarian sister. When he saw what it would be used for later, meetings of civil rights activists and my personal activities he would be enraged. However, while I lived in the caravan at Dunree I called regularly to visit my mother and aunt in their farmhouse in Lifford and to do some chores for them there. A few days after my uncle's funeral I arrived to find my Aunt Martha alone, and in extreme distress. I was sure it was something I had done. It usually was. But then she told me that my Aunt Lizzie, the oldest member of my mother's and aunt's family, had died. With my Aunt Martha staying behind to look after things I drove up to my dead aunt's house outside Castlefinn. My mother was already there.

I tried to imagine what could have happened. My aunt's death coming so soon after my uncle's seemed a terrible coincidence. Aunt Lizzie was the oldest of the family. My mother was the second oldest and was closer to her than any of the rest of the family. She would be devastated. And my Aunt Martha had just lost her husband and now was losing a sister all in a few days. And then there was my civil rights activity coming on top of that. It was one blow after the other for my mother and aunt.

My Aunt Lizzie lived in a small cottage. It had no amenities and was owned by a local farmer. Her husband was dead. He had owned no land and worked in a local mill. He was one of the few Protestants in the area with no property of any kind. My Aunt Lizzie and he had had three sons. Two had emigrated to get decent jobs, one to England and one to Australia. The other and youngest worked for the local farmer who owned the cottage in which they lived. My aunt was not happy with him working in that low paid hard job with no future, and living in a house that was tied to that job. My aunt's house and living conditions had barely improved from the house and living conditions of her own father and mother, of my mother's father and mother.

I pulled up at the cottage. There was smoke coming out of the chimney. There were cars outside. Mourners were arriving. My Aunt Lizzie was well liked and respected. My mother opened the door. 'Oh John. Poor Lizzie, her life is over. It is wild for her. Come on in. God bless her and all of us.' My Aunt Lizzie's son was standing behind my mother. I shook his hand: 'Robert, I am very sorry about your mother.' 'Thanks, Thanks.' He was weeping.

There were a few other people in the small kitchen. It was the main room in the house. The wood-burning stove was lit and it was warm. There was a small bedroom off the kitchen and my mother took me into it and said: 'John, it is not just that your Aunt Lizzie is dead. It is worse. She took her own life. She went up to the lint dam and threw herself in and drowned herself. I cannot believe it. Poor Lizzie. And the boys. She was seen out on the road late one other night. She must have been working up to it. Maybe your uncle's death pushed her over the edge. And then last night ... Ah John, poor Lizzie. The poor boys.'

I was silent as I listened to my mother. I thought of my aunt dying with that cold water engulfing her and filling her lungs and wondered if she had changed her mind at the last minute and maybe tried to get out again. I thought that my mother must be feeling very bad that she was not there to stop my aunt killing herself. That my Aunt Lizzie had not felt confident enough in their sisterhood and close enough to her in life to talk to her about her troubles and instead go off alone and throw herself into a cold lint dam. I myself felt terrible that I was not there for my Aunt Lizzie.

I asked my mother why my aunt would have done such a thing. My mother looked at me and seemed to be deciding what to say. 'John, Lizzie was ... John you do not know how hard a life she had. I ... look ... John, John. Your Aunt Lizzie was tired of her life, she had so much suffering, and they had so little, at least we have the few fields, and then she was very concerned about Robert not having a good job. Part of what made her do this was to free Robert from having to stay here in that job so they could still have a house to live in. Robert in his kindness and loyalty felt obliged to stay and work in that job because the house they lived in was owned by the farmer he worked for. It was tied to the job.' I could not answer my mother. I admired the courage of my aunt and her willingness to sacrifice herself for her son, her strength to end her life because she thought that this would make things better for him. I respected her courage. She was a heroine.

'John, you know what she did? She left out towels to dry herself. And wee envelopes with the few pence she owed the grocer and the butcher. She was as honest as the day is long all her life and to the very end. John you did not know your Aunt Lizzie very well. She was the best one of all of us. And she had the hardest life. And then she had to end like this. I cannot bear it.' My mother leaned forward in her chair and held her head in her hands and wept. I could not comfort her. I could not hug her. Trying to stand against the pressure to accept my family's ideas tended to make me withhold open expressions of solidarity and sympathy. I was worried that the more open comfort and support I gave my mother and my family the more susceptible I would be to their efforts to make me think and live the way they wanted me to think and live. I was afraid to show my feelings for my mother and my family in case this would rise up against me. I was trapped with my mother as I was with my uncle. Trapped by my fear that if I expressed too much caring and sympathy to her and my family members this would weaken me and make me susceptible to their pressure on me to go back and adopt their ideas again. I was not strong enough and mature enough to be able to properly comfort my mother there at that time of her need and at the same time be confident that this would not weaken me in my struggle for my own ideas and way of life.

As I stood there with my mother telling me about my Aunt Lizzie's qualities and how she was so honest, I was also thinking would the Protestant shop keepers say to my Aunt Lizzie's family do not worry, keep the few pence. After all she was one of their own. I thought they would not. The 'one of your own' pretty much stopped where the money started.

I would later find out that my Aunt Lizzie was my mother's half-sister. My mother's mother, also my Aunt Lizzie's mother, my grandmother, had been hired out to a farmer who had raped her and made her pregnant. She had then been married off to my grandfather. He was much older than her. This marriage was arranged by the church to which she and her rapist both belonged. This church wanted to cover up what had happened. My Aunt Lizzie was then born and after her three more sisters and a brother.

My Aunt Lizzie and my mother and her sisters and brother had all been indoctrinated into believing that any woman, who had sex outside of marriage was a sinner. No exception was made for sex in the form of rape as was the case with my grandmother when my Aunt Lizzie was cenceived. In the old pre-Christian Irish society with its Brehon laws rape was openly recognized and outlawed. Under these old laws rape was defined not only as sex with the use of force but also it included a man telling a woman lies to have sex with her. Christian Ireland was a major step back in this area of life. The thinking that was imposed by Christian Ireland meant that my Aunt Lizzie and her siblings always had a conflict of ideas within them. On the one hand they knew that their mother had done no wrong. That Aunt Lizzie was as good as any of the rest of them. On the other the Christian churches told them that there was wrong. In reality that there was something lesser about my Aunt Lizzie. My mother and her sisters and brother kept what happened to their mother in the case of my Aunt Lizzie's parenthood strictly to themselves. But this did not mean it did not bring them pain, it did not bring them contradiction and confusion. And on top of that in spite of others outside the family knowing what happened to my grandmother my aunts and uncle tried to keep it a secret inside the family. I thought again how cruel this Christian society was.

My mother treated my Aunt Lizzie with great kindness. Always trying to help her as much as possible. Our family was better off with our few fields and my mother would give my Aunt Lizzie some food, a chicken, a duck, eggs, a loaf of her home baked bread. But most of all my mother helped my Aunt Lizzie with her care and warmth and support. Never a bad word would cross her mouth about Aunt Lizzie. It was only many years later that I found out what that rapist farmer had done to my grandmother and that the rapist was my Aunt Lizzie's father.

As I thought about my Aunt Lizzie's decision to kill herself I wondered if anybody had suggested she come and live with us at our home place at Lifford. She could have done so. There was enough room. This would have freed up her son. It would have been a good solution. Why had I not suggested it? I had never thought of it. I was ashamed. I was too busy thinking about civil rights and socialism to think about this as a solution to my Aunt Lizzie's problems. I was not even aware she had these problems. When I would later think about this I was astounded thinking about the rigidity of my and my family's thoughts at that time. My Aunt Lizzie moving to live at Portinure would have been the ideal solution but nobody brought it up. And this included me.

Aunt Lizzie's funeral had less of the ceremony of my father's or my uncle's. But more people expressed how much she had meant to them in their lives. It had more warmth. It was more a women's funeral. One Catholic lady came to me and told me how when my Aunt Lizzie had worked as a servant in a big house she would secretly save food and give it to her, the Catholic lady, when she was hungry. I was proud of my aunt.

My Aunt Lizzie worked in the big houses all her life as a servant for the rich. They all praised her as a very good servant, this meant she accepted her meagre wages without complaint, did what she was told, and kept quiet about what she saw going on. But it was their system that kept her poor and which eventually drove her to her terrible death. I thought of this as we buried her.

I noticed there were none of these rich people whose houses she cleaned and food she cooked at my aunt's home during the wake or in the graveyard at her funeral. It was not that they would have been unwelcome. In fact given the conservative views of all the rest of my family they would have been very welcome. Their presence would have even been seen as an honour. It was that they wanted to stay warm and comfortable in their own homes murmuring about how good a servant my Aunt Lizzie had been and drinking tea out of their china cups, tea prepared now by newer and younger servants and going on about 'poor Lizzie'. Or maybe now that she was dead they would be calling my aunt 'Elizabeth' to give the pretence that they respected her.

There was another reason these people did not come to my aunt's funeral. By not coming they were saying and letting everybody else see that they considered themselves better than my aunt. They were too good to come to my aunt's wake or funeral. They did not have to come. They were too good to come because my aunt was 'only' a servant and also because of her birth origin. They gave their other servants time off to come as their proxies. My hatred of these people and their class and their system and my commitment to my revolutionary views were strengthened. If my Aunt Lizzie had been one of, what they would have considered one of their 'own class', or one of their 'betters' they would have been there. I seethed as I stood at the graveside and thought about these people.

The events and circumstances of my aunt's life and death strengthened my revolutionary views in another way. As well as the rich types for whom she had been a servant not attending her funeral, there was the role of the more right wing religious people in her church. They did not want my aunt to be buried in the church graveyard because she had taken her own life. This was cruel. But my Uncle Pat, the brother of my Aunt Lizzie and my mother and Aunt Martha and Aunt Rebecca, had influence in the church and in organisations such as the Orange and Masonic Orders. Through this he was able to oppose these people and my Aunt Lizzie was buried in the church graveyard. I thought about it. To get buried where she wanted my uncle had to fight the right wing in his and my aunt's own church to make this happen. I was glad I had broken from the poison and cruelty of religion.

My uncle, Patrick he was called, but more often Pat, he was my mother's brother. He was like myself the youngest in the family and the only boy. He had been pushed to get a better education and so a better job than any of his sisters. He had achieved this. He had not deviated from the intended path like I had done. My Uncle Pat, as I called him, was the treasurer in the local Protestant-owned woollen mill and a member of the Masonic Order. I used to visit him on the occasional Sunday night and we would argue strongly about ideas and politics. He was a good-hearted man but like the rest of my relatives and like just about all the population, Protestant and Catholic, he was sectarian. On this occasion of the death of my Aunt Lizzie and her burial place he acted very properly.

Seeing this hypocrisy and the class prejudice in the Protestant population concerning my aunt and her death strengthened my opposition to all religions. I knew the Catholic Church was just as bad if not worse than the Protestant religions. They made couples involved in mixed Protestant-Catholic marriages make a vow that any children would be brought up Catholic. They blackmailed their members with the threat of 'hell' to toe the line. The celibate priests harassed women who were married and did not have children to 'do their duty', that is have children. I increasingly opposed and had contempt for all religions. I used to provoke the religious people I argued with by asking them what they would do if Muslim people were going to take over in Ireland. Would they get over their Catholic-Protestant antagonism and unite. They would just look at me. The idea was something they had never considered. It was totally outside their conception. What had Muslims to do with religion? Religion was Protestantism and Catholicism.

Many years later I would hear the following from my sister who had heard it from a former neighbour of my Aunt Lizzie. My Aunt Lizzie had some neighbours who were just about as poor if not poorer than her own family. She wanted to send them some of her wee scones. The children of this family went up and down past my Aunt's house on their way to and from school. She wanted to send the small box of scones down with them. But she was worried they would open the box and eat all the scones and there would be none for the rest of the family. So she told the children that in the box were some small birds that their mother wanted to have in the house as pets. And that if they opened the box the little birds would fly away and die in the cold weather and their family would not have them as pets. So the children did not open the box. What imagination, what intelligence, what humour, what a wonderful woman was my Aunt Lizzie. That such a wonderful woman would see no other way but to end her life in a cold lint dam was a major condemnation of the society in which she and we lived.

The deaths of my aunt and uncle did not interrupt my work in the civil rights movement or the Derry Labour Party. In fact they hardened me and strengthened my commitment. They also drove me to try and understand more. My thirst for knowledge was so great I drove to Dublin, found the Communist Party (CP) bookshop and bought twenty copies of Connolly's *Labour in Irish History*. I brought these back, kept one for myself and gave the rest to other members of the emerging civil rights movement. I wondered at the attitude of the CP. I was a young man from the North. I had driven all the way to their shop in Dublin and bought twenty copies of Connolly's *Labour in Irish History* yet they did not even ask my name. I would later learn that all Stalinist organisations such as the CP were afraid of anything they were not sure they could control and this especially meant the youth.

My involvement in the Derry Labour Party increased my understanding of the way things worked. I learnt that the trade unions were the basic organisations of the working class and that workers' common economic conditions tended to drive them together into the trade unions. I had always been against sectarian division but I now learnt how this could be overcome, how best it could be fought. I learnt that it was not just a question of fighting for unity of Catholic and Protestant but what was necessary was to fight for unity of Protestant and Catholic workers against all the bosses Protestant and Catholic, and against both sectarian states North and South, and against the British capitalist system and the Irish capitalist system and all of their divide and rule policies. I came to understand that it was the common conditions of all workers, both Protestant and Catholic, which were the key to success in the fight against the system and against sectarianism. I learnt it was a class question.

I increasingly saw how the class and economic and political issues related to the civil rights struggle. I was approached in Strabane by a leading Orangeman. He had been a friend of my uncle and father. In spite of being, rather because of being, a Protestant, and a leading Orangeman, he was the buyer for the biggest potato exporter in the area who was a Catholic. He attacked me. 'Your father would turn in his grave if he knew you were running about with them civil rights Fenian scum. When you lie down with dogs you get fleas.' I replied: 'You have your job with that Catholic businessman because you are a Protestant and an Orangeman and this allows you to buy the Protestants' potatoes for your Catholic boss. Do not talk to me.' He had no answer except a red face which looked as if it would explode. His sectarianism was rooted in his wallet. When it came to making money it was okay for these elements to collaborate with Catholics.

Sometime later I was arrested and held in the Strabane police barracks. While there I was looking out the window of the cell and I saw this man's boss, the Catholic potato exporter, standing in the alley talking to a group of British soldiers and Northern Ireland police. He reached into the back of his big expensive car and handed them over two bottles of whiskey. It was not hard to see what was going on. He was bribing them to look after his interests. He owned a number of pubs in the riot-torn Catholic areas. I was seeing that to the wealthier people property and wealth were inexorably intertwined with religion and when it came down to it, property and wealth and whatever was necessary to hang on to these came first.

CHAPTER 15

THE BOGSIDE UPRISING

EVERYBODY KNEW SOMETHING was going to happen in Derry on 12th August 1969, the day of the annual march by the Protestant organisation the Apprentice Boys. It was decided to set up the Bogside Citizens' Defence Association (BCDA) in advance. This was formed on a street corner in the Brandywell. By that time I was an active member of the Young Socialists and I was elected a member of the BCDA as a representative of the Young Socialists. I had by that time been helping to set up branches of the Young Socialist organisation and of the Labour party throughout the North West. This was also a factor in my being elected to the BCDA.

The divide and rule religious sectarianism was working as I was the only person from a non-Catholic background on the committee. By that time I was an atheist. The left sectarianism was also working as the only other socialist present at the meeting to form the BCDA tried to keep me from being elected onto the committee. The CAC had by this time atrophied as the struggle had moved to the streets where the members of that organisation, who did not like to throw stones, did not have much of a presence.

On the night of 11th August, I was in Derry with other members of the Labour Party Young Socialist branch. A group of Catholic youth from the Bogside had gathered on the edge of the the Fountain, the small Protestant enclave within the city walls. They were intending to attack it. We went up to see if we could stop this. The dim streetlights and the rain cast a dull depressive atmosphere. We were wet and uncomfortable. The Fountain and the Bogside both lay under the falling mizzling rain and the weak yellow lights. But the Fountain sat on the top of the hill and inside the city walls and the Bogside sat at the bottom of the hill and outside the city walls. An accurate illustration of how things were in the North.

'Hey boys, how is it going?' The young people turned to see who we were.

'Who the fuck are you? What do you want?' 'Nothing, just seeing what is going on.' 'We are going to get these Orange fuckers that is what is going on.' 'Why would you do that? They are only working people like us. There is plenty wrong in this city but it is not the people in The Fountain who make the decisions.' 'Working people? I am not a working people. Me da is not a working people. We have never had a job. Them Protestant fuckers get first whack at jobs and everything else, well that is going to stop.'

We went back and forward like this for a couple of hours. Working class unity did not get much response because most of the young people had never had a job, many of their parents had never had a job, never mind worked with Protestants. But our arguments had some effect and slowly the Catholic youth drifted off. We had prevented an attack on The Fountain. This was good. As I left I thought about the many Protestants who attacked me for being a traitor to my Protestant background, for supposedly being against Protestants. Many of them would later say I should be shot. Some of them even tried to make this happen. But there were none of those heroes there that night stopping the Catholic youth from attacking the Fountain. I was.

With this threat to the Fountain over I drove down to my caravan at Dunree Fort. The sun was coming up behind the hills to the east behind me. It was a beautiful dawn. I could hear the waves breaking on the shore. I could smell the North Atlantic as it pushed up into the Lough Swilly. I was at peace and glad to be alive and feeling good that I had been part of stopping the attack on the Fountain. I sat for a while on the step of the caravan looking out over the ocean and absorbing the dawn and thought again about what I had been part of the night before. It was a good thing we had done. I also felt the continued peace of now knowing my place in the world. I made myself a sandwich and some hot tea.

As I sat there, my wee Jack Russell dog, the wee ratter, was with me. I had him from before I went on my travels. My family had looked after him when I was away. One of their many kindnesses to me. He was, as usual, looking for some bits of my sandwich. But he was also looking for companionship. That morning, as was very common, he sat with his backside against my ankle looking out at what was going on. Maybe a rabbit. Every now and then he would turn his head and look up into my eyes. When he would do this, I would feel he was putting his all into seeking a deeper connection with me. I felt so bad that I could not talk to him. That was one of the most peaceful moments of my life.

I awoke around noon the next morning, left my wee dog with a local lady who liked to look after him and headed back into Derry. Arriving on the outskirts of the city I felt a calm, like people were keeping off the streets. Parking my car on Northland Road I walked down William Street to the Bogside and into a mass uprising against the police and the state and events that would change the North and myself forever.

It was mostly young men and boys at that stage. They were confronting the police and the Apprentice Boys marchers with stones. The police were trying to escort the marchers along their usual route which was on the edge of the Bogside. This march always and naturally caused resentment as the Bogside residents rightly felt that it took this route in order to make clear who was boss. While this was true it was usually reluctantly tolerated. However this year was different. The Bogside youth attacked the march and the police backed up by forty or fifty Protestant civilians counter-attacked the Bogside youth with batons and stones.

The Bogside fighters were not intimidated. Were not America's black youth fighting their racist cops, were not the Vietnamese fighters taking on the US military, were not workers and peasants and students all over the world fighting their capitalist and Stalinist regimes? Here in the Bogside the fighters, even if unconsciously took their place in the uprisings of the world. They were part of the worldwide uprisings. Back and forward the battle raged. As it became clear that the youth were not going to be crushed, more people of all ages, reinforcements, came from the Bogside and down from the Creggan and joined them. The Bogside uprising was on. History was being made. The old balance of forces, the old structures of the Northern state were cracking. The people of the Bogside and Creggan had had enough.

Not being from the Bogside or being one of its directly discriminated against residents I did not initially have their extreme rage. It was not my house that was under attack. It was not me who could never get a job. As opposed to my experience, the people of the Bogside had suffered the discrimination and poverty and repression of the Northern Irish state for decades. The full reality of the situation was brought home to me by a woman who came out of a small store. She was in her forties. She joined in stoning the police and cursing them with the most extreme ferocity. 'I've waited too fucking long for this,' she shouted as she threw the stones. Spittles of rage flew from her mouth. Her face turned bright red with her rage. When a policeman was hit with a petrol bomb and went up in flames she shouted at the top of her voice in celebration. The intensity of her anger made me understand the seriousness of the events in which I was involved, helped me see the powerful hatred of the majority of the Catholic population for the Northern state, helped me see that this uprising would not be ended with some cerebral discussion over what was fair and what was not fair. This was an uprising by people who had been living under an unjust system and state for a long time and they were going to fight.

This woman's rage also made me understand that I needed to be prepared to listen and learn from people like herself. Not be frightened away by their rage. I am proud to say I was not. On the contrary, I recognised the righteousness of her anger and learnt from it. This hardened, sharpened, my fighting spirit, my cutting edge, my commitment to struggle, my commitment to revolution. That lady took her place along with Marty, Verdes and Spanish in my education.

The Catholic Bogside and Creggan had the worst unemployment and poverty in the city. Its only sizeable factory had just closed down with the workers turning up for work one morning to find the doors closed. They did not even get a day's notice. This increased the anger in the area against the system. Not a single Catholic worked in the Guildhall, the city hall. On top of this Derry was passed over for Northern Ireland's second university which was established instead in the small Protestant town of Coleraine. And at any sign of protest against these injustices, this discrimination, the fist of the Protestant state was sent to put it down. The people of the Bogside and Creggan were saying no more.

Along with other members of the Young Socialists I took up a position stoning the police from an alley leading on to William Street. The night before we had helped stop a threatened attack on the Protestant Fountain, now we were helping stop an actual attack on the Catholic Bogside. On both occasions we were doing the right thing, we were stopping working class neighbourhoods from being attacked. As I took part in that action there on William Street I thought of the many sectarian Catholics around Lifford and Strabane who knew me and scorned me for not being Catholic. There were none of them there defending the Bogside. I was.

As the battle escalated a small petrol bomb factory was set up. The workforce was mainly women in their forties and fifties. Their concentration and work rate was impressive. There was a happiness, a joy even, in them, along with an intent seriousness, as they liberated themselves from decades of discrimination and being treated as second-class citizens both as Catholics and as women. Many of them worked in the shirt factories and were the main breadwinner in their homes. This gave them confidence, skills and the ability to work together as a team. They were applying their life and work experience to this new task of operating the petrol bomb factory. After all it was not that much different from working together to make shirts.

More young women joined the fighting on the streets. I was standing beside one, she was a member of the Young Socialists, when a large stone thrown by a Protestant civilian who was fighting on the side of the police struck her in the ribs. She went down with a scream of pain. Myself and a few others carried her to the first aid station which had been set up and was being worked by volunteer nurses, doctors and women from the area. Another young woman, an American who had come some weeks earlier to see what was going and was caught up in the uprising was overcome by the CS gas that the police had started to use and I also helped to carry her to safety. Those who went down with the CS gas or by being struck by rocks or batons were rescued by the participants in the uprising who would rush forward and drag them away from the attempts of the police to arrest them.

As we were throwing the stones and petrol bombs word came that the petrol bomb factory was running out of petrol. Along with another member of the Labour Party I got my car and we drove out to a petrol station on the Letterkenny road. But what the ... ? It was closed, locked up. We looked at each other. What were we going to do now? Then we burst out laughing.

There we were taking part in an uprising against the state. Just about one of the most serious action you could take and we were worried about a locked door at a petrol station. Looking around we found a couple of big rocks, hefted them up and threw them through the glass doors of the station, turned on the power, helped ourselves to all the cans we could find, filled them with petrol and drove back to the Bogside. The ladies stepped up production. The petrol filled bottles were loaded into milk crates and rushed to the front by younger legs. The front was the Rossville Street flats. The petrol bombs were thrown from the top of these down on to the police and their supporters below. They would come flying down with their flaming tails rejoicing.

As the uprising went on the police began to fire canisters of CS gas. When these would land the white gas would come fizzing out stinging and blinding the eyes. The entire area was a great violent drama. The CS gas canisters flying from the police and landing with their fizzing white tails, petrol bombs flying down from the top of the high flats with their multi-coloured flaming tails, stones and rocks being thrown at the police and outside attackers from the defenders of the Bogside and Creggan, and the police and their supporters responding by throwing stones and with baton charges, yes a great violent drama.

To try and deal with the CS gas, myself and another Young Socialist member drove out to a Catholic convent, broke in and stole all their jute sacks. The owner of the petrol station from whom we had stolen the petrol was Protestant. The owner of the convent was the Catholic hierarchy. We laughed together with each other how we were non-sectarian in our struggle. Protestant or Catholic it did not matter to us, to help the uprising we would steal from either. I tore my pants climbing over the wire topped gate to the convent and for the rest of the uprising did not look too respectable. But then respectability was not what was needed in the events of the time. Bringing the sacks back we soaked them in water and spread them around the war zone. The idea was that whenever a CS gas canister would land we would rush and throw one of the sacks over it. This manoeuvre was not very successful as we did not have enough sacks and more importantly the canisters usually started spewing out their gas before we could get to them. Also with the exception of the petrol bomb making factory and the carrying of the crates of petrol bombs to the top of the flats there was no real coordination of the overall uprising of who would do this, who would do that, no real division of labour.

The uprising went on for five days. There was a feeling that it had to be kept going in solidarity with Belfast where people, mainly in the Catholic areas, were being killed both by the police and sectarian loyalist groups. In an effort to get help and keep the uprising going I phoned an activist I knew in Strabane and he organised a rally and mobilisation outside the police station there. This pinned down the Strabane police so they could not come to Derry as reinforcements.

There was also humour in the uprising. A man with drink in him and a lit cigarette in his hand came to offer his help in making petrol bombs. He could have blown the whole place up and burnt everybody. The ladies chased him away and he was most indignant that his help was refused. Then, three days after petrol bombs were being used by the hundreds, a member of a left wing group in London arrived with a crudely drawn diagram of a petrol bomb on a crumpled sheet of paper. Pompously he took it from his hip pocket and tried to hand it to the ladies. On it he had written 'Molotov Cocktail'. The ladies in the petrol bomb factory looked at him like the poor man needed help, his mother, God bless her, should come and take him home out of harm's way, and then that Molotov business, what kind of a name was that, was he a communist or what, some sort of a Russian. Then there were the young students who arrived from the continent to help. The local people put them up in their homes. But they would not let them sleep together. What kind of an uprising was this? The local ladies who were making the petrol bombs and challenging the capitalist state would not let them sleep together! Sure that should have been half the fun of the whole thing. Then there was the overdressed government minister from the South who sneaked into the area to see what was what. By chance he ended up talking to a few of us more left wing people. Nervous and not knowing what he was really doing he handed over a fifty pound note supposedly to support the uprising but also it was clear to make sure he would get out of the area safely. We looked at the fifty pound note. When he left it was used to produce leaflets attacking the government in the South.

I had another interesting and educational experience during the uprising. I was increasingly interested in finding out about Marxism, what it was etc. During a lull in the fighting I saw a young man whom I had been told was in a marxist group standing watching the fighting in a doorway. I went up to him and very politely said: 'Excuse me, I heard you are a Marxist. Could you tell me what that means.' He drew himself up and looked at me and pronounced to me: 'Marxism is dialectical materialism.' I had not an idea what he was talking about. I responded: 'Well in that case why don't you go and f... yourself.' Many years later I would understand the importance and excitement of grasping dialectical materialism but that was an example of how the sectarian organizations claiming to be marxist put people off Marxism. He wasn't even taking part in the fighting and he could not even tell me what Marxism was.

During the days of the uprising and for some time afterwards I stayed in the home of a fellow member of the Young Socialists. I learnt more about the life of the Catholic working class in the North of Ireland. The man of the house was a skilled electrician. But he could not get work in the North. He had to go and work in Scotland. He was only able to come home to be with his family two weeks in the year. I could see how difficult this was for his family. Another thing I saw that was not right about this Northern sectarian state.

The Bogside uprising was no skirmish. Thousands of people participated. Over 1,000 people were injured in the fighting. Over 350 police sustained serious injuries. The Battle of the Bogside as it came to known was a real mass uprising. The genuine article. This is what I was part off.

Towards the end of the fifth day the police were exhausted and the B Specials, the part-time Protestant and mainly rural state militia, armed with 303 rifles, were called up and ringed the Bogside. These bitter, siege mentality, mainly rural people had no idea who their real bosses were or what the balance of forces were or what was and what was not possible. As they saw it things were simple, they were there to shoot the Catholics, Fenians, Taigs. They would soon put an end to this disorder. A massacre was on the cards. If this had taken place it is unlikely that I would be writing this book.

If this had taken place the fighting would have spread to the South and Britain and upheavals would have been inevitable in the US and Australia and other countries where there were large Irish populations. England, Scotland and Wales, all their major cities had large Irish populations or populations of Irish descent. This was the importance of the Bogside uprising. It had the potential to become a world-wide crisis for British imperialism. I was involved in an event of world significance.

Faced with this threat the London government ordered the Northern government and state to pull back and sent in the British Army to take control. This was a major development. For the first time the Northern sectarian state had been pulled out of direct control of the Catholic population in the main cities of the North and direct control had been given instead to the British Army. The Protestant state and most Protestant people were enraged as they saw this as giving in to the Catholics.

Most Catholics on the other hand saw this as a victory. British soldiers were welcomed with cups of tea in the Catholic areas. Nobody thought it was the start of a thirty year war between the self-styled Irish Republican Army (IRA) and these same soldiers. Very few people thought that in a matter of months these soldiers would, on the orders of London, be imprisoning without trial hundreds of activists, at first Catholics and later Catholics and Protestants, and torturing them in prison cells and prison ships.

Not wanting to stir up more trouble immediately the British state did not, for the time being, try to enter the 'No Go Areas', that is the areas which were encircled by the barricades that had been thrown up in the fighting in Derry and Belfast. The Southern state wanted nothing to do with intervening in the North, just wanted to leave it to the British government. A Southern government minister actually said that the North had to look after itself. So the 'No Go Areas' in many cases came under the control of local committees. The Bogside came under the control of the BCDA.

The membership of the BCDA, while all from a Catholic background except myself, had a mixed political composition. The majority was Republican or nationalist in outlook and was under the influence of the Catholic hierarchy. The Republicans were mostly old timers and right wingers. There was one Republican, an impressive young man called Johnny White, who was on the left. He, and another local man and revolutionary socialist Eamon McCann, also from the Bogside, and I were part of the tiny left wing on the committee. Eventually the only millionaire in the Bogside, the owner of a string of betting shops, would become a member to see for himself what was going on and to try and strengthen the right wing.

The BCDA was something new for me. Until then I had lived a life of individualism, that is making decisions on the basis of my own individual experience. But the BCDA was a collective body which, in spite of its stresses and strains and differences and limits, had been put in place to try and represent a whole area. It took its decisions by democratic vote. I learnt a lot from this experience and not only about the democratic and collective process. But also about the lives of working class people as they brought their problems to the committee to try and have them solved. Their housing problems, their problems with crime in their area, any and all kinds of problems, all would end up at the BCDA office.

In times past there had been mass uprisings of working class people such as the Paris Commune in 1871, the Russian Revolutions in 1905 and 1917, the Limerick workers' uprising in 1919 and many more. Many of these had thrown up what were known as communes, or soviets' or workers' councils. One was the 1919 Limerick Soviet. The distinctive feature of these communes, soviets, councils was that they were made up of elected representatives mainly from the working class, and this meant in most cases directly from the workplaces. They were the elected organs of power of the working class. They were not made up of representatives of the ruling classes or the middle classes. The BCDA did not have representatives from the workplaces. There were very few workplaces in the Bogside. The BCDA was not a soviet, not an organisation of the working class. It was a sectarian-based community committee on which all classes of the Catholic population were represented and in which the nationalist republican organisations, and the middle class Catholics backed by the Catholic hierarchy were dominant.

The main issue of dispute on the BCDA was over the barricades that had been erected in the uprising and remained up around the area. These were patrolled by self-appointed young volunteers who decided who could get in and out. The right wing wanted the barricades brought down because they wanted their class to be able once again to have unchallenged control and speak definitively for the area. They wanted the area to be returned to capitalist state control whether that was the Northern Protestant state or the British state. Either of these was preferable to them than the area being under the control of local youth and workers on the streets. This was the position of the majority on the BCDA, but they could not say so openly.

In spite of mumblings to the contrary designed to cover their tracks, the Republican movement also wanted the barricades to be brought down. They wanted them down so they could implement their own agenda for the area without regard to the wishes of any democratic or even partial democratic body such as the BCDA. The Republican movement was dictated to by the IRA which was organised on an undemocratic, militaristic basis. It was this structure that made decisions. This was undemocratic, its structure was similar to the undemocratic top down structure of the capitalist armies. The left, including myself, wanted the barricades kept up so decisions could be made as democratically and as collectively as possible by and for the whole area, so that the local population could have as much input as possible. We wanted to extend and make the BCDA more democratic and more working class based. We wanted to move to where there were elections in every street and workplace and delegates from these elections to make up the committee.

It became obvious that the situation, that is the two competing outlooks (those who wanted control of the area to continue in the hands of the locally elected committee, the BCDA, as opposed to those who wished to see control of the area put back in the hands of the capitalist state) could not exist side by side for long.

The right wing had a majority on the BCDA to take down the barricades. But they were cautious about using this majority. They feared that if the barricades were taken down and this was followed by a new attack on the area they would be blamed. But eventually they screwed up their courage and pushed through a vote to have them removed. The minute the vote was taken and the majority position to take down the barricades was passed, the meeting broke up and all sides rushed to the main barricade on William Street. There was already a group of people at the barricade intent on enforcing the decision of the majority of the BCDA and taking the barricade down. Amongst those were a number of dockers who were amongst the better paid of the Catholic working class. They had obviously been organised in advance by the Catholic hierarchy and its supporters and business types to provide the forces to carry out the BCDA decision.

This group started to shout at those of us who were against taking down the barricade that we were communists and should get out of the city. I got into a confrontation with one of them and called him a Catholic B Special. He pulled a long knife which was wrapped in newspaper from his inside pocket and we struggled as he tried to stab me. Other people rushed and separated us. The barricades remained up for a time but the momentum behind them was gone.

As the forces on the BCDA fragmented into their different opinions and objectives and as the IRA, without any reference to any democratic will of the local population, launched its military offensive, the mass movement that erupted in 1968 and 1969 was undermined, the mass of the population removed themselves from the streets. The military offensive of the IRA appeared to offer a way forward to sections of the Catholic youth, and at the same time discouraged the older and wider sections of the Catholic population from mass direct action and in this way undermined the movement. Rather than try to deepen and extend the democracy that was reflected in the BCDA and which was the essence of the mass uprising itself, the IRA sought to undermine this and get control into its own undemocratic hands. This was a very negative and damaging step.

Instead of trying to extend the BCDA to a delegate from every street and workplace, the IRA moved to undermine the BCDA and launch their own military offensive which was under the control of their own undemocratic military structure. Instead of trying to involve, for example, the ladies who had run the petrol bomb factory directly as elected representatives on an extended BCDA committee, instead of trying to get delegates from the shirt factories that existed even though these factories were outside the area most of their women workers lived in the area, instead of trying to get delegates from every workplace in the area, instead of setting up a youth wing of the BCDA, the growing Republican movement controlled by the undemocratic IRA sought to undermine the BCDA and to themselves undemocratically control things. This was a very mistaken and undemocratic approach. It helped undermine the BCDA. It helped undermine the mass movement. If the opposite road had been taken, that is to deepen and extend the democratic and working class base of the BCDA, this would have made it possible to reach out to the then existing non-sectarian peace committees in Belfast which were trying to stand against the sectarian pogroms there. This could have made possible, or at least have given some possibility of a united working class movement.

The declining involvement of the mass of the Bogside and Creggan population in the struggle would eventually, over a period, allow the British Army to move in and take down the barricades. The false policies and promises of the IRA were an important factor in undermining the mass movement. They made their promises and advocated their polices to the Catholic youth. They promised the Catholic youth that an offensive military campaign could defeat the British Army and unite the country. These promises could not be and were not fulfilled. However, they attracted a section of the Catholic youth and led them down the wrong path.

After years of discrimination and repression, the Catholic population of the North had had enough of discrimination and repression. It was only right that the civil rights movement took mass action to end this. Instead of recognising this and making changes for the better, the Northern state, backed by the British state, tried to beat the movement for reform off the streets and launched a vicious attack on the Catholic areas. This created a justifiable demand for defence. This was reflected in the rise of the peace committees in Belfast. More generally it resulted in the spontaneous demand in the Catholic areas for defence. The Bogside uprising and the street battles in west Belfast were defensive movements of the Catholic population. What was taking place was a mass democratic defensive uprising of the majority of the Catholic population in these areas. I, by taking part in the Bogside uprising, took part in this defence. I was right to do so. Unfortunately the undemocratic IRA, basing itself on this genuine and understandable demand for defence launched its military offensive to try and drive out the British Army and unite the country. This military offensive was never going to succeed. I spoke in opposition to that military offensive.

I was not clear on all my ideas by any means. But I was clear on one thing. The country could not be united nor British rule ended by a military campaign based on the Catholic population. The Protestant population, with its back to the sea, if it was threatened with being forced into the Catholic dominated, Southern, poverty-ridden capitalist state with its lower living standards, would fight. And they would not be defeated. This was my thinking at the time and after the Bogside uprising and it has remained my thinking ever since. The country could not be united, the country could not be changed for the better for all working class people, British imperialism could not be defeated, Irish capitalism could not be ended, unless a united working class movement was built and this meant winning over a large section of the Protestant working class, meant uniting the working class Protestant and Catholic. This was, to use a capitalist phrase – the bottom line. This was where I stood and was to stand.

The BCDA straggled on for a period. Before it disappeared altogether it met with officers of the British Army. I was present at this meeting. A row of British officers sat behind a long table facing members of the BCDA. From the look on their upper class British Officer faces it was clear they thought we should be shot rather than discussed with. Nothing came from this meeting. I asked the officers at this meeting was it not the case that anything they agreed to could be overturned by their superiors later. They agreed this was so. My question was accurate but it did not help to take things forward. Nothing that could have been said at that meeting could have taken things forward. The future was being prepared outside that room. There was a moment of humour at the meeting. Well humour for all but the British Army officers. This was when an elderly man, a long-time member of the IRA, rose and addressed the top British Officer by saying: 'speaking as one military man to another.' The BCDA contingent went into near hysterical laughter while the British Officers looked like they would have a collective heart attack.

Around this time a meeting of people from left wing and Republican groups met in a small hall in the Bogside. There was a discussion on whether or not to try to acquire guns to defend the area. There was no agreement. One reason was because young people were already being recruited and given military training by the IRA and agents of the Southern State in Donegal and the Brandywell area of the Bogside. As part of this the IRA wanted to control any guns that might come into the area. They did not want any democratic committee to have any say. They wanted their own undemocratic military structured IRA to control any arms. Another reason nothing came of this meeting of left wing and Republican groups was that socialists like myself understood that the priority was not to acquire guns but was to develop a programme and strategy that could unite the working class, Protestant and Catholic, including on issues such as defence.

Caught by surprise by the uprising in the North, initially there was confusion and division in the Southern ruling class. One wing around

Government ministers Blaney and Haughey, motivated by political ambition and their determination to keep the uprising in the North from spreading to the South, armed and helped develop forces within the IRA. This facilitated a split in the IRA and the development of what became known as the Provisional IRA or the Provos. A condition of providing weapons and support to this group, that is the Provos, was that they would not conduct any armed struggle against or within the Southern state. The other wing of the Southern ruling class around Lynch, and this was to become the dominant wing, moved decisively to work with the British government and to leave it and its state to handle events in the North.

The Provisional IRA had increased resources, mostly initially provided by the Blaney/Haughey forces who were a minority in the Southern government. As the increasingly strengthening Protestant paramilitary forces continued to let off bombs in Catholic areas and in the Republic, and as they, along with the Northern police and the British Army attacked the Catholic areas and killed Catholics, there was an increasing demand in the Catholic areas for defence. Because of the weakness of left forces of which I was part, and because of the refusal to lead of the trade union and Labour leaders, no mass united working class movement for defence was built, so the inevitable result was the IRA with its false methods and promises and its offensive military campaign stepped into the vacuum in the Catholic areas and the Protestant paramilitary organisations such as the Ulster Volunteer Force and the Ulster Defence Association with their anti-Catholic violent sectarian methods stepped into the vacuum in the Protestant areas.

I increasingly understood that the struggle had to be spread to the South and if any progress was to be made, a united working class struggle North and South had to be developed. To this end, as well as helping to build Labour Party and Young Socialist branches in Donegal in the South, and Tyrone and Derry in the North, I took the initiative to organise action over the border at the Donegal County Council meeting in Lifford. Along with some young socialists and other activists we called for more jobs and services North and South as well as an end to the sectarian state in the South and an end to the sectarian state in the North.

I understood that the South was a sectarian state similar to the North. The Protestant population in the South were a discriminated against minority as was the Catholic minority in the North. However there was a very significant difference. The Protestant population in the South were so small relative to the overall population of the state it did not threaten the existence of the state as the larger minority of Catholics in the North threatened that state. Because of this, the discrimination against Protestants in the South was not so vicious and all pervasive as was the discrimination against the Catholic minority in the North. But nevertheless if the struggle against the sectarian state in the North was to succeed there had to be a struggle against the sectarian state in the South. There had to be a struggle for the rights of the Protestant minority, the non-Catholic minority, in the South, there had to be a struggle against the dominating role in the South of the Catholic hierarchy and the political forces and state over which it was so influential, there had to be a struggle against the sectarian poverty-ridden Catholic state in the South. It was not realistic to expect the Protestant population of the North to take action to end the Protestant sectarian state in the North and its discrimination against Catholics and say nothing about the Catholic sectarian state in the South. I saw this and tried to start such a struggle by organising action at the Donegal County Council meeting in Lifford, that is, in the South.

I organised members of various left and radical groups to picket one of these meetings. We called for an end to the sectarian state in the South as well as the sectarian state in the North and for jobs and services for all. We had arranged for the press to be present. When the councillors went to lunch we occupied the council chambers in Lifford, barricaded the doors and handed out a statement of our demands to the press. These included demands for more jobs, better wages, better social services in the South and also an end to the South being a sectarian Catholic state. We had decided to be non-violent, get arrested and then use our trial as a platform to further spread the struggle to the South.

When the councillors came back, they and the Gardaí broke down the doors and attacked us with their fists. We tried to remain peaceful. But as he was being beaten one of our protesters turned round and shouted at me: 'Fuck you Throne and your peaceful protests', and launched into a councillor with his fists. Fighting intensified between us and the Gardaí and the councillors. I got singled out for some of the worst attacks as the Catholic councillors and Gardaí were sectarian and particularly enraged at me, from a Protestant background, acting against the Catholic Southern state.

We were arrested and taken to the barracks. After being held for some time from our cell we could hear the sergeant talking to his superior officer in Letterkenny. 'What, let them go? But they took over the council chambers. They broke the law. They were violent.' There was silence as he listened to his superior. 'Okay, Okay. Whatever you say. You are the boss. I will let them go.' And that is what happened. And with our release went our chance to get into a court in Donegal and use it as a platform for spreading the movement into the South.

As usual there were always the moments of humour and levity in the struggles. At this time, four leading members of the Irish Labour Party visited the Bogside. Three of them were members of the Southern parliament. They arrived looking totally out of place. Their fancy suits set them apart from the residents of the Bogside and especially the denim clad youth who had until a few days before been fighting the police on the streets. I was on the delegation that met these Labour leaders. By accident the BCDA members present were mainly on the left wing of that organisation. We had nothing to say to each other, we were from different worlds. But both sides felt they should go through the motions.

We took pleasure in sitting them and their fancy suits scrunched together on a too small couch in the headquarters of the BCDA. You could see their indignation at the seating arrangements. They were not being treated with the 'respect' they thought they deserved. I on the other hand thought this was exactly what they deserved. They could not get out of the place quick enough. I later heard that after they left they immediately met with representatives of the Catholic hierarchy and the Catholic middle class and got the line from them. The headquarters of the BCDA at the time had received a lot of used clothing and foodstuffs as people from outside the area thought we were starving and without a shirt on our backs. Unfortunately there were some fleas in these supplies. We laughed as we hoped these Labour Party leaders in their fancy suits would have picked some up and taken them with them to the bishop's palace and back home to their fancy homes in Dublin. I would in the future meet these Labour Party leaders, these political fleas, in my struggle against social democracy in the South.

CHAPTER 16

LABOUR LEADERS ABDICATE
– REPRESSION
– SECTARIANISM
– FILL THE VACUUM

FROM **1968** to 1970 there was a movement in Ireland to change things for the better. During those years the working class in the South shared first place with Italy for the highest number of strikes per head of the population of any European country. The Irish working class was fighting to improve their lives. Along with the industrial battles in the country there were the movements for civil rights, women's rights, housing and jobs.

In 1969 the Southern Labour Party moved left and stood on the slogan: 'The Seventies will be Socialist.' It won its highest ever number of votes, partly because it had grown and had the resources to stand more candidates than ever before but also because there was a rising left wing mood in the country. 50% of Dublin's youth said they would vote Labour if they were the age to vote. In the North, Labour candidates and left wing socialist and civil rights and socialist candidate Bernadette Devlin between them won 20% of the vote. New Labour Party and Young Socialist branches were springing up North and South. In Donegal, one of the areas where I was active, twelve new Labour Party branches were formed between 1968 and 1969.

I concentrated on helping to build these Labour Party and Young Socialist branches. I did so in Donegal, Tyrone and Derry. Labour Party branches were set up in Stranorlar, Letterkenny, Lifford, Omagh, Strabane, Coleraine and other areas. I worked to link these with the already established branch in Derry. I organised a meeting in Strabane to set up a Young Socialist branch. In an effort to have a non-sectarian branch I went to my old school and asked could I put up posters for the meeting? The headmaster said if he put them up he would be fired. The sectarian tentacles were everywhere. In spite of that, two hundred mainly youth attended this first meeting and sixty joined up on the spot. I was the only person from a Protestant background in attendance. That is how effective was the sectarian divide. These Labour Party and socialist groupings were non-sectarian and working class in their outlook but unfortunately they were overwhelmingly from one side of the religious divide, from the Catholic population.

I was approached at this time by the secretary of the Northern Ireland Labour Party to be their organiser in the western counties of Northern Ireland. But they had one condition. I had to organise to undermine Bernadette Devlin. I told them to get lost. I was insulted that they would even think to make such an offer to me. They were trying to recruit me to use against Bernadette Devlin whom they saw as a political threat. But also they had by that time decided to go for the Protestant vote and for this reason also they were against Bernadette Devlin. I reported this sectarian offer to the Strabane Labour Party and the Strabane Young Socialists and the members of these organisations demanded disaffiliation from the NILP. So these sectarian geniuses, not only did they not get me to help them fight Bernadette Devlin, but they lost the potential base in the Strabane area where there was, at one point, sixty members in the Young Socialists and over thirty in the Labour Party. I had been trying to get these organisations to affiliate to the NILP. The sectarian right wing outlook of the leaders of this party would eventually reduce it to just about nothing.

The rising movement of working class struggle and for civil and other rights from 1968 to 1970 was not the only development at this time. There was also a counter movement. There was the attack by the police on the 5th October march in 1968. Then in the first days of 1969, students marching for civil rights from Belfast to Derry were brutally beaten by loyalist farmers, police and B Specials at Burntullet Bridge outside Derry. I saw one of my former schoolmates amongst the attackers. There was the pogrom against Catholic areas in Belfast. These sectarian attacks were organised by right wing loyalist politicians such as Paisley and Craig and by sections of the Northern state. Of course these Protestant politicians did not take part themselves. At the same time the small Protestant paramilitary organisation, the Ulster Volunteer Force, was stepping up its assassination of Catholics and setting off bombs both in the North and the South.

Then on 15th and 16th August 1969 even greater sectarian events took place with pogroms mainly against Catholic areas in Belfast. 1,820 homes were burnt, 1505 of them Catholic, the rest Protestant. Seven people were killed, five Catholics and two Protestants. An all-out sectarian conflict threatened. However, just like when the rise of the more left and civil rights movements took place earlier in the 1968/1969 period and were confronted by sectarian forces, these sectarian pogroms and forces were also confronted by forces moving in the opposite direction. Northern Ireland was at a fork in the road. Would it go forward to sectarian conflict or would the working class be able to unite and go forward in united struggle for its own common interests as a class?

On 15th August, the same day that the sectarian pogroms were raging in Belfast, 4,000 mainly Protestant workers at the Belfast shipyard held a meeting. They passed a resolution to 'maintain peace and set an example for the rest of the Province'. At the same time a gathering of 2,000 workers, mixed Protestant and Catholic, took place at the Michelin Factory at Mallusk. Its spokesperson said: 'If Protestant and Catholic can work together, why can they not live in peace together?' This made perfect sense to this worker and also to myself. At another factory in the Belfast area a mixed workforce of Protestant and Catholic workers physically protected their workplace against sectarian gangs and forced the owners to pay them for the time they spent doing so.

There were other occasions around this time when workers expressed their opposition to sectarianism. Three hundred and fifty shop stewards met in conference and called for working class unity. A conference of delegates of the 40,000-strong Confederation of Shipbuilding and Engineering Workers called on the Irish Congress of Trade Unions to act to 'defend its members and for defence organisations to be set up'. The Belfast Trades Council passed a resolution for unity of the working class and to 'win the workers from the sectarian demagogues whose only objective is to keep workers divided and vulnerable to attacks made on the trade unions and workers' standards of living.'

These pronouncements by the various sections of the organised workers' movement were significant. They showed the mood that existed amongst a section of the organised workers, both Protestant and Catholic. They showed the road that could have been taken, they showed that there could have been an alternative to sectarian division, an alternative of working class unity. However, passing resolutions for peace, while positive, did not meet the needs of the situation at a time when hundreds of people in sectarian gangs were roving Belfast and burning people, mainly Catholics, out of their homes because of their religion.

Resolutions and words were not enough in that situation. What was needed was actual organised physical mass action to stop the sectarian pogroms and killings. Along with some other Young Socialists with whom I was discussing and working at the time we campaigned for the trade unions to set up a trade union-based defence force. But while sections of the organised working class spoke for united action for defence, their leaders refused to act to bring this about. As a result these calls for united action against sectarianism from sections of the organised working class and also from ourselves came to nothing.

The trade union and labour leaders refused to act and build an organised trade union defence force because they could not see themselves playing an independent role from the capitalist state. They could not see that the working class could build an alternative society to capitalism. They thought that any attempt of the working class to try and do so would lead only to chaos and also to a threat to their own relatively privileged positions. This is why they let down their members and the working class, it was because of their wrong political views and ideas as well as fear of losing their privileged positions. I had a different problem.

I was still a very active member of the NILP and Young Socialists even though these organisations were shrinking rapidly. Inside these organisations there was a handful of us, half a dozen or slightly more who were in discussion with the London-based, left wing group The Militant. These discussions helped us to see that our task was to campaign for united working class action against sectarianism, against state violence and to change the North and Ireland as a whole in the direction of socialism. But there were only a handful of us. While the trade union and labour leaders let down the working class because of their false policies, we were not able to show a way forward for the working class because of our miniscule resources. And as the Republicans and Loyalists gained strength and sectarianism gained strength our ability to gain more resources weakened even further. While our little revolutionary socialist nucleus survived and continued to fight for our ideas we were not able to gain any significant new forces. We never came anywhere close to be strong enough to influence events. Our half a dozen people who by that time were coalescing on the left of the Labour Parties and Young Socialists, were just not enough. The Northern trade union leaders with their quarter of a million members had the resources to show a way forward for the working class but because of their false ideas they refused to do so. We had the right ideas to take the movement and society forward but because we were so small we were not able to do so. As a result the road of working class unity was not taken.

What was needed was for the trade union and labour leaders to actually organise the working class against sectarianism. This would have meant organising united working class mass rallies and strikes against sectarianism. At the same time setting up united working class defence squads around the non-sectarian unions, the trades councils, the union branches, the workshop and shop steward committees and also in the schools and colleges. Then using their 250,000-strong union membership organised as they were in mixed Protestant and Catholic trade union branches and trades councils to pull these forces into cohesive united action, create an alternative non-sectarian movement and physically drive the sectarian forces of the streets.

At the same time this movement could have appealed to the rank and file of the British army. Calling on its rank and file to demand to be withdrawn from the war zone, from the North, and the danger into which they had been thrust. Calling at the same time for the rank and file to have trade union rights and the right to elect its officers. And on this overall programme and strategy organised real action and appealed for support to the hundreds of thousands of union members in the South and millions of union members in England, Scotland and Wales.

Such a lead by the trade union and labour leaders could and should also have been linked to the call for unity of the working class on the economic and social issues. A guaranteed job for all at trade union pay and conditions, equal rights for women, equal pay for work of equal value, women to have control over their own body, a guaranteed affordable home for all, free health care, free education, full free care for the unwell and elderly. This movement and these demands could and should then have been linked to the need to end capitalism and for a democratic socialist society in Ireland and Britain. In this way a united movement could have been built. Tragically the union and labour leaders who controlled the workers' organisations refused to give such a lead, to take such action and so for this reason the North descended into decades of sectarian war increased sectarian division and segregation.

Refusal of the labour and trade unions to act in this way and give a lead was shown in the words of NILP leader Vivian Simpson. He stated: 'Let us be absolutely clear about this. There will be no Armageddon between capitalism and socialism in the North.' This statement showed that he knew that a united, working class, socialist option potentially existed otherwise why would he have felt he had to speak against it? This statement and the thinking that lay behind it was treason as far as the Northern working class was concerned. Given this refusal to lead of the trade union and labour leaders and with the coming apart of the old Northern Ireland state it meant that the descent into sectarian conflict was inevitable.

The refusal of the trade union and labour leaders to act was criminal. Even when sections of the working class were able to temporarily escape the stranglehold of their own leaders and briefly organise non-sectarian united working class calls and actions, these leaders carried on with their refusal to lead. This was never more obvious than with the spontaneous rise of the peace committees in Belfast in 1969. These were united committees of Protestant and Catholic workers and residents which patrolled the streets, which did actually take action.

A survey carried out by the three main Belfast papers at the time reported that there were peace committees in over twenty areas of the city. The Belfast Trades Council in a statement said: 'The people in practically all areas of the city formed their peace committees composed of Catholics and Protestants.' Even in the most sectarian areas these were set up. They developed in the Catholic Markets area and the Protestant Shankill area and according to the Scarman report of the time these committees 'worked together'. Some were quite developed. One such committee in Protestant East Belfast had its own daily publication. Loyalist sectarians ordered Catholic workers out of their homes in this area. When this happened this newsletter stated: 'Stay. We will protect you.' This was a genuine movement of united working class people from below to try and impose themselves on the situation and cut across the slide to sectarianism. It was a very admirable development. It was the only hope for the North. It showed not only the potential for working class unity but actual working class unity against sectarianism. What was needed was the full power of the 250,000-strong trade union movement to be integrated with these peace committees. But the trade union leaders continued to refuse to take action.

This movement could have been developed and could have stopped the slide to sectarianism. It could have organised and provided a way forward for the tens of thousands of working class youth and workers who were trying to figure out a way to avoid a sectarian holocaust. The quarter of a million trade unionists in Northern Ireland were in mixed Protestant and Catholic integrated unions. There were around thirteen trades councils organised in the main cities and towns. These were also mixed and integrated across religious lines. There were three quarters of a million trade unionists in the South of Ireland. There were millions of trade unionists in England, Scotland and Wales. This force could have stopped the drift to sectarianism and civil war. But this did not happen. The reason it did not happen, was that the initiatives from some sections of the working class against sectarianism and violence, such as the peace committees, were not pulled together and developed by the leadership of the trade unions and the labour movement. After initially boasting about the peace committees the trade union leaders very quickly realised the danger they represented to their positions and the capitalist system they supported. They realised they might get out of hand. They might act independently. So true to form the trade union leadership ran for cover while at the same time repressing the action of their own members. It stood by and let the peace committees die, let a vacuum develop and inevitably the sectarian forces fill this vacuum. The result of the refusal to lead of the trade union and labour leaders was that sectarian conflict engulfed the North. 1972 was to see the highest number of sectarian killings of the entire Troubles.

I was fully behind the united action of the peace committees and the call from various workers' trade union organisations for united action. I believed the peace committees and the calls for united working class action were the way to move forward. On the bigger questions such as the ultimate solution to the issue of the border, the relationship with Britain, I believed in changing the South and making it a democratic socialist society and changing the North and making it a democratic socialist society. Ireland could therefore have become a democratic socialist secular society governed by a democratic workers' body on an all-Ireland basis. And along with this I believed in changing Britain into a democratic socialist society and moving to a democratic socialist federation of Britain and Ireland.

I believed that this objective would only be possible through an all-Ireland socialist revolution which would spread to Britain, or a socialist revolution in Britain which would spread to Ireland. I worked on this basis, against nationalism, against unionism, against British imperialism and for a socialist federation of Ireland and Britain.

There were many forces who opposed the idea of working class unity, a trade union defence force, or the peace committees, saying that any effort in this direction would only make things worse. Better to leave it to the police. Or better to help arm the Catholic areas against the Protestant areas or help arm the Protestant areas against the Catholic areas, I was in none of these camps. I believed working class unity was the only solution and also believed that it was possible. Were the trade unions not united, did we not see the calls for unity from various trade union bodies, had we not had the peace committees? This was my way, my idea was to build on these elements of workers' unity that were showing themselves. Events would prove that sectarianism developed and defeated attempts at working class unity. But this did not mean that working class unity was not the way to go. The problem was the leaders of the workers' organisations prevented this from taking place.

As well as the refusal to lead of the trade union leaders, there was one other factor that accounted for the working class not being able to change the situation for the better. There was no organised opposition of any significance within the unions or the labour movement to the pro-capitalist, social democratic and sectarian leadership. If there had been sizeable squads of organised workers, a sizeable network of workers, in the workplaces and the ranks of the trade unions with an independent life from that of the trade union leaders, with a programme to end capitalism, and if these had been linked together against the employers and the rising sectarianism and instead for working class unity and a good life for all, then there would have been a chance that the blockage of the union leaders could have been overcome and the working class could have found its way to its feet and given a way forward. But with the conscious, organised, pro-capitalist, leadership at the top of the trade unions and the labour parties, and the absence of a revolutionary or even anti-capitalist independent alternative in the ranks of the unions and labour parties and the workplaces, the tendency against sectarianism and for working class unity was blocked. As a result sectarianism and reaction climbed into the saddle.

With the organised working class movement giving no lead against sectarianism and repression, the peace committees withered and died and the vacuum in the North increased dramatically. This vacuum was filled by sectarian organisations. Tens of thousands of Catholic youth joined the IRA as the sectarian pogroms developed and even more so when hundreds of Catholics were interned without trial in 1971, and when this was followed by the Bloody Sunday massacre in Derry in 1972. After these events there was no turning back. The movements towards working class unity were pushed to the one side and died. The peace committees, the calls for the trade unions to provide defence were no longer heard from any significant section of the trade union or working class movement. My tiny voice and those of the few others with whom I was working in the Labour parties and Young Socialist branches, and which called for working class unity were not heard.

The bringing in of internment in 1971 was initially aimed at the Catholic population. This was a major blow to any movement towards working class unity as it was a huge recruiting tool for the Irish Republican Army. And as this force grew so also did the Protestant paramilitary groups. Sectarianism was gaining strength by the day. Working class unity was being weakened by the day. In 1972 with the massacre of Bloody Sunday in Derry by the British Army thug regiment the paratroopers, so many Catholic people, mainly youth, surged to join the IRA that it had to close its doors.

In 1971, I was organising against internment in Strabane. I tried to get a rent and rates strike started in Strabane. I also was central in organising a one-day general strike against internment which shut down that town. I also was central in organizing a demonstration against internment in Strabane. I explained that while it was being used against Catholic workers at that time it would be used against all workers and the labour movement in the future. This was shown to be correct as when the Troubles developed, significant numbers of Protestants were also locked up. I invited Bernadette Devlin to speak at this meeting against internment and she came. She was very obviously pregnant at that time and she was not married. The Catholic Church hierarchy and the right wing Catholic nationalists used her pregnancy to attack her when the main reason they were attacking her was because they opposed her socialist views and they were frightened of the base of support she had. She climbed slowly up the steps of the town hall to speak. I was waiting on the platform for her. At first there was only a subdued applause. Then the large crowd caught itself on and erupted with a powerful welcome. It was saying you are okay Bernadette, pregnant or not. I was proud to be part of that movement that day.

Other than Bernadette I was the only person on the platform. The 'lapsed' Protestant, now revolutionary socialist and atheist from across the border in Donegal, and the pregnant Bernadette. It was not impressive. I took the mike and by way of explanation and in front of the crowd I criticised the local, conservative, Catholic, political forces in the town for refusing to help me organise the meeting.

During that rally against internment the British army shot a young man dead. This was the first killing by the British army in the town. The war had come to Strabane. The ranks of the local Provisional IRA were further filled.

As the meeting wound down a woman, the mother of a Young Socialist member, ran from her house and shouted to me that she had heard over her radio that I was to be lifted and interned. The Northern state were after me because of my activity opposing their repressive rule and at that particular time the introduction of internment. I ran out the Urney Road to get down to the river to swim over to Donegal and the South of Ireland. On the way I met my second oldest sister and her husband in their car. They craned their necks and glowered at me. Pulling off my clothes and holding them in one hand above my head I jumped into the river and began to swim towards the other bank. The water was cold. A helicopter appeared above and soldiers reached down and tried to grab me. I was a good swimmer and I was able to submerge and come up for air and submerge and come up for air and in this way stay out of their reach. The conflict had not reached such a pitch yet where they felt politically comfortable going over into Donegal to get me so they turned around and I escaped. I concluded that my sister and her husband had reported where I was.

I was not overly worried about being interned for my own sake. It was the effect on my mother and aunt that concerned me. They would have seen it as their duty to come to visit me and they would have been the only Protestants, the only non-Republican persons, visiting a relative. This would have been very hard on them. I was very worried for their sake that this might happen.

As the repression and internment and Bloody Sunday filled the ranks of the IRA that organisation stepped up its military offensive, setting off bombs and killing members of the police and part time Ulster Defence Force. At the same time the Protestant Ulster Volunteer Force stepped up its military offensive setting off bombs North and South and killing Catholics. The deaths caused by the IRA's military offensive were Protestant. The deaths caused by the Protestant paramilitary groups were Catholic. The state forces were mainly killing Catholics. They were also helping coordinate the killing activities of the Protestant paramilitary groups against Catholics and republicans. Sectarian killings and sectarianism were increasing by the day. It was these sectarian forces and the sectarian British and Northern states that were calling the shots on the streets of the North. Things were going from bad to worse.

Republicanism and Loyalism and sectarianism had deep roots, and they had resources. When the trade union and labour leaders refused to give an alternative, refused to unite and mobilise the working class, refused to coordinate the peace committees, when there was no revolutionary united Protestant and Catholic organisation with significant roots to influence events these forces filled the vacuum. These sectarian forces on both sides were armed and they were using these arms. The trade union movement confined itself to passing resolutions, setting up talking shops, mouthing platitudes and leaving the streets to the British and Northern state forces and the paramilitaries.

The working class as a class became more and more divided and irrelevant as a class and as an independent force which could influence events in society. An even greater weakening and dividing of the working class came later with the cleavage between Protestant and Catholic workers in the North which resulted from the Ulster Workers' Council strike in 1974. This was part strike and part intimidation. It was organised by the Protestant paramilitaries. These, then mass organisations, had developed amongst the Protestant working class as the sectarianism had increased and the Protestant population feared they would be pushed into a united Ireland. The Ulster Workers' Council strike was against any deal that would have given the Southern government any say in what happened in the North. It was also against Catholics taking part in any power sharing agreement in the North.

My friend and Comrade Bill Webster and I produced a flyer against this strike and we went into Protestant East Belfast and distributed it on the streets. I do not know how we got away with it. It was either an act of extreme heroism or extreme lunacy. I do not know which. But I can say that none of the other forces on the left who opposed the strike were there. For fear of their own safety they conceded the Protestant areas to the Protestant paramilitaries.

After this strike's successful action the Protestant and Catholic populations retreated even more into their respective religious bunkers.

Attempts by workers to unite against sectarianism such as the 1969 Peace Committees no longer existed. Sectarian division was consolidated. The opportunities that existed from 1968 to 1970 had receded into the past. A new period had opened North and South. It was a period of reaction.

Initially the civil rights movement had taken up the justifiable grievances such as discrimination against Catholics and working class Protestants. And attempted to do so by mass non-sectarian means. But the British state, the Northern state and the Northern and British ruling class initially sought to get away with making minor changes, and along with this dividing the movement and beating it off the streets.

The result was predictable. With the experience of decades of discrimination and under the hammer blows of internment and Bloody Sunday, and with the illusion that with their increased forces they could end British rule in the North and unite the country, the IRA stepped up its military campaign. At the same time tens of thousands of Protestants joined the Protestant organisations such as the Ulster Defence Association, the Loyalist Association of Workers, and the Ulster Volunteer Force. They were motivated by their fear of losing their marginal privileges, of being forced into a Catholic-dominated united Ireland and also by the offensive military campaign of the IRA as shown in such events as the Claudy bombing. Events hurtled down the sectarian road.

I continued to stand for the position I had from the beginning, that was, that the IRA's offensive military campaign was based on a seriously mistaken view of the situation. I continued to understand and strongly argue that the Protestant population with their back to the sea and offered only the IRA's option of a Catholic dominated, poverty-ridden capitalist state in the South being extended into the North, would fight. Any serious development that would look like it could force them into a Catholic dominated, sectarian, poverty-ridden capitalist united Ireland, they would fight and this would lead to civil war and repartition. This in turn would be accompanied by a major disruption of capitalism and would not be tolerated by British imperialism. I continued to see and strongly argue that British imperialism would put its forces into combating the rise of the IRA and eventually all the paramilitary groups. British imperialism would not let a civil war develop in Ireland. British imperialism would eventually use the term, 'an acceptable level of violence' to describe what they could attain and would accept in the North in their struggle with the IRA. This is what happened over the next thirty years. British imperialism was able to prevent an all-out civil war developing in Northern Ireland and prevent such a situation from convulsing Irish emigrant populations internationally. I could see this and I could also see that the campaigns of all the paramilitary groups would end up as catastrophes for all workers, Catholic and

Protestant alike. They would increase sectarianism and further divide and weaken the working class. And this is exactly what has happened.

Over this time I came to have a better understanding of how British imperialism saw and sees sectarianism. British colonialism and later British imperialism established the sectarian divide in Ireland. They deepened this divide in Northern Ireland after the establishment of that state. Sectarianism was and is essential to British imperialist and capitalist rule in Northern Ireland. The ruling capitalist minority and British imperialism can only continue to rule if the majority, that is the working class, are divided. Sectarian division is essential to capitalist rule. You cannot have capitalism in Northern Ireland without sectarianism. However British imperialism and capitalism as a whole, unless they are threatened with revolution, want the sectarian division, want sectarianism, to stay at a certain level, they want it to simmer, they want it kept on the low burner, they do not want it to boil over. They want it strong enough to kep the working class divided but they do not want it to boil over into open armed conflict as this could threaten their whole set up, threaten their property, threaten their profits, threaten their control. What happened as the early 1970's unfolded was that the sectarian division which British imperialism had kept simmering from the formation of that state began to boil over. British imperialism moved to get it back to simmering, get it back on the low burner. They achieved this. Sectarianism continues to be strong enough to divide the working class but not too strong as to threaten British imperialism's property, profits, and control. British imperialism at least for the time being has maintained its divide and rule sectarianism and so its control. Sectarianism for the time being simmers, does not boil over. But this is not the end of the story. While there is the veneer of power sharing of working together on the surface, the last decades of conflict has driven sectarianism and segregation along religious lines deeper into the foundations of the North. If sectarianism boils over in the future it is liable to be a different story. It will be a lot more difficult to get it back on to the low burner, back to the simmering.

At no time did I give any support to sectarianism or to the methods of struggle of the paramilitary groups, either Republican or Loyalist. At no time did I give any support to the British or Northern or Southern states. I stood for a united trade union defence force, a united and independent working class movement, socialism in Ireland and Britain and internationally. A small number of us, less than ten, were evolving around these ideas at that time. I was part of that nucleus. Some of the members of this small group were part of the London-based organisation known as The Militant, or as it was known to its members, the Revolutionary Socialist league. This is how things stood as 1971 and 1972 unfolded and as I tried to catch my breath to see where I was.

CHAPTER 17

CLIMBING A CLIFF FACE

THERE WERE MANY different forces seeking to fill the vacuum in the North at that time. I sought to have my voice heard amongst these, I tried to convince the youth and workers I could reach that the problems, repression, sectarianism, poverty, unemployment, discrimination, could not be solved on a capitalist basis whether by the capitalist forces of the British or Northern or Southern variety. My starting point was that there was no solution on a capitalist basis. There was no solution on the basis of negotiations between the various sectarian and capitalist forces. The only solution was on the basis of working class unity and socialism and internationalism.

At the same time I sought to convince the workers and youth I could reach to oppose repression, but to do so by mass action of a united working class and link this to the struggle for socialism, that is to unite the working class in a struggle to change the North, to change the South and to change Britain. This would have given the movement a way forward. The problem was this was a long-term strategy and along with this my resources were minute. At the same time, the Catholic youth were enraged by the repression and discrimination and wanted action then and there. And again who was I? I was just some individual from a Protestant background who was working with ten or so fellow thinkers.

Who was I with my long term strategy? I was irrelevant. While agreeing on the need for working class neighbourhoods to defend themselves, I opposed the offensive military campaigns of the Provisional IRA, the Official IRA and the Protestant paramilitaries. All of these I could see would only lead to sectarian conflict and a weakening of the working class.

In 1969 I met a young Strabane man called Jim McGinn and recruited him to socialism and the Strabane Young Socialists. He was an excellent young man. He had intelligence, energy, drive, fight and was full of laughter. I can still see him walking down the main street in Strabane in his best suit with a girlfriend on each arm and all of them laughing together. I lost touch with him for a few months. Then he came to see me. We sat and talked in a small café in Lifford as we were both wanted by the state in the North at that time.

Jim got straight to the point. 'I have left the Young Socialists. I have joined the Provos.' That is the Provisional IRA. I tried to talk him out of it. 'Jim, Jim their campaign will never work. The Protestants will fight and the British will back them. And not only that I know you. You will be out there in the lead. Jim you will be dead in six months.' He responded: 'Nah, I have to join up. There are too many of the lads inside. I cannot do nothing while they are in there. Anyway look at what those cops and soldiers and the loyalists are doing to us. We cannot do nothing. Talking is not enough. I cannot let my friends down. I have to join.' I tried again to convince him but he rose from where we were sitting in that small café and that was the last I saw of him.

A few months later he was carrying a bomb across Claudy Bridge and it detonated and he was blown to bits. Whether it was the British army or others who detonated that bomb was never known. He was too left wing for some in the Republican movement, a movement which with its undemocratic military structure did not tolerate opposition. The Republican movement at that time, both wings, was dominated by their military structure which was based on the undemocratic military structures of capitalist armies. That is its discipline was based on commands from unelected leaderships, commands that were enforced as in capitalist armies by force and the threat of force. Discipline in healthy revolutionary working class movements is based on consciousness, on democratic discussion and democratic decision making not on commands from above, on threats from above.

On one occasion I was walking with Jim and one of his friends in Strabane. I was arguing socialism and atheism. His friend was not saying much. Jim turned to him and said: 'Mickey, you are the kind of boy Throne does not agree with. Come on speak up. Better still show him what you have in your coat pocket. Come on. Show him.' His friend reluctantly pulled out a set of rosary beads. Jim laughed at him and said: 'See Mickey, that is what Throne thinks is bad about us. We are all only a bunch of Catholics. We do not leave any room for the Protestants or for atheist people like him in our movement.'

I attended Jim's funeral which was held from the home of a Republican in Lifford. As I stood waiting for the cortege to move off, a man who was new to the Republican movement and who was organising the funeral called me up and asked me to carry the coffin which I did. This was very unusual as the funerals of Republicans are jealously guarded as they provide opportunities to build the movement, to strengthen the emotions and traditions around Republicanism. I would later find out that there was conflict within the Republican movement, between its old right wing Catholic wing and some new forces such as Jim and others who had joined recently and were more socialist, more Che Guevara inclined. I was also to find out later that there was discussion in the Provos about me carrying the coffin and that violent action should be taken against me. But this came to nothing. There was something unusual about Jim's death and his funeral and me being asked to carry his coffin. These were unusual times. New organizations were developing, old organizations were going through change. Alternative ideas in some of these organizations were not welcomed, were discouraged and not always democratically.

Jim's trajectory was shared by many other Catholic youth. Under the impact of internment and the sectarian repression of the Northern and British states, the Young Socialists collapsed. When internment was brought in, the Strabane Young Socialists went from their approximately sixty members to three overnight. I was one of the three. While I maintained my socialist position and never had anything to do with Republicanism, the majority of what had been the membership of the Young Socialists either dropped out of political activity or joined one wing or other of the Republican movement.

The Young Socialists were also attacked by the Catholic hierarchy. One young female member who was very active in the Strabane branch was particularly targeted. She was a very bright and vivacious and lively young woman. She not only disagreed with the Catholic hierarchy's politics but also their anti-women and anti-sex hypocrisy. On one occasion a local priest went to her school, took her from her seat, brought her to the front of the class, and in front of her fellow students ordered her to stop being involved with the Young Socialists and to have nothing more to do with me. This type of bullying was par for the course for the Catholic hierarchy. Any radical movement that looked like developing they moved to squash it. As a result movements for change, having nowhere to go in the trade union and labour movement went instead to the Catholic sectarian republican movement. The Catholic hierarchy had blood on its hands. In this case this young woman refused to bend to the bullying of the Catholic hierarchy and went on for the rest of her life to represent workers' interests.

The Republican movement had split in 1969 into two wings, the Provisionals (Provos) and the Officials. The Republican movement was always splitting because their ideas did not correspond to reality, and so it could not achieve the aims it set for itself. It was a like a truck hitting a wall. It would inevitably shatter and split again and again as its wrong policies came up against reality. Stuck in its backward tradition, it could never see that what caused its continual splits and crises were its wrong ideas. Ideas and policies that did not correspond to reality meant that different views and conflicts were inevitable. Their wrong ideas meant that again and again they broke their neck against reality. But in spite of this, circumstances in the wider society in the late 1960s, early 1970s, allowed both wings of the IRA to grow and develop for a time. With the anger against repression and with both wings claiming the tradition of the IRA and offering the armed struggle, both wings were able to build a mass base in the Catholic areas.

A section of the Southern capitalist class for a time gave some qualified support to the Provisional IRA and its political wing Sinn Féin. And when it came to a choice between the Provisionals and the Official IRA and its political wing Sinn Féin – The Workers' Party, with the latter's more left ideas, with its Stalinist ideas, the Catholic Church hierarchy were on the side of the Provos. Initially there was little difference between the two IRA wings. Both carried out offensive military campaigns for a time. Both saw their ranks filled by the thousands as internment and Bloody Sunday took place. Both wings took advantage of these masses of youth who wanted action. As they did they once again dragged out the discredited ideas and methods of republicanism and nationalism and individual terrorism. These had been shown time and time again to lead to sectarianism and defeat. They had led to the division of the country in 1921, to a civil war amongst Republicans themselves at the same time. These methods facilitated the creation of the sectarian state in the South which in turn helped Loyalism justify the sectarian state in the North. I could see that these methods were and would always be a failure. Both wings of the IRA would go on to play negative roles. The thousands of Catholic youth who were to join them were to be disillusioned by the failure of their false promises, their promises that they could break the will of the British state to stay in the North, that this in turn would force the Protestant population to negotiate and from this they could get a united Ireland. This was a pipe dream. What I and the rest of our small nucleus said was correct, that if it came to any threat that the British would pull out and the Protestant population would be faced with being forced into a Catholic-dominated, poverty ridden, capitalist all-Ireland, then the Protestant population would fight.

The peace agreement signed thirty years later by the Provisional IRA confirmed this position. It was a defeat for that organisation and showed that the promises the IRA, both wings, had made to the Catholic youth had been false. That is the promises that their methods could defeat British imperialism and unite the country. Neither of these objectives were achieved. In pursuing their military campaigns, which led to their defeat, the leadership of the Provisional IRA and also the Official IRA wasted a generation of the Catholic youth. And where did their strategy leave the Provisional IRA itself? It ended up in the embrace of the party of the right wing sectarian bigot Paisley. They not only gave up their sectarian offensive military campaign which they should never have started in the first place, but in doing so they moved not to the left and working class unity but to the right and to the embrace of Paisley and right wing capitalism and imperialism.

The leadership of Sinn Féin, the political wing of the Provisional IRA, try to claim that their offensive military campaign was worthwhile. They point to the increased numbers of Catholics in civil service and public sector jobs in the Northern state. They point to changes such as more housing for Catholics, reforms in the voting system, changes in policing, consultation between the governments in the North and the South. But the door to these reforms was opened overwhelmingly by the mass civil rights movement and the Bogside and West Belfast uprisings of 1969, not the Provos offensive military campaign. It was the mass marches of the civil rights movement, the victory of the Bogside uprising over the police, the mass uprising in West Belfast which forced British imperialism to intervene directly and force reforms, it was these movements which cracked the repressive sectarian structure of the Northern state.

The Provos point to the peace agreement as a great victory for them. So one of them gets to sit as deputy minister in the North and implement the capitalist policies dictated from London. There will be consultation between Catholic and Protestant political parties in the North on policing and other issues. But it will still be capitalist state forces, anti-working class state forces that will wield the fist. There will be consultation with the Southern government on secondary issues but on the issue of any change in the position of the border, any change to a united Ireland, the Protestant population still have a veto.

On one occasion I met a supporter of Sinn Féin at a social function. She was one of the middle class types in the Catholic population who had benefited from the concessions made to the Catholic middle class in the peace agreement. She explained to me in a whisper that she and her family would not have got anything if it was not for the Provos' military campaign. Of course neither she nor any member of her family ever fired a shot. She made sure her children were safely abroad getting a good education and good jobs while the Provo working class rank and file were dying on the streets in the North or in Long Kesh prison camp.

And any gains that were made, have to be weighed against the following. After more than thirty years of the Provos' military offensive, the North is more segregated today than it was fifty years ago. 90% of social housing is now segregated and 93% of children are in segregated schools. From 1984 peace walls have gone up from twenty-two to either forty-eight or eighty-eight depending on what way they are counted. The working class as a whole is more divided than ever before. A generation of Catholic youth and workers have been sacrificed to a failed strategy and one which I and the small nucleus of fellow socialists with whom I was working understood would fail from the beginning.

The Provisional Republican leaders and their supporters made grandiose claims for what their military campaign could achieve in its early days. But the peace agreement is an acceptance that it failed. They implicitly accepted this when they called it off. A difference must be made between the mass movements for civil rights marching behind songs such as We Shall Overcome, and the Republican campaigns singing Nationalist songs. A difference must be made between mass defensive movements to defend neighbourhoods such as the Bogside uprising against the attack by the police and sectarian forces and the offensive military campaign of the Provos and for a while the Officials. The offensive military campaigns of the Provos and for a while the Officials were disasters from the word go, but what is even worse is that the Provos continue to refuse to admit that their offensive military campaign should never have been carried out, that it was a mistake in the first place. This refusal to face up to reality, this prancing about in the company of US and British and Unionist and Southern Irish capitalist politicians, this posing as big shots who knew everything about everything all the time, leaves the door open to these sectarian methods of republicanism and individual terrorism to rise again.

Brendan Hughes, the now deceased leading military activist of the IRA in Belfast, was one of the few of the Republican leaders prepared to be honest. Before he died he said 'the IRA's military campaign as everything has turned out, was worth not one death.' But the present leadership of Sinn Féin, such as Adams and those around him, and especially the opportunist gombeen men and women who have jumped on the Sinn Féin bandwagon hoping for financial and political benefits, have not been prepared to admit this. Instead they give a wink and a nod to the IRA's sectarian offensive military campaign and use the publicity and resources it brought them to move to the right and into capitalist politics, Stormont, the White House, Dáil Éireann and the board rooms of Irish and US capitalism.

The danger of refusing to admit that the Provos' campaign was a failure is that in the future when economic times become worse, the false ideas and methods of Republicanism and militarism can get a mass base once again and a new and even worse sectarian conflict can erupt in the North. And this time, given that the North is more divided along sectarian lines than ever before and given the deepening of sectarianism over the thirty-year war it can result in all out civil war, repartition and hundreds of thousands being driven from their homes. Rather than a united Ireland, a newly divided Ireland after a civil war, after 'ethnic cleansing', an Ireland with an even smaller rump of a Northern statelet, could be the result.

A difference must be made between the offensive military campaigns of the Provos and also for a while the Official Republican movement and the right of working class neighbourhoods to defend themselves. As a member of the young socialists I helped stop Catholic youth from attacking the Protestant Fountain area in Derry on the night of August 11th 1969. In the days following I helped defend the Catholic Bogside area from attacks by the police and Protestant sectarian gangs. Working class people have the right to defend themselves. And there was a powerful demand in the Catholic areas for defence as the Troubles exploded. But the way to organise defence was, as I and the others with whom I was involved argued, through a united working class movement, through a trade union based defence force. Through following the example of the non sectarian peace committees of 1969. Tragically the Provos based themselves on the mood for defence in the Catholic areas and from this launched their offensive military campaign. This was a catastrophe. And while the military conflict has for now mostly ended, seeds have been sown which can lead to even an greater sectarian military conflict in the future.

For a time the other wing of the IRA, the Official IRA also had a substantial base. At one time in the early 1970s it had fifteen clubs in Belfast alone, thousands of members and a military wing. The Official republican movement and the Official IRA had been taken over by a Stalinist clique which believed in the stages theory, first a democratic Northern Ireland, then a united capitalist Ireland and then the final stage a socialist united Ireland. When I first heard this put forward by one of their leaders at a meeting in a house in the Brandywell, Derry, I could not believe anybody would take it seriously. That the Protestant population would sit around passively waiting for a democratic North, then sit around again passively waiting for a democratic united capitalist Ireland, and then sit around again passively waiting for the final stage, a socialist united Ireland? It was ludicrous. But it was believed and fought for viciously by the arrogant cabal of Stalinist intellectuals who took over the leadership of the Official Republican movement. This cabal also for a time had influence in the capitalist media in the South of Ireland.

The Official IRA at first did not confine its activity to expounding this, what was known as the Stalinist stages theory, they also for a time had their own offensive military campaign. Inevitably it became more and more sectarian. I was approached, presumably because I was from a Protestant background, by a leading figure in the Official IRA at that time and asked for my opinion as to how I thought the Protestant working class would see it if they killed a leading Protestant politician and businessman whom my uncle had known. Would Protestant workers see this as a sectarian act or as an action against an employer, a boss, a businessman, that is as an act against a member of an opposing class or as a sectarian act? I told this person that in the climate of the time it would be seen as a sectarian killing and would deepen the sectarian divide and they should not do it. The Official IRA went ahead and killed this businessman and inevitably Protestant workers saw it as a sectarian act and the sectarian divide was deepened.

In 1972 the Official IRA called off their military campaign as they could no longer ignore the reality that it was seen as sectarian by the Protestant working class. They fell back on their Stalinist stages theory that the struggle in the North was in its democratic phase. This in reality was a similar position to that of Simpson of the Northern Ireland Labour Party where he said there would be no Armageddon between socialism and capitalism in the North. Many of the most energetic and committed youth who joined the Officials when they had their explosive growth in the 1969/1971 years were looking to take on capitalism, were looking to fight for socialism, but the leadership of the Officials, just like Simpson, in spite of using a different excuse, refused to offer the youth, refused to offer their membership a socialist alternative. The result was disillusionment and a spiralling down into splits and irrelevance with the Officials making their own contribution to the setting up of other republican splinter groups and the wasting of a generation of the Catholic youth. The Stalinist ideas of the leadership of the Officials were responsible for this.

Stalinism, through its taking over and domination of the Official IRA, shared responsibility for the catastrophe that would develop out of the Northern struggles, both the military and political catastrophes. While the Provisional IRA leaders ended up in the arms of Paisley and British imperialism, some of the most prominent leaders of the Official movement, the Stalinist wing, ended up in the leadership of the Southern Irish Labour Party and in Coalition with Fine Gael, or in the bureaucratic leadership of the trade unions, and from both these positions, they cooperated with the carrying out of major attacks on workers' living standards on behalf of world capitalism, the IMF, the EU etc. They were still at the capitalist stage you see. So therefore their position was the movement had to accept the dictates of capitalism. Stalinism, like nationalism and republicanism, played a disastrous role in the movement to change Ireland for the better. The Stalinist clique of intellectuals which took over the Official republican movement thought they knew everything. This was far from the case. Their destructive role should not be forgotten.

While the vacuum was being filled in the Catholic population by republicanism, it was being filled in the Protestant population by the Protestant paramilitaries and organisations such as the Ulster Defence Association, the Ulster Volunteer Force, the Loyalist Association of Workers, all of which for a time had a mass base. All of which were right wing and sectarian in their policies. It was these organisations which came together in 1974 and organised what was called the Ulster Workers' Council Strike. This came about when the Protestant organisations were at their height. After that these organisations lost their mass base. This did not mean there were no longer Protestant paramilitary forces.

There were the various forces such as the viciously sectarian Ulster Volunteer Force, the Red Hand Commandos, the Shankill Butchers. These smaller organizations were much less under the influence of the Protestant working class population as a whole and as a result were much more viciously sectarian and murderous. Their policy could be summed up as kill the Catholics. The Protestant Ulster Volunteer Force had been setting off bombs and killing Catholics even before the civil rights movement had begun. As the civil rights movement took on mass proportions this organisation and other Protestant paramilitary organisations carried out the most horrific killings and torture of Catholics and even on occasion some Protestants who would not toe their sectarian line. A section of the Protestant youth and workers were drawn into these organisations and had their lives destroyed.

Right wing Protestant death squads were recruited from these Protestant paramilitary organisations by the British Military and the Northern police and these targeted and murdered Catholics. They were also used by the British state in such events as the Dublin and Monaghan bombings. These bombings killed dozens of civilians in the South of Ireland. The purpose was to warn the Southern population to stay out of the North. Many of these workers and youth who went through these Protestant organisations and manipulations by the British and Northern states degenerated into drug dealing and other criminal activities. A whole section of the Protestant youth was wasted.

As well as the false policies of the trade union leadership and of republicanism both wings and of the Protestant organisations, there was another reason why the movement in the North took the sectarian road. This was the role and policies of the leadership of the original civil rights movement. This leadership was a mixture of right wing Catholic business people, under the influence of the Catholic hierarchy, the right wing republican movement and the Stalinists in the Official republican movement with their stages theory. These all agreed that the civil rights movement should call for equality but nothing more. It should not ask for better wages and jobs and houses and conditions for all. The Catholic business people did not want wages and jobs and housing and conditions on the agenda. Their own workers might take up these issues and this might harm their profits. When the civil rights movement was not calling for more jobs, more and better housing, better wages, better opportunities for all, it did not have anything to offer Protestant workers. It was inevitably seen by Protestant workers as wanting to take away their marginal privileges and give them to Catholics. This strengthened the elite's strategy of divide and rule, strengthened sectarianism and further confirmed Protestants in their siege mentality.

Some of us challenged this approach. I helped organise a large public meeting in Strabane in 1969. I was able to arrange for Bernadette Devlin, Eamon McCann and myself to be the last speakers at this meeting. We called for the civil rights movement to organise not only for an end to discrimination and for one person one vote, but for jobs for all, homes for all, better wages and conditions for all, and in this way have a chance to unite the working class. We also called for socialism as the only way to achieve these objectives. At that stage in the movement we did not give anything like sufficient emphasis to fighting for gender equality, to fighting against the special oppression of women. Working class women, Protestant and Catholic, were discriminated against both as workers and as women. If we had given more prominence to the fight against the special oppression of women this would have helped, but given the overall situation would have been unlikely to have been able to unite the working class and cut across sectarianism. But this was no excuse for this issue not being put at the front of the movement. This was a bad mistake.

At this meeting in Strabane and in general in the civil rights movement people like myself were condemned for our effort to expand the demands of this movement to ones which would have attracted workers of all religions, of no religion, and of all genders and sexual orientations. We did not have the resources to win the civil rights movement to our position. So it carried on to become insignificant and the North proceeded further down the road of the military campaigns of the paramilitary organisations and the repression of the British army, the Northern state and the Southern state and into decades of sectarian conflict. It was ironic. I had to stand against the stream in my fight against the dominant ideas of my Protestant family and background. I also had to stand against the stream in fighting the anti-socialist ideas in the civil rights movement. Standing against the stream in my Protestant background toughened me to stand against the stream in the civil rights and labour movement.

The policy of plunder and repression and divide and rule of British colonialism and British imperialism over centuries was to blame for the sectarian conflict in Northern Ireland. These forces had 'planted Ulster', they had played the 'Orange Card' for centuries and they were playing it again. They had nourished and cultivated sectarianism and divide and rule. They had created the sectarian Northern state. The policies of Republicanism and Loyalism and Nationalism and the civil rights leadership played into the hands of British imperialism and their divide and rule strategy of sectarianism and repression. But the sectarianism had been consciously and deliberately created and fostered by British imperialism. This was the reality of things. This was who was to blame when it came down to it.

But who was to blame for causing the sectarian catastrophe was only one side of the question. There was also who was to blame for the catastrophe not being averted, who was to blame for there not being a united working class movement to solve the problems. While British imperialism and its policies over the centuries were the cause of the problems in Northern and Irish society, the reason the problems were not solved lay elsewhere. They were not solved because of the refusal of the labour and trade union leaders to lead. That is, they were not be solved because of the refusal of the leadership of the working class, the only force that could solve the problems of society, to lead that class to change society.

This refusal of the leadership of the working class to lead was the decisive reason the rising movement of struggle that was beginning to take shape in Ireland, North and South, from 1968 to 1970, could not find a way forward. These leaders, their refusal to lead, was to blame for there being no solution to the problems, was to blame for the North sliding into sectarian conflict.

The reason the leaders of the workers' organisations, the trade unions and the Labour Parties, did not lead was because they did not believe the working class could build a new society. Never for a second did they consider that they themselves could lead the working class to build an alternative to capitalism. So instead of taking the movement forward from the starting point of the united peace committees and the workers' meetings, from the organised workers united in the unions North and South and in Britain, they insisted that responsibility for events in the North remain with the British army and the police in the North; with the Southern Army and Gardaí in the South; and with the capitalist classes which controlled these forces. Because increasing numbers of workers and youth were losing confidence in these state forces, the result of the trade union and labour leaders' refusal to lead left a huge vacuum. And into this vacuum, stepped sectarianism and the sectarian organisations.

It may be thought that in my story I put too much emphasis on the role of the trade union and labour leaders. But look at it this way. Every city and every sizeable town in Ireland North and South has a trade's council. This is a central body which brings together delegates from all trade unions in its area. These bodies are linked together through the country. Then there are all the particular unions with their memberships. The membership of the unions and the trades' councils in the North was mixed Catholic and Protestant. These bodies were also linked together in the Irish Congress of Trade Unions. In the late 1960s there were around 1 million members in the trade unions in Ireland. Potentially the most powerful force in the country. It could stop and start production and the entire workings of society. But this is what precisely frightened the trade union and labour leaders. They did not want to stop and start production and society. They wanted nothing to do with such activity. They wanted to leave everything in the hands of the various capitalist classes but with capitalism offering a dead end to the majority of the Irish population North and South then there was again, we are back to it again, the vacuum. The trade union and Labour leaders can be compared to the attack dog that did not attack, the watch dog that did not watch. So other forces filled the vacuum. Nationalism, Unionism, Republicanism, Loyalism, Sectarianism.

In this situation with the working class in the North thrown back and increasingly divided by the refusal to act of the trade union and labour leaders, my difference with these leaderships became more sharp and more clear. None of these forces believed that the working class could take power and build an alternative to capitalism, build a new society. They believed that any attempt to do so would only lead to chaos and to a threat to their own positions. Therefore at every turn about, the labour and trade union leadership sought to prevent the working class from taking independent action against capitalism and the status quo. Their role was one of counter-revolution.

I, on the other hand, believed that with the proper leadership and organisation the working class could take power and build a new society. Not only that, but I believed if the working class did not do so, there would be very serious consequences, and not only in Ireland but internationally. I fought at every turn to build an independent movement of the working class to end capitalism. As opposed to the position and role of the trade union and labour leaders, which was one of counter revolution, my position and role was one of revolution. This was the chasm that existed between us. Concretely in the North and Ireland as a whole, the trade union and Labour leaders looked to the capitalist class and capitalism to deal with the crisis while I looked to the working class nationally and internationally, to establishing international socialism, to deal with the crisis.

In pursuit of my goal I believed that a fighting, organised, working class movement and Party had to be built, one that was prepared to confront capitalism and the capitalist state. And confront it not only through propaganda and demonstrations and mass general strikes, but if necessary with arms in hand. For the trade union and Labour leaders this was extreme madness. They were totally committed to capitalism and the capitalist state. They could see no alternative. So at every turn they sabotaged any independent movement of the working class and any movement to end capitalism and establish socialism.

While the union and labour leaders refused to organise and lead its membership to try and take control of the situation, the Republican and Loyalist organisations did not. They consciously selected, organised and trained activists for their sectarian military and political campaigns. The British and Northern Irish states, while having their own existing state apparatus, also selected and organised forces to fight for their ends. The British and Northern states selected and recruited and organised death squads out of the sectarian Protestant organisations. The most sectarian of these were taken to a British military camp in Wales for training and then returned to the North to kill.

However, it would be inaccurate to say that the union and Labour leaders did not select and organise forces at all. The problem was they selected and trained forces not to mobilise but to demobilise the working class. They moved against any worker who wanted to take offensive united working class action against sectarianism and capitalism. At the same time they selected and promoted those whom it could control and keep in line with its policies of doing nothing and leaving it up to the capitalist 'powers that be'. They selected and trained a full-time apparatus to fit into the world of management and the state, fit into negotiating behind closed doors, fit into playing golf with management and staying as far away as possible from any effort to organise the working class to act independently. This was what they did when they should have been selecting and organising activists and workers and youth in every workplace, union branch, working class community, school and college into a combative force to fight for working class unity, socialism and internationalism.

The overwhelming majority of the leadership of the mass workers' organisations in Ireland were right wing, sectarian, social democrats of either the Catholic or Protestant variety. As social democrats they believed there was no alternative to capitalism. They took their ideas from the capitalist ideologues, the capitalist class itself and from its political and religious mouthpieces and organisations. The Catholic hierarchy dominated the Catholic social democrats who sat in the leading bodies of the trade unions and the Labour Parties. The Protestant churches and Orange Orders with their links with the British Crown and British imperialism dominated the Protestant wing of the union and labour bureaucracy which sat in the leadership of the unions and Labour party in the North.

But whether Catholic or Protestant, the union bureaucracies all had one thing in common, they believed there was no alternative to capitalism, they believed the working class could not build an alternative society. The result of these ideas and leaderships dominating the workers organisations was that the working class was prevented from uniting in a mass movement which could have taken the situation forward and changed things for the better. As a result the opportunity that existed in the period from 1968 to 1970 was lost. This refusal of the Labour and trade union leaders to lead meant that the catastrophe of violence and sectarianism which developed in the North in the decades that lay ahead would not be avoided. The leaders of the trade unions and the Labour Parties were to blame for not showing a way forward. They looked for a solution on the basis of capitalism when there was no solution on the basis of capitalism.

There was no solution on the basis of capitalism not only because of the contradictions of capitalism in Ireland but also because on a world scale, capitalism was in crisis. The ruling capitalist class worldwide could only hold on to power by increasing divide and rule and repression. This was doubly so in Ireland where capitalism was weak. Capitalism in Ireland meant a poverty-ridden, sectarian Catholic state in the South and a poverty-ridden, sectarian Protestant state in the North. The degrees of poverty and sectarianism might vary but fundamentally capitalism could not eradicate these evils. Sectarianism, poverty, repression, chaos political and economic, were endemic to capitalist Ireland.

Opportunities do not last forever. The opportunity for the working class to unite and build on the possibilities of 1968 to 1970 receded into the past. It was replaced by its opposite, the tendency towards division and retreat. The belief that capitalism was the only system was the dominant ideology North and South. Capitalism owned and controlled the means of production, distribution and exchange, the mass media, the education and health systems, capitalism was the dominant ideology of the churches, this gave the capitalist classes North and South huge influence over ideas and consciousness. Capitalism also controlled the State and legal systems. And it used all these instruments to conduct the most determined struggle for the consciousness of the working class and to hold onto its power. To end this would have demanded an organised and centralised and conscious democratic effort by a mass united working class revolutionary movement. This did not exist. So the working class was unable to see itself as a class, see itself as a class for itself, act as a class for itself, and take on its enemy, the capitalist system and capitalist class and confront the sectarian conflict which was developing.

Even at this early stage in my political development I could see that the only power that could take on and defeat the capitalist and sectarian forces was a united working class, organised and consciously fighting to take power into its own hands. This was my starting and finishing point. I stood for a united working class consciously fighting against capitalism, consciously organising to take the power from the capitalist class and consciously fighting for a democratic, socialist society. There could be no solution to any of the major problems facing Irish society on the basis of capitalism, or on the basis of nationalism or republicanism or Loyalism.

I never supported any of the sectarian options or any of the sectarian organisations or campaigns or actions. I always opposed all repression by all the capitalist states no matter at whom it was aimed. I maintained my position that there was no solution for the problems in Ireland except on the basis of independent, united, working class action, an end to capitalism, the socialist revolution and the spreading of the socialist revolution internationally. I have maintained my position of organising for working class unity and socialism and internationalism. I believe that events have shown that the positions I have held have been correct. To those who would claim that the various military campaigns were the way to go I would pose this question. Is the working class in Northern Ireland today stronger and more united than it was in the 1960's? There is no doubt that it is weaker, that it is more divided, nationalism and loyalism have greater roots, British imperialism remains in charge. This is the way to judge the events, the policies and roles of the various organizations which had influence over the past decades.

PART 3

WHAT THEY NEVER TELL US

CHAPTER 18

CAPITALISM – WHAT IT IS AND HOW IT WORKS

A s I WAS PARTICIPATING in the struggles around the Bogside uprising I realised that on many occasions and on many issues my knowledge was lacking. I concluded that I needed help. The civil rights movement and the uprising in Derry had confirmed me in my belief that working class people would fight to change their lives for the better and that my place in the world was to participate in these fights on the side of the working class. And as all the best people and the best ideas I met in these movements were against capitalism and for socialism and for working class unity, I came to oppose capitalism and to see myself as a socialist and for working class unity and socialist revolution. But while this was all well and good I did not have a rounded out understanding of how capitalism worked, or what a socialist world would look like or how it could be brought about. When I had been trying to understand things earlier in my life I had gone abroad. So I decided it was time for me to take another trip. In the spring of 1970 I left for London to discuss with socialist groups. In doing so I entered a world of ideas, debates and Marxist literature.

This time in London was for me one of the most exciting and important periods in my life. It was the time when I made progress in clarifying my ideas. It is not that difficult to describe my evolution in my earlier years in a way that is familiar to all, it is not that difficult to describe dramatic events like the Bogside uprising in an interesting way. However describing the evolution of my thinking on the more complicated ideas I was then tackling is more difficult, and describing my struggle for and understanding of theory is more challenging still. However I appeal to my readers to stay with me. The new understanding that I accessed at this time was way more than worthwhile for me. And if I can describe it in any kind of an accurate and living way it will also be more than worthwhile for all. Without the new understandings that I gained over this period I would not have survived as a revolutionary. My fighting spirit would have been broken by the ups and downs, the victories and the defeats of the years ahead.

What happened in my time in London with my discussions and reading and study can be summed up in this way. I was able to make conscious the instincts and the semi-conscious understandings that had accumulated in my head from my life's experiences so far. I was able to become a conscious revolutionary. This was a major qualitative breakthrough. A whole new world opened up to me. My ability to continue as a revolutionary was made possible. Please, readers, fight your way through this more dense and more difficult section of my story so you can share what I shared and so that you can also live your life as a fighter against capitalism. Please also make allowance for the fact that I might not be able to explain things as clearly as I would wish.

Class hatred, Marx said, was the basis of wisdom. I could understand this. I had class hatred, I hated the capitalist class and its allies. I had a deep-rooted hatred of capitalism. This motivated me. It drove me to seek wisdom. I nurtured my hatred of capitalism. However if I was going to keep fighting throughout my life I would need more than class hatred. If I was going to pick myself up and take up the fight again after I and the workers' movement suffered inevitable defeats and setbacks, I would need more than class hatred. I would need to understand how capitalism worked and why it could never solve the problems of society and how and why if it continued to exist it would destroy life on earth as we knew it. I would also need to understand that there was an alternative, that is, international socialism, what international socialism would look like and also that there was a force, the international working class, that could bring this about.

I would also need to understand how the working class could do this, could take power in society and build a new world. I needed this knowledge if I was to dedicate my life to the struggle to end capitalism, if I was to commit my life to this goal, and if I was to convince others to do likewise. These were the issues I needed to understand. I struggled to do so in my time in London. And I made progress on that front.

I was first attracted to Marx for a very basic reason. Marx was hated by all the forces that I opposed. This was good enough for me to start with. But along with this I had read that he had predicted that capitalism would evolve into greater and greater concentrations of wealth in the hands of fewer and fewer corporations. I could see this taking place before my eyes.

If he was right on this, what else was he right on? Arriving in London I visited his grave at Highgate Cemetery and was astounded and also inspired by the continual stream of visitors from all lands and of all races who came to pay their respects. Why would people from all corners of the world keep coming to the grave of a long dead man in a broken down London graveyard, if he did not have something important to say.

I had been in London before. But this time I arrived with different eyes from when I had visited previously with the Boy Scouts' troop. On this occasion, when I watched the boats on the Thames I thought of how in past centuries they had sailed and slaughtered and plundered and returned with vast amounts of the wealth of the planet, which were then poured into the coffers of the British ruling class. I imagined the British ruling class looking into the holds of their returning ships and seeing the loot they had forcibly stolen from foreign lands and thinking how they could live in luxury on it and build their power with it. I looked at British imperialism's palaces and museums and centres of art. I thought how these were built with the plunder it had violently seized abroad, combined with the plunder it had violently seized at home from its own peasantry, feudal and working classes. While being repulsed by how this wealth was acquired I took advantage of it being gathered in the one spot and visited some of these palaces and museums and centres of art.

I also came to understand that London had many sides to it. It was not only British imperialism's centre, from where the looting of its vast wealth was organised and much of it stored, and from where it had dominated the world for a century, it was also from where the London working class played a leading role in the building of the First International, the first mass revolutionary international organisation of the working class, The International Working Men's Association. I was not only ready to learn what I needed to learn, I was also in the right place to do so.

But while my priority in London was to learn, I first had to get a job and somewhere to live. I went to work with London Transport driving one of their big red double decker buses. I think it was the number seventy-two. However my head was so full of the search for revolutionary ideas it had no room for negotiating the busy streets of London in such a vehicle. I quit and went to work with the park district. This was less stressful, cutting grass, and digging flower beds, more like my work on my uncle's farm. I was earning and I had time to think. My friend Cathy Harkin from the Derry Labour Party arranged for me to have a room in the apartment of the socialist member of parliament Bernadette Devlin. This not only left me with a place to stay but also put me at the centre of left wing political life. I attended meetings of various left groups and individuals.

One of the largest of the left groups at that time was the Socialist

Workers' Party (SWP). One of its leaders, Paul Foot, came for a discussion with Bernadette Devlin. He was trying to recruit her to his organisation. I sat in on that discussion. Bernadette asked him why he wanted to recruit her. I was astounded at his reply. 'Because if we recruited you we could raise a lot of money.' Incredible. Make money out of her?

I would later visit Bernadette in prison in Northern Ireland. I was accompanied by a leading member of that same organisation in the North. I suggested to Bernadette that I would work to build an organisation for her in the towns and villages of her constituency. I could make enough to live on from my various activities while I did this, if she could give me enough for my travel expenses. She said yes and instructed the member of the SWP who was present to give me the money. Outside the prison I asked this person how we would coordinate this. He said he was giving me no money because if an organisation was built it would control her. This organisation was afraid of the working class, it put what it saw as its own interests above that of the working class. I was to come to understand that this was typical of left sectarianism. I wrote off this organisation.

I had previously had discussions with one of the other more sizeable left groups, the Socialist Labour League (SLL). It was also centred in London. I had met it before in Derry and I had attended one of its meetings in Dublin which was attacked by another left wing group. More left sectarianism. I was prominent in the fighting to defend the meeting. As soon as the fighting was over and the attackers were thrown out of the hall, the leader of this group, Gerry Healey, came over to me. This was the first time we had ever met. Obviously impressed by my fighting ability he said to me: 'I want you to join us and take charge of security.' I could not believe what he was saying. Join? Take charge of security? It was like he had an army. And asking me to join and do this, somebody he did not even know, I could have been anybody, a police agent, anybody. It was ridiculous. I took his invite as a condemnation of his organisation. Like I had done with the SWP I wrote off this organisation.

Fortunately the SWP and the SLL were not the only left groups. If this had been the case I would have been in trouble. There was also The Militant Tendency or The Militant. It was also known to its members as the Revolutionary Socialist League. I had met and discussed with some members of this group when they had visited Derry previously. It was the smallest of the main left groups but it impressed me the most. I met on numerous occasions with its most influential and founding member, Ted Grant. Ted had kept the basic ideas of revolutionary socialism alive in Britain in the post-war decades. He had fought for the ideas of Marxism and always did so with an orientation to the working class. He did not look over his shoulder at the students or left petit bourgeois and academics, he looked over his shoulder and judged his ideas on the basis of how they interacted with the working class. By his struggle he provided a lifeline for me and for many others. He helped me understand the world and how to conduct a struggle in that world. He helped me to find my place in that world. In spite of the differences we would later have it would be hard for me to overstate the contribution he made to my life. I met and discussed with him many times when I was in London.

I also met and discussed with his assistant Peter Taaffe, another capable and knowledgeable revolutionary. I had previously met and discussed with him when he had visited Derry and I was impressed with his knowledge and analysis of the Irish situation. Just as I did from Ted, I learnt a lot from him. In spite of the unprincipled and treacherous and dishonest role he would later play in trying to drive me out of revolutionary work, I owe him also for a better understanding of the world and my place within it.

Unlike the other left groups, The Militant was not carried away by the events in the North of Ireland. Unlike the other left groups, while opposing the role of Loyalism and the intervention of the British Army, The Militant openly opposed nationalism and with it the IRA campaign, standing instead, as I did, for working class unity and socialism. This attracted me towards them. They helped me anchor myself against the rising tide of sectarianism and militarism that was taking place in the North.

I was also drawn to The Militant because they helped me with another problem I was grappling with at that time. I was a member of the Northern Ireland Labour Party (NILP). There were still good workers in that party and it had the affiliation of a number of trade unions. However it believed that capitalism could not be ended, just reformed. I disagreed. I believed that capitalism had to be and could be ended, could be overthrown. I believed that socialism could be established. The Militant resolved this issue for me by explaining its 'entryist' tactic. This was that I could still fight for my revolutionary socialist views and organise around these a caucus, a tendency, within the existing party, the NILP. This could be done while denying I was part of an organisation, rather just a tendency. This was what was known as entryism. I would later carry out such work in the NILP and the Irish Labour Party.

The Militant helped me in another important way. It explained to me that capitalism in the post-war decades had experienced an economic upswing. This had strengthened illusions amongst the working class in the advanced capitalist countries, and also in Ireland, that capitalism could deliver the goods. This was one reason why there was a certain base of support for capitalism amongst the working class. The Militant explained that when this period of economic upswing would come to an end there would be a change in the consciousness of the working class and the work of fighting for socialism would be made more easy. While this was a bit overstated, it was basically correct and it allowed me to maintain my belief in the working class, in socialism and to continue my struggle to convince others to fight for socialism.

As well as the discussions with The Militant, the readings I did at this time were very helpful to me. I had read some of Marx, Engels, Lenin, Trotsky and Luxemburg when I was living in my caravan on Inch Island and at Dunree Fort on Lough Swilly. I read more of these in Bernadette Devlin's flat in London. When I read the Communist Manifesto by Marx and his collaborator Engels, more scales fell from my eyes. It explained that society was divided into two great classes, the capitalist class and the working class. The capitalist class ruled through its ownership of capital. It had accumulated this capital initially in the most savage and brutal manner, slaughter, genocide, torture, slavery, plunder, mass theft. By these means, which Marx described as the primitive accumulation of capital, the capitalist classes accumulated capital which it was then able to invest to build war machines to seize more capital and also invest to develop its means of production, distribution and exchange. And from this, accumulate more profits and wealth. And from ownership of the means of production, distribution and exchange and the rent, interest and profit it was able to extract from this ownership, it was able to control the state apparatus, the military power, the political system, the mass media and the legal system in whatever societies it ruled. From this position of ownership and control it exploited and suppressed the mass of the population of the world, that is, the working class and what was left of the peasantry.

The Communist Manifesto also explained that the working class was the other main class in society. Its dominant characteristic was that while the capitalist class lived off its capital, the working class lived of the sale of its labour power. It depended on the sale of its labour power to exist. Getting a job was central to the working class. Getting a job or not getting a job meant the difference between being able to sell its labour or not sell its labour, to live or not to live. The working class was enormous in size. It was spread all over the world. It kept the wheels of the world economy turning. Without the working class society would grind to a halt. Being in this position, that is, providing the muscle and brain for production, distribution and exchange, meant it had the potential to determine how the world economy and society worked. It meant it had the potential to reconstruct society on a new basis. It was the class which, if it acted consciously as a class, could change the world. It was the progressive class of the time. The readings and discussions I had around this issue of the class nature of society gave a stronger foundation to what I understood about my experience of being declassed in my time in Ireland after I had returned home from my travels.

The other important step forward for me, and which also came from my discussions and readings in London at that time, was getting a grasp of how capitalism worked and how socialism would work. But before moving on to explain what I learnt about how capitalism worked I feel it is necessary to say this. Marx in his writings went into great detail on the workings of capitalism. He did this with the help of his friend Engels. Engels worked in the factories owned by his family. In this way he shared and observed the workings of those factories, the capital on which these factories was based and the workers and the consciousness of the workers in those factories. This was invaluable to Marx and his studies and writings. Along with Marx, Engels developed the ideas of scientific socialism which was the term they preferred for the ideas and conclusions they drew. Today there are many learned people, academics and otherwise who concentrate on and write about and seek to explain the detailed workings of capitalism on a daily basis. What is important to see is that while these people can play an important role it is neither possible nor necessary for every worker or revolutionary to be able to understand every detail of capitalist economics, to follow every twist and turn, every intricacy, every theoretical detail of how capitalism works from day to day.

It is not necessary and it will never happen that every worker, every revolutionary will read Marx's *Capital*, or his *Grundrisse* from cover to cover. I have not done so. I have read Engels on Marx's *Capital*. I have read some of the pamphlets of Marx such as 'Wages, Prices and Profit', 'The Eighteenth Brumaire', and others, but I have not read *Capital* from cover to cover nor *Grundrisse*. I never will. I do not have the years left. I acknowledge this reality. I read the main capitalist publications regularly and follow developments. I regularly refer back to and read again some of the basic documents of Marxism. I regularly read some of the more erudite and capable Marxist economists of the day. But if I thought that I and every worker and revolutionary had to or could read all the works of Marx and Engels and follow every daily intricacy of the unfolding of capitalism, if I thought I could, if I thought I had to, if I tried to make every worker and revolutionary think they could and think they had to, this would not lead to the strengthening of the revolution but the opposite. For all revolutionaries, for all workers to try and read all the works of Marxism, to understand every twist and turn of capitalism would be trying to do the impossible. To think this way would tend to lead to the working class and activists becoming intimidated by this task. As Marx said we have to recognise necessity, or I would put it recognise what is possible and what is not possible. If we try to do the impossible we will only produce demoralisation and or distortion in our work as revolutionaries.

This is a dangerous, although in my opinion an absolutely correct conclusion. Dangerous because it could lead to workers and revolutionaries with less time to read and think about capitalist economics to conclude that they had to leave the most complex issues up to some elite few. This is not the case. But this danger must be recognised. Part of guarding against this danger is to recognise there will be times, such as perhaps when there is a sharp turn in the economic situation, when the balance of the work of all members of a revolutionary organisation, would have to turn towards seeking to clarify as much as possible the immediate and medium term economic developments. At such times a healthy revolutionary organisation would bring together the knowledge of those of its members who were most up on the study of economics along with the day-to-day experience of the organisation as a whole and especially the day-to-day experience of the workers in industry who would be most up on the day-to-day workings of capital on the shop floor and in the workplace and merge these together and in this way have the best chance of clarifying the developing processes.

At such times there would have to be a conscious turn by all members to give greater priority, even at times to put aside other work and study the economic situation and the Marxist classics. The specialised knowledge of those who had read and studied the Marxist classics would be invaluable in this but so also would be the day-to-day experience of the workers on the shop floor who would be experiencing and seeing on a day-to-day basis the tos and fros of the capitalist economy. Every worker revolutionary will not have the time to read all of the works of Marxism or follow the daily detailed intricacies of the capitalist economy on a regular basis. The revolutionary who has the time to do this is unlikely to have the day-to-day experience of the worker on the shop floor, the worker in the productive process, the worker who daily stands in front of and interacts with the dead capital of the machine. The task is to build a collective organisation which brings together the varied experiences and knowledge, which recognises that as in production so in clarifying ideas a division of labour is necessary. Most revolutionary organisations pay lip service to the role of the working class. But when was the last time we have heard of a revolutionary socialist conference having as its main speaker, a worker from the shop floor explaining his or her day to day experience with the bosses, that is with capitalism, his or her experiences with the machines they work, the changes in the machines and the way these work, the development of robots, the new technology, his or her workplace experience against the background of the fundamentals of Marxist theory? The various experiences and different specialised knowledges have to be married together, the experiences in production have to married together with the theoretical explanations and conclusions of Marxism.

Before I go on to try and explain the basic fundamentals of capitalist economics to the extent that I have came to understand them from my readings and discussions in London, and from my life experience, I would also like to say this. It is not just a question of only understanding economics. It is a question of understanding political economy. This means that the various ups and downs, the various twists and turns of the capitalist economies cannot be separated from political developments. All you have to do is think about how a political crisis affects the world's stock markets and the different world currencies and the willingness or unwillingness of the world's capitalist classes to invest. Along with this all you have to think about is how an economic crash affects political developments. To keep our feet in the struggle to end capitalism we have to recognise that it is political economy, not economy, on which we have to base ourselves.

With these comments I would like to try and explain what I learnt from my discussions and readings on capitalist economics in London at that time. What I learnt was the basic fundamentals, the basic contradictions of capitalism. Understanding these basics, these fundamental contradictions of capitalism has been sufficient to allow me to keep my feet on the revolutionary road. An understanding of these fundamentals is also sufficient for all workers to keep their feet on the revolutionary road. We do not all have to have read Marx's *Capital* from cover to cover. The fundamentals are enough. The fundamentals I came to understand were as follows.

I came to see that capitalism was a system of production based on private ownership. And inevitably from this a system addicted to, the pursuit of rent, interest and profit. And that this rent interest and profit came from the unpaid labour of the working class. The capitalist class, by owning the means of production, distribution and exchange, and from this the state apparatus, is able to force the working class to accept a situation where it is not paid the full value for its labour, where some of the value of the wealth it creates goes unpaid, instead is pocketed by the capitalist class. This unpaid labour is the basis for the class struggle and class conflict. This is the reason the working class rise again and again to confront the capitalist class. It wants to be paid the full value of its labour. This is why class struggle is inseparable from capitalism, the working class is not paid the full value of its labour. Capitalism's rent, interest and profit is the unpaid labour of the working class.

This reality explains why the ideas of the mass workers parties such as the social democratic parties, in the English speaking world mainly called Labour Parties, are wrong. These parties believe there can be peace between the capitalist class and the working class. But this is not so. The reason is simple. The capitalist class live off the unpaid labour of the working class. And as nobody likes to work and not get paid for the full value of their work, of what they produce, the working class rise again and again to try and get the full value of its labour. This is why there can be no permanent peace between the classes. Under capitalism the class struggle is inevitable.

My readings and discussions also helped me to understand that while the struggle between the two main classes is the main conflict in society, there are conflicts within capitalism itself. The capitalist classes in the more developed capitalist countries, that is the imperialist countries continually keep their foot on the neck of the capitalist classes in the less developed countries of the world from which it loots and plunders and accumulates wealth. This means continual colonial wars and invasions and occupations of these countries and continual uprisings and wars of the working classes and peasantries of these countries against capitalism's invasions and occupations. It also means continual conflicts between the more developed capitalist countries, that is between the imperialist countries themselves as they fight each other over access to the markets and resources of the less developed countries.

An inevitable feature of capitalism is the nation state. Capitalism originally developed within national boundaries. However, as capitalism has developed, its means of production and its system have outgrown the different national boundaries. Capitalism has to go outside its national boundaries for markets and resources. Part of the reason for this is that each capitalist class does not pay its own working class the full value of what it produces so the working class in any given nation state cannot buy all that it produces so each capitalist class has to sell its surplus product elsewhere. All the various national capitalist classes have to do this. Have to seek markets and resources outside their national boundaries. This means non-stop, inter-capitalist struggles for markets and resources. This inevitably means conflicts and wars between the various capitalist classes. At times such as in the decades after World War II, some progress was made by capitalism in an effort to overcome these national boundaries. But there has been only temporary and partial success on this front. This temporary and partial success was reflected in the development of world trade agreements and the development of formations such as the European Union. However this development is coming to be seen as a temporary and partial phenomenon. Even in this period of the development of world trade, in the period of the development of technology and worldwide communications, the latter as never before, there continues to exist the nation states and the barrier of the nation states to capitalism developing as a stable world system. The nation states will, the nation states are, reasserting themselves now as the crises of capitalism deepens. Capitalism, while it could for a while partially overcome the barriers of the nation states, as it enters into periods of slower growth this tendency is beginning to be reversed and once again national boundaries will more decisively reassert themselves and with this national conflict will increase.

The capitalist class is not omnipotent or united. Capitalism is not a stable system. Periodic crises is its norm. At times these crises reach such an intensity that they can only be 'solved' by capitalism going to war amongst itself. This was the case with the first and second World Wars. These were fought over market share and access to resources and markets in the advanced capitalist world as well as the world as a whole. The nation states exerted themselves, made various alliances and went to war. As well as the conflicts between the various capitalist classes and their nation states, there is also the continual competition between the different sections of capitalism within the various nation states and internationally over which section of the capitalist class can get the greatest share of the profits.

These many contradictions of capitalism mean that capitalism is always prone to wars, conflict and instability. Private ownership, the nation state, profit being the unpaid labour of the working class, capitalism cannot overcome these contradictions, cannot overcome the crises that flow from these. This is why there has to be the international socialist revolution.

Competition within capitalism is inevitable and non-stop. This competition between the various capitalist entities force these to continually increase the size of their production units, to try and drive their rivals out of business. They have to continually increase their investment in machinery and in the amount of raw materials they use relative to what they invest in labour power. But these raw materials and machinery, what Marx called dead capital, are not sources of rent interest and profit. It is only from labour power, what Marx called living capital, that rent interest and profit can be derived. But capitalism in competition within itself, in its struggles to outdo its rivals, has to invest more and more in raw materials and machinery which do not produce rent interest and profit, relative to what it invests in labour power, which does produce rent, interest and profit, therefore a crisis of profitability again and again tends to develop. That is, its rate of profit, not necessarily its mass of profit, but the proportion of profit relative to its overall investment, declines. There are many other contradictions in capitalism but this is the central economic contradiction that it faces and however long it tries, however it twists and turns to try and escape from this, the contradiction of the tendency of the rate of profit to fall expresses itself. This tendency is inseparable from the capitalist system of production. It can on occasion be thrown back but it will always reassert itself and lead to crisis after crisis. And it also means that again and again the capitalist class have to launch new offensives against the working class to try and prop up its rate of profit. Conflict between the various capitalist classes, between the various capitalist corporations and economic sectors, between the capitalist class and the working class, all are inseparable from capitalism. Capitalism is a system of conflict and crisis.

At first I had a hard time getting my head around these ideas of dead capital and living capital and the rate of profit. Then I read where Marx said that it was easier to understand concepts and processes if we could visualise them and also if we could think in mass terms. I envisioned a small mountain of iron ore. If nothing was done to this, if labour power was not applied to it, could not be applied to it, it would just sit inert, unchanging, not increasing in value or producing new value. If labour power could not be applied to it it would be of no value. Nobody but a deranged speculator with more money than sense and more than half drunk would want to buy a mountain of iron ore on the moon. Labour could not be applied to it. It would have no value. If capitalism had a mass of machinery sitting in some factory, but if nothing was done to this, if labour power was not applied to this, if labour power could not be applied to it, and this mass of machinery was not set in motion, if it was not oiled, not maintained, it would not create new value nor would it increase in value. It would only be if labour power was applied to the machinery that there would be an increase in value. Nobody but a deranged speculator with more money than sense and more than half drunk would want to buy a machine stuck on the moon. Labour could not be applied to it. It would have no value.

The transformation of the ore, the starting and maintaining of the machinery, and from these the production of commodities for which there was a demand, and from which capitalism could make a profit, this was only possible by the application of labour power to the process. Only labour power could dig the ore out of the ground and transport it to where it could be used to make steel or other products. Only labour power could set in motion and maintain the machinery to where it could shape products for which there was demand. What was common and central to the change in both the raw materials and the machinery was the application of labour power. This was what was essential if the dead raw materials, the dead machinery, could be turned into products, into commodities for which there would be demand, products which capitalism could sell and from which capitalism could make its rent, interest and profit. This was not contradicted by the use of ever more developed machines, even the most advanced robots. The robots, like other machines, were only stored up labour power, dead capital. This central contradiction, the relationship of dead capital to living capital, and from this the tendency of the rate of profit to fall, meant that the capitalist class had to continually attack the working class to try and prop up their falling rate of profit. This inevitably meant that the class struggle was continuous and inevitable. It could change in intensity but it would always be present.

While the tendency of the rate of profit to fall was the central economic contradiction of capitalism, there were other and related contradictions. The capitalist class owns the means of production, distribution and exchange, and from this controls the state apparatus and so on. From this position of power it is able to force the working class to accept less in wages than the full value of what it produces. Capitalism has to pay its labour power something, enough to eat and reproduce itself at the workplace, to do its work. But this is different from paying it the full value of its labour. Capitalism is in a continual struggle to pay its labour power as little as possible, always less than the full value of its labour, and still have it alive enough to produce, and at the same time make as much rent, interest and profit as possible. This struggle over the unpaid labour of the working class is inseparable from the capitalist system.

And from this the following contradiction flows. As the working class is not paid the full value of its labour it cannot buy back all the goods that it produces. There is therefore the tendency towards over production and/or overcapacity. That is a situation where there is the tendency towards a surplus of goods in the market place or/and a surplus of capacity in the production process. This leads to the continual recessions and slumps as capitalism closes factories, fires workers, in an effort to sell off, or burn off its over produced goods and its overcapacity.

Capitalism tries again and again and in different ways to overcome its tendency to over-production/overcapacity. It prints money which has no backing in reality. It goes into debt. It loads up the working class, the middle class, the world's governments and cities and its own corporations with debt. This allows the economic system to go further than its own limits for a time. But as any person knows, debt has to be paid back or the debtor has to default. When the debt is no longer sustainable the system snaps back within its own limits and slumps, recessions, wars, revolutions are the result. This, I came to understand, was the situation presently facing the world economy.

As well as debt and credit, capitalism tries other ways to overcome the tendency to over production over capacity. It has developed a massive armaments industry, that is, the production of scrap metal, armaments, which it continually destroys in wars, this is sometimes referred to as the permanent arms economy. The production of weaponry contributes nothing useful to society, instead it wastes society's resources. It uses resources, it produces its military goods, which do not contribute to the needs of society. It is utterly wasteful, increases debt, increases inflation, utterly useless. When was a tank or a submarine or a fighter plane, or a machine gun ever seen building a road, a bridge, a house, a hospital, a school, or feeding a child?

So as well as the tendency of the rate of profit to fall which is the main economic contradiction of capitalism, there is this tendency towards over-production/over-capacity. These two contradictions of capitalism keep pushing that system into crisis after crisis, into recessions, upswings, booms, slumps, wars, revolutions. It cannot overcome these contradictions. Wars, slumps, booms, revolutions, wars, slumps, booms, revolutions, these were and are inevitable with capitalism as it twists and turns to survive. These crises of capitalism have been particularly prevalent in the last century and into this new century as capitalism comes towards its end, as it threshes ever deeper into its existential crisis.

As the years went, on a new feature of the crisis of capitalism entered my consciousness. I was not sufficiently aware of it in that time when I was to trying to clarify my thinking in London. Nor was The Militant. This is climate change, global warming, pollution, the cutting down of the world's forests, that is, the rapidly developing destruction of the environment. In the coming years I would come to see that if capitalism continued climate change would destroy life on earth as we knew it. Capitalism cannot solve this crisis of climate change. If capitalism continues then life on earth as we know it will be destroyed either by climate change, pollution, drought, all results of the profit-addicted, mad capitalist system. Or as conflict between nations increases it will be destroyed by nuclear war. Capitalism has not produced tens of thousands of nuclear warheads for nothing. Capitalism is a system of war. These nuclear weapons have temporarily held capitalism back from all out world war as with the nuclear weapons that now exist such a world war would destroy the human species including the capitalist classes. But capitalism is a system which has its own insoluble contradictions and one of these is that it is a system of war. And it is also a system that works behind the backs of its own ruling class. If capitalism continues, life on earth as we know it will be destroyed, if not by climate change then by nuclear war. Only the international socialist revolution can preserve life on earth as we know it.

Of course capitalism does not just sail along, only interrupted every now and then by its own internal crises and contradictions. It is also continually confronted, continually challenged, again and again by the working class as this class rises against its exploitation, against not being paid the full value of its labour. After all people do not like to work for nothing. However while the working class repeatedly rises in struggle, as long as it does not take into its own hands the means of production, distribution and exchange, as long as it does not smash the capitalist state apparatus, the capitalist class and end capitalism, it is forced to yield, and the class struggle continues. This struggle will rise and fall in intensity but it will continue as long as capitalism continues. This continual class struggle between the working class and the capitalist class in its many and varied forms, as well as the related and continual economic and political crises of capitalism, are the dominant and permanent features of the period of history in which we all live. This is the big picture.

This struggle between the classes is not confined to a peaceful exchange of views over dollars and cents. In conflict after conflict the working class, while on many occasions starting out from the economic issues or democratic issues, moves on to the larger issue of who runs society. It comes to see that a tiny minority, that is the capitalist class, is a dictatorship over society. In such situations, and on occasion after occasion, the working class seeks to, has sought to, move on to take matters into its own hands, to attempt to carry through a revolution and end capitalism, to build a new society and a new world.

The recorded history of the human species is the history of class struggle and of revolution and counterrevolution. It is the history of the ruling class of the day trying to maintain power and look after its own interests being challenged by a new emerging class seeking to take power and build a new society in its own interests. In the present period in which we live it is the history of the ruling capitalist class seeking to hold onto power and the exploited working class, sometimes consciously, sometimes unconsciously, seeking to end this situation and take power into its own hands.

In the course of this continual struggle in this existing present period of history, the ruling capitalist class, when seriously challenged, seeks to put down the working class through bloody counterrevolution. This on occasion takes the form of dividing the working class along nationalist or racist or religious or gender lines and throwing it against itself in mass slaughter, for example the World Wars. It on occasion takes the form of fascism where sections of the more backward layers of the working class and the middle class are organised and thrown against the working class in its effort to end capitalism, in its effort to bring about the revolution. It on occasion takes the form of military coups. What all these methods have in common, and demonstrate, is that capitalism will not give up its power, its rent, interest and profit, without a struggle. The working class have to understand this reality. What is needed is the overthrow of the capitalist class. This is the lesson I learned from my discussions, my readings, my thinking when I was in London, when the lessons of my own experiences were made conscious by these readings and discussions and thinking.

My readings and discussions and thinking in London not only increased my understanding about the big political and historical and class issues. An unexpected and other positive side effect of my increased class consciousness was that I was able to more clearly see the situation in which my family existed. As small farmers, small property owners, my family were not part of either of the two main classes in society. They were part of what

I came to describe as the middle layers in society. These middle layers also included middle-sized business people and to some extent the so-called professional classes. Not being part of either of the two major classes in society my family tended to be continually crushed between or to be continually vacillating between the two major classes. This meant that they consciously or unconsciously felt, and correctly so, that they had little power, that they could not change society. This affected them politically and psychologically. Not having the power of being in either of the two great classes, not being in a class which had the power to take society forward, they tended to be insecure and susceptible to all kinds of backward pressures and confused ideas. I came to see that my family's position in the Orange Order and their strong adherence to Protestantism was an attempt to gain some power and security in society, and not only on the economic front but also on the psychological front.

It was not only that they were part of a religious minority in Southern Ireland but that they were part of the middle layers in society, not part of either of the two major classes. This was a tragedy and a source of insecurity and pain for them all their lives. It was also central to our interfamily struggles. I was fortunate in that I was able to separate myself from this intermediate class into which I had been born and join the struggle of the working class, the progressive and potentially most powerful class in society in this period of history. When I was able to do this and also develop and believe in and work for revolutionary ideas and working class revolution my insecurity and confusion ended. Unfortunately for my family they were not able to make this break.

As I understood the class nature of society, and the period I was in, I increasingly dedicated myself to becoming a participant in the working class and to helping it in its struggles. I rejoiced as I became more and more clear of my role and place in society. I was able to see myself as part of the great working class, the new emerging progressive class, which held the future of society in its hands. I moved decisively and consciously out of the class into which I was born, the rural small farmer class, or as it could be called the rural petit bourgeois, I moved away from the period when I was declassed. I moved decisively into the working class. Of course moving from one class to another means serious stresses and strains, personal as well as social, it is a struggle. But overall and without any qualifications it was a huge step forward in my understanding and also in my confidence in myself as a person. To be consciously part of the class whose responsibility it was to take society forward, which had the potential to take society forward, was an honour and a privilege and placed me in the forefront of society. I no longer had any up and down days. I knew who I was, what I was, I was balanced and focused in my life.

MATERIALISM
— HISTORICAL MATERIALISM
— DIALECTICAL MATERIALISM
— DIALECTICS
(DON'T PANIC, THEY ARE 'ONLY' WORDS)

IT WAS A SUNNY DAY. I was cutting the grass at a school in Hammersmith. That is where I made another breakthrough in my understanding. I had learnt a lot as I had grasped the basic conclusions of Marxism, a lot of answers to a lot of questions. But that morning I realised that these conclusions and answers were not Marxism. Marxism was much more than that. It was a method of thinking, a tool, which if used properly, could allow me, myself, and all who grasped this method of thought, to analyse and understand processes, to understand the world, and to work out answers to questions ourselves. There in Hammersmith, cutting the grass with that old lawnmower, a new light went on in my head. I entered further into my new world.

In my new readings and understandings I went travelling again, but a different kind of travel. On this journey I came upon not new places, but new words, new phrases, new terms, new concepts, a whole new way of thinking. I came upon a whole new vocabulary. Words and expressions like materialism, historical materialism, dialectical materialism, dialectics. While very intimidating to me at first, understanding these new terms and what they represented was to become amongst the most important and exciting revolution in my thinking.

The struggle to understand these new words and terms and concepts was not easy. But it was much more than worthwhile. It allowed me to understand how history developed, not just over a century or two, but over countless millions of centuries. It gave me a glimpse into the universes, the countless numbers of galaxies, and these over literally countless millennia of centuries. These terms, 'materialism', 'historical materialism', 'dialectical materialism', 'dialectics', all new words to me, were shorthand. I did not know what they meant. They intimidated me at first. But I did not hesitate. I had learnt a lot from my discussions with The Militant and from reading the Marxist literature. I was confident I would not be disappointed in my effort to grasp these new terms and concepts.

Materialism was not too complicated. It was to understand that the world was made up of matter and matter only. To understand that there were no ghosts or spirits or inexplicable non-material entities or creatures. No god who lived forever, floated about forever, in some heaven in the sky or some devil who lurked forever in some hell below our feet in the centre of the earth. All was matter. Not that this meant that all was easily explainable, far from it, but it was to understand the essential reality that all was only matter. And to understand the world and ourselves the search had to be directed towards understanding matter and how it existed and how it was transformed. And how also it was never destroyed, only transformed. And never fixed in place or time, always in motion. The world, all, myself, ourselves, could be described in the most basic terms as matter in motion. Matter in motion, this was the bare bones term which best corresponded to reality.

Even the most seemingly non-material entities could only be explained by a materialist approach. Our thoughts, our emotions, these seemingly non-material entities were but the products of, part of, the material world in which we existed. This material world entered into our brains through our senses, eyes, ears, touch and so on, material entities all, and on into our brains which in turn was also matter. The most complex of matter on the planet but matter nonetheless. In our brains the material world became our thoughts. Our ideas and thoughts and emotions were impulses and observations and experiences which arose from our interaction with the outside material world, entered into our brain through our senses and in this way 'we thought' and 'created'. The trillions of experiences of our daily lives and the trillions of daily electrical charges and chemical reactions in our brains, all material, came together and so came about the thoughts and ideas and emotions of every creature on the planet. At root all psychology, all thought, all emotion was physiology, was material, was matter. What a new and exciting world I was entering. The blindfolds kept coming off.

Historical materialism was not that complicated either when I got the hang of it. I thought about it in terms of my uncle's farm. What demanded the least effort to most efficiently grow the greatest amount of potatoes? What demanded the least effort to most efficiently build the fences, the byres, the dwelling house, to make clothes for our backs and shoes for our feet? What demanded the least effort to develop the productive forces? Historical materialism explained that the system that could best deliver on these tasks, that is best and most efficiently deliver the material necessities of life, tended to become dominant. It only made sense. People would want to produce as much as possible with the least effort. If, on my uncle's farm, there was an easier and a more productive way to grow potatoes, or to build a byre, a barn, a dwelling house, or dig a drain, this would, over a period be the way it would tend to be done, rather than a less efficient way. It would not necessarily always be the way it would be done but it would be the way in which it would tend to be done over time. The more inefficient way, the more unproductive way would tend to become discarded. The more efficient way would tend to become the norm through a process of selection based on experience. This was historical materialism. This material way of looking at things explained how history developed. It was not the nonsense about kings and queens and lords and ladies and knights and popes, it was about what system could best develop the productive forces and provide the necessities of life for the greatest number of people with the least effort. The kings and the queens and the popes and the masses had to be seen in the context of this historical materialism.

But it was not a simple or straight line process. Historical materialism explained that when a system, or a ruling class in that system, prevented progress on the material front and whenever another system existed or had the potential to exist, one that could do better on the material front, then society entered ferocious struggles of the most violent character with the more progressive system trying to replace the old. This was the process of history, this was how history developed, it was a process of revolution and counter-revolution. The old system trying to hold on to existence with everything it had, that is counter revolution, the new system fighting ferociously to come into being with everything it had, that is revolution. This was how history developed. This was historical materialism.

I came to see that this was like the process of evolution in nature. Not only human society but all life on earth developed in this fashion. The most efficient species, the most efficient within each species in terms of developing and surviving, would tend to out-do other species, other members of their own species, and so survive, and so re-produce, and so evolve, and so evolution. I was coming to understand that I had been right all those years ago when I thought against the indoctrination of the preachers and Sunday school teachers that Darwin was correct. I was learning by leaps and bounds. But the finishing line kept moving. This I was to also learn. The finishing line would always keep moving. After all everything was matter in motion.

The more I learnt the more I realised that my method of thinking continued to be inadequate. If I was to fully understand I would have to become more conscious about all the ins and outs of my method of thought. Here I came to the dialectic. I would have to more thoroughly understand the whole issue of dialectics, to more fully learn how to use this tool, this method of thought, dialectics. This was an entirely new word and concept to me. I was reared to think that the way things were was fixed and could not be changed. Historical materialism showed this was not the case. There were many different systems throughout history – primitive communism, slavery, feudalism, capitalism and hopefully in the future there would be socialism. I was also reared to think that if by some miracle there was to be any change in what existed it would be in a simple, one-directional fashion. But this too I was to come to see by the study of history and in particular, by the dialectical materialist study of history, by the study of dialectics, was not the case. Through understanding dialectics I was to come to see how things actually changed.

Dialectics, this new word, this new concept, demanded and got my attention. The dialectical way of thinking did not contradict what I had learnt in relation to how history developed with one system being overthrown by another. It just explained the complexity of, and the contradictory way, the dialectical way, through which this came about. As I began to read and discuss this dialectical method of thinking I took another step higher on my ladder of understanding. And another horizon came into view. It was like when I had first grasped the historical materialist way of looking at the world. Understanding the dialectical way of thinking was another new and exciting leap forward in my consciousness.

The main component of dialectical thinking was that everything was always changing and developing. Myself, my world, the universe, the universes, were always changing and developing. Dialectical thinking was a conscious recognition of this reality. It was a superior form of thinking to that which I had been taught, that is, to formal logic. Formal logic taught that things were fixed and that was that. This is what the society I was brought up in taught me, what my family was taught and in turn taught me. Nothing could be changed just knuckle down and accept things. When of course this was not the case. What existed at any time was not fixed, rather it was always in the process of coming into being, maturing and passing away. Everything was in a continual process of change. Nothing was fixed.

I was beside myself with excitement as I grasped this. It consolidated my atheism. If everything was always changing and developing there could be no god who existed forever, there could be no God. I was right. I was more secure in my atheism. And not only that, this understanding confirmed my conviction to fight for revolution. If everything was always changing and developing there could be no system or regime that could last forever. That opened the door wider to revolution. There could be no regime that lasted forever. This also explained why capitalism fought this method of thinking in relation to politics and history. If everything was always changing, if everything had a beginning a middle and an end then this meant that capitalism also had a beginning and a middle and an end.

The capitalist class could not accept this reality. As the ruling class they had to cling on to the belief they were fixed and permanent and would rule forever. They might reluctantly accept that their system had a beginning but under no conditions would they accept that it, and they as a ruling class, had a middle and an end. This left the capitalist class in essence blind. This explained how they could fight to keep in place a system which if it was kept in place would destroy life on earth as we know it, and that included destroying themselves, the capitalist class. Their inability to accept dialectics as a form of thought left them blind. It led them to glorify the idiot Fukuyama at the US State Department who after the collapse of Stalinism declared the 'end of history'. That is, that capitalism had triumphed and would last forever.

But a dialectical method of thinking was more than saying that all was always changing. Dialectics also explained how things changed. As a method of thinking which corresponded to reality and reflected that reality, it explained how things changed. It explained that change did not take place one plodding foot after the other in an endless, one single direction line. No, dialectics was a method of thinking, which as it corresponded to the reality of the world, explained that all change was uneven and contradictory. It took place by means of steps forward and steps back steps back and steps forward. Becoming conscious of this new reality, that all change was contradictory and uneven further allowed me to understand history and my own world.

Many centuries previously there were the development of societies such as the Mayan, the Khmer, the Roman, the Greek, and others which were more advanced than other existing societies of the time. There were also the old societies of which practically nothing is known, such as the societies which built Grianan Fort in Ireland and Stonehenge in Britain and many other such structures throughout the world. These societies reached significant heights of knowledge, in science, architecture, agriculture, astronomy. Steps forward for the time. But these societies all fell and their great buildings and burial tombs and knowledge were grown over by the jungles, buried by the deserts, sank into the oceans, or were destroyed by barbarian tribes which were economically and culturally less developed than they. Development was not in a straight line. There were steps forward and steps back. Under certain circumstances, materially and scientifically and culturally more developed societies could find further development blocked and could fall back. The laws of development expressed themselves as tendencies not iron laws, and as a result development did not take place in a straight line. The tendency for a society to go forward in a certain way did not mean there was an iron law that would make this definitely so. There was only a tendency for it to be so. Tendencies could be and were on many occasions cut across. Progress was on many occasions cut across and blocked, more advanced societies could be destroyed and replaced by less developed societies.

The Mayan empire expanded past its limits to where it could no longer feed its huge urban populations. There was no class or force in that society capable of solving this problem. The result was that in order to feed and clothe and shelter themselves, the peoples of this culture were forced to desert their great cities and return to the jungles and to a more primitive way of living of hunting and gathering which was materially and culturally below that in which they had previously existed. Their cities and other architectural and scientific achievements collapsed. The Khmer Empire was based around an extensive irrigation system of canals and waterways. These silted up and there was no class or force in this civilisation which could solve this problem and that society also collapsed and was replaced by a less advanced culture. The Roman Empire over-extended itself in non-stop wars against its slave population, and in wars to conquer and hold new territories. Internally it was based on slavery. Its slave population had no incentive to develop the means of production, to develop the productivity of that means of production, there was nothing in it for them, there was no class or force which could resolve these contradictions so this empire could not go forward and ended up being overthrown by the less developed barbarian tribes from the north. And its great achievements were lost. What all these societies had in common was that as they entered into the crises of their own internal contradictions there was no other class, or force, that could step in and resolve these contradictions and take these societies forward.

So historical materialism, while being essential to understanding history, had to be seen in a dialectical fashion. That is that things did not develop in a straight line, that things developed through steps forward and steps back. That while overall there was the tendency for those societies which could best develop the productive forces and the material life of their populations to come to the fore, nothing was guaranteed. It was a tendency not an iron law. I came to see the importance of thinking in terms of tendencies not iron laws. The tendency towards this, the tendency towards that, the interruption and throwing back of the tendency towards this, the tendency towards that, this was how things worked and this was the way my method of thought was developing.

I also came to understand the concept of what, again in shorthand, was known as quantitative and qualitative change and how this related to the tendency towards this, the tendency towards that. For example, water in a kettle could be heated and heated with no change in quality for a time. That is, it would remain water. But when the water reached boiling point then a qualitative change took place in the process and the water changed into steam.

Again dialectics explained the complexity of change. Not only that change did not take place in a straight line, and steps forward and steps back, but also through quantitative change becoming qualitative change. This dialectical understanding was very important in political struggle as it explained that systems, regimes, could appear to be fixed until they reached a certain point and then a qualitative change could take place. For example, anger amongst a working class could develop for decades and not express itself decisively but then at some stage it would reach boiling point where qualitative change took place and change and revolution were placed on the agenda. Northern Ireland in 1968 was such an example of qualitative change. The explosion of the civil rights movement was a qualitative change in Northern Irish society. Quantitative and qualitative change meant that processes of change would tend to take place in the form of long periods of seeming stability on the surface, while under the surface the tensions were building and these at some stage would explode to the surface. In other words, a qualitative change would take place.

I looked at my family increasingly in a dialectical materialist manner. I looked at my family in the old way, the formal logic way, and then in my new dialectical materialist way. My family owned their small farm since at least the early 1800s. Nothing is known before that. But they thought of themselves and their ownership of the farm as fixed, as permanent. Or at the very least they wanted it to be fixed and permanent. They were committed to making it fixed and permanent. But the world, their world, was not and could never be, fixed or permanent. It was always ever changing. My family lived in an ever-changing environment. But in relation to their farm they thought they owned it and that was that and they looked to this being so forever. That I would take it over, settle down and with some woman have children and they in turn would have children and so the small farm would be in the family forever. But that was not going to ever be the reality and so they kept being bumped up against this reality, bruised and damaged by this reality. Their life was made much harder by not having a dialectical view of their world, by trying to make their world permanent and fixed.

I originally thought my family were fixed in their personal ways and with their personal traits and that was that. I originally thought I too was fixed in my ways and that was that. And that it was just the way it was for my family and I to all come into conflict with each other and that was that. But that was not that. With my new way of thinking, my dialectical materialist way of thinking, I was able to come to better understand the reality of life. And as part of this I was better able to come to understand my family, better able to understand myself and thus better able to learn to try and live with them in less conflict.

I looked at an example of formal logic versus dialectics. I thought of the sports days we had when I was at school. The high jumps. We would run at the jump, leap off the ground and try to get over the bar. If a photographer took a shot of the jumper at the height of his or her jump, it would look like the jumper was not only not moving, but was defying gravity, in fact that gravity did not exist. This shot would not in and off itself be wrong. The jumper was actually defying gravity. But the shot was wrong in this way. It was incomplete. It was leaving out the ascent of the jumper from the ground and the inevitable descent of the jumper back down to the ground again. The dialectic taught me to see that nothing could be properly understood 'in and of itself'. All had to be seen in context, in a process of change, in processes of interacting changes, in processes of quantitative and qualitative change. My whole world began to look different. The reality of the jumper was his or her ascent and descent, it could not be the fraction of a second when they appeared fixed at the height of their jump. Like the jumper all things had to be seen in context and as parts of processes and processes in motion.

I looked to apply this method of dialectical thought to the capitalist world and my own personal world in which I had to exist. Capitalism in the 20th century was a system on its last legs. It was a system of climate change, environmental destruction, pollution and world wars, slumps, non-stop repression and exploitation and poisioning physically and mentally of the working class and peasantry, a system desperately fighting to hang on to power and existence. The revolutionary Trotsky described it as being in its death agony. It was ripe to be overthrown. The class whose responsibility it was to carry out this task was the working class. But this class had a leadership that rather than being committed to overthrowing capitalism was committed to propping up capitalism. The result was the working class was not able for the moment to overthrow capitalism. So history, society was temporarily stuck. But this was not the end of the story. As I had learnt as I grasped the historical and dialectical method of thinking nothing was fixed, nothing was permanent, everything was always changing. Something in world capitalism would have to give.

The working class again and again rose against capitalism and tried to build a new revolutionary leadership which could allow it to overthrow capitalism. The most important effort to do this was carried out under the leadership of the Bolshevik party in Russia in 1917. Capitalism and landlordism were ended in that vast country. A qualitative change took place. But this revolution took place in an economically and culturally backward country with a small working class and along with that it was isolated. No other successful revolutions took place in advanced capitalist countries which could have come to the aid of the Russian revolution. So with the revolution isolated in a backward country, the working class lost power to a caste of bureaucrats, to a dictatorship, under the leadership of Stalin. Over a period of time this caste dragged the economy into stagnation, surrendered to the international capitalist class, and capitalism was restored. History took one partial step forward with the 1917 revolution, then one full step back with the restoration of capitalism. The tendency towards ending capitalism expressed itself in the 1917 Russian revolution but the achievement of this tendency was thrown back with the restoration of capitalism in the former Soviet Union again as the 20th century came to an end. Nothing develops in a straight line, the dialectic in all its power. The qualitative step forward in 1917 was negated by the qualitative step backward as the 20th century came to an end and capitalism was restored.

I came to understand more and more important conclusions that flowed from a dialectical method of thinking. To think more about the reality that things were always moving and changing and developing. This applied to the hardest diamond and to the softest petal of the most fragile flower. No matter how fixed things seemed this was an illusion. It was necessary to take a real genuine grasp of history to see this. History was not a thousand years, nor a million, it was all of time and existence. It was necessary to see this to understand how the hardest diamond had something in common with the most fragile flower. They were both always in a state of change. Whether it was a few days or a few millennia it was always the change. It was a question only of the tempo of change.

Another thing that flowed from a dialectical method of thinking was that because change tended to be uneven with steps forward and steps back and steps forward and steps back, this meant that in just about all circumstances we had phenomena which were made up of contradictory elements. That is, made up of components from when history, when processes, were taking steps forward and at the same time made up of components from when history, when processes, were taking steps back. The shorthand for this was the interpenetration of opposites. To understand such phenomenon it was necessary to analyse them from a dialectical point of view, in other words, to identify and separate the contradictory and changing elements, see which represented the steps forward, the progressive movement, and which represented the steps back, the reactionary movement, and then to base ourselves on the progressive elements.

The restoration of capitalism in the former Soviet Union was a victory for capitalism, but it was a step backward in history. I was able to survive this step back with my revolutionary ideas and commitment intact. I was able to do so because of my grasp of the method of thinking of historical and dialectical materialism. Different societies had existed before. More advanced ones had given way to less advanced ones. Then new more advanced societies had emerged to take society forward once again. The restoration of capitalism in the former Stalinist world was not the end of the story. History did not travel in a straight line. The working class would fight again to build a new world. And it could still succeed. I based my life and struggle on this understanding. But I did not leave it there. With the help of the dialectical method of thinking I was also able to deal with the possibility that the working class could also fail. There was nothing automatic about success. The working class taking power and building a new world was a tendency not an iron law.

Another aspect of achieving a dialectical method of thinking was this. A person could achieve a knowledge of the components of the dialectical way of thinking could be able to apply this knowledge in their actions and life. However this same person could lose this knowledge or could lose the ability to apply this knowledge to their actions and life. There were many reasons for this. A person could suffer damage and demoralisation from personal or political defeats. From these they could conclude that nothing could be changed so what was the use it would always be like this. Like everything a knowledge of dialectics and the ability to apply dialectics was not fixed.

It was the case that a person could learn the components of dialectics but be unable to apply them. Or be able to apply them for a time and then lose this ability or partially lose this ability. A person could learn to be a nurse, a carpenter, an electrician, a surgeon, a whatever but might not have the ability to successfully apply this knowledge and be a good nurse or carpenter or whatever. Or could have this ability for a while but could have an experience in their life which would damage them and result in them losing this ability. Nothing was fixed.

As I became more familiar with the dialectical way of thinking and as in the future I would spend many hours discussing this with people whom I was trying to recruit to revolutionary work I noticed an interesting phenomenon. This was that people who did not have a sense of humour tended also to be people who had great difficulty in grasping and more importantly applying the method of thought of the dialectic. I would read that Lenin had said that revolutionaries needed to have a sense of history, a sense of proportion and a sense of humour. Maybe this was what he was talking about in terms of the sense of humour. I wondered what was humour, what was laughter.

I came to think about it in this way. Humour is rooted in contradiction. The yarn starts by taking the listener along a certain path, his or her emotions follow the story along that path, he or she is prepared for that path, he or she builds energy and emotion along that path, but the punch line takes the listener and throws him or her off that path and on to another path. The result is that the emotional and intellectual energy that was building in the listener taking him or her along that path can no longer go along that path. But this energy has to go somewhere. This energy explodes in the form of laughter, faster breathing, sounds from the throat and chest, shaking and other physical movements. This, what is known as laughter, is the explosion of energy as the listener tries to handle the trauma of being thrown on to the new path. Laughter is the release of energy which flows from the contradiction which is at the heart of the yarn, which is the punchline of the yarn. Even the term 'punchline' gives it away. Being punched from one path to another. A shock, a trauma. Laughter makes us feel good as it releases the pent up energy. It is also good for the health as it reduces the stress and tension in the body and mind. I thought of people whom I was convinced would have lived longer if they had been able to laugh.

But humour, laughter is not only the telling of jokes. It also flows from observation of the contradictory nature of life. From observing and seeing the staggering complexity and contradiction of life. And shaking ones head, curling up ones lips, letting the energy out, the energy that is created as we observe this contradiction and complexity, letting this energy out in the form of the peel of laughter at the wonder of it all. For this to happen demands not being frightened by the contradiction and complexity of it all. Not being frightened when we see events, when some comedian or comedienne describes events in which we see ourselves and our own experience.

Perhaps those who are not able to laugh are intimidated by the complexity and contradiction of life, instead want life to unfold in a straight line, that is, those who are unable to laugh are unable to see the dialectical, the contradictory nature of life or if they can see this, are frightened by this and paralysed by this. I felt deeply sorry for these people. Humour, laughter is one of the greatest blessings of being a human being. Maybe this is also one way the drink comes into it, where the drink can make people feel good. Well until the hangover. But that is the complexity of it all also, the dialectic of it all also. The drink unshackles the mind to let it see and rejoice in the contradictions and complexities of life. To not be frightened by these. Then comes the hangover that is the reminder that everything has to be seen in context, that everything has a price.

I wondered to myself could any other species laugh. Maybe that was the difference between the human species and other species, not the nonsense about humans having a soul, but humans being able to laugh. I was years later to see the actor and comedian Robin Williams go into a cage with a giant silverback gorilla and with the greatest caution and gentleness begin to tickle the gorilla. Slowly gradually the gorilla responded and began to tickle him back. Before long they were rolling round in the cage tickling each other. And while I could not say the gorilla was laughing there was an expression of happiness on his face. This made me think. There were different kinds of humour and laughter. Was this humour of the gorilla the result of perhaps at first thinking that Williams was going to attack him and this built up his fight or flight energies and then when he saw that Williams was not going to attack him this energy had to go somewhere and it went through him physically showing his happiness and tickling Williams back and putting this laughter expression on his face. That seemed to me close to laughter.

Then there was the other thing. I would later have a wee Chihuahua dog. The smartest dog I ever had. I would pretend to fight with it, push it around, grab it by the tail, it would try to fight me off, grab me with its teeth. His actions were ridiculous given how tiny he was compared to myself. Neither of us would hurt each other. It was play. But every now and then it would reach a stage where Shorty or as I would sometimes call him The Short, could no longer hold all the energy I was provoking in him within the bounds of play, within the bounds of not seriously trying to bite me. But he would not want to bite me. At such times he would take off and run at top speed round and round the house. Letting off this energy. Maybe that was his equivalent of my laughter. Or maybe when I talked to him and he wagged his tail. Maybe that was the equivalent of his smile.

Then there was another thing. Sometimes when in the kitchen making my food and The Short was at my feet waiting with optimism for something to eat, I would talk to him. Sometimes I would make up a joke and talking out loud tell it to myself and to him. Sometimes it would be a story. Sometimes it would be a sentence. A play with words. Then I would laugh at my own joke. Or was I laughing at the idea of me making up a joke and telling it to a Chihuahua who did not know what I was saying. I would never really be able to understand what was going on in this case. This laughter is a complicated one. The dialectic no doubt. I mourned for those who could not grasp the dialectic, who could not let the dialectic into them, who could not laugh.

But back to the greater and immediate world forces and the dialectic. As I struggled to understand this existing world I had to take into account the developments in the huge country of China. A guerrilla army had ended capitalism and landlordism there. Again a variation on the 'norm', not the working class but a guerrilla army had ended capitalism and landlordism in China. It established a society where the economy was nationalised, similar to the Soviet Union. It was also similar to the Soviet Union in that it was a society which was ruled by a bureaucracy, that is it was a dictatorship. But in spite of being a similar economic and political system to the Soviet Union it entered into rivalry with the Soviet Union bureaucracy and the Soviet Union. This conflict between these two powers was sufficient to prove that neither of these societies were socialist societies. If they had been socialist societies they would have worked together to build a socialist world not been at each other's throats.

The ending of capitalism and landlordism in China having been carried out by a guerrilla army meant that the working class were not in power. In fact this guerrilla army on coming to power slaughtered urban workers who sought a genuine democratic workers' state. The Chinese working class could not take power into its hands. As the 21st century unfolds, China shows the tendency towards the restoration of capitalism. It is not clear if this tendency will develop all the way or will be cut across by a new uprising of the working class which would take China forward to a new healthy democratic socialist workers' state. Again the dialectic, the steps forward, the steps back. I would have to continually follow the always changing events and try to be prepared.

Again and again we have the vicious exhilarating twist of the dialectic. Stalinism seized power from the working class in the former Soviet Union and for a half century or more defended the nationalised economy, that is to say, prevented capitalism from being restored. During its period in power it also prevented feudalism from being restored. With feudalism no longer an obstacle, could the new Russian capitalist class develop a new capitalist economy which would be vibrant and have a healthy vibrant home market? This was a question I pondered. If, as seemed possible, the Chinese elite, which was emerging from the Chinese Stalinist bureaucracy, continued on their way toward capitalism, could they perhaps establish a new vibrant capitalist economy? After all feudalism was no longer an obstacle as it had been ended by the Stalinist regime which came out of the guerrilla army. So neither in the former Soviet Union nor in China was feudalism an obstacle to the development of capitalism. So could healthy capitalist economies develop and open up a new period of capitalist development worldwide? Could things work out dialectically in this way?

I concluded it could not for a number of reasons. One was the state of capitalism worldwide. It was increasingly experiencing slower and slower growth rates and it was increasingly in competition with itself both in terms of the major corporations and the nation states. This was in spite of developments like the EU where some national borders were temporarily and partially overcome. I believed these would be shown to be temporary contradictory developments which would not last. On top of this, new wars, not just proxy wars of the imperialist powers, would evolve. A new nuclear or partial nuclear war was on the cards on the basis of capitalism. They did not have their tens of thousands of nuclear warheads for nothing. Such a development would for certain cut across any new world economic upswing. The extent of a nuclear war or a partial nuclear war is shown by a recent study which estimated that 1 billion people internationally would die if there was a nuclear war between Pakistan and India. Imagine the result of a nuclear war between the major nuclear powers. And such a war is inevitable if capitalism lasts. A new modern vibrant world economy with new vibrant Russian and Chinese capitalist economies is not on the cards.

There is also the cataclysmic crisis of climate change and pollution. The potentially powerful Chinese working class are being choked to death with the air that they breathe and the water that they drink as capitalism threatens to reintroduce itself. At the same time corruption on a massive, unprecedented scale is developing as the new aspiring elite in China rob the country blind in an effort to accumulate and seize the capital to make themselves the new dominant capitalist class in the world. This corruption is inseparable from the accumulation of private capital which is taking place in China. The entire capitalist world, including the advanced capitalist countries such as the USA, are all experiencing the catastrophe of pollution and climate change. It looks like the rising Chinese capitalism is coming on the scene too late. And of course there is the existence of the huge and new and fresh Chinese working class. This Chinese working class will seek to put their hands to the plough and turn over the soil of their world and seek to carve out a place for themselves in a new socialist China. That will shake up the world. China cannot give a way forward to world capitalism by developing a new vibrant capitalist China.

Neither can the new capitalist, the new imperialist class which has come to rule Russia open the door to a new vibrant Russian capitalism with a developed home market which could allow for a new phase of capitalist upswing worldwide. The new brutal capitalist class which has seized the country's economy after the collapse of Stalinism is based mainly on the countries natural resources rather than a developing balanced capitalist economy. On top of that the extreme inequality that exists in Russia between the new capitalist class and the working class will sooner rather than later result in huge uprisings by the working class. There has already been large demonstrations against the corruption of this new capitalist class, there have movements for democratic rights, and movements on the issue of housing. Economic crises, exploding class conflict, this is the future for the new capitalist Russian state. It cannot provide any way out for world capitalism.

As I considered these developments, and as I came to better grasp the method of thinking of dialectical materialism, I thought more about the old advanced societies which, because they had no class or force to take them forward, collapsed and were replaced by less advanced societies. I thought more about the lessons of these developments and whether something similar could happen in the present epoch. I concluded the answer was a definitive 'yes'. If the working class could not build a revolutionary leadership and end capitalism then capitalism would come to an end. But the question was how and what would replace it? History taught it could be replaced by a less advanced society. But I concluded the threat on this occasion was not just a less advanced society.

This time it would be much worse than when the old societies of the past collapsed and were replaced by more primitive forces and systems. This time capitalism had the science and technology to do one of two things. The dialectic again. This new science could be either very progressive or very reactionary, all depending on the context in which it would develop. It could help build a new world of undreamt of plenty. Or it could destroy life on earth as it presently existed in a holocaust of climate change, pollution, nuclear war, civil wars, mass starvation, floods and drought. Life on earth as we knew it could be destroyed. The human species could be wiped out or left as a few deformed gibbering scatterings here and there on the planet.

Materialism, historical materialism, dialectical materialism, dialectics, I was grasping these concepts, these methods of thinking. I was arming myself with these. They were explaining to me that a new world was possible where people could live well, but they were also explaining to me that life on earth as we knew it could be destroyed. I was being armed and warned and forewarned for the future. I was being prepared to step up my fight to build a new leadership of the working class, the progressive class, which could take society forward, build a new international socialist world and give a future to all. I was understanding that life on earth could be wiped out unless capitalism was ended and this could only happen if a new mass revolutionary international organisation of the working class was built. Now I really knew my place and role in the world.

My grasp of materialism and dialectics did not end on that serious and sombre note. It also further opened up to me the worlds of literature and art and psychology and personal relations and also dare I say it, science. Instead of seeing everything as fixed, instead of seeing everything as this is this and that is that, instead of seeing things as being just one thing, instead of seeing things in isolation, instead of being unable to see where things came from and what elements of different worlds they contained, I came to see things in context and also as always changing and developing, as containing within themselves many different elements of many things. I came to see that I had to view all as part of a process, part of many interlocking processes, as part of many interlocking always changing processes. I came to see that I had to view anything that was said or done not just in and of itself but by whom it was said or done, why it was said and done, where it was said or done, when it was said and done, and on and on and on. That all had to be seen in context and in an ever moving, ever shifting context, in fact, in ever moving, ever shifting contexts of ever changing time. And not just be seen in a one-sided way but in a many-sided way, not just in and of itself but to see that anything that was done, anything that was said, must not be seen in a simple, one-sided way. What an exciting world I was coming to inhabit. It was like swimming in a great ocean with great huge waves raising me up and surging me forward and back and up and down and below the surface and above the surface and forward and back in never ending movement and change. I was beside myself with excitement with my new method of thought. The tides flowing and ebbing, the waves crashing and withdrawing, the oceans calm and rough, how great it was to be alive with my new knowledge.

My new dialectical materialist method of thought also allowed me to see and understand my family in a whole different way, how they were, how they came to be what they were. I came to empathise with them and on occasion when on my own I would weep for them. I came to see them also in context.

And myself. That was harder. I could understand where I had come from, the contradictions and experiences that had shaped me. I also understood I had to struggle to be a revolutionary. I also understood I had to be strong to be a revolutionary. But not only that, I had to be harder with myself than with others. If I empathised with myself too much, 'understood' myself too much, I would maybe end up a small farmer in Donegal. Not a revolutionary socialist. It was the contradiction of the dialectic. I had to fight the ideas of my family but I had to empathise with them. I had to fight the ideas which sought to conquer me but not empathise too much with myself personally as this could make me soft and incapable of being a revolutionary. It was the magical, contradictory, explosive shooting stars of the dialectic.

On other fronts, a grasp of dialectical materialism also enlightened my world, made it more exciting, more beautiful. Van Gogh again. Now with my grasp of dialectical materialism I could go some way to understanding where he came from and how he came, what had formed him. I read his book of letters to his brother, *Dear Theo*, I looked at the prints of his paintings. I would later see his actual paintings in Amsterdam and Paris. I saw them with a totally different eye. Were his great swirly brilliantly coloured starry nights not the endless universes in which we lived? I would learn later that astronomy and physics would see what they saw in their telescopes and through their studies as corresponding to Van Gogh's great swirling skies. Van Gogh had 'nailed it'. Van Gogh's paintings, the paintings of this man of 'exaltation', the paintings which he said 'came to him as in a dream', were the real reality.

And Joyce's *Finnegans Wake*. Words and half words and strings of letters which did not even make words in any traditional way of understanding. But which corresponded to the thoughts conscious and unconscious in our heads, thoughts forming and merging and re-emerging in our heads. Was this not like the great swirling universes of Van Gogh's night skys? Only in this instance Joyce took what entered into our eyes and ears, what came together in our brains, both consciously but perhaps even more importantly unconsciously, and put this down, not like Van Gogh in paint and canvas but put its down in words and half words, in the particular order of the words, in strings of letters. It took Van Gogh in his times of exaltation to capture the real reality in paint and on canvas. It too Joyce in his times of exaltation to capture the real reality in the words and 'words' in the pages of his books. It was said that Joyce on occasion would pass out as he struggled to capture the real reality in his words and strings of letters. I could understand that. Consider these words of Joyce: 'I see the ruin of all space, shattered glass and toppled masonry and time one livid final flame.' Such staggering shocking beauty, such a correspondence with the threat to humanity from nuclear war. This, I imagine, like Van Gogh with his paintings came to Joyce as in a dream.

Then there was Einstein. Without any formal training in art or literature I had a hard time grasping the greats in these fields such as Van Gogh and Joyce. My situation was even worse when it came to science, to physics. But even there with my understanding of dialectics I was able to get a half a sliver of a glimpse of what Einstein was saying. Space, time, all related to one another, weight, gravity, all related to one another, and not only that as all things were always and ever changing so also were space, time, gravity. There were no permanence, there were no fixed straight lines. All was relative. There was no permanent fixed force of gravity. Now time not fixed, that was hard but I fought with it. The excitement of it. That Einstein was something. Spent his life proving that the dialectic applied to all.

As I grasped the dialectic I thought more about music. Especially what is called classical music. As a child I thought that the conductor of an orchestra just stood up in front of the orchestra and waved his or her baton as a way of egging on the musicians. Then with my grasping of the dialectic and thinking more about music I came to understand that the conductor was pulling together the various parts of the orchestra, combining them with their various sounds, relating them to each other, combining them into one wondrous whole. Well wondrous if the conductor was good at his or her job and the musicians likewise. I thought about the orchestras as similar to the way the world working class could work together. I had a friend who was a conductor of an orchestra and who wrote a paper on the relationship of colours to music. Everything was related, everything was related in a dialectical way. I wished I could play the violin. Now playing the violin, there was a dialectical process. The 'dead' instrument the violin, the hands and head and ears and life experience of the player, the head of the composer, possibly long dead, who composed the music, the mathematics of composing and writing down the music and merging this with the feelings and emotions and not only the feelings and emotions of the composer him or herself but also the feelings and emotions of the players and the listeners. The players, the composer, the audiences all their past experiences and immediate moods and consciousness, all merged together to produce the sound.

I thanked the lot of them, Marx, Engels, Lenin, Luxemburg, Trotsky, Van Gogh, Joyce, Einstein. I thanked all those in the cultures of the old societies in Africa, Asia the Americas the recordings of whose knowledges has all but been wiped out by the savagery of capitalism and imperialism. I thanked those who had developed the conscious understanding of the method of thought known as dialectical materialism, this way of thinking that I was increasingly grasping and which was continually, and more and more, opening my eyes. I was more and more able to see that the struggle was to understand what was in the heads of these greats by seeing how it had got there, that is the role of all life, human and all life, in providing the raw material which allowed these greats to understand and fight to express.

I was also more and more able to see what was in my head and how it had got there. In all cases it was the material world outside, outside my head, and reflected as thoughts inside my head. This was what it was all about.

Again I wished I could play the classical violin. Again I wished I could better understand what Van Gogh said when he said that painting would become more like music than like sculpture. Play the violin and with the greatest gentleness come to those notes, produce those notes that brought the whole world and all life to our immediate existence and presence. Produce those notes that made us on occasion sit motionless and on other occasions twist to try and let them into us and transform us if only momentarily.

Dialectics and getting even a sliver of a fraction of what Einstein was saying gave me a clue to the biggest picture of all, that is the universe or rather the universes, and the galaxies. I was walking back to Bethnal Green tube station in London one day when it hit me. The scientists said that the evidence from the telescopes and satellites showed that the planets and stars we could see were rushing apart. But if everything was always changing and developing where did the expanding universe of which I was part fit in, if everything changed not in a straight line but in a contradictory fashion, steps forward and steps back, where did the my expanding universe fit in? It could not keep expanding in the one direction forever. This would deny dialectics. It was then I understood.

If our universe was expanding then the universe or universes next door must be contracting. Wasn't everything always moving and changing and developing? Wasn't everything matter in motion? Then this must mean that our expanding universe must be forcing the next door universes to contract. There could not be just one universe ever expanding in one direction. That was it. There were a never-ending number of universes and galaxies some expanding and some contracting. The, whatever they were, the universes, the galaxies, had no beginning in space or time, they were endless in their contracting and expanding in their space and time. This was the world I lived in. It had no beginning or ending in time and no beginning or ending in space. Momentarily I felt a bit unimportant to say the least.

Another thought came to me. Inevitably our universe would at some time reverse itself and contract. Would we all be crushed up into tiny pieces? I laughed to myself. I would be long gone by then. This understanding of the universes and galaxies was frightening and exhilarating and staggering and challenging all at the one time. But that was my world. And I embraced it and smiled and bared my teeth at it all at the one time. I laughed out loud in excitement and wonder. I looked around me to see did anybody see me do so as I descended the stairs down to Bethnal Green tube.

I glorified in my new understanding. My consciousness was in consonance with the universes. I was exhilarated and delighted. The big picture was a wonderful thing to have a hold of. I thanked the world in which I lived for teaching me to think in a dialectical materialist manner. I thanked my experiences for helping me to see that I lived in a dialectical materialist world and how the dialectical materialist manner in which this world existed was reflected in my brain and in my thoughts and consciousness. This is what and who and how and where I was.

CHAPTER 20

IRELAND AND THE THEORY OF THE PERMANENT (OR UNINTERRUPTED) REVOLUTION

WHILE CELEBRATING my new consciousness I was reminded that I was not as smart as I thought I was. And also that knowing something and applying that knowledge in practice were not the same things. I was speaking at a meeting in London one evening when I was approached by a young man. He said: 'I was interested in what you had to say. I am wondering what is your position on Ireland and Trotsky's theory of the permanent revolution?' I was struck dumb. This was the first time I had thought of Trotsky's theory of the permanent or uninterrupted revolution in relation to Ireland. It was like the time the young man in Canada had asked me about Joyce. I had said who is Joyce? I had never heard of him. I was humiliated and enraged at my ignorance. Out of my readings and discussions that flowed from this humiliation I learnt about Joyce. And out of my humiliation at not being able to answer this young man about Trotsky's theory of the permanent or uninterrupted revolution and Ireland I learnt about Ireland and the theory of the permanent or uninterrupted revolution. I owe that young man a debt. Just like I owe that young man in Canada a debt. Humiliation, like almost everything else, if responded to properly can be a helpful experience. Again the dialectic.

I had learnt that society, that history developed on a materialist basis, and that in the present period capitalism was struggling to maintain its hold over society and keep the working class down. At the same time the working class was striving unconsciously, and on occasion consciously, to rise up and take power. I had also learnt that there were different levels of development in different societies. The capitalist classes in the economically advanced countries, the imperialist countries, had emerged first and carried out their tasks, that is, ended feudalism, unified their national territories, distributed the land to the peasantry, built modern home markets and a world market, established powerful military machines and went out and dominated the rest of the world. The result was that the capitalist class and the capitalist systems in the less developed countries such as Ireland were restricted in their development. Trotsky described this as the law of combined and uneven development. A capitalist world existed. But the component parts of this capitalist world, while combined, were unevenly developed within this capitalist combination.

The capital and power of the advanced capitalist, the imperialist countries, penetrated the less developed countries, keeping the local capitalist classes weak. At the same time this penetration strengthened the working class in these countries through the industries it developed there. This working class, along with the working class which worked in infrastructure and other sectors in these countries, was strengthened and the result was that this further frightened and intimidated the local weak capitalist class, further undermined its confidence and capability.

So in the countries where capitalism came late on the scene of history, such as Ireland, the capitalist class was not able to carry out its historic tasks. Weak and dominated by British imperialism and threatened by its own working class, the Irish capitalist class was not able to carry out the tasks of its own capitalist or bourgeois revolution. These tasks of the Irish capitalist class were as in other countries which were dominated by imperialism: to overthrow and drive out imperialism, to unify the national territory, to end feudalism, to develop modern capitalist agriculture and to build a modern economy and a modern home market.

Trotsky, in his theory of the permanent revolution, concluded that in societies such as Ireland that came late on to the scene of history, the capitalist class could not carry out its tasks, could not carry out its revolution, so as a result these tasks had to be taken on by the working class. The working class had to take power, and carry out those tasks of the capitalist or bourgeois revolution that were in its interests, these were ending feudalism and driving out imperialism. But Trotsky also explained that the working class could not stop there, it had to move on directly, uninterruptedly, to carry out its own socialist tasks. These were to take the dominant sectors of the economy out of private hands, out of the hands of the capitalist class and imperialism, and put them under the collective democratic ownership and control of the working class and on this basis develop a democratic socialist economy and while doing so simultaneously spread its revolution internationally. It was a brilliant flash of thought, a brilliant colliding of the synapses, a product of a moment of exaltation of Trotsky. With it Trotsky was able to avoid being imprisoned by the mechanical method of thought which saw the stages of development which had been the experience of the advanced capitalist countries being looked to as examples that had to be followed mechanically by all countries. It was also an example of how Trotsky used the dialectical method, change takes place, but not always in a straight line, not one plodding foot mechanically plodding after the other.

As I grasped Trotsky's ideas I realised that I had instinctively been to some extent working along the lines of the permanent revolution in Ireland but did not know it. As I thought more about this I realised that while I had an understanding of the dialectical method there was also the question of how conscious I was of using this method and my skill in using this method. I need to improve in both these areas.

In spite of what Trotsky said about the inability of the capitalist class in countries such as Ireland, which were dominated by the powerful imperialist countries, to carry out their tasks, in some countries, one such was Ireland, some of these tasks had been carried out or partially carried out. How was this so? I was back again to the dialectic, to the uneven manner in which things changed and developed.

In the latter half of the 1800s, the British capitalist class was fighting on three fronts, warding off its rivals internationally who were trying to end its domination of the seas and its number one place in the world; keeping down its own working class which was trying to rise to its feet through organisations such as the Chartists and the new trade unions; and at the same time fighting against the Land League, that is the peasantry in Ireland. Fighting on all three fronts was too much for it. So British imperialism retreated from one of them. It bought out, subsidised the buying out, of the Anglo Irish landlord class in Ireland and ended feudalism there. It did this through the passing of the Land Acts. The Irish capitalist class were not able to carry out its task of ending feudalism in Ireland so another class, in this case the British imperialist class, for its own reasons stepped in and carried out this task of the Irish capitalist class. Again I was confronted with the twist of the dialectic.

Ending imperialist rule, unifying the national territory under its own control, that is the national question, and building a modern home market and economy, these were the remaining tasks of the Irish capitalist class, part of the Irish capitalist or bourgeois revolution. Between 1916 and 1922 the uprising and War of Independence were faced with achieving these tasks. But in these struggles the weak Irish capitalist class was either missing or even at times supporting imperialism. These battles were fought on a nationalist basis by a section of the working class, the remnants of the poor peasantry and some intellectuals. This war ended with a civil war, and a partial and limited independence for the twenty-six Southern counties while the Northern six counties remained directly controlled by British imperialism. Irish capitalism was proven previously to be unable to end feudalism and was now showing itself also unable to unify the national territory. But this did not mean that nothing changed. Feudalism was ended by British imperialism when it bought out the Anglo Irish landlord class and it lost direct political and military control of twenty-six of the thirty-two counties of Ireland in the War of Independence.

While it could not unify the national territory or drive British imperialism from the Northern six counties, the stunted weak Irish capitalist class tried to develop a modern economy and home market in the twenty-six counties it did control. It tried to do this by keeping out British and foreign capital. The result was a disaster. The weak Irish capitalist class did not have the capital or the resources or the skill to compete on the world market and to develop the economy and build a modern capitalist country. In the four decades after it gained its independence, Southern Ireland sank further into stagnation and extreme poverty. Over this period one of every two Irish workers had to emigrate to find work. As well as being unable to end feudalism, as well as being unable to unify and make independent its territory, Irish capitalism was unable to carry out this other one of its tasks, that is, develop a vibrant healthy capitalist economy and home market.

In the 1960s, Irish capitalism admitted defeat, took down its capital controls and grovelled at the feet of British and foreign capital, invited in foreign capital, and at the same time opened up trade with the Northern six counties. The result was some economic development but with a mountain of debt and eventually a collapsed economy. Even with the help of foreign capital and the money that came later from the European Union and with setting extremely low tax rates for foreign capital the Irish capitalist class would prove itself unable to develop a vibrant modern home market and economy.

The Celtic tiger would come decades later. It gave the illusion of success. It was based on subsidies from the European Union, low taxes for, that is the bribing of, foreign companies and a mountain of debt. As the world economy went into recession in 2008 the Irish economy was exposed for the shell game it was. It collapsed under its mountain of debt, fell into recession, and the country was left with new roads and big houses which their owners could not afford. The failure of Irish capitalism to build a vibrant and modern and internationally competitive economy remained.

As a result, when the Troubles broke out in the North in the late 1960s, weak Irish capitalism was faced with elements of the capitalist or bourgeois revolution still to be resolved. These were an underdeveloped economy dominated by imperialism and a divided country with a section of it under direct control of British imperialism. The tasks of unifying the national territory and driving out imperialism and developing a vibrant modern home market and economy were and would remain, beyond it. The weak economy in Southern Ireland was no attraction to the Protestant working class in the North and along with other things cut across any effort to unite the country. Irish capitalism with its weak economy and its inability to provide for its own working class was terrified to try and unite the country and instead left British imperialism with its political and military might to control things in the North. The theory of the permanent revolution applied dialectically was a great help to me.

It explained that I was right in my conclusion that the Irish capitalist class, no wing of it could play a progressive role. It could not drive out imperialism, unite the country or develop the economy. It explained to me that the only progressive class in Ireland was the working class. It was the only progressive class because it was organised throughout the whole island in its unions, it was objectively united in its common interests for better wages and conditions. And it could only achieve these ends of better wages and conditions if it united and fought together. The theory of the permanent or uninterrupted revolution helped me to understand that the working class had to be united in struggle and take power into its own hands and overthrow capitalism and establish a socialist society and go on to spread the socialist revolution internationally, only this would solve the country's problems. As I understood this I realised that I was standing in the traditions of Trotsky.

However, the more I understood Trotsky's theory in the years ahead the more I came to realise that there was one area to which I, and also The Militant, with whom I had been discussing and eventually joined, had not been giving enough emphasis. This was the international aspect. Trotsky had explained that the working class in the less developed countries had to take power and carry out the capitalist tasks and move on immediately to the socialist tasks if the problems of those societies were to be resolved. He also explained that the revolutions in those societies had to be spread internationally. At the time of the Russian revolution he and Lenin both said that unless the revolution was spread to the advanced capitalist countries such as Germany, it would not survive. In fact both of them said they would sacrifice the Russian revolution if this would mean a successful revolution in the more advanced capitalist economy and society of Germany. It took longer than these revolutionaries thought but what they feared was exactly what happened. The Russian revolution was isolated in a backward country, cut off from the revolutionary upheavals and the working class in the advanced capitalist countries and as a result capitalism was restored to the former Soviet Union. Again the dialectic, steps forward and steps back.

While I had always raised the need to link with the working class in England, Scotland and Wales and internationally in my work, neither I nor The Militant gave enough emphasis to this aspect of our ideas or raised it in the proper way. We tended to speak of the international aspect of our work more in terms of solidarity and workers' unity in the interests of solidarity, not in terms of the process of revolution in England, Scotland, Wales and Ireland and internationally. The issue was not just seeking solidarity between the working classes in all these other countries, it was the struggle to bring about the socialist revolution in all these other countries including Ireland.

I was later to change my position in relation to the socialist revolution and Britain and Ireland and borders. I maintained my position of the need to have the socialist revolution in all these countries. I also maintained my position on the objective of a socialist federation of Britain and Ireland. However I reviewed the issue of the borders within such a federation. I came to believe that if the socialist revolution developed first and was successful in England, the economically and politically and militarily most powerful country, and swept over the borders into Scotland, Wales and Ireland it could be possible to go directly to a Socialist United Ireland within a socialist federation of Britain and Ireland.

However if this was not the case and if the socialist revolution did not take place first in England Scotland and Wales and spread to Ireland, other possibilities would have to be considered. British imperialism with the backing of Irish capitalism would try and put down any revolution in any of these countries but especially Ireland, through divide and rule. Specifically it would as shown historically try and turn the Protestant worker against the Catholic worker in Ireland and drown the revolution in a sectarian blood bath. It would use these measures to stir up division in Scotland, Wales and England also where there were large Irish background populations and differences in religion and nationality. In this situation, to call in advance for a Socialist United Ireland could be to assist capitalism to deepen division and put down the revolution in sectarian conflict and civil war in Ireland. So I changed my position.

I increasingly felt that in order to undermine capitalism's sectarian divide and rule strategy, it would be best to raise the demand for a socialist Federation of Britain and Ireland within which the borders would be determined by events and democratic discussion and interaction. Leave open what would be the internal borders. One of the possibilities would be a socialist federation of Ireland and within the Northern part of the federation guarantees of the rights for the Catholic minority and within the Southern part of the federation guarantees of the rights of the non-Catholic population, Protestant, Muslim, atheists, etc. Atheists were becoming a significant section of the Southern population. And of course within the Northern part of any federation the rights of Protestants would also have to be guaranteed.

In such a federation, especially within a Northern Ireland socialist state, the possibility of the establishment of cantons based on the different religious groupings in the North would have to be a considered. A form of cantons already existed in the North, as was shown with the different villages and neighbourhoods with their different flags and painted sidewalks. Cantons existed in Switzerland with different linguistic and ethnic and national groups having their own areas and local legislative bodies within the overall country. This might be the best way of standing against capitalism's efforts to derail the socialist revolution by using the Orange card, by whipping up religious sectarianism, by divide and rule, by cultivating the siege mentality of the Protestant population by drowning any attempt at a workers' revolution in a sectarian blood bath.

One result of my inadequate emphasis and slant, of The Militant's inadequate emphasis and wrong slant on the international aspect of the struggle, was I and The Militant tended to be always on the defensive, always explaining that we were neither unionist nor nationalist, when we should have been making the case much more strongly that we were internationalist and for the revolution in Ireland, England, Scotland and Wales and internationally and the order in which it would develop was immaterial to us. In fact we should have been going even further and saying that if it was a choice between the socialist revolution in Ireland and the socialist revolution in England then we would chose the socialist revolution in England, the much more economically developed and powerful country with the much stronger working class.

As I read and discussed more, I realised that two leaders of the movement in the 1916–1921 struggle for independence were groping towards aspects of Trotsky's theory of the permanent revolution. One of these was James Connolly, the most important, the most theoretically capable, the most determined of all of Ireland's workers' leaders. He explained, as he put it, that the 'cause of Ireland is the cause of Labour and the cause of Labour is the cause of Ireland'. And most importantly, he pointed out the weak cowardliness of Irish capitalism when he wrote: 'Irish manufacture was weak, and consequently had not an energetic capitalist class with sufficient public spirit and influence to prevent union.' The 'Union' he referred to was Ireland being ruled directly by the London parliament and British imperialism. He was saying here that Irish capitalism could not throw out

British imperialism. This was in line with Trotsky's theory of the permanent revolution.

Unfortunately Connolly would yield somewhat on this position when he took part in the premature uprising of 1916. But in spite of this his ideas were so threatening to Irish capitalism as well as to British imperialism that in spite of him being wounded he was taken out, tied to a chair and shot. The leaders of the Irish capitalist class such as William Martin Murphy supported his murder. In fact called for the British military to continue with the executions of the leaders of the 1916 uprising because they said the worst of them, that is Connolly, was still alive. Rather than leading the Irish national revolution, Murphy and his class, the Irish nationalist capitalist class, who had starved the Dublin workers back to work in the 1913 lockout, bayed along with British imperialism for Connolly's blood. That they did so was a further confirmation of Trotsky's theory of the permanent or uninterrupted revolution.

Another leader of the forces fighting for independence in that period was Liam Mellowes. In a debate from his prison cell with the extreme right wing Catholic nationalist and supporter of capitalism de Valera, he wrote the following: 'Under the Republic, all industry will be controlled by the state for the workers' and farmers' benefit. All transport, railways, canals, etc., will be operated by the state – the republican State – for the benefit of workers and farmers. All banks will be operated by the State for the benefit of Industry and Agriculture, not for the purpose of profit making by loans, mortgages, etc. That the land of the aristocracy (who support the Free State and the British connection), will be seized and divided amongst those who can and will operate it for the Nation's benefit.'

In this statement, Mellowes leaves no doubt he was looking to move beyond capitalism. Like Connolly he wanted the struggle to go on to where it ended capitalism. Like Connolly, he too was groping in the direction of the permanent revolution. It is no surprise that he, like Connolly, was also taken out and shot. In his case by the other wing of the so-called independence forces, the Free Staters, who represented the weak Irish capitalist class and who wanted to make a deal with British imperialism and to maintain capitalism.

There was another important aspect of the developments at this time which was related to the weakness of the Irish capitalist class and which would go on to shape the Southern Irish state and also affect the Northern state that would develop in the decades ahead. Irish capitalism was very weak in the new Southern state. It had played practically no role in bringing it about. It had little authority. It needed and sought allies. It looked to the hierarchy of the Catholic Church for allies. In return for the hierarchy of this organisation preaching and organising for capitalism through its huge apparatus and resources at every turn, in return for this hierarchy helping put down any left movement wherever such appeared, a deal was done with the new ruling capitalist class in Southern Ireland which gave the Catholic hierarchy enormous power and influence in the new state.

It was given control over the schools, hospitals, social legislation, given women and children as slaves to work in their laundries and earn them money, given control over young people imprisoned in industrial 'schools' and so on. Things even went so far that the Southern state in its constitution would declare itself to be a Catholic state. It was the weakness of Irish capitalism that allowed, in fact promoted, the Catholic Church hierarchy to become so powerful in the South. It is no exaggeration to say the Catholic hierarchy became a central component of the ruling class in the South of Ireland. The weakness of Irish capitalism and its deal with the Catholic hierarchy were part of what led to the monstrous crimes of that organisation that have recently been uncovered. In all condemnation of these crimes, Irish capitalism must also be pointed to as sharing the responsibility. It was Irish capitalism's weakness that led to its deal with the Catholic hierarchy and which gave the Catholic hierarchy the power and opportunity to carry out these crimes.

This deal between Irish capitalism and the Catholic hierarchy also fuelled the arguments of the Protestant organisations in the North that the South was a Catholic sectarian state and assisted the Northern Protestant elite and British imperialism to convince the Protestant working class that the North should be a Protestant state for a Protestant people. This stoked the fires of the sectarian conflicts that were to come and strengthened British imperialism in the North. The weakness of the Irish capitalist class and its inability to carry out its tasks, and the deal it made with the Catholic hierarchy as a result, remain major factors in the troubles, economic, military and political of Ireland to this day.

My experiences over the 1968 period, my readings and discussions in Ireland over this period and in London in 1970 made things clearer to me than ever. The problems and crises in Ireland and internationally could not be solved on a capitalist basis. Only the working class, by carrying out a revolution and taking power and establishing a democratic socialist society in Ireland and spreading this internationally could solve the problems. And this could only be done if a mass international revolutionary organisation was built. This was the task. And towards achieving this task I dedicated my life.

In the course of my discussions and readings in London I learnt that in the past the working class had built international organisations to overthrow capitalism. These were known as the First, Second, Third and Fourth Internationals and came about over the period of the last half of the

1800s through the first half of the 1900s. All had some achievements but all failed in their attempts to overthrow international capitalism and take human society forward into a new historical phase, into a new socialist world. I resolved to try and help build a new international that this time would not fail. I returned to Ireland with this objective. I knew what I had to try to do.

However I also knew I could not build such an International on my own. I did not have the knowledge or resources. I had to join some existing organisation. This consumed my mind as I returned home from London in the autumn of 1970 and was to be a central part of all my thinking and of my work in the civil rights movement, the trade union and labour movement and the movement against repression in that period and the years ahead. How to build a mass revolutionary international, this was no small challenge, but it was what history demanded and therefore it was what I had to attempt.

CHAPTER 21

THE COLLECTIVE POWER – THE COLLECTIVE BRAIN OF THE WORKING CLASS

(HOW A SOCIALIST REVOLUTION CAN COME ABOUT – HOW A SOCIALIST SOCIETY WOULD WORK)

WHILE FIGHTING to understand capitalism, to understand the method of Marxism, to understand the big picture, I also tried to understand the concrete reality of my present world and the tasks I faced. If I was to convince others to help build a revolutionary socialist organisation and fight for socialism I would have to have a clear understanding of how a socialist society could be brought about and how it would work and what it would look like. For some reason this was an area where The Militant and all the Marxist groups were weak. I never had a single discussion on this issue with any group. Maybe it was that they did not think, consciously or unconsciously, they would ever get there? This was not good enough for me. I was changing my life, breaking my relations with my family and milieu to fight for the revolution. If I was going to do this I would have to know specifically how this could be done, have to know specifically how a new society would work. From my own readings and thinking about things and looking at events such as the Paris commune, the soviets' or workers' councils in the Russian revolutions, the Limerick soviet or workers' council, I became clear.

278

History showed that when the working class rose to its feet it sought to establish its own organisations, the Paris Commune in 1871, the workers' councils or soviets in Russia in 1905 and 1917, the Limerick soviet or workers' council in 1919, there were many other such examples. These were made up of elected representatives of the working class, in most cases overwhelmingly from the workplaces. These were the democratic working class centres of power, the organs through which the working class sought to take power away from the capitalist class, the organs through which the working class sought to express itself and rule, the organs through which and on which it would build the new society. The conclusion of Marxism was that it was on these organs of power, on these democratic organisations of the working class that would be built the new socialist world. I agreed with this. These organisations were the forms of rule of the working class. On occasions the peasantry, where they existed, had also thrown up peasant councils and sought to fight for their interests through these. With proper leadership from the working class through its workers' councils, these peasants' councils could be drawn together with, and under the leadership of, the workers' councils.

History showed that when the capitalist class was challenged it would resort to the most violent means to stay in power. It had used the most ferocious methods to get power and it would use the most ferocious methods to try to hold on to power. The working class had to learn from history and prepare. It had to arm itself theoretically, historically, organisationally and militarily. It had to educate itself as to what capitalism had done to get power and to hold power and it had to take measures to see that the capitalist class could not succeed in using these methods again to stay in power. It had to educate itself as to what the working class with the support of the peasantry did on the one occasion when it did take and hold power for a time, that is, in the 1917 Russian revolution. The working class had to have a knowledge of and a sense of history. It took capitalism five or more hundred years of the most violent slaughter and struggle to establish itself as the dominant system on the planet. The working class had only been trying to establish its system, international socialism, for less than two hundred years. It could not be judged to be a failure no more than capitalism three or four hundred years ago could have been judged to be a failure. The fact that no single country in the world came up to the standard, existed as a model, for the democratic international socialist model I stood for was not an argument for the failure of socialism. Time, history, had yet to make their judgement.

The working class had to draw the lessons of history. It had to arm itself, not only programmatically and theoretically, but also militarily and physically to be prepared to take on the capitalist class and its forces.

Capitalism did not come to rule the world using pacifist methods. Peaceful change would be preferable but such a view was not realistic, not shown to be correct by history. Capitalism took power using extreme violence, it would try to hold onto power with extreme violence. The working class, while arming itself theoretically and programmatically, had to also arm itself in other ways.

The Militant, in its correct objective of connecting with the existing consciousness of the working class and with its main base in Britain, put forward the demand for an enabling act to be presented in parliament by any Labour government. This enabling act to take over the 500 corporations which dominated the British economy and so open the door to socialism. This was correct as far as it went but it was incorrect in that The Militant left it there. The Militant did not explain that such a step would be met by the full power of the British and international capitalist class, it would seek to use all its power, including military power to prevent such a step. While supporting and putting forward this demand for an enabling act I always explained that this would not be tolerated by the British ruling class, or any ruling class, and such a step would have to be accompanied by the building of workers' councils in the workplaces and working class communities and the linking of these together to take on the capitalist reaction that would inevitably come. The Militant leadership in its correct aim to connect with the consciousness of the working class was making an opportunist concession to that consciousness. Instead of just in my own work putting forward the need for the building of workers' councils etc., when I later joined Militant I should have taken up a struggle in that organisation to change the policy of that organisation in that area. It was a mistake for me to think that as long as I was not making this concession, as long as I was explaining the need to build workers' councils etc., that was good enough, that things would work out. This was a mistake. I should have conducted a struggle within The Militant on this issue. I would later think that the fact that the main leaders of The Militant were based in Britain, with its relatively peaceful class relations was a factor in The Militant making this mistake.

I came to understand that the working class had to see that it had to seek to split and win over at least some sections of the state apparatus of capitalism, the armed forces and police, it had to win over scientists and others who had their fingers on the buttons of the nuclear and other weapons in order to disarm these weapons, it had to win over sections of these to the mass international revolutionary party of tens and hundreds of millions that it had to build. This mass international revolutionary party of tens and hundreds of millions had to learn these lessons and draw the necessary conclusions and build a mass fighting international organisation of tens and hundreds of millions to end capitalism. This mass revolutionary party, if it was built, would be the organisation through which the working class would end the rule of capitalism and imperialism and take the power into its own hands. It would then be able, by linking the workers' councils, and where they existed, the peasants' councils, together internationally, build a new democratic structure of power. This one based on the working class and peasantry and not the capitalist class.

Through its own democratic bodies, the workers' councils, and linking where they existed, with the peasants' councils, the working class would take the wealth of the world out of the hands of the capitalist class, out of private ownership, and collectivise it under working class ownership, control and management. The international working class, through its own organisations, the democratic workers' councils, linked together worldwide, and working with the peasants' councils where they existed, would have available to it the knowledge of what resources existed in the world. It would also have available to it the knowledge of what were the needs of society worldwide. Who better to know this than the working class and peasantry who produced and consumed the world's resources and products? These councils would link together on a world scale, and using the new technology would be able to work out what resources were available and what needs existed and with this knowledge could draw up a democratic, international, socialist, sustainable plan to meet these needs. The new technology, the new methods of communication would make this possible as never before. Different parties would exist which would discuss and debate the priorities for this new international socialist world order.

No more capitalism, no more private ownership of the means of production, distribution and exchange, no more capitalism with its falling rate of profit, with its addiction to profit, with its continual internal contradictions and wars and slaughters, with its destruction of the environment, with its climate change, with its destruction of the world's species, no more a tiny ruling class spewing out divide and rule to stay in power and to divide the majority, these evils would be ended. They would be ended because they were rooted in private ownership and capitalism and so when these were ended then the evils that flowed from them would also be ended. There would be no more nation states, no more national economies, no more anarchy of profit-mad capitalism, no more wars, no more destruction of the planet through climate change and pollution and the threat of nuclear war, but an international, democratic, collectively-owned, sustainable world economy.

Given the new technology and communications systems, all the people of the world could be involved in the discussions to draw up this international democratic world economy and plan. This plan could then be broken down economic sector by economic sector, industry by industry, workplace by workplace, community by community, worker by worker. Everybody would have a voice in assessing what resources were available and what needs existed and what were the priorities of production. And what should be the priorities of distribution. Everybody would have a voice in drawing up and implementing a democratic, international, sustainable plan; everybody would know what was possible, what was needed, what work they themselves had to do every day if the objectives of the democratic plan were to be reached. And also would know what would be possible if the objectives of the plan were met, what improvements in life such as a shorter working day, more and better housing, more resources for health care, education, for the arts, the better life for all that would be possible if the plan's objectives were met.

Working in this way, consciously discussing and deciding on the day-to-day work and life of society through its democratic workers' council structures, and where they existed peasant structures, an international network, consciously assessing and adjusting on a daily basis could be created. On this basis, it would be possible to bring into action as a conscious entity, as the central conscious entity which would determine the workings of the world, the collective brain of the working class. It would be possible to activate this collective brain in the task of democratically deciding how society would be run. Not a few billionaires running things, not some bureaucratic apparatus, not some billions of individuals trying to influence things on an individual basis, but the great collective democratic human brain, the great collective brain of the working class determining how things would work. Neither one political party deciding all as was the case under the Stalinist dictatorships but many political parties putting forward their views on how the international collectivised world economy would work, its priorities etc. Like all brains in all creatures including especially the human species the collective brain of the working class would not be some grey uniform entity but would be one living brilliantly coloured organism in continual living activity and creative explosive interacting thought and adjustment and decision making. This would be the future if there was to be a future for the human species and for life on earth as we know it. What a vision, what a step forward, the collective human brain, the collective brain of the working class. The collective brain of the working people of the world working and running things collectively. And of course in multi-colour and in interacting and clashing thought and this reflected in many parties and organisations of the working class.

Such a process would also be how the alienation of the working class which existed under capitalism would be ended. A socialist world based on a democratic, sustainable, socialist plan would be capable of assessing the resources of the world and drawing up a plan for how these resources should be used and for how the fruits of such a plan would be distributed, and capable of drawing up a plan for our daily work and the distribution of the product of that daily work. The world's population would all be involved in adjusting the work rate, the hours of work, the priorities. Society's work rate, society's priorities, society's distribution, all would be decided democratically by the collective brain of the working class. We would no longer be alienated from the fruits of our labour. We would no longer see the products we made, the services we provided disappear into a system over which we had no control. No the fruits of our labour we would know where they were going to and we would know how they related to how many hours a day, how many days a week we should work. We would decide collectively what labour we would carry out, how the fruits of that labour would be distributed, this was the way the alienation that existed under capitalism would be ended. This would be more possible today than ever before given the explosive development of new technology and communications of the past decades.

In those societies where there was a significant peasant class, they also (on the basis of revolutionary events, as has been shown in the past) have tended to throw up their own peasant councils. These would have the knowledge of what was available in their economic sectors and also what was possible. They would have the knowledge of older and other ways of agricultural production which had existed or were being wiped out by capitalist profit-mad methods. The food, the water, the air are all being polluted. The peasant class, working together collectively with socially responsible scientists rooted in the working class, and the peasant class, and with the democratic, collective brain of the working class could open up a whole new sustainable world of agriculture. They could bring together the old traditional ways and merge these where it was possible and conducive to health and sustainability with new ways and the world's population could be fed, the world's resources could be sustained and the world's non-human species could be treated in a humane fashion.

From this new way of working in society, a new consciousness would evolve. All would become conscious of the workings of society and their place in that society and the decision making process that existed and in which they would play an equal role to everybody else. Care for all would come to be understood to be a superior way to live rather than the savage individualism, racism, sexism, nationalism, ageism of capitalism. The tendency towards a new collective consciousness already existed in the working class and in the new society, with the collective ownership, with the democratic, collective, international decision making process this would be encouraged and developed and express itself and become the dominant tendency in the new society. This new consciousness would evolve on the basis of the collectivised and democratic and international material conditions and foundation of production and control and management and distribution and exchange. An international socialist world with an international collectively owned, democratic, sustainable, socialist plan would give rise to an international, collective, democratic, socialist, consciousness. On a grand scale, social conditions would determine social consciousness. This would become the ethos of the new international, democratic, sustainable socialist society. This was my international, socialist alternative.

Alienation could be ended in this new socialist world. With the new technology and with the international unified democratic workers' and peasants' councils all people would be able to be part of the conscious international collective drawing up of a democratic socialist sustainable world plan. All would be part of deciding what that plan should be and what our daily work should be to meet that plan, and how the fruits of that sustainable plan should be distributed. All would be part of working together consciously with all the working people of the world. Everybody's everyday work would be able to be seen as part of the international, democratic whole, seen as part of the best way for all to live, part of being best for all and for the planet. No more would any individual be alienated from their world or their work or the product of their work and the rest of the species and what the human species produced. All would be a conscious integrated part of their world. The collective human species giving rise to the moving into action of the collective brain and the collective consciousness.

An essential part of the ending of the alienation that existed under capitalism would be that the international working class and the world's population would be able to see what was being produced, how much was being produced and how this production should be distributed. And as part of this see what work time would be necessary to produce what would be necessary to satisfy the needs of the world's population and the planet. On this basis the international collective brain of the working class, working through the network of workers' and peasants' councils would be able to decide the length of the working day. In this way everybody's work rate would be able to be linked to society's and the planet's needs. And with the new technology, with the ending of the waste and corruption and destruction of capitalism the working day for all people could be reduced. The world's population would no longer be alienated from what it produced. The world's population would be able to see what was being produced and from this would be able to determine how long it had to work every day for all to have the best possible life. Working people would no longer be alienated from their work and the product of their work.

My understanding leapt forward by the hour. It was the summer of 1970. I was twenty-six years old. I was in London. It was the greatest of times for me. I was so excited I could barely contain myself. Every day I saw better who I was and what was my role. I was a fighter with the international working class to over throw capitalism and to take over and collectivise the wealth of the world economy under workers' management and control. I was no longer declassed. I was an international socialist revolutionary, a builder in the fight for an international, democratic, socialist, sustainable world. At last I knew the tasks of history, knew the tasks that faced the human species, knew my own responsibility as part of this. Knew my place was as part of the working class, fighting with the working class to change the world. I was home at last. I celebrated.

Now that I was certain I knew my role in the world I had a drink of alcohol for the first time. I had a few whiskies for the first time. Along with a female friend and Comrade we had a few wee Powers. Personal restrictions, some that I did not even know I still had, were swept aside in an explosion of energy. For the first time, my physical and psychological and political being combined in unrestrained sexuality and laughter. It was good to at last know my place in the world. It was good to be an international socialist revolutionary. It was good to have a whiskey. It was good to no longer be afraid to be free. This feeling was real and powerful. But in spite of all my recently acquired understanding I was still being a bit un-dialectical, a bit one-sided. Yes, I was more liberated than ever before but as I should have known from my understanding of the dialectic, from my new consciousness, nothing unfolds in a straight line, all phenomena had their positives and negatives, all phenomena has to be seen in their all-sided completeness. I would learn more about the negatives later. In the meantime I rejoiced in the positive, that is, my new understanding of how the world worked, what was the alternative to that world, and what was my place in the struggle for that alternative.

PART 4

TO THE GRINDSTONE

CHAPTER 22

THE LEAVING – THIS TIME FOR GOOD

WITH MY STUDIES and discussions over, I returned to Ireland. I did so convinced of the need for the world socialist revolution, with my view of how this could be brought about and as part of this, the need for myself to help build a revolutionary international organisation. There were still a few loose ends poking at me about building the revolutionary international, but the overall objective was clear. In the meantime I had to make a living. I caught the tail end of the fishing season, did some odd jobs carting goods for local farmers and merchants, did some work around what was now my mother's farm and continued with the smuggling. I lived in my caravan and had to pay no rent. I more than got by.

My main preoccupation was trying to think further about the whys and wherefores of building the international revolutionary organisation. I struggled for a time with my motivation. I would be giving up the good money, my big car, my caravan, my boat, and being able to get up every day and look out across the ocean and see its tides and waves and smell its smells. And have my friends come visit.

I worried was I thinking about giving all this up because of some remnant of unconscious Christian guilt about helping the poor. I felt I had to be acting for the right reason. But the more I thought about it the more it became clear. Every day the world brought new information to me through my senses. This told me that capitalism threatened life on earth as we knew it. The information I received also told me that millions of people in many parts of the world were fighting this threat and trying to change things for the better.

So I had a choice to make. I could deny the cruel realities of capitalism. I could ignore all the struggles that were taking place against capitalism. But if I did I would have to block out the information that came into my senses every day. If I did I would need some way to do this, some place to hide from this information. Knowing Irish society at that time this would most likely have been in the bottle. Or it could have been by developing cynical, stupid ideas, blaming the world's problems on people of other races or religions or nationalities or sex or sexual orientations rather than capitalism. Or it could have resulted in some sort of mental disability as I tried to deny what my senses told me.

I imagined myself in my fishing boat one night and hearing of a new attempt at revolution somewhere in the world. How would I react to that? It would depend. If I had decided not to be part of the movement for change I would have to close my mind. I would have to shut out the inspiration that such a struggle would threaten to give me. In doing so I would have to kill off the best part of me. So that was it. Involving myself in the movement for change, joining a revolutionary collective organisation would not be a sign of some remnant of Christian guilt but would instead be enlightened self-interest. Being part of a revolutionary movement, of a revolutionary international to fight to end capitalism was not only best for the working class struggle and for humanity but also best for me. It would strengthen and develop what was best in me. Being part of a revolutionary international organisation of struggle and moving away from individualism was best, not only for myself, but also to the extent that I could influence things, was best for the working class and for humanity. It would mean that I would be in consonance with the needs of the world and of history.

Once I became clear on this it was easy to decide what organisation to join. The Militant was head and shoulders above the others. It unconditionally opposed imperialism and capitalism and Stalinism, it unconditionally opposed Nationalism, it unconditionally opposed Loyalism, it unconditionally opposed the IRA campaign and stood instead for working class unity, socialism and internationalism. It was far superior in its ability to explain ideas, to orient to and connect with the working class. I called Ted Grant in London from a coin box in the Bogside and told him I was going to join. When I told Ted that I was formally joining in my mind's eye I could see him rubbing his hands together and over the phone I could hear him chuckling with glee. So I became part of what was known as The Militant, an international, revolutionary, socialist, organisation.

As I made this commitment to join Militant I continued with my political work locally in the civil rights movement and the remnants of the Labour Parties and the Young Socialists. But pressures were building. A letter was sent to my mother's address. It contained a passport-sized photo of myself with a printed code number across the bottom. It was from a police file. There was an unsigned note with it. 'Be careful we found this on one of the Prods. They are after you.' The Prods was a nickname for Protestants. This meant I was being targeted by the Loyalist death squads which were becoming active at that time in assassinations. I was to hear that some local loyalists were discussing amongst themselves and saying I should have been shot a long time ago.

One day I was driving from Strabane to Derry and in the boot of my car I had posters for a meeting at which Bernadette Devlin was to speak. I was stopped by a patrol of the Ulster Defence Regiment, (UDR) that is, the part-time police. It would have been more accurately named the Protestant Defence Regiment. Its membership was sectarian to a person. Some of them were former schoolmates of mine and one of them was my brother-in-law. He swaggered over to the officer in charge and said: 'Do you want some help with this boy.' This was the man I had loaned money to some years before to buy a site on which to build a house for him and my sister.

It was a beautiful summer's day. 'Stand over there and put your hands up and do not move,' the officer, a local farmer, growled at me. 'You,' he said to my brother in law, 'go back to your place.' To one of his other underlings he said pointing to me: 'If he moves shoot him.' I thought of the posters in the boot. If they saw them they might lose it. I thought that maybe I would die that day. I looked out over the River Foyle flowing towards Derry and the North Atlantic Ocean. It was okay. It was a beautiful place and day to die. It never occurred to me to pray to any god for help. I was proud. I was a fully convinced atheist.

But I did not need help from any god. There was a soccer match in Derry that day and supporters of Derry City were driving down from Strabane. The UDR patrol stopped them when they got to the roadblock at which I was being held. These supporters being Derry City fans from Strabane were all Catholics. They got out of their cars and gathered on the road confronting the UDR patrol and started to shout. 'Hey what are you doing with Throne? Leave Throne alone.' The officer of the patrol hesitated for a few minutes and then said: 'Okay move on.' And under his breath: 'We will get you next time.' I drove off passing my scowling brother-in-law as I did. I had been saved, not by any god but by Strabane workers.

I was constantly in danger of being arrested at this time. My photo was on the wanted list at the military checkpoint between Lifford and Strabane. I was not too worried about being locked up. What I was worried about was the affect this would have on my family, especially my mother and aunt. They would feel they would have to come and visit me. They would be doing so along with other mothers and relatives who would all be Republicans. This would be a very difficult for them. I wished that my family and I had similar views and could be united and I could have their support. I envied the Catholic youth in the civil rights movement and socialist groups whose families stood with them. This was not the case with me. I felt terrible for my mother and aunt and the pain I was causing them. But I had no choice. I had struggled too much to find my place in the world to throw this away now. I was an international revolutionary socialist and I was going to help build the revolutionary socialist international.

But I was committing myself to this work against an extremely difficult objective situation. The movement of 1968 to 1970 had been blocked and thrown back. *We Shall Overcome* had been replaced with *Sean South from Garryowen* and *The Sash my Father Wore*. There was a stampede to sectarianism on both sides of the religious divide. Building a movement based on working class unity and socialism and internationalism was just about impossible. At this time also my own safety became increasingly threatened. I was particularly hated by sections of the rising Protestant sectarian elements who saw me as a traitor who was selling out to the Catholics. They saw me as a white person would have been seen in the southern US who supported and was involved in the civil rights movement there. I had to decide what to do.

It was a brisk spring day in 1970. The buds were coming out on the hedges and trees. The farmers were ploughing and getting ready to plant. I drove up the Coneyburrow Road from Lifford, turned right up the Haw Lane which took me to the top of Croaghan Hill, the highest of the hills around. In the old days fires were lit on the top of Croaghan and other hills down to Derry to warn of the approach of the Vikings. I briefly wondered how the locals got the fires lit. They would have had no matches. But understanding that was not a priority for me that day.

I had fought against the ideas of my family. This had hurt them and myself very much. I had fought against the ideas of the Protestant milieu and culture into which I was born. I had fought against religious ideas of all kinds including the just about all-pervasive Catholic religion in Southern Ireland. None of this had been easy. Then I had went abroad in an effort to find an alternative. All this had hurt my family. When I returned for a time I was lost, I was in danger of sinking into an aimless life. I could not see any alternative. But eventually with the help of international events, the worldwide struggles, with the help of the Bogside Uprising, with my studies and readings and discussions of Marxism, I found my way to the struggle against capitalism and to becoming an international revolutionary socialist. I was pleased at this achievement. However it had not been easy. For my family it had been extremely wrenching.

As I sat there up on the top of Croaghan Hill I thought about what I had decided to do with my life. I thought about my mother and aunt who lived in the small farmhouse down on the side of the hill and whom I visited regularly. They could not in any way understand what I was doing. They could not be expected to understand. My activities were inexplicable to them, I brought them only pain. Now I was going to have to leave the area and them altogether and this would bring them even more pain. I needed to help build the international revolutionary organisation and I could not do this running about Lifford, Strabane and Lough Swilly. And I could not do it if I was shot in the head. I had to move. I had to leave them. I had to leave them alone in their little farm house. I grieved for us all.

I grieved also at having to leave the beauty of the rivers and valleys and the hills. I grieved at having to leave the three rivers, the smell of the heather, the grass and the trees, the powerful crooked oaks, the straight limbed mountain ashes, the year-long green firs, the badger's den, the rabbits' holes. I grieved at having to leave my mother and aunt to fend for themselves But I had to do what I understood history demanded, I had to do what I understood I had to do, that is try and help build the revolutionary socialist international.

I grieved also at having to leave my two dogs behind, the sheep dog and the wee ratter. I always had a sheepdog and a wee ratter. We spent a lot of time together both when I was working in the fields and when I was living in my caravan and fishing on the Swilly. They would stand with their front feet up on the rim of the boat looking out over the water. On occasion if they saw a fish they would even jump in. I would have to reach over, getting soaking wet in the process and pull them back in. I would be cursing them while at the same time laughing at their audacity. Now what would I do, I would have no dogs.

I sat up there on the top of Croaghan and stroked them as they lay with me for warmth. I looked over at the ruins of an old house where an old lady used to live. She was a relative of my family. When I was a child I developed mumps. I was taken to her and she put a rope halter round my neck and led me to where a solitary tree stood in the middle of a field, led me round the tree three times and back to her house. The tree was known as The Fairy Tree. The story was fairies danced around it at night. Naturally I did not believe this but my mumps did go away. Now I was going into the modern world of international socialist revolution and dialectical materialism. No longer to live amongst the rivers, hills, valleys, trees, fairy trees, or my two dogs. Mangled words of an old song drifted in and out of my head. Not going to live on a farm anymore. Have a head full ideas, they would drive me insane.

I drove back down from Croaghan Hill and over to the house of my mother and aunt. They were at home, working in the kitchen baking bread and cleaning up. When I came in they stopped made tea and set me down some food to eat. They looked at me. I saw it in their eyes. What hurtful news was I bringing them this time? I told them that I had to go and live in Dublin as I had to try and organise a revolutionary socialist international. And it was for them just 'blah ... blah ... blah ...'. They had no concept of what I was talking about. A revolutionary international. I had already broken their hearts by rejecting all they had worked to give to me. What could they do? They could only endure the pain and hurt. The pain was also in myself. I rose from their table and left the kitchen and the house and drove away, taking another and qualitatively greater step out of their lives. Their faces and eyes attempted to hold on to me and the life they had hoped would be for all of us.

CHAPTER 23

DUBLIN

IN CONSULTATION with leading members of The Militant in London I moved to Dublin in 1971. Dublin was the biggest city in Southern Ireland. Its population was almost as large as the rest of the country combined. It had a strong working class tradition going back to the 1913 Lockout. My move there was to build the revolutionary organisation. I believed that capitalism and Stalinism were destroying life on earth as we knew it and that these systems had to be overthrown. To do this a new mass revolutionary organisation of the working class had to be built. And not only that, the clock was ticking. I believed that capitalism and Stalinism had to be overthrown in the next five to ten years. Setting myself this rigid timetable was a sign of my inexperience and my not applying the method of dialectical materialism in a proper manner. However this belief and timetable dominated my move to Dublin and all aspects of my life.

I saw myself as playing a central role in building the new party of revolution in Southern Ireland, as helping to bring together the most combative, thinking and conscious workers into a revolutionary organisation, that is The Militant, and in helping this layer of workers orient to and integrate with the broader mass of the working class and in this way build a mass revolutionary party of the working class. The way I saw it was that there was nobody else in Dublin or Southern Ireland who had the ideas of Militant so I believed there was nobody else who could start this task. I saw it as my responsibility.

I was driven to fight for this objective by the experiences I had gained and the struggles in which I had participated. It felt as if my entire life – the many debates and arguments I had had with my family, the things I had seen when I travelled the world in search of knowledge, the violence, fear, anger and street politics I had seen and in which I had participated in the Bogside, the facing death or at least physical violence from 'my own', the armed Protestant militias such as the UDR and others, all my readings and discussions of Marxism, all of these had prepared me for this time in Dublin laying down the foundations for the revolutionary organisation. Everything was coming together. The ideas and method of Marxism and these experiences had shown me my role in life. I was unshakeable in my determination to build the revolutionary organisation.

The first thing I needed to begin this work was a paper around which I could organise. With a paper I would have to write articles on events and this would develop me. I would have to do research and think about issues and develop my writing skills. I would have to listen more carefully to workers and readers of the paper and test the ideas of the paper and any nucleus that I could build in discussions with these workers. I would be forced to defend the ideas in the paper in discussions with its readers. I could sell this paper and this would allow me to meet with more people and put forward my ideas. I was the first member of The Militant in Southern Ireland. There were around ten members in the North. We did not have enough resources to produce our own paper. So for a time I used the paper of the British Militant group. It was called The Militant and it was produced and printed in London and copies were sent over to Dublin and Belfast.

Every Friday and Saturday night I took a city bus out to the outskirts of Dublin, Finglas, Ballymun, Tallaght, Kimmage, Dundrum, and more, a different route every weekend. Getting off at the last stop I would walk back along the bus route going into every pub and selling. Dublin was a smaller city then. The pubs would be full to the brim of people throwing back their pints and whiskies and vodkas. Given the events in the North there was a lot of interest in ideas and politics. Often on these nights, especially if it was wet and drizzling, as this reminded me of Donegal, I thought of how I, from a small farmer, Donegal Protestant, Orange Order background, ended up selling a revolutionary socialist paper in the working class pubs and streets of Dublin. I especially enjoyed selling in the pubs in the Coombe, old working class Dublin, where I would be faced with discussion, questions and from the older ladies teasing.

As well as these regular paper routes I sold at strikes and union halls, at the General Post Office on Saturday afternoons, at political meetings and demonstrations of radical and left groups and Labour Party and trade union meetings. With all these sales and discussions I met new people and tried to convince them of the ideas I held. I asked those who were most interested would they take part in regular discussions. Selling the paper, meeting and discussing with people, asking them for donations, eventually I was able to pull together a small discussion group which met weekly. We discussed current events, history, theory, capitalism, socialism. The first of the show was getting on the road.

In these discussion groups I explained that Militant was a cadre organisation, that is, an organisation of dedicated people which while not yet even within shouting distance of carrying out the socialist revolution was committed to that objective. I explained that a cadre was somebody who dedicated their life to bringing about the socialist revolution and that is what I was asking them to do.

The training of cadres meant educating ourselves by reading and discussing but also meant intervening in the struggles of the working class and discussing with the working class. It meant being conscious of the need to have a dialogue with, to listen to, as well as talk to the working class. The task of this dialogue was to exchange ideas, policies etc. for Ireland and internationally and also to explain the general principles that dominated our work and also to learn from the workers.

The general principles we fought for were that we did not believe capitalism could solve the problems of society so we never supported capitalism or its ideas or institutions. On the contrary we believed that only the working class, by taking power and establishing socialism internationally, could solve the problems of society. Therefore at all times we fought for international socialism and for the building of independent, international, revolutionary, working class organisations and institutions. We stood on a different foundation from capitalism, we stood for international democratic socialism and the overthrow of capitalism worldwide.

I also tried to train myself and those I was able to bring around me to keep up with the propaganda and ideas of our enemy, the capitalist class, to know what they were thinking. This involved reading the serious capitalist press and journals. Members of our little working class nucleus could often be seen walking around with copies of the Financial Times under their arm.

I also explained that given the mood in the country at the time, the sabotage of the movement by the Labour and trade union leaders, the increased sectarianism, the movement to republicanism and loyalism, the withdrawal of workers from the mass strike action of the earlier years, the decline of the left in the Labour Party, that our cadre organisation could only expect to recruit and build in ones and twos at that stage. We could not expect to build a semi-mass or mass organisation or expect to influence events in the near future. This was also part of being a cadre organisation, working out the most likely developments, trying to estimate the tempo of events, pacing ourselves for the long haul, if it was going to be a long haul.

The composition of our little group was mainly working class. We did not look to the universities although we did recruit some important members from these sources. We wanted to have our roots firmly in the working class and not in the student movement and academia. So our orientation was to the working class in the workplaces, the rank and file of the trade unions and Labour Party, the pubs, the streets. It was from here I recruited some new members.

Our weekly meetings were introduced by a participant who would speak for up to an hour and then there would be discussion. It was not discussion in the real sense. It was putting the line of The Militant. If people did not agree they tended not to come back. This form of 'discussion' would cause major problems in the future but in the meantime in spite of this incorrect internal life and method of discussion the organisation inched forward. This was because the 'line' of The Militant in general corresponded to the objective needs and potential of the working class, to the history of the working class and on this basis it was able to attract small numbers of workers and youth.

At the weekly meetings there was always a business section. This lasted half an hour or so and dealt with paper sales, finances, people we were discussing with, whom we called contacts, and how to try and take these discussions forward and get these contacts to join the organisation, to become as we called them, 'Comrades'.

We also held public meetings under the name of Militant with members speaking from the platform and the floor and getting this experience. These were especially helpful in giving members experience as there tended to be non-members present who would ask questions and disagree. Members spoke for the ideas in the Labour Party and trade unions and gained experience in this way also.

Gradually the small nucleus increased in size. With this came more members prepared to sell the paper and so more sales and income from sales. With this also came more donations from these new members. With these increased resources we were able to produce our own paper by the end of 1972. On my proposal it was called *Militant Irish Monthly*. I was able to increase my own sales of this paper to the respectable number of 400 per issue. Having our own paper was a big step forward. Progress was being made.

But even with this progress The Militant in the South was still really only a set of ideas and a handful of members. This was what I was asking people to join. I had a hard neck on me. But I committed myself to this work with all my resources. I ignored the difficulties, the fact that we were so small. I also ignored, was not even conscious of the importance of the fact, and the difficulty that flowed from this, that there was no tradition of Trotskyism in Ireland.

This lack of a Trotskyist tradition was a serious obstacle. There were traditions of Nationalism and Republicanism and Loyalism, with their organisations and institutions and music and marches and version of history. There were the various religious traditions with large buildings in every city and town and hamlet complete with full-time organisers, the priests, clergy etc., who made propaganda for their ideas and capitalism. The way these institutions supported capitalism was by never mentioning it, instead explaining all by referring to their various gods, heavens, hells and so on. There were the songs and poems and heroes and the music of Republicanism and Nationalism and Loyalism and Unionism and Catholicism and Protestantism. These were everywhere. When the leadership of the working class refused to lead, these traditions inevitably filled the vacuums that were left. It was only in the late 1960s that a few small groups calling themselves Trotskyist emerged. They were never more than a few dozen in membership. They were very quickly subsumed by their opportunist policies, especially the concessions they made to Republicanism.

Tradition is not often thought about when speaking of political struggle but it is of great importance. Pubs were the centre of social life in Ireland. But there were no pubs that sang the songs, that kept alive the poems and stories of the heroic Trotskyist fighters against Stalinism and capitalism. The opposite, these were either totally ignored or were vilified by all the capitalist forces of whichever religion and also vilified by the rest of the so-called left, the social democracy, the left republicans and of course the small Stalinist organisations. As there was no tradition of Trotskyism the reality was we were starting from scratch. In fact worse than scratch as the tiny sects that called themselves Trotskyist were either opportunist, or sectarian or ultra-left, or a continually shifting combination of all of these. To the extent that they were known they got Trotsky and what was known as Trotskyism a bad name.

But this was not our biggest problem. Nor were our ideas our biggest problem. Our biggest problem was our tiny forces. Many workers agreed with the ideas of working class unity, socialism and internationalism, but even the most conscious workers, perhaps especially the most conscious workers, had difficulty in seeing how we could, with such minute resources, bring about the change we advocated. The forces against us, capitalism, social democracy, that is the Labour Parties and the trade unions leaders, Stalinism, the churches, Republicanism, Loyalism, other left forces, these were seen as just being too strong. Workers correctly saw the task we were asking them to take on was gigantic. Only the most audacious and determined were prepared to sign up.

But in spite of this we got enough people around to formally start a branch in Dublin in 1972. With the branches in Belfast and Coleraine/Derry, by 1972/73 we had three branches in Ireland. The branches in the North were developed mostly around people who had been recruited when they were students in Britain and who then moved to live in the North.

This progress was made at a time when the forward movement of 1968 to 1970 had been blocked and thrown back, when this was being replaced by the ideas of Republicanism, Loyalism, Nationalism and sectarianism. But it was a complex period. At the same time as this was going on and the movement was being thrown back, there were many workers and youth who had been stirred into political thought for the first time by the previous years' events and were looking for an understanding. It was amongst these layers that we began to get some results. But again the problem was that our organisation seemed just too small for the task it was setting itself and to which we were asking our contacts to commit themselves. We were asking them to change their lives, to become activists in their workplaces, unions, communities, schools and colleges. We were asking a lot. Given the overall situation and the extreme scarcity of our resources this was too much for all but a tiny few. But in spite of this we did get a small nucleus together.

As I sold the paper and intervened in the workers' movement, especially on the streets and the pubs, I came to know and to like the Dublin working class and its intelligence and humour. I came to know of Behan. I read *Borstal Boy* and the passage where he criticised the priest strengthened me in my opposition to all organised religion. I was moved by his poem 'A Jackeen's Farewell To the Blaskets'. On the basis of reading this poem I would later visit the Blaskets. The raging Atlantic, the jagged rocks and the tiny patches of soil on the islands would overwhelm me with sadness at the hard lives of the people who had to live there, with anger at the system that forced them to live there and determination to try and end that system. Behan had lived for a time in a house near where I lived in Dublin. Locals were looking to put up a plaque on the wall of the house. They asked me would I plaster the base for the plaque. I did so. It was an honour.

I visited Kilmainham Jail. I was enraged when I saw what had been done to the prisoners there. I wept when I saw the spot where the socialist James Connolly had been tied to a chair and shot.

My will to fight was strengthened both by the beauty of the Blaskets and the harsh power of Kilmainham's monument to repression and injustice. My will to help build the revolutionary nucleus, which was my task, my objective in life, was strengthened. Nothing else took precedence. I would allow nothing else to take precedence. To build the revolutionary nucleus, all must be pushed aside to achieve this task. I grew more and more committed to this belief, to this task.

CHAPTER 24

A STRATEGY

I DID NOT CONFINE my work of building to seeking out ones and twos here and there and recruiting them to the nucleus. Along with The Militant in London and the other few members in the North of Ireland, we sought to work out a view of what we thought would happen in the future, to where the working class would move, where the great class battles would take place, where working class consciousness would move out of these battles, where new left forces would develop. And we tried to draw organisational conclusions from this. That is, draw conclusions as to where to place our tiny forces to be in a position to build out of the coming struggles and any coming new left movements.

We concluded that the working class, as it came under the blows of capitalism, would move to the organisations it had created in its past struggles, move through the channels it had carved in previous struggles. Like a tide that came in and out it would tend to use the same channels. These in our opinion were the Labour Party and the trade unions. The workers had formed the trade unions out of great strikes and struggles of the past and out of the trade unions had formed the Labour Party. The trade unions were affiliated to the Labour Party, sending delegates to all its conferences and helping fund its activities. Because they were formed out of working class struggles, the Labour Party and the trade unions were workers' organisations. Their programmes and their policies were capitalist but their base was in the working class, they had been formed by working class struggles. Due to this base and history we concluded that as the class struggle unfolded, this would be reflected inside these organisations and a left wing would develop. And further concluded that if we put our resources inside these organisations we would be able to get our ideas a wider hearing and so build our organisation.

A left wing had developed in the Labour Party in the late 1960s early 1970s. But when the party refused to rule out coalition with right wing parties, the youth of this small left wing walked out of the party. This was a mistake. If these forces had stayed in they could have influenced larger forces in the party who would become opposed to the Party leaders' right wing policies in the future. I was not part of Militant at that stage but I did not walk out of the party. I stayed and fought.

The leadership of these organisations, the Labour Party and the trade unions, were right wing social democrats. They believed that capitalism could never be ended. They believed that at best a minor reform might be possible here or there. But in reality at that time when capitalism was on the offensive against the working class, social democracy, because it believed in capitalism, helped that system attack the working class and helped crush any idea of a socialist alternative. Social Democracy was against socialism and in favour of capitalism. It was a counter revolutionary force.

Believing that there would be an increasing conflict between the rank and file and the leaders of the Labour Party and the rank and file and the leaders of the trade unions as workers' living standards were attacked, we concluded that we would get a hearing for our socialist ideas. As a result of these conclusions our strategy was to join and stay and fight for our ideas in these mass organisations of the working class, the trade unions and the Labour Party. This strategy of putting our forces into the larger party, the Labour Party, was known as 'Entryism'. The idea was to fight for our socialist ideas inside this larger workers' organisation, against the social democratic, capitalist ideas in the Labour Party and also the trade unions and in this way build our nucleus. The Labour Party leadership knew me from Donegal and Derry, knew that I was a capable organiser and that I was a revolutionary socialist who opposed their views so they told my local Labour Party branch, the Crumlin branch, not to let me join. But Crumlin was an independent-minded, working class branch and accepted me as a member. The Labour Party leadership claimed we were a separate organisation and should not be allowed into the Party. We insisted we were a 'tendency' and not an organisation. This was not the case. We were an organisation or at least in the process of becoming one.

It was not so simple for the Labour Party leaders to oppose us. They were dedicated to capitalism while many of the rank and file members of the Labour Party genuinely saw themselves as being for socialism. And the trade unions which were affiliated to the Labour Party, while not socialist, were continually coming into conflict with the bosses and the demands of their capitalist system. These were problems for the Labour Party and trade union leaders, contradictions they faced, and this allowed us to get an echo amongst Labour Party and trade union members for our socialist ideas.

We were not loyal to the Labour Party leadership or their social democratic pro-capitalist policies, which they foisted on the Party. But we were loyal to what many members of the Party thought the party should stand for, and these were the ideas of its founders, the socialists, James Connolly and James Larkin. On this basis we were able to put down roots.

Our prediction that when the working class would move into struggle it would move to its traditional party the Labour Party and to its traditional organisations, the trade unions, was not correct, at least not in the short and medium term. The extreme right wing policies of the Labour Party's leadership and its entry again and again into government with the extreme right wing party Fine Gael, turned the workers off that party and the collaboration with management policies of the trade union leaderships in the national wage agreements alienated workers from the unions. Most who were in the unions stayed in them but were inactive and few new members joined.

However, in spite of this mistaken view, our work in fighting the social democratic ideas in the Labour Party and the trade unions gained the organisation some new members, raised our profile, and gave the base to proceed to build as an independent revolutionary group, but our view of how the Labour Party and to a lesser extent the trade unions would develop was wrong.

I joined the Crumlin branch of the Labour Party in 1972. Crumlin branch was for a time one of the most active and political branches in the Party. This was mainly because of my role. Every monthly meeting was convulsed with discussion and debate as I would bring a resolution for consideration. This allowed me to fight for my ideas, to allow them to be heard and in this way to recruit people to the organisation. The leader of the branch, a conservative Catholic worker was advised in his struggle against us in regular secret meetings with the national leadership of the party. Just as we organised to fight for our ideas in the Labour Party so did the right wing leadership.

I was proud to be a member of the Crumlin branch. At its height it had over twenty members, eighteen of whom were active trade unionists in their workplaces. There was also an elderly lady who came to every meeting with a large shopping bag. Nobody ever knew what was in it. She was mentally challenged. But she always had something to say, either about some problem in her neighbourhood or about some national or international event. She saw the monthly meeting as very important in her life, a place where she could express herself and have her say about her world. When she spoke the branch listened to her with the attention. Watching this take place I developed great respect for this lady and for this most thinking section of the Dublin working class.

The workers in the Crumlin branch did not always agree with me by any means. However they listened to me and honestly debated with me. They were active in their workplaces and listened to what their fellow workers had to say and brought this with them to the branch meetings and into our discussions and debates. These workers were a microcosm of the more conscious workers in Dublin. I was always less than fully confident of any particular idea until I first raised it at the Crumlin branch and heard the views of its members. It was one of my sounding boards, one of the places I learnt a lot, one of the most important places where I developed a dialogue with the working class.

Amongst the first people who joined the nucleus in Dublin were members of the Labour Party. There was a debate at the 1973 Labour Party conference. Sectarian violence was tearing the North apart at this time. I moved the following resolution to the conference:

'Conference recognises that the spate of sectarian intimidations, beatings and murders being carried out almost daily in the North underlines the complete inability of the so-called security forces to safeguard the lives, jobs and homes of ordinary working class people be they Catholic or Protestant. Conference recognises that only the people of the areas involved can protect themselves and their neighbours from sectarian attacks and therefore calls on the Labour movement, as the only organisation capable of mobilising both Catholic and Protestant workers, to immediately convene conferences of street committees, tenants' associations, together with local shop stewards and trades councils in all working class areas as a first step towards the building of an armed trades union defence force. Conference further recognises that such a force, based upon and under the control of the trade unions, if linked to a clear programme of socialist change spelled out by the leaders of the labour movement, would alone be capable of weeding out sectarianism and at the same time ending the present system of economic exploitation of Catholic and Protestant workers.'

This resolution sought to recognise the reality of the time. The workers' movement North and South had been thrown back, repression by the state forces was on the rise, sectarian paramilitary groups and violence were on the rise, this resolution was an attempt to convince the working class, at least those sections of the working class that we could reach, that they should seek to unite and take action and try to put their imprint on the situation. This resolution was good as far as it went. It had no chance of being implemented given that the workers' movement had been thrown back. But it was the correct position to take and it was the only way that the slide to sectarianism and increased repression could have been stopped. So we were correct to put it forward.

But the resolution was not perfect. It was good as far as it went. It opposed the sectarianism and violence of the various sectarian individual terror groups. It explained that only the united working class could stop this. But where it was weak was while it gave no support to any state forces it did not sufficiently state its opposition to the British Army and state forces in the North and their repression and violence. In my daily work and discussions I and our little nucleus always opposed the British Army's presence in the North, and when the British Army was sent into the North in 1969 The Militant, unlike some other left forces, had opposed this development. But this resolution, written by the leading member of our group in the North did not sufficiently clearly express this position. In the future it came to be well known that the British Army and all the state forces, as well as being directly responsible for internment and for Bloody Sunday in Derry, were also involved in organising and assisting the development of Protestant sectarian death squads and in infiltrating the Republican groups and being involved in assassinations in and through these also. This should have been boldly explained in this resolution.

The Labour Party leaders organised all their resources to defeat this resolution. They saw it as a challenge to their do nothing position on the North. The Labour Party leader Corish had earlier said the North had to look after itself. These leaders needed to crush this resolution to show they were serious about this, that their position really was to let the British State and Army and the Northern state control the North. They wanted to show that they were keeping out of it, that they had no intention of building an independent working class movement to deal with the crisis in the North.

The Labour Party leaders removed all other resolutions on the North from the conference agenda to let mine stand alone against their resolution. They selected leader after leader to attack the resolution and me. They were terrified it might pass and they might come under pressure to do something. The result was a predictable and, from their point of view, a successful outcome. My resolution was defeated with over 1,000 votes against and only 12 for. The social democratic leaders had won. They had kept their organisation and themselves out of any struggle to provide a solution to the North and out of any independent working class action. Part of the reason they had won their vote was also because the Party's members had no confidence that they and the working class could take independent action. The vote was a sign of the weakness of the working class movement.

But I had not lost totally. Of the twelve conference delegates who voted for my resolution two were skilled industrial workers who were soon to become members of Militant. One of them was an electrician and one a carpenter. From the point of view of my entryist tactic, moving this resolution to the Labour Party conference was therefore a success. The working class alternative had been raised and two new members, and two industrial workers at that were won to our little nucleus. Progress was being made.

As I continued to fight for our ideas in the Labour Party I ran for election to its Administrative Council, that is, its leading elected body. It was elected at the annual Labour Party conferences. As my ideas and our group and myself became better known, my vote increased until I was elected in the latter half of the 1970s. This was a big step forward. It gave our nucleus a bigger platform. It gave us more authority. It allowed party members and others to see our small nucleus was a serious group that could take on and gain victories over the social democracy. This in turn helped us to recruit new members to our nucleus. Joining us no longer seemed such a hopeless cause.

Given the role of the Labour Party and the trade union leaders in the so-called austerity attacks on the working class over recent years, it is hard to believe there were healthy branches made up of serious workers in the Labour Party and the trade unions at that time. But this was the case. It was only when the leaders of these organisations took on openly and brutally the role of helping lead the attacks on the working class that were demanded by the so-called austerity programme of international capitalism, that these organisations degenerated to the extent that they did.

CHAPTER 25

ON THE BUILDING SITES

WHILE I WAS WORKING every minute I could spare to build the revolutionary nucleus, I still had to make a living. I went to work on the building sites working for a while as a labourer to a friend of mine from Strabane who was a plasterer. This work was never too pleasant, cold winds, the wet running down your neck and up your sleeves, cracked knuckles and joints, a sore back, it was not a picnic. But there was a certain satisfaction to seeing my friend leave the walls with straight edges and smooth. It was in a way a type of sculpture work, a type of art.

After my friend returned to Strabane I continued to work on the building sites and picked up enough plastering skills to get work as a plasterer. I worked on a number of small sites and then got a start on a big one. There was no shop steward, that is, elected representative, for the plasterers on the big site. In my union inexperience I did not give much thought to why this was the case. At midday we would take our break and eat our sandwiches in a half plastered house. At one of these I proposed we needed a shop steward. This was agreed and I was elected.

All the plasters except myself were working on the 'lump'. That is, instead of getting paid a fixed wage they were paid for how many houses they plastered. They got more money this way but they were burning up their human capital, their bodies, at a terrible rate. I refused to work the lump because it encouraged an 'every man for himself' approach (there were no women plasterers), made union organising more difficult, and increased the divisions between the labourers and the plasterers. The plasterers' union did not admit labourers. The plasterers and the labourers did not even eat their sandwiches together. I opposed this – another form of divide and rule.

As well as representing the plasterers I began to organise the labourers. I should not have been, but I was surprised when one of the members of my own plasterers' union told me straight out that I should not do this as it was in the interests of the plasterers on the lump that the labourers remain unorganised, that is weak, so they could be made to work as hard as possible and without any rights and have to do the plasterers' bidding.

My surprise at this view of the plasterer showed the uneven level of my development at that stage. I was developed theoretically to the point where I was driven to build the revolutionary organisation. But I was not immune to a certain wishful thinking where the working class itself was concerned. When I looked at workers I was always trying to find their desire for working class unity and revolution. And it has to be said most times convincing myself I saw this where it did not exist. I was underdeveloped in that I did not sufficiently listen to and see the negative side of the workers, especially the workers on the lump. One of these workers objected to me taking on the foreman as he said he wanted to be a foreman himself someday. I thought I could mobilise and get support from these workers when their priority was getting as much work as they could and as much money as they could in the immediate term. I overestimated the extent I could rely on these workers in the future when push would come to shove.

I held a weekly lunchtime meeting of the plasterers to ask what issues they wanted me to take up with the bosses. I did not see it but the reality was most of the plasterers did not want me to take up any issue, just wanted me to let them get on with working as hard as they could in their lump system. I was only in the shop steward position a few weeks when the two full time bureaucrats of the plasterers' union arrived. Some informer of the boss or the other workers had told them about me. The leader and head of the union was a little dried up stump of a man happed up in a long thick overcoat and wearing a cloth cap. The other was his flunkie who trailed along after him and was hunched over from years of bootlicking. They were a sorry looking pair of so-called workers' leaders.

'Who the fuck do you think you are? Calling meetings here. You are not in the fucking Bogside now you know. If there are any meetings that need to be called I will call them.' His flunkie drew on his cigarette and nodded his head in silent agreement. He kept blowing out the smoke from his cigarette for emphasis.

I replied, 'I was elected by the members here. I never take up any issue unless I raise it with them first and get their approval. Is that not right men?' I turned and asked the members. There was silence except for one man called Tom who spoke and backed me up. 'Well I am telling you this stops now. You are finished as shop steward.'

I had been put in my position democratically and was now being removed bureaucratically. I spoke; 'I know what you are doing. You are removing me as shop steward so they can fire me. You are only a scab.'

He rushed at me and I at him. The members held us apart. He frothed at the mouth shouting: 'You do not call me a scab.' Even as right wing a bureaucrat as he was he was angry at being called a scab. Those were the good old days when the word 'scab' was still considered an insult. He went off shouting over his shoulder: 'You are out.'

The mainly rural workers with their earnings from the lump in mind gave me no support. They did not want any trouble so they kept their mouths shut. Rather than seeing me as fighting for them I came to realise that they saw me as causing trouble, disrupting the job, maybe ending the lump and having all of them working for an hourly wage and as a result, as they ruled out a united struggle of all the workers against the boss, they saw my activities as threatening a reduction in their income.

I was fired the Friday following the visit from the two union bureaucrats. On Monday I put a picket on the site demanding my job back. Initially the plasterers did not pass. Then the same two union bureaucrats arrived in their car and told the workers that there was no 'all out picket' so they were to go to work. Given the nod by the bureaucrats the workers did what they wanted to do anyway and passed my picket and went back and took up their tools.

The 'all out picket' was a new agreement between the union leaders and the bosses whereby a strike by any union would only be supported by all unions if the leaders of all the unions met beforehand and agreed to do so amongst themselves, and then instructed their members to support the strike. The whole idea was to reduce strike activity and to take decisions out of the hands of the rank and file and also to allow the leadership to more easily base themselves on the less advanced, less combative workers. It was the end of Larkinism, the sympathetic strike, which was named after the union leader James Larkin, and which had grown out of the class battles such as the 1913 Lockout. Larkinism was when all workers were expected to automatically support other workers when they would strike. It was rooted in the consciousness of the workers, it was formed by the class battles they had fought. Under the pressure of the bosses the union leaders were now destroying this consciousness and weakening the working class. The idea of 'one out all out' was being destroyed. Workers' solidarity was being undermined. I was a casualty.

I got jobs labouring on other sites. I could not get back plastering. The word was out to keep me away from that trade. I kept going to the union hall when members were there and demanding something be done about my firing. The two bureaucrats hid behind their office door. Then a lawyer with connections to the company from which I had been fired waited outside my door one morning and sidled up to me and offered me money to let things go. I told him to clear off. The whole thing came to nothing as the union bureaucrats had a meeting with the bosses and said the case was closed. I was told in advance by a sympathetic member of another union about this meeting and tried to attend but was locked out. I smiled ironically to myself. I was a sort of an individual version of the 1913 Lockout. I was locked out too but this time not by the bosses but by my own union leadership. I did not have enough of a base in the union to fight a prolonged battle and so was defeated.

I learned a lot from this experience. One thing was the importance of judging the consciousness of the different layers of workers. In this case I had tried to launch an offensive on the site when the consciousness and balance of forces were not there for an offensive. The workers did not want to fight and I was trying to make them fight. This was a good lesson. And not only for small struggles such as on this site or in any workplace but it was a lesson which applied also to the whole issue of revolution. You could not force the working class to carry out a revolution if it did not want to. You could help the process. You could observe and judge the mood and but you had to also see that other factors which you did not control, that is what were referred to in revolutionary circles as objective factors, influenced the mood of workers and the working class and therefore the possibilities.

I learned you had to assess the workers' economic conditions, the wider economic and political background of the working class as a whole, the consciousness of the working class and the workers in your own workplace and trade, to assess how many, if any, good fighters you had around you, and from this work out tactics and strategy. Just because you wanted to fight the bosses did not mean it was always a good idea to try to launch an offensive against the bosses. The balance of forces had to be taken into account.

I also learned that the working class was not perfect. I learned that it could and did at times let you down. I was further confirmed and further educated in my understanding that there were different layers in the working class and different shifting moods in the working class. I learned I had to apply my dialectical method of thinking to the concrete situation in which I was involved. These were very important lessons I learned from this struggle. I grew in experience and consciousness. I gained very important experience but I did not recruit any new members to our group from this struggle.

Losing my job did not have much effect on my daily life as I was able to get regular jobs labouring. The wages were lower but not dramatically so. A few weeks after I was fired I drove out to the old site from which I had been fired, parked my car in a side street, and went through the half built houses breaking off the copper pipes which I sold to a scrap dealer. This subsidised my income for a week or two. I smiled to myself as the pipes cracked and my bag filled up. I cursed the bosses and the union bureaucrats. I whispered gleefully to myself in the darkened houses. But while pleasurable, this showed that I had still not fully broken from my semi-criminal or as I had learnt to describe it my semi-lumpen past. This was not good.

There had been one worker on the site who had supported me. His name was Tom and he was a traveller who lived in a caravan on Sundrive Road dump. He was interested in my ideas. But he had seen too many broken promises in his life to commit to any organisation. His experience also told him that the working class would not fight. Seeing what happened to me did not change his mind, on the contrary. He asked me to his caravan for food. I knew he was testing me to see if I would eat in his traveller's caravan home. I did so unhesitatingly. His wife Margaret had prepared a stew with herbs that she had gathered from the hedges. It was very good and I ate my fill. I also helped him by going with him to a pub from which he was banned because he was a traveller. We caused a row and got the owner to back off and let him in. In the course of this struggle I met old man Bewley, the owner of the famous Dublin coffee shop and who was a supporter of the travelling peoples' cause. He asked me about my overall political ideas and how I saw things being changed. I said I could not see a peaceful change. He looked at me and shook his head in sadness.

Back on the labouring meant back on the cement mixer. I would start this up first thing in the morning, make sure there was fuel, get it going and throw in the mix. I liked the thudding noise of it. When each load was ready I would tip it out on a large flat piece of plywood and shovel it into a bucket. I would then carry full buckets to where the plasterers were working. Sometimes this was inside and sometimes it was outside, sometimes it was on the ground, sometimes it was up a ladder to a scaffold. There were other times I would be mixing plaster for finish work and I would do this in a large pail with an iron plunger which I would thrust up and down until all the lumps were gone. It was hard work. But I liked hard work. It was therapeutic. It was callus work. And my hands were increasingly calloused hands. Playing the violin was pushed further over the horizon.

CHAPTER 26

EXPANDING: STRENGTHS – WEAKNESSES – PRESSURES
A FULL-TIME REVOLUTIONARY

WORKING ON THE SITES I discussed world and national events on a regular and serious basis with workers. I had to listen more carefully to those to whom I sold the paper as I saw and interacted with them every day. I had to think of historical events and theoretical concepts which shed light on the events of the present and bring these all together in my discussions and in the paper in a way that these workers found interesting. I grew along with the paper.

The main people involved in starting and producing the paper were Gerry Lynch in Derry, Bridget O'Toole, Alex Wood, Gerry Dawe in Coleraine, Peter Hadden and Eileen Cullen in Belfast, Finn Geaney, Pat Smyth, Jimmy Kelly and myself in Dublin. These were also amongst the founding members of our small nucleus or as it was now referred to, as 'the group'. Being a member meant fighting for the ideas of our group, helping produce and write for the paper, selling and raising money for the paper and paying regular weekly amounts of money to the group.

We recruited more new members at this time. Some came from the Labour Party and some not. It was hard. We had to pull together people who were individuals a year or two before and transform them into a collective grouping. But I was determined to build and make workers see the correctness of my ideas even if it killed me. As it turned out it nearly would. But that lay ahead.

I had to work on the sites to pay my bills. I had to keep building our paper and our small group. I was fighting on too many fronts but I did not recognise this. When things got very hard I would always fall back on words of Trotsky: 'You can have a revolutionary who is smart, you can have a revolutionary who is not smart, but you cannot have a revolutionary who is not prepared to fight to overcome obstacles.' So I bared my teeth and dug in to overcome obstacles.

In doing so I left myself too little time for theoretical study and development. It is true that every day I tried to read two serious capitalist papers, The Financial Times and the Irish Times. This was supposedly to see what the capitalist class were thinking and how their system was working. But while this was part of it there was also that I was reading these papers a bit too much to get information to back up the already fixed and rigidly held analysis of myself and The Militant.

I tried to make up for my lack of reading and study of theoretical material in two ways. I regularly attended the meetings of the Central Committee of The Militant in Britain and while at these was able to take part in discussions with members some of whom were more theoretically developed than I. I also lived on theoretical credit built up from previous periods of reading and study and discussions. But still too little time was being left for my own reading and theoretical development and this was a serious mistake.

I was insufficiently developing myself on all fronts except one, that was the organisational side of building the revolutionary group. My life was focused overwhelmingly on this one thing. All was subordinate to this. I was becoming politically deformed. I did not know this. I was building and that was that. Were the results not there to be seen? Were we not growing, new members, a paper, a small group that met weekly with committed participants? Progress.

Those who came around our group at this time were dedicating themselves to a hard road. They were fighting for working class unity, socialism and internationalism. These were not wildly seen to be practical, to be achievable at that time to put it mildly. Those who joined us did so because they believed in and were prepared to fight for these ideas against the stream. They were good people.

I was so determined to build the group that I would on occasions drive around on the nights we had meetings and collect anybody who had showed any interest in our work. This was extremely stressful and exhausting. I would get off work on the building sites, come home, clean up, go and collect those interested, go to the meetings at which I played a central role initially and then drive most of those present home again. But we did grow, even if it was slowly, even if it was just about imperceptibly, even if it was like climbing a cliff face.

During this time I was living in a house in Crumlin. It was used as the headquarters for the group. When we had our own paper it was produced initially from there. Our discussion meetings were held there. Noel Browne, the well-known former Member of the Dáil, the Irish Parliament and minister for health in a previous government, attended a discussion there as he was initially interested to hear to our ideas. Also at this time I was travelling to the North for weekend discussions to help coordinate our work and if I had any resources to help the work of the members there. I had an old Opel car and drove round the long way through Sligo and Donegal Town and into Derry the back way through the Brandywell and the Bogside. I was worried that if I used the shorter route through Omagh and Strabane where I was better known, I would be under threat from the sectarian Ulster Defence Regiment and the Protestant militias, not far from being the same thing at that time. This was a long haul of over four hours, hard after working on the sites all day.

On my return from the Derry weekend meetings and discussions I would call and see my mother and aunt in Lifford. They lived alone in the old farmhouse. My sister Mary and her husband and family would visit regularly. My mother and aunt would always have a supply of bread and eggs and cakes for me to take back to Dublin. I felt very bad seeing them there alone and recognising that it was I who was responsible for this and for them feeling that I was so much in opposition to what they believed and stood for and for which they had worked all their life. Not understanding or agreeing with my ideas it was inexplicable to them why I would not accept their farm and come and have an easier life. It was extremely hurtful to them. I was rejecting all they had worked for, all they lived for, all they had accumulated to give to me. I was rejecting it all. What I was doing was extremely hurtful to them. I had to harden myself further.

Usually on these visits my mother would have many complaints and many chores she wanted done. These would normally be about the problems she had and how she would not have these if I were at home. This was true. If I had been at home I could have solved a lot of her problems. These were usually things like broken fences, leaking roofs, neighbours who were trying to get one over on her, the doings of the chickens and ducks and turkeys. On occasion I would do some of these jobs, clear a blocked drain, cut an overgrown fence, but I would always be mumbling to myself in rage about what had this got to do with building the international revolutionary organisation.

My mother could not see I could not stay with her and my aunt on their farm, that this was impossible. She could not see that if I gave up my life's work, if I became a farmer in Donegal, I would not be me. I would have to fundamentally change and diminish myself. And I would have to blame somebody or something for this. Inevitably I would sink into drink and blame somebody or something, probably her. We would be in continual conflict. She would not accept this and instead wanted what was not possible. I thought again of what Marx said that freedom was the recognition of necessity. There was no way I could live the life my mother wanted me to live. But she could not accept this 'necessity' of my life, of our lives. So our relations could never be 'free'. We were locked in, bound together in, an irresolvable contradiction, in irresolvable conflict. But for my mother there were no such things as irresolvable contradictions, irresolvable conflicts, just problems that were there to be solved. So our conflict was never ending.

My mother and I were regularly in disagreement about money. This became worse when I became a full-time organiser with the group. She instinctively knew that I was being paid less than a pittance. She always wanted to give me money from her pension and what she earned from her farm animals and her land lettings. I would always refuse. This was very hurtful to her. But I saw it as making sure I maintained my independence from the old ideas and traditions and family pressures.

On one occasion my mother was particularly hurt. It was when I was moving the resolution for an armed trade union defence force in the North at the Labour Party conference. I had nobody to second this resolution but I walked up toward the front of the conference hall anyway hoping for the best. On the way I saw a man called Johnny Byrne who had lived for some time in London and was sympathetic to the ideas of Trotsky.

I asked him to second my resolution. He agreed. But he was not prepared and so asked the conference to support the resolution because I was a Protestant and knew what I was talking about. I wrote a letter to the Irish Times correcting this and saying I was not a Protestant but an atheist and Marxist. This letter was printed in that paper and also read out on the RTÉ news radio programme the following morning. My mother always listened to this news and so heard my letter and my name being read out. The RTÉ news was saying her son was an atheist and a Marxist. Now the whole country would know. It was close to the ultimate blow. There was a chasm of pain between my mother and me.

It seemed that whatever I did to ease this pain did not work. I had a little Jack Russell dog in Dublin for a time. It was a bit of a charmer. It was hard for me to look after it with my work on the sites and my political work. So I decided to give it to my mother and aunt. I hoped that they would get comfort and companionship from it. But it was not to be. The next time I visited it they told me that it had killed all their ducks. One by one it worked its way through them. It seemed there was nothing I could do to help things between my mother and aunt and I.

Building the organisation in ones and twos when I was for a while the main person in the South was no easy task. As well as maintaining and developing my ideas, I had to be consistent and never miss an opportunity to meet and discuss with people who were interested. Time after time I would have an arrangement to meet somebody for a discussion and they would not turn up and my time would be wasted. I had to develop a thick skin as well as recognise that people had all sorts of pressures on them and were not as driven and single-minded and with the same priorities as me.

My work was not helped by my left sectarianism. This included treating all other left groups as useless and refusing to work with them. I thought and The Militant thought we knew everything about revolutionary politics and were right on everything. I was also on occasion ultra-left and this too hurt my work. This ultra-leftism would result in me overestimating the consciousness of the working class, such as I did on the building site. I would put forward tasks, ideas and demands that workers did not see as in any way possible to be attained. Especially given our tiny forces. These mistakes hampered my work.

However it would be wrong to interpret this approach of myself and The Militant to other left groups as just some arrogance. What was at its root was the correct belief that revolutionary organisations always had to orient to the working class as the working class was the only force that could change society. And as far as I could see, and rightly so, the other left groups in Ireland at that time did not orient to the working class. Most of them looked to the left intelligentsia for ideas and leadership. While they may have, like the Official Republicans did, sought to recruit in and build from workers in the unions and workplaces, they would seek to sneak into positions in the union bureaucracy and at the same time they maintained their view that their leaderships would come from the left academia.

This was a major mistake. It was shown in later years when many of these left academic types in the Official Republican movement would go over into the ranks of the social democratic pro-capitalist leadership of the Labour Party and the trade unions. An orientation to the working class does not only mean an organisational orientation, that is, working in the trade unions, the factories and workplaces. It also means putting out the ideas of the organisation in the working class and having them genuinely tested in the working class. That is listening to what the working class has to say about them and making adjustments while at the same time maintaining the revolutionary principles. Militant was not perfect at this but was more correct on this than any other left group. This allowed us to stand against the left academic, the trade union bureaucratic pressures that afflicted other left groups, it was not a question of The Militant and people like myself just being arrogant and thinking we and only we were correct because we were special, it was because we held on to this correct idea that revolutionaries had to orient to the working class in a genuine and thorough way, have a dialogue with the working class, yes fight for our ideas in the working class but also learn from the working class.

In spite of the weaknesses we had in The Militant, we were the best of the left groups and our work was going forward. The greatest strength of Militant and myself was that we most determinedly maintained our orientation to the working class. This allowed us to resist at any time supporting or making concessions to capitalism, republicanism, loyalism or nationalism. At all times we stood for the independence and unity of the working class, an end to capitalism and Stalinism and an independent, democratic, socialist world. My work in building Militant in Dublin would be an important part of bringing together what would be the first small nucleus of what would later become for a time the most influential Trotskyist group in Ireland.

However the organisation I was building and I myself were making mistakes. Amongst these was our tendency towards left sectarianism. There were a number of kinds of sectarianism. One was the religious sectarianism between Catholics and Protestants. This religious sectarianism is not what I am talking about here. We were never guilty of that. What I am talking about here is left sectarianism. There are a number of varieties of this. In general left sectarianism is where an organisation puts what it sees as its own interests, gaining more members, more resources, above that of the interests of the working class. We were not so much guilty of this at this time, though in later years after I left Ireland, the nucleus I helped build would move in this direction and in so doing do serious damage, breaking up organisations such as the United Left Alliance, and so helping prevent left groups and activists working together as a united front. Along with this, and also at a later stage, The Militant in Britain allowed its left sectarianism to cut across the potential of the anti-poll tax movement to be developed into a powerful, organised, anti-capitalist force.

But even when I was still a central part of the group in Ireland we were not innocent when it came to another variety of left sectarianism. We treated all the other left groups as 'sects' and referred to them as 'sects' and would have nothing to do with them. We should instead have recognised that these groups existed and would be around, and that their approach was damaging, and while holding to our principles we should have conducted an open struggle against the left sectarianism of these groups to limit the damage their left sectarianism did. We should have identified left sectarianism, explained what it was, pointed it out to workers and explained how damaging it was. We should, and also in front of the working class, have confronted the membership of the left sectarian groups and those who came around these groups and demanded they quit their left sectarianism. It is unlikely that this would have had much success with the hardened members and especially the leaderships of these groups but by not doing this we were leaving left sectarianism unchallenged and allowing more youth and workers to be mis-trained by the left sectarian groups or be put off by these left sectarian groups.

And it must be said put off also by our treating all the left sectarian groups as 'sects' and just dismissing them. By doing so we too looked as being left sectarian in the eyes of workers and youth who came around us in struggle. Openly and publicly identifying and opposing the left sectarianism of these groups would have been a more constructive way to work. It would have had a better chance of allowing us to interact with the more reasonable, the less sectarian individuals in and around these groups to jointly fight left sectarianism. This would also have given a road forward to the many people who had gone through these groups and been put off by their left sectarianism. Instead, by treating all other groups as sects, we too were seen as sectarian. And by condemning all other left groups as sects and having nothing to do with them we were not fighting left sectarianism, we were ignoring it.

Then there was ultra-leftism. This is where an organisation sees its policies and work, draws up its policies and plans its work without taking into account the consciousness of the working class, and in so doing overestimates the consciousness of the working class. I had been guilty of this on the big building site where I worked. I had not sufficiently or accurately understood the consciousness of the workers on the site and so I tried to lead them on a road along which they were not at that time prepared to travel. I learnt from this. My work on the building site had been ultra-left, that is I tried to open up an offensive against the bosses when the workers were not ready to do so.

However the most important mistake that the organisation was making was that it had a deformed internal life. This was mainly the result of the organisation's incorrect view of the tempo of events in the world at that time. We thought that Stalinism and capitalism would soon collapse and the world socialist revolution, which would be led by our organization, would take place in five to ten years. This five to ten years and ourselves leading the world revolution view not only dominated the organisation's political view but also its internal life.

It created an internal culture in which there was no genuine atmosphere of critical thinking and exchange of ideas. We 'knew', or rather more accurately the leadership 'knew', what was what and raising any alternative ideas or questioning was seen as wasting time that could be better used building. After all we only had five to ten years. The result was the emphasis in internal life tended to be the leadership working out ideas and taking these to the membership. In virtually every case the position of the leadership was accepted by the membership. This was a very serious mistake but it was not obvious as long the organisation could point to examples of where its analysis was being borne out. This resulted in every event where the working class took the slightest step forward being exaggerated, and every event where it was being thrown back being underestimated or even ignored. Not only our small Militant group in Ireland but the larger Militant group in Britain for a long period refused to accept that the British miners' strike had been a major defeat. This was a very serious mistake. I more than share the responsibility for this mistaken balance and these mistakes in the internal life given my position in the leadership of the group at the time. In the future this mistaken balance would lead to catastrophic consequences.

We were also making other mistakes. One very serious mistake was the incorrect balance on the issue of the special oppression of women, the insufficient attention to the special oppression of women. From when I was in my early teens and looking around me in my home in Lifford, I had always been struck by how the women in society were in second place. Men dominated in capitalist society. I was increasingly concluding that no healthy society could be built on this basis. I thought about the very inadequate emphasis Marxism, including The Militant, gave to this. I tried to understand how capitalism had managed to make women second class citizens. I struggled to understand this as the revolutionary socialist writings and material had written so little on this topic. It was only many years later that I was able to half understand this.

I came to understand that part of the rise of the capitalist class to power demanded a number of things, including divide and rule along racial, national and gender lines. A major part in this was the special oppression and subjugation of women. This special oppression of women was not only a question of divide and rule to control but it was to force women to carry out vast amounts of work, in some cases for no pay or in cases where women worked for a wage their wage was always less than that of their male counterparts. Women, giving birth to the next generation of workers, women working in the home and bringing up the new generation of workers were, with few exceptions, paid nothing for this essential task. I concluded that as a revolutionary fighting for an alternative society it was a priority to fight for gender equality and against the special oppression of women on all fronts in this new society. I saw it as being of the same priority as fighting against racial and national oppression. The fight against all these divide and rule ideologies and tactics and injustices was essential if the working class was to be united and capitalism overthrown.

While in the main Militant had the formerly correct position on the special oppression of women, and while we stood for women to have the right to choose to not have a baby or choose to have a baby, and free and hygienic facilities and the material necessities required for whichever of these they chose, we did not give anything like enough emphasis to this issue. Neither I, nor the organisation, took part in the direct actions of the women's movement to bring contraceptives into the South of Ireland. This was a mistake. If we had then the organisation would have become more conscious about the special oppression of women. We would have learnt from this movement and the women in this movement. It would have shaken up the male domination that existed in society and was reflected in The Militant.

There were very good combative women members of Militant at all levels. But the majority of the leadership was male. This did not result from any conscious policy to keep women down, but it resulted from women not starting from a level playing field in society with men and The Militant not taking conscious steps to correct this. This was a mistake.

Later our group was elected the majority on the leadership of the Labour Party Youth section – Labour Youth. When this happened we did not act correctly on this issue of the special oppression of women and the right to choose. We acted in an opportunist fashion. While Militant itself maintained its correct position on a women's right to choose and openly argued for this position, it did not try to commit Labour Youth to this position as we feared this could lead to that organisation being disbanded. This was opportunistic and unprincipled. We were not trying to convert Labour Youth to the women's right to choose while thousands of women a year were going to Britain for abortions. A fight to commit Labour Youth to a women's right to choose would have helped strengthen this struggle in Ireland and would also have helped give the opportunity to women members of the group to play a more leading role.

While The Militant had the correct position on a woman's right to choose, many young male workers, when we first met them, had to be convinced. Within the organisation we conducted a struggle to convince these young people. We put emphasis on the right to choose actually meaning the right to choose, that is the right not to have a baby and full, free, hygienic facilities to have an abortion and the decision to be made by the woman and nobody else. But we also said the right to choose meant the right for all women to if they wished have a baby and if they chose to do so there must be full free health care and medical facilities, a secure and full-time job for all women at a living wage and with full maternal and paternal rights and childcare facilities at work, home and in the communities, free and professionally staffed. This was a correct position. We held this position in Militant Irish Monthly and our own organisation but did not try to commit

Labour Youth to this position. Not trying to commit Labour Youth to this position was opportunism.

On one occasion in Dublin the group was having a discussion on this subject. There were about thirty members present. Some of the young male members, when we would meet them first, were opposed to women having the right to having an abortion. Some were present at that meeting. I was arguing against their position. In the middle of the exchange of views a young woman member stood up and announced that she had had an abortion. I can still see her there, standing strong and defiant and speaking out. I will always respect her for what she did. She was doing what the group should have been doing in Labour Youth and in society as a whole, openly standing for the right to choose, challenging anybody who denied women the right to choose. Our group should have taken an example from this young woman and openly and defiantly fought to commit Labour Youth to the position of the women's right to choose. It did not. By not doing so along with letting down women, it also did not inspire women members to play a more leading role in the group.

Then there was the vicious oppression, the slave labour, of the Catholic Church and the state in the Church-run laundries. I knew of these laundries but I did not give sufficient thought to what they were. It was only in later years that I, and the organisation, would come to be fully aware of the conditions that existed in these institutions. I would later find out that after I became the first full-time organiser for the organisation in Ireland and we had a headquarters in Dublin City Centre, I passed one of these slave labour laundries every day on my way to and from work and did not even know. I should have known. The Catholic Church ran these laundries and forced women to work for nothing or next to nothing and to live in shame. They also took the children from the young women and gave them away or sold them and kept their destination secret from their biological mothers. It was close to what slavery had been like in the US.

The Catholic Church also ran what were called 'industrial schools'. These were prisons for young people who had committed some petty crime. These prisons were usually down in the country and were run by tyrannical priests. There was much physical and sexual abuse. One leading criminal in Dublin who himself had gone through one of these schools said many of Dublin's leading criminals had done so also. In colourful language he explained that he himself and many of his fellow criminals had been made what they were 'by those mad monks in the bog'.

More recently we have seen the criminal actions of the Catholic and also the Protestant hierarchy in burying the bodies of young children in mass graves. These were children whose mothers had their children without their sexual relations being 'blessed' by these self-appointed religious institutions; and of course where no money and power were exchanged to the churches' benefit. The result was these children were seen by the religious organisations and by religious society as inferior and were neglected. Thousands of children died of such neglect in the religious-run institutions.

Insufficient attention was also given to the role of women in The Militant itself, and in the revolutionary left and the labour movement in general. It was easy to criticise capitalism for discriminating against women but what about my own organisation and all the revolutionary organisations and the wider labour movement? With practically no exception men led these organisations. In that sense they were almost exact mirror images of the Catholic and Protestant churches. We did not sufficiently recognise that there was not a level playing field between men and women in the revolutionary and labour movement just as was the case in capitalist society. We did not discuss this and did not take action in the organisation and in the labour and left movement to try and correct this.

I would later come to consider that if we had to estimate which gender was the stronger, male or female then it would be hard not to conclude that women were the stronger. Their central role in the reproduction of the species, the suffering involved with this, the change in their bodies and minds as they reproduced, the demands that were made of them as they nurtured and looked after and brought up the children, I would come to conclude it would be hard not to think that these experiences did not make women the stronger gender.

Another issue that the organisation was wrong on at this time was gay rights. I personally had broken from this prejudice many years before as I explained in my encounter in Toronto when I was twenty. The group itself stood against any discrimination against gay people. However this was a very contentious issue in Ireland of that time. And again we acted in an opportunist fashion when we got control of Labour Youth. To my shame and the shame of the organisation we did not take this up as an issue in Labour Youth and fight to commit Labour Youth to this position. In fact we argued against taking it up as we said it would be used against the Labour Youth organisation by the Labour Party leadership, possibly be used to dissolve the Labour Party Youth. This was unprincipled and opportunistic. It was the old 'end justifies the means' corrupt way of looking at things. In struggling for our position on this, that is not to commit the Labour Youth to fight for the rights of gay people, reactionary homophobic arguments were even used on occasion.

The organisation was also wrong on its attitude to members from middle class backgrounds. Many members from such backgrounds had committed themselves to the organisation and gave it a lot. But in many cases they were seen as in some way not of the same calibre as members from working class backgrounds. In spite of being from a small farmer background this was not applied to me. This was for a number of reasons. I was not from the professional middle classes, I had done blue collar work in my working life before I was a full-time organiser and also I had been the first member in the group in the South and played a leading role. The way the other members from a more middle class background were treated was a weakness and an injustice to these members and did damage to the organisation. It prevented members from this background play a more leading role and this weakened the organisation.

While the organisation was growing it was doing so in a period of serious reaction with only a small number of branches North and South and with these strengths and weaknesses. Its main strengths were its orientation to the working class and its generally correct, though way out in terms of tempo, revolutionary perspectives and ideas for Ireland and internationally. Its main weaknesses were its tiny resources and the mistakes explained above.

In terms of the bigger picture, our main weakness was that we did not recognise and draw conclusions from the fact that we were faced with a veritable hurricane of reaction in Ireland which was going to stretch out for decades ahead. We were making the mistake of being unable to correctly analyse the actual world around us, both in Ireland and internationally, and see this reality. I was so determined to build the organisation I would not give any countenance to the possibility that the objective situation could be so bad.

The working class in the South of Ireland was for the most part, inactive. Disillusioned by the union leaders' collaboration with the bosses in the national wage agreements and the Labour Party leaders' participation in Coalition with the right wing Fine Gael, it was being driven back. In the North, sectarianism and division were going from strength to strength and the working class could barely be said to exist as an organised active entity. Republicanism and loyalism were filling the space.

Death squads increasingly developed from the Protestant paramilitaries in the North. British intelligence and the Northern police force were instrumental in helping their formation. To some extent these operated under the direction of the British and Northern state and an organisation which came to be known as 'The Committee'. This was an organisation of top British and Northern Irish police and military elements and top Northern Protestant business people. These squads were organised to kill IRA members and also ordinary members of the Catholic population to intimidate any who might consider supporting the IRA. The Northern-based sections of this Committee also saw its role as being prepared to take unilateral action and go for an independent North in case the British government was prepared to make a deal with the South and withdraw. We still stood for a socialist united Ireland, an end to the poverty-ridden, Catholic-dominated South, an end to the poverty-ridden Protestant dominated North, a socialist united Ireland as part of a socialist federation of Ireland and Britain. We did not support the idea of any kind of independent North as we considered that this would only increase sectarianism and lead to civil war and ethnic cleansing in the North.

In this very difficult situation, I and the other members of The Militant were working nonstop to build our small group. Events seemed to show that what we stood for was impossible. The workers' movement was giving no lead. The religious sectarian organisations had mass bases. The trade union and Labour Party leaders were sabotaging any movement to independent working class action. However I believed in the ideas. I believed that our way was the only way the problems could be solved. So I bared my teeth and got on with the work. We gradually inched our way up to twenty members and increased resources. We achieved this with countless discussions, countless paper sales, fighting for our ideas in meetings and strikes and struggles. With all our mistakes we were building a fighting cadre nucleus.

In 1973, the organisation managed to get together the resources to hire a full-time organiser. The London leadership of The Militant wanted this to be Peter Hadden, who was based in Belfast. He had been recruited by that London leadership when a student in England, he had a higher theoretical level than I and as well as this the London leadership of Militant were more confident that he would go along with their views. However the majority of the organisation in Ireland preferred myself to be the full-timer. I presumed they did so because I was better able to work with people than Peter Hadden, better able to give room for others to develop, not so arrogant. So I became the first full-time organiser for The Militant, now the Socialist Party in Ireland. Borrowing a page from the book of Stalinism, the leaders of the Socialist Party of today write this role I played out of their history.

When I went full-time I worked just about seven days a week and sixteen hours a day to build the organisation. I continued attending the central committee meetings of The Militant in London. I would take the boat to Holyhead on Thursday night, connect with the train to London and return the same way on Sunday night. There were many rough crossings on hard chairs. I looked forward to the warm comfortable seats on the train through north Wales. Getting back into Dublin and having a hot whiskey in a pub was an oasis.

Returning from one of these trips I was up on the bow of the ferry from Holyhead when it dawned on me. Things had changed. I would normally have been worried that when I returned the entire group would have collapsed. But now I realised that we would still be functioning, our paper would still be coming out, we would still be involving ourselves in struggles. A small cohesive nucleus of an organisation had been built. This was a great relief. A milestone had been reached.

This progress was mainly due to there by then being enough committed and experienced members to set up internal structures. At its annual conferences the group elected a central committee. This met every three months to discuss what was going on and to set tasks and objectives. This body in turn elected a smaller Executive Committee which met weekly.

We also developed an all-Dublin regional committee with the full-timers from Dublin and with delegates from all the city's branches. With more members and these paying weekly contributions we could afford to and did take on more full-timers. We set up caucuses for the youth work, trade union work and women's work. We were developing an organisational structure, a spine, around which the organisation could grow. All was no longer resting on a couple of peoples' shoulders.

The paper came out every month and its contents improved. Finn Geaney and Pat Smyth were to a great extent responsible for this. Another reason the quality of the paper improved was as we recruited more workers, and learnt how to discuss and listen better, we were better able to cover national and international events. Over this period the paper went from four to eight pages.

We continued to recruit more new and serious members. A woman member, Deirdre Dagger, herself a serious and committed member, met Dermot Connolly on a pub sale. He was a thoughtful and intelligent worker who was a helper on a truck. We discussed the transitional programme pamphlet by Trotsky. Early in the discussion he asked if there was an organisation such as the 4th International which was referred to in the back of this small pamphlet. I said yes and asked him to join. He did so very quickly after that. He would go on to be the main Southern member of the organisation after I left Ireland in 1983. He would later spend time in prison for his struggles against the attacks on the working class. He also went on later to see through the false internal life of the organisation, leave the organisation and, along with his companion Joan Collins, who became a member of parliament, go on to play an important role in revolutionary politics.

Finn Geaney, originally from Limerick, had worked in London and been in the organisation there. On returning to Dublin he played a major central role in the organisation. For some time he edited the paper, was the organisation's treasurer, was active in the organisation, worked at his teaching job and had a family, all at the same time. I never understood how he could do it. He was central to the development of the group in this period.

Sometime earlier Anton McCabe had joined the organisation. I met him when I was attending a Labour Party meeting at University College Dublin (UCD), He was a committed, thoughtful and intelligent member who maintained his revolutionary ideas, who became an active trade union member and would go on to become an excellent writer. He participated in student struggles and also along with myself, in the struggles of autoworkers' occupations and strikes.

Through him I met Joe Higgins who was also a student at UCD. From a rural small farmer background like myself he listened to our ideas on socialism, history and internationalism. Then he asked what was our programme for small farmers? I explained. By taking over the dominant sections of the economy and building a democratic socialist society we would be able to reach out our hand and give support, cheap loans etc. to the small farmer sector of the economy and integrate them into the economy and socialist society. He joined the organisation and went on to play a major role. When I left Ireland I proposed the organisation put him forward for my place on the Administrative Council of the Labour Party. My proposal was accepted and he was elected by the Labour Party conference. From this position, to which I had previously been elected, his prominence in Irish left politics came about. He would go on to become a member of the Irish and European parliaments.

Unfortunately while keeping up his struggle against the bosses and their system, and he must receive credit for this, he was not able to stand against the later to develop unprincipled, undemocratic internal life of the organisation. To keep his leading position in the organisation, and his positions in the labour movement as a whole, he supported my later expulsion from that organisation and also stood by and let other good members who were independent in thought be driven from the organisation. However when he joined, he strengthened the organisation.

It was our position at the time that the working class when it moved, would move to the Labour Party. At a meeting before I left to work in the CWI internationally and in order to see the strengths and weaknesses of the members, I raised the possibility that this might not happen. The reaction was very interesting. Dermot Connolly was able immediately to participate in an exploratory discussion of this possibility. Joe Higgins sat in shock, not able to contribute in any way, as the perspective we had was questioned. Joe was not able to adjust to turns and twists in the class struggle, he would continue to need others to orient him when events changed the ground on which the organisation had to work.

Jimmy Kelly, the electrician and leading member of the electricians' union I had met at the LP conference when I moved the resolution on a trade union defence force for the North, had also joined. He would play an important role in the organisation and its role in the trade unions. He brought other members of his family into the organisation with him. He would become one of the most experienced and active trade union members of the organisation.

Two young Dublin workers also joined at this time. Ted Gannon, an electrician and Mick Carbin, who worked in the post office. They were from the central Dublin working class, both were intelligent and thoughtful workers. They strengthened the organisation. Ted Gannon would go on to serve on the Labour Party administrative council as the representative of Labour Youth. Unfortunately both would later leave the organisation. We also recruited workers such as the pipe fitter Clem McCluskey and young students and workers such as Mick Barry.

Young women workers and students such as Norma Prendiville and Angie O'Leary and Audrey McCready had also joined the group. These members along with Bridget O'Toole and Eileen Cullen and Carmel Gates in the North helped increase the number of women in the organisation and the strength of the organisation overall. Norma Prendiville would become a full-timer and played an important in the organisation. However, unfortunately, after I left and unknown to me, she came under attack by the male egos and the controlling method of The Militant leadership both in Ireland and Britain and was driven out. She would go on to play a leading role in the trade union movement.

From the mid-1970s on, I began to increasingly travel and build outside Dublin. The organisation being unable to afford a car, I would hitch hike. I made regular trips to Cork and Galway. By leaving Dublin at 7.00 am on a Friday morning I would be able to get to Cork in the early afternoon and spend the rest of the day and evening and next day selling papers on the streets and in the pubs, staying in a filthy guest house overnight and hitching back on Sunday. We eventually got a small branch in that city.

I also began to hitch to Galway. I met and over some years recruited Emmett Farrell. He was an outstanding activist who had allowed his home to be used as the family planning centre for Galway. He was way ahead of the organisation on the emphasis he gave to that issue at that time. He tested our ideas through long discussions. When he joined he was very committed to the organisation and went to South Africa and played a role building in the underground there before returning to Ireland to play a leading role in revolutionary politics to this day.

He and others such as Laura and Ken Cooke opened the door into the Galway Labour Party and the university where I spoke at many meetings and was to meet and discuss on a number of occasions with Michael D Higgins, the future President of Ireland. Gerry Dawe the well-known poet originally from Belfast, was also a member in Galway for a time.

The group was spreading throughout the country. We had a number of branches in Dublin city, a branch in Cork and Galway, branches in Belfast, Derry, Ballymena and Coleraine. In spite of the ebbing tide of the workers' movement as a whole we had grown from the dozen members in the early 1970s to close to 100 members. This was a significant achievement. We had also become better known, regularly having letters printed in the capitalist press and appearing on TV. We were making progress. We had established a small revolutionary nucleus. But it was like climbing a cliff face.

CHAPTER 27

MY SYSTEM PRESENTS ITS BILL

As I HITCH-HIKED the country to do my work, I would on occasion be left off on a quiet stretch of a country road. When this happened I would find a small clump of trees or a quiet spot by a stream, climb over the hedge and lie down in the open air and rest and sleep. I carried an old rainproof ground sheet to lie on to keep dry. The smell of the grass and leaves would sooth and comfort me. These were some of the most pleasant moments of my life.

I had fought to get away from my home in Donegal, from the ideas and traditions with which I was raised. But I missed the countryside and nature of Donegal. I yearned for the trees and fields and rivers and lakes and the sea. There was an ache in me for these. I felt for the majority of people in the world who had never or would never see the ocean. But giving up these things was part of the struggle to build the revolutionary organisation, giving up things that were part of me. Lying down and resting in the fields when I was hitching was an attempt to make up for my missing the countryside and nature and rivers and oceans of my younger days, and to make this sacrifice bearable.

I tried to give myself similar breaks when I was in Dublin. If I had a few hours free on a weekend I would take the bus out to Enniskerry. From there I would walk up into the Wicklow hills and have a picnic, sometimes by myself and sometimes with a friend. I would light a fire and cook something or have some bread and cheese. Like my rests on the road these were peaceful interludes in nature which helped me endure the relentless battle to build the organisation.

I was not celibate or without relationships in these times. But I always kept any relationship within certain boundaries. My priority was to build the revolutionary organisation. I could not see how this could remain my priority if I had a permanent relationship. I was still acting like I did with my family, keeping people at arm's length, even though I now knew my place in the world it seemed that I could not let go of the old ways, that is, keeping myself independent of others and of any committed relationships. On a number of occasions I would have a relationship where my friend made clear she would accept the kind of relationship that she thought would be possible for me, that is to say, me giving priority to building the revolutionary party over any relationship and she would help me with my work. But I could not accept this. I did not believe it would be that simple. I believed that any relationship I would have would tend to develop into a closer and closer relationship. That if this happened I would not be able to accept that I was not pulling my weight in the relationship and so the relationship would become impossible.

One day in the summer of 1977, I was thirty-four years old, I was at a meeting of the executive committee of the group. The meeting was in the middle of discussion when some words burst out of my mouth. They were not formulated consciously in advance in my brain and then spoken. They forced themselves out: 'I cannot keep on working at this rate.' Everyone present turned and looked at me in surprise. Nobody spoke. I also said no more, just pretended nothing had happened. Everybody else did the same. We continued with our discussion.

That night I went to walk home. The closer I got to my house the more anxiety and fear took over. I realised I was terrified of getting there and going to bed and to sleep. It was only then I remembered the dreams and nightmares of the night before. They were not narratives. They were bleak colours, harsh textures, jagged edges, non-organic substances, metals. I felt I could not go to sleep and go through this again. But I could see no alternative to trying to escape into sleep?

I lived at that time in a small one-story, two-bedroom house in a cul de sac in the Coombe. It had been built for brewery workers many decades before. It had a fireplace. I lit a fire to see if the heat and comfort from this might make me feel better. I always liked lighting fires, seeing the flames take hold. I put the kettle on the stove in the kitchen. I wished I still had my dogs. I needed something living to be around. By my own choice I did not have a human being.

The fire, the tea making, the sitting down and looking at the fire did not work. I held my head between my hands to try and press out the fears. I needed to sleep or I would not be able to do my work. I had some Powers whiskey and got it out and had a glass. I dragged out the mattress from the bedroom and put it on the floor in front of the fire. Hopefully the fire would not set light to the mattress and burn me, instead it would take the oxygen out of the air and with the Powers help me sleep.

Eventually I half dozed off. I kept waking again and again. I kept looking at the clock but it was as if its hands were stuck. What was I going to do? My head was screaming. I had to sleep. I kept thinking of the morning. I would have to go to work.

In the morning I went to the doctor round the corner, an old man with Einstein hair. I described my symptoms. 'What do you do for a living?' I told him about my work and my driven attitude to organise. He then asked me: 'Have you had any major traumas in your life recently?' I told him about my struggle with my family over the years and my commitment to my work, and the pace of my work. I did not tell him about the death of another person for which I had been at least partially been responsible. My extreme interpretation of what was necessary to build the revolutionary organisation contributed to that death. I dealt with my guilt over this by baring my teeth and declaring that nothing would stop me building the revolutionary organisation. This guilt was to congeal in me and would permanently stop my being from properly functioning. This guilt entered into the centre of me and would affect, would damage me for the rest of my life.

The doctor's diagnosis was that I was mentally and physically exhausted. He said: 'I will give you something to slow you down, to help you be less driven as you put it. But also I want you to take up something like yoga so you can begin to change your lifestyle.' I thanked him and left with a prescription for Valium. I threw it in a rubbish bin on the way back to the house. As I saw it I was not going to go on the dope. I did not consider having an occasional whiskey as dope.

At that time our headquarters was in Abbey Street in the city centre. I had to go in and help with the paper and discuss the day's work. I could not avoid this. I was determined nobody should know I was not well. I was ashamed of what I saw as my weakness. I thought the doctor was right and I was mentally and physically exhausted. But I was not going to admit this. I bared my teeth. Nothing was going to stop me building the revolutionary international.

I steadied myself and got the bus down to the city centre and our headquarters. There were other full-time members already there. I was usually first. I was together enough so that nobody noticed anything wrong with me. I was a good bluffer. 'So shall we get started?' We went through the agenda and allocated tasks for the day. I was to do research for an article. I said I would be at the library and if I got good material I would go straight home afterwards. This was so I could get away but nobody took it as strange.

I took a long cut home through the grounds of Trinity College with its grass and trees and old buildings. When I had been working in construction

I had helped build an addition to the college. Walking through the grounds and thinking about this gave me back some balance and confidence. I thought about being mentally and physically exhausted. I realised I was in this condition not just because I was working too hard, not just because I had brutalised my emotions to get where I was, it was also because I was unrelentingly focused on one thing, building the revolutionary organisation. When I lay down in the countryside, when I walked in the grounds of the college and saw the old buildings and trees, this exercised a different part of my brain. My brain was not only overworked, but it was also focused on only the one thing, day after day, night after night – build the revolutionary organisation and through this extreme concentration and focus as well as the over work it was being thrown out of balance, it was being overheated.

If my brain was not to seize up altogether I would have to allow it to engage in other things. I would have to have different activities, different hobbies. Perhaps go to the theatre, to the movies, read poetry and literature. I would have to take up painting, sculpture, some sort of creative activity not just building the organisation. To heal I would have to get a more balanced approach to the nonstop work of building the revolutionary organisation.

I was as bad as my family now, maybe even worse, even more addicted to work than they had ever been. And in my case I had an even more narrow, harsh field of work. Nor did I have my father's Aberdeen Angus, my uncle's horses, my mother's butter making, my aunt's flower garden, I had no art in my life, I would not allow myself to have any art in my life. I considered it would only take up my time. But if you deny yourself something you need badly, this does not mean your need goes away. It will just assert itself in another form. That was partially what was happening with me. Focus only on the drive to build the revolutionary organisation, my refusal to allow any creative urges other than building the revolutionary organisation to develop, my refusal to allow any serious personal relationships to develop, only build and build the revolutionary organisation, this was the combination that was bringing me down.

And not only was I focused on work, and only work, and only the most narrow view of what that work was, but there was the nature of that work. I had to continually organise and motivate people. I had to convince them to change their way of living, change their lives. I had to convince people we could change the world. I had to convince people the struggle to build our organisation was worthwhile when just about all the other forces in society were telling them the opposite. I had to lift many of these people up on my shoulders. This was nonstop. This was exhausting. Fighting to convince people that what we were seeking to achieve could be achieved. This was taking from me and giving to them. This struggle never ended. It had drained and exhausted me.

One example of this was two members, good workers. I knew that every now and then they would have doubts and want to give up. I would always know when they were approaching this point as they would be very friendly and ask could they come round to my house for a chat. I would always say yes sure but I would know what was coming. I would serve them tea and cake and then I would start on about how well our work was going, how we were building, talk about this new young member and that new young member, and emphasise even over-emphasise all the positives in our work. By the time I was finished they did not have the heart to tell me they wanted to leave the organisation. I would then ask them what was it they wanted to talk about. They would usually say they just wanted to see if I was okay and then they would leave. I would be exhausted after such interventions and this one was by no means the most difficult. Recruiting and keeping members in the organisation took a powerful toll on me. Of course this did not apply to all the members of the organization but it did to a not insgnificant number.

I thought more about these issues as I walked on towards my home in the Coombe. I thought of having different hobbies and interests. I was convinced that this would be a good thing. But the problem was this would take time away from building the revolutionary organisation. This was not on my agenda. Things were not going to be simple.

As I thought further about things I realised that it was not just a political question. I was not taking into account the personal, that is not allowing any personal relations to develop, and in particular my struggles to break from my family's ideas. I considered these were just things that had to be done. So how could they be bad for my health?

I had not yet got a full grasp of the dialectic, the positive and the negative in my personal world. I was very underdeveloped in my understanding and thinking about the relationship between my health, mental and physical and psychological, and my political world at that time. My illnesses and experiences would later educate me. They would teach me that even fighting for the right things, in my case to understand my role in the world and to be active in pursuing that role, that is building the revolutionary international, while positive and necessary, could also be and in my case was, damaging. And especially as was the case with myself and my tendency to extremism, if fighting for these things was pursued in excess, pushed to an extreme, it could seriously damage me. It was as in all things a question of understanding the different contradictions in my life, seeking to reduce the conflict between these contradictions to a minimum while not turning myself into an inert creature. It was a question of balance and context. I had to continue to be a revolutionary but I also had to be able to live and have an emotional and psychological balance that would allow me to function. I was not able to do this.

I was thinking about these issues as I walked through the grounds of Trinity College, across the cobble-stoned square and up to Nassau Street. I thought more about my non-family personal relations. They had a role in this too. Just because I did not allow personal relations to develop did not mean that I was celibate. I had women friends. We played together. In a number of cases some of my women friends would want a more permanent relationship than I. But I had to build the revolutionary international. I did not allow these relationships to develop. I thought again about the song I would sometimes sing to myself when I was alone. It was Bob Dylan's 'It Ain't Me Babe'. This about summed it up.

These relationships were like the relationship I had with my family. I would, while allowing them to develop to a point, always halt them and stop them at a certain stage, so they did not obstruct my struggle to build the revolutionary international as I saw it. I was incapable of seeing that a good relationship with another revolutionary would be a help to building the revolutionary international and to myself. I was too scared by my experience with my family to consider this. This way of conducting myself was hurtful to my women friends and seriously damaging to myself.

My reaction to the ending and break up of relationships was straight out of my by now well used play book. The one that I had used with my family and their ideas and their pressure to have me involved in their Orange Order world and their farm. I bared my teeth and moved on. I conducted a war of terror against my emotions. I had to build the revolutionary organisation. Nothing was going to stop me. I put my ended relationships into what I thought was a closed compartment in my head, this compartment was labelled: 'Above all else the task is to build the revolutionary organisation, all must be sacrificed to that. Keep this compartment closed.'

There were numerous files in that compartment. My relations with my family, my relationship with Barbara, my relationship with the beauty and peace of Donegal and the rivers and fields and sea of that county, all were in that compartment. Sacrificed to my need to find my role and then to fulfil that role, as an international socialist revolutionary. 'Above all else the task is to build the revolutionary organisation, all must be sacrificed to that.' I had fought long and hard to find my way to this conclusion and there was no way I would abandon it. This was my life. I had no doubt that this was correct for me so how could it harm me? How could this way of living damage my health?

I was naive about life and health in those days. I did not see that doing the right thing for yourself and society was not simple. If you did this to excess then it could spring back and hit you in the face, it could damage you. It was a question of balance. I had fought for and came to understand my role in the world, I had fought to build the revolutionary organisation which

I came to understand was my role in the world, but I had done so to a degree that I had done a lot of damage to others along the way. And inevitably done a lot of damage to myself also. It did not matter that where I had to start from, that is from an Orange Order family in rural Donegal and so my struggle was particularly harsh, had inevitably to be particularly harsh, this did not matter – the reality was that damage was done. These experiences all contributed to the mental and physical crisis I was now in. But then maybe considering where I came from, the only way for me to get to where I had to be was to fight to the excessive, the extreme, degree I did and to endure the damage and the wounds. Did I have any choice? I was not convinced I had.

So I did not change my lifestyle or priorities in any way. I remained convinced I was doing the right thing and it was still five to ten years to the revolution, there was no time to lose. I would think of my different relationships and the hurt I had caused to others and myself but I would also think that given my level of understanding and my past experiences, could some sort of damaging relationships have been avoided? I told myself no. I could not afford to think otherwise. Some wreckage, some damage was inevitable on the road from Orange Order small farmer Donegal to international revolutionary socialism.

I had developed a relationship with a woman friend some time before my illness struck. Her husband was well off, with a business in the retail creative field and he was quite well known, appearing on television on occasion. We met at a Spanish class which I had been attending to learn the language in anticipation of doing more international work. She was a practicing Catholic. After we had gone out for some food and a drink a couple of times she said she wanted me to accompany her to a place that was special for her. I agreed. She drove to a large square building in an expensive neighbourhood. We got out and she led me to a small door in a high wall of this building. She rang the bell. A tall man in a monk's outfit answered. He obviously knew my friend and he welcomed her.

With my friend in front we followed him down a narrow corridor to a small room and he left us alone. The room was a small chapel. My friend took my hand and led me to one of the row of pine wood seats. She sat down and then knelt forward and bowed her head and closed her eyes in prayer. I sat on the seat respectfully observing what she was doing. After a few moments she raised her head and looked at me. Her eyes were shining and she seemed to have taken a step which opened up some new path for her in her life. Her expression seemed to say that she now knew what she was going to do and she was content with her decision. She took my hand and stood up and raised me with her. We left the chapel and the building. We went to my small house and for the first time we enjoyed each other physically. My friend had obviously made her peace with her god in that small chapel, maybe even 'married' me in her own way.

But in the future I even broke this relationship. I would not let it last. I would not bend enough. After all I had to build the revolutionary organisation. I would later think of her superior method to mine. She had bent. She had taken me to her little chapel. She had perhaps discussed her situation with the monk who had let us in. When she had bent forward with her head bowed she had probably 'discussed' her situation and her decision with her god. She had not asked me to say a word. Just be there with her. She had said her words. Then she had, against her Catholic marriage vows and beliefs, had a relationship with me for some time. But for me it was still building the revolutionary international and all had to be sacrificed to that. So I ended the relationship. I hurt her and I hurt myself. I apologise to her in my mind. In what I saw was the interest of building the revolutionary international I hurt my friend and hurt anybody who came close to me and hurt and damaged myself. This was not good.

My health crisis continued in the weeks that followed. I continued to have difficulty, sleeping, reading, crossing roads, judging distances and speeds. I should have taken the Valium the doctor prescribed me as this would have given me a temporary respite, given my system a time to rest. But I did not. Instead I bared my teeth and I bluffed my way. The members of the organisation did not know of my crisis. As well as learning to better judge distances and speeds and cross roads, I was able to organise myself to prepare for meetings and intervene at these. I learned to read more slowly. I was not so much getting better, as stopping a further slide downwards. But that was something.

Some months of this and I asked the organisation for a couple of weeks off. I had never asked for time off before. There was full support for this with members declaring that I should have had time off long ago. After all it was years since I had started as a full-time organiser for the group. I borrowed a bike and loaded up a few clothes and took the train. I had the loan of an old broken down caravan in Kerry. It was autumn and the site was empty except for this wreck. There were square marks on the grass of the site where the other caravans had been in the summer. These accentuated my aloneness. The first night the winds blew and the windows and doors on the caravan rattled and I did not get a wink of sleep.

I left the caravan the next morning and set off to cycle up the coast staying in youth hostels and meeting people from different countries. Talking to them about their different countries and worlds and their ideas took some pressure off my head. Meeting with all the different people from different countries in the hostels was allowing my brain to cool somewhat and more of a balance to develop.

The countryside was beautiful with its rocky terrain, the purple heather and the black bog, the ocean and the lakes and rivers and the rocks. I would get of my bike and pick and eat the ripening blackberries from the hedges. I swam in the lakes heated by the sun shining on their waters and reflected up again from their rocky bottoms. I spent time in Connemara. I came to feel that it was here, in the West of Ireland, especially in Connemara, with its rocks and bog, with its soil that was made of seaweed dragged in from the sea by the starving people in the past, that my atheist's spirit was most at home. I felt some peace.

It was autumn. I cycled up and down the west coast, from Kerry, up into Clare, into Galway, back down south again following the coastal roads and staying in the hostels. I went inland to Yeats tower. By then I accepted that though he came to be influenced by the extreme right in his later years he could still put together great combinations of words, great truths. 'Things fall apart the centre cannot hold.' My own centre was not holding too well. There was an odd crack developing in my own tower.

I spent a day in a small village in Clare. There was a forge there where the blacksmith was shoeing a horse. It reminded me of my holding my uncle's horses while he shoed them. It reminded me of when I was a schoolboy and called into the forge on the way home from school and pulled the bellows for the blacksmith. I stayed the entire day with this blacksmith standing in his doorway looking out over the river flowing past. He smoked, we talked between his spells of work, his clanging of his hammer on the red hot metal and the anvil. We looked out over the river that flowed down in front of his forge. When the time came for him to close up and go to his home we shook hands and parted. I had had a peaceful day and my head was more cooled and balanced.

I spent a week in a youth hostel outside Killarney in Kerry. On my first day there I found the ruins of an old church with a graveyard. There were many old fallen over gravestones and graves. One grave was covered with a large flat stone like my family's grave in Lifford. There were a few dried up human bones under this stone. For the week I stayed there I cycled the roads and lanes in the area for the first half of the day. In the afternoon I ate in the quiet comfort of the dining room of Muckross House, with its linen tablecloths and its view of the lawn stretching down to its small lake. After my meal I would go to this graveyard and crawl under the large gravestone and sleep amongst the bones. Only years later did I wonder what that was all about. Was I unconsciously trying to make it up to my family for all the hurt I caused them? Sleeping amongst old bones in an old grave like that of my family's grave in Lifford. Maybe I was having the illusion that I was at last resting in peace amongst my own family. But this was an illusion. However in spite of this these were peaceful interludes among the bones.

As I returned to Dublin I was still having damaging dreams and sleeping badly. But I was no longer on the verge of collapse or unable to judge distance or read a book or a newspaper. I had halted the plunge downwards. I had been on the edge of complete physical and mental disintegration but this was no longer the case. I had pulled back from this abyss, back to an acceptable balance and relationship with the physical world and with my mental and psychological and political worlds. This was no small relief. However having said all that and although I did not realise it to any extent fully at the time, permanent damage had been done to my health and this would never be reversed. But able to function once again I returned to my full-time organising work.

I did so thinking my crisis was just a question of the effect of over-work, of over-focus on one task, of insufficient rest and relaxation and of the damage done by past experiences such as the struggles with my family and in my political and personal life. And it was all of these. It was no accident my health crisis came when it did, after years helping to drag the first nucleus off the ground, after years of standing against the stream, after years in which I put too many demands on myself and others. But in later years I was to learn that my health crisis was much more than that. I was to learn that I had fundamental organic chronic health problems, such as a non-functioning thyroid gland and non-functioning adrenal glands. These illnesses I had inherited from my father. I had other health problems also. These came from the many concussions and injuries that I had received from my younger days. I would also develop epilepsy. When these health problems would develop further in the future I would come close to death on many occasions. I would suffer more than I had done in my health crisis of the 1970s.

CHAPTER 28

WORKING CLASS NORTH AND SOUTH – EFFORTS TO RISE

THE 1970s was a decade of increasing sectarianism and near civil war in the North, a decade when the working class became more and more divided. However there were a few occasions when it did try to rise to its feet. After a series of vicious tit for tat sectarian killings in the North in 1976, a small movement of workers took spontaneous action. Demonstrations took place in Derry, Lurgan and Newry. Five thousand workers, Protestant and Catholic marched together in Derry against sectarian violence. Bus drivers went on strike after one of their members was forced to drive a bomb on one of their routes. Women workers in Derry went on strike when a bomb was left near their workplace. Derry had its first May Day march since 1920. Nine new trade union branches affiliated to the city's trades' council. After a vicious sectarian attack in mid-Ulster, the Mid-Ulster Trades' council called a strike. The union bureaucracy as usual came out against it but the mood from below amongst public sector workers especially was so great that they had to back down and they were forced to call a strike and demonstration in Belfast. These movements of workers from below against sectarianism forced the union leaders to pretend to take some action.

They set up the Better Life For All (BLFA) campaign. BLFA committees were established thought the North. However, true to form, the trade union leaders who were forced to set up the BLFC refused to confront in any real way the violence and repression and sectarianism, the most immediate issues of the day, and more than that they sabotaged the BLFA. The result of their sabotage was that the BLFA movement withered and died.

However, in spite of the refusal to lead of the trade union and labour leaders, the tendency of working class people to reach across the sectarian divide and to try and deal with the problems they faced tried again to express itself. This time it did so through what became known as the Peace Movement.

Three young children were killed in a car crash when their car was rammed by another car which was being driven by IRA members and which had been shot up by the British Army. In response working class women marched from the Catholic Falls area into the Protestant Shankill area, and from the Protestant Shankill area into the Catholic Falls area protesting against sectarianism and repression. These working class women from both religions welcomed and greeted each other and marched together. This movement had the potential to transform the situation in the North.

For the briefest of few weeks it showed what was possible. In one area of Belfast it drove away paramilitary groups who were trying to hijack cars. At the same time it repelled British Army patrols which were trying to raid houses. It was very significant that they drove away the British Army patrols as well as the paramilitary groups. They acted through their 'whistle patrols', which summoned people, overwhelmingly it was women who acted, by whistle from their homes to take over the streets, in other words, they mobilised working class people to take action and impose their will on the situation. Imagine what could have been possible if the trade union leaders had brought their organised membership onto the streets along with the women-led Peace Movement. Many of the participants in the Peace Movement were either in the trade unions or had family members in the trade unions. With 250,000 union members in the North a powerful movement could have been built which could have transformed the situation.

But just like they had done with the BLFA campaign, the trade union and Labour leaders, the right wing, male-dominated, union leaders refused to put their forces to help the Peace Movement. Instead, like every spontaneous movement of workers on the streets and workplaces to unite and build an independent movement, they sought to undermine it. They came out with their usual platitudes about peace but held their members back and let the upper middle class politicians and the British state take over the Peace Movement and defang it. When this happened there were no more whistle patrols. The leaders of the peace movement were flown round the world and flattered and the movement was demobilised. Once again the trade union and labour leaders had betrayed the working class and their members and allowed sectarianism and state repression to rule. The last thing these leaders wanted to do was to build and mobilise a united working class movement.

Our organisation intervened in these movements. But our resources were miniscule. What was necessary was a united working class organisation with hardened tough fighting cadres with a determined, conscious leadership which could have taken to the streets and workplaces, physically stopped the sectarians and worked with the rank and file of the BLFA campaign and with the Peace Movement. And at the same time appealed to the rank and file of the British army. Such a force did not exist. Wherever we could intervene we argued for this alternative but we were too small to bring it about.

Further towards the end of the decade and into the 1980s, there were movements of the working class on bread and butter issues. These efforts took place through the rank and file of the trade unions. The Dublin Trades Council organised a strike against the Pay As You Earn (PAYE) unfair tax system in the South which was loaded in favour of the better off and property owners. Close to 300,000 workers marched in Dublin, Cork, Waterford, Limerick, Galway, Sligo and other towns. This was the biggest workers' demonstration in the history of the Southern state.

In Dublin, at a meeting of between 150,000–200,000, the leader of the Dublin Trades Council took the mike. Would there be a miracle and would she call for organising fighting workers' groups in the work places and rank and file of the unions and build on this huge movement and go on the offensive? Unsurprisingly, it was not to be. She took the mike and sang a song. And not a song of the workers' movement but the whining, religious, passive, reactionary song One Day at a Time Sweet Jesus. Yes one day at a time and sweet Jesus. Once again there were the religious ideas permeating the workers' movement and steering it away from the combative anti-capitalist road.

The PAYE strike and demonstrations were not the only development in the workers' movements at this time. There were also the occupations of a number of plants. These were a direct challenge to the bosses' ownership and control of the workplaces. In the early 1980s there were at least twelve workplaces occupied in the South, from Dublin to Cork to Kerry to Clare to Galway. At around the same time there were four workplaces occupied in the North including one in Protestant East Belfast. These could have all been pulled together into a united movement.

The bosses' magazine, Irish Business, stated at the time: 'With three major successful sit-ins under their belts, the sit in tactic by early 1983 had achieved a certain respectability and had demonstrated to be a sure winner. What was more natural but that it would be used again?' It should have been but the union leaders prevented this from happening.

Major struggles took place in the North and Britain over this period. Workers took action against the London government's wage controls and to support the health workers' struggle. There was the Liverpool City Council struggle, the miners' strike and later the anti-Poll Tax movement.

18 million people were to refuse to pay the poll tax. This struggle was led by The Militant and was victorious in bringing down Thatcher. Many non-payers went to jail.

In the North the movement in support of the health care workers' struggle for better wages resulted in the first ever general strike of a united workers' character in the North. 40,000 Protestant and Catholic workers took action side by side on the picket lines.

However these struggles North and South were not able to overcome the accumulated previous defeats of the workers' movement, the refusal of the workers' leaders to lead, the lack of a mass fighting, organised alternative in the working class and the period of division and reaction that existed. In Britain the miners' strike was defeated and this threw the British and Irish working class even further back. Not even the victorious anti-Poll Tax movement which took place later could change the overall situation.

The lack of a semi-mass or mass revolutionary alternative in the working class was central to the inability of the working class to show a way forward. It was to creating this alternative that our and my work was directed. We failed in this for a number of reasons. Mainly, the tiny resources we had when the movement was at its height and its most progressive in the period 1968/1969. We were starting from way behind events. And we were never able to catch up. Related to this were the roots and traditions Republicanism and Loyalism had amongst significant layers of the population. Most of all of course was the pro-capitalist policies of the trade union and Labour Party leaderships which prevented the working class movement from finding a way forward.

The Militant leadership in Britain was also not blameless. It would not let the anti-Poll Tax movement evolve organically into a permanent mass force taking up all the issues facing the working class and with its own internal democracy and decision making process organised on general anti-capitalist ideas and methods and within which a revolutionary, democratic non-sectarian current with a much more open and democratic internal life could have been built. The Militant's inability to do this cut across the potential of the anti-Poll Tax forces to develop as a genuine, permanent, semi-mass or mass anti-capitalist fighting force which could have developed as an objective force in the class struggle in Britain and in turn affected events in Ireland, and which could have allowed the working class to begin to put its imprint on the situation.

The movement of the working class that had tried to find its feet again in these struggles North and South and in Britain was once again choked into submission by its own leaders who were working arm in arm with the capitalist political parties and forces. The Militant played a role in this also by its left sectarian policies in the leadership of the anti-Poll Tax movement.

Two obstacles, the refusal to fight of the pro capitalist leaders of the unions and labour parties and the left sectarianism of The Militant when it was in the leadership of the anti-Poll Tax movement blocked the working class from putting its imprint on the situation.

That it was the refusal of the trade union and Labour leaders to mobilise the potential of the workers' movement which held the movement back was shown by some developments and opinions in the South. The Southern Economic and Social Research Institute did a poll on peoples' attitude to the ownership of industry. 40% were in favour of industry being nationalised, that is taken out of private hands. This was when no mass party or union was campaigning for this alternative. This was extremely significant and showed the potential for an anti-capitalist movement. At the same time the Labour Party membership voted for the nationalisation of natural resources and the finance houses. Even after years of sectarian conflict in the North and the right wing policies of the Labour and trade union leaders North and South, there was still a significant left consciousness in the South. I continually criticised the Southern trade union and Labour Party leaders for underestimating this consciousness of the working class. They vehemently disagreed. They could not afford to agree. If they admitted what I said was correct then they would have had no excuse for refusing to mobilise the working class.

While 40% of the population of the South were in favour of industry being nationalised, that is moving in the direction of socialism, what were their leaders saying? I had a sufficient base in the Irish Labour Party at the time to be invited by the Dublin Regional Council of the Irish Labour Party to debate with the general secretary of that Party, Brendan Halligan. Halligan stated: 'Capitalism will remain. Socialism was neither socially acceptable nor would be implemented.' So according to the general secretary of the Labour Party, the Party of Connolly and Larkin, the party which supposedly stood for socialism, socialism was not acceptable and would not be implemented. Coming from the man who was in reality the leader of the main political workers' organisation in the South this was open conscious treason. This statement from Halligan clearly showed that he was a participant in some kind of an outfit which discussed these issues of capitalism and socialism. Some kind of an anti-socialist outfit. And he was secretary of the Labour Party which was supposed to be socialist. The plot thickens. Who educated and indoctrinated Halligan and the Halligans?

Halligan was a conscious pro-capitalist bureaucrat while at the same time being the dominant figure in the workers' political organisation, the Labour Party. From this position he believed and openly stated that socialism was not acceptable. From where did he get this? He got it partly from being part of the pro-capitalist social democracy nationally and internationally. At its conferences and through its connections it taught him that only capitalism was possible and acceptable. He believed this and fought for this.

But it would be wrong to think that social democracy was the only influence on Halligan and his fellow Labour Party leaders. The Catholic hierarchy worked consciously to indoctrinate their members to believe that capitalism was the only alternative and help them get into positions of influence and power where they could fight for these ideas. Especially into positions to hold back the working class movement, that is into leading positions in the trade unions and Labour Party. Halligan and the rest of the labour and trade union leaders, with very few exceptions, fought for pro-capitalist ideas which they shared with and partially got from the Catholic hierarchy.

In contrast to what was being said by Labour leaders such as Halligan, here is what a worker in a tire factory in Finglas had to say: 'There is enough brain power on the floor to run the industry more efficiently and more responsibly than existing management.' Unlike the Labour and trade union leaders and bureaucrats, this worker believed that the working class could run industry. What a condemnation of the Labour and trade union leaders. What a confirmation of our position that if the union and Labour leaders would lead a battle against capitalism, they would have received support.

The workers' movement both North and South was sabotaged on all fronts. In the South the union leaders came to an agreement with the employers and the government to establish National Wage Agreements. These agreements restricted the right to strike and excluded the most active and militant workers from decision making and involvement. The Catholic hierarchy preached support from its pulpits for these agreements. The result was the undermining of workers' struggles with days lost on strike falling from 1 million in 1970 to 277,000 in 1971.

There was also the sabotage of the union and Labour leaders on the political front. Again and again the Southern Labour Party leaders took the Party into coalition with Fine Gael, then the most right wing of the two bosses' parties, a party which had roots in the fascist movement of the 1930s. This disillusioned the working class and left many of them seeing no reason to vote for Labour. After all if Labour was going into coalition with Fine Gael, what was the point in voting Labour?

Fine Gael made clear where it stood on these coalitions. One of its leaders of the time stated: 'There will be no compromise on fundamental issues or our principles. Fine Gael are prepared to forego office rather than compromise on the fundamental elements of the programme we have put forward and for which we have sought support. I give this unqualified assurance that the programme which we implement in government will be the Fine Gael programme.' In other words it would not be the Labour programme.

In the North, the trade union leaders sabotaged the trade union struggles by going along with the anti-union laws and wage controls and attacks on conditions coming from the London government. On the political front the leaders of the Northern Ireland Labour Party counted heads, saw there was a majority of Protestants and took a sectarian Protestant position. They also made clear they would not mobilise the working class. As already stated one of their leaders, Vivian Simpson, put it bluntly: 'Let us be absolutely clear about this. There will be no Armageddon in Northern Ireland between the forces of capitalism and socialism.' He was reassuring the capitalist forces in Northern Ireland and Britain that they had nothing to fear from the Northern Ireland Labour Party and he was making it clear to any workers who might be listening that they would get no help to fight capitalism from the Northern Ireland Labour Party.

This statement by Simpson, the Labour leader in the North, was in line with that of Halligan, the Labour Party secretary in the South. They both came out openly against socialism. These statements showed that the anti-socialist ideas of these leaders, their sabotage of the movement, were not the result of individual mistakes on their part.

They were the result of the conscious pro-capitalist views that they held and which they got from the capitalist institutions which dominated the state and society, from the pro-capitalist social democracy to which they belonged and from the churches to which they belonged. These people were conscious supporters of the capitalist class and their system. As such they blocked the working class movement from going forward. They, and the rest of their bureaucratic caste, which sat on top of the working class organisations were, more than any other force, responsible for the inability of the working class to prevent the sectarian violent catastrophe which developed.

If it was not one thing that weakened any attempt to build a united workers' fighting movement it was another. For some time there had been a struggle by Republican prisoners in the Northern prisons for political status. These prisoners insisted they were not criminals but political prisoners. Thatcher's government refused to recognise them as such and the prisoners launched a hunger strike. The Provisional leadership was initially against this but the prisoners forced it on them.

The first hunger striker to die was Bobby Sands. He had many Protestant friends when he was young. He was a poet and writer who went on to become a military activist in the Provos. He was one of the many youth who could have been won to a revolutionary, united, working class movement if the trade union and Labour Party leaders had offered one, or if ideas like ours had had a semi-mass or mass base. But with no such alternative he went on to the dead end of the Provisionals and to starve himself to death.

100,000 people turned out for his funeral. All over Ireland H Block committees were formed and demonstrations and marches were held. These committees were called H-Block committees after the cell blocks in Long Kesh prison which were shaped like the letter H. Prisoners and hunger strikers were elected to parliament. The Provos, building on the sympathy for the hunger strikers and using the sectarian divide developed a mass political and electoral base.

I met with former prisoners at that time to discuss what was what. From this Finn Geaney, on behalf of our organisation, moved a resolution to a Labour Party conference. This did not support the IRA in any way but did call for reforms in the prisoners' conditions as well as the setting up of workers' committees to decide who was a political prisoner and who was not. We were not prepared to campaign for sectarian killers to be designated as political prisoners. We moved similar resolutions to union branches. Unsurprisingly the Labour Party and union leaders mobilised against these resolutions and they were defeated.

The way in which the H Block struggle was conducted by the Provo leadership increased the sectarian divide in the North. The Catholic population moved further to support Sinn Féin. As prisoners died a wave of emotion swept the Catholic population. Walking home in Dublin one night I met a man from Strabane. I had worked with him on a building site some years before. He took me by the lapels and began to weep. 'Throne, Throne. They are dying. These are better men than the ones in 1916.' And he staggered away down Abbey Street.

As Sinn Féin became a mass force out of the hunger strikes, at the same time the Protestant population moved further to support the Loyalist parties, especially Paisley's so-called Democratic Unionist Party. The North was becoming more divided along sectarian lines than before. The workers' struggles in the South had failed. The workers' struggles in the North likewise. North and South the working class was unable to put its imprint on the events. The situation travelled on down the sectarian road and the decline of working class struggle. The result was our struggle for working class unity and struggle remained extremely difficult.

Yet in spite of that our little group continued to make incremental progress. In spite of everything the organisation not only held together but even experienced some growth. Its strength, above all else, was its political ideas. Working class unity, socialism and internationalism, these ideas were sufficiently attractive to enough people to bring small numbers of new members into our group and to keep us going. Our weakness was our miniscule size which led workers and youth to conclude that while our ideas were good there was no way we could implement them. However we continued to exist and even to grow slowly. But it was a bitter, bitter struggle.

CHAPTER 29

A SMALL NUCLEUS

EVER SINCE I had begun my work with The Militant in Ireland I had made clear that whenever we had a solid nucleus established I wanted to go abroad and help build in other countries. Part of my thinking was that I believed that a successful organiser was one who could replace him- or herself. The leading organisers in The Militant in Britain were opposed to this view. They saw themselves as being in their positions for life. I thought this was an un-Marxist and bureaucratic view. But as resources were few and as I was proposing to move to London and help with the international work and then help to build in the USA and Canada, and because I had helped bring about some success in Ireland, there was no open resistance to my proposal.

As I prepared to leave I proposed and it was accepted that Joe Higgins take my place on the Administrative Council of the Labour Party. I was the first member of Militant on this, the leading body of the Labour Party. I had been elected at a Labour Party national conference. Ted Gannon was also on this body as a representative of Labour Youth. Labour Youth had been set up by that time on the basis of a proposal I had moved to the Administrative Council of the Party. By the time I left Ireland we had been elected as the leadership of Labour Youth.

I proposed that Dermot Connolly should take my place as the central person in The Militant in the South. He was a committed revolutionary, had roots in the working class and was a critical thinker. My proposal of Dermot Connolly was resisted by the leadership of The Militant in London because like with myself when I went full-time, the London leadership wanted somebody more pliable and compliant to their wishes and they saw this as being Joe Higgins. They were right in their view of Joe Higgins as being more compliant but wrong in wanting such a person to be the central figure in the organisation.

The growth of The Militant in Ireland in a period of the ebbing tide of the working class movement was a significant achievement. It was due to the efforts and struggles of every single member of the organisation over the years of its existence. No single individual should receive sole credit. Such credit must go to all whether they remained members of Militant or not. The present leadership of Militant or as it is now known, The Socialist Party, tries to write off the members who are no longer with the organisation and deny them their role. You will search in vain for any mention of myself and many other formerly leading members in the material and websites of the Socialist Party. We have been erased from history. This is one of the methods of Stalinism, the writing of people out of history.

Being elected to the leadership of Labour Youth was a big step forward. We had defeated the Labour party leadership to win this struggle. This increased our authority. It showed that we were a serious organisation that could fight and have victories over the Labour Party and social democratic bureaucracy. It also allowed us to hold many of our events, marches, debates, conferences etc. under the official name of the Labour Party Youth. From this position we were able to organise and lead a 500-strong, mainly youth march in Dublin against unemployment. The composition of the march was impressive. There were twelve Labour Youth banners from the South and six Youth for Socialism banners from the North. It was a non-sectarian, all-Ireland, working class youth march.

Also on the march were banners from the Antrim Labour League, the Labour Women's National Council, the Dublin, Bray, Galway, Letterkenny, Ballymena Trades Councils, the ITGWU, ETU, ATGWU, IMETU, POWU, AUEW trade unions, the Bolton Street Students' Union, the College of Commerce, Rathmines Student Union, the Dublin Unemployed Group and Militant Irish Monthly. Of course, because of their left sectarianism, none of the other left groups took part. And because of our left sectarianism we made no effort to get them to take part.

While we had many banners from the workers' movement we did not have even a fraction of the mass membership of the organisations these banners represented. We did not sufficiently consider what this meant. We were overestimating our base. Yes it was good what we had gained but as far as the mass of the working class was concerned we had no influence. It was good that we had many banners of trades councils and trade unions on the march but we did not reflect on the fact that we had only a miniscule fraction of the membership of these organisations, maybe not even a miniscule fraction of these organizations on the march. We did not discuss that the overwhelming majority of the working class and youth were not on our march and the reasons why and what this meant for our organization.

As well as our base in the South and leadership of Labour Youth we had small non-sectarian youth and working class groupings in the North. They were organised as Socialist Youth and the Labour and Trade Union Group. Through these bodies we were able to organise over 100 non-sectarian mainly youth in Belfast on a march for jobs. There were also marchers from the South present on this march.

The Labour and Trade Union group in the North, of which we were the leadership, had eleven branches at the time and supporters in other areas. This stood for a mass Labour Party in the North. At its conference in 1980, it had delegates from five trades' councils and many unions as well as youth organisations North and South and visitors from Britain. With our lead the Labour Party conference in the South passed a resolution supporting the Labour and Trade Union Group in the North in its struggle for a mass Labour Party. These were good achievements but again we were not able to mobilise anything like the mass membership of the workers traditional organisations. Again, as with our march in the South, we did not consider the significance of why the overwhelming majority of the working class were not on these marches.

At this time we held annual summer camps. These were attended on occasion by 200 to 300 youth from the North and South and internationally. They were non-sectarian. Every morning there would be political discussions, every afternoon would be sports and every evening political debates. They were very successful in bringing youth together and showing that revolutionary socialists were not dried up nerds. Also at this time we organised a speaking tour for Peter Taaffe, one of the leading members of The Militant in Britain. Meetings were held North and South. 300 people attended in total.

But the greatest indication of Militant's increasing influence and resources at that time was the organising of a meeting to which Militant Irish Monthly, under the banner of Labour Youth, invited Tony Benn, the left wing Labour leader from Britain. The Labour Party leadership with one exception, Michael D Higgins, now President of Ireland, gave no support to this meeting. It was held in Liberty Hall and organised entirely by Labour Youth, that is in reality by The Militant. Over 2,500 people attended. Instead of the one hall that was booked it filled three halls linked up at the last minute with a PA system and even with this, hundreds could not get in. It was one of the largest, if not the largest, indoor Labour public meetings in Irish Labour history. And it went off without a hitch, in organisation and security it ran like clockwork. It showed what was possible.

These marches and this larger meeting with Tony Benn alarmed the social democratic and capitalist forces. At this time I received a package in the mail containing a copy of a document which had been sent to the Labour Party leadership. There was no information as to who had sent me this package. The document offered the Labour Party leadership tens of thousands of pounds if it removed the Marxist leadership from Labour Youth and expelled Militant from its ranks. I was on the Administrative Council, the leading body of the Labour Party at the time. At the next meeting I threw this document down on the table and demanded answers. The Labour Party leadership were dumbfounded as it had no idea I had this material. The money was to come from a social democratic organisation which was a CIA front and which worked in the international Labour movement. The Labour Party leaders claimed they had no knowledge of the document and that was that for the time being. But we were being increasingly noticed.

The pro-capitalist social democracy and its backers internationally were not the only right wing institutions that were paying more attention to us at that time. The Catholic Church also tried to move against us. It sent a group of young Opus Dei members into Labour Youth. They were smug middle class types. They did not expect to be confronted with the confident socialism and atheism of the majority of Labour Youth. They expected to meet people they could intimidate with reference to the Pope and him supposedly being the representative of some god on earth. They soon became demoralised. It was one thing to speak from a pulpit when nobody could put alternative views. It was another thing entirely to debate democratically.

Along with these developments documents would come out later which showed that my home was watched by the police, my phone was tapped and the neighbour next door had been recruited by the Garda as an informer. The state was also taking increasing interest in our small group.

As I prepared to leave in 1983, I thought about how far we had come since 1971 when we had only myself in the South and around ten members in the North. The membership by 1983 had reached close to four hundred in Ireland as a whole with over two thirds of these in the South. We had branches in over twenty-five locations and individual members in other areas. We had members in up to twenty trades' councils and caucuses in a number of trade unions. We were the leadership of Labour Youth in the South, had two members on the Administrative Council, the leading body of the Labour Party, and we led Socialist Youth and the Labour and Trade Union group in the North.

As the organisation grew it attracted more than its share of personalities. From the straight laced to the overly fond of the drink. From the members who could laugh to those who thought to do so was a waste of time and resources. After all there was the five to ten years. I would consider again my observation that those who could not laugh were those who had the most difficultly in grasping the dialectic.

There were many characters. There was one member who when his girlfriend was in a car crash and in hospital felt so sorry for her he asked her to marry him and then came into the headquarters the next day asking me how to get out of it. There was a strong, tough young Dublin woman who fought determinedly and vocally at all times for her views. There was a young woman from a rural background who was as tough and humorous as the rest of them. There was the member from an upper class liberal background who was not afraid to speak his mind and fight for his ideas. I was very encouraged with the diversity of the organisation.

As we grew and became an organisation of hundreds, the social aspect of our work increased. Meeting like-minded committed fellow socialists on a regular basis at sizeable social events was a big attraction. We were able to hold large socials. Ted Gannon brought a bus driver who was an accomplished blues singer to socials in Dublin on a few occasions. The singer was overwhelmed by the response. It was connected to our politics. We were all products of the Black revolt in the US in one way or another. Listening to this man play the blues and looking at the dancing, singing, laughing members of the organisation and their friends as they responded was a great pleasure and satisfaction. I felt that I was finally away from my rural, loyalist background and had become an international socialist revolutionary in all ways, politically, culturally, socially and personally. In later years I would remember these nights and the members who participated in them and think about how the lives of these people would turn out. Some would turn out positive and some when I heard about them my heart would break.

At that time there was a member of the group from Chile. She and her daughter had to flee their country from the right wing coup of Pinochet and they came to Ireland. We were friends. She was a classical musician. At one of our socials and after being asked to by myself she took the stage without a mike and began to sing. There were about 100 people in the hall with their drinks and glasses clinking and talking and laughing and making noise together. But gradually the trained voice of my friend singing her classical music brought quiet until not a sound could be heard. I was proud of this Comrade who had escaped death at the hands of Pinochet, who had become a world class classical musician and I was proud of the working class Dublin audience who recognised they were hearing something special and who went silent in their respect and appreciation.

We were a team that worked hard and fought for our ideas and were making progress. We were a team who would go out together and have our music and laughter and socialising on a Saturday night and get together as Comrades and friends. We were a team that would on occasion hire a bus and visit the large monuments at Newgrange. One of our members who worked in the National Museum gave the organisation the guided tour. So even though the objective situation in which we were working was difficult it was not a bad time for the organisation.

Young people especially were essential to the development of the organisation. The young members were also the ones to get the most out of it. Going on to the streets, to meetings, into pubs to sell papers was new to them. Having to discuss with those who bought the papers was also new. Having to respond to serious discussion as well as to the banter and teasing that they inevitably received, even on some occasions the abuse, helped these young people to develop as revolutionaries and as human beings. In later years when I returned to Ireland I would be pleasantly surprised to see how many of these members were active in the unions, the media, education, former members who had cut their teeth in the ranks of the organisation and in working to build the organisation.

There was reason to be confident that we had a sufficient nucleus upon which could be built a semi-mass, even a mass force of workers and youth based on the ideas of working class unity, socialism and internationalism. There was sufficient reason to be confident that on this base we could build the Irish section of the revolutionary international. I had come to Dublin with this objective. I felt good as I prepared to move to work as an International full-timer in London and to enter a new phase of my life.

I had left Ireland in 1965 when I was twenty to try and better understand the world. I had left again in 1970 when I was twenty-six to try and develop my ideas in discussions with left groups in London. Now it was 1983 and I was leaving again at the age of thirty-nine, this time with an understanding of my place in the world and as a leading member of a small international revolutionary organisation. I was a revolutionary going to help build a mass international organisation to overthrow capitalism. Things were good.

Just before I left Ireland I was speaking at a meeting in Dublin. As it was about to begin the door opened and members of the organisation from the North came in. This was a surprise to me. The meeting had been secretly turned into a farewell and thank you event for myself. I was presented with a gift, a boom box. I hid my thoughts about this. I saw it as an insult. What about a painting or piece of art or a piece of sculpture that I could treasure. Was my cultural level so low, my contribution so little, that it was a symbolised by a cheap boom box? I was told that Peter Hadden, the leading member in the North, had suggested the boom box.

This same person made a speech about my role and how I represented the all-round Bolshevik, theoretically, organisationally, politically, capable and determined, a complete revolutionary. This assessment was not repeated when a few years later this member would play the leading role in blackmailing me out of any connection with the work in Ireland. But that was in the future. I was leaving having played a central role in building a substantial revolutionary socialist, a Trotskyist, nucleus, in Ireland.

This was the truth. And this truth had to be looked at with an optimistic eye, recognising the important gains that were made, and recognising also that I had played a central role in making these gains. But the truth is many sided. I had not succeeded in building a semi-mass or mass organisation of revolutionary workers and youth on a revolutionary socialist programme and strategy, with roots in both the Protestant and Catholic working class. I concluded and I believed correctly so, that the main reason for this was that the forces against me and against our tiny group were just too powerful at that time. We were working against the stream, standing against the tide. Divide and rule and repression had worked too well. Along with that the majority of the working class could either get enough to eat or were able to emigrate. So when the Labour leaders would not lead the dominant view was that there was no alternative to capitalism, and along with this there were the traditions and organisations of Loyalism and Republicanism and religion which filled the vacuum.

But could we instead have filled the vacuum? Could we have built a force of tens of thousands out of the civil rights movement and mass strike movements of the late 1960s and out of the strikes of the late 1970s and early 1980s? To carry out the revolution in Ireland, an organisation of tens of thousands of revolutionaries organised in the one organisation would have been necessary. Could we have built this and done so on a revolutionary socialist and internationalist basis? Could we have brought together a force of tens of thousands of workers and youth, Protestant and Catholic and with this prevented the rise of the sectarian forces, prevented the divide and rule and repression of capitalism and imperialism North and South? I concluded that because in the late 1960s when the movement was exploding and thousands were looking for revolutionary organisations to join, we did not exist, that we could not have done so.

We had only a dozen people in our group in the beginning of the 1970s and the workers' movement and the civil rights movement were already ebbing and sectarianism and the sectarian organisations were rising. We had come too late on the scene and with too few resources. Tens of thousands of youth were already, if unconsciously, demanding a revolutionary organisation by the 1969/1970 years. But it is necessary to question. Along with putting forward the generally correct ideas, working class unity, socialism and internationalism, and allying this with politically and physically arming our small forces and trying to do so on a strictly hard line workers' unity basis, and defence of working class people, both Protestant and Catholic basis, could we have succeeded in building a mass united working class movement? I concluded we could not have done so. We just did not have the resources, the numbers. Nor were there Trotskyist traditions on which we could have built. Our dozen members was not even a drop in the ocean.

If we had tried to take military action in defence of the working class and working class unity with the tiny resources we had, the state and the sectarian armed groups would have taken action against us and would have wiped us out. The idea of working class unity was disappearing like snow off a ditch. And we had only a handful of members. On my initiative we discussed at one meeting in Belfast whether we should begin to rob banks and get resources to buy guns and in this way and along with our policies try to offer an alternative to the most militant youth and workers to defend working class neighbourhoods and fight for working class unity and socialism. We correctly concluded this would be a mistake as we would be wiped out and also that even if we were not such steps would totally deform the internal life of our group as those who would be robbing the banks and getting the money would begin to determine policy. It was correct to see that all we could do at that time given our minute resources, was stand against the stream, fight for our alternative ideas, and try and build more forces around these ideas. If we could be successful in this then we could move on to build an actual united, working class, armed, semi-mass and mass force. But this was beyond our reach at that time and we saw this. We did what was possible with the tiny resources we had to hand. In the meantime, the tens of thousands of youth and workers rushed past us into the existing sectarian organisations, some left and some right. We were right to recognize what we could do and what we could not do. By doing so we survived as a small nucleus.

It was an achievement that we recognised what was possible and what was not possible. This was good. But it would have been better if we had more consciously discussed this reality and recognised our weakness. This would have prepared us better for the struggles ahead. It would also have helped us see that an organisation of tens and tens of thousands was what was necessary, not a few hundred or even a few thousand. This could have been more openly recognised. If it had been it would have helped us keep our feet more firmly on the ground and more specifically to avoid left sectarianism and ultra-leftism and opportunism. It would also have helped us see that the internal life of our small group was not such as to make possible our growth into an organization of tens of thousands. But all in all we had achieved something important. We had laid down the nucleus of what would later, for a time, become the most important Trotskyist group in Ireland.

Leaving Ireland was painful. I did not discuss my going with my mother or my aunt. What I was doing with my life made no sense to them. To leave Ireland for what? To build the revolutionary organisation on a world scale rather than work on their debt free small farm. There was nothing to discuss. We were in different worlds. To break from my family and their ideas in the past, to break from the country that I knew and in which I was reared and for which I had such feeling, I once again cauterised and stunted my emotions my feelings. More damage. Once again, more rupturing, more brutalising, more terrorism against my emotions and feelings, as I left the country where I had been born and whose colours and smells and shapes were part of me. But as I saw it these had to be given up for the revolution. Had to be given up to work for the cause in which I believed and which strengthened me and which overall gave me a good life.

PART 5

DEFEATS UNSHACKLE MY THINKING

CHAPTER 30

THE COMMITTEE FOR A WORKERS' INTERNATIONAL (CWI)

I JOINED THE MILITANT GROUP in 1971. It had a couple of hundred people in Britain and around ten in the North of Ireland. By 1974 it had members in over a dozen countries and was able to hold an international conference and form an international group which called itself the Committee for a Workers' International (CWI). I was a delegate to this founding conference from the Irish section. The CWI (also called by its members, The International), would grow to over thirty countries and 14,000 members in the years ahead. The CWI was funded by its national sections which in turn were funded by their memberships' subscriptions and fundraising activities.

The CWI's largest section was in Britain. At its peak its British section had up to 8,000 members, had representatives in parliament, in city and town councils, was for a time the main force in Liverpool city council, the main left force in Scotland, was the effective leadership of the country's main civil service union and it had led the anti-Poll Tax movement that had brought down Thatcher.

The CWI met in conference every summer. This conference, which was made up of delegates from all its sections, elected an International Executive Committee of around thirty (IEC). This body, of which I was a member, met every three to four months to oversee the work of the organisation. It elected an International Secretariat (IS) of six people which ran the organisation on a day to day basis. After I moved to London I was also a member of this body. It was a lot different from driving a tractor, ploughing fields, digging drains, milking cows and poaching fish in Donegal.

Moving to London allowed me to become more familiar with the main people in the CWI. There were two leading individuals. Ted Grant had been the central figure in a small revolutionary socialist group back in the 1940s. From this developed The Militant in Britain and from this developed the CWI. By the time I moved to London Ted was in his middle age. But it was one of his eccentricities that he would never admit his age. It seemed like he believed that if he did not do so he would live forever. In some fields, while a most capable dialectician, he had difficulty in applying this method of looking at things to himself.

Ted had the highest theoretical level and was the most respected member of the CWI. He had played the main role in establishing a new analysis of the world situation after World War II. Trotsky's perspective of a new mass revolutionary international which would replace the social democratic and Stalinist internationals after World War 2 ended had been proven wrong by events. It was Ted who mapped out a new world analysis. This was an extremely important achievement.

Ted saw that after the World War, a period of economic upswing lay ahead in the capitalist world. He saw that this would strengthen the leaderships of the mass workers' parties of social democracy and of Stalinism in the advanced capitalist countries. He also considered that it would strengthen the trade union bureaucracies in these countries, as these organisations would be able, given this capitalist upswing, to deliver more goods to at least a section of the working class in these advanced capitalist countries. He also saw that these bureaucracies would be able to at least some extent hold back the working class in the less developed capitalist countries from working and fighting through their workers' organisations, where these existed and thus the struggle in these countries would be liable to take different routes such as guerrilla warfare and conventional warfare such as in China and Vietnam.

Ted also saw the temporary strengthening of Stalinism and the Stalinist bureaucracies in the Soviet Union and in China after the Chinese revolution. Ted designated these Stalinist regimes as proletarian Bonapartist regimes. That is to say, regimes where the rule of the capitalist class had been ended, where the economies were nationalised and planned however not controlled by the working class and not organised on the basis of workers' democracy but by Stalinist castes, Stalinist dictatorships, of one kind or another. Examples of these were the Soviet Union and Eastern Europe. Another example of such a regime was China, where after 1949 capitalism and landlordism were wiped out, but not by the working class but by a guerrilla army, which conducted guerrilla warfare and also conventional warfare. Another example of this was to be Vietnam which defeated French and US imperialism through guerrilla and conventional warfare.

Ted based himself on the view that the world situation, that history, was facing a race between a workers' and democratic socialist political revolution in the Stalinist countries which would keep these economies nationalised and planned, but change them to where they were run democratically by the working class, and a socialist revolution in the West which would take these economies out of the hands of the capitalist class, out of the capitalist system, and move to societies which would have nationalised economies run by the working class as democratic socialist societies. Ted and the CWI saw history at that time as being a race between which would come first, the political revolution in the East against Stalinism and which would establish workers' democracies, or the socialist revolution in the West against capitalism and which would establish workers' democracies. And whichever came first would spark the other and lead to a world revolution and the end of capitalism worldwide. Ted set himself and the CWI the task of leading this world revolution. The CWI, all of us, had big plans.

This analysis sufficiently corresponded to reality, and to the aspirations of sufficient numbers of workers for a sufficient length of time to allow the CWI to grow and develop. But events would show that this analysis was not correct and so the CWI was building on sand. It was building on sand because its world view was wrong. In a mistake of historic proportions the CWI did not see the restoration of capitalism in the Stalinist world and so it was not prepared for this step back in history. This mistake was made by all leading members of the CWI, including myself.

Ted's, and the CWI's main weakness in terms of method, was the unconditional way in which it approached the existing world situation and the perspectives for the world situation, that is what was likely to happen in the world. Ted and the CWI thought we could see the future with just about certainty, that we could be just about unconditional in relation to what lay ahead in the world. This was a serious mistake, so serious, it would later shipwreck the CWI. But that was in the future. Ted's general view of events that he laid out in the 1950s sufficiently corresponded to reality for a few decades to allow the CWI to grow and develop. It was an important achievement. Only later would the mistaken perspectives and the mistaken method become obvious and decisive.

I learnt a lot from Ted. I also personally liked him. He was a funny and eccentric man. Of course like everybody he had his weaknesses. While he had been the most successful person in the British Trotskyist movement in the 1950s and 1960s in working out the new world situation after World War II, and for that he deserved great credit, there had been other very capable members in the Trotskyist movement in that period. But Ted tended to run the show himself. Genuine collective leadership was not for him a priority. This was a serious error.

Another of Ted's weaknesses was that, like the majority of the rest of the International Secretariat of the CWI, he would not admit to ever making any mistakes. This was very damaging to the CWI. When a person or organisation cannot openly and honestly admit their mistakes they cannot learn from their mistakes and correct their way of thinking and working. This is a real weakness in an organisation or individual. It set the CWI up to where it found it very difficult to face up to the mistake it made by not being open to the restoration of capitalism to the former Stalinist world. This was no small error in method. Collective leadership and admitting mistakes were not for Ted or the CWI.

I personally have a lot to thank Ted Grant for. He kept the basic ideas of Marxism alive and by doing so held out a lifeline to me and to many others. Later when things would go bad in the CWI and I would find myself on the other side of issues from Ted I went to see him in his apartment in London. I was on my way to catch a flight to the USA. I knocked on his door. He opened it. I said: 'Ted, I want to thank you for helping me understand the world and so making my life better.' He replied rubbing his hands together: 'You see we were right on everything all along.' I replied, 'Ted, Ted but we did not even see the restoration of capitalism into the Soviet Union,'

'What time is your flight?' Ted responded, 'surely you must be going. You would not want to miss it.' And he ushered me out the door. After all his achievements he was not able to face up to and admit this major mistake that he and we all had made. I walked down to the tube station. I thought of this man and his life and how he was living in this tiny apartment in London as his years moved on. I felt a deep sympathy for him.

Peter Taaffe was the second leading figure in the CWI. He, like Ted, had a high theoretical level and he was a good organiser. I learnt from him as I did from Ted. However he, like the rest of the IS, including myself, held rigidly onto the old view of the world when this no longer corresponded to reality. He, also like Ted, did not see the need for a genuine, collective leadership. The difference between him and Ted was while Ted thought he should and would be the leader for all time, Peter Taaffe thought he should push Ted aside and take over and be the leader for all time.

Peter Taaffe was just as bad as Ted in another area. He would never admit to ever making any mistakes. As with Ted this was very damaging to the CWI. And as with Ted this was an un-dialectical, un-Marxist approach. Peter Taaffe was also an insecure individual. Having never made the breakthroughs in insight that Ted had in the years following World War II, he did not have the confidence that Ted had. One form that this took was that he sought to control all that he touched, he kept this well-hidden but it was his method nonetheless. This also was very damaging to the CWI. It made it impossible for it to develop as a mass force and with a collective leadership and an organic and democratic internal life.

When I arrived in London Peter Taaffe suggested that I should be the secretary of the CWI. I turned this down as I did not know what was expected of this position and I did not know if I would be capable of doing the job. I later concluded that he suggested this because he saw me as a bit of an independent thinker and strong personality and it would be better to have me close to him so he could keep an eye on me and from his point of view hopefully mould me and control me. When I later found out he would go on to run a secret undemocratic clique within the organisation, I concluded he had then been feeling me out to see if I would be a candidate for that. I am proud that I turned down his suggestion that I become the secretary of the International and even more proud that in later years he never asked me to be part of his secret, undemocratic clique.

Other leading people in the International were Roger Silverman, Alan Woods and Lynn Walsh. Being newer to the International than Ted Grant and Peter Taaffe, they accepted the leadership of these two members. Between Alan Woods and Lynn Walsh there was a continual unhealthy immature competition.

Along with this neither of the two of them recognised the privileges they had in life. They had gone to university in the early 1960s, the decade of revolution. They immediately met and were trained by Ted Grant and became part of the organisation from a young age. Not only did they not recognise they had these privileges and advantages but they did not recognise that with the strengths that came from these also came weaknesses. As with Ted Grant and Peter Taaffe, they did not recognise the dialectic as it applied to their own lives, that is, that with strengths come weaknesses. The positive and the negative. Their weaknesses included lack of direct experience in the working class, a refusal to admit it when they made mistakes and a tendency to think that modesty, humility, were only for others. They also, like Ted Grant and Peter Taaffe, did not give any priority to building a genuine collective leadership.

Roger Silverman was the first secretary of the CWI. He had a high theoretical level and I was to also learn from him. He was much more open to admit the mistakes we had all made and on this basis he and I were to become closer as the crisis in the CWI developed. I found he had a better grip of some of the ideas and tasks and mistakes the CWI had made than the other leading people but I also thought that he would not fight sufficiently hard to get the CWI to recognise these.

The other major weakness of all these leading people in the CWI was an insufficient consciousness in relation to the special oppression of women. All of them believed most of them consciously some unconsciously, that women were not as capable as men. There was just about no talk of Rosa

Luxemburg. There was no recognition that women did not start from a level playing field and that the organisation should have discussions and policies to ensure women members could play their full role, could realise their full potential.

When I first joined the CWI I was speaking at a British conference. I was sharing the platform with Peter Taaffe. A woman Comrade spoke and said there should be childcare facilities. There were none at Militant events at that time, that is how bad it was. This woman Comrade got no support from the leadership. Peter Taaffe whispered to me: 'There she goes again. She is only a petit bourgeois.' So in the mind of one of the two leading members of the British Militant and the CWI to ask for childcare was 'petit bourgeois'. I suppose the thinking was the little woman should stay at home and look after the children. I replied: 'It does not matter what she is, she is right on this.' He kept quiet. I made a mistake, I should have stood up and openly supported that Comrade and put the issue before the membership. I am ashamed that I did not.

On another occasion I was at a meeting of the IS. The women's department in the British section had recently set up the campaign against domestic violence. It was a spectacular success winning increasing support at a rapid rate. I said how great this was and how it was especially good that it was the women's department itself that had taken the initiative rather than having to wait for action by the British EC or IS. At this Peter Taaffe literally screamed that it was not the women's department that had set up this campaign it was the British EC. He could not tolerate the idea that the EC, and as he saw it, himself, was not responsible for every good idea and initiative. And in particular he could not tolerate the idea that it was women members who had led. It was not long before the leading women members in the women's department left the organisation. No wonder.

On one occasion I spoke out at a major event of the CWI against the sexism in the organisation. It was an international conference. Some women members came to me and complained about how some male members were treating them. These male members were trying to get together with them personally in a most disrespectful manner, and if they did get together with them they afterwards ignored them. I stood up at the international conference and condemned this. The response was an uncomfortable silence from everybody. This was another sign of the CWI at that time not being prepared to discuss the special oppression of women and of sexism.

The leading members of the International were complicit in not taking on the sexual oppression. I was to hear later that when a female member went to Peter Taaffe and complained about another leading member sexually assaulting her, Taaffe told her to deal with it herself. On another occasion, a leading female member asked Peter Taaffe his opinion on whether it was better for members to be married, to be in permanent relationships or not. This member was directing this at Peter Taaffe who was married and whose companion looked after him and saw to his every personal and domestic need. He got out of answering this by saying it was up to every person to decide for themselves. This allowed him to ignore the fact that if one partner in a relationship did the domestic and personal tasks for the relationship that person could not play their full role in revolutionary work. When cornered on the weakness of the CWI on this front these leading members, especially Peter Taaffe would fall back on the excuse that these were the times that were in it, this was the objective situation, we could not fight on all fronts at all times and many more learned sounding, but dishonest, excuses. Hiding behind the objective balance of forces, using the objective balance of forces as an alibi for not confronting the special oppression of women and its effects within the CWI. The CWI did not have this approach in other areas of its work.

While recognizing these weaknesses this is not to say in any way that the CWI was all negative. After all I joined it rather than any other left organisation. Its main strength was that it sought at all times to try and clarify perspectives, that is what was likely to happen in the world. Then base themselves on that analysis. As Trotsky had put it, the art of revolution is to analyse the objective situation and on this basis decide on what subjective action is to be taken. The CWI did this. As a result, and in spite of its major mistakes in the late 1980s and 1990s it tended for a period to have a much better idea of the objective situation and how and where to work than any other left group.

When I discussed with the left groups in London in 1970, The Militant was the smallest. The others had grown much more out of the mainly student anti-Vietnam War movement. Militant had taken part in this but it did so while maintaining its general position. This was that it would not be the students that would change the world but it would be the working class. And while the working class in Britain at that time were not showing signs of great activity this would change. Therefore it was vital that the revolutionary forces maintain their orientation to the working class. The Militant did this, standing against the stream, recruiting small numbers of workers and also students and educating them for the working class battles ahead. These battles, The Militant said, would take place in the trade unions and Labour Party, the traditional organisations of the working class.

It was this emphasis on perspectives, and also this orientation to the working class that was Militant's great strength and which resulted in it being head and shoulders about the rest of the left groups. When the anti-Vietnam War movement receded with the ending of that war, when the student movement declined, the British working class began to move in strikes of miners, engineers and others. When this happened, the other left groups which had not prepared for this, in particular not prepared for the new movement of the organised working class, went into crisis. The Militant on the other hand, along with this new rising of the working class, began to grow and develop and became the biggest and most important revolutionary left group in Britain. An emphasis on perspectives, an orientation to the working class, an ability to stand against the stream when events in society were not going well, these were the strengths of Militant.

But it also had its weaknesses. It took me some time to see these and recognise the seriousness of these weaknesses. The longer I worked out of the International centre the more I came to dread returning to London from my trips. At first I considered that maybe I had come to hate London. I looked forward to my visits abroad to get away. Then it dawned on me it was not London I hated, it was the British and CWI centre.

There was no democratic collective atmosphere. The British Executive Committee (EC) was dominated by Ted Grant and Peter Taaffe, and it ran the show. Not being able to admit their mistakes, any alternative view was seen as a challenge that had to be crushed. Alternative points of view were not welcome. As a result there was no genuine exchange of ideas, there was no intellectual curiosity, there were no theoretical sparks flying. Lesser mortals were in general afraid to challenge the orthodoxy. Every time I entered the centre I felt like a weight was descending on my shoulders.

On one occasion on behalf of the US members, I raised about the cover of the British theoretical magazine on which there was a design related to an article about China. It did not portray Chinese people in a flattering light. A Chinese-American member in the US said it was racist. I raised this with the British section in the international centre. I expected there to be a comradely exchange of views and the opinion of the Chinese-American member to be given serious consideration.

But I was wrong. Backed by the EC, the editorial department refused to accept there was anything to the concerns of the US member and myself. Again and again I discussed with them. I tried all my approaches, from my most diplomatic to my most firm. But they would not budge. According to them there was nothing wrong. Eventually all I could get out of the discussion was they said well if you think there is something wrong with it then you think there is something wrong with it, we do not but you can think what you like. I was astounded at this attitude of the British centre backed up by the British EC. This was indicative of the approach of the centre. Never admit to any mistakes and stall and then put together a combination of words to confuse. I was extremely frustrated the more I saw the way things worked.

Then there was the British section itself. When I was in London between trips, I tried to keep up with its work. After all it was the largest section of the CWI. I did this initially by trying to have discussions with the general secretary of the section, Peter Taaffe. He would not discuss, instead he would send me down the hall to discuss with his secretary. He seemed to think it was beneath him to discuss with me. In spite of my efforts, I could not get the problems of the British section discussed on the IS either. It was off limits. It was the territory of Peter Taaffe and Ted Grant. I was in a very different situation from when I worked out of Dublin. There I had been at the centre of building the Irish section, but then and in spite of living and working out of London I could not even get a discussion about the British section with Peter Taaffe, one of the two leading members of that section. I was becoming more and more frustrated, increasingly wondering why this was so.

The leading people of the CWI had drawn wrong conclusions from the Russian revolution. They had concluded that because Lenin was essential to victory in 1917, there always had to be a Lenin, a one-man show, and a Lenin who never made any mistakes. (Never a one-woman show.) And of course in their thinking it was always one of themselves who had to be the Lenin and who would never make any mistakes. I agreed that Lenin was essential in 1917, but I believed that this should have been seen and recognised as a terrible weakness forced on the Bolsheviks by circumstances and steps should have been taken in the work of the CWI to oppose this being repeated in the CWI by consciously and deliberately taking steps to build a collective leadership.

I increasingly saw the steps that should be taken should amongst other things seek to avoid the same one or two people doing all the main tasks, doing all the main introductions to discussions, writing all the main articles. I increasingly saw building a collective leadership as democratically deciding from one meeting to the next who would do the introductions at the next meeting, who would write the main articles. I also saw it as encouraging an atmosphere of democratic discussion and debate and exchange of ideas and probing and disagreement on ideas. I had been surprised when I first joined The Militant about the lack of this approach. I raised this a few times with Peter Taaffe and Ted Grant and on one occasion proposed an alternative slate at a CC in an attempt to get a discussion and more collective approach going. But I did not take it to the wider membership and make a struggle for it there. And then after raising this issue a few times l mistakenly let it go. After all we were growing and things seemed to be going well. This was a mistake I made.

My increasing disenchantment with the London centre was held at bay by my many trips abroad. In preparation for these trips I would have discussions with leading members on the IS. The problem was the IS and I still had the wrong view of the world at this time and I was taking this wrong view with me. This was serious. I was not preparing the sections of the CWI I was visiting for the coming events such as the restoration of capitalism in the Stalinist world and the wave of reaction that would follow. I was still preaching the CWI's old line, capitalism was in such a crisis that there was no possibility of the restoration of capitalism in the Stalinist countries, five to ten years to the world revolution. This was good for recruiting mainly young people in the short term but it would lead to catastrophe in the medium and longer term.

One of the ways I kept my sanity in London was by walking home from the organisation's centre through the parks and canals. I would see the children playing soccer. I would see the families as they took their pleasure in the parks. I would pet the peoples' dogs as they romped panting and jumping. As I did so I would remember the nature and fields and roads of Ireland. London's parks helped me survive. I did not have any spare money as I was living on the pittance of a full-timer's wage as I had been doing in Ireland. But this did not bother me as I was so committed to my revolutionary work that I did not consider non-political activities, social entertainment activities. My living expenses were funded by the CWI as were all my travel expenses. I was a full-time organiser funded by the CWI, my travels were on behalf of the CWI and funded by the CWI.

CHAPTER 31

TRAVELS

I MADE TRIPS to many different countries while I was based in London. I visited Greece regularly. The section there had about 100 members when I first started making my visits. But with no cohesive leadership. The leading member would on occasion stay away from meetings where controversial decisions were to be taken. His companion knew him better than I and took me aside and told me he was not capable of doing what I wanted him to do. But I just went ahead. I was going to make him lead whether he could or not. Of course his companion, she was right. I was wrong. And I was wrong in another way than just my estimation of this Comrade. He had many good qualities but was not able to play the central role. I should have focused more on building a collective leadership of which he would have been part.

I made visits to the Cyprus section. The membership there had been sharpened politically by the Turkish invasion of the North and the division of the country. I found them to have a high level but with one exception not prepared to commit themselves to full-time revolutionary work. I made visits to the North, that is Turkish Cyprus, as Greek Cypriots were not allowed to travel there. The CWI section was all Greek Cypriot. Eventually the Northern authorities figured out I was discussing with left wing people in the North and banned me from travelling there again.

In Northern Europe there tended to be a different kind of section and membership. Recruited mainly from the youth of the social democracy and living in countries with higher living standards they tended to be younger and less tough. I made many trips to Belgium, the Netherlands, Germany, France, Italy, and Spain, holding discussions with groups and individuals in these countries. These discussions were either in English or there was translation. These Northern European sections were made up of genuine and committed members but at that stage, as was the case with all the sections of the CWI, with the exception of the British section for a time in the struggles in Liverpool, Scotland and around the poll tax, they were too small to have any influence in the working class.

I made a trip to India which allowed me to better get to know Roger Silverman, another member of the IS. He was based there and attempting the Herculean task of building a nucleus in that huge sub-continent. The climate alone was a brutal challenge. I visited Bangalore, Madras, New Delhi, Kanpur, Calcutta, Bombay and participated in discussions with Roger and the activists he had around him. On the way into India I was arrested by the police and held for questioning. As well as trying to get information out of me about the political objectives of my visit they wanted a bribe. The interrogation was aggressive but not violent. Eventually I was released without a bribe.

I stayed with Roger and a very poor family in Kanpur. We slept on blankets on the clay floor. In the morning we washed in the courtyard where young children threw buckets of water over us as we squatted. They laughed with delight seeing us squirm. And probably with being allowed to throw water on white foreigners.

India was a cultural and climatic shock. At some of the discussions the heat was so great that people would take a glass of water from the table and pour it over their heads. At one meeting I looked out a window and saw women in saris carrying bricks in boxes up rickety ladders to bricklayers in over 100 degree heat and under a brutal sun. We the revolutionaries were indoors discussing around a table.

The streets were packed with people with whole families living, sleeping, washing and cooking round a fire-filled bucket on the sidewalk. They would hunker down on their knees and with their long clothes hanging down around them as cover they would wash themselves out of another bucket. They seemed to be amongst the cleanest people I had ever seen.

At night the noise in the cities was horrific. I did not know it then but it was made worse for me because of my health problems. The noise was a combination of non-stop traffic, people talking and shouting and others chanting their religious incantations. I did not know how Roger stuck it.

Roger was a learned Marxist and I gained and learned from our discussions. But while learning from him I felt that he tended to be too optimistic in assessing new people we would meet.

I also travelled to Sri Lanka and discussed with the section there. On the way back I was held by the country's police as they thought being from Ireland I might have had connections with the Tamil Tiger guerrilla movement. They were more aggressive than the Indian police and they banned me from returning.

One day while there I went for a swim. Again and again the waves threw me back on the land. There were shacks along the beach. The people who lived in these were extremely poor. One family invited me in. They had a hollow cement block on the ground as their 'stove'. Into this they put some sticks they had gathered and lit them and boiled water and made tea. I took the small can of the liquid they offered me. I was traumatised by their poverty and lack of belongings.

I made a trip to Brazil. It was very different from my trip up the Amazon twenty years before. This time I was in Brazil's cities, with their huge urban concentrations. I was delighted by the racial diversity of the working class population. It was not just different races but a mixture of racial backgrounds within different individuals.

This two-year period when I was based in London and making trips to different countries was a preparatory period for me to work and build in North America in 1985. I made many visits there over this period. I would fly into Atlanta, Georgia on Eastern Air Lines, and from there travel to many other cities on each trip.

The CWI had individual contacts in New York City and Boston. I would visit and discuss with them and try to get branches set up. I also followed events and travelled to intervene in different strikes and struggles in areas where we had nobody. I was doing the kind of work I had done in Ireland and other countries, only now I was doing it in the huge cities of the most powerful country in the world. As well as visiting New York and Boston, I visited Detroit, Minneapolis, Chicago, Austin, Los Angeles, San Francisco, Seattle; and in Canada – Vancouver, Toronto and Montreal.

My focus on these visits was to try to develop individual members to where they could build local groups and branches. I was continuing with my approach that the role of leadership was to help in the development of new leaders who could replace themselves.

For the two years from 1983 to 1985, I was working out of the International centre in London. I mostly concentrated on the European countries mentioned and the USA and Canada. The work in these areas made some progress.

My travels over this period included some of the richest countries in the world and some of the poorest countries in the world. Seeing this inequality strengthened my hatred of capitalism, strengthened my belief in the need for revolution and strengthened my drive to build the CWI. The way I saw the world revolution happen was that the CWI would become strong enough to take power in an important country and this would put our International on the map as the most successful and authoritative revolutionary force on the globe. This in turn would draw to us tens of millions of the best revolutionary workers and youth internationally and we would build the new mass international and take power worldwide. Like a repeat, only more successful, of the development of the Bolsheviks, when they took power in

Russia in October 1917 and this then gave them the authority to set up the new third International with its tens of millions of members.

I looked forward to being in a position to challenge capitalism for power as part of a mass international in five to ten years. However I, and the International were to put it mildly, insufficiently reflective of the times that were in it and what we were doing. We were still operating on the five to ten year plan to world revolution. But the ten years were already well gone. This was never mentioned. It was just ignored. It would have been seen as a betrayal to raise this mistake. But five to ten years to the revolution no longer corresponded to the reality of the objective situation. But not only that, the world objective situation, instead of helping us to put the five to ten years to the revolution on the agenda, was by then moving decisively in the other direction. It was moving in the direction of counter revolution. And the CWI was blind to that. I was blind to that. I was travelling the world with this wrong view. Taking this wrong view with me. Talk about being wrong. Ignoring mistakes when they were made, even such major mistakes as the five to ten year timescale was part of the wrong method of the leadership of the CWI.

My own personal strength and the strength of the CWI compounded the weakness that flowed from our mistaken perspectives. We remained very determined and very unconditional and unquestioning concerning our world view. We knew what was going to happen and that was that. There was no attitude, no atmosphere of scientific probing discussion and debate. It was the five to ten years. We were far too unconditional in our world view and opinions. The result was we did not notice that the world was changing around us in a fundamental way.

My own personal strength added to this mistaken balance. I had a strong will. I applied this to what I thought was the essential task, that is build the CWI so as to be able to take power in the next five to ten years. But the priority task for the CWI at that time was not to build its numbers, it was to reorient itself, to correct its world analysis and bring itself into consonance with the new world situation. So my strong will, rather than helping the development of the CWI, was helping to divert the CWI from what should have been its absolute top priority, that is, examining the new processes then becoming dominant in the world, the changing events, the new situations, openly owning up to past mistakes, and from this preparing the CWI for coming events. As mentioned before Trotsky said the art of revolution was to combine an understanding of the objective situation with subjective action. As every year went by and the world objective situation changed and we did not adjust our analysis of that objective situation, there developed an increasing disconnect between the analysis of the objective situation and our subjective action. Inevitably something had to give, something had to snap. My will and drive to build the CWI into a mass international organisation increasingly turned into an obstacle and a weakness in the work. And so contributed to the CWI snapping. But that was in the future. In the meantime I was heading for another collapse in my health.

CHAPTER 32

ILLNESS AGAIN

THE REST OF MY STORY will suffer from my deepening health crisis. The more I travelled to different countries the more stress I was putting on myself and the more I damaged my health. I was increasingly experiencing blackouts. A number of times I came round in emergency rooms of different hospitals in different cities not knowing how I got there or what happened. The IS of the CWI knew I had this health problem as I had a blackout at an international meeting.

The doctors referred to these black outs as Transient Ischemic Attacks. TIAs. They were minor strokes. The doctors did not know what caused them. Coming together with the effects of my previous concussions, I was not in great shape. In the years ahead I would be diagnosed with hypothyroidism, Addison's disease, hypoglycaemia, cancer and epilepsy. I would only be able to remain alive by taking fifteen tablets every day and eating healthily. I did not think of myself as chronically, seriously ill, but this was the reality. However in spite of this it never crossed my mind to give up my revolutionary work. My family had taught me that if there was something wrong with me to 'just get on with the work'. I looked at the people who were in the CWI who had no problems with their health, and who had never had the conflict I had to break from my past. I thought how little they knew about the difficulties of life. And in many cases how they lacked real strength of will.

Over a period of twenty years I would have nine different surgeries. The most serious was one for cancer, one to cut into and open my skull to lever broken facial bones back into place, and another to repair my right scapula which had been broken during my first very violent epileptic seizure.

My health situation brought with it all kinds of adventures. On one occasion while on a trip to the US I was trying to meet some people to build a branch in Seattle. I took the night off and went to see an old black and white movie of the life of French singer Edith Piaf. I had a TIA, that is, a small stroke, in the cinema. I slumped forward in my seat semi-conscious for most of the movie. I then regained sufficient consciousness to stumble out with the rest of the patrons. I did not know who or where I was. I managed to cross the street to a park. It was a soft, wet Seattle night. I sat down under a tree. For a time I thought I was in France in the 1930s.

On another occasion, again in the US, I was driving on Highway 1 from San Diego to Seattle. I had a TIA while driving but was able to pull the vehicle off onto the grassy shoulder. I opened the door and fell out unconscious. I came round to look up to see a cop poking me with his boot. He thought I was drunk or on drugs. When he saw I was 'only' ill he turned and left me lying there. It would take me days to get over these TIA episodes.

It was at this time that I came to realise that my health problems were not just over work. I was walking to the underground in London shortly after I moved to live there. I saw a doctor's shingle hanging from some railings. It triggered the memory of my father who had died young and whose thyroid did not work. I went in and asked to have my thyroid tested. A very kind older lady doctor said of course and took some blood. The next day I left for Brazil to visit a socialist group.

When I returned there were a number of messages from the doctor. I called. 'You have to come in right away. You are the worst case of hypothyroidism I have ever seen.' My thyroid gland was not producing sufficient thyroid hormones and so my metabolic rate was much too low. My whole system was getting slower and slower. I was exhausted all the time but I just thought this was normal. To do otherwise I would have seen as weakness. The doctor put me on Synthroid, a replacement for the hormone my thyroid was not producing. I told her I had been running and taking cold showers to try and stimulate my system. She held her head exclaiming: 'Running. Cold showers. It is a wonder you are still alive.' I felt somewhat better after I began to take the hormone but I could tell something was still not right.

I tried many ways to deal with this. When travelling to meet members in sections I would often say I was getting in later than I actually was as this would allow me to rest at the airport or bus or train station before the local members would come to meet me. Sometimes I would be so weak I would have to find some building such as a bus station, a library, and on occasion even a church and go in and sleep. But in spite of all these problems I continued with my work of helping to build the International.

I tried alternative medicine as a means to deal with my health problems. I got tested for allergies. The clinic was on the south coast of England. The lady put me on a strict detoxification diet for a week. When I returned she made me lie down on a couch. She had a number of small pieces of foodstuffs in a plate on the counter beside her. She made me raise my arm and hold it vertical as she tried to push it back down horizontal along my side. I was able to resist her pressure. Then one at a time she inserted a small piece of different foods into my mouth each time applying pressure to my arm. The first food she inserted was a piece of apple, then a piece of pear. I was able to continue to resist her pressure to push my arm down. Then she put a piece of bread into my mouth. My arm collapsed under her pressure. She went, on cheese, again my arm collapsed, a piece of bacon, again my arm collapsed. The same with some other foods. I asked her what was happening. She explained.

'When your arm collapses this means you are allergic to those particular foods. When I put these foods into your mouth your system understands that it is going to have to gather its resources and rush them to your digestive system as these foods are now in your digestive system. Your system has to work extra hard to deal with these foods every time you eat them. So the resources of your system are taken away from your limbs and also your brain and sent to your digestive system. As a result you no longer have enough resources for your limbs and brain.'

The doctor then looked in my eye with a torch. She said: 'You like the sea.' I said, 'I am not answering that until you tell me why you ask it.' I knew how much I liked the sea. She explained that my system had a hard time with my sodium potassium balance. So it tried to deal with this by pushing salt into the various nooks and crannies of my body. She said she could see this when she looked in the irises of my eyes. But still my system needed salt. So when salt from the sea air landed on my skin my system felt that maybe it was going to get some salt, some relief and it temporarily felt better. So it seemed it was not only that I loved the beauty of the sea but it was also that it made me feel physically better. The doctor gave me a diet to follow. But because I was continually travelling from place to place I was unable to follow such a strict and unconventional diet so I continued with my health crises.

I was later diagnosed with Addison's disease where the cortex of the adrenal glands is impaired. It affects the sodium potassium balances in the system and can lead to death. It was this sodium potassium imbalance that the alternative medicine doctor saw in my eye. I was diagnosed with Addison's by a blood test. I told the conventional medicine doctor who diagnosed me about the lady who looked in my eyes with a torch. The conventional medicine doctor said: 'I have no idea how she could have made that diagnosis by looking in your eyes.' I should have listened more to the alternative medicine doctor.

During this time it became more difficult for me to sleep. I would wake up three or four times every night. The positive side of this was if I wanted to get up at a particular time I could tell myself to do so and exactly at that time I would wake up. But the negative side was that I was not sleeping deeply. I was inflicting more damage on myself. The concussions, the hypothyroidism, the untreated Addison's and hypoglycaemia, the build up to what would later be epilepsy and cancers. Overall I was seriously ill. However I continued my work in the International.

It will not only be my health crises that will damage the rest of my story. For a time I was to be staying in a house in Chicago. The lady who owned the house was very right wing in her views. From a small town some distance from Chicago she sought to find a role for herself in the fringes of business in that city. In doing so she became most ferocious in her attitude and most right wing in her views. She suspected my political views. On one occasion when I was on a trip she snooped amongst my things and took boxes of my note books and threw them in the trash. These contained details of my trips and discussions I had with people I met. This was to be a blow to my writing my story.

I also lost access to other material which would have helped me write this book. When I would later be expelled from the CWI that organisation refused to give me copies of the written reports I had made of all my trips. I had initiated this practice in the CWI, that is, that everybody would give written reports of any trip they made. But because I came to disagree with the majority in the IS of the International at a later stage and they undemocratically expelled me, they refused to give me access to the reports of my own work, which I myself had written and which were in the files in the London centre.

These reports contained the discussions that took place on my visits and the discussions I had with the other members of the IS when I would prepare for and return from these visits. Of course as time was to tell the perspectives discussed between us at that time were wrong. This was the main reason the IS of the CWI would later not give me my reports. These reports would have shown without question the mistakes that I myself had made. But more importantly for the majority on the IS, the reports would also have shown the mistakes made by the majority of the IS. This was not acceptable to the majority of the IS. They could not own up to their own mistakes. They would not give me my reports.

CHAPTER 33

WRONG METHODS – MISTAKES OF MY OWN

HELPING TO PUT TOGETHER a revolutionary organisation is no easy task. It involves a correct view of the world, a correct view of the alternative we wish to fight for, a correct view and relationship with the working class, the force that can bring about this new world. It also demands the willingness and ability to see when mistakes are made, recognise these mistakes and draw conclusions. And of course it involves bringing together many individuals with all their individual experiences, positive and negative and fusing these into a collective whole with the one objective. Part of this is handling all the egos involved.

After moving to London, I naturally maintained contact with the organisation and with friends in Ireland. I also attended the Irish caucus meetings at the IEC. Sometime after leaving Ireland I received a letter from a full-time member who was the editor of the Irish paper in Dublin. He had previously worked in the organisation in Belfast. This letter was unsolicited by me. In it this talented full-time member complained that the leading member in the North did nothing but criticise him and gave him no room to develop.

This complaint had credibility with me as I had seen this leading member in the North criticise this Comrade's work in front of others and in a way which was humiliating and unhelpful to that member and the work. I had seen this leading member do the same to others, usually to the most talented and committed members who could have played a leading role in a genuinely collective leadership. I suspected that he consciously or unconsciously criticised these particular members precisely because they had the most ability and were most capable of playing a leading role. If they had been encouraged to do so this would have meant that he himself would have had to change his way of working and accept being part of a collective leadership rather than running a one-person show.

I had previously received complaints from four other members of the organisation about this leading member. These complaints were along the lines of him being over-bearing, insensitive to the membership, not listening sufficiently to the membership, not encouraging a new layer of leadership to develop, and always wanting to have his own way. Peter Taaffe had described him to me as 'imperious'. I found him to be arrogant.

I believed a number of things in relation to leadership. I believed the leadership had to have a high theoretical level. I believed to be effective, leadership had to be 90% by example. I believed it had to be prepared to openly admit its mistakes. I believed it had to be able replace itself. And I believed leadership had to be genuinely collective. I was very clear on the first four points of these criteria for leadership and I practiced these in my work. On the fifth point, the need for a genuinely collective leadership, while I was groping towards it and while I had raised it on occasion with leading members of the CWI, I did not see it as so central as it was and as I was to see it later. And in particular I did not see it as being as central as it was in this situation which was then developing with this leading member in the North. Nor was I clear on how the approach of the CWI as a whole was far too centralised; and the internal life, and in particular the life of the leadership, was insufficiently self-critical and probing. As a result my ability to deal with the crisis I was about to face was weakened.

It was also weakened by the perspective of the CWI that we were five to ten years to the revolution and the need above all else was to build and build and build and that any questioning and debate just got in the way of this. There were no discussions on this mistake because the majority of the leadership of the CWI and the internal culture of the CWI did not recognise that they ever made mistakes. How could something that did not happen be discussed? I had been part of the drive to put this emphasis of the five to ten years in place so I bore part of the responsibility for this mistaken emphasis of the work and the crisis that was to develop.

I responded to this letter I received from the Irish member by saying that we should proceed with caution as we tried to resolve this as I had experience with the member involved in the past and had never known him to admit to having ever made any mistakes. Proceeding diplomatically and with caution would be the best way to have any chance of preparing the ground for a democratic, comradely exchange of views and perhaps getting this member to reconsider his way of working rather than him to immediately dig into an aggressively defensive position.

I returned from an international trip to an attack upon myself by the majority of the IS and the member who had been the subject of the complaint in Ireland. Bob Labi, a full-time member who worked with me on the IS, in reality his role was to spy on me and keep his eye out in general and report everything back to Peter Taaffe, had gone into my private files and taken out the letter from the member who had complained about how he was being treated, and my response to this letter. Both were private letters. But without consulting me they had been handed around to all IS members and also forwarded to the member against whom the complaint had been made. Old scores and jealousies were involved here. During this time, when I was away, the rest of the IS had discussed the issue amongst themselves and with the leading member in the North of Ireland. I was not present for these discussions. My letter where I said that we should proceed with caution was also shown to other selected members outside the IS and twisted to say that I was trying to undermine the member against whom the complaint had been made. The idea was to slander and undermine me with these members, isolate me from these other members, before I got a chance to put my side of the story. I would later understand that this was done because I did not fit into the culture of the IS which among other things looked for each member to back up any other member who was criticised regardless if the criticism was right or wrong.

It was portrayed that the whole dispute had arisen because I was trying to undermine the leading member in the North. When in fact the issue had arisen because members had complained about the leading member's attitude to them and the membership, his attitude of not helping them to develop into positions of collective leadership, in fact he did the opposite. Why should I try to undermine the leading member in the North? I had already left Ireland. The reality was not that I was undermining this member but it was that he was undermining the members who had made the complaints against him, he was preventing a genuine collective leadership from developing. That is he had undermined these potentially leading members and weakened the leadership of the organisation. Needless to say when the majority of the IS were spreading the slander about me, supposedly undermining this leading member, they did not mention the complaints from the other members against this leading member.

As I expected, but hoped would not be the case, this member denied that any single one of the complaints raised against him had any validity. Not only that, but he attacked me for not trying to get the five members who had complained about him to withdraw their complaints and even attacked me for getting the letter as if I had any control over that. This was what I worried would happen when I spoke of the need to proceed diplomatically and with caution to try and prepare the ground to resolve the issue.

There were complaints against this member by other members in his own area and I was being attacked for not trying to stop these complaints and for not automatically defending him! This was not a correct approach, it was an injustice to the members who had made the complaints and it was an injustice to me. And it only encouraged this member in his wrong methods. And on top of that it strengthened the wrong internal life and culture of the CWI.

On occasions previously I had to have discussions with this member about different issues and his way of working and approach. One was precisely this issue of his not praising and encouraging newer and younger members. On another occasion he said he wanted to step back from his leading role in the work in the North because of a personal relationship he was having at the time. I discussed this with him, stressing very strongly his responsibility to the organisation. After this discussion, which included an older and wiser member than myself, this older member said to me: 'You know he will never forgive you for that. For seeing him when he was weak.' I thought no more about this at the time. I should have.

This leading member in the North against whom the complaints had been made, was a theoretically developed member. His theoretical level on some issues was higher than mine. But on other necessary criteria for leadership and for building he was wanting. He refused to admit his mistakes, he did not believe in the need to encourage other members to develop, he did not believe that one of the tests of leadership was could we develop other members to replace ourselves, he did not believe in a genuinely collective leadership. He saw the North of Ireland where he was based as his territory, he was the leader and that was that.

I had left room for and encouraged people like Dermot Connolly, Finn Geaney, Joe Higgins, Ted Gannon, Norma Prendiville, and others in the South to become leading Comrades and form a collective leadership. I proposed and organised that these members would write major theoretical articles and in this way develop themselves as I developed myself. I had left the country and this left room for these and other members to lead. However in the North there was not a selection of members for leadership, there was not an encouragement of members to develop into leading members on an equal basis.

One of the issues I had tried to discuss with the leading member in the North was that of making mistakes. I considered it my responsibility to not only admit my own mistakes but to openly admit to these. I considered that this was the only way that the organisation could learn. I considered this the responsibility of all members if the organisation was to grow. The leading member in the North, like the majority of the IS, did not share this approach. In fact when I would raise this issue of admitting our mistakes he would become openly hostile as if I was attacking him. After all he thought he never made any mistakes. So therefore why would he discuss the issue? This left a resentment in this member against me.

There was another occasion when I had a conflict with this member and where he had to back down. Needless to say he was very unhappy about this. It was where at a summer camp a leading member in the North had struck his partner. I brought this up on the central committee of the Irish section and demanded that this member be removed from his position as a member of the central committee. The leading member in the North tried to defend this member, saying that the female member had provoked her partner who had struck her by going to a party on her own. I very strongly opposed this and insisted on my position that the member involved be removed from the central committee. This was accepted. The leading member in the North had to back down. Never being wrong on anything he did not like this. It increased his resentment of myself.

However I myself was making a mistake at this time. I had no problem in bringing out and openly discussing my own mistakes. This I did. I saw it as not only being the right thing to do but as a way to show an example and try to get other members to do the same. But the problem was I was not insisting on bringing out the mistakes of the organisation as a whole, the mistakes of other members, such as the leading member in the North and the majority of the IS. I was not bringing these out for open discussion within the membership as a whole. I did not do this for a number of reasons.

In relation to the situation with the leading member in the North one reason I did not insist on this being brought out amongst the full membership was that I anticipated that the response of the leading member in the North and the rest of the leadership would be to deny that any mistakes were ever made. I concluded that this would result in turmoil and division inside the organisation and this would be very damaging, especially because I thought the priority was to keep the emphasis on five to ten years to the revolution and related to this the need to build and build and not be diverted by other, what I incorrectly saw then as secondary issues, such as the nature of the internal life and collective leadership. Again the wrong perspective, the five to ten years to the revolution and related to this the wrong organisational internal emphasis, these were central parts of the problem.

As it became clear that the leading member in the North was aggressively defending his way of working, four of those who made the complaints went silent, and the fifth, who had written me the letter of complaint went on to leave the organisation. So I was left alone in the middle of this conflict which had been started by the wrong methods of work of the leading member in the North and the complaints of the five members about these methods of work. But the main reason I was left isolated was that there was a culture inside the organisation of trying to keep differences between the leading members, especially differences on internal organisational questions, also mistakes made by leading members, away from the membership. And I, in spite of raising the issue now and then with other leading members, went along with this. I made a serious mistake in doing so.

I should have taken the issue openly to the entire membership. This would have been very difficult for those who had made the complaints as they would have faced the full wrath of the leading member in the North and he would have been backed up by the majority of the IS. This was one of the reasons I did not take the issue to the membership. However it was not the main reason. The main reason was the existing culture in the organisation of keeping such things quiet so as not to 'disrupt the work'. I should have stood against this culture. It was true that if I had taken the issue to the full membership and looking back at how events turned out if I had done so the people who made the complaints would probably not have stood by them but it would at least have given these members who had made the complaints an opportunity to receive the input of the membership and have more of a democratic atmosphere around them. It would have also given the entire membership the opportunity to collectively think about the issues and give their opinion and make their decisions.

I should have taken the issue into the entire membership in the most open and direct fashion for another reason. If I had done so it would have been an example to the membership and organisation as to how disputes should be handled. It would have made the internal life of the organisation more healthy. This was the main general lesson I learnt from this struggle. That is, that all conflicts and problems and crises in revolutionary organisations should be confronted openly in front of the entire membership and in front of their working class periphery. Any attempt to cover these up, even if people think they are doing so for good reasons such as not to disrupt the work, or to shield the organisation from scandal is always wrong, would always be doomed to do more damage to the organisation and to all concerned. This is what I learned from these events.

I should have understood that confronting the issue openly in front of the entire membership was what would have been in the best interests of the organisation. But I did not. I did not see that there were times in a revolutionary organisation when an internal struggle is in the best interests of that organisation. I did not see that there are times when unity is made the top priority. I did not see that there were times when the boat needed to be rocked. I did not see that this was one of those times. The organisation needed to be confronted with its mistaken internal methods and forced to face up to these. I did not act properly and see that this was done.

If I had taken the issue out to the entire membership and conducted a struggle, the organisation would have gone through a serious internal debate and would therefore have been much better prepared for the battles that lay ahead, the debates, the disagreements, the faction fights, the split, the corruption of the internal life. But having said this, and to be realistic, it is most likely I would have been driven out of the organisation at that stage rather than being driven out some years later. The reality was the internal life was already on the way to being seriously undemocratic and nobody was going to be allowed to challenge it and survive. However this does not change the fact that I should have taken the issues out into the membership and forced an open debate. Whatever the result would have been, whether I would have lost or not, whether I would have been driven out at that stage or not it was the right of the membership to hear what was going on.

The reality in the CWI at that time, was that when the majority of the leadership thought it was best organisational disputes between members were held behind closed doors and the membership kept in the dark. And this was what happened here in my case. This was very damaging to the organisation. It excluded the membership from having an input and an opportunity to solve whatever problem existed. It damaged the membership as it kept them from taking part in all discussions, having this experience, growing and developing and realising their full potential. The entire organisation and membership would have learned and developed much more if they had participated in all discussions and debates. I made a serious mistake in not taking the issue openly to the entire membership.

Not taking the issue out openly to the entire organisation was very damaging both to the organisation and to myself for an additional reason. This was because there was already a clique in the organization which was in the process of being developed. This was developing around Peter Taaffe. He saw it as to further his own ambitions in the CWI. He took my conflict with the leading member in the North as an opportunity to strike at me in the organisation and to further bring together his clique. And this is what happened. It is always and for all reasons a mistake not to bring issues out openly to the full membership. Peter Taaffe used his inside knowledge of such secret internal conflicts to increase his own influence and leverage inside the organisation.

This mistaken method of work of not admitting mistakes and covering up for each other was shared by all members of the IS but for different reasons. Myself and Roger Silverman thought this was the correct way to work. The rest of the IS and the leading member in the North had this approach because they wanted to protect their positions in the organisation. They wanted to make sure that any complaints were made against them, or if their work was questioned in any way, that the rest of the leadership should circle the wagons and defend them right or wrong. I began to get a half glimpse of what was going on. Leading members were expected to defend other leading members when they came under criticism or when they made mistakes and the favour would be returned when and if necessary. You scratch my back, I scratch your back. It was an old boys' club. I was not doing enough back scratching. But I only got half a glimpse of this reality. I did not want to face up to the fact that the organisation I had joined and to which I had given and was giving so much was internally undemocratic and on the way to being corrupt.

I was not able to face this fact for a number of reasons. It never occurred to me that members would act in their own personal interests, in the interests of their own personal position in the CWI. My own struggle to break from my past to be a revolutionary did not allow me to see that others could be revolutionaries and also have their own petty individualistic ambitions such as was the case with the leading member in the North and with Peter Taaffe. And at the same time I was influenced by the fact that we were growing and gaining strength and did this not show the method was correct. And then again there was still the albatross around the organisation's neck of the five to ten years to the revolution and the wrong priorities and balance this brought to the organisation's work.

With the rest of the IS, with the exception of Roger Silverman, behind him the leading member in the North then proceeded to drive me out of any connection with the Irish work. This was the same member who had travelled to Dublin for my going away event and made the speech about how I was the all rounded revolutionary and the important role I had played in building the Irish section. He was singing a different tune now when his own work was being discussed and criticised. Now I had to be slandered and discredited and driven out.

He demanded that I be banned from attending the Irish caucus meetings which took place at international meetings. He backed up this demand with the threat that if I was allowed to attend he would not attend. By this threat he blackmailed the IS. The IS incorrectly allowed itself to be blackmailed. This was undemocratic. I protested. But as I had already left Ireland I thought why have a major fight on this, so under protest I mistakenly accepted being driven out of having any connection with the Irish work and section to which I had given so much. The reality was that what was needed was precisely a battle in the organisation on this and the entire issue.

Being blackmailed out of the work of the Irish section by this member with the support of the majority of the IS, with the exception of Roger Silverman, sickened me. But as I considered the CWI still far and away the best of the left groups and it was still 'five to ten years to the revolution' I carried on with my work and membership of the CWI. I did not anticipate that this difference in method between myself and the majority of that organisation would rise again in the future and with much more serious consequences. It would be dragged out and lied about in the coming faction fights and struggles in the CWI. Both the faction around Ted Grant and Alan Woods and later the faction around Peter Taaffe and Lynn Walsh would say I had been forced to leave Ireland because of this issue. This was a lie. I left Ireland on my own proposal to work in the CWI. The conflict over the issues of the mistakes of the leading member in the North took place after I had already left Ireland. It could not therefore have been the reason for my leaving.

I was to find out that some years later a member of the IS, who was an unquestioning servant of Peter Taaffe, raised with an Irish member that maybe one of the other leading members in the North was no longer up to the job. In other words what I had been wrongly accused of in relation to the leading member was actually considered by the clique that was developing around Taaffe. I would also learn later that the clique around Peter Taaffe which would come to lead the CWI moved secretly in the German section to remove the then leading member in that section, a female working class Comrade, and replace her with a student member. It would take me some years to see the depth of the false methods and in fact what in the future would become the outright corruption of Peter Taaffe and the clique he gathered around him.

CHAPTER 34

US CAPITALISM – GUNS OR BUTTER

ROM 1985 on, my work became concentrated in the USA and Canada. I made regular trips to these two countries to the exclusion of any others. Ever since joining the CWI in 1970 I had made clear that if the work was successful in Ireland I wanted to attempt to organise in the USA. The CWI saw the importance of North America. The leadership of the CWI had seen the success of my work in Ireland and in my time visiting other sections. They had also, if the truth be told, understood that the attacks of the leading person from the North of Ireland on myself had not been warranted. The leadership of the IS had played the role they did to defend their own positions and their own way of working which was that the leading members should back each other up if criticised, whether the criticism was right or wrong. So the concentration of my work in the USA and Canada was without any opposition, without any open opposition anyway. I looked forward to this new challenge. In preparation I immersed myself in the history of these countries. What follows are some of the conclusions I drew.

The Native American and Inuit people were the first known inhabitants of this huge land mass. They travelled, traded, hunted and gathered from coast to coast and the Arctic to the gulf. They were a multitude of different tribes, mainly of hunters and gatherers who lived collectively within themselves and had many different languages and cultures. Their world, a type of primitive communism, with an estimated 60 million people, was to be destroyed by developments in another continent.

Small elites in Europe accumulated large amounts of capital by seizing the land and wealth and surplus product of their own peasant, feudal and working classes. Transforming this into capital they financed expeditions led by members of their own elite to plunder the globe. Wherever they went they measured up the land and resources and labour power and with swords slashing and crucifixes flying seized these and took them into their own private hands.

What was to become the United States of America and also Canada had vast tracts of highly productive agricultural land, it had mineral and oil wealth in great amounts – these were all privatised and stolen by these newly arrived capitalist and slave-owning elites. This was done through violent occupation and genocide against the native people and by violent oppression of all working people. The US ruling class was, from the beginning, a brutal and violent class, it came to power through brutality and violence and genocide.

The US ruling classes did not come to North America alone. From previous invasions and plundering of Africa the elite that was to go on to form the US capitalist and slave-owning classes brought with it tens of millions of Africans whom it had forcibly seized in Africa. The US elite then made these people work without pay for up to three centuries. Some studies estimate the amount owed to African Americans in unpaid back pay for their time during slavery amounts to at least $20 trillion dollars. Some estimates are much, much, much greater. It is undoubtedly the case that it is much, much, much, greater. These unpaid wages of the African American population under slavery were very important in laying the foundations, in accumulating the founding capital for US capitalism. In this process of establishing US capitalism there were other murderous legacies laid on the back of the African American people. They and their children were bought and sold, they were raped and lynched and their bodies burnt in public ceremonies. The destruction and damage and cruelty was close to unimaginable and was built into the foundations and traditions of US capitalism and US society to this day.

African American people were mainly forced to work in cotton. This crop filled the pockets of the new American elite. It also fed the rising industrial power in Britain, fuelling the industrial revolution in that country and the development of capitalism worldwide. The rise not only of US capitalism, but also world capitalism drew much sustenance from the unpaid labour of African American workers, known as slaves, in what was to become the US. When I would later spend time in the poor neighbourhoods of South Chicago and other US cities and saw the poverty there I would think of what had been stolen from the African American people and how the poor neighbourhoods in South Chicago were directly and conversely related to the mansions in New York, London, Paris etc.

The US elite had established their independence in a war against the British ruling class in the 1700s. In the 1800s, the slave-owning section of the US ruling class challenged the capitalist section of the US ruling class for power. The capitalist class, with the help of the slave population, crushed the slave owners in a ferocious civil war, carried through to the finish its own revolution and established itself as an independent, economic and political and military force. Along the way it destroyed in genocide the Native American population and took their land. It invaded and seized part of Mexico and suppressed the Mexican population in what was to be the USA. It bought Alaska and the area around what was to become Florida. As it expanded it needed more labour, so it imported the poverty-stricken masses of Europe. Initially some of these were also held as slaves. Tens of millions came either voluntarily or involuntarily. These workers, along with the African American workers, both when they were slaves and after they were 'freed' after the civil war and the Latino workforce and smaller Asian American workforce provided the labour power for US capitalism.

As its power increased at home, US capitalism strode out onto the world stage, pushed aside all rivals, invaded countries in every continent and seized resources and markets. This process continues to this day and remains the number one source of world instability and what is referred to as terrorism. The American historian William Blum recently published an updated summary of the record of US foreign policy from 1945 to the present. He showed that since that year, the US had 'tried to overthrow more than fifty governments, many of them democratically elected; grossly interfered in elections in thirty countries; bombed the civilian populations of thirty countries; used chemical and biological weapons; and attempted to assassinate foreign leaders.' This is world destabilisation, slaughter and terrorism on a massive scale. Through a combination of these methods and its economic strength, US capitalism surpassed Britain in the early decades of the 20th century to become the number one world power.

Its dominance allowed US imperialism to loot much of the rest of the planet. This in turn affected the balance of class forces at home. When faced with challenges by its own working class, this looted wealth allowed US capitalism to make concessions to sections of its own working class and reduce the class tensions. These concessions went mainly to a small layer of the European American skilled workers who were given higher wages and benefits and easier access to jobs than African American and Latino American and Asian American workers. This gave an additional material basis for the divide and rule and racist policies of US capitalism.

Along with this process, when workers' struggles would develop, these were initially mainly in the east of the continent where US capitalism first established itself, and from where it was possible for a time for workers to move west and south into partially open territory, the Native American people having been cleared from these lands through genocide. The class tensions were reduced in this way also.

These special features helped US capitalism maintain its dominance over its own working class and to keep the balance of power between the classes in its favour. These were major factors in the US working class being the only working class in any industrial country that did not build its own mass political party. They also partially explain the relatively low class consciousness of the US working class.

However, in spite of all this there remained a tendency towards struggle and towards unity of the working class in North America. This frightened the capitalist class. So they passed laws to make inter-racial marriage and relationships illegal. They consciously and deliberately divided the working class and as part of this carried out special oppression against all the racial minorities and against women. They funded and organised the right wing racist terror groups such as the KKK. After the civil war, when slavery was made illegal, they made sure the new state continued to remain racist and the African American people to remain super exploited. They also increased their effort to separate the white working class, especially in the South, from the African American working class. They stepped up their strategy of divide and rule racism and sexism and brutal repression. Using religion and others means they made every effort to increase the division between the genders and the different sexual orientations.

However, the US capitalist class had a problem that would not go away. This class was and would always be a small minority of the population. When a small minority rules a majority, in order to hold on to power, it has to divide the majority. In my native Ireland the divisions were around religion and gender. In the US there were many more opportunities for division. There were the Native American, African American, European American, Latino American, Asian American people and there was of course also gender. No other country had such diversity and thus also such potential for divide and rule. It was much worse than Ireland. While all the different peoples, races and genders were hurled against each other to allow the minority capitalist class to divide and rule, due to their size in the population, due to the fact they could be identified by the colour of their skin, and due to their importance in the economy, African Americans were especially brutally targeted and discriminated against and repressed.

The economic contradictions of capitalism, as well as the need of the capitalist class to keep the balance of forces in its favour, combined to make it necessary for the US capitalist class to divide the working class. Capitalism could not tolerate full employment. If all workers had jobs they would have increased power and they would push for higher wages and better conditions. This would tend to eat into profits and it would also increase workers' class and political consciousness and so would tend to shift the class balance of forces in favour of the working class. So US capitalism, through the manipulation of its monetary system, that is by raising or reducing interest rates, by increasing or decreasing the money supply, thus affecting the speed at which the economy could grow, always kept tens of millions of workers, usually at least 6%, and on occasions double and more than that, of its workers unemployed. This was deliberate. To get acceptance for this it used repression and especially racist repression and racist propaganda.

This had a very negative result for working class people. With only 5% of the world's population, the US had 25% of the world's prisoners. No other country in the world came close to having so many of its population locked up. The US ruling class spewed out racist propaganda to 'explain' this, falsely claiming that its huge prison population, the vast majority of whom were African American or Latino, was because of the existence of the large minority populations in the country. The real reason was the conscious and deliberate policy of keeping millions unemployed in a society which had practically no social services. And doing this to weaken the working class and keep the class balance of forces on its side thus increasing its profits.

To back up repression and its divide and rule racist propaganda, US capitalism made sure its incarceration policies were racist. African Americans were imprisoned at six times the rate of European Americans. European American workers were bombarded with the propaganda that this inequality proved it was the fault of the African Americans themselves. Left out was the history of African Americans not being paid for 300 years, the higher unemployment rate in African American areas through investment decisions made by the mainly European American capitalist class, and the brutal and discriminatory laws and repression. This racist propaganda and these racist policies of repression lowered the consciousness especially of the European American working class.

The more I carried out organising work in the US, I came to see that as well as keeping control through these racist policies, US capitalism was increasingly stepping up its repression in general and strengthening its state apparatus. The police forces in every city and state were being equipped with full body armour and large armoured vehicles. These were later to appear on the streets at the time of the Occupy and anti-racist and anti-police brutality movements. This increased repression was also shown in the surveillance of just about every phone and computer in the country. The reason for the strengthening of the state apparatus was because the US capitalist class no longer had the wealth to continue as in the past.

To keep its position in the world US imperialism had bases in up to two hundred countries and the amount it put into military spending was greater than its next ten rivals combined. Spending on arms and military technology is in reality spending on scrap metal. It will be destroyed either in war or by becoming obsolete. It does not contribute to the needs and good of society and the human species. US imperialism wasted a lot of its productive forces in the production of scrap metal, that is, weapons of war.

US imperialism saw itself as having the right to intervene anywhere it thought its interests were threatened and where it could do so. It also had to always have a war or proxy wars or propaganda wars going to justify its military spending and to lower the consciousness of its own working class. Until the collapse of Stalinism it was the war against 'communism', that is Stalinism, after that it was the war against Islam, the war against terrorism, the war against drugs, there always had to be a 'war'. These 'wars' were necessary to keep the US working class supporting their own capitalist class and saluting the flag and justify the spending on arms. But these wars cost money.

The collapse of the Soviet Union did not lead to the new capitalist class which arose out of the collapse of this former Stalinist power lying down in front of US imperialism. Out of its collapse arose a new imperialist power, Russia, and a number of smaller capitalist powers over all of which US imperialism sought to dominate. These myriad of new states caused new problems for US imperialism. There was not a 'new world order' with the US sitting comfortably in the saddle as US imperialism predicted. There was a new world disorder. Within this there was also the rapidly rising power of China. So US imperialism, rather than having less fronts on which to fight after the collapse of the former Soviet Union, had more fronts on which it had to fight and so needed not only to continue with its military spending but in fact even increase its military spending.

Also at this time, the US regime was bogged down in one of its longest ever wars and entanglements in the Middle East and Central Asia. It was increasingly challenged in Africa, Latin America, Asia, Europe and Central Asia. It had Putin's and China's ambitions to contend with. In spite of facing this it was not prepared to withdraw from any of its positions. It has been top dog for a century. It was not prepared to give this up. Its whole system and apparatus was built on it being number one. Its whole economic, political and military system was based on it being the dominant power. An important part of its economy was its military spending. It was not going to give up its number one position in the world without a fight.

But it faced a major problem, what could be called a 'guns or butter' problem. It could not afford to maintain its number one position in the world with its hundreds of military bases, it could not afford to keep its military spending at the level it considered was necessary and at the same time keep its own working class on the living standards to which it was accustomed and which it expected would continue. It could no longer afford guns and butter. Its efforts to push this problem off into the future was shown by the massive debt that it had run up over previous decades. It was reduced to ruling the world with money borrowed from countries such as China which was at the same time one of its main rivals. US imperialism understood this and so it made a decision. It launched an offensive to take back all that had been gained by the US working class in the movements of the 1930s, the post-Second World War period and in the 1960s. President George W Bush stated this openly. So did his vice president Cheney.

Cheney, one of the most arrogant and stupidly outspoken representatives of the most ruthless section of the US ruling class, thinks his class can say and do what it likes. He played a leading role with his lies and policies as vice president in taking the US into the wars in Iraq and Afghanistan. He was at the centre of events leading up to 9/11 which he blamed on Iraq when Iraq had nothing to do with it. But this meant nothing to Cheney and his section of the US ruling class. US imperialism wanted to invade Central Asia to seize its resources and to try and contain Russia and China, and so 9/11 was used to create the mood at home to allow them to do this.

Cheney threatened Democratic Party Senator Wellstone with serious repercussions if he voted against the war in Iraq. He also ordered him to stop 'poking his nose' into 9/11. Wellstone refused to back down and a few days later he and other members of his family were killed in a small plane crash. Wellstone's family banned Cheney, at the time vice president, from attending his funeral. They were making clear what they thought about Cheney and any role he might have played in their family member's death.

Recently Cheney, on behalf of his class explained how he and they saw things. He stated emphatically and publically that social spending, such as food stamps, had to go and the savings had to be used to fund the military. This is the essence of the offensive of US capitalism. Cut the living standards of its own working class at home to fund its imperialist wars and occupations abroad. Cut the butter to allow it to be able to continue to afford the guns. This is what is reflected in the increased militarisation of the cops and the US state. This increased militarisation is preparation to allow the US capitalist class to cut its own workers' living standards, to cut the social safety net, to the extent that one exists, and cut further into the real wages of all US workers in order to be able to keep funding its international position. US capitalism knows the US working class will fight against being driven back to the poverty of the 1930s so it is preparing its state apparatus to fight its own working class.

I could see that that this meant that a break in the situation, in the equilibrium, in the class balance of forces in the US lay ahead. The equilibrium, albeit limited, of the past decades could not last. The main feature of this break, of this ending of the equilibrium, would be the US working class rising to its feet. It would not accept being put on rations without a fight. It would not accept being put back to the living standards of the pre-1930 period without a battle.

While being confident of this analysis and these conclusions I was aware that this break still lay ahead. The big battalions of the working class, organised and unorganised, had not yet decisively moved. They were discontented, even angry, with their lot, but with their leadership in the trade unions being as it was, they could not see how to fight and win, so they mostly, but not totally, remained waiting and watching. They were getting by, most of them were still able to make ends meet by working harder, working longer hours, more than one job, going deeper into debt, trying to survive through such individual efforts. They did not want to risk losing what they had. It would be when they could no longer get by, could no longer keep their heads above water by such individual efforts and within the system, that the big events would happen and things would change in US society, when the break in the situation would come. While I remained convinced that this analysis was correct, what I and the CWI got very wrong was the tempo. This break in the situation would take much longer than we thought.

With the possible exception of a major climatic or environmental disaster or partial nuclear war internationally, either of which would qualitatively affect the mass consciousness in the world and in the US, I considered that the rise of the US working class to its feet would very possibly be the main event of the coming decades. The world's number one economic and military power, the world's main source of aggression and war and occupation, when this force could no longer play this role because its own working class refused to pay the price in sweat, blood and treasure, this would change the world balance of forces. Part of this would be a dramatic increase in the class consciousness of the US and world working class.

Different countries, cultures and classes have different traditions. The US capitalist class had and has a tradition of extreme brutality and violence and racism and sexism. It is continually at war, either directly or by proxy. It is the only capitalist class that has dropped atomic weapons on civilian populations. It carried out genocide against the Native American population. It has the brutality and violence of slavery built into its system. It has the tradition of violence against its own working class when it has tried to organise also built into its system. It has the tradition of assassinating members of its own class when they would 'get out of line'. It is prepared to kill and brutalise large numbers of its population to achieve its ends, in the form of the mass hunger in the US, the lack of access to health care, the mass incarceration, the mass doping through prescription drugs and illegal drugs, the throwing of its youth into endless wars, the use or tolerance of tactics such as 9/11. The US capitalist class was and is a violent, brutal, criminal, ruling class. I absorbed this reality as I worked in the US. I was convinced there would be no peaceful road to socialism in that country.

CHAPTER 35

US WORKING CLASS

W HEN TRYING TO BUILD a revolutionary nucleus in the US as well as studying the history of the US capitalist class and US capitalism, I studied the history and tradition and role of the US working class and of its leaders. While there were around 300 million workers in the USA, there were only approximately 14 million workers organised in the US trade unions. The trade union members were diverse in race and gender. They were organised in many different unions which were coordinated in the American Federation of Labour-Congress of Industrial Organisations. (AFL-CIO) These unions organised their members in the workplace and in city-wide labour councils. Their members had many interests in common: wages, conditions, jobs, benefits, housing, health care, education, repression, racism, sexism, democratic rights, the environment, war and peace. In spite of the small numbers relative to the working class as a whole, there was great potential for the trade unions to build a powerful, united movement against the bosses capitalist system.

But the problem was as elsewhere – the leadership of the working class. In this case it was the leadership of the trade unions as there was no Labour Party or workers' party. The role of the leaderships of these unions, of these organisations of the organised working class was directly related to the consciousness of the working class. These trade union leaders would not organise and unite the working class in struggle against capitalism, so this inevitably had an extremely negative effect on the consciousness of the working class. The reason the leaders would not lead was as elsewhere. The union leadership believed in capitalism and in the case of the US, believed in and supported the capitalist party, the Democrats. They did not believe the working class could act independently and build a new society. This was the major reason for the logjam which prevented the US working class from fighting and which allowed the balance of class forces to remain so much on the side of the capitalist class. There was also of course the privileged positions, high wages and benefits, secure jobs and in some cases the outright corruption of the union leaderships which cemented these leaderships in their alliance with US capitalism. However negative and all as these factors were and are, the decisive reason the union leaderships refused and refuse to mobilize and lead the US working class was and is that they do not believe there is an alternative to capitalism, and they believe that any effort by the US working class to build an alternative would lead to chaos and also of course would threaten their own privileged positions and their control of the 14 million strong US trade union movement.

The break in the situation would come in the future when US capitalism would move even more decisively to cut the living standards of its own working class. When this would happen, when this whip of the counter revolution would be laid more decisively across the backs of the US working class, then the shift in the class balance of forces to the side of the working class would begin. Such an offensive against the working class, such an attack on the working class, was not wanted by me. I did not want to see the US working class suffer more than it was suffering already. But such increased suffering was made inevitable by the role of the trade union leaders. Because they would not lead and organise, the working class would only be convinced that they had to take serious action and organise against the system after suffering defeats and suffering at the hands of the capitalist offensive. It was the refusal of the trade union leaders to lead that made inevitable the defeats and increased sufferings of the working class that lay ahead, sufferings and defeats which would transform the consciousness of the US working class. However such a break in the situation still lay in the future. The balance of class forces still lay with the US capitalist class. Convincing workers to organise for a socialist revolution was not going to be easy.

When US imperialism was defeated in Vietnam, it regrouped and with the coup in Chile launched a new international offensive. Part of this was going after its own working class at home. Its first decisive step was against the Professional Air Traffic Controllers' Organisation (PATCO) in 1981. These union workers went on strike for better pay, more jobs and a shorter work week, the opposite to what the bosses' butter-cutting offensive demanded. Reagan, on behalf of his class decided upon and carried out on behalf of this class, the deliberately provocative action of firing all the strikers, replacing them with non-union workers and banning them from working in their profession again. This was unprecedented in the decades of the post-war period. Reagan and his capitalist class threw down the gauntlet to the US working class.

This was not just any strike. The *Wall Street Journal* explained its significance. It wrote: 'the PATCO strike has to be defeated for all sorts of reasons that have absolutely nothing to do with relations between the Federal Aviation Administration and PATCO. The defeat of PATCO is related to the more important issues, commitments to rebuild military strength, to restore the dollar to soundness, to cut taxes and regulations, to resist Soviet imperialism and to curb the wild ascent of federal spending.'

This was no beating about the bush. After the defeat in Vietnam, after the economic crisis of the early 1970s, and with the rising US debt, US imperialism was moving to rebuild its economic and military strength at home and internationally. It was moving to decisively get back in the saddle again. And this meant taking on its own working class. PATCO was a turning point in the strategy of the US capitalist class, in the US class struggle in the post-World War II period. US imperialism was moving decisively to take away the gains that had been won by the US working class.

Along with the attack on PATCO US imperialism set up the North American Free Trade Association. This allowed capital and goods to move with little restriction between the US, Canada and Mexico. This gave the much more powerful US capital access to the cheap labour in Mexico and the markets of all three countries. It also cut into the jobs and income and power of the US working class. Also at this time US capitalism and its international collaborators moved to so-called global capitalism, that is, the removal of restriction after restriction and regulation after regulation on the workings and movement of capital anywhere in the capitalist world. Capital was to be allowed to go anywhere it liked, do anything it liked, and in the process of this unrestricted movement, this unrestricted competition, the conditions of the US working class and the working class internationally would to be driven down to the lowest existing level. The race to the bottom was on. The capitalist offensive was on.

This offensive against the US and the international working class took place when Stalinism was collapsing and new resources of capital, raw materials and labour were becoming available to the capitalist world economy. There were also the breakthroughs in new technology. While its contradictions continued and even worsened, these developments combined to give US capitalism a temporary boost. These events also for a period weakened any belief that existed amongst the working class in the US and internationally that there was an alternative to capitalism. The result was the balance of class forces, both in the US and internationally, was pushed even further in favour of the capitalist class. This was what was happening when I began my systematic work in the US in 1985. The offensive of capitalism internationally and in the US was gathering steam. Organising for socialism was not going to be easy.

The role of the leaders of the working class in the US, that is, the leaders of the trade unions, was central to the class balance of forces. These leaders, as was the case elsewhere, had been completely cowed by the capitalist offensive. They had been committed to capitalism before but they had now become absolutely unquestioning and willing and cooperating partners with capitalism in its offensive. This offensive and the refusal of the workers' leaders to oppose it, in fact their willing cooperation with it, made for a powerful ebb tide pushing back the US working class.

This advance of the capitalist offensive was not inevitable. The PATCO strike need not have been defeated. The union leaders in the US could have called work place and union, local and regional, and labour council meetings, explained what was involved and how it was necessary to force the bosses to retreat by stopping production by mass general strike action and occupying workplaces. They could have organised workers' squads in every workplace and union body dedicated to halt and throw back the capitalist offensive by mass direct action of a united front, and general strike and occupation character. They could have taken this offensive out to the unorganised workers and brought them into the unions. No more protests and whining about how bad things were but actual fighting squads of workers on the offensive in their own interests and to improve things. The World Trade Events in Seattle which came later, showed what would have been possible. Youth and workers took to the streets and physically fought the cops. Such an approach by the union leaders could have led to organising the unorganised, throwing back the capitalist offensive and pushing forward the building of an offensive of the working class itself, and the building of a mass workers' political party.

Instead the heads of the unions ordered their members to pass the PATCO picket lines. Instead of fighting, the union leaders consciously decided to let PATCO be defeated so they could prove their reliability to US capitalism and cosy up even closer to the capitalist Party the Democrats, and further consolidate their policy of the team concept. The team concept was collaborating with the employers in the workplaces and working with the employers' party, the Democrats, in politics. It did not mean team work with the rest of the working class it meant team work with the capitalist class. Instead of unity with the rest of the working class against the bosses, it was unity with sections of the capitalist class against other sections of the capitalist class and other sections of the working class. These policies undermined the independence and militancy of the US working class.

The President of Phelps Dodge explained the thinking of the bosses in relation to their offensive and to the class balance of forces at that time. He said in an article in The Wall Street Journal in 1992, that his mining company in Arizona had: 'led the way in the copper miners' strike in AZ in 1983. We created a new approach to labour. It was followed all over. Suddenly people realised you can beat a union. Time was big unions were considered invincible. We demonstrated that nobody was invincible.'

In this same article in The Wall Street Journal there was an interview with a United Auto Workers' Union leader. He was asked about the role of his union's leadership in the Caterpillar strike where it had ordered its striking members back to work when the company began to bring in replacements for the strikers. He explained this by saying: 'we were not going to commit economic suicide.' It never occurred to this union leader, or if it did he never acted to bring it about, that the workers could have occupied the plants, physically taken on the replacement workers and the state and spread the strike and won. The union officials at this strike even went so far as to walk up and down the edge of the sidewalk keeping their picketing members from blocking the roads and the scabs. They did the bosses' and the cops' jobs for them. They should have been sworn in and given uniforms.

These articles in The Wall Street Journal, the main public mouthpiece of the bosses, were very significant. They contained this quote about the PATCO strike, they contained this quote from the Phelps Dodge president and counter-posed it to the quote from the United Auto Workers bureaucrat. They explained the wider significance of the PATCO strike. The Wall Street Journal wanted to make sure its readers saw what was going on. That the bosses were on the offensive and winning and the union bureaucratic leadership were a bunch of wimps on the retreat against this offensive and could easily be defeated, and in the process their members could also be defeated.

Of course this was not passively accepted by all sections of the working class. There were many strikes by different groups of workers throughout this period, airline workers, Greyhound workers, industrial workers of all kinds and throughout the country. There was the strike of the P9 local against Hormel and the Pittston miners' strike both of which drew mass solidarity across the country. There were the two solidarity days with workers' marches in Washington involving hundreds of thousands of workers. There were movements in defence of the rights of women which involved hundreds of thousands of demonstrators in Washington. There were the mass uprisings of youth in inner cities such as Los Angeles. There was the potential to build a powerful workers' offensive.

The union leaders had all the facts at their fingertips to build a mass offensive movement. From around the end of World War II to 1980, productivity gains and US workers' wages had risen about in tandem. But from 1980 to 2008 productivity rose by 75% while average wages rose by only

22%. So during the thirty years to 2008, workers were paid for only 30% of the rise in productivity. With facts like these the union leaders could have built a movement of workers capable of blocking and throwing back the bosses' offensive and launching an offensive of their own.

One group of workers in the P9 local in Minnesota made a heroic effort to stop the bosses' offensive. In 1985 they rejected the bosses' demands for concessions and went on strike. They appealed for support across the country and internationally. Three hundred union locals in North America sent material support to the strike. Forty two independent P9 support groups were set up throughout the country. Tens of thousands of workers came to the town to demonstrate their support. Local solidarity committees drew in families and children to the struggle. To prevent the strike from winning the leaders of the union to which the strikers belonged, the United Food and Commercial Workers removed the leaders of the local who were leading the fight, and replaced them with other leaders whom it controlled and who obeyed the union leaders' orders to accept the bosses' demand for concessions. In this way the strike was sabotaged and ended.

The leadership of the strikers' international union, led by Bill Wynn who was paid over $200,000 a year could not afford to let the workers at P9 win. If they had done so this would have proven that concessions did not have to be made to the bosses' offensive. It would have proven that strikes could win. This would have undermined the entire propaganda and strategy of all the union leaders which was that there was no alternative but to give in to the bosses. The union leaders dressed up their 'strategy' in a fancy term: 'controlled retreat'. Of course at times it might be necessary to retreat to better position the movement for a new offensive but this was not what the union leaders were doing. They were in full retreat with no thought to preparing the movement for an offensive of its own at any time. In fact it was not even full retreat, it was full surrender. It was fleeing from the scene of battle. The UFCW union leaders were so determined to end the strike, so petty in their sabotage of the strike, that they ordered the sandblasting of the huge mural which supported the strike which had been painted on the wall of the Labour Centre in the town. No union trades' people in the area would do this so the leaders of the local who were put in place by the leadership of the union to sabotage the strike had to do the job themselves.

Other groups of workers tried to move in the same direction as P9. One was the Pittston miners. They occupied their workplace, they appealed for support for their struggle nationally, they set up a camp for strike supporters, they ran a candidate for the state legislature and had him elected. 40,000 workers travelled to the area and surrounded the occupied mine in support. This action could have been built upon. It could have won. But as with PATCO, as with P9, what terrified the union leaders was that if any of these strikes had won this would have exposed the leaders' whole 'strategy' which was based on their false claim that the workers could not win and so concessions had to be made. Their strategy was based on their belief that capitalism was the only system, its offensive was unstoppable and so defeats had to be accepted. And anybody in the union movement who thought that victories were possible had to be isolated and crushed. The union leaders, as they had done with P9, isolated the Pittston strikers and made sure that they did not win, that they did not provide an example to other workers, that they did not expose the cowardly surrender strategy of the union leaders.

But there was another factor which allowed for the success of the bosses' offensive and which allowed the union leaders to go along with this bosses' offensive and to crush the P9 and the Pittston workers. While there was great support for the P9 and Pittston strikes and other strikes there was no organised cohesive mass or semi-mass organisation of fighters amongst the rank and file of the working class that had a conscious alternative to the bosses' offensive and to the capitulation of the union leaders. So in spite of their courageous and militant actions the P9 workers and the Pittston workers and other workers who took strike action such as in a prolonged strike in Decatur Southern Illinois did not have the support they needed. They and the many other workers who acted against the bosses' offensive at this time, because there was no organised semi-mass or mass anti-capitalist or even just anti the bosses offensive movement, were unable to achieve victories in their own struggles and from this lead the working class as a whole to defeat the bosses' offensive.

There were tiny left groups which existed and claimed to stand for the working class and for the overthrow of capitalism. They veered between sectarianism and ultra-leftism and opportunism, had no base in the working class, and where they had any influence for a time they only harmed the movement. Out of the P9 strike there arose an attempt to set up what was called the 'National Rank and File Against Concessions'. This met in conference. This conference could have laid the basis for a real opposition movement in the unions to the capitalist offensive and their sell-out leaderships. However this potential step forward was wrecked by a small sect, the so-called Communist Labour Party. Sectarian to the core, this sect secretly sneaked its people into positions of leadership of this effort and instead of trying to help it grow and fight the bosses it sought to use it to get members of its own sect into positions in the trade union bureaucracy. Another self-styled revolutionary group, or to be more accurate sect, the Socialist Workers' Party put resources into solidarity for the P9 strike but only to further its own interests. It would not fight the union bureaucracy as it thought this would cut across its efforts to get its own members into positions in this bureaucracy. It refused to share its sizeable contact list with the P9 strikers but wanted access to the P9 strikers' solidarity list. The so-called Communist Party also played their role undermining the P9 strike and in preventing the building of the National Rank and File Against Concessions. Their method of undermining the potential movement was to continually cast doubts on the strategy of the P9 strikers, claim they were dividing the trade union movement, and all this in the interests of their strategy to cosy up to the union bureaucracy, support the leadership of the AFL-CIO and to ingratiate themselves with the capitalist Democratic Party.

This lack of any semi-mass or mass alternative to the pro-capitalist, pro-concessions union bureaucracy was an important factor in the thinking of all workers, especially organised workers and especially the most conscious organised workers. I became friends with a Belfast man who had emigrated to Detroit. He was a leader of the opposition in the United Auto Workers. He took me to a meeting of an opposition caucus of the most skilled workers in General Motors. They worked in the design and tech centre where they developed the prototypes for the cars of the future. They were amongst the most skilled and highest paid of the US working class. We discussed the class struggle, Ireland, the Vietnam War, when they had walked out of their plant against the war. These were very intelligent and thoughtful and skilled and well paid workers. I raised directly the need for them to organise for direct action against the bosses' offensive, against the corporations and their system, that is, organise as a cohesive force and along the lines of preparing for tactics such as the workplace occupations, the street fighting, the three big strikes of 1934 which had blocked the bosses' offensive at that time, sparked off a new offensive of the workers and opened the door to the increase in union membership from around two million in 1930 to twelve million in 1940.

These workers listened to what I had to say. But their eyes glazed over when I raised the need for they themselves to seriously organise for an all-out fight using the tactics of the '30s, the mass occupation of plants, the taking on in battle the cops and scabs who were used to break the strikes. I could see that they were thinking that they would have to take on the bosses and their state, and not only that but take on their own union leaders and build a new leadership. It might have been a different story if their own leaders had been prepared to fight but they were not. It might have been a different story if there had existed a semi-mass or mass force within the ranks of the unions and in the workplaces which was prepared to take on the bosses but there was not. So what I was proposing was too much. I could see that they were thinking that maybe I was wrong and they would get by. After all they had been getting by pretty good up to then. And who was I, just some crazy Irish revolutionary. I did not recruit any members, not even my Belfast friend, from that meeting.

But I learnt something from this discussion. I learnt that with my, in reality, non-existent forces, and given the treacherous role of the union leaders, it would be very difficult to build any sizeable revolutionary nucleus from the most skilled and highly paid layers of the US working class at that stage. Workers, and especially skilled and blue collar workers, had a significant appreciation of their power and that they could bring the economy to a halt and so tended to be more cautious than white collar workers, than students and youth precisely because they had this power. The dialectic again, their greater power and their greater consciousness of that power together with their understanding of the role of their leadership made them more cautious about using that power. For the students and sections of the youth who did not have that power they tended to be less reluctant to act, at least initially. There was also of course the fact that most of the more skilled and organised workers still had a half decent living standard.

While recognising this consciousness of the working class and especially the organised working class, I continued to make a special effort to involve myself with union activities in an effort to more clearly understand the mood and consciousness. The meeting with the General Motors design and tech workers was very helpful in that it showed me that even the most thoughtful workers, maybe particularly the most organised and most thoughtful workers, given the role of their leadership, given the lack of any semi-mass or mass alternative in the working class, and given their in most cases half tolerable wages and benefits were not at that stage prepared to fight in the way that was necessary. My conclusion was that my work would be slow and steady, and in particular, building in ones and twos and probably not amongst the most skilled workers in the early stages, probably more amongst the youth.

Nevertheless, I intervened in as many of the big strikes as I could. A Greyhound strike stands out. It was a hot humid night in San Francisco and there were hundreds of strikers. We were gathered to try and close the depot and stop the buses that were being driven by strike-breakers. The cops were there on one side keeping the gates open and workers were there on the other trying to close them. Pushing and shoving both sides tried to achieve their objective. I saw the cops catch a small Latino American worker and break his arm with their clubs. The fact he was small, the fact he was Latino American, the fact the cops and the majority of the strikers and the strike breakers were mainly European American were all bundled up in this. It was also a sign of the times that this Latino American worker who had his arm broken, would later be recruited into the ranks of the union bureaucracy. Rather than reward him with a fighting winning strategy, the union bureaucracy rewarded him with a desk and a suit. And along with that none of the self-styled revolutionary groups could recruit him. And this included ourselves. Our alternative, build the revolutionary nucleus, just seemed too unrealistic to him.

Visiting picket lines and strike meetings was vital education for my work and development. I would introduce myself as a trade unionist and activist from Ireland. Ask what the strike was about, express my support, suggest that I could get messages of support from other countries and other locals in the US and Canada. I was doing what the union leaders should have been doing, going on to the picket lines with the workers and linking them up with workers nationally and internationally. I would also listen to the workers and see what they had to say, what they thought about their struggle and could they win etc. I was developing and training myself further in union work in the US.

I would attempt to sell our paper. Its name, Labour Militant, was a good name for selling on picket lines and in general, and usually after some discussion and being seen to be prepared to listen to the workers it was possible to sell a few copies. Some workers would express enthusiasm for the idea of themselves being a 'Labour Militant', but this was in the main superficial, the majority of workers would listen and observe and keep silent. They were not sure it was a good idea to be a 'Labour Militant' even though they were on the picket line. They felt being a 'Labour Militant' could isolate them and make them more of a target for the bosses and union leaders. But occasionally I would get the ones and twos who would be prepared to meet and discuss and even occasionally the one or two whom I could convince to take the ideas more seriously and commit themselves to become a revolutionary and a member.

I would regularly explain the history of the US workers' movement. Explain that the present defeats and the refusal of the union leaders to lead did not mean there had never been great movements and victories of the US working class. There was the eight-hour day movement in the 1880s; there was the rise of the craft unions in the American Federation of Labour around the same time; there was the rise of the Knights of Labour also around the same time; there was the rise of the Industrial Workers of the World in the early 1900s; there was the temporary rise of Deb's socialist party at the same time; there was the rise of the Congress of Industrial Organisations and the mass workplace occupations in the 1930s. The rise of the Congress of Industrial Organisations made dramatic and permanent gains and also forced the other union Federation of that time, the American Federation of Labour, to drop its openly racist policies. There was the strike movement in the post-War period which won gains, and then in the 1960s, the great African American revolt and women's movement. Time after time the US working class and specially oppressed groups fought and time after time made progress. To many workers I was bringing this knowledge for the first time and this was attractive and inspiring to them.

But I was also explaining that times were different now and these gains of the past were being rolled back by the capitalist offensive. The decisive reason for this was that the union leaders would not fight. I would therefore explain that we had to base ourselves, not on the methods of defeat of the union leaders, but on the methods of struggle that had achieved the victories in the past. The methods of the 1930s in particular; the methods of the three big strikes of 1934, Minneapolis, Toledo, San Francisco; the occupations of 1936, which turned the balance of forces on to the side of the workers at that time. Great class battles would come again and the task was to be ready for them. And to build for these and out of these.

But while I was right in this explanation and this work I was making a mistake in another area, I was making a mistake in relation to the big picture. And this was the most important issue.

Neither I, nor the CWI, recognised the real world balance of forces nor the full extent and power of the capitalist offensive. We underestimated the determination and organisation of the capitalist class. Even more important than that, we did not see the events that were unfolding in the Stalinist world, which would lead to the collapse of Stalinism and how this would add impetus to the capitalist offensive. We did not see the spurts of economic growth that were to come in the capitalist world. We did not see how much of a factor the new technology would mean to the capitalist world economy. We underestimated capitalism. And we were over-optimistic about the tempo of the struggle of the working class and the movement to come. This wrong world view would have very serious repercussions in the years ahead. But that was still ahead.

The small group I was helping to build did not have the resources to travel and take our ideas to, and meet the workers involved in most of the struggles that were taking place. We would try and overcome this by meeting them when they were on speaking tours. However in the main struggle of that time, that of the P9 local in Minnesota, Richard Mellor who was part of our little group, was able, because of his union base, to get a P9 striker into his labour council, the Central Labour Council of Alameda County. The union bureaucracy and its supporters tried to stop the P9 striker's case being heard. Richard fought them. The role of the left groups was exposed at that meeting. Not one of them would second Richard's motion to let the P9 strikers' case be heard because the leadership of the P9 strikers' international union, the United Food and Commercial Workers had by that time withdrawn its official support for the strike and declared the strike to be over. These lefts would not support Richard's effort to allow the P9 striker to be heard because they did not want to alienate themselves from the union bureaucracy. This was par for the course for most of these left groups. Richard was only able to get the P9 striker's case heard because his motion to do so was seconded by another union member. This union member was not a member of any left group. But he played a better role than any of these left group people. This was a good illustration of how so many of the left groups who are in any way active in the union movement, because they do not want to alienate themselves from the union bureaucracy, end up abandoning the workers in struggle. A worker who was not a member of any left wing group was prepared to support Richard in his struggle to have the P9 striker be heard, while the left including the so called Communist Party were not.

However, I and our small group made a mistake at this time. I was travelling round the country meeting workers and young people in struggle. I was orienting to the working class and this was correct. I was helping to produce a paper explaining the need for democratic socialism and putting forward a programme on which the working class should fight. But my approach was too general, insufficiently targeted. While there were many other major strikes against the bosses' offensive over this period, the strike of the P9 workers was the most important. As the full-time organiser of the CWI covering North America I should have moved to and lived with and worked with the P9 strikers for the entire duration of their strike. I would have met and better absorbed the consciousness and mood of the strikers and their families and also the mood and consciousness of the tens of thousands of workers who came to the strike in solidarity. Working in a non-sectarian way, listening to the ideas of the workers, absorbing the mood of the workers, helping in the day to day work of the strike, getting support for the strike internationally, I could have built respect amongst these workers. I would have learnt from the strikers and their supporters.

If I had moved to live there for the duration of the strike I could also have organised other members of our small group in other areas, not only to orient to the strike by building support in their own areas, but also to come and regularly visit and stay for prolonged periods amongst the strikers and their supporters. In this way our small group would have developed with a more working class core and experience and consciousness. This approach would have hardened up the members of the group who were from a more student and middle class background. It would have given them a more working class consciousness. It would have helped them to see the need while fighting the bosses to also fight the union leaders. This would have been enormously helpful in the struggles that were to come in our group when later the majority bent to the pressure of the union bureaucracy in what was to develop as the Labour Party Advocates. My refusal, and the refusal of the other members who did not capitulate to the union bureaucracy in the Labour Party Advocates was, amongst other things, due to our experience in fighting the bosses and with this fighting the union bureaucracy. Due to our having been hardened in these struggles and having a better understanding of the role of the union bureaucracy. Due to our having a more working class consciousness.

It is also probable that it would have been best to temporarily suspend the production of the group's paper and instead to put our resources into producing a regular P9 solidarity bulletin which would have been primarily based on supporting the P9 strikers but which would also have had theoretical and historical material. This journal, which should have been produced and distributed for free, would have been able to get a hearing amongst the P9 strikers and their families and also it would have been possible to get it into the hands of workers who came from other parts of the country in solidarity and they would have taken it back to their areas and so the ideas would have been spread. We were making a fetish out of producing a general socialist paper and to always sell that paper as opposed to producing a journal for the most important struggle of the time and distributing that journal for free. This was a mistake. If we had not made these mistakes we could very possibly have built a socialist grouping amongst the strikers themselves and amongst their supporters. The P9 strike was the most important strike and attempt by the US workers to throw back the bosses' offensive. It would have been better to have centred our work at that time in that struggle. Doing so would not have meant that we would have had to give up on building a socialist current with knowledge of history and theory. This could have been done at the same time as we would have centred our work in the P9 struggle.

This would have been the right thing to do. It would have been in the best interests of the striking workers and the working class as a whole and in the best interests of our small group. But even if we had taken this approach we could not have affected the outcome of the P9 strike. We did not have the resources. We were not part of a force of tens of thousands of combative experienced workers with roots in the work places and in the broader masses of the working class. Without this we would not have been able to convince any significant numbers of workers that the capitalist offensive could be halted and thrown back and convince them to put themselves on the line to achieve this. We would not have been able to convince them that the obstacle of the union leadership could be overcome. The lack of leadership from the union bureaucracy, but also the lack of a mass fighting opposition alternative in the working class, these factors were decisive in allowing the bosses' offensive to continue. There was also the sectarianism and ultra-leftism and opportunism of the left groups. The false methods of these groups cut them off from the working class. When they did get any chance of having an affect their weaknesses either paralysed or more often resulted in them undermining the workers' struggles. There was also the fact that we were so small that we had no influence in the working class. These factors, but most especially the betrayal of the union leaders, were the decisive factors that resulted in the defeat of the P9 workers and other strikes and these defeats in turn allowed the capitalist offensive to roll on.

The responsibility for the defeats of the working class lay first and foremost with the union leaders who controlled the mass union organisations and their resources. After that the responsibility lay with the many workers who, while seeing the crisis around them, buried their heads in the sand and convinced themselves that everything would be okay, convinced themselves they did not have to educate themselves and organise and act. Responsibility also lay with the many left groups who refused to admit to their false methods and correct their way of working, a way of working that cut them off from the working class and made them ineffective in the class struggle.

In spite of these difficulties, especially the continuing offensive of the bosses, I still held to my fundamental understanding: the task was still to help build a mass revolutionary international to overthrow capitalism. And my work was still to try and establish a small revolutionary nucleus in North America which, along with my fellow fighters in the CWI internationally, could help build an international organisation of tens and tens of millions of workers. Failing health, practically no resources, the opposition from capitalism, the opposition from the pro-capitalist Trade Union leadership, the massive anti-socialist propaganda, the low class consciousness of the US working class, our own mistakes, none of these could be allowed to stand in the way. I had to continue with my struggle to influence and raise the consciousness of the working class and to build a revolutionary grouping.

CHAPTER 36

ANOTHER SMALL NUCLEUS

IN THE LATE 1960S, due to the anti-war movement, the Black revolt, the women's movement, an estimated 500,000 workers and youth in the US considered themselves to be revolutionaries. This may be a high estimate. But even if the number were half that, this was a substantial number. The central question therefore was this? Where did these people go? Why had the left groups that claimed to be revolutionary not been able to bring these, or at least a significant proportion of these forces together and orientate them to the mass of the workers and build a semi-mass or mass revolutionary force in the US working class? There was of course the objective situation. The fact that US capitalism was able to keep its show on the road economically and militarily was a factor. So also was the unattractive nature of Stalinism both the Russian and Chinese varieties, and its counter revolutionary policies. And of course there was the powerful counter-revolutionary role of the trade union bureaucracy. But there was also the combination of opportunism, ultra-leftism and sectarianism of the left groups. The combination of the mistaken methods of these groups prevented these left forces from building a base in the working class. That there is something seriously wrong with all these left groups is shown by the fact that there are more people who consider themselves revolutionary socialists outside these groups than inside them. Some of the weaknesses and mistakes of these groups were also shared by the CWI of which I was part.

But I did not see this reality. Instead I set to work with my rigid formula for the world and for building. The first step was to produce a paper. The first thing I did when I began my trips to the US was to work to this end. We called the paper *Labour Militant*. Its sub title was: 'For Labour and Youth –

working class unity and socialism.' And its first headline was 'End the dictatorship of big business'. It covered strikes and workers' struggles. It was edited and typeset in the apartment in which I stayed in New York City, and printed over in New Jersey. I took the camera-ready copy over by bus to New Jersey and collected and brought back the printed copies. I compared that drab industrialised part of New Jersey to the green fields and the glinting rivers and beauty of Donegal.

This was the second paper in which I had played a central role. A woman member moved from Boston to work full-time in producing the paper. This woman member had joined the CWI after meeting and discussing with a South African member who had studied in Boston for a time. Two student members, one originally from Greece and one from England, were also very involved. The Greek member had been a member of the CWI in Greece before moving to the US. These and a few other members made up the tiny nucleus of which I was part as we moved to produce the paper.

In spite of its over-optimistic slant, *Labour Militant* was not a bad paper. It dealt with the issues facing the working class: wages, jobs, trade union struggles, housing, health care, repression, racism, sexism, the dead end offered to youth, international and national issues. However it was weak in its coverage of the environmental crisis that capitalism was creating. The paper dealt with theory and history, it put forward a socialist alternative. It had articles on capitalism and socialism and Stalinism. It had articles from correspondents in other countries such as Canada, South Africa, Ireland and Britain. With its help more people were drawn around us. We expanded.

I was travelling back and forward to London regularly for the International meetings of the CWI. When I was in the US, I was working like I did in Ireland only on a much bigger area. I was selling the paper, and discussing with people I met and who were interested. I asked them to sell the paper for us and to give us donations. I involved them in getting regular weekly discussions off the ground. Our main tool for development of this work, as had been the case in Ireland, was the paper.

The roots we were putting down in the East coast, New York and Boston were mainly amongst white-collar workers and students from the colleges and universities. It was easier to build amongst these layers at that stage. Even though I explained how serious the class struggle was and to what I was asking them to commit themselves, they had a hard time in grasping this reality. Blue collar workers and especially blue collar skilled workers understood this much better because they understood they could bring the economy to a halt but paradoxically this also meant that in the main these workers were more difficult to convince to be part of our nucleus.

However we were not only building amongst white collar workers and students on the East coast. I visited the San Francisco Bay area where I met three experienced union activists and blue collar workers. One was a carpenter, one a heavy equipment operator, one a phone company worker. At this time also, two members had moved from New York to Seattle. One of these members was a carpenter. One was a technician in the health field. We were expanding but we were doing so on a certain class basis. The east coast where we had the most members was mostly white collar and students and the west coast mostly blue collar and experienced union activists. This difference would become very important at a later stage.

One of the blue collar workers in California who had joined us was Richard Mellor. He had emigrated to the US from England in the 1970s and worked for a water company, the East Bay Municipal Utility District (EBMUD) that served three million people or so on the east side of San Francisco Bay. Richard worked in the maintenance department as a plumber fixing leaks and installing water services and was also active in his union, local 444, which was affiliated to the American Federation of State Council and Municipal Employees (AFSCME) that was emerging as one of the largest and fastest growing unions in the US at that time.

EBMUD had a large and diverse workforce, including workers at the main sewage treatment plant for East Bay, and Richard worked in the largest corporation yard based in Oakland, called Central Yard. It was also the most diverse because it was based in Oakland, the major East Bay city. Its membership was African American, European American, Latino American and Asian American. It also was diverse in terms of gender.

The workers at EBMUD had two locals, one for the blue collar workers and one for the white collar workers. Richard was to become the leading activist in the blue collar local and in the organised workers in the workplace overall. His joining our group was an important breakthrough. In 1985, in what was another big step forward, Richard was one of the main leaders of a strike of his workforce. Richard had built a close relationship with an African American worker Marvin Cain. Marvin was a strong working class union activist and fighter.

Marvin helped me understand the racism in the US and also the high consciousness of many African American workers. On one occasion I was sharing with him my ideas on the need to end capitalism and what steps I believed would be necessary to achieve this end. Marvin listened and looked at me. Then he took his forefinger and pointing and putting put his forefinger on his arm he said; 'well that sounds okay but there is only one thing. You see that, I am black. They would shoot me'. Then he paused and again looked at me and said; 'Come to think of it they would shoot you too'. Marvin understood the way things were.

Richard was on the negotiating team along with Marvin so their relationship was important. This was the first strike in which we were able to play a leading role. Below is Richard's brief summary of that strike. Richard wrote at the time:

'I believed the only way to win the strike was by appealing to the rest of the trade union movement and other sections of the working class. Through this method, mass pickets could be applied. I suggested that the white collar local in EBMUD and my local the blue collar local should unite in a joint struggle. At the same time I suggested that we had to draw the unemployed on to our side so they would not be used to break our strike. To this end I called for a shorter work week and more jobs. Unfortunately the union leadership, particularly at the District Council level, was tied to the management and the team concept so were opposed to this approach and undermined any joint mobilisation of the two locals and the unemployed. The result of the strike was a draw. Management got some of what they wanted and we were able to prevent them from getting all they wanted. If the union leaders had not stifled our struggle and instead mobilised the union movement and the unemployed, the outcome could have been very different.

If the leaders of our District Council AFSCME DC 57, and the leaders of the white collar local had adopted the same approach of broadening the struggle to the rest of the movement and our communities, and mobilised the union movement and the unemployed, we could have made gains. We could have demonstrated to workers in other unions and workers in no unions that unions could make gains and were worth joining. Instead faced with a leadership that was against uniting with the blue collar local, the members of the white collar union passed the picket lines with the exception of one unit at the water treatment plant.'

This report of Richard correctly explained our approach to strikes and workers' struggles. In leading this strike Richard was helped by John Reimann, a carpenter, and by then a member of our group. He was also from the Bay Area and was an important addition to the group when he joined.

This strike was extremely important in building our small group. It inspired members in all areas where we had a few members. It went some way to temporarily strengthen the understanding of the more white-collar section of the group on the East coast in relation to union work and the importance of getting a base amongst, and the possibilities for getting a base amongst, blue collar and industrial workers. It strengthened the small nucleus we had in the Bay Area and it helped give our paper a more working class foundation and orientation.

In my work in North America I was travelling pretty much non-stop throughout the US and Canada. As we produced the paper in New York I spent more time there than anywhere else. I found the city just as fascinating as I had when I was there on my trip twenty years before. Its great racial mixture excited me even more now that I knew so much more about racism and the history of different peoples. There were daily papers in over twenty languages in the city. I would sit on the subway and look at the different peoples reading all their different language papers. I was not in Lifford anymore. There was the great energetic movement of people, traffic and goods as before. I was also much more personally and politically mature and theoretically developed and so could understand what I was seeing and experiencing to a greater degree. However, obsessed as I was with building the revolutionary nucleus, I did not take advantage of the city's great museums and art. It was not only that I was so concentrated on my political work but it was also that with my meagre pay from the CWI for working as a full-timer I could not afford the museums and art galleries and concerts.

As well as playing a central role in producing the paper in New York City, I was involved in daily discussions with members and contacts and also visited strikes and struggles of one kind or another. We set up a club at Hunter College. The student base there was overwhelmingly working class and most of them had part time jobs so this was not just student work but also work with lower paid and part-time workers. I also intervened regularly at New York University speaking at meetings, selling the paper and discussing. I was able to speak to classes and to student clubs at both these colleges on many different topics.

The response was varied. There were always a few cynical and hostile students who would argue against socialism and Marxism, claim that the US was wealthy because of the 'work ethic', never any mention of slavery or the looting of the land and the genocide of the Native American people, or the exploitation of the working class. I was astounded to find a group of students who considered themselves on the left and who had read on dialectical materialism but who scoffed at it as useless. They were unable to apply it, so in their arrogance they blamed the method of thought not their own lack of ability to apply the method of thought.

I intervened with a group of hotel workers who were on strike. They were mainly Latino American workers. They were militant and very verbal in support of their strike but many were undocumented and were worried they would be arrested and deported.

I became involved in a small strike of blue collar workers. Its workforce was a mixture of Latino American, African American and European American workers. They were mostly unskilled. The skilled workers, mostly European American, were organised in a union but the other workers were not. The skilled, organised workers were better paid but still not paid the full union rate for their trade. I continually tried to unite the workers to fight for a wage increase that would have brought all their wages up and would have brought them all into unions.

In this struggle, as in all union struggles, I came up against not only the employers but also the union officials. In this case the only workers who were unionised were the skilled workers. Their officials just wanted to cut a deal that they could justify to their own members. Their thinking was that they would be better able to get a wage increase, or to be more accurate, limit the size of any wage decrease, for their own members if there was no increase for the non-organised workers. They saw the size of the pie as being fixed and if the unskilled and unorganised got more there would be less for their members. They were opposed to looking at the employers' profits and seeing what could be taken out of those to bring all workers' wages up. The union officials saw the profits of the employers as sacred, as not being on the table when negotiations and struggles would take place.

I spent a lot of time discussing with and consolidating the members and eventually we had a number of branches in New York City. But my work was not confined to New York. As the nucleus there grew I travelled more, sometimes by plane and sometimes by Auto Drive Away. Auto Drive Away was a system where people or companies who wanted a vehicle transported across country would go to this company 'Auto Drive Away' and leave their vehicle with them. Then people like myself who needed transport would go to Auto Drive Away, leave a deposit and drive the vehicle to its destination. I travelled many of the highways of the North America in this fashion, sometimes sleeping in the vehicles overnight.

From New York to Chicago, to Seattle, to San Francisco and San Diego, to Texas, to Los Angeles, San Diego and Florida, to Toronto and Montreal. I travelled the length and breadth of North America. My days on the road gave me time to think about my work. They allowed me to see the different parts and cities of the US and the different peoples. They allowed me time alone when driving. Also time alone when I would need to rest from driving and I would pick a beautiful spot and pull over and let the environment come to me. I would sit or lie and take in the beauty of nature.

The first time I crossed the Mississippi I tried to go down to its banks and rest and look at it and think of its historic role. But I could not get down to its banks. Eventually I took a dirt road down parallel to the river. A few miles along this I came upon a farm house. I stopped and knocked at the door. A lady came out. I said, 'Excuse me, I wonder if I could walk down through your fields and see the river. I have heard about the Mississippi all my life.' The lady asked me where I was from. We talked. Then she said I will take you down. She drove her pick-up truck from her barn and took me down. We sat under a large spreading tree by the river bank, the sun was shining.

On another occasion I had to make a trip from Chicago to Los Angeles and again used Auto Drive Away. I made a detour through Little Rock, Arkansas. When I was young, I was inspired by the fight to integrate the high school there. On entering the outskirts of the city I stopped at a traffic sign and rolled down my window and asked two African American ladies in the car beside me did they know where the high school was. They immediately said, 'Follow us,' and zoomed off at high speed. I could hardly keep up. After some twenty minutes they pulled over beside the school and we all got out of our cars.

I explained: 'I watched your struggle to integrate the high school here when I was young in Ireland. It helped me live a better life. Thank you.' The two ladies stood very straight and proud. 'It was nothing, we were only doing what was right.' 'No it was not nothing. It and all your struggles changed the world, changed my world. Thank you.'

'Aw we were only doing what was right.' In spite of what the ladies said I could see they were very proud of what they had done and appreciated what I said. I was honoured to be with them.

Initially while working in New York one issue continually frustrated me. Again and again I was told not to go to Harlem as I would get into trouble. This was not advice I was inclined to take. After all I had been from a Protestant background and went into the Bogside. The fact I was white was not going to stop me from going to Harlem. One evening I was standing on 50th Street and 5th Avenue. I had had enough. I went straight to the subway and took it north to 125th Street, the heart of Harlem. There was not another European American face to be seen.

I had heard of a restaurant which sold Southern food. I saw its sign and went in and ordered beans and corn bread. The food was delicious. There was not a hint of unfriendliness. I soaked up the food and the atmosphere. Soaked up the animated talk and buzz of the African American patrons. It was somewhat similar to the atmosphere of a pub at home. After I ate I went out to take a walk. I saw a notice for a meeting for a moratorium on evictions. It was just starting.

There were about fifty people at the meeting. I was the only European American present. Initially I sat and listened. The meeting was very working class but the chairperson and platform were clearly middle class. After some time I put up my hand to speak. The chairperson dismissed me with a wave of her hand. 'This is for Harlem residents, for African Americans. You cannot speak.' I objected and said it was a public meeting so I should have the right to speak. The chairperson, thinking she would have the backing of the audience, after all they were all African American like her, stood her ground.

Then an African American woman in the audience spoke up. 'Let him speak. He has as much right to speak as anybody. We did not fight in the '60s to keep people quiet.' Others in the audience spoke in her support. I was impressed and humbled by the democratic approach and courage and solidarity of the African American working class woman in the audience as compared to what I would later learn was the middle class Black nationalist people on the platform who were running the meeting. The effects of the 1960s Black revolt were powerful and lasting. The platform had to back down and I got speaking. Unfortunately I did not get any permanent contacts out of that meeting. The gap between the audience and I in age, race and background was too great. But more than that, the alternative of revolutionary socialism probably seemed to have no relevance at that time to these peoples' lives.

Building the group was not a worked out, rigidly maintained, orientation to struggles. There were also random opportunities that would come up. I would hear of people interested in the group in different ways. Sometimes people would meet the CWI when they travelled to countries where it already had sections. Sometimes people heard of us by word of mouth and contacted us. The odd person who was already a member of the CWI in other countries moved to the US and Canada and this also helped. Slowly and surely we were putting down a small network, partly based on orienting to workers' and youth struggles in the major cities, and partly working with individuals with whom we would get in contact in one way or another. I also organised people to attend conferences and events of the CWI in other countries and they could see our successes. This would give them more confidence they could build in North America.

I was travelling throughout all of North America. I would at times stay in peoples' homes. I would at times stay in hostels when I visited cities where there was nobody I knew to put me up. Some of the hostels were rough. I stayed in one in the Midwest where I had to jump from my bed in the middle of the night and throw out an intruder who was trying to steal my things. After that I always slept with my belongings between my body and the wall.

I preferred to stay in hostels as I could cook there and this allowed me to better control my diet. I had been told by the alternative medicine lady in England about my allergies but partly because I did not have the will power and partly because I was not able to live in one place and control my day to day life enough, I only half thought about the allergies. But there were ones such as to processed foods, the oily and chemical foods, the dairy products that were very severe and would make me fall asleep or become semi-conscious and I would have to try especially hard to avoid these foods. But it was very difficult to do this when I would be staying in people's homes. I would find out later that the Addison's disease that I was eventually diagnosed with made me extra prone to having allergies. Health-wise I was not a great specimen.

Staying in the hostels also meant that I could better determine my own schedule and take a rest when I needed it without feeling impolite or ungrateful as I would have if I had been staying in people's homes. I tried to hang on to my health by eating well and trying to get a rest now and then. But this was not easy as I was still pretty much on the seven days a week, twelve hours a day routine.

I remained as driven as ever to build the revolutionary organisation. The truth was that it was really only when I had my health crises, my TIAs, my small strokes, that I had any spells of rest and these were not really rests, more recoveries as I would be trying to overcome the damage done by the earlier TIA. After each of these I had to concentrate and drive myself to my limits to do my work. It was not a walk in the park.

Throughout this period I was the first full-timer for the CWI for North America. During this time, and doing this work, I maintained regular contact with the London centre of the CWI by phone calls and written reports. I would also fly back for the International Executive Committee meetings which took place around every three months. These would help me a lot politically as I would be able to participate in the international discussions and hear reports from sections in different countries. But they meant a lot of flying and more stress. I was to fly back and forward across the Atlantic dozens of times.

As we built our resources it was decided to move the headquarters of the group to Chicago. It was more central and cheaper. I based myself there rather than New York. Lisa and Rob, the two leading members who lived in Seattle also moved there to live. I increasingly spent more time in Chicago. Lisa and Rob had been very successful in their work in Seattle building a branch and a 250-strong Youth Defence Campaign. (YDC) The YDC was a youth organisation which focused on the issues of youth, jobs, education, police brutality, racism, sexism and opposed these through direct action tactics.

None of us were looking forward to moving to Chicago. With the exception of the area around the extremely expensive downtown Lakeshore Drive area, Chicago was an ugly, flat city. Seattle was a beautiful city with its Puget Sound and its mountains. New York was New York.

I went to Seattle to drive across country in a truck with the furniture and belongings of Lisa and Rob. Rob was coming later. It was winter. Lisa and I drove east on the highway. Snow was falling as we made our way up the Cascade Mountains and climbed towards the Rockies. It was beautiful. As we climbed the Cascades we wondered why motorists were putting chains on their vehicles.

But when we crested the mountains we no longer wondered. I was driving. The truck began to slide downward on the snow-covered road. It was headed toward the side of the road beyond which there was a sheer drop down into the valley miles below. I said: 'Lisa, get your boots on, your coat. We are going to have to jump.' Meanwhile I was trying to get the truck steered away from sliding over the cliff's edge. Things were looking very bad. Miraculously the tires began to grip and very gradually I managed to get the truck turned to the centre of the road, then the other side of the road and then slid it into the bank which sloped up to the mountain top above. I switched off the engine and sat there. Both of us were in silent shock. We had almost died.

We sat looking at each other for a few moments. Saying nothing. Then a knock at the window startled us. It was a man holding up a set of chains for the truck's tires. I opened the door. Did we want to rent them until we got to the bottom of the mountain? Capitalism was working. The demand for the chains was there and the local entrepreneur provided the supply. He put on the chains, followed us down, we paid him and he took the chains back at the bottom of the mountains. And on we went.

I helped with the work in Chicago while still continuing to make trips around the US and Canada. In Chicago our little group became involved in a defence campaign for youth who had been the victims of police violence at a rock concert. It also campaigned around the case of a woman who was a victim of domestic violence raising publicity and money for her cause. When we had arrived, the branch had two members who were active in their union and some work was done there. Through these campaigns the group began to get some contacts and develop paper sales and get invited to speak at meetings in schools and colleges.

Lisa and Rob used the experience they had gained with the YDC work in Seattle to set up a similar group in Chicago and we expanded this to other areas. In Seattle the youth work had been linked up with the United Food and Commercial Workers' union. After meeting and discussing with an official of a local Lisa and Rob were asked to speak at a meeting of members and agreement was reached to try and recruit the youth to the union. But the reality was the union leadership only paid lip service to this and left it to the YDC to try and recruit the youth. The Youth-Labour Organising Committee was formed but the union leadership was afraid of it and starved it of resources. They also stood in the way of this initiative developing by their refusal to fight for gains for the youth, better wages, jobs, free education, an end to police harassment, racism and sexism, etc.

But in spite of this, the YDC made gains in Chicago and throughout the USA and Canada. By the end of 1987 it had branches in Oakland, Chicago, New York, Boston and Toronto. It was the centre of the group's activity for a time. I travelled to many cities, especially Seattle, to help with this work. As the YDC evolved we changed its name to Youth Against Racism and Poverty (YARP) to make more specific and concrete what it stood for. YARP took up the slogan 'Jobs not Drugs'. Along with this and the demand for a higher minimum wage it appealed to the youth.

YARP organised demonstrations on youth issues, held regular meetings, gave out flyers, discussed with people and set up YARP branches. It continued to go to union locals for support. At one stage six union locals were, at least formally, supporting YARP in Seattle.

YARP also took up the fight against racism becoming involved with the campaign to release Dwayne Holmes, a young African American man who had been framed in California for a $10 robbery, and when he began to organise a gang truce in prison the prison authorities came down on him hard. They did not want their divide and rule strategy to be disrupted. They did not want any gang truce. Our group also linked up with a man who was on death row in Indiana who was a socialist. Unfortunately all his appeals and our campaign failed and he was killed by the state.

The group put down roots in Canada through YARP and connections were made with the New Democratic Party youth. Branches were established in Calgary, Edmonton and Toronto. I travelled there regularly and discussed with young people. The group was strengthened when Steve Pybus joined YARP and also the group. Steve was a construction worker in Canada who played a leading role in his workplace and union and the New Democratic Party, and wrote for Labour Militant and attended our meetings in the US.

The group also did international solidarity work. Mainly through Richard's union local AFSCME 444, we campaigned for the release of trade unionist and socialist Mahmoud Masawra who was imprisoned in Israel. This was so successful that the Israeli trade union federation, the Histradut, complained to the AFL-CIO.

As well as the youth work, our group had consistently campaigned for the working class to have its own political party. In spite of our small resources we were able to take some steps in this direction.

On 13th May 1987, we held a meeting in New York and set up the Campaign for a Labour Party (CLP). 100 people attended to hear Bernie Sanders, the former mayor of Burlington, Vermont and a US Senator who then described himself as a socialist and more importantly then called for a Labour Party. He also at that time claimed to be independent of the Democratic Party. This would later change. Also speaking at this meeting were Terry Fields, a member of the British Parliament and member of the CWI; Steve Pybus, President of Calgary McCall New Democratic Party and member of our small group in Canada; an Eastern Airlines striker; and Vinita Seward who had worked on Eugene Debs campaigns. This was a success and strengthened our work to build a Labour Party.

I had heard that the leader of the Oil and Chemical Workers' Union, Tony Mazzocchi, had been calling for a Labour Party. He agreed to meet. Along with Alan Akrivos the Greek member of the group in New York we met him in a small coffee shop in Manhattan and I explained that we were in favour of a Labour Party and could we work together. After our discussion he said he would speak at a meeting for a Labour Party, but on one condition: it had to be organised by an official body of the trade union movement.

We turned again to Local 444 of AFSCME, Richard's local. Richard was the only member who had a strong enough union base to organise such a meeting. Richard leading the previous strike in his workplace and then being the only member who could organise a meeting for a Labour Party showed that Richard had the main base, the deepest roots, of any member of the group in the workplace, in the unions, in the working class. Richard moved a proposal to his local to organise this meeting and the membership of Local 444 agreed. With this decision by Local 444, ten other locals endorsed the meeting. So too did District Council 57 of AFSCME. Richard and John Reimann gave out thousands of flyers. Richard's and John Reimann's years of work in the labour movement gave the meeting credibility. So also did the presence of Tony Mazzocchi. Around one hundred people attended, mostly blue-collar workers. It was a success.

At this meeting myself and Richard and John Reimann spoke and we popularised the idea that the bosses had two parties, the Republicans and the Democrats, the workers needed one of their own. This was to become one of the slogans of the Labour Party Advocates (LPA) which was set up by Tony Mazzocchi after this meeting. He said that the 444 meeting was so successful that it convinced him to take this initiative. We explained that to be part of and build the LPA you did not have to be a socialist. You just had to oppose the bosses' offensive, give no support to the capitalist Democratic or Republican parties and work to build a Labour Party. The LPA was a united front based on these positions.

The afternoon of the day of this meeting myself and other members met with Tony Mazzocchi. It was December 1989. Stalinism was collapsing. He did not want to talk about the meeting. He wanted to talk about the collapse of Stalinism. He listened intently to our views and to our explanation of what Trotsky had said would happen to these societies if they remained isolated. His interest showed how much the change in world events, that is the collapse of Stalinism, was having on consciousness. Tony Mazzocchi would have had no interest in our views on Stalinism or on Trotsky previously.

The LPA held another meeting in New York some time later with over 200 in attendance. Numerous meetings followed throughout the country in the Bay Area, Seattle, Boston, New York, Los Angeles, etc. At most of these, LPA chapters were formed. In June 1996 a conference in Cleveland announced the formation of a Labour Party. The majority of the members of our US group said the Labour Party had arrived. But Richard Mellor, Lisa Hane, John Reimann, Rob Rooke and I did not agree. We explained in fact the opposite was happening. We explained that the machinations behind these meetings were trapping the LPA behind the AFL-CIO leadership's policy of not running in elections, leaving the unions links with the Democrats intact and in fact killing the LPA and the so called Labour Party.

Our tiny group had made gains organising the meeting at Richard's local and by convincing Tony Mazzocchi to set up the Labour Party Advocates. However that was the limit we could achieve with our resources at that time. The more the LPA showed its potential the more it frightened the leadership of the AFL-CIO which was determined to cling to the Democratic Party. This leadership gave Mazzocchi an ultimatum. Either they would launch an all-out assault on the LPA, move to prevent any of the AFL-CIO unions or locals from formally supporting it, or the LPA would agree not to run candidates and agree not to call for the unions to break from the Democrats. Unfortunately the majority of the LPA caved in to these top union leaders. This was all they needed. As long as the LPA did not run candidates or try and break the unions from the Democratic Party it would die at its own hand. And this is what happened.

After the meeting at Richard's local and the setting up of the LPA, many left groups and individuals who had not been active in the Labour Party work until we had organised the successful meeting with Tony Mazzocchi at local 444 jumped on what they thought was going to be a bandwagon. When they did, they supported the deal between Mazzocchi and the AFL-CIO leaders not to run candidates. They did so to try and preserve their cosy relationship with the union leaders. But their opportunism only helped ensure that there was no bandwagon. By their actions these lefts helped kill the LPA.

My political life at that time was concentrated in the USA and Canada. I was still a member of the London-based International Secretariat of the CWI and I made regular trips to London and discussed and interacted with the CWI members there. With the exceptions of these trips back to Europe to international meetings, I worked in the US and to some extent in Canada over this period. I also made a couple of trips to Mexico. By the latter half of the 1980s, that is, after around five years of working mainly in North America, we had branches in New York, Boston, Philadelphia, Chicago, Los Angeles, The Bay Area of California, Seattle, Toronto, Vancouver, and individuals in other areas. We had a few contacts in Mexico. We had a regular paper and a number of full-timers funded by the membership. Members like John Reimann had become full-time organisers. The group met regularly locally and nationally. We were known as The Labour and Trade Union Group and were the US affiliate of the CWI. We were making progress.

However everything was far from well. The hopes that most of the East Coast membership had for the LPA were dashed and followed by disappointment when it did not develop. It was the East Coast leadership and membership who had illusions in the LPA, who had thought the announcement of a Labour Party at the Cleveland conference actually meant what it said. The failure of the LPA took place at the same time as the continuing success of the capitalist offensive and the restoration of capitalism in the former Stalinist world was gaining strength. To the limited extent that the LPA was known amongst workers, its failure threw the mood of these workers further back. The combination of these developments had a negative influence on the majority in our North American group, especially on the more student and middle class members and white collar workers in the North East. They found it harder to see how they could make progress. They became desperate to remain on good terms with the LPA leadership, and hold their positions in that organisation. To this end they further played down any differences with, they refrained from putting any alternative to, the approach of the LPA leaders. They became increasingly opportunist.

The greatest number of people in the organisation in North America was based around NYC, Boston and Philadelphia. They were mostly white collar workers or students. There were a number of disagreements between them and the more blue collar, experienced union activists in the West coast and myself and Lisa and Rob in Chicago. One of these disagreements was on the LPA but there were others.

North East members such as AA and TW, were leading members in New York City and the north east. But these members had no experience in union work or in fighting in workplaces. They had no experience in baring their teeth and standing against the stream when it came to the working class movement in full retreat. They did not have experience in the trench warfare of the shop floor. Instead of digging in and fighting in the difficult situation in which we were working they became even more conciliatory to the leadership in the LPA and the trade unions. In the union work, a leading member and collaborator of theirs in Boston refused to fight the demands of the bosses and the union leaders to bring in flexible work rules to the workplace. That is, he refused to defend the conditions and work rules that had been won in the past through struggle.

The world was a cold place for revolutionaries at that time. The task was precisely to stand against the stream. The times needed strong fighters. AA and TW and the people around them had done good work in the group in the past but as the situation became more difficult they were not up to the task. Under pressure of an increasingly difficult objective situation they wanted a place to cozy up to some other body for warmth. The majority of the east coast leadership of the group were in this category. They tried to make peace with the LPA leadership. In reality to surrender to the LPA leadership. They did not make clear that while we were in a united front with these leaders on the need to build a Labour Party we had significant differences with them on other issues. Making this clear would have demanded a strong and skilful stand but if such a stand had been taken the organisation could have helped the best of the LPA members to see a way forward and also won to our little group some good people from the LPA when it would later collapse. But instead of this the majority of the group increasingly conceded ground to the LPA leadership and to the general mood.

I opposed this concentrating of the work in the LPA and the concessions being made to its leadership. I advocated that the organisation should orient to the stirrings that were taking place amongst the youth and some workers in society. This was scoffed at by the majority. Where were these stirrings? I was shown to be correct when later the Occupy movement developed and when the events in Seattle around the World Trade Organisation took place, when whole new layers of anarchist type youth took part in these events in Seattle. But because the majority of the leadership and the US section were stuck in the Labour Party Advocates, the opportunities that existed and was shown in these events were missed. I also advocated the setting up of minimum wage committees to fight for a $10.00 minimum wage and equal pay for all. This was also rejected. Years later long after this majority would collaborate with the IS majority in expelling myself and others from the CWI in the US they would take up a minimum wage campaign such as we had advocated.

The political difference over the Labour Party Advocates should have been dealt with openly and honestly. However this did not happen. The majority of the leadership in the east coast who were making these concessions to the LPA leaders did not have the confidence to fight openly for their position. They made every effort to hide it from the rest of the organisation. Led by the majority of the IS, especially Lynn Walsh who was based in London but making secret trips to the US under the orders of Peter Taaffe, they held secret discussions and set up a secret combination within the organisation to organise against us. They increasingly and secretly attacked those of us with whom they disagreed and they did so behind our backs and on a personal and dishonest basis. I was increasingly prevented from participating in the work in the north east. Members such as AA and TW were particularly dishonest, unprincipled and disloyal to the organisation and the democratic rights of the membership at this time.

This political disagreement in the US group was taking place at the same time as the majority of the IS based in London were considering driving me out of the organisation. The majority of the IS wanted me out of the International for different reasons from the majority of the North American section. The majority of the IS wanted me out because I insisted on discussing the mistakes all of us had made and were making, mistakes such as not predicting the return of capitalism to the Stalinist world and not predicting the spurts of growth in the capitalist world in the 1980s and 1990s, and not seeing the effects of the new technology on the world economy. The majority of the leadership of the IS was not prepared to admit these, or in fact any, mistakes. And I, by insisting on admitting that I had made these mistakes, we all had made these mistakes, and insisting we had to discuss these mistakes and was there a mistaken method in the organisation which led to these mistakes was seen by the majority of the London-based IS leadership as undermining their attempt to portray themselves to the membership as the great leaders who were always right. The majority of the IS also remembered that I did not fit into their 'you scratch my back I scratch your back' way of thinking of the majority of the IS. This had been demonstrated previously in my struggle with the leading member in the North of Ireland.

The reason the majority in the North American section wanted me out was different. I, and the other members who would be expelled, Richard Mellor, Lisa Hane, John Reimann, and to a lesser extent Rob Rooke were pushing the majority to stand up and put an alternative to the Labour Party Advocates leadership and the union bureaucracy and some left hangers on who by then dominated that leadership. The majority in the North American section were not capable of taking this road given the hostile climate generally and their demoralisation which resulted from this hostile climate. There were other secondary reasons such as personal ambition. But the main issue was they were too weak to stand against the stream.

A secret combination of the IS majority based in London, and the majority of the top leadership in the East Coast in the USA, organised their secret meetings. From these they orchestrated a campaign of lies and slanders and organisational initiatives against those of us with whom they disagreed. Secret trips to and from Europe and the US were made to select an alternative leadership and hold individual discussions with selected members in North America to explain to them that they would soon be the future leadership and we would be out. They told these members, whom they correctly felt they could manipulate, that we were holding them back and they should be the leadership and not us. They told the people they wanted in their camp that we would not listen to them. Peter Taaffe made one last try to win me over by suggesting to me that if I agreed to John Reimann being removed as a full-timer then I could stay. I was insulted and strongly refused and told him so. I pointed out that John Reimann had taken the risk of going to the Chiapas uprising and the Los Angeles uprising on behalf of the organisation and I would not stab him in the back.

This political weakness and shift to the right of the majority of the leadership of the organisation in the east coast of the US and in Canada, became very evident after we were expelled. The name of the paper was immediately changed from Labour Militant to the vague liberal title *Justice*. The IS then became worried as it saw their collaborators moving much further right than they had anticipated. Things were going too far. There was also the fact that the new leadership they were preparing had all participated with the IS majority in the corrupt, undemocratic methods used against us and so was tainted, stained, corrupt themselves. The result was the IS moved to put in place a new leadership.

The new leading member the IS majority selected was based around a student from a liberal arts college. And unsurprisingly, a male. The last leading person the IS majority wanted was a worker hardened in struggles on the shop floor and the unions, one who could fight for his or her position. So predictably they looked for a student with no such experience and no base in the working class on which he or she could stand and fight for their position. They found one. The five people who would later be expelled were all workers with experience in blue collar jobs and unions. The members such as AA and TW who made such a campaign against ourselves for supposedly being top down did not object to the IS majority taking this top down secretive, corrupt, undemocratic action to expel ourselves and to select this new leader. How could they, they had participated in the same secretive, corrupt, undemocratic actions against ourselves? The result was they were too weakened by their own past actions in manoeuvring against us to stand up to the corrupt methods of the IS majority leadership to place their own chosen one in the leadership. They ended up being bitten by their own dog. But these dirty machinations did not surface immediately. They were temporarily postponed by other events.

CHAPTER 37

THE WRECKING OF THE CWI

WHILE THESE DIRTY METHODS were going on unbeknownst to me, I got a phone call from London. It was no coincidence that it came at the same time as the differences were developing in the North American work and the secretive manoeuvrings which had been going on between the main leaders of the US group in the north east and the majority of the IS. For myself and the other members of what was to become the minority faction in the US, this phone call was a bombshell. There was a split in the International. Until I got this call I had known nothing of this. Even though I was a member of the IS I had been kept in the dark.

Peter Taaffe and Lynn Walsh were leading one faction in this split in the CWI and Ted Grant and Alan Woods another. Such a split was unprecedented in the organisation. It was the chickens of our wrong perspectives and our refusal to admit we had had these wrong perspectives, our refusal to face up to our mistakes, coming home to roost.

The Ted Grant/Alan Woods faction initially refused to face the fact that we had all been wrong in saying that capitalism would not go back to the Stalinist world and wrong also in expecting a new and deep economic recession in the capitalist world in the immediate future. Desperately this faction clung on to the old, wrong ideas until events made this no longer possible.

The Taaffe/Walsh faction recognised more quickly that capitalism was being restored in the Stalinist world. I was in agreement with this faction on this. Of course the Taaffe/Walsh faction did not mention that like the rest of us they had ruled this out for their entire political life until that point.

While I agreed with the Taaffe/Walsh faction that capitalism had gone back to the former Soviet Union, I had an important difference with them in that they would not openly admit this major mistake. They refused to discuss it. On one occasion Peter Taaffe said he had earlier 'set a hare running' on the possibility of capitalist restoration. Nobody could find where this hare had gone. The way Peter Taaffe made this claim said it all. He did not say at what meeting he had said this, he did not show where he had written it in a document, he could not because he had never done so, but rather he claimed he had 'set a hare running'. He was trying to cover up his mistakes. It was impossible to find any tracks of Peter Taaffe's hare.

The Taaffe/Walsh majority on the IS moved on to try to discuss the new world situation and ignore the past mistakes. This is why I was so unacceptable to them. I was not prepared to be quiet about these mistakes we had all made. I had to be silenced. But for the moment they needed me. Action against me would have to be delayed for the moment.

There was another difference between the two factions. The Taaffe/Walsh faction said that the mass social democratic parties had become completely bourgeois parties and there was nothing to be gained by working within them. They said that parties such as the British Labour Party had been transformed into capitalist parties such as the US Democratic Party. From this analysis they moved to decisively turn away from these and set up new 'parties'. This faction, which was by then the majority in the international would go on to set itself up as 'Socialist Parties' in most country where it had any kind of a membership, posing as the parties that would become the mass workers' parties in the future.

Because I agreed that capitalism had gone back to the Stalinist world I became part of the majority faction. I also agreed it was better at least temporarily to move away from the total concentration of our work being in the social democratic parties as for the moment there were more opportunities to build in that way. However I did not rule out working in the social democratic parties or in new mass parties again as I thought that new movements of the working class when they would arise would again have an effect on at least some of the old traditional parties while at the same time throwing up new parties.

The majority of the leadership of both factions turned the tactic, of working or not working in the mass parties into a principle. The majority insisted on the need to break completely and immediately from work in these parties, while the minority insisted on the need to stay in them at all costs and forever. The debate on this became known as the debate on the open turn, that is, whether or not to turn away from the mass parties and openly declare ourselves as new workers' new Socialist Parties. The majority had this latter position. Like with the case of not seeing in advance the restoration of capitalism to the former Soviet Union and not openly admitting to this mistake the leadership of the majority of the CWI who were now writing off the mass traditional social democratic parties also ignored the fact that for decades we had been saying that the working class would turn again and again to these parties. Now the majority of the leadership of the majority faction in the CWI were saying these parties were capitalist parties just like the Democratic Party in the US. More refusing to face up to past mistakes, more damage being done to the CWI.

It would have been possible to have avoided a split on these issues if the internal life had not been so sectarian and with its secret cliques with their own agendas, agendas which were based on the desire of the majority of the leadership of both factions to split. The differences could have been debated and clarified and an agreement made to continue to work together on the position of the majority, which was to leave the mass social democratic parties, or to have a different tactic in different countries, as opposed to having a single unified tactic for every country. Open work could have been carried out while at the same time aiming united front propaganda to the ranks of the social democratic parties, and any other mass parties that might arise, while putting the resources of the CWI into building independently. A small group, a small fraction of our resources, could even have been left inside the mass parties to work and observe. If, as was to be the case with Jeremy Corbyn in Britain later, events threw up opportunities in the social democratic parties, or if new parties were thrown up in the future, then resources could have then been put into these parties by one or more of a number of tactics.

While I became part of the majority faction, I was more flexible than the leadership of this faction who ruled out ever being part of the old traditional parties again. I said there were many tactics, open work, entryism, fraction work, united front work, and at different times and countries different tactics were appropriate.

Understanding such tactics and terms is a challenge for the 'lay person', the non-revolutionary or those coming to revolutionary work. 'Open work' is working openly as a revolutionary organisation stating openly and publicly that you are a revolutionary organisation. 'Entryism' is when a group denies it is a separate revolutionary organisation in order to be able to clandestinely put its forces into another larger organisation's structure in order to try and convince the members of that organisation of the need for revolution. 'Fraction work' is secretly sending a fraction of the forces of the revolutionary organisation into a mass party while simultaneously maintaining an open organisation. 'United front work' is working openly and independently as a revolutionary party or grouping while at the same time working arm-in-arm with another workers' organisation or other workers' organizations on a few basic demands on which there is agreement. While taking my place with the majority faction of the international in favour of the open turn, I had these qualifications.

It would also have been possible to avoid a split on the events in the Stalinist and former Stalinist countries. The developments in these countries could have been discussed and observed and given time to unfold. Factions could have been set up to discuss and examine this issue. Different opinions could have been debated and openly printed in the organisations press. The CWI had no resources of any significance in these countries so it could do little more than observe and comment in any case. Time could have been given for events to clarify the situation, meanwhile discussing the different possibilities and allowing time and events to clarify the perspectives.

But the majority of the top leaderships of both factions in the CWI were driven by their own sectarianism and egotism and ambition, they were determined to have their own organisations, they were determined to split the CWI. As will be explained later in the report of a then member of the CWI who was for a time part of the Taaffe/Walsh clique, the Taaffe/Walsh group had their own secret clique going for years. It met secretly before all important meetings to discuss what it would do and say. At the same time a former member who had the ear of what was to become the Grant/Woods group would later report that for years Ted Grant had been pushing Woods and others to work with him for a split. The secret cliques in the leadership of both factions was responsible for wrecking the CWI. I am proud I was never part of any of these two undemocratic, secret cliques.

I went back to London as soon as I heard about the development of the two factions. I discussed with Peter Taaffe and heard his faction's view. I told him I could not take a position until I heard the other view. He was clever and said of course, of course. He knew from past experience it would be counterproductive to appear to be excessively pushing me or taking me for granted. I met with Ted Grant and Alan Woods and right away Alan Woods made a mistake. Rather than discussing the issues, his first words were that if I did not join them, the majority would have me out in no time. I was insulted. He was suggesting I should take the view which would best secure my place in the organisation, that is that I should be an opportunist only looking after my own position. Put off by this and not agreeing with their positions in general I then openly and formerly became part of the majority faction.

I played an active role in the faction struggle, travelling to many countries to debate the issues. I was active in the majority faction which retained the name the CWI. The CWI split, the majority retaining the name the CWI and the Grant/Woods faction splitting off to set up their own organisation which they called the International Marxist Tendency. I remained living and working out of London throughout this period. For a while I shared an apartment with a member of the CWI in Greenwich and for a while I lived in a small studio apartment in West Ham. I continued to receive my income from the CWI as an organiser for the CWI. I travelled to many sections, Germany, Belgium, the Netherlands, Italy, Greece, the USA, Canada, to put my understanding of the views of the majority. The US and Irish sections with which I had been most associated both supported the majority position in the debate.

After the split I spent a lot of time working out of London attempting to help build the new CWI. In anticipation of their splitting, the majority of the leadership of the CWI around Taaffe and Walsh had been secretly securing the legal rights to the names and finances and properties of what had been the old united CWI. This was a stab in the back to all those thousands of members who had sacrificed to accumulate those resources over many decades. It also proved that this clique had been planning to split the CWI all along.

During this time after the split, one of the most important initiatives I was involved with, in fact was in charge of, was organising an anti-fascist march in Brussels which mobilised many thousands. It weakened the fascist movement in Belgium for a time. Many activists from the British section of the CWI came to this march. They wore their anti-Poll Tax shirts and carried the crude wooden clubs which I had got from the owner of a timber yard in the city. This man never asked me why I wanted these pieces of planks. He would look at me suspiciously every day but always hand me over another armful of discarded bits of planks. With the mostly British contingent in the anti poll tax shirts and their wooden clubs in the lead the march was an impressive sight. While doing this work I lived in Brussels, sleeping mostly on the floor of a garage.

However, I continued to have a serious problem over this period during and after the split. I still wanted to discuss the major mistakes we had all made in how we had seen world developments and even more importantly was there a mistake in our method that led to these mistakes. However I could not get these issues discussed. The leaders of the then CWI would not admit they had made them. They blamed everything on Ted Grant. After some time trying in vain to get such a discussion, I resigned from the IS and on my own initiative proposed that I concentrate again on working in the USA and Canada. This was February 1994. It was on my own proposal I had left Ireland to work in the CWI. Now and again on my own proposal, I was leaving my work at the headquarters of the CWI working in the international as a whole to go back to concentrate in working in the USA and Canada. Unlike the majority of the other leaders of the CWI I was not paranoid, I was not personally ambitious, I was not clinging on to my seat in my own little section, afraid to move in case I lost control of something.

In my resignation statement I explained that I had been on the IS for ten years but could no longer accept the refusal of the majority of the IS leadership to admit to and discuss its mistakes, such as where we had ruled out capitalism returning to the Stalinist world and the spurts of economic growth in capitalism in the 1980s and 1990s and the effect of the new technology, and also the rise of China. And our other mistake of just about ignoring the unfolding capitalist caused crisis of climate change, pollution and environmental distruction. And also where we had adamantly insisted that the working class would move again and again to their old traditional organisations. I wrote in relation to the British section: 'There appears to be the lack of an atmosphere of open, comradely, critical assessment, including self-criticism of the work of all Comrades ... I believe the real danger to the organisation, after incorrect theory, perspectives, policies and programme, is if issues and differences of party organisation are not dealt with openly and on the bodies of the organisation.' I made this statement because I could see the deepening crisis and collapse in the British section and I could not get serious discussion on this with Peter Taaffe or on the IS or the IEC.

When I was making this statement, thousands were walking away from the CWI, demoralised by its wrong perspectives and its unhealthy internal life, but more especially its refusal to admit to and draw lessons from its mistakes. Hundreds remained in the CWI but did not insist on discussing its wrong perspectives or its wrong internal life and so did not make healthy the unhealthy internal life of the CWI. I was not in either of these categories. But I was not clear on what was happening and it was not correct for me to resign from the IS and go back to concentrate my work again in the US. I should have made a bigger effort to remain on the IS working out of London and clarify my thinking.

I was reluctant to come to the conclusion that there might be something much more fundamentally wrong with the internal life of the CWI, with the CWI overall. I resisted accepting that the organisation, to which I had given so much, could be as undemocratic and wrong in its methods as it was beginning to seem to be the case. I shied away from accepting this for as long as possible. This was a mistake. I was not convinced by the accusations of Ted Grant and Alan Woods that Peter Taaffe was leading a clique because, as I told them, if he was, they were also. I tried to hold on to the conclusion that the problem was only the false perspectives, the five to ten years to the revolution, and from this the need to build and build and not 'waste time' discussing differences. I had been part of this mistaken approach.

However while trying to cling on to this idea and trying to correct the perspectives and from this correct the internal life and have more discussion and debate, I was more and more pushed to consider a more serious conclusion. Could there be an undemocratic, corrupt clique in the CWI? Could there be a grouping which, instead of having the interest of the whole organisation and the revolution at heart, instead secretly sought to further its own interests and positions? Was it possible that on this point Ted Grant and Alan Woods, who made this accusation against Taaffe and Walsh, were more right than wrong? But while increasingly considering this possibility I fought against accepting it. And after all, as I was to find out, Ted Grant and Alan Woods had their own clique also.

So not able to see what was what, not able to fully understand what was going on, and after raising many times that I wanted discussion on our mistakes and was there a mistake in our method which led to these mistakes, I resigned from the IS and returned to concentrate my work again in the USA and Canada. My aim was to try and clarify my thinking on our mistakes, including in our internal life and at the same time build a healthy organisation. I intended to fight for my ideas and a better understanding through my work in the US and Canadian sections and my membership of the IEC. But others had different ideas. The IS/majority had already set in motion steps to expel me from the organisation.

In the early summer of 1994, Peter Taaffe toured the US and Canada. It never occurred to me that he was doing anything but seeing how the work was going. At around this same time Lynn Walsh was continuing with his trips, some secret and some not secret. The purpose of these trips was to clandestinely select and discuss with and groom weak members of the US section to become what the IS majority saw as being an alternative leadership to myself and other leading members such as Richard Mellor, Lisa Hane, John Reimann and Rob Rooke, members who did not agree with the concessions of the majority to the LPA leadership. The five of us were to become the minority faction in the US section and in the CWI. An important part of the work of the Taaffe and Walsh effort was to slander and lie about me. I was said to be one of the snakes who had been cast out of Ireland. It was said that I was a gangrene that had to be cut out of the organisation. At the same time, resources were being held back from the centre in Chicago. During this time also obstacles were put in the way of me participating in or being told about the work in the north east. Secretly the ground was being prepared to expel me, close the Chicago HQ and move the centre back to New York.

The majority of the IS was putting together an unprincipled, secret combination of the IS majority clique based in London and the majority of the North American organisation leadership which was capitulating to the leadership of the LPA. This was an unprincipled combination for a number of reasons. It did not fight on the real issues. That is, on their position on the LPA. They could not because the IS were more in agreement with us, what was to become the Minority faction, on this than they were with the majority of the US section. So because the IS majority itself thought more as we did, that the majority in the US were making too many concessions to the LPA leadership, they tried to keep discussion away from this issue. This was dishonest and opportunist. Walsh in an unguarded moment said to me that he had criticisms of the majority's positions on the Labour Party Advocates but when asked to repeat this at a conference so it could be discussed he refused. So they cobbled together an unprincipled combination based on the accusation that we in the leadership of the North American section would not listen to the membership. Instead of an open honest discussion on how to work in the LPA where we had differences with what was to become the majority faction, they made the issue that we would not listen to the majority. The issue was we did not agree with the majority and we had the right to do so and say so. But no, the IS majority and the majority in the US section made it an issue of us, the minority, not being prepared to listen to the majority. In reality we were being denied the right to disagree. This allowed the IS Majority and the US majority to avoid the uncomfortable fact that on the issue of the LPA the IS majority were more in agreement with us than they were with the US majority.

A statement from JB one of the leading members of the IS/majority/US majority combination in Boston, the member who would not fight on the shop floor, openly stated the dirty unprincipled manoeuvres that were going on. He said that he and the rest of the participants in the secret, unprincipled combination needed time to prepare the International for the expulsion of such a long time member as myself. This made clear that secret, systematic discussions about expelling myself, discussions which excluded myself, were going on before the proposal to expel me was ever raised openly. They had decided to expel me, set about preparing the ground for this, and later come up with 'reasons'. This statement also made clear that the majority were not prepared to openly discuss the differences we had, not prepared to put these in front of the membership for their consideration, instead they we were manoeuvring to get time to discuss individually with people about how nasty we the minority were, and how we needed to be expelled.

We would later make contact with a member who had been a leading international full-timer in the CWI. He knew about and was part of the Taaffe/Walsh clique for a time. But he saw through its methods, courageously broke from it, and wrote openly of his experiences. His report showed the extreme degeneration that had taken place.

In his report he wrote:

'Comrades didn't know but the split was being organised by both factions secretly, long before open factions developed. I was part of a secret, shadow IS chaired by Taaffe, which operated entirely independently of the structures of the CWI and, indeed, of the British section and took totally independent decisions from the legitimate bodies. It wasn't a faction initially, simply a secret group around part of the leaders deciding how to manoeuvre against Grant and Woods and use others, like John Throne and Roger Silverman, as temporary tactical allies.

John and Roger were regarded like outsiders and unreliable misfits, who didn't fit in and couldn't be trusted. They were both evaluated and talked about in the same manner comrades sometimes rather haughtily discuss potential new contacts for joining the organisation. Their strengths and weakness were discussed and it was evaluated what they were capable of, what their political level was, what sort of commitment they had and any problems they might pose. There were lots of personal jibes against both of them, attacks on their record as full-timers, dismissing their work and devaluing their contribution. I was told that they'd passed their prime and weren't up the tasks of the moment. Roger's work in the Indian sub-continent was rubbished and the work of John in the US was equally dismissed as a failure.

This was all part of an attempt to consolidate me and a few others. In a cult, it's a psychological tactic. The insults at others are part of your initiation into the secrets of the high priests, to flatter you and make you feel important by implying you were a better comrade than the two of them put together. The tone was already one of "they were expendable", but that for the moment they had to be mollycoddled into supporting us to defeat Woods and Grant. Had Roger and John sided with Grant and Woods, Taaffe knew his group would have been seriously undermined in Britain and internationally. In my opinion, the future expulsion of John and the removal of Roger from the leadership was already planned at this time in broad terms and they had already decided to look for the opportunity to get rid of them once the split had been carried through.

Even after the Woods/Grant split, I think we all remained a little naive and trustful. Perhaps, we felt that most of the problems stemmed from the IMT (the Grant/Woods faction) and that after the difficult and unpleasant affair of the split was over, things would be better, even much better than before, and open and honest discussions would flourish without any dirty tricks. We were wrong, of course. Looking back, it is ironic, just after Militant had been the focus of a witch hunt by the Labour bureaucracy, a similar "witch hunt" took place inside Militant's own ranks with the aim of also extinguishing free debate and democracy. Who was more ruthless is anyone's guess. The witch hunt spread internationally through the CWI and, on the same criteria, those who posed a potential threat to Taaffe were likewise removed.'

This report of this Comrade was an accurate description of the undemocratic destructive wrecking activities that had been carried on by the clique around Peter Taaffe.

CHAPTER 38

EXPELLED – A BADGE OF HONOUR

GAINST THE BACKGROUND of these events in the CWI I was again concentrating my work in the USA and Canada. As I did so I struggled to draw conclusions about the organisation of which I was a part. While concerned about what was going on with the internal life in general, and while trying to understand the problems and the causes of these, I had no idea that the knives were out and I was one of the main targets. I continued to cling on to the belief that a comradely debate and discussion could be held in the organisation.

As I did so I struggled with the events and crises that had developed in the CWI and in my life as part of that organisation in the last years. However, I never questioned my decision to be part of that organisation or to be a full-time worker for the socialist revolution. While on occasion I would miss the countryside and the laughter and culture of Ireland, I never regretted leaving there to do international revolutionary work.

However I did draw lessons from the past. In the past struggle with the leading member in the North of Ireland and the majority of the IS, I made the mistake of not taking the issue to the membership. I did not make that mistake again. This time, along with Richard Mellor, Lisa Hane, John Reimann and Rob Rooke, we set up an open faction. It was known as the minority faction. I announced its formation and existence openly at an IEC meeting. By forming and openly announcing the existence of this faction we acted in a principled fashion. Unlike the clique around Taaffe and Walsh who hid their secret organising for as long as possible, and who had the objective of expelling us, we were open about our faction and our objective was to build and improve the CWI. We fought openly for our ideas. Our faction was based on our differences with the US majority over the LPA work and over the false internal life of the CWI overall, especially its refusal to admit to its mistakes.

On concentrating my work again in North America I increasingly found that the differences that had been developing between the east coast organisation and the west coast and myself were increasing. With a few exceptions, the membership on the east coast were increasingly pessimistic about any possibility of struggle developing outside the LPA. I raised the need to orient to other developments, especially some stirrings amongst sections of youth. I continued to raise the idea of setting up $10.00 an hour minimum wage committees and working through these. This approach of minimum wage committees was adopted years later by the CWI in the USA. It had good success. It should have been adopted much earlier.

While I was striving to build the CWI in North America, the majority of the North American leadership was working in collaboration with the majority of the IS to undermine my work and expel me from the organisation. The majority of the IS knew its position was unprincipled and corrupt. I again asked Walsh to bring out what he had previously said were mistakes of the US majority in relation to the LPA work but he refused. On another occasion Walsh had said to me that the CWI was bureaucratic centralist, not democratic centralist, but again when I asked him to say this and discuss this openly in the organisation he refused. Walsh was, on occasion, incautious and would say what he really believed, only not in front of the membership. On another occasion he said that he did not care if the CWI lost its entire membership in North America outside of New York. In the most undemocratic and most damaging way he kept these criticisms he had of the majority in the US section and of the work of the CWI as a whole from being discussed in the organisation. If he had raised them openly there might have been some chance of correcting the organisation.

Peter Taaffe was the central and most corrupt figure in the unprincipled combination between the IS majority and the majority of the leadership in North America and the corruption of the CWI's leadership and the wrecking of the CWI. I had earlier written a document on the LPA and given it to him for his opinion. He said he agreed with it. But when it became clear that the way to get a majority against me in the North American section so I could be expelled was to ally with the US majority in spite of their wrong position on the LPA, he no longer supported my document. While Peter Taaffe was the central figure in this corruption of the CWI, his method was to get others as much as possible to do his dirty work. He tried to avoid being seen as moving against any members or member in case he needed to try and work with them later. Under the impact of the mistakes we had all made and in relation to himself under the impact of his refusal to admit to these mistakes, Peter Taaffe had become a thoroughly unprincipled and corrupt individual.

Peter Taaffe sent Walsh to North America to do his dirty work. He also sent a Swedish full-time member. Between them they carried out a dual attack on myself and the members who would not go along with them. Behind my and our backs they said such things as we were finished, our work was a failure, that I had been put out of Ireland because of my way of working. Openly they said we would not accept the democratic will of the majority. We continually asked them to give examples of this but they were unable to do so. We had to go and that was that. The real reason was that we would not keep quiet about the mistakes we, including ourselves had all made, while the majority of the leadership fought to maintain that they had never made any mistakes that they were the know-it-all, always right brigade.

This was the background to the North American conference of the CWI in New York in the summer of 1996. Peter Taaffe made sure he was not there. He sent his representative Walsh instead. This conference was alien to anything any of us in the minority faction in the organisation had ever seen. We had never been treated in such an unprincipled fashion before, even in our struggles with the social democracy. We were shocked and nauseated by the approach of the leadership of the majority. It became immediately obvious the conference had been organised secretly and undemocratically in advance to be a non-stop assault on our views and on ourselves personally.

Member after member of the majority combination condemned us and did so mainly personally. Walsh directed the tired elements in the American group and orchestrated the destruction of the section. The IS majority wanted us out so it could rebuild the section in its own image, that is unquestioning of the international leadership and never admitting to any mistakes. This was the essence of the destruction of the section. Unquestioning of the international leadership and refusal to ever admit mistakes. The IS and US section majority had to expel us at all costs. This was their way of doing so. That is by destroying the US section.

It was only at this conference that we, the minority, realised the depth to which the US majority and the IS had sunk. We found out that the IS majority faction had been telling the International that they need not read our material or discuss with us as we were going to split. This was a very big obstacle to having our views heard, and also a lie as was shown by the major efforts we would later make to appeal against our expulsion and stay in the CWI. The leadership of the majority in the CWI also refused to circulate much of our material. We had announced our faction at an international meeting. We had an open faction and therefore the right to have our material circulated. But most of our written material was not circulated.

The conference in New York was a conference of an unclean, corrupt, alien organisation. We were attacked non-stop from beginning to end and then we were expelled. The excuse given was we had broken so called 'democratic centralism'. To try and 'prove' this the IS majority, along with the majority of the US leadership, consciously and deliberately wrecked the most important union work of the section. This was in Richard's union, AFSCME, the American Federation of State and County and Municipal Employees. It was the biggest public sector union in the country. And the work in this union was the most successful union work of the organisation in the US and it was gaining strength.

With the authority of leading the 1985 strike behind him, with the experience of his day-to-day work representing his workers and with the help of the organisation, Richard had gone on with others, some members of the CWI and some not, and developed an opposition in his union around a magazine called AFSCME Activist. This had grown to where it was being sold in ten states and becoming the opposition voice in the union. It was a united front magazine, that is, it was not a magazine of the CWI, but a magazine of those who supported its basic demands which were a commitment to fight the bosses' offensive, election of union officials and build a Labour Party.

As part of driving us out, the IS in conjunction with the US majority wrecked the AFSCME Activist. This was important to them as it was Richard who was the main person in AFSCME Activist. They were not prepared to have a leading member of the minority faction leading the most successful union work. To achieve their ends and expel ourselves, the IS of the CWI in combination with the US majority created a deliberate provocation. They ordered Richard to hand over the magazine and all its addresses to the organisation. The magazine and its addresses were not Richard's to give. It was a united front magazine. We refused. The majority at the time were refusing to sell the magazine and to hand over money from former sales. And they also voted against electing non-CWI people on to its editorial board.

We, the minority faction, on the other hand put the interests of the working class movement above the interests of the organisation or of our faction and refused to hand over the addresses. As a result the IS/US majority faction accused us of breaking so called democratic centralism. The IS/Majority/US Majority faction consciously and deliberately destroyed the rising opposition voice in the biggest public sector union in the US in pursuit of their own sectarian interests. But they did not care. Their corrupt factional interests came first. Their attitude was to hell with the interests of the workers, their faction came first, Peter Taaffe's domination of the CWI came first. Their demand that Richard hand over the addresses was to allow them to be able to portray the minority as not complying with so called democratic centralism and so 'justify' expelling us.

It was no accident that in their attempt to drive us out, the IS majority and US majority leaderships targeted Richard and the AFSCME union work. Only Richard had a sufficient base in his union and workplace to hold the Mazzocchi meeting that led to the development of the LPA. Richard had the main union base of any member. He had run for Oakland City Council and won 6% of the vote. As well as his refusal to go along with the dirty, dishonest methods of the IS/US majority combination, Richard had too big a working class base to be tolerated. He had to go. The reality was that the IS and US majority were afraid of members who were principled and who had a base in the working class.

Another dirty provocation and lie was created to slander us and try and justify our expulsion. It was over the organisation's headquarters in Chicago. When the HQ was being bought, the organisation did not have the money for a mortgage. Two members of the minority faction who were later to be expelled, took out a mortgage in their own names. This was a big risk for these members. As the expulsions took place agreement was reached between the minority and the majority in the US section for the majority to take over the mortgage and the house. But Walsh insisted on this agreement being broken. He and the majority tried to dump the house on the two minority members who were responsible for the mortgage.

The CWI majority lied about this and slandered and accused us of not being prepared to hand over the house. This was a lie. The reality was the majority wanted to dump the house on the two minority faction members and do as much damage to the minority as possible. During this whole period Walsh and the IS majority accused me of trying to swindle the International financially and get the house. Eventually I confronted Walsh at an international meeting of the CWI and he was forced to admit to that meeting that this was not true and that the organisation had got the market price for the house. This did not stop the majority from accusing me of 'stealing', of 'embezzling', their words, money, from the CWI over the house, for decades to come.

I had been active in the workers' and revolutionary movement for almost thirty years at that time. During these years I had many ferocious struggles with social democracy, Republicanism and Stalinism and different left sectarian groups. But never in all these struggles had I ever been accused of being financially dishonest. But here in this organisation to which I had given most of my adult life, as soon as there was a disagreement I was accused of 'stealing', of 'embezzling' money, of being a thief. This was the method of Stalinism without the violence. I had been a full-time organiser living on next to nothing for over twenty years. And I was expelled and fired from full-time work without a pension or a settlement of any kind. All I got were lies and slanders and filth heaped on my name. And leading this vicious injustice were Peter Taaffe and Lynn Walsh. Such an outfit could only build a corrupt and degenerate society.

Not content with these slanders the IS majority and their supporters in the US spread the lie that I had AIDS which they claimed was a result of what they dishonestly and falsely claimed was alleged sexual promiscuity. This was a lie. They based their lie on the fact that I had become emaciated in the recent years. Losing up to fifty pounds in weight. This was because I had Addison's disease which had not been diagnosed. When it was diagnosed and I returned to my normal weight the lie was no longer repeated but of course there was no apology or retraction made. The IS majority and US majority were utterly corrupt.

On the Sunday morning after we were expelled at the conference in New York, Richard and I were walking down Fifth Avenue in Manhattan. We met a lady leading a Jack Russell dog. 'Could I pet him please?' I asked. 'Of course.' He jumped around full of excitement and enthusiasm as is the way of the Jack Russell. I felt I was coming up for air again, I felt like I was being cleansed. I thanked the lady and the dog. The dirt of the conference and its demoralised, politically degenerate participants was fading away.

Only one Comrade would put us up for the night. Richard and I stayed in her apartment in Brooklyn. That evening we went out to a pub. Sitting at the counter of a packed, noisy working class bar, a free drink came around for everybody. It was a Polish man celebrating his birthday. Everybody raised their glasses and shouted and toasted him. Then a little later another free drink. Again he was toasted. Then a scuffle started at the top of the bar. It was the man who had bought the drinks. The lady owner had two other customers grab him and throw him out. What the hell was this? We were not happy. After all we had just been thrown out of something ourselves.

We asked the lady who owned the bar what was going on. She answered in an angry tone. 'It was his birthday. And there he was. I let him buy one round for the bar. I did not want to but I let him buy another round he was so determined to anyway. Then he wanted to buy another. He wouldn't have had a cent left. That wasn't going to happen to anybody in my bar.'

There we were, Richard originally from England and I from Ireland, as we saw it from more humane, less corporate-dominated cultures, but here we were seeing the good hearted, the generous side of America, the working class influenced side of America. We contrasted it to the demoralised corrupt people who made up the majority combination in the CWI who had just expelled us. After a few moments the man who had been thrown out put his head round the door again. Looking sheepish he asked could he come back in again. The lady behind the bar said: 'Okay but no more buying drink.' Thrown out of a pub for buying drink! US capitalism had not totally destroyed the US working class. It was a wonderful night. Everybody in the bar, including ourselves, laughed and sang and shouted with the man who had been let in again to continue with his birthday celebrations. The whole bar competed to buy him drink. We were recuperating from the dirt of the conference and the organisation. Like we did when we petted the wee Jack Russell on Fifth Avenue, there in that pub in Brooklyn we shook the dirt of the corrupt CWI off our feet. I was very glad. I was very proud. I threw back an Irish whiskey with my head held high. I was not ever in, and even better had not ever been invited to be in, the corrupt gathering of the IS-dominated majority of the CWI and its weak supporters in the US and Canadian sections. Here I was at home with the working class with all its positives and negatives, with all its life. And I was clean.

We went back to the apartment of the Comrade who was letting us stay. We told her what had happened. A man was thrown out of the bar for trying to buy drink. We all began to laugh. We fell on the floor laughing in our joy for life. We were alright. We had given most of our adult life to an organisation that had betrayed its own stated principles but we were alright. Our revolutionary spirit and our ability to laugh were intact. Our belief in the need for revolution was as strong as ever. Our commitment to fight for that revolution was as strong as ever.

It was our constitutional right to appeal against our expulsion. We attempted to exercise this right. We were barred from attending conferences in Ireland and England and internationally to explain our side of the case and appeal against our expulsion. In the IS/majority/US majority clique we were dealing with liars and maneuverers of the most unprincipled types. In Chicago, one of their supporters who had been meeting secretly with the IS majority faction was promoted in the organisation in return for his support in expelling myself and the other members of the minority faction. He sold his soul for a higher position in a corrupt organisation. This was typical of this clique.

I went to see Joe Higgins, a leader of the Irish section whom I and Anton McCabe had recruited to socialism and the CWI and who, because of this, would become a future member of the Irish and European parliaments. We met in Buswell's Hotel in Dublin. I did not ask him to support my political position but only to support my democratic right to appeal against my expulsion. He sat there clutching his CWI documents to his chest and looking with his tightened face at his future in front of him. Then he blurted: 'I will not. You got yourself into this mess, you can get yourself out of it.' I will never forget those unprincipled words, that unprincipled, tightened, guilty, ashamed face of a man I had recruited to socialism and with whom I thought I had been a friend. I told him he was participating in an injustice and he jumped up and ran from the hotel, scuttling from his shame and betrayal. I looked in disbelief and contempt after him as he scurried off clutching his cowardice and opportunism and his lack of principle and his CWI documents to his chest. It seemed that as long as he clutched these documents to himself they would act like a breastplate and protect him from his own behaviour.

Joe was doing as he always did when it came to himself and the internal life of the CWI. While he fought the bosses and deserved credit for that, when it came to fighting for the rights of those who had different views in the CWI he would not do so. In the internal life of the CWI, Joe Higgins looked after number one. He sold his soul to the leadership of the CWI. He parroted the lies against me and supported the expulsion and slandering of myself and the minority faction. Unless he changes his ways and openly owns up to the role he played, these injustices will forever be a stain on his record.

One of the most glaring examples of how corrupt the CWI had become was the control commission. The control commission was a body elected at conferences and its membership were not members of any of the leading bodies of the organisation. It was supposed to be called into action when there were difficult disputes and its role was to investigate and make a report to the full organisation. We called for the control commission to investigate our case. We were confident that if this body met, the dirty tricks and lies and slanders and undemocratic methods would be exposed.

But the problem was that the majority of the IS and its partners in the US and Canada were just as confident that if the control commission were called in to investigate, all the dirty tricks and lies and slanders would be exposed. So the leadership of the CWI not only refused us our right to appeal against our expulsion but also refused to call into action the control commission to investigate what had gone on. The CWI had become a corrupt and undemocratic organisation in its internal life.

We acted in a principled fashion in this internal struggle, openly explaining our ideas, openly announcing our faction to fight for these ideas. I am proud of how we acted. I did not make the mistake I made in the struggle around the complaints against the leading member in Northern Ireland when I went along with not putting the issue to the full membership. This time I and the other minority Comrades announced our position and faction and published documents explaining our position. We had learnt from the past. But the problem was that as we acted in a principled manner, openly setting up and announcing our faction and seeking to put our position to the membership of the CWI, the leadership of that body undemocratically refused to allow us to do so. They banned us from appealing against our expulsion, they banned the membership from hearing our point of view.

Our expulsion was not inevitable. We could have hidden our ideas. We could have adopted ideas we did not believe in and gone along with the IS/majority combination. We could have stopped insisting that our mistakes of the past be openly discussed and owned up to. We could have given up and walked away. We could have sold our souls. But the members of the minority faction, including myself, would not do it. I personally would not do it. I had not fought loyalism, nationalism, republicanism, Protestantism, Catholicism, and all the other ideas that had threatened me when I was young, to sell my soul at that stage to a bunch of corrupt individuals masquerading as revolutionaries. I was a principled revolutionary socialist and I remained so.

Continuing leading members of the CWI froth at the mouth with rage when they hear my criticisms. They seriously underestimated my tenacity in fighting against my expulsion and against the injustices they carried out against me. But what they do not see is this, when it comes to trying to preserve as much as possible of all the hard work that all the members and former members put in to building that organisation, I have been acting much more positively, more correctly than any of those who sit in that organisation with their mouths closed or who justify my expulsion.

There is no possible way that the CWI, or its Irish or any section, or any of the self-styled revolutionary socialist organisations that presently exist, will become a semi-mass or mass organisation with their present internal life. The larger these organisations become the more differences and debates will inevitably arise. This is not only healthy, not only inevitable, but also necessary for a developing semi-mass or mass organisation. And if the internal life of the CWI is not changed to where it will be able to have a democratic and healthy internal life and tolerate different views and different factions, and openly admit its mistakes, the future of the CWI and all the self-styled revolutionary left organisations will be one of splits and expulsions and fragmentation.

Just take some examples in the CWI. Our minority faction in the US was expelled, Dermot Connolly the leading Southern Irish member after I left Ireland could no longer tolerate the corrupt and undemocratic internal life and left, Finn Geaney could not tolerate the corrupt and undemocratic internal life and left, Joan Collins and Clare Daly, leading women members and members of the Irish parliament, were not prepared to tolerate the corrupt and undemocratic internal regime and left, and of course hundreds walked away when they saw what was going on and also saw that the majority of the Socialist Party, the CWI section in Southern Ireland and CWI leadership were not prepared to admit to and face up to their mistakes.

The case of Dermot Connolly and Joan Collins, Dermot and Joan are partners, in particular illustrated the corruption and the thinking of the leadership of the Socialist Party the Irish section of the CWI and of the CWI itself. Dermot and Joan had 'flaws' as far as the CWI leadership was concerned. These were that these Comrades were independent thinkers and they had a base in the working class. Dermot and Joan were able to be part of and play leadings roles in meetings of seven to eight hundred working class activists in the Crumlin area against the bin tax, a new tax which was taking more money out of the pockets of working families by making them pay for getting their garbage collected. In this struggle Dermot was imprisoned for disobeying a court order and blocking a garbage truck. While in prison, Dermot's partner Joan, presently a member of the Irish parliament, was not contacted once to see how she was, how Dermot was, did she need anything. Not only that the Socialist Party the Irish section of the CWI of which Dermot was then still a leading member, refused to take part in a demonstration to the prison, claiming they were too busy. They even refused to allow the Socialist Party banner to be used on this demonstration. The mass meetings of working class activists in the Crumlin area of which Dermot and Joan were part discussed the struggle against the bin tax and democratically decided tactics. These did not always coincide with the 'directives' handed down from the Socialist Party headquarters. This was not acceptable to the leadership of the Socialist Party/CWI. Their position was that Dermot and Joan should try to impose the party's tactics on the movement. When Dermot and Joan correctly refused to do so the Socialist Party leadership backed up by the CWI refused to organise against Dermot's imprisonment. This was outright betrayal.

There were two reasons the leadership of the Irish Socialist party and the CWI acted the way they did with Dermot and Joan. One was that they did not want independent thinking people in the leadership of the Irish section. The other and related reason was they did not want people with a base in the working class, people like Dermot and Joan, in the leadership of the Socialist Party. As elsewhere they wanted compliant individuals who would take orders from the CWI leadership in London. So they promoted a young member who had no experience in the class struggle, no base in the working class and who for reasons of personal ambition went along with orders. With the support of better known members of the Socialist Party, members like Joe Higgins and Ruth Coppinger, both members of the Irish Parliament, the CWI leadership got their compliant leadership in their Irish section. But as the saying goes and will be born out, is being born out, be careful what you wish for.

I am acting more in the interests of the revolution and the working class, and in building a healthy revolutionary organisation, more than any of those who justify the corrupt internal life of the CWI or who kept and keep quiet in the face of the corrupt and undemocratic methods of the self-styled revolutionary organisations. If members of the CWI want to give that organisation a future, they have to conduct an internal struggle to change the internal life of that organisation. It would be more in their line to do this than to slander and lie about me. They should take their head out of the sand. It will take an international organisation of tens of millions, perhaps hundreds of millions to overthrow capitalism. There is no way an organisation of such a size can be built unless there is open debate, democratic rights and genuine faction rights, unless there is a genuine collective leadership, not a Peter Taaffe dictatorship, and unless there is an end to slander and lies. The CWI as it exists at present does not fit this bill. Nor do any of the other self-styled revolutionary organisations.

CHAPTER 39

DEMOCRATIC CENTRALISM – COVER FOR A MULTITUDE OF SINS

MY EXPERIENCE with the CWI did not in any way shake my commitment to building a nucleus that would hopefully be able to contribute to the building of a revolutionary international. It remained clear to me that international capitalism could not be overthrown without the working class being organised in a mass revolutionary organisation of tens and hundreds of millions. It never occurred to me to give up the struggle to this end. I came to see all those who said they were against capitalism, but at the same time would not build an organisation to fight against capitalism, were not facing reality. The task was to build, to organise. Capitalism had its huge organisations, economic, political, propaganda, military – these could not be defeated without the working class having its own mass revolutionary international organisation. To believe otherwise was to live in a fantasy world. I was not impressed with the approach of those who claimed to be against capitalism but who would not organise.

This did not mean I expected everybody to be a full-time revolutionary. This would not only be unrealistic but it would also make it impossible to carry out the international socialist revolution. It was only the working class as a class that could carry out the international socialist revolution. This class had many different layers. Some more advanced and thinking layers, some more combative and active layers, some more cautious layers, some more backward layers. It would only be when significant sections of these layers would come together to fight capitalism that victory could be achieved. In the process of building to this end it would be necessary for full-time organisers, writers and activists to be developed. But not everybody could, for personal or family reasons, be a full-time organiser. But more than that, not everybody should be a full-time organiser. The revolution needed workers permanently working on the shop floor and in the work places. But the revolution also needed a full-time apparatus dedicated to the fight against capitalism. Organising against capitalism was the task of all workers, some would do this in their workplace and union, some in their schools and colleges some in their communities and some would do it as full-time organisers for the revolution. But what was not acceptable in my eyes was not to organise to end capitalism.

The membership of the CWI, before the split was around 14,000. After the split and the departure of the International Marxist Tendency, as Ted Grant and Alan Woods called their group, and the years of demoralisation that followed for many of the former members of the old CWI, the combined membership of both groups dwindled away to the hundreds. The split was not a positive development to put it mildly. I tried to understand why it had taken place and what mistakes had been made.

The main reason for the split was the CWI's view of the world no longer corresponded to reality. It was clinging on to 'five to ten years to the revolution' when such a prospect was totally excluded. Not only that, but the world situation had become one of reaction with capitalism being re-established in the Stalinist world as the 1980s came to an end as the 1990s unfolded. The CWI acted like the tide was still flowing in its favour when it had turned and was flowing against it. The historical process had been thrown back. The workers' movement had been thrown back, but the CWI acted as if it was still going forward. The result was the CWI broke its neck against the movement. This, and the refusal, the inability, of the CWI to understand this, to honestly face up to this were the main reasons for the wrecking of the International.

The period of world reaction that came with the collapse of Stalinism was a turning point in world affairs. It shifted the balance of forces between Stalinism and capitalism and between the classes. It would have caused problems for the CWI no matter what. However, what turned things into a catastrophe and caused the split and the collapse in membership of the CWI was that its wrong worldview came together with its incorrect internal life. This incorrect internal life combined a number of features.

One was the internal life did not encourage questioning and debate and probing of ideas. We 'knew' everything. We 'knew' that Stalinism and capitalism were both about to collapse. We 'knew' it was a race between the political revolution in the East which would over-throw Stalinism and replace this with a democratic socialist system and the socialist revolution in the West, which would overthrow capitalism and replace it with a democratic socialist system. And we 'knew' that then the world would surge forward on an international socialist basis. We 'knew' it was five to ten years to the revolution. And not only that, but we 'knew' that only we could lead this revolution, and so we had to get on with it, with organising, recruiting, raising money, etc. etc. We 'knew' all this.

So stop questioning, stop probing, get on with the 'work', sell the paper, read what you are expected to read, raise money. In this way the CWI was driven headlong over the edge of a cliff. I was as responsible as anybody else for this catastrophic mistake. In fact, more responsible than most as I was a member of the IEC for all of this time and a member of the IS for part of this time. This combination of a wrong view of the world, and the wrong internal life was what led to the shipwrecking of the International.

The mistakes in the world view and the internal life resulted in, were part of, a generally incorrect method. In particular the CWI was far too unconditional in relation to the tempo of events, and in fact in predicting events in general. Marx, Engels, Lenin, Trotsky, Luxemburg had been much more conditional in how they saw history unfold. However, even they were very wrong when it came to the tempo of events. Capitalism lasted much longer than they anticipated. It is still with us. But it was not only a question of tempo. It was also a question of not basing ourselves on the dialectic when developing perspectives. History took a step forward when the working class took power in the Russian revolution and ended capitalism and landlordism in its territories. But history took a partial step back when the working class lost power to Stalinism. Partial because while the working class lost political power the economy was not restored to private hands, to capitalism. But then as the 1980's ended and the 1990's unfolded history took a full step back when capitalism was restored. Marx, Engels, Lenin, Trotsky, Luxemburg and the CWI did not anticipate such developments. History, like all processes, does not move in a straight line. We in the CWI, the great believers in the dialectic, were not able to apply the dialectic in this new period. We were basing ourselves on the belief that events would develop in a straight line, straight ahead forward to world socialism. The wishful thinking of the CWI was directly related to it not being able to apply the dialectic.

Any organisation will inevitably make mistakes. However the CWI compounded its mistakes by being so unconditional, overconfident and arrogant. It and we acted like we knew everything about everything and all other left forces were 'sects', and their ideas rubbish. One result of this wrong way of working was it was much harder for the CWI to be self-critical and see and accept when it was wrong and to make changes. Such an internal life based as it was on these 'certainties' made it very difficult for genuine internal debate and questioning and clarification of ideas and correcting ideas. It also meant that any change in the ideas inevitably lagged far behind events. This would be fatal for the International.

As well as being far too unconditional about events, there were other mistakes in the method of the CWI. The majority of the leadership around Peter Taaffe thought they were the teachers of the membership. It held a monologue with the membership, not a dialogue. The arrogance of this majority of the IS was astounding. After the split, when the organisation was trying to work out an analysis of the new world economic situation, Walsh was given the task to lead on this front. This was another example of Peter Taaffe not knowing what was what but not being prepared to say so and therefore giving Walsh the task, letting Walsh hold the bag while he himself observed and bided his time. Let it be Walsh who threw up the ideas to be batted around and rejected or accepted as the case may be. In this way Peter Taaffe could sit back and appear all knowing. This was not a principled way to act. If it was not for all his dirty tricks and never being prepared to admit his own mistakes it would almost be possible to feel sorry for Walsh. But you make your bed. Walsh took to discussing with a member who worked in a major high street bank. He would then come to IS meetings and present the ideas that came out of these discussions as his own. I objected and said the International should have these discussions and try to work out the new world view itself. Walsh's response was that he 'did not have time to give seminars to the IS.' When this was his view of his relationship to the other members of the IS, imagine his view of his relationship to the membership. Walsh and the majority of the IS did not see the membership as a whole as a living, breathing, thinking resource out of which would come ideas and clarification of events. They saw it as being there to be taught.

Better late than never I came to see that the internal life of the organisation was much too top down. That is, all ideas were expected to start at the top and be handed down. The majority of the leadership did not share its views with the membership until it worked these out amongst itself first and only then presented them to the membership. This approach discouraged the membership of the entire organisation from independent, democratic discussion and debate and critical thought. It prevented the potential of the collective membership from being realised. Why go to all the trouble to figure things out for yourself when you could have them handed to you on a plate. I was guilty of participating in this false method for most of my years in the CWI.

For my first twenty years in that organisation, we explained the correct idea that while there was an economic upswing in the capitalist world, this would come to an end and when it did the class relations would change and there would be an upswing in class struggle. This did not seem to be contradicted by reality, in fact it seemed to be confirmed by events such as the 1968 French general strike, so I saw my task as being to convince the membership of this, to put the line. I was guilty of using all my resources to drive home this idea to the membership. My strength in being able to convince people of ideas became a weakness when I was convincing people of the wrong ideas, and when this strength discouraged people from thinking for themselves. All the leadership of the CWI saw this as the way to build the organisation, saw that the way was to convince people that the revolution would come, and soon, and so join up to help be prepared. As Ted Grant had told me when I first became a full-time organiser, I had to always be optimistic. This was a one-sided, non-dialectical piece of advice. Yes, always be optimistic but also always seek to be realistic.

The internal life of revolutionary organisations from the time of the Bolsheviks was described as 'democratic centralism'. This term and method had its roots in the Russian revolution. It supposedly meant that a living, breathing, thinking membership would, after full democratic discussion, come to majority decisions, and these decisions would be implemented, but with minority opinions having the right to continue to have their views heard. This sounded good, but the world balance of forces, the tasks and pressures of revolution and counterrevolution, and the rise of the Stalinist counter-revolution continually challenged this method.

The experience of the Bolsheviks took place in a specific context. The Bolsheviks were no sooner in power than they had to defend the revolution against the right wing armies from within Russia as well as the invading imperialist armies. In these the most conscious revolutionaries and workers who would have been best able to fight to keep the revolution healthy and democratic, were either killed or militarised. This weakened the traditions of the working class, and the working class itself. At the same time, the economy of the new workers' state was devastated by war and famine. Mass starvation and mass slaughter was the experience. Along with this the revolutions in the more advanced countries such as Germany were defeated and the Russian revolution and the Bolsheviks were isolated. The working class in Russia had been a very small minority to begin with but at the end of the civil war it was even smaller with many killed and many militarised in the course of the civil war. Along with this the majority of the population had always been the peasantry and sitting on top of this the anti-democratic forces of the landlord class and Tsarism.

These realities opened the door to the rise of a bureaucratic caste within Russia. It crept into positions of power in the economy, the military and politics. It replaced world revolution with so-called socialism in one country. This meant no socialism in any other country, nor for that matter in Russia. It led to unprincipled deals with imperialism. It led to the crushing of all attempts at revolution at home and abroad. As part of this, the then ruling

Stalinist caste also moved to crush all alternative views in society and in the Bolshevik party. It presided over a vicious dictatorship both in society and the Bolshevik party. In the 1920s and in the 1930s, it slaughtered the best of what was left of the revolutionary forces in Russia.

As part of this, all the democratic norms that existed in the Bolshevik party when it was healthy were crushed. This was done under the name of so-called democratic centralism, but the truth was this new party, the leadership of this new party, while still calling itself democratic centralist and communist, was a dictatorship, both over the country and also against all alternative views within its own ranks.

In the capitalist world in the post-World War II period, the post-War economic upswing strengthened the mass parties of social democracy and Stalinism. The working class in the advanced industrial countries, in the main did not see the need for the socialist revolution as they were getting by in the economic upswing. This isolated the self-styled revolutionary left groups, which claimed to be Trotskyist, from the fresh democratic breeze of mass movements of the working class in struggle and as a result these organisations, as had been the case with the social democratic and Stalinist organisations earlier, also degenerated. Their degeneration was assisted by the fact that they modelled themselves on what they thought was the Bolshevik Party, but not the Bolshevik Party in its healthy period, but when the Bolsheviks were well on the way to degeneration as Stalinism took over the Soviet Union and the Bolsheviks themselves. The CWI was no exception to this process which affected the self-styled revolutionary left groups. It was only a matter of degree.

The CWI view of the world that it was on the verge of a new world capitalist crisis and/or the overthrow of the Stalinist regimes, and their replacement with democratic socialist societies was always incorrect. But this only became undeniable with the collapse of Stalinism in the late 1980s early 1990s. It was only when Stalinism actually collapsed and was replaced not by democratic socialism as the CWI had been predicting, but by capitalism, that the wrong internal life of the CWI surged to the forefront and became absolutely dominant. It was only when it became obvious that history was not only not about to take a new step forward, rather it was in fact taking a step back with the restoration of capitalism in the former Soviet union, that the wrong internal life of the CWI expressed itself decisively.

The internal culture of the CWI had been wrong all along, all members, including myself were wrong on this. However as long as we could convince ourselves that we were still heading for a new period of revolution and as long as the organisation was growing this did not seem to be a problem. But with the collapse of Stalinism in the former Soviet Union in the late years of the 1980s and the early '90s, and its replacement with capitalism, things changed. The result was questioning and doubts inevitably and correctly were expressed inside the CWI. This questioning was inevitable and healthy. In this new situation the false world view, the false internal life could no longer be ignored. It erupted like a volcano and the crisis and split was on.

In my years in the CWI I had occasional doubts about what was known as, what was practised under the name of democratic centralism. On my first year on the British section's leading body the central committee, in the early 1970s I had put forward an alternative slate to the proposed slate of the outgoing leadership. Leaderships were elected by the undemocratic slate system. That is the outgoing leadership would propose a slate of members for a new leadership. This would inevitably be the old leadership with at best one or two new members added on or taken off. This was undemocratic as it tended to result in the old leadership, with only the odd occasional exception, re-electing itself.

When I proposed my alternative slate, it was rejected. But it was not only that. It was the reaction it caused. It was rejected with such a negative response from the leadership that I mistakenly concluded that there must be something I did not understand and I did not again propose an alternative slate. I should have stuck with my instincts in this case. The method of the leadership of the CWI was also to talk to people who had their own resolutions for conferences and try and convince them not to move their resolutions. Such resolutions coming from the membership were seen as disrupting the teacher's curriculum. I did not agree with trying to talk people out of putting alternative resolutions or positions to conferences, and after mistakenly doing so on two occasions, when asked to by the leadership, I did not repeat it. I was wrong in not openly conducting a struggle against this false slate method, this talking people out of moving alternative resolutions. The internal life of the organisation would have been entirely different and more healthy if the norm had been that all branches could have felt confident that they could have put forward their own resolutions, their own proposals for the leadership bodies within the organisations' structures up to and at the national and international conference level without being moved against, and if there had been an open method of electing the leaderships.

On a number of occasions in my early days in The Militant organisation when I had disagreements on issues, I did raise them openly. At a conference on Ireland when Peter Taaffe said our position on withdrawal of the British troops from Ireland was a conditional demand, I openly spoke against this and said it was not conditional. I was the main speaker on the platform at that conference along with Peter Taaffe. He did not respond and so there was no debate. Not responding was another way of not discussing or of not accepting mistakes and continuing with the same policy. I also raised, at an international conference, and again as a platform speaker, the incorrect way in which some male members were treating female members. Again because nobody spoke either for or against what I said there was no debate.

The longer I was in the CWI the more I tended to fit into the culture of do not rock the boat, it was only five to ten years to the revolution, get on with building, do not take internal organisational differences issues to the full membership, this would only hinder the work. There was also the fact that Ted Grant and Peter Taaffe and those around them had, between them, an overall greater knowledge than I and so I was not always confident of my positions not always confident to take them to an open debate and struggle in the organisation. Part of the reason for this was that the Ted Grant/Peter Taaffe leadership would not share their reasoning on issues, share their method of thinking on issues, sought instead to only share their conclusions. Their attempt to monopolise their method of thinking out of specific issues gave them a much more dominant position in the organisation and worked against the organisation being healthy and democratic.

On becoming a member of the organisation, while I was able to build and develop the organisation, I was still dependent on the organisation's leadership as a whole for my theoretical development. I was insufficiently, theoretically, independently developing myself and this was not improving much as I put the emphasis in my work on building and organising. This was a serious mistake I made over these years. I gave insufficient attention to my own theoretical development and so was overly dependent on the accumulated theoretical and historical level of the older existing leadership and so insufficiently spoke out on issues where I had doubts and/or disagreements.

As the split in the CWI unfolded and I more clearly saw the method of the majority of the IS leadership which was known as democratic centralism, I came to reject this method of organising. I came to conclude that this method of organising known as democratic centralism was incorrect, and not only that but that this method of organising was extremely damaging to the workers' movement. It had been used to justify the internal life of all sorts of organisations such as the murderous, reactionary Stalinist organisations, as well as the sectarian, ultra-left, self-styled revolutionary groups. It was a method that justified organisations with undemocratic, and eventually corrupt internal lives such as the CWI. It was used to cover a multitude of sins. I discarded this wrong method of organising which was known as democratic centralism.

There were various reasons it took me so long to see the incorrectness of what was described as democratic centralism. One was that while events in general confirmed our view of the world and that the world revolution lay ahead, there were no great debates or differences in the organisation. And as a result of this, the false methods which lay under the surface were not often exposed and not often used. And on top of that leading members who would tend to act in a democratic manner, when the organisation was in the main unified, when its ideas more or less corresponded to reality, when it was going forward, could when our wrong world view became undeniable, and inevitably differences developed, and they would be unable to clarify their thinking, they could change. In their confusion and inability to develop a new analysis, and crucially admit that this was so, leading members could on such occasions abandon their previously more democratic methods of work and instead turn to wrong methods of work and act in an undemocratic way. Like in all aspects of life things were not fixed in the internal life of the organisation or with individual members. I struggled to become more skilled in consciously applying the method of dialectics to organising. The method of thought that explained that all things were always changing and not in a straight line but through contradiction and steps forward and steps back.

So I eventually came to reject the method of organising which was described as democratic centralism. This was a big step forward for me in my work. But rejecting the method of organising known as democratic centralism did not solve the problem of organisation. The task of history remained to build a mass revolutionary international organisation of tens and hundreds of millions of working class people and fuse them together into a collective, conscious, democratic, fighting force which could end capitalism and build a new democratic socialist world. Capitalism could not be overthrown without such a structure. It could not be overthrown on an individual basis. An international, collective, democratic organisation of tens and hundreds of millions with a healthy internal culture and life was necessary. I came to the conclusion that what was described as 'democratic centralism' was an incorrect method of organising.

My own evolution to becoming a revolutionary involved moving from acting as an individual to what I understood as becoming part of a collective democratic organisation and process which based itself on general political principles, such as overthrowing capitalism, establishing international revolutionary socialism, building an independent working class movement, building on general organisational principles such as honest and open discussion and exchange of views and decision making based on democratic majority opinion, combined with the rights of minorities to have their say and organise for their views. I came to regard the highest achievement of humanity in this period of history would be such a collective democratic decision making organism based on these principles. In a way, such an organisation would be the frontal lobe of the collective brain of the working class.

I came in my rejection of what was called democratic centralism to conclude that such a complex task as building a mass international organisation could not be described by a couple of words such as was attempted to be done by what was known as democratic centralism. The correct approach was to reject any attempt to describe the method of organising with a few words but was to understand and describe the correct method of organising as a set of principles. These principles being full democratic discussion, decisions to be made by majority opinion, full rights of minority opinions to be expressed and heard and organised for. Rather than seek some neat couple of words to describe the method of organising these principles had to be explained and the organising work to be based on these.

But things could not be left there. The dialectic again. Change. Different circumstances, different objectives, all had to be kept in mind. While continuing to base ourselves on the above principles it also had to be recognised that at different times there would be different emphasis in the work. It would at times of great opportunity be necessary to have all hands on deck to take the opportunity, all strength at the point of attack to make the breakthrough. There would also be times when the movement would be under severe attack and threat of being destroyed that it would again be a time for all hands on deck, all strength at the point of defence if the movement were to survive.

In other words there would be different balances in the revolutionary organisation at different times. However the general principles as outlined above would be maintained. Great opportunities or great risks did not justify the setting aside of these principles rather demanded even greater application of these principles, that is full democratic discussion right of minority views etc. I came to question the decision of the Bolsheviks to ban factions at the height of the civil war. I was no longer sure it had been correct. If there are different opinions there will be factions either formal or informal. Different views will express themselves and rightly and inevitably so.

To take a step forward to understand the type of organisation that was necessary I had to remove a major block from my mind. Up until that point I incorrectly saw a properly functioning revolutionary organisation as one which came out of every conference united on everything down to the smallest detail, which was at all times unified down to the smallest detail. I had to change and I did so. And when I did I was euphoric with my new way of looking at things and my new way of working. I came to see that a revolutionary international of tens and hundreds of millions could not exist without differences. Differences were inevitable. It was not a problem or something to be stood against. And not only that, it was necessary to see that differences were not only inevitable, but they were necessary, they were to be welcomed. If they did not exist the organisation would not be healthy. The international organisation had to see its internal life as being able to allow internal differences and disputes, even further, not just allow, but welcome these internal differences. Instead of seeing an organisation as being successful only when it was based on complete unity, it had to be seen as being healthy only when it had internal debate and differences and was able to live and fight and struggle and survive while still holding such differences, in the sense that they could have them and still work together to overthrow capitalism.

I took on board what the founders of revolutionary socialism had to say about organisation. Engels said that internal 'struggle' was the law of development of the revolutionary party. Lenin insisted that when members had differences they must put them forward for debate. He insisted it was their duty to spell out, to write down their differences, present them to the party and in this way the party would be educated by the exchange of views. He also insisted it was the duty of the Party to share its ideas and opinions and debates with the people as a whole. He had this to say: 'We Social Democrats resort to secrecy from the Tsar and his bloodhounds, while taking pains that the people should know everything about our Party, about the shades of opinion within it, about the development of its programme and policy, that they should even know what this or that Party congress said at the Congress in question.' Yes Lenin said the 'people', not even just the working class but the 'people should know everything about our party'. How different this approach was to the approach of the CWI and to that of all the self-styled revolutionary socialist groups presently existing. Trotsky said that the healthy period of Bolshevism was a time of factions and even factions within factions. Marx and Engels debated publically with all the forces in and around the First international of which they were part. I came to understand that the duty of the revolutionary party was to precisely outline its differences in front of the working class, openly share its differences with the working class, so the working class could examine the alternatives and decide which way forward it thought was correct. Hiding differences, distorting other faction's positions, these were betrayals of the working class. These put roadblocks in front of the working class clarifying its analysis, its programme, its strategies, its tactics, its thinking.

The CWI never had an internal life which was anything like this. Any alternative ideas to those of the leadership were seen as a threat to be crushed by fair means or foul. As I saw through the incorrect method of what was described as democratic centralism, which I and the CWI had practiced for decades, a whole new exciting approach to building opened up to me. It took my expulsion from the CWI for me to understand this. My expulsion was a positive development in my revolutionary work. It made me more cautious and questioning of my own approach to working out ideas and drawing conclusions. This was good. I also came to remember again what had at one time been a saying of the CWI that debate is good. It is the revolutionary organisation sharpening its knives for the fight against capitalism. Unfortunately in the CWI, in that period when the perspectives of that organisation were shown to be incorrect, when the majority of the leadership refused to admit its mistakes, debate meant from the majority of the leadership's point of view the sharpening of knives to be used not against capitalism, but against anybody in the organisation who had a different point of view.

My new way of looking at organising was in line with the dialectical method. Nothing is fixed, everything is always changing, all is in a process of struggle and change and development. The revolutionary organisation could not be correct at all times. The revolutionary organisation could give no guarantees. Great events and struggles would throw up great mass revolutionary formations. In these would be great debates and struggles and differences. There could be no guarantee that the revolutionary organisation would be correct, would be up to the task. This would only be determined as the revolutionary organisation faced the explosive events of the process of revolution itself and as this happened the revolutionary organisation would inevitably go into great paroxysms of debate and struggle as it tried to grapple with the great events and chart the way forward. This was the reality. The method of the majority of the CWI leadership was not this. The method of the majority of the CWI leadership was that it knew all and that complete unity was necessary, that complete unity was possible and desirable. These were concepts that were totally wrong. The revolutionary organisation was a living breathing organism, had to be a living breathing organism, as such it had to have great debates and struggles, it had to precisely because it was a living breathing organism. It was like all other life forms, it had to develop through a process of evolution, a process of struggle, a process of the fittest, in this case the fittest ideas, and the fittest ideas as they became developed in interaction with the working class in struggle. The method of the CWI was never this. Rigid total unity, was the approach. This was entirely un-dialectical and un-historical. It made for an organisation that was and is incapable of becoming a mass organisation, leading a great, mass, breathing, full of conflict and struggle movement, leading a revolution. The self styled great dialecticians, the majority of the leadership, who led the CWI were being totally un-dialectical.

In seeing through the false method of organising that was described as democratic centralism I increasingly looked for a different formulation to describe the method of organising which was best for a revolutionary organisation. For a time I considered the term 'democratic collectivism' to describe what I now believed. I considered this as a way to describe the revolutionary organisation as a collective organisation rather than an organisation which was led by the nose by a leadership which was elected by the so-called slate system, itself an undemocratic incorrect method. However I was not happy with this formulation, democratic collectivism. It did not recognise that there would inevitably be, that it was also necessary for there to be, a hardened experienced leadership in a revolutionary organisation. However I could not come up with a better formulation. I concluded that the key was not the formulation, but the key was to explain the various aspects of organisation and also that different emphases were necessary at different times. That any talk about internal organisation had to begin with a discussion on the objective situation both of capitalism and the consciousness of the working class, on the state and resources of the organisation, the immediate needs of the organisation and from this the principles of organisation and the balance of organisation that was necessary at any given time.

I saw the main task as being to move away from an organisational method which was that of all the organisations that claimed to be democratic centralism, a method which in reality was just a tipping of the cap to democracy but which in reality was a method of organising where the centralist leadership decided things in advance and amongst themselves and then went out and fought the membership to get them to accept the leadership's positions. The form of organising that I now consciously fought for was where the membership at all levels looked at and proposed various alternatives, where a culture was created where any member or group of members could put their alternatives in front of the membership and the working class and have them discussed without being portrayed as enemies of the organisation. Out of this would come a more clear leadership, a more sharpened leadership, a more sharpened cutting edge in the revolutionary organisation, a more flexible, questioning, thoughtful, probing membership and leadership. Around these ideas I sought to help build a new healthy culture for a new revolutionary movement.

The Stalinist regimes that developed internationally under the impetus of the Soviet Union had state power. Other Stalinist regimes such as China would also develop. The Chinese regime also had state power. These regimes were totally contrary to the ideas and methods of Lenin and the Bolsheviks in their healthy period. They suppressed all opposition using mass murder and repression. The CWI did not have state power. It did not suppress opposition by violence. It did not have the resources to do so. But it used the resources it did have. It created an anti-democratic culture, one that discouraged debate and discussion, it lied about and slandered and expelled any serious opposition, or made it just about impossible for any serious opposition to play a role in the organisation. It was Stalinist without the state power and violence. I concluded that what was known as democratic centralism had to be identified for what it was, a reactionary way of organising which had arisen out of a specific period of a devastated and isolated Russia and when the international revolution of the working class was blocked.

In concluding that the method of organising known as democratic centralist had to be rejected, and that there had to be a much more collectivist culture and leadership, I also concluded that this could not be left to chance. I concluded there had to be a conscious and open stand taken against any one person or a couple of persons dominating. A healthy organisation as opposed to an unhealthy organisation had to take measures such as democratically deciding on who should give introductions to discussions, who should write documents, and who should do so based on striving to consciously develop a democratic collectivist internal life and culture and leadership. The same person doing introductions at every meeting, the same person writing all the major documents, the same male ego, or for that matter, female ego, ruling the roost, this way of working had to be openly discussed and opposed.

I came to look at the issue of a collectivist and diverse membership and leadership in this way. It could not be left to chance. Democratic decisions had to be taken keeping in mind the need to develop, to have a collective leadership, keeping in mind that different people should be selected to give introductions and write documents. I had already been doing this in the couple of years before I left Ireland as I prepared to leave. But with the crisis which erupted in the CWI and the split which resulted from this I then became more conscious of the need for this approach overall and conscious of the need to build a collective leadership.

I came to work consciously to apply the same approach to the issue of gender balance in the organisation at all levels. I concluded that domination of the organisation's leading bodies by males meant there was something wrong. I came to conclude that if this was the case, conscious specific action had to be taken to correct this. There had to be an open recognition that women in society, especially women workers in society, in general did not start from an even playing field, and that steps had to be taken to make up for this. I concluded that if it was the case that there was an uneven gender balance whether in the leadership or in the membership, that this had to be discussed and specific concrete action taken to correct this. There had to be an open and regular discussion and culture of increasing gender balance consciousness in the revolutionary organisation. This would involve the organisation being more conscious of the special oppression of women and fighting with more emphasis against this special oppression, and taking organisational steps to combat this special oppression within its own ranks. And along with this organisational steps to combat special oppression against those with different sexual orientations.

I came to conclude that while an exact one for one quota system was not essential that the gender balance had to be continually looked at and action taken to correct imbalance when necessary, to see that the process was moving in the correct direction. In contrast to this approach, the old CWI leadership said that capitalist society repressed women and it was idealistic to think that the revolutionary organisation would not reflect this. They came out with other statements which while correct in the abstract, but in the context in which they were being raised and the way in which they were being used, and by whom they were being used, were in fact just clever sounding phrases to cover the tracks of the male dominated leaderships. These leaderships would say that the tool, in this case the revolutionary organisation, did not resemble the product it was formed to bring into being. The hammer did not resemble the box it was used to nail together. These were alibis that the male-dominated leadership used to justify their refusal to take action to deal with the male domination of the organisation. This was a particularly insidious method of defending their hold on leadership. They were providing clever arguments which taken in the context of the organisation made it possible for members, especially the male membership to justify not conducting a struggle to change their own consciousness and conduct. In the small organisation that I was involved in setting up after my expulsion, *Labour's Militant Voice*, we recognised this as an important issue and before that organisation imploded, we were moving in this direction. In an effort to increase the consciousness on the need to fight against the fact that women members did not start from a level playing field we held a conference where all the introductions and all the summing ups were done by women members. Some sort of approach such as this is more important now than ever as fifty per cent of the world's factory workers are presently women. There will be no successful world revolution without women playing a leading role.

I moved to take the same approach to racial and ethnic imbalances in terms of organisation. There had to be open discussion on these also and how the racist and sexist and ethnic and national oppression and the divide and rule policies of capitalism on these issues put roadblocks in front of all minority groupings, in front of all specially oppressed groupings and made it more difficult for these groupings and people from these groupings to play an equal role in society and in organisations including revolutionary organisations. This weakened the working class in struggle. Such discussions would have to involve not just a head count of how many people of different gender and racial and ethnic backgrounds were in what positions in the revolutionary organisation and taking organisational steps to get a balance, it more importantly demanded clarification and discussion and decisions in relation to what struggles to take up to fight against racism and sexism, including the discrimination against people of different sexual orientations, and how to take up all these struggles, give more emphasis to all these struggles and as a result change for the better the composition and understanding and consciousness of the organisation on these fronts.

I came to conclude that the ongoing life and composition of the revolutionary organisation had to be continuously evaluated and guided. That from one meeting to the next, from one written document to the next, different people should be asked to write these documents. At each national and international meeting a democratic decision should be taken as to who would do the introduction at the next equivalent meeting, a democratic decision should be taken as to who would write the coming necessary document and documents. This would not necessarily mean that a different person would play such a role on every occasion but that the process should be one where there should be a consciousness of the need to organise in a way as to help all members of the organisation to develop and play the role including a leading role as their capabilities allowed. This would mean that every introduction to a discussion that every writing of a document would not necessarily be done by the most capable person. Thought had to be given to helping newer and less experienced people develop, giving them not just the room but also help them get the opportunity to develop. I came to believe that such an approach was necessary if a genuine collectivist organisation with a healthy internal life and a diverse, collective leadership and which realised the full potential of its membership was to be developed.

I also came to understand that for an open democratic internal life and for an organisation to be able to genuinely act collectively and democratically there had to be no secretive internal life. There might be a detail here or there that would have to be kept secret for security reasons. But the overall approach of the organisation had to be open. And not only open within its membership, but also open in its interaction with the working class. As Lenin said: the life of the party had to be made known to the 'people'.

This meant the revolutionary organisation had to continuously interact with, have a dialogue with, share its opinions and its differences with, and very importantly ask advice from, and listen to the working class periphery in which it worked. The revolutionary organisation had to have a practice of sending its members out consciously to ask its working class periphery its opinions on issues that were being discussed in the organisation. That is, genuinely have a dialogue with the working class, not just try to tell the working class what was what. When discussion and debate and differences developed in the revolutionary organisation, these had to be shared with and opinions had to be sought from the working class within which the organisation worked and struggled. In its healthy period the Bolsheviks printed their differences in their public papers and distributed these openly amongst the working class. In today's world the ideas discussions and debates of the revolutionary organisation have to be shared on the Internet and elsewhere. Given the development of the Internet and new communications systems they will be anyway whatever the wishes of the organisations involved.

Along with these methods, and this was also vital, there had to be the willingness to admit mistakes, in fact there had to be a determination to admit mistakes, in fact not just to 'admit' mistakes but to identify and explain mistakes and see that recognising and understanding mistakes were in fact essential to the development of an organisation. Mistakes were inevitable, this had to be understood, but not only that, mistakes, if recognised, were openings to allow the organisation to see more clearly. To paraphrase Joyce, mistakes, if responded to correctly could be portals of discovery. This was the only way the organisation could learn. If an organisation did not admit its mistakes it could not learn from them. On a regular basis the written material of the organisation should be read and discussed specifically from the point of view of seeing where the organisation had been wrong, not as tended to be the case to only be discussed to see where 'it was right'. Instead of what was the norm in the CWI and in all self-styled revolutionary groups where every meeting was dominated by congratulating itself on how correct it had been on everything since the last meeting, there needed to be a move at all levels to regularly discuss where the organisation's material and documents and predictions and programme and demands had been wrong in the previous period. This needed to be a permanent feature of the life of any revolutionary organisation. Cheerleading and continually clapping oneself on the back for how 'right' we were on everything was not the basis for building a healthy revolutionary organisation. Regular meetings to discuss the mistakes of the revolutionary organisation as well as its correct actions and ideas were essential.

Such an approach of course would, on occasion, bring the organisation into conflict with some egos, especially male egos. But I remembered what Trotsky had said in this regard. And I came to fight for this in my work. Trotsky had said that to be a strong revolutionary it was necessary to have a strong ego. But he had gone on to say that what was essential was that all egos be harnessed to the needs of the revolution and the revolutionary organisation. I understood this as saying that unless the egos were harnessed to the needs of the revolution and the revolutionary organisation then they would be continually in conflict and would be destructive to the revolutionary organisation and the revolution. I understood this to mean that unless the egos were harnessed to the needs of the revolution they would not be able to be brought together as a collective force to take the revolution forward.

To be able to harness the ego to the needs of the revolution and the revolutionary organisation demanded the ability to be self-critical. If the ego was such as to create all sorts of conflicts and lead its owner to think he or she knew everything and did not need to act collectively and listen to others and be self-critical, this had to be recognised. This did not mean always agreeing with others by any means, but it did mean listening to others in a genuine way. It also meant members looking at their own behaviour in a genuine and self-critical way. Were members lying around and doing nothing to help the revolution, were they strutting around arrogantly thinking that everything they did, just by the fact that it was they who did it, was helping the revolution, these were the kind of things had to be considered. I myself became more self-critical and more committed to listening to others and fighting for such a culture in my revolutionary work.

For me these were some of the general principles of what I came to see as a healthy method of organising. Some of the principles which I saw as replacing the rigid top down, over-centralised, undemocratic structures and culture and slate system of what was described as democratic centralism, and to be the foundation on which I increasingly came to build. But in doing so I also came to understand, as mentioned above, that internal life was like all things, not fixed. At different times, different balances were necessary. At times the balance of the organisation's resources had to be overwhelming directed towards discussion and clarification of the ideas, the programme, strategy and tactics. At other times the balance had to be in the direction of moving the resources into concrete action to either take the organisation forward in an offensive or to defend it and possibly retreat and hold itself together if it was on the defensive or under serious attack or threat of attack. It was as with everything in life, a dialectical living process. The ability to identify what period the organisation was in and what emphasis of internal life was necessary was essential to success. In the building of the revolutionary organisation there would have to be emphasis on giving all the opportunity to lead and develop. But there would be times such as a revolutionary situation when the organisation would have to act with what it had and whoever was the most capable would have to lead. Of course in saying this care would have to also be taken as the gender bias could also result in seeing who was the most capable in a biased manner. It would also be the case that great events would show great ability in people who until then would not have shown this ability and this would have to be recognised and room would have to be given for such people to play their full role. Great events could also show great weaknesses in people who had previously played leading roles. It was essential at all times to seek to identify the phase through which the organisation was passing and adjust.

In the years up to and after the split in the CWI, its worldview became more and more out of touch with reality. Therefore the internal balance that was necessary at that time was to open up the organisation and mobilise the entire membership in discussion and debate in order to correct and clarify the ideas and analysis. The organisation's internal life needed to be opened up to the greatest possible degree. Let a thousand ideas bloom should have been the approach. Mobilise the collective experiences and knowledge of the entire organisation to clarify the perspectives and ideas. More consciously listen to its working class periphery. To create the right atmosphere for this there would have had to have been full, unconditional admission of the major mistakes we had all made, especially the leading members and bodies of the organisation would have had to openly discuss and outline their mistakes and why they thought they had made them. This would have been necessary in order to encourage the greatest possible involvement of all of the membership to discuss these mistakes and the lessons of the past, to turn to the literature and experience of the movement, and develop a new world view. Think of how inspiring and encouraging it would have been for the entire membership, and in fact how it would have drawn in and more fully involved whole new layers of members, if the leadership of the CWI had openly and honestly and publicly announced that they had made serious mistakes and the organisation was now moving to an open and full and frank discussion on these mistakes, the reasons for them and how it was going to try and avoid then in the future. Rather than damaging the CWI this would have been enormously positive. It would have unleashed the energies and knowledge and input of the entire membership to a degree never experienced in the past. But not only that it would have drawn towards it the best elements in other revolutionary organisations and the many potential revolutionaries who would not join a revolutionary organisation because they saw the unhealthy internal lives of these organisations and organisations who thought they knew everything about everything. Now this would have been real leadership.

Instead of this happening, the opposite occurred. Driven by their own petty ambition, by their reactionary determination to hold on to their positions, the Taaffe/Walsh leadership and their followers combined to insist they had never made any mistakes and from this went on to clamp down on internal discussion. They had never made mistakes. It was all the fault of the Ted Grant/Alan Woods faction. This unprincipled, factional and personally ambitious response combined with the wrong worldview went on to shatter and demoralise the majority of the membership of the CWI. Instead of thousands of views flourishing and healthy, democratic and exciting debate erupting and the organisation being built anew, and on a much more healthy and democratic basis than in the past, where the ideas would be clarified and the internal life of the International made better than ever before, thousands of members walked away in demoralisation and disgust, and the International shattered into pieces. A similar process developed in the International Marxist Tendency which was the split off around Ted Grant and Alan Woods. When Ted Grant died, Alan Woods became the member who knew everything. He made just about every main speech, wrote just about every main article, saw women as unable to play a top leading role, the lot. Needless to say there was demoralisation and continual split offs and expulsions from that organisation also.

The split of the CWI was a step back. However having said this it does not mean that on every occasion a revolutionary organisation can avoid a split or should try to avoid a split. There are times when a revolutionary organisation is faced with a situation where it is best to split. For example if a revolutionary situation was developing and a significant section of the revolutionary organisation refused to see this and to face up to its responsibilities, then it could be justifiable to split the organisation to assemble as many forces as possible to take the revolution forward. Similarly if an ultra-left faction developed in a party and tried to take the working class into a premature clash with the capitalist class then it might be necessary for the revolutionary party to split to hold together as many forces as possible to hold the working class back to avoid it or its leadership being destroyed. There could also be a situation where an organisation could be so bureaucratic and undemocratic that internal debate and discussion was impossible, so in that situation also it could be necessary for the healthy democratic forces to split away. I came to see that no rigid formula was possible. What was necessary was to analyse the objective situation, the balance of forces, especially the consciousness of the working class, the relationship of the revolutionary organisation to the working class, all its layers, and along with this the resources and power of the revolutionary organisation and its chances to be able to take power and from this to decide on programme, strategy and tactics and also on the balance of internal life. For this to be achieved, a healthy democratic internal life was essential. Having said all this and having what I think is correct, bent the stick in the direction of criticising the false internal lives of the self-styled revolutionary groups of all stripes with their emphasis on leadership, it is necessary to see that at times, such as in a revolutionary situation the revolutionary organisation would have to assess its resources and its most capable and determined forces would have to provide the leadership and seek to take the revolution forward.

I was to come to understand the mistaken method of what was known as democratic centralism through a number of experiences. These included my struggle around the issue of the complaints of and about the leading member in the North which had taken place earlier. They included the split in the CWI and also my own expulsion from that organisation. Perhaps the most important general lesson I learnt was that all differences and debates had to be held openly and involve the entire membership and with all documents and alternative views open to the membership and also open to the working class. This was why when it became clear there was a significant difference between myself and the four other members of the minority faction with the rest of the International, we immediately and openly set up and publicly announced the formation of our faction and what we stood for. I did not make the mistake I had made before during the struggle around the accusations made against me by the leading member in the North when I had not conducted this struggle openly and throughout the entire membership of the CWI.

In concluding it was correct for myself and the other Comrades to form a faction at that time, I also concluded that I could see just about no occasion when it would be correct to ban factions. Factions were when groups within a party which agreed on the general policies of the party but had disagreement on this or that particular policy would come together on their own to discuss their difference or differences and organise to put them forward in the party. I concluded that it was incorrect and also in reality impossible to ban factions. If there were serious differences they would reflect themselves either as formal or informal factions or the issues involved would be insufficiently discussed and along with that there would be splits. The banning of factions even though the leadership of the CWI never said they were banned, they just made their existence impossible, or made up an excuse as they did in our case to expel us using the lie that we had broken so-called democratic centralism that is their commands, inevitably meant that the working class who were in touch with the organisation did not get the chance to consider the various views and opinions. This was a disservice to the working class, even a betrayal of the working class. It also meant that people with different views from the leadership of the CWI were given no choice by that leadership but to split from or resign from the CWI. When I and the other members of the Minority faction refused both of their 'offers', that is we would neither split or resign they were forced to expose themselves for what they really were and expel us. And expose themselves even further by denying myself and the other members of our faction our right to appeal.

It was not just the wrong world view, or the wrong internal life that led to the wrecking of the CWI. There was also another factor involved. And this was no small detail. In fact it was so strong that it was able to stand against the democratic tendencies and instincts of the members. This was the outright conscious corruption and ambition of a small number of members of the leadership of the organisation, represented by and organised in the clique around Peter Taaffe and Lynn Walsh. This was a corrupt clique. It stopped at nothing short of violence to get its way. It came close to that when, on one occasion, Peter Taaffe took a young female Comrade into a room and smashing his fists on the desk told her he would 'crush' (his word) her if she did not go along with his orders. Lies, slanders, secret meetings, secret organising, saying behind their backs that members who had given their whole adult lives to the CWI were passed it, useless, had stolen money. The majority of the leadership of what was left of the wreckage of the CWI had degenerated into a corrupt, undemocratic, bureaucratic clique. The crisis of the CWI was not just a wrong view of the world, not just an undemocratic internal life, not just the wrong method of so-called democratic centralism, it was also the existence of a corrupt, secretive clique around Peter Taaffe and Lynn Walsh.

While I had participated in the wrong method of so-called democratic centralism which was practiced in the CWI and is still practised in the CWI, and while I was and am partly responsible for the serious mistakes arising from this wrong method and balance, in my own defence and with complete certainty, I can say that I never took part in any of the secret, dishonest corrupt cliques and their slanders, lies and expulsions and denials of members' rights such as their right to appeal against their expulsion. This is proven by the fact that none of these secret cliques ever invited me to join them. These corrupt cliques did not trust me to be corrupt.

I remember the precise moment when I understood with absolute certainty that what was known as democratic centralism as practiced by the CWI and all left groups was a false method. I was denied my democratic right to appeal against my expulsion by the CWI leadership and I had been flyering CWI conferences and branches to demand my right to appeal against my expulsion. It was 1996. I was standing outside the Irish section's conference at the North Star Hotel in Dublin asking for my right to get in to appeal against my expulsion. Keeping me standing outside, the Irish leadership huddled amongst themselves and I presume phoned London and asked for their orders. The result was the decision not to let me in and to be heard. Just imagine that, I had been the first member of what was to become The Militant, later the Socialist Party that is the CWI, in the South of Ireland. I was the first full-time organiser of the CWI in Ireland as a whole. And I was not allowed into that conference to explain why I thought I should not be expelled and to appeal against my expulsion. There and then I fully and consciously decided that I would never again help to build an organisation like the CWI with its false method of organising known as democratic centralism. There and then I broke decisively and consciously and absolutely from the false method known as democratic centralism; there and then I was completely and absolutely convinced that so-called democratic centralism was a system of organising that leant itself to be, that tended to be, reactionary and rotten and corrupt; that instead of getting the best out of people it tended to get the worst out of people. I decisively broke from it, shook the dust of my feet and walked away.

As I carried out my struggle to get the right to appeal against my expulsion I travelled to different sections and contacted different members. One member of the International stood out at this time. Bill Webster who lived in Derry came to Chicago to see if what was being said about me was correct. Bill and I had been through a lot. We had flyered East Belfast in the teeth of the sectarian Ulster Workers' Council strike. It was Bill who had been with me when I discussed with the leading member in the North and strongly pointed out that member's responsibility to remain playing a central role in the organisation. And it was Bill who had said to me that that member would never forgive me for seeing him when he was wavering. When Bill came to Chicago to discuss with me about my expulsion and to see if what he had been told about me was correct, he concluded I was being lied about and slandered and went back to Ireland and resigned from the CWI. Bill was a principled man. It was not an accident that Bill was from an industrial trade union background. Bill's resigning in protest from membership of the CWI over how it acted in relation to myself did not prevent that organisation from claiming him as a loyal member when he died. That organisation would sink to any depths to try and enhance its reputation, even to claiming the body of a dead man whom had long since resigned in protest from its ranks. It was Joe Higgins who at Bill's funeral dishonestly claimed Bill for the CWI. The CWI and Joe Higgins could not even let a dead former Comrade be treated with honesty and respect. Even in death Bill exposed the false and corrupt method of the CWI.

The Irish section of the CWI held a conference around this time and one of the agenda items was my expulsion. I was not informed of this conference and so was not in attendance. This was part of the CWI denying me my right to appeal against my expulsion. The leading member in the North led a lying and slandering attack on me. Three members of the organisation at that time in Ireland opposed my and our faction's expulsion. They were Jimmy Kelly, Emmett Farrell and Martin Walsh. I appreciate their support.

When Bill had visited me in Chicago, he and I went to my favourite Jewish deli up in Highland Park. It was the early afternoon and as usual it was full of Jewish families, grandparents, mothers and children. I liked the life and energy. Bill did too. I said to him. 'Comrade' that is the way we addressed each other, 'Comrade, just think, the dirty Nazi degenerates who slaughtered little children like these and the millions of Jewish people and the Roma, the mentally and physically challenged people, anybody they did not think was a healthy member of the so-called Aryan race, and also the millions of socialists and communists German and non-German. Those Nazis were the scum of the earth.'

Bill looked up at me over our bowls of red cabbage soup. The tears came into our eyes and we wept silently for the slaughtered victims of the Nazis and their capitalist backers. There we were, an Irishman and an Irish-based Liverpudlian, weeping together for the victims of the Nazi capitalist-inspired slaughter, and specifically at that moment as we looked around us in that Jewish deli, we wept for the Jewish victims. Then we wiped our eyes and our weeping turned into a mixture of laughter and tears as Bill said: 'If you went round this place and asked people did they think that there could be two people, one an Irishman and another a Liverpudlian who lived in Ireland, sitting here crying about the fate of the Jewish people under the Nazis, they would never believe it.'

We drifted into silence. Then Bill said: 'Hey John, remember that day we went into east Belfast during the Ulster Workers' Council strike and gave out flyers against the UWC strike. We were calling for working class unity.' 'I do Bill,' I replied. I was proud I had been expelled. I was proud I had rejected the false method of what was called democratic centralism. Principled strong Comrades such as Bill respected me and the stand I had taken and this was what mattered above all.

My expulsion from the CWI and its denial of my right to appeal against that expulsion proved a number of things. The so-called democratic centralist method of the CWI had been shown to be unable to accommodate another point of view when that point of view was strongly fought for. It was shown to be unable to admit its mistakes. There could be no doubt about these realities. They were not just proven by my expulsion but they were proven by the many excellent people, former members of the CWI, excellent revolutionaries who had walked away from that organisation yet continued in their struggle against capitalism.

Out of the CWI I had to think about my expulsion and how to deal with this and my new position in the world. Had my work as a revolutionary socialist been a waste? Had my life been a waste? How did I go forward from there? How did I view what had happened? I drew some conclusions. The perspectives had been wrong and for this I was partially responsible. When this was proven we had to be honest and admit this. I did so and sought answers. But the majority of the IS with the exception of Roger Silverman and I, did not. Their response was to cover their tracks by amongst other things slandering me and driving me out, side-lining Roger Silverman, blaming Ted Grant. I could have gone along with their dishonesty and lies and corruption and been accepted. I did not. I had acted with principle and in what was the best interest of the revolution. This was the correct thing to do.

But what about all those years and work I had put in? I had no regrets about this either. I had helped spread socialist ideas in Ireland and internationally and this was a good thing. It was true these ideas were finding it hard to grow for the time being, but their day would come again and the contribution I had made would be a small help.

I kept my feet on the ground by reminding myself of how I had become a revolutionary in the first place, reminded myself of what I had decided that morning of 6th October, 1968, when I went to see Cathy Harkin in the walled city of Derry, that morning when the streets were strewn with rocks and bottles from the previous night's battle with the police. That morning when I had vowed that from then on, everything I saw I thought was wrong I would try to speak and organise against, and everything I saw I thought was right I would try to speak and organise for. That morning I had adopted these as my guiding principles and they remained my guiding principles. I had stood on these principles both inside and outside the revolutionary organisation that I had joined. I was satisfied with myself. These principles kept me going as I was being expelled from, slandered and lied about by the organisation to which I had given so much.

When I was expelled from the CWI I was written out of its history. But not only that. With the exception of a very few people with whom I was close friends and who were strong characters I was shunned by the members of that organization. These people also would be removed from the CWI in one way or another in the future. The truth was that the cultish tendencies that had existed in the CWI but had not become dominant then did become dominant. It became a cult. A cult around Peter Taaffe and in each section around the various chosen ones who were the chosen ones because they were prepared to take their orders from Peter Taaffe. Like other cults anybody who did not go along with the thoughts of its leader was driven out and shunned. It had become a cult and like all cults it was corrupt. And like all cults it sacrificed it members rights, it covered up abuses such as abuse against women members, in what it saw was the interest of the cult. I took my expulsion as a badge of honour.

My expulsion from the CWI was liberating. My struggle within and my expulsion from the CWI liberated me from the rigid, unconditional, unquestioning line and method of the CWI, and as a result I became much more flexible and capable in my thinking. I was able to continue as a revolutionary socialist and a more effective revolutionary socialist. My expulsion was inevitable because I stuck to my principles. I was proud that they had to expel me. They had to precisely because I stuck to my principles. I was partly in debt to my family for understanding the need to have principles and standing by these and for toughening me to be able to stand for my principles. Given the corruption of the CWI, my expulsion was the best thing that ever happened to me. My expulsion unshackled my experience and knowledge from the censorship, from the 'line' of the CWI. I became intellectually unshackled.

Of course this did not mean there was no down side. I had to try and follow events and keep an understanding of world events and how I should react to world events. I had to continue to be an active international revolutionary as world events unfolded and do so without the help of being part of an international organisation. It was not easy as I was very much isolated compared to my years in the CWI, when I would meet every three months in conferences with people from over thirty countries and hear reports and take part in discussions with people from these countries. I tried to deal with this problem by setting up a new revolutionary group with the other expelled members of the minority faction and some new young people we had met. We called ourselves Labour's Militant Voice (LMV).

CHAPTER 40

LABOUR'S MILITANT VOICE

L ABOUR'S MILITANT VOICE was to be short-lived. That it came about at all was a tribute to the tenacity of those of us who had been expelled from the CWI and our determination to build a revolutionary nucleus. It was correct to fight for this objective, it never occurred to me not to, but there were too many factors working against LMV to allow it to develop. No longer a full-time organiser for the CWI, I no longer received any income. I wanted to continue to do some work for a time in North America to try and help establish a new nucleus, so gathering together some money I bought an old pick-up truck and went to work moving furniture, art and antiques. Through my battle to make a living moving furniture with this old pick-up truck, through my lying in hospital beds fighting to stay alive as my health worsened, through my struggle to keep my spirit and humour intact, I did not stop my work of trying to build a revolutionary nucleus. This remained the centre of my life. I bared my teeth, swore at capitalism, at the labour bureaucracy, at the bureaucracy in the CWI, and maintained my struggle.

But I was doing so with a different emphasis. I was giving attention to learning the lessons of the past. I moved on from what was my tendency before, which was, through the force of sheer will and by repeating a few basic ideas, to recruit and build. With LMV I set about seriously examining the work I had done in the past and the mistakes made. Not that all my work had been made up of mistakes but a balance sheet had to be put together and conclusions drawn. This was the importance to me of LMV. It was a transition into a new, more reflective, approach to my work, a transition to a new period when I sought to look at the lessons of the past and draw conclusions and work in a more effective way. This was done not by retreating into study, but by remaining involved in struggles while at the same time continually seeking to examine and draw conclusions from these struggles.

To this end myself and the other members of LMV took a hard look at our work and set out our priorities. These were continuing to intervene in the working class movement, to look at these interventions not only with a view to building, but also to see what mistakes we had made in the past, what mistakes we had not made and make the necessary adjustments to our work. To intervene in the movement we needed a public face. To this end we produced a small journal which we called *Labour's Militant Voice*. Richard set up a Blog and we called it and our other Internet profiles 'Facts for Working People'. We selected this name so it would have no traces of the sectarianism and ultra-leftism that put working people off, names such as revolutionary this and revolutionary that. This was one of the corrections we made to our work. We wanted to be sure we moved away from sectarianism and ultra-leftism. There were two kinds of sectarianism. One was the sectarianism of putting the imagined interests of the revolutionary group above that of the working class, not putting the interests of the working class foremost. The other was the internecine squabbles amongst the self-styled revolutionary groups. We moved to avoid both.

For a while, LMV survived. However, in spite of our best efforts we could not overcome the major problems we faced. We were forming our tiny group when the capitalist offensive was still at full tide and when the world balance of forces were moving further in the direction of capitalism. Along with this we were still bruised from our battle in the CWI. And we were isolated in one country. But we did not hesitate. We turned outwards to try and hold what we had and to build. As we did so and as we drew conclusions from this work we were able to rescue out of our years of work a small nucleus of a few people. This was the importance of LMV. It was a bridge toward a healthy questioning nucleus, to a nucleus which saw as central to its existence the clarifying of our ideas and methods of work, a bridge towards a more healthy method of work.

In my old days in the CWI, I and the CWI thought we I knew everything and were always right on everything. My experience going through the wrecking of the CWI and in building the LMV made me see I did not know everything. Realising I did not know everything allowed me to know more than I did before. It was a liberating experience, a big step forward. But it came, as all important progress does, through struggle, steps forward and steps back. It was an exciting and also a challenging time. It was also not easy.

The strongest base of LMV was with Richard and his roots in his local 444 of the union the American Federation of State Council and Municipal Employees' in the Bay Area of California. John Reimann also had a union base in the Bay Area in the carpenters' union. We were further strengthened in the Bay Area when Rob Rooke moved there and became active also in the carpenters' union. Through this we were able to play a leading role in a carpenters' strike.

5,000 construction workers walked off the job. Workers marched from one site to another closing them down. The huge site at San Francisco airport was closed. This strike won increased pensions. The leading role played in this strike by Rob Rooke and John Reimann showed that we had retained our fighting spirit. The strike was sparked off when union members stormed and occupied a union meeting. This was led by Rob Rooke and based on his experience working in the Ontario Coalition Against Poverty and their direct action methods. This strengthened the direct action aspect of our work, no longer just patient explanation and discussing in ones and twos, but also direct action where we had the resources.

However, we were not able to build new forces for LMV out of the important role we played in this strike. The main reason for this was the overall objective situation. That is, the mood in the world and in the working class and youth at that time. As far as the left movement and as far as our tiny group was concerned, the consciousness of the working class was an objective factor. Meaning that the way the working class looked at things was being shaped by major world events, the world economy, the fact that most workers in the US were still getting by, the collapse of the Soviet Union, the refusal to lead of the union leaders. These events convinced the working class it could not bring about a socialist revolution or even in most cases wage successful struggles. This objective situation and the consciousness that flowed from it was not such as to allow us to convince the relatively well paid carpenters whom we were able to get involved in this strike that revolution was necessary and to join our tiny revolutionary organisation.

But there was another reason we were not able to build out of the leading role we played in this strike. We were not able to run a candidate from the strike in the local city elections which followed the strike. John Reimann, who had been the elected leader of the strike committee, and who had been living in the area for many years, was the obvious candidate. But after initially agreeing to run he pulled out, stating unilaterally and undemocratically to the rest of us in LMV that the issue was not up for discussion. He instead and incorrectly made a priority out of trying to use legal action to get back into the union from which he had been expelled for his role in the strike. He did not succeed with this legal action and remained expelled from the union. Rob Rooke, in spite of playing a similar, if not even more important role, in initiating the strike by leading the direct action which broke up the meeting of the union leadership which was making the concessions to the bosses, was not expelled from the carpenters' union.

Some of us in LMV drew lessons from this experience. One was that the work of John Reimann in his union was ultra-left. His personal position left him in a better economic position than most of the other carpenters in his union and so he tended to ask them to make sacrifices he could afford to make because of his better economic position but which they could not afford to make. This tended to isolate him in his union.

This strike showed that there were still opportunities for our work. This was confirmed by the battle around the World Trade Organisation meeting in Seattle in 1999. The union leaders brought some of their members on to the streets for what they intended to be a peaceful gathering to let off steam. They were joined by hundreds of young people, who had been organising in loose, decentralised, anti-capitalist groupings. These were mainly anarchist type groups. They were the types of stirrings amongst the youth I had been pointing to and trying to get the Labour Militant to turn to before I was expelled. The leadership of Labour Militant instead sat in the dying LPA. So they missed this important development. They missed putting down roots in the new stirrings of the youth and they missed the battle of Seattle. This was a very serious mistake the Labour Militant majority made. This also meant they missed being able to put down roots amongst these youth which would have allowed them to play a role later in the Occupy movement.

In Seattle the youth and sections of the workers united and physically fought the police in street battles. This terrified the union leaders. It was there that Sweeney, the leader of the AFL-CIO got down on his knees on the platform and prayed. No doubt asking his god to help him undermine his own members' struggle. You need to use your imagination to think about the kind of mentality and political ideas of this union leader, this leader of millions of workers in the economically and militarily most important country in the world, that he would do this. Tens of thousands of union members and youth were fighting the cops to close down the meeting of the World Trade Organisation which represented the major forces of world capitalism and was meeting to further plan the offensive against the international working class, and thousands of workers and youth were fighting against this on the streets. And what did he do?! He got down on his knees and prayed for his members to stop! It reminded me of the union leader in Dublin, when at the head of Ireland's biggest ever workers' march, instead of giving a fighting lead to the workers, she sang the song *One Day at a Time Sweet Jesus*. Like with Sweeney and his praying in Seattle, these were examples of religious ideas, in her case singing a religious song, in his case praying, blocking the workers' struggle.

LMV did not have the resources to intervene in this struggle in Seattle. We could only observe and try and draw conclusions. And this is what we did. The main conclusion we drew was that in spite of our tiny resources we had to try to get involved in these type of movements especially of the anti-capitalist youth. We also strengthened our conclusions that where we had the resources we had to build in ones and twos and where possible help build squads of fighting workers amongst rank and file union members and workers in the workplaces. This was the alternative to the pro-capitalist union leadership like the Sweeney's.

The Seattle events were accompanied by a movement of youth throughout the country. It went under various names. The Direct Action Network, Action Councils, Rising Tide, later the Occupy movement. All these names were indicative of spontaneous struggle from below. These were the stirrings from below of which I had been speaking. The Occupy name came out of the increasingly used tactic of occupying various capitalist institutions and events. This movement, mainly of anarchists, threw up the idea of targeting the 1%, that is the rich. That is to fight against the 1% and fight instead for the interests of the 99%. This way of posing the issue, that is targeting the 1%, corresponded to the consciousness of sections of the youth and the working class and was to enter into the mass consciousness being used by rank and file working class people throughout the country as they moved into struggle.

This slogan, that is opposition to the 1% increased mass consciousness against the rich. The anarchist-type groups which came up with this way of posing the issue deserve the credit for doing so. This slogan increased class consciousness in relation to the role of the rich in ruling the country and this was good. However it did not raise consciousness in relation to the ability of the working class to overthrow the 1% and run the country. Neither did the form of direct action advocated by these groups raise the consciousness about the need for the working class as a class, and the ability of the working class as a class being the only force that could change things fundamentally. These youth groups did not seek to involve the working class, instead sought to mobilise the more middle class youth and also to avoid articulating demands such as for better wages, free health care, free education, affordable housing etc. Such demands would have tended to draw into struggle layers of the working class.

Nevertheless opposition to the 1%, mobilise the 99%, were slogans which took the movement forward at that stage. They were positive transitional slogans for the time as they linked with the existing consciousness and helped bridge the gap, make the transition, between that consciousness and the understanding of the role played by the ruling minority elite who controlled the country. This slogan was not developed by the self-styled revolutionary left, neither of the so-called Stalinist, Soviet or Maoist variety, or the so-called Trotskyist variety. It was developed by the newly developing anarchist type groups. The long established self-styled revolutionary, self-described Marxist groups were too rigid and stuck in the past, too ultra-left and sectarian, too inflexible to develop this slogan.

Neither was it developed by the old CWI nor our own LMV. Another conclusion we in LMV drew out of this was to be less sectarian to other groups and listen more. And also give more thought to the existing consciousness and to avoid being ultra-left. 'Down with the 1%' was a lot more accessible to the existing consciousness of the working class than the idea of nationalising the commanding heights of the economy.

I gave more thought to how to relate to and intervene in movements. I concluded that every movement for change was assaulted by different forces, came under different pressures. There were of course the capitalist forces and their agencies and the pro-capitalist union bureaucracy. But also every movement for change was threatened by the ideas of ultra-leftism, political sectarianism and opportunism. I came to examine every movement against this background, came to seek to stand against these threats and also to identify which of these threats was most dominant at any given time.

Ultra-leftism was putting in front of the working class demands, strategies and tactics which that movement could not see as achievable. The result was that instead of helping the movement go forward, a roadblock was created in the path of the movement. I concluded that I had to give more thought to the consciousness, assess what was possible and base myself on this, try to take the movement forward on this basis. This did not mean never raising the issue of capitalism, of the need to end capitalism, but what it meant was that if the movement was not ready to end capitalism, but was ready to strike a blow at the attacks of capitalism, then it was ultra-left to try and commit the movement to ending capitalism. The latter could be raised, it could be explained that in the last analysis this would have to be faced up to but in the meantime a united front of forces to take on capitalism's attacks would be an important step forward. It would increase the understanding of the working class and strengthen the movement of the working class.

It took the new movement of mainly anarchist youth from below, to develop these concepts of the 1% and the 99% which corresponded to the consciousness of large sections of the US working class at that time. These conceptions entered the mass consciousness of the working class and changed this mass consciousness for the better. They increased anti-capitalist consciousness. They went a small way to challenging the capitalist offensive. We in LMV recognised this reality, were self-critical in doing so, recognising that we had not developed the 1% slogan. In recognising this we took another step forward in learning the lessons from the past, into a new and more exciting future for our small nucleus, towards having a healthier, more self-critical internal culture.

Arising out of the events of the WTO battle in Seattle, a movement took shape around the country. In Chicago where I was spending time, up to 200 people met regularly for a period. They called themselves the Direct Action Network. (DAN) I was still healthy enough to play a role in this. Just about all left groups and individuals were drawn in. There were also some workers from community struggles. The trade union movement with its 320 locals in the Chicagoland area and its half a million members affiliated through their unions to the Chicago Federation of Labour was blocked by its leadership from participating in this. It was absent as usual. DAN involved itself in protesting the World Trade Organisation and global capitalism and in taking up local issues such as attacks on public education.

In the middle of these events the World Trade Centre was hit. The timing was very suspicious and very helpful for US imperialism which wanted to create a mood at home to allow it to invade central Asia, seize its resources, contain Russia and China and increase repression and cut the living standards of its own working class at home. Some sections of the US ruling class had, at the very least, some prior knowledge of the attacks on the Twin Towers and the Pentagon and allowed them to go ahead. US imperialism understood that they had to take on their own working class. Along with creating the mood for war and invading central Asia, the Twin Towers events allowed the US ruling class to put increased resources into its state apparatus at home for this purpose. This became evident when the Occupy and anti-racist and anti-police violence movements developed later. Immediately, these were met with tens of thousands of cops in full body armour and military vehicles. These did not develop overnight. They had been prepared in the previous years. Many of the vehicles had previously been used in places like Afghanistan where US imperialism was fighting for its interests and these were then brought home to push through the attacks of US imperialism on its own working class and youth. The decisive sections of US capitalism knew they had to cut the living standards of their own working class if they were to be able to afford their world role and had been preparing their state apparatus for this task.

In the Direct Action Network in Chicago some youth tried to commit DAN to supporting the attacks on the twin towers in spite of the 3,000 people dead, the mainly 3,000 US workers who were dead. This was another example of ultra-leftism. I took the lead in most strongly opposing this approach. On behalf of LMV I proposed that DAN should condemn the attacks, condemn those who carried them out, but make clear the reality of who and what were ultimately responsible for these attacks: this was the foreign policies of the US government which were dictated by the major US and other corporations which, by looting and repressing the Middle East, had fuelled the fires of anti-US sentiments and anti-US organisations in that area.

The US corporations were robbing the world, and especially the Middle

East. They were supporting the most reactionary ruling classes throughout all the underdeveloped countries and condemning the majority of the world's population to poverty and repression. These policies created rage against US imperialism and out of this and with the help of related sinister forces came the Twin Tower attacks. I explained that the way to stop such attacks and to have security for the US population and the world's population was to halt the plundering and wars against and occupations of the Middle East and the former colonial countries by US and world Imperialism.

I also proposed that DAN, while taking this explanation out to the youth and working people should link the plundering of the Middle East and other super exploited countries by the US corporations, to the attacks on the US working class by these same corporations. And from this try to unite the working class in the Middle East and the US and internationally for a struggle against the corporations and their profit-addicted, capitalist system, and on these policies seek to build a united front of mass direct action struggle. With the help of some other experienced activists this policy at least formally was to become the policy of DAN in Chicago.

The old organisation from which I had been expelled was still in a state of semi-demoralisation as its LPA strategy was failing and so it was not able to intervene in DAN. The CWI leadership had to eventually move against this rightward movement of that group. This did not stop them continuing their attacks on me by condemning my participation in DAN which was one of the largest youth movements for decades. Their two Chicago members were not able to work in this living movement of youth and workers so as part of their continued slandering of me they condemned me for doing so and for putting forward these policies.

In the course of this work I met some young people. Two of these, a young woman and a young man temporarily joined LMV and gave it some extra resources. We were hanging on to existence by a thread. But we were learning, we were fine-tuning our approach.

Around this time we heard of a change in tax policy over the state border from Chicago in Indiana. Taxes on the corporations were being reduced and those on households increased. We travelled down to intervene. There was a meeting of around 700 people in a school auditorium when we arrived. The speakers on the platform were the same politicians who had voted for the pro-corporation tax change. They were trying to obscure and justify their role. Nobody was challenging them. It was a time to put up or shut up. I stood up in the meeting and began to shout over the speakers on the platform so everybody could hear me. 'You voted for these changes. Tell the people that. You should not be up there. You voted to reduce the taxes on the corporations and increase them on the working people. Let working people speak.' People started to shout support for what I said and some also began to shout against the platform speakers. My intervention turned around the mood of the meeting. I had a hard neck on me, a revolutionary socialist Irishman shouting in a school auditorium in a small suburb in Indiana.

Over a few weeks we were able to get support to take up the slogan 'Can't Pay Won't Pay' in relation to the tax increases on working people. We led a small movement for direct action against the forces and people who had voted for the tax change, where we could we named these people. We picketed their homes, neighbourhoods, workplaces, businesses, churches and clubs, giving out flyers explaining what they had done. We called for all contact with those who supported the tax changes to be cut off. That is that they should not be served in shops, gas stations, restaurants, repairs should not be done to their homes, to their automobiles etc. In other words we called for a boycott of all who had supported the tax change. Or in other words a complete withdrawal of all labour from the people and class who had made the tax change. We were, in effect, calling for selective targeted strike action. We also organised a car caravan through the area with the slogan 'Can't Pay Won't Pay'. We won a small improvement in the tax changes.

While our work in the 1% movement and the DAN movement had helped us develop a better understanding of the importance of and the way in which to stand against ultra-leftism, the work in Indiana helped us and LMV develop more experience in, and fine tune our understanding of what was known as united front work. And as part of this, helped us to be more conscious of the need to, and the way to stand against ultra-leftism and sectarianism. United front work is where forces and individuals from different backgrounds, with different political views on other issues, can come together and fight together on one or two common issues. We proposed and won support for a united front against the tax increases around the slogan 'Can't Pay Won't Pay', and for direct action to fight for this. No lobbying of the Democrats or the Republicans, but mass direct action. We did not question whether the people involved in the 'Can't Pay Won't Pay' united front were Democrats or Republicans or anything else. This would have created a road block to building a united front movement. The criteria for being part of the united front we were able to build, was did people support the 'Can't Pay Won't Pay' position, and very importantly, did they support the tactic of mass direct action to win this. Our experience in this struggle helped us to better understand how to build united fronts and bring different forces together, how to stand against ultra-leftism and sectarianism which made successful united front work impossible.

Around this time there was a movement in California to defend public education and to oppose any increase in student tuition. This also involved united front work and given the large numbers of left groups in California, also involved a serious struggle against sectarianism, ultra-leftism and also opportunism. We held regular conference calls between myself in Chicago and other LMV members in California and worked out our policy and demands. No cuts of any kind in education, no increase in tuition, these were our main demands, the demands of the united front direct action movement we sought to build. These demands recognised the existing consciousness of the movement and the need to take that movement forward. State-wide demonstrations were planned for 4th March. The union leaders had seen this movement develop and were moving to take it over and make it acceptable to their Democratic Party pals, that is, to get it to accept cuts in education spending and an increase in tuition. We moved to prevent this by setting up alternative centres of struggle. On my proposal, we called them March 4th committees.

The idea was that these democratically elected committees would be made up of representatives of the students and parents and all workers in education. And with this composition would have a chance of preventing the movement being dragged into the bureaucratic structures controlled by the union leadership, who worked under the orders of the Democratic Party leadership. We successfully led the movement to set up these committees in some different areas of the state. We were helped in this struggle when Richard got a resolution along these lines passed by his local. It was referred to as the Mellor resolution.

However not only did we have just about no real resources to conduct our struggle. We had many different forces against us. The most powerful of these was the trade union leadership and their concessionary, and opportunist policies. This concessionary and opportunist approach of the trade union leaders was based on the idea that there was no alternative to capitalism and as a result they were always looking for a way to defang and demobilise any movement of struggle. On practically every occasion they sought to do this by advocating concessionary policies. That is, by taking any opportunity they could find to concede to the employers and the system, of course by doing so they sold out the interests of the workers and students.

This movement to defend education in California was not successful. Its defeat was caused more than anything by the refusal of the trade union leaders to mobilise the hundreds of thousands of members in its ranks and link these in struggle with the hundreds of thousands of students and parents and community activists to defeat the tuition increases and any cuts in education. The movement from below was against the attacks on education, the union leadership were caught between this and the push by the capitalist class to cut education spending. This is where the concessionary policies of the trade union leadership came in. They intervened to undermine the movement to defend education, that is, to block the movement from below from defeating the attacks. The union leadership used their resources to contain the movement to what was acceptable to the capitalist forces. Some of the self-styled revolutionary groups, which in other cases would be ultra-left or sectarian, joined the opportunist union bureaucracy and covered up its role. Opportunism, that is, undermining the struggle of the working class and youth against capitalism, capitulating to the attacks of the capitalist offensive was not confined to that of the trade union bureaucracy.

In this struggle we also had to deal with the sectarian policies of most of the left groups who were involved in the movement. Their priority was not to win the struggle, their priority was to use the movement to recruit new members, that is to say, they put what they saw as their own interests above the interests of the struggle. This was the essence of left sectarianism. Every action, from where a demonstration should be held, every demand no matter how small and detailed, was fought for by these different sectarian groups from their own sectarian point of view, in other words, from what they thought would best allow them to recruit new members to their group.

We in LMV came out more clearly than ever before and spoke against this left sectarianism and also ultra-leftism where it appeared, and watched carefully that we ourselves did not practice these false methods. I spoke openly of how I had been left sectarian in the past and how this had been damaging for the movement. We called out the other groups and individuals on this and asked them to join us in struggling to change the movement and defeat left sectarianism and ultra-leftism. Unfortunately while this approach attracted a few people into the ranks of LMV we were not successful in preventing this scourge from damaging the movement.

This was the first campaign in which we became fully conscious of the need to openly identify and campaign against left sectarianism. Before we had tried to ignore the left sectarian groups dismissing them all as 'sects'. But this meant we were allowing sectarianism to continue unchallenged. This approach meant we were in reality ignoring left sectarianism, not fighting left sectarianism and the damage it did to the movement. Our new approach of explaining how we in the past had been left sectarian, of now identifying and naming left sectarianism, not attacking the left sectarian groups individually, but identifying and attacking the scourge of left sectarianism in general wherever it existed, and from this taking up an open struggle against this sickness, was an important step forward for us.

Through LMV we also intervened in a struggle in Alameda in the Bay Area of California, to defend Section 8 tenants from losing their homes. Eighty families were involved. We advocated and organised direct action. By targeting and picketing the homes and businesses and churches of people who were involved in taking these decisions we were successful in defending the homes of these families. This was an important achievement and an extremely important gain for these families in their daily lives. Along with the small improvement in the tax changes we had gained in Indiana this showed that our method of struggle could have victories, that even in this climate of the capitalist offensive, gains could be made. We pointed out what could have been possible if the union leaders, with control of the apparatus of the unions had been prepared to fight.

Around this same time we also organised small but successful struggles in Los Angeles. We helped low-paid, mainly women, garment workers organise and through direct action get better pay and conditions. We also opposed racist material on a shop front and forced the owner to take this down.

We also intervened in the catastrophe of Katrina, the hurricane in New Orleans. We were still able to afford a full-time organiser at that time and this person went to New Orleans, slept in a tent and helped people get re-housed. This person was a good fighter and became prominent and respected in the struggles there. In the other areas where we existed we raised and got support for the displaced people in New Orleans. We helped and intervened in this way to the extent our resources allowed. However this was not all that was to come out of the correct decision we took to send our full-time organiser to intervene in the New Orleans area around Katrina.

As is always the case when big events such as Katrina take place, the revolutionary movements and groups are challenged: is their way of working correct, do they have to change their way of working, their slogans, demands, etc. The result of the effect of big events can be positive or negative and in many cases both. In the case of LMV and Katrina it was both. While the intervention in Katrina clarified the pluses and negatives in our small nucleus and some of us were able to grow from this and this was positive, the negative was that it led to the end of the nucleus of the LMV.

It came about this way. The balance of the work of the full-time member in New Orleans became a subject of discussion and eventually debate. Along with others, I felt while the full-time member there was doing very good work in helping people get re-housed and helping build the wider movement and intervening in a non-sectarian manner, he was insufficiently paying attention to another aspect of the work. Yes he was helping the general movement, helping people getting re-housed, but there were also many people from around the country who had travelled to New Orleans to help and who were also looking for a way to fight the existing society. There were of course also the many New Orleans residents who had seen the way that capitalism had treated them, was treating them and were enraged and who were open to an anti-capitalist explanation. I felt that the full-time member we had there did not sufficiently seek out these most conscious activists in the movement who wanted to take the fight further and explain to them the ideas of revolutionary socialism and build our small revolutionary group within the overall larger united movement, build the revolutionary nucleus. We had a number of discussions on this issue. There was no agreement as the full-time member remained convinced of his position. So we decided to have a discussion on the issue at a coming LMV conference.

John Reimann, one of the leading members in LMV, a member who had been a full-time organiser in the CWI and had played a positive role there and who had up until that time played a positive role in building the LMV, this member demanded that he should be the one to debate this issue with this full-time member. Others like Richard Mellor and myself, while in agreement with John Reimann on the general issue, disagreed with him being the person to debate with the full-time Comrade. We had experience of this member's tendency to go for the jugular in debates. To seek to show he was correct rather than clarify the issues and to seek if possible to unite around an agreed position.

We were making a real effort to learn the lessons from the past. One of these lessons was the need to discuss issues with the entire membership and also to discuss issues, especially differences in a comradely tone. With the exception of this member, there was agreement on the need for a comradely tone. We also wanted to convince the full-time member of what we thought was the right approach without destroying his morale. However this other member said he did not give a 'f**k' about the full-time member's morale. The majority of us opposed this member being the person to debate with our full-time member who had been in New Orleans.

As this issue was developing we were considering how to deal with what we considered other mistakes we had made in the past. One was paying insufficient attention to fighting sexism, and from this the need in LMV to have a better gender balance at all levels of the organisation. We held a conference at which it was decided that all the speakers would be women members. We also put gender equality higher on our agenda and consciousness. We stated our objective was to achieve as close to a 50/50 gender balance at all levels of the organisation as possible. We said if we were not showing signs that we were moving significantly in this direction then we would have to consider and discuss if we were working properly and make greater efforts to focus on correcting our work on this front.

We also saw that the most experienced people in LMV were mostly, though not all, older white males. We moved to try and change this by having more campaigns and involvement in the struggles against sexism, racism, mass incarceration, police brutality and violence against women. We had experience in these fights, including the fight against racism and mass incarceration through past campaigns with young prisoners with whom we had worked. One of these became a leader of a gang truce in the California prisons and another one of them died in the electric chair. We concluded that to the extent we had the resources, we had to try and step up the emphasis of our work on these issues. It was thought that campaigns on such issues would increase the consciousness of LMV on these issues and also bring into our little group more people from these backgrounds and struggles.

We also thought more about the actual overall concept of leadership. We concluded that leadership in the past had been thought to be too much as teaching the membership. We looked at ways to change this by trying to have more young members in leading positions and doing more of the speaking at conferences etc., and having a more collective leadership. I reminded myself and others that when I had joined Militant in Ireland I did many introductions at meetings, and many of these introductions were to put it kindly, less than adequate. But this was part of how I developed. I looked to give newer less experienced members in LMV the same opportunities I had when I joined in Ireland. I was given these opportunities by chance rather than by design. It was that we were just beginning then in Ireland, there were not experienced members there and by luck we were distant from the leading people in London. If I had joined in London I would not have had the opportunity to develop in the way that I had in Ireland as the more experienced people there would have tended to fill the space into which I was able to develop in Ireland. Drawing conclusions from this experience I at this time as we tried to build LMV said that I did not want to run for the leading committee, it was called the coordinating committee, to give more room to younger and especially women members to be elected.

We moved to try and correct what we saw as weaknesses in LMV many of which were hangovers from the time some of us had spent in the CWI. This meant changes in the roles of especially the older and more experienced members. However as we did so, our actions were misinterpreted by the member who demanded that he be the one to debate the member who had been working in Katrina. As a result new and very serious tensions arose. This member was unable to see the needs of the organisation as a whole and to subordinate his ego and ambition to those needs.

He opposed the changes we proposed to try and counter the effects of the reality that the playing field was slanted against women members both within society and within LMV. He opposed LMV holding the conference at which only women members would do the introductions and concluding remarks at all the sessions. He said these measures and the measures we were taking to bring more younger and more women members on to the leadership, to build a more diverse leadership, were directed at pushing him out of the leadership and out of the organisation. This was untrue as all the rest of us older European American male members, including myself, were stepping back to try to make room for newer and younger members and more women members in the leadership.

Ignoring this reality this member insisted there was a 'cabal', his word, working to push him out of LMV. He also interpreted the opposition to him being the person to debate the full-time member on his work in New Orleans as him being pushed out of LMV. He refused to see that we were trying to improve the workings of the organisation and learn the lessons from the past and this inevitably meant change. The accusation that we were trying to push him out was shown to be incorrect by amongst other things, the fact that after the carpenters' strike we wanted him to run for election to the city council.

This member had many good qualities. He had a lot of energy and drive, a knowledge of theory and history, a willingness to challenge long-accepted ideas. However, as all of us did, he had negative qualities. For example one of my negative qualities is that I have a tendency to focus too much on the organisational. I was helped in combating this weakness when I was expelled and we as a small nucleus had to rely on our own resources to develop perspectives and theory. This other member's weakness was he was ultra-left in his union work as was shown by the fact that after decades of work he was expelled but could not fight this as he had no base in what had been his union local over decades.

Another weakness of this member was on the issue of tactics in relation to working in the movement or working with other people on the left. Rather more than a weakness on tactics it was that he did not seem to even consider that the issue of tactics existed. He had one tactic. This was to approach any movement or individual and seek out some mistake they were making, or that in his opinion they were making, and hammer this to death. Never seek to see on what points there might be agreement and then seek to build on these and on the issues there was disagreement, discuss these in a comradely manner and see if these differences could be resolved, or if not lived with. This approach of this member would result in his being isolated in and cut adrift from every grouping he would seek to work with in the future.

One other serious weakness this member had was a very over-developed and unharnessed ego, combined with a sectarian personality. During the years when the CWI was growing and gaining strength, it had a lot of authority. And I, as the main person of the CWI covering North America, also had authority. This restrained these negative qualities of this member. But as the CWI collapsed so did its authority and so did mine. The result was that this member's ego and sectarian personality exploded into the vacuum that developed. The weakened authority of the CWI and of myself was no longer capable of harnessing this member's ego, or restraining his sectarian personality or preventing him from exercising his wrong approach to working with other people and forces.

This member became convinced that he should play the leading role in LMV and he pushed to make this happen. This, at a time when the rest of us were pushing for nobody to play the leading role, instead to develop a collective leadership which would be newer and younger and more diverse. Along with this because of his weaknesses he was not capable of playing the leading role. Due to the political and organisational conclusions stated above, and the health problems of Richard and I which were getting worse, there was nothing we wanted and needed more than new and younger people to play leading roles.

Richard and I wanted a collective leadership with a newer and more diverse composition. We were opposed to one person playing the 'leading' role. But we could not convince this member of our views. Richard and I had many discussions to try and convince him that he was not being pushed out. The reality was that his struggle against allegedly being pushed out was a struggle by him to take over the leadership of LMV. Not fully knowing himself what he was actually doing, he became very confused.

In spite of insisting he was being driven out of the organisation, he announced he would not run for election to the new coordinating committee of LMV. Richard and I pleaded with him repeatedly to change his mind and to run for election. He was much physically healthier than either Richard or I, we also wanted to decisively convince him he was not being pushed out of the organisation so we discussed with him again and again to try to convince him to stand for election to the coordinating committee. This was exhausting. At the last minute he agreed. The election took place. He was not elected. He had undermined his own position in the group. Then, while at the same time complaining about not being elected, he announced that he had not voted for himself. His behaviour undermined his credibility.

The discussion was still going on about the intervention in Katrina. This member continued to demand that he do the lead-off in the debate with the full-time member over his intervention there. When we did not agree, he said he would not come to the conference unless he got his way. He put a gun to our head. We could not tolerate this blackmail. We said so. He refused to concede. We still wanted him in the group so we voted to suspend him for six months and have a discussion then, when hopefully things would have cooled down and also have become more clear. He refused to discuss at the end of the six-month period and as a result took the decision to have nothing more to do with LMV. The role played by this member over this period was one of the factors that led to the end of LMV.

Another member played a significant part in the ending of the LMV. This was Rob Rooke, a member, a carpenter, he had played a leading role in the carpenters' strike and was still active in his union. He fought the bosses. He was not ultra-left in his union work. These were strong points that he had. However his weakness was that he was not prepared to conduct a struggle when necessary within the revolutionary nucleus. He saw the other members of that nucleus as his friends and wanted always to be friends and to be liked by these people. It is good to be friends. It is good to be liked. But these factors have to be seen in context. It is more important to be prepared to fight for the ideas you think are correct. Not in a sectarian way, but in a firm way. Richard and I stood firm on our positions, how to work, how to fight racism, and others. This member wanted no part of this struggle. He opted out. By doing so he played a significant role in destroying the nucleus of the LMV. This member would later re-join the CWI which had expelled and abused him verbally in the most dirty way. I discussed with him and said I had no problem with him rejoining the CWI as long as he did so on a principled way. That is by insisting they discuss their disgraceful action in covering up the abuse of one of their female members by a male member. By discussing how he himself had been told that if he was prepared to blame myself for all the problems of the CWI in the US he could remain a member. But he of course knew that if he had insisted in discussing these issues, especially the covering up of the abuse of the female member, the CWI would never have let him rejoin. By rejoining the CWI in this manner he made himself a captive to the leadership of that organisation and also contributed to the further degeneration of that group. And on a personal note he broke off relations with myself in the most hostile and nasty manner. He who had always said that I had played such an important role in his life. Of course if you act in an unprincipled manner you do not want to have anything to do with people who point this out. As with all the other members of the CWI who had acted in an unprincipled manner when myself and others were expelled he had to hide his role from himself and this meant cutting off all relations with myself, to have anything to do with me was to be reminded of the unprincipled role he had played. He was not running from me he was running from his own unprincipled past actions.

Another factor in the collapse and the end of LMV was the health of some members such as myself and Richard and also our age. Richard had a heart attack. I had many different health crises including many epileptic seizures. One of these left me in a severe coma which threatened to be fatal. I also had a number of Addisonian fevers which threatened to be fatal and for which I was admitted numerous times to hospital. Tested for infectious diseases, put in quarantine and so on. These illnesses of both of us added to the difficulty in keeping LMV together.

So in spite of being active in these several struggles, we were not able to build LMV, not able to keep LMV together. The ebb tide of the objective situation, what we had been through in the CWI and then LMV, and then our health and age were just too much. So LMV collapsed. After all these years, Richard and I and a few other members were left on our own. We had maintained our struggle against capitalism and for revolutionary socialism, we had not been bought, we had not been beaten, we remained revolutionary socialists organising for the socialist revolution. After all we had been through, this was not a bad achievement. In spite of our isolation we were still active revolutionaries.

Throughout all these struggles, to build the CWI, within the CWI, to build the LMV, within the LMV, to try and hold LMV together, Richard and I became the closest of Comrades and friends. Richard is an outstanding revolutionary. Nobody I know draws greater creative energy from the working class in all its richness and contradiction. Along with this he turns his hand to whatever the struggle demands. When we were expelled and through the experience of LMV and its collapse, the priority was to maintain our orientation to the working class movement, to keep our connection with the working class, to discuss with and listen to the working class, to identify the phase through which the movement was passing, to draw the lessons from the past, to develop a programme and strategy and tactics based on this orientation, and based on listening to the working class.

As my health worsened Richard had to carry most of this burden. He continued with activity in the struggles of workers and youth. He maintained his contact, political, social and personal, with many of the workers he had worked with in EBMUD. This was of great importance in helping us maintain our orientation to the working class.

Richard taught himself Internet skills and set up our Blog. We called it weknowwhatsup.blogspot.com. This was a spectacular success, reaching close to 1.5 million page views at the last count and over 4,000 followers. The success of the Blog was due, more than anything, to the role of Richard as editor and the main writer. He is an excellent writer, able to make complicated issues simple while at the same time expressing the anger of the thinking worker. Richard's skills, will to fight, refusal to give up, epitomised the statement of Trotsky. To sum up what Trotsky said: You cannot have a revolutionary who is unprepared to bare his or her teeth and fight to overcome all obstacles. Richard is prepared to bare his teeth to fight to overcome all obstacles.

Richard epitomised another saying of Trotsky. That is that revolutionaries needed a strong ego but that they had to be able to harness their ego to the needs of the revolutionary movement and the working class. Richard's ego was not in any way weak, but it was harnessed to the needs of the revolutionary movement and the working class. Whether an ego is weak or strong is not so much the issue. Even those with a weak ego but who believe in a better world can play a role. It is a question of whether or not the ego is harnessed to the needs of the revolution and the working class. If it is so harnessed then the stronger it is the better. If it is not so harnessed then the stronger it is the more damage it can do. The dialectic again.

Richard and I would talk at least once a day on the phone. Sometimes after he has been to his local pub we would share what went on. This way I could go to the pub without going to the pub. Richard is partly Irish in background. He worked on blue collar jobs with Irish labourers in the building sites in England. I am Irish, I worked at blue collar jobs or as a full-time revolutionary all my life. Both of us have been committed revolutionaries for the majority of our adult lives. We have a common outlook and sense of humour.

We share many things. We share the insight into capitalism and the hatred of capitalism; we share the commitment to international democratic revolutionary socialism; the determination even at these late years in our lives to learn lessons from the mistakes we have made; and to help build a revolutionary international. We also and most importantly share the belief that the working class can change the world. We believe in the working class. And one other thing we share: the bourgeois have not bought us, they have not broken us, nor have their agents in the working class movement. Nor has the sectarian now corrupt leadership of the CWI. This was not a bad achievement after all these years. We bare our teeth and fight capitalism and its agents. We also laugh together at life and its great magnificent contradictions and at its most nuanced and delightful twists and turns. While fighting capitalism we, as they would say at home, have the craic.

Richard and his companion Joanne have a dog to which they are deeply committed. They look after its every need and exercise it daily. This also helps Richard with his health, helps him from a repeat of the heart attack he had some years earlier. Unsurprisingly, the dog is a Jack Russell.

This is where I stood politically and personally as LMV came to an end. As over forty years of being in revolutionary organisations came to an end. Still a committed revolutionary but without a revolutionary organisation. It was time to start again. But there was also the issue of making a living now that I was no longer a full-time paid revolutionary.

PART 6

A SENSE OF HISTORY –
A SENSE OF PROPORTION –
A SENSE OF HUMOUR –
TOOLS OF A REVOLUTIONARY

CHAPTER 41

MY MOVING 'CAREER'

IT WAS 1996 when I was expelled from the CWI and fired from my organising job. I was fifty-two years old. I was weighing up going back permanently to Ireland or working in the USA a little longer to get a new nucleus off the ground in that country. The CWI had cast me off like a piece of dirt. I received no pension and no health care. When I was landed with a huge hospital bill the CWI refused to pay. Lynn Walsh, on behalf of Peter Taaffe and the CWI, said that I had not told them in advance that I was going to have my my epileptic seizures and glandular failures. It was as if my twenty-five years of work in that organisation never existed. If you had a disagreement with the CWI and fought for your position, solidarity and loyalty and decades of work counted for nothing. Any weakness its leadership could find in you they tried to exploit to break you. In my case, amongst other things, they tried to use my health problems. They made a mistake. In spite of never paying my hospital bills the CWI did not break me.

Being fired from my organising job changed my life in one way but not in another. The centre of my world remained organising to build a revolutionary nucleus. I remained, above all, a revolutionary. From when I got up in the morning to going to bed at night, this was what was on my mind. Whenever I had a spare moment I was either reading to keep up my understanding for this task or I was discussing with workers and youth to try and convince them to work together with me in this task. My life revolved entirely around building the revolutionary nucleus. This remained my priority. There was only one difference. I was no longer paid a wage to do this. So while carrying on with my revolutionary work as the central task of my life, while trying to decide whether to move and base myself permanently back in Ireland, in the meantime I had to make a living.

I had never finished Secondary School. I had no qualifications recognized by the capitalist economy, no skilled trade qualifications, no degree, that were recognised in the US. Some friends who were teachers tried to talk me into bluffing my way into that profession. I turned this down as I saw it as unprincipled and that I would be acting in a fraudulent manner in relation to my students.

When I was doing my political work in New York I had seen a sign on a post: 'Man with a Van $40 an Hour'. I must have had a premonition. It stuck in my mind. I got together enough money to buy a used pick-up truck. I bought it from an African American man who was a mechanic and owned a small auto shop. We became friends as we shared experiences. We had both grown up on small farms, he in Louisiana, I in Donegal. We laughed together when talking about crawling under the chicken's roosts to collect the eggs, and about the strong women our mothers were, and how they did not spare the rod when they thought we needed it. And what it was like moving to the big city.

I posted flyers in the coffee shops, 'Man with a Van $40 an Hour'. Within days I was inundated with work. I was no longer a mover of ideas and people. I was now a mover of objects – furniture, antiques, art. I very soon built up a customer base of dozens of people and small companies who regularly used my services. I then had two identities. 'Man with a Van $40 an hour' – this was the way of paying my bills. My other identity, the one that was the essence of me, was international revolutionary socialist, nothing an hour.

My moving 'career' was to last for ten years. It was hard work. It only came to an end when my health collapsed. I was driving on the Elgin O'Hare expressway outside Chicago with a load of furniture and I had a transient ischemic attack (TIA), in other words, a small stroke, and blacked out. The van went out of control, crossed over the central bollard and went careening down the expressway the wrong way. The honking of motorists coming the other way brought me round sufficiently to allow me to get the van pulled back across the bollard again and onto the right side of the expressway. Along with my epileptic seizures, that was the end of my driving and my moving business. But before this happened I had many experiences and adventures and I made a living.

I had different types of jobs and clients. Jobs that were not too hard and jobs that were backbreaking. It was not easy but it was a living. And there was the other side to it. Along with my political work, it gave structure and discipline and balance to my life. Together these two activities kept my mind active and challenged. I had to work to a schedule arranged with clients. I had to think out how to load items onto the truck, how to unload them, how to see they were not damaged. This was good for me. And all the time I was looking at my clients, the jobs, the areas I worked in, and thinking about them politically and in class terms. I was gaining more knowledge and education and a more balanced view of life.

I remembered what I had realised when I had been physically and mentally exhausted. That it was not only because I had been working seven days a week, twenty-four hours a day, but it was also that I was focused on only one thing – building the revolutionary organisation. While this was still the central task of my life it was no longer the only one, now I had furniture, art, antiques to move, I had clients to work with and please, I had a whole different series of tasks out there that I had to carry out. This was good for me. It gave me a better mental and physical balance.

I had many different clients. The lady who owned the high end antique store and had me bring her a case of red wine every week or two. She liked the wine and the talk. She laughed when I first met her and she asked me what did I think of the result of the Chicago Bears National Football League game and I said I was not interested in a bunch of millionaires throwing around an inflated piece of skin. I supposed she laughed because she realised she was not interested either and also at how badly she had misjudged me, thinking I fitted into the US male stereotype. Then there was the other lonely elderly lady antique dealer whose main reason for hiring me was to have a chat. She found any excuse to hire me even if it was to move only one small chair. Then there were the other two ladies who also liked their glass of wine and one day when I brought them a painting they told me they liked my ass. Laughing and giggling these ladies were characters. There were the many artists I moved from the Art Institute and the Three Arts Club. There were many young students who had me move them from their apartments. There was the young Korean student of photography who, after having me move her stuff, did a photo shoot and biography of me for her university class. When her parents visited her from Korea they very kindly and respectfully came to see me and thanked me for being good to their daughter. There were the two artists who painted the plastic cows which were screwed into the sidewalks of the city at the time. I delivered these cows too. I got work in many sectors of the art world, collecting and moving paintings, and sculptures. Framing shops hired me to collect from and deliver to their customers. I got work hanging paintings in the homes of people who hired me to move the paintings. I was told by a gay couple whose paintings I hung that I had a good eye. I was not sure what to make of that. Especially given they way they giggled amongst themselves when they told me.

I got regular work with a number of charity organisations. One was a Jewish agency which collected and delivered furniture, clothes and goods from better off, mainly European American people in the richer suburbs of the North Shore and the Loop, and delivered these to poor people who were mainly African American in the South side.

I saw the rich lifestyles in the North Shore and the poor life styles in South Chicago. I had little contact with the mainly European American working class neighbourhoods in the rest of the city and the suburbs. They were not throwing much out nor where they getting much charity, nor were they moving art and antiques. The people in these areas mostly thought they were too good to take charity. This attitude was a load of the back of the rich. I also had little contact with the Latino people who either did not have much to throw out or did not know of the existence of these type of charity places.

I was thinking about all this one morning as I stood on North Avenue and Hamlin in west Chicago. It was a brutal, hot, humid Chicago day, only 7.30 in the morning but the clothes were already sticking to my back. There was never such weather back home, when the sweat oozes out of you even if you are not moving. I wished I was in Donegal with it raining from grey overcast skies, with grey rocks sticking up through the ground, with grey rivers and lakes, and the rocky shores being pounded by the grey Atlantic. And where on the better land to the east there was the green grass. I cursed to myself. Why was I here in this flat ugly city with its scorching summers, its freezing winters and where it was a miracle if you ever got a half decent day in between. I spat on the sidewalk in contempt at myself.

It was the last decade of the twentieth century. The previous two had changed the world. Mine included. The arrogant corporate criminal capitalist class with their mad blind addiction to profit, wealth and power were back rampant in the saddle again and riding roughshod over just about the entire planet. Big money ruled again okay. History had taken a step back when capitalism had re-established itself once again in the former Soviet Union. And there I was on North Avenue with my beat up pick-up truck. But as I thought about it I felt good. My spirit was intact, more than intact. I scorned capitalism and its temporary victory. I spat on the trade union and Labour leaderships. I spat on the bureaucrats in the CWI who had tried to break me. Things would turn around. The dialectic would come to the rescue. I laughed defiantly to myself and in the face of the temporary victors. My time would come. I spat again on the sidewalk and on all of them. I just had to keep making a living and stay alive long enough for the tide to turn.

With the change in the world I had gone from flying from country to country organising revolutionaries, to driving around Chicago as 'Man With a Van - $40 an Hour', moving furniture, art and antiques. I had to laugh to myself. It was the only way. And anyway my flyers were all over the city's coffee shops, I was getting jobs hand over fist and making enough money to live on. I was also meeting more people from different walks of life and this was good. I was one of the lucky ones. Yes I too had been thrown into the new triumphalist capitalist world but I was more than getting by. With that and my continued belief in and ability to fight for my revolutionary socialist ideas, life was good.

However my life was not a picnic. Many of the jobs I had to take meant carrying heavy furniture up two or three flights of stairs by myself. I was six foot tall and strong but this was still tough. I often had to carry steel-framed, fold-out couches on my back. I was not twenty any more when I carried the 112 pound bags of oats and wheat up the stone steps to my uncle's barn. Now I was in my fifties with serious health problems.

When I started the moving I knew I had hypothyroidism and was being treated for that. But I did not know I had Addison's disease so I was not being treated for that. Nor did I know I had hypoglycaemia. Nor did I know I was soon to have cancer and would develop epilepsy. It was a struggle. But there was nothing I could do but grit my teeth and bear it. My mother and family had taught me well. You have to work. Hard work never killed anybody she always said. Even though this was not true I thought this way also. It was the best way to survive.

I preferred the moving jobs that I could do alone. These allowed me to fix my schedule better to my liking and better decide when I started and stopped. They also helped me to better carry out my political work. Between jobs I sat in coffee shops, read the main capitalist papers, followed events, wrote articles and flyers on my laptop, and communicated with Richard. The coffee shops were the centres of much of my political work, where I read and wrote. I also frequented the upscale health food stores and ate their free samples, anything to save a few dollars. It was also the pleasure of getting something for nothing from the corporations, this itself a small blow against their capitalist offensive.

The corner of Hamlin and North Avenue where I stood that morning was five blocks from where I lived on Keystone Avenue. It was a tough, low income neighbourhood, mainly Latino Americans, with some African Americans and a smattering of European Americans who had not yet fled to the suburbs or could not afford to flee to the suburbs. There were, to all extents and purposes, no Native Americans anywhere in the US cities. The estimated 60 million of them who had lived in North America when the European colonial powers had arrived had either been slaughtered *en masse* in the genocide following the invasion, or died of starvation or disease. The few that survived were in the main imprisoned in reservations. Nor were there any Asian Americans in this neighbourhood. They were mainly either around Chinatown or in the suburbs.

I liked the racial mix and energy of where I lived. I disliked the conservative, frightened, mostly European American suburbs with their closed doors where just about nobody knew or spoke to each other. But three young people had been shot dead in a gang war on my block in the first six months I lived there. Another young man had fired shots at the house next to ours because his girlfriend who lived there had dumped him. He was a bad shot. Three of the bullets came through the wall of our house, into the sitting room, blew the back of a chair and went through Lisa's record collection. It was close. I refused to throw myself to the floor. I cursed the shooter. To myself I said I am not getting down for anybody. Not too smart, but my dignity was intact.

On another occasion I was walking home from the local pub. It was a bitter cold winter night. Snow lay on the ground. I wore a long coat with the hood up. The street went under a railway bridge. As I crossed under the bridge two young Latino men jumped out behind me. 'Hey. You'. I stopped. Looking round I could see from how they were dressed that they were gang members. They each had a hand inside their coat. It was obvious to me they were seeing if I was from a rival gang trying to take some of their territory. Very quickly I pulled down my hood. They saw that I was white. So not from a rival gang. In that area the gangs were either Latino or African American. They said okay and turned away back up to their look out spot. This was all part of the energy of the area.

Working for the Jewish agency that day, I was collecting furniture, clothes, canned food etc. from the North Shore. This particular sweltering day was the first time I needed help from another person for a job. There were two big fold-out couches with metal frames and a large refrigerator and other bits and pieces to collect and to deliver to a third floor. The lady in charge of the agency ordered me to get somebody to help. I knew she was worried if I was injured I would sue. We were in the land of the personal injury attorney. No to collective action, yes to get yourself an attorney and sue and the attorney got a cut and you got a cut. Individual action, not collective action ruled.

Across the road from where I was standing was a 'Labour Ready' centre where people who needed work and people who needed workers met up. The Labour Ready outfit got a commission. They were notorious low pay, no benefit, rip-off centres which were owned by the most exploitive types. These Labour Ready outfits saw their job as to get workers who were desperate ready to be super exploited by people who needed labour. I was once invited by a friend to a party in the home of a man who owned one of these Labour Ready places. He lived in luxury. On the other hand, the people who used outlets such as his were the poorest workers and especially the newly arrived Latino American workers.

African American workers had enough centuries of working for nothing to easily submit to what these places offered. Also most African American workers had enough of an established family back-up network to help them out. European American workers too usually had enough of a cushion and enough contacts and opportunities to avoid these places. I would regularly see the poverty stricken, mainly Latino American workers as they lined up for the work. I tried to imagine their lives and how they got there.

Most likely they were a thousand miles or more from home. Many of them had probably crossed the dangerous fields and deserts of Central America, Mexico, and the US, were preyed on by the human coyotes and the US and Mexican cops. The women especially would have been prey for the rapists and abusers. Then it would have been riding the rails north to Chicago. And when they arrived most likely did not have a cent in their pocket and for some of the young women maybe pregnant as a result of rape. Waiting in terror to see if their period came. It was a nightmare. I wished I could have got these young women to speak and write of their experience. But legal oppression and religious oppression kept their mouths shut. Many of these workers would have no documents. Living in economic and legal and personal insecurity twenty-four hours a day, worried about being arrested, their lives and families torn apart, with the threat of being sent back to their home country at any time. What a life. And not to mention what a life for their families back home. If they died on their journey north their families would never know what happened to them. Was their decomposing body lying in a ditch in some desert being picked to pieces by the birds or torn apart by animals?

All my life I either had something in my pocket to get by or I was in a position to borrow something from somebody. I was never completely broke. Not like so many of these poor mainly African American and Latino American people. Paid less than minimum wage, many of the Latino Americans who had no papers were cheated out of their pay altogether, forced to huddle up in overcrowded, bug-infested houses because they could not afford an adequate home, I tried to imagine what it was like but I could not. My imagination was not up to the job.

But it was not the Latino American world I was about to enter that day, it was the African American world. As I stood across from the Labour Ready, a tall African American man came up my side of the street. I moved closer to him. 'How are you doing, sir?' I said. He looked at me suspiciously. 'Aright,' he said curtly, weighing me up. He was about my own height. He did not look like he ate too much or too often. 'I am looking for somebody to help me with some work. Would you be interested?' He did not beat about the bush. 'Not if you pay what they pay,' he said gesturing to the Labour Ready. I was impressed with his directness and consciousness. I looked him in the eye and said: 'No, I have a different way of paying.'

I had been thinking of this since I was told I had to get help. I did not want to be exploiting anybody. In my younger days in Ireland I had poached fish. There had to be two people for this work and there had to be a boat and nets. Payment was organised on a third, a third, a third basis. The man who owned the boat and nets got a third of the catch for these, that is for his ownership of the capital equipment. It was always a man. He also got another third for his own work. The other worker, also always a man, got a third for his work. So I had decided that I would get a third for having the truck and getting the job, another third for my work and the other worker would get a third for his work. Just like home and the poaching. My consciousness when I had been poaching back home was not sufficiently developed to think about there being no women in the fishing.

I explained my one third, one third, one third payment method to the man. He looked at me again, wondering if there was a catch. That was natural. I was a European American man 'offering' him work. Was it going to be different this time, would he get paid and how much would he get paid? European Americans offering work or forcing work on African Americans had not been a great experience for African American people in the past. There was the three hundred years of slavery when they got paid nothing. It would be neither natural nor smart to be too quick to say yes. Every day I would see the wee buckshee sewer cleaning outfits, a European American man with his pick-up truck and an African American man. It was always the European American man who owned the pick-up driving and looking down the hole and the African American man down the sewer in filth to his eyeballs looking up.

'How much are you getting for the job altogether?' he said. 'It will depend how long it takes. With the two of us I will be charging $60 an hour and this will mean you will be getting $20 an hour.' Hesitating for a few minutes and clearly thinking about what I had said, he eventually decided to take a risk and replied: 'Aright.' 'My truck is over here, up Hamlin.' I could see him looking with less than confidence at my white Ford E 150 with its rough body and the bullet hole in the panel below the driver's door.

We got in and headed for the Northern suburbs. In spite of it being only 7.30 am the city was long awake. The streets were filled with traffic, the sidewalks were alive with school children with their backpacks going to school and the expressway roared with trucks and cars going and coming to and from the city. US capitalism made its workers get up earlier than any other country I had ever visited or lived in. It trained the school children to do the same. What a place? The sun was barely up but the workers and even the children were up.

There was no other advanced capitalist country in which the corporations, the capitalist class, were so dominant. The refusal to fight of the trade union leaders and the related factor of the low level of consciousness of the US working class allowed the class balance of forces to be so much on the side of the capitalist class. Due to this, the capitalist class could enforce its will to a very great degree. This was noticeable everywhere, in how early people went to work, in the long hours worked, in the speed of work, in the manner in which people were treated while at work, for example no stools to sit on at the cashiers' desks, in the way in which the society was laid out, built in the main around shopping malls to suck the money out of people's pockets, rather than around centres which grew out of the natural way in which people would have wished to live and relate. This was why people were up so early when my new workmate and I headed for our job.

With the exception of the expensive area around the lake downtown, Chicago was an ugly city. Elsewhere the houses were overwhelmingly wood-framed and drab. The streets were mostly on a North–South, East–West grid system. This added to the city's lack of charm. There were a few streets that ran East/West round the bottom of the lake through the city centre area and at an angle on towards the North West and back towards the South East. These had been the original trails the Native American people and the first European American settlers had used. These were a bit of a help.

I thought more as I drove. What the hell was I doing here in Chicago? I knew, or rather I thought at that time, it was probably only temporary until I returned to Ireland again but still. I was a man for the ocean and here I was, whether I went east or west, north or south, the ocean with its ocean waves and tides and smells were 1,000 miles away. The Great Lakes with their fresh waters, their lack of ocean smell, their lack of tidal movement, for all their size, were no substitute. And the whole area was as flat as a pancake. There was not a hill or a mountain of any substance for as far as you could go in a day. If I went over a bump on the road it was like an erotic experience. If there was a slope I would get excited as I thought maybe I was home again. It was only bearable because I knew that I had ended up there because I refused to give up the struggle to build a viable revolutionary nucleus. I could of course have left and went somewhere by the ocean in Ireland or another country and built a nucleus. But I had started here in the US and I could not find it in me to quit. And the US coastal cities were much more expensive places to live than Chicago. The pleasure of living by the sea or any pleasure would always come second in me to building the revolutionary nucleus. I did not have much understanding for anybody who put their own pleasure or satisfaction above building the revolutionary nucleus.

'I am Sean. What do they call you, Sir?' 'Perry.' 'How are you doing?' 'Aye.' 'Are you originally from Chicago Perry?' 'Aye.' It was going to be a long day if Perry said nothing but 'aye'. 'I am from Ireland. I have been here for over fifteen years now. I was around New York City for a few years and then came to Chicago. That New York is a great city.' 'Why did you come here then?' So Perry did say more than 'Aye'. And it sounded like he was defensive about Chicago. I would go easy. 'I worked as an organiser for a radical organisation and they sent me here as it was the biggest industrial city in the middle of the country.'

Perry said nothing. He was being careful not to give too much away, especially to me, a European American and a stranger, cautious almost to the point of being antagonistic. And anyway, what was this about working for a radical organisation.

'I heard that Louis Armstrong came to Chicago from the South. I have great time for Louis Armstrong. Old man river. That old sun it has nothing to do but roll around heaven all day. I can just see it. Working in the fields in the terrible heat and then looking up and seeing the sun 'doing nothing'. I read that Chicago was so bad for black people at the time that Louis Armstrong and his friends piled into an old car one day and headed for New York and the centre of world jazz moved with them. That was some loss for Chicago. But it deserved all it got if it was that racist. He could sing, and play the trumpet. Aye. Send down the cloud with a silver lining and ... I am bad at remembering the words of songs.' Perry just looked at me. There was no way he could be anything but surprised at an Irish man and Satchmo and jazz and blues and criticising Chicago and racism and liking New York all in the one package. Who knows what would come next? But I was sending him a message, letting him know that I was not a racist and also that I was not an idiot who thought Chicago was a paradise.

After twenty minutes on the expressway heading north towards Milwaukee, I took the turn off east on Lake Cook Road to Highland Park for our first pick up. But I was going to have something to eat first. My favourite Jewish deli outside of New York was in that suburb. Thinking that Perry might have no money I said: 'Perry I need to get something to eat. I will buy you breakfast.' He said nothing just looked straight ahead. I suppose what he saw as a European American man whom he had just met buying him breakfast was another surprise. Maybe he had been girding himself up to work all day on an empty stomach. He probably did not know what to make of it. Things were getting stranger by the minute.

We parked and entered the Jewish deli. It was the one Bill Webster and I had gone to. I liked the place for more than the food. The majority of workers behind the counter and on the floor were Mexican Americans. The owners were Jewish. But the Mexican American workers were involved in all the jobs including the cash register. Most European American-owned businesses would not let the Mexican American workers near the money.

They served the food, cleared the dishes or cleaned the floor. The workers in this deli were obviously trusted. They must have been halfway well paid. Usually the bosses figured out if the trade-off was worth it. Pay a little more so that the workers had enough to survive and wanted to stay in the job and so conclude that it was not worth the risk to steal or pay them so little and make more profit but risk the workers being tempted to steal. I was very pleased to see that for the first time there was now a young African American woman working in the deli.

Perry and I went to the counter to order. I had seen the Mexican American man on the register many times before. He had lost a lot of weight. 'How are things with you?' I said. 'Good. Good. What can I get you?' he replied. 'Are you alright?' I said. 'You have lost a lot of weight. Are you okay?' 'Yes, yes, I alright. No problem. But thanks for asking. What can I get you?'

America. What a country. Again we were back to the dominance of the corporations. The pressure was always on to keep working at top speed. Workers were allowed no time to say hello and have a chat. The corporations dominated in the US more than any other advanced capitalist country. They kept their lash continually and incessantly on the workers' backs, speeding them up, whipping them on. And so everybody was always in a hurry and just about everybody was forced to be impolite and undiplomatic. This man was given no time to say hello to me. At home in Ireland we could have had a bit of a chat. Personal relations, social relations, these were continually damaged by the whip of the profit-mad bosses and their system. US working peoples' personalities were continually under assault by the dominance of the corporations.

I thought about the mechanic I used. He owned his own shop. But even he was under the whip of the corporations. When I knew him first and I would call to get my truck worked on and I would begin the conversation by asking him how he was he would either not answer me or cut me off. His attitude was he had no time for small talk. But this was his own shop so I would not back down and every time I called I would ask how he was and wait to he answered. After a time he got the message and would say he was alright and he even came to where he asked me how I was. We eventually became friendly. But it was hard work. I had to break down his attitude that was related to speeding up his work rate so as not to be driven out of business by the big corporations and their car repair chains. I thought about my first years in the US when I would experience such interactions and how I thought everybody was insulting me.

The man behind the counter in the deli was doing his best to be polite. His Mexican American culture helped him, but this was coming under the hammer of the US corporate culture and from his boss. He knew what was expected; take our orders and get us moving on as fast as possible. 'People are waiting to get served. Keep that register ringing.' I could hear the owner thinking from where he stood behind the glass where he was supervising the making of the bagels. Under my breath I cursed the bosses and their bagels and their corporate culture and their pressure to work harder and harder and tell me I could not have a chat with this man. I cursed the boss behind the glass. What about a chat? What about a decent humane interchange of hellos? But I could not get this man into trouble so I chatted no more, just gave the order for Perry and I. The worker was probably working two jobs to make ends meet. I could not put him at risk. My consciousness of this and my solidarity put me under the corporate lash too.

I suggested to Perry he order a feta cheese omelette and veggie hash, my own usual. I also ordered a small table-full of toast between us. When the food was brought I could see Perry was pleased with the choice. He ate and never spoke and when I saw how hungry he was I got another arm full of toast and marmalade and strawberry jam. He ate firmly, neatly and with careful manners. We had some feed. I was stuffed full by the end of it. The food pressed comfortably against me from the inside of my belly. And the coffee was in me hot and warm. For some reason I thought of my mother and uncle and aunt, they had never had a cup of coffee in their lives. Only tea or a glass of milk or buttermilk. But back to the present, yes the food was good. Just the job I thought.

'Okay Perry. Will we make a move? Was your food okay?' 'Aye. Good. Thanks.'

'My pleasure. I never come up here to Highland Park without having a feed at this deli.'

The pick up we had to make was at a large expensive house. It was a big load, couches, a fridge, a stove, two microwaves, two chairs, bags of clothes and a few boxes of kitchen utensils. Perry and I studied what was there. 'What do you think we should put on first Perry?' I believed in involving people and learning from people. Perry was surprised at not being ordered what to do, instead being asked his opinion and I imagine especially being asked his opinion by a European American, by a white man. He hesitated and then said: 'Maybe the stove and fridge and heavier bits.' And that is what we did.

You get to know a lot about a person when you do heavy physical work with them, especially lifting things together. Do they try and lay the weight off on you and not do their share? Do they take their share and make it easy for you to work together? Do they run at it and grab their end and risk hurting both of you? Perry was balanced in his approach, taking his share in a careful way so that neither of us was in danger of being injured. My respect for him increased.

The couches were at the far end of a long living room with a bare hardwood floor. I went to get the two-wheel dolly to wheel them out. When I got back Perry had put a thick moving pad on the floor, tipped one of the couches up on it, and pulled the pad and the couch across the hardwood floor to the door. It slid along so easy on the moving pad on the hard wood floor. It did not damage anything. There was no risk that the dolly's wheels or iron base would leave any marks. I would have never thought of doing it that way. Perry knew more about moving than me. And he had the confidence to go ahead and do it his way. I was very pleased.

There was a lot of racist America's story in Perry and me and the moving of that couch and my little moving outfit. Perry was more skilled and knew more about moving than I. But I was the one that was able to get my hands on the money, the capital, for a truck and this meant I was earning more money than Perry. It all came back to Marx and access to capital. It made no difference that Perry knew more about moving than me, he could not get the capital for a truck. I could. Perry could not get the capital for a truck because of centuries of slavery which meant that most African Americans had not been able to accumulate capital over the centuries. It was probable that Perry did not have family members or other contacts from whom he could borrow the capital, again because of years of slavery. I on the other hand was able to get the capital for the truck.

This was what made all the difference. It was economics. But it was also economics where the African American working people were shafted most, where they had been paid no wages for three hundred years, where racism was a central part of the economics. It was like when I said to the African American man that it was not a question of colour when it came to African American people being treated worse meaning it was a question of capitalism and divide and rule and cheap labour. This African American man turned to me and said: 'Naw, it is a question of colour.' And rubbing his finger and thumb together in the universal gesture for money he said: 'It is green.' He was right. He understood way better than the big shot economics academics.

Malcom X had said that working for three hundred years and getting paid no wages had consequences which lasted for centuries. The legacy of slavery lived on. Perry was continuing to suffer from it. I had never been a slave nor had my family to my knowledge. Even the impoverished conditions of the life of my family in their small holding of land in Ireland had left them with a few pennies. If there had ever been slaves in my family background it was many centuries back and it lasted a lot less time than slavery had lasted for African Americans. I was privileged over Perry. Slavery was over, the black revolt had made some gains, but African American people, especially African American working class people like Perry, were still suffering from its affects, still having great difficulty in accumulating any significant amounts of capital, never mind even a roof over their head. Those slave-owning degenerates, this former slave-owning country, my teeth ground with rage as I thought about the whole thing.

The person at the house where we were doing the pick up was a tall slim lady. Her sallow skin and curly black hair and the suburb we were in made me think she was Jewish. She watched us as we loaded up. I was thinking she was maybe worried we would steal something. I mean, an African American and an Irishman, not a great combination, in fact altogether potentially a bad lot. You would have to watch them. Was this what she might be turning over in her mind?

I had gone out with a Jewish lady like this once. She was very attractive and very confident of herself. A mixture of being brought up in an upper middle class household, taught she was from the chosen people, being very attractive and intelligent and being positively affected by the women's revolt of the 1960s and 1970s. We eventually broke up as she would think if I was a moment late for a date this was an act of extreme discourtesy seeing she was so special. Or if I was exactly on time she would see this as a sign that I was committed to her for life. I mean how could it be anything else seeing she was so special. When all that was involved was the pressure or lack of pressure of work. Then, when we would have our debates she would always try and win, no matter what the subject, by calling me anti-Semitic. I could not take it. For this and other reasons we broke up. But she was a character and through our relationship I came to better understand more aspects of the Jewish world.

I broke the tension that existed as a result of the Jewish lady of the house standing watching us. 'How are you doing today then Mam?' I was not afraid to break the class divide and speak to her in a familiar way. Nor was there any race divide between her and I to break. No European American mob would come running to lynch me and hang and burn me from a tree. I was not in danger. As I was a European American man, it was more acceptable for me to be a bit forward with a European American or Jewish woman. The lady was surprised at my confident and even slightly sexually provocative tone. But she recovered herself and responded well, a hint of a smile and a raised eyebrow. I admired that. 'I am fine thank you.' We talked back and forth. She seemed to get to enjoy, even be proud of the unusual situation where she was conversing with two strange men, one of whom was African American and both blue collar. Even though Perry never said a word she would probably boast to her friends later about how brave she had been. Why did Perry say nothing? I knew why. It was the centuries of racism. Perry was being cautious. I did not have to be.

When we got back to the warehouse in Chicago the lady in charge pointed out other items and we added these to the truck for our delivery and the lady gave me the address. It was down on Armitage and Kimball, not too far from where Perry and I both lived. The house was a three level wooden frame in bad shape. It needed painting, siding and gutters. I rang the bell.

I was surprised when a European American lady answered the door. She was in her late fifties, obviously a working class woman who had worked hard throughout her life. Her hair was grey and her face deeply lined. Her hands were big and rough with large knuckles. Immediately I felt for her. The sound of kids erupted from a back room and with a clatter of feet four young children, the oldest about eight, charged into the kitchen to where we stood. One of their parents was obviously African American. Perry and I allowed no expression on our faces.

'What is the best way to bring this up Mam? The back porches or the front stairwell?' 'Whatever is best with you, well maybe the back porches so nobody complains.' 'Okay.' More city stress, more capitalist overcrowding, always having to try not to annoy the neighbours.

I backed the truck up the alley and we went to work, unloading and carrying everything up the three flights. It took a while and it was hard work. As we moved in and out I heard the lady calling at the children. She had a Southern accent. 'Where are you from originally Mam?' I asked. 'South Carolina.' 'I have never been there. I hear it is nice.'

She was going to answer but the screaming kids overwhelmed her. We finished unloading and went to leave.

'Will you take a glass of water men?' She probably wanted to keep us round for a few minutes to exchange a few words and dilute the pressure of the children. And as a working class woman she would know the need for a regular drink as people worked.

'Yes please Mam. That would be good. It is thirsty work carrying up them stairs.' 'So where are you from? I hear an accent.' 'I am from Ireland.' 'I hear it is beautiful.' 'Aye it is not bad. Okay.' 'I am from an Irish background myself. The old ones used to talk about it. Not that they ever saw it. But they wanted to. I wish I could make a trip. But with these young ones,' and she gestured to the children, 'that is not likely now.' 'They are lively young ones I can see. They will keep you going. Thank you for the water Mam. I hope that you will find what we brought useful.' And we left. I felt a terrible sadness that this woman would never be able to see Ireland. It was not right.

As we drove I thought about the home we just came from with the older European American lady from the South, now living in poverty in Chicago, and looking after four young children of mixed race. Ever since that day I wondered did she cope, whatever happened to them all? I also thought of her courage. Probably her daughter was the mother, came to Chicago, had a family with an African American man, then something happened and the lady we had just met came to Chicago to look after the children. That woman was a heroine, a woman of loyalty and duty. But this corporate, racist society would never recognise her as a heroine, would never give her any awards. There should be awards for such women. Working Women of the Year, Women of Duty of the Year. Caring Woman of the Year.

The agency had another job for us that day. We had to collect the belongings of another woman and move her to a different place. She lived in one room in a single family home. She was a large African American young woman, clearly not well off. 'Is it all to go?' I asked the lady when we arrived. 'Yes everything. I am moving to my aunt's.'

We loaded up and off we went, down into the heart of the South side. Down past where the cops had murdered Fred Hampton. The population on the streets and sidewalks was completely African American. The south side was in reality a great African American city of its own of around two million. The lady sat in the centre of the front seat of the truck between us. I should not have let her because if anything went wrong she could have sued me. But she did not seem to have any other way to get to where we were going.

We arrived at her aunt's small, run-down wooden house in a very poor neighbourhood. I thought of the swanky house where we had done the pick up on the North Shore earlier in the day. The young woman knocked on the door. There was no answer. She knocked again and again, but each time nothing. She sat down on the porch steps and started to weep. 'What is wrong Mam? Do you think she is out or just cannot hear us?' The lady looked up at me. Her ragged clothes, her unkempt hair, her wrinkled face, her large body, I felt a great sorrow for her and a great solidarity with her. 'No she is in there alright. She just does not want me to stay with her.' Perry stood silent watching. What were we to do? We could not carry her belongings around in the truck.

'What do you want to do?' I asked. 'I do not know what to do,' she replied. 'You knock again. I will call the agency and see what they say.' The agency answered: 'Just leave her stuff off there at the house. We have done what we can.' 'We are to leave your things here. But where will we leave them?' The lady went into an even more terrible fit of weeping. Perry and I were helpless. Then she gradually quieted down. 'Put everything here under the porch. She will have to let me in when she sees my stuff is all here.'

And that is what we did. We drove off leaving her sitting on the porch surrounded by her belongings and locked out. How was she going to get help to carry them in? Like I did with the other lady and the four children I would always wonder what happened to her. Daily painful tragedies, tragedies of poverty and social and personal crises like these were non-stop in the poor neighbourhoods of Chicago and in my work. I was getting a more thorough and class-based education. I wished I could have introduced this lady to the lady I had met earlier in the day who was looking after the four young mixed race children. In a different world they could have helped each other out.

With that job we were finished for the day and I drove Perry home. 'Perry if I need another man again are you interested?' 'Aye.' 'Well then how can I contact you?'

'Come and get me where you drop me off.' 'But Perry I need to know in advance if you are available. Do you have a phone?' 'Naw, no phone.' No phone in an American house. Perry really was poor. 'Over there, left on Potomac. There just at that white car. That is my place there, with the brown porch.' 'Okay then Perry, when I need a second person I will try and get you. But are you sure there is nobody I can call who could get you a message.' 'Aye wait my sister.' And he gave me his sister's number.

'Here is your money Perry.' As usual I had got paid in cash by the agency. We had worked five and a half hours but I fiddled it up to six. At $60 an hour this meant the agency was giving me $360. One third of this was for Perry. I gave him his share, the $120. 'I hope you think this is fair Perry,' I said as I gave it to him. 'Aye. I do. Thank you, boss.' He was so glad to get the money that his reserved demeanour temporarily cracked and he called me 'boss'. It was out of character for him, entirely different from his proud and dignified manner of the rest of the day. I was humiliated for him. 'Perry, please, do me a favour. Do not call me 'boss'. We work together and my name is Sean.'

I could see he was bewildered. A European American man who did not want to be called 'boss'. But from his expression I could see he liked what I had said. He nodded his head.'Perry I will be seeing you most likely in the next few days.' 'Aye. And thanks,' he said holding up the money. 'This is good. For the last week I had to borrow from my mother to buy cigarettes. Can you think how that makes a grown man feel?' Perry was sharing his feelings with me. I was honoured. I tried to imagine having to borrow from my mother as I turned the truck and headed back in the direction of my apartment. That would eat at a person.

A few days later I had another job from the same agency for which they again ordered me to get another person. I had called Perry's sister and she had said she would get him the message. I drove down to his house. As I got out of the truck, gunshots came from across the street and men and a young woman scattered in all directions. It was a skirmish in a gang war. I sheltered behind the truck.

I knocked on the door. A tall, light-skinned African American woman answered. As I always did when I saw a mixed race American I thought of how there were lots of mixed race Americans but very few mixed race marriages or relationships. And this was even more the case in the past. The explanation was overwhelimingly the raping of African American women during slavery. Like Perry his companion was very thin, only in her case her thinness looked unhealthy. Not like Perry's who just looked like he did not get enough to eat. A long loose dress hung from her thin shoulders. 'Hi. How are you? Is Perry in please?' As I was asking I could see that there was not a stick of furniture in the room behind her. I thought of how badly nourished both Perry and this woman looked and on top of that the room had no furniture.

Perry came through from a back room. He was back to his non-talkative self and seemed uncomfortable with me being at his door and seeing his home and the woman. 'How are you Perry?' I asked. 'Aright.' 'We have to collect a few things and take them to the central storage.' I made sure to tell Perry in advance what the job was. When you did not know what the job was you could not pace yourself. This became more important as people got older and had to conserve their energy and resources.

We pulled up to the house where we were to collect the items. It was a two level in good shape. I rang the bell and a lady came to the door. 'Hello Mam, we are here to collect the things for the agency.' 'Och sure, come in, come in.' I could not believe it. I was listening to a west of Ireland accent. I thought about Connemara and Lough Corrib and Galway. I missed Ireland badly. I missed the West, Dublin, the lot. There were times I missed it so bad I ached, and times when I was driving home after a hard day's work I would howl in anguish. It was not easy being an emigrant. That was how the Irish pub owners made their money.

The lady with the Galway accent pointed out the pieces. We set the fridge on our two-wheel dolly and bumped it down the stairs to the street, over and on to the truck. Soon we had finished loading. But I was not going to miss the chance of having a few words with somebody from home.

'Where are you from then Mam? Somewhere in the West I think?' The lady looked at me. 'I thought I heard a bit of a Northern accent with you. I am from Galway. Connemara.' 'Connemara, there is no place like it. I went camping there when I was young with a girlfriend and there was nothing but rock. We could not get the tent pegs driven in. The old ones had to bring the seaweed from the sea to make the soil between the rocks to grow their spuds. It is spectacular, the lakes, the sea, the mountains the heather, the rock hedges, the history, it is the place.' 'Where are you from then?' she asked. 'Donegal, east Donegal. It's nothing like Connemara. Have you been out here all your life Mam?' 'Naw, I came here when I was in my early twenties. There was nothing at home then. Not like now.'

As we talked in the woman's kitchen Perry stood in the doorway without saying a word. 'Here, where are my manners? You will have a cup of tea?' In the Irish way the first response was to refuse but in a way that invited a further offer. I would always get mad when as was usual, Americans never offered twice, usually never once. I responded in the Irish way. 'Naw, naw, Mam, sure we would not want to be putting you to any trouble.' 'Sure it will be no trouble at all. Sure come on now, it is not often I get to have a chat with somebody from home. It will be a pleasure.'

It was the conversational and diplomatic skill of the Irish. A skill which was that of the Irish born and raised, not the Irish American born and raised. Living under a repressive system for centuries, the Irish-born learnt how to speak indirectly, diplomatically. After all if you were too direct with the landlord or the British officer it could mean imprisonment, deportation or execution. So it was always better to be indirect and diplomatic. Irish Americans who were born and brought up in the US, no longer under the same degree of oppression, had mainly lost that skill. Our hostess, born and having spent her early years in Ireland, had not. We were being offered tea in a way that was being presented as if we took it we would be doing this lady a great favour. What could we do? We had to do the lady the favour.

'Well if you are sure Mam. We would not want to be putting you to any trouble. But sure it would be good as you say to have the chat with somebody from home.' The lady answered. 'Sure that will be very good. Well have a seat will you please.' Then realising that it might appear we were excluding Perry from our conversation she turned to him, 'Yourself sir, there up at the top of the table,' directing Perry to the best seat in the kitchen. She was being careful to see that he would not feel less important because he was not Irish or European American. Perry was very careful as he sat down. He said nothing, not looking at either of us, acting most mannerly and unobtrusive. I was very aware of his presence and hoped he felt welcome.

The woman kept on talking about home as she made the tea. She went to a cupboard and took out a scone of bread, some butter and a square of Irish cheddar cheese, traditional Irish country fare. I thought of my mother. The lady cut the cheese into slices and set it down on a plate on the table before us. Perry and I were eating together for the second time. Maybe I could put a bit of weight on him at this rate. 'My mother taught me you should never let anybody out of your house without giving them something to eat,' the lady said. I laughed with delight and replied: 'My mother taught me the same thing.' The poverty and the hunger in the history of the Irish.

The lady poured the tea into three large cups on saucers in front of us and sat down along with us at the table. She pushed over the jug of milk and the bowl of sugar. 'Now sir,' she addressed Perry, 'please eat up.' I thought as I sat, that given that Chicago was the most racially segregated of all of the major cities in the US, this was possibly the first time that this Irish woman had an African American man sitting down to eat in her home. I had seen too much racism amongst the Irish American population not to be proud of this woman. She was acting impeccably. Perry was getting treated with the utmost hospitality, respect and politeness. Some racists would not have had an African American in their home never mind drinking out of their cups. 'Sorry, I should have told you our names. This is Perry and I am Sean.' 'I am Kathleen.' We all said we were pleased to meet. Or Kathleen and I did and Perry said something which was not audible. He nodded his head forward in a gesture of acknowledgement of his welcome and the introduction.

'So Sean do you have a family over here?' 'No, I do not,' I answered. 'What about you Perry? Do you have children?' Perry kept looking away for a time but then his good manners turned his head back and he said, 'I do. I have two boys.' 'Well that is good, it is good to have a family. How old are they?' Perry hesitated and then said: 'They are twelve and thirteen.' 'Just getting to be a handful I would say.' Perry was having difficulty in speaking. He almost seemed to be choking up. I was getting ready to step in and rescue him thinking he might be insecure about how welcome he was and how his experience with his children might be misunderstood or might be of no interest to his European American audience.

I was very pleased when he spoke out. Maybe because it was about his children that he felt he had to speak. 'Yes they are alright. I am trying my best with them. They live with their mother. She has a good job as a nurse at County. They always have a lot of questions for me when they visit. I do not know what to tell them. If I tell them about the things that were done to us in the past maybe they will get so mad they might go out and get themselves into trouble. On the other hand should they not know these things? I do not know what to do.' Kathleen was silent. I said 'Perry you have to tell them, they have to know their history. Just like us Irish have to know our history. For a long period the Irish were put down also, not anything like as bad as your people, but not good.' Perry said nothing. I had not thought of it in this way before. That if you told your children the truth, told them the real history, told them how they and their people had been so badly treated, that this could threaten their future and lives.

The conversation came to a halt. It had taken a serious turn very quickly. Maybe Perry was worried he had said too much. I asked the lady: 'What about you Mam, do you have a family over here?' 'I do. If you go to the sessions you might know my daughter. She plays the fiddle. She composes music too. She wrote the music there for a film. Aw she is a great success. Sure money just sticks to her.' I smiled at this great expression. Through meeting this lady I would later be contacted by her daughter to move her fridge. We spoke about Irish music, Irish America and racism. I told her how I admired her mother's hospitality to Perry and I.

We cleaned up the bread and cheese had another cup of tea, thanked Kathleen for her hospitality and left. I was proud of this Irish woman from Connemara. She had made Perry feel he was wanted. There was not a hint of racism in her welcome. Reaching Perry's home I gave him his share of the money and dropped him off. 'Thanks for the work.' 'No problem Perry. Thanks for the help. I will call you when I need another man again.'

Parking the truck I went up to my apartment. The full moon was shining through the skylights. It was beautiful. I put on a small light by the tape player and the CDs. I found Sam Cooke and flicked it forward to where he sang 'Change gonna come'. What a song! There were none like it. I wept as I sat in the chair, looked at the moon, listened to the Sam Cooke man and thought about this country. How many of the most talented and strong of the African American people were murdered? Sam Cooke also. What a waste. What a dirty, racist, vicious country. How had Perry survived? Would his sons survive? I wept further. I had changed in my weeping from the days of my father's death. Now I was able to weep but mostly, though not only when I was alone.

I got up, groaning. My legs and arms were sore. I was too old for this work. Groaning when you got up or sat down was like the creaking of an old machine. I swore to myself as I thought of capitalism. I went on swearing as my sore limbs and having to carry heavy weights made me think of the organisation to which I had given my adult life and which had now left me making a living carrying things on my back, a beast of burden. I shook my head in almost disbelief and let Sam Cooke do his soothing work.

Then I heard the dog at the back door. It belonged to a neighbour. When he heard me come home he would romp up the back outside stairs to greet me. We would wrestle on the floor in play. He would catch me with his teeth but never close them on me and I would hold him by the neck and throat but never hurt or choke him. He was part German Shepherd and part Chou, the shape of a German Shepherd and the red colouring of a Chou, a beauty, and made even more attractive because one of his ears flopped forward while the other stood up straight. I would later feature him in a photo with myself in the inside cover of a book I was to write. After our wrestling bout he lay down with his head on my feet and his tongue out panting. I thought about dog's skins being used for the most delicate leather work in the old days because they had no pores as they sweated through their tongue when they panted. With no pores the sewing thread did not so easily pull through the skins. Humans could be cruel.

I took off my clothes and got into the shower. The tension began to leave my body under the impact of the water and as the sweat and dirt washed off me. Slowly I could feel the healing hydrotherapy envelop me. There was nothing to beat a shower. I had been in my early teens before I ever had one.

We did not have water in our house back in Ireland before that. I thought of my family's home. I dried myself and felt better. Rubbing my skin hard with the towel until it was red. But that was another thing about getting old. It was harder to get all the nooks and crevices dried out properly. You had to twist round and with the joints getting stiffer this was not always pleasant.

I cooked myself a feed of potatoes, hummus, salad and fish. It was what I had in the fridge. That was another thing. We did not have a fridge in Ireland when I was growing up. I shared some of my food with the hound as I called him. He was always in luck when I was cooking as I would feed him pieces of raw carrot which he liked. I would also give him some of my own cooked food when I sat down at the table and ate. I had to watch as he would take the finger off me. The hunger was on me that night. The dog did not get so much. He was focused on every mouthful hoping for the best. When I was finished I let him lick the plate. Then I washed it, got up, and went to bed.

My job the next morning was collecting two pieces of art from a high-end dealer. I did not need Perry. This dealer liked the drink and the smell of whiskey was always on him no matter how early I arrived. His home was a multi-million-dollar three-story stone house in the city by the lake. It was like the big brownstones in New York City. In this case the centre of the house had been gutted and spiral staircases went up inside on to landings and doors opened from these into different rooms. It was impressive. Itself it was a work of art. He stored some of his art in a storage space he rented. But much of it hung on these walls. He would bring his most valuable and trusted customers to his home and let them see these pieces, selling one every now and then and replacing it with another from his storage.

That morning I was collecting an Andy Warhol and an old master, I did not know who the old master was. I thought how come there was never any talk of old mistresses in the context of art. The dealer had no idea I was not insured to carry such valuable works. I suppose it never occurred to him I would take such risks. These two pieces together were worth tens of millions of dollars. I also wondered why he did not worry I would hit him over the head and steal them. Maybe it was the whiskey. I said nothing. It will be alright I would say to myself under my breath. I would not damage anything, including his head. And anyway where could I sell them?

I wrapped the two pieces in large thick pads, loaded them up and headed for the south west suburbs. He rode with me in the truck. We took the 290 expressway. It was busy. A big silver Mercedes flew past me and cut in. I cursed the driver for cutting me off, for his or her wealth in this land of great poverty, for them and their tinted windows and their lack of compassion for the poor. Driving at top speed past poverty-stricken, violent south Chicago. Mercedes degenerates.

'Do you follow the basketball Sean? That is where we are going to today. Our buyer plays for the Bulls.' 'No I am sorry, I do not know much about it.' 'Then you probably do not know the man we are delivering to this morning. He might be the next Michael Jordan.' I did not say to this bourgeois man that I did not like Jordan because he would not meet the workers who came to Chicago to get support for their struggle for better pay and conditions in the sweat shops in Asia where his Air Jordan shoes were made. 'He is one of the top players at the moment. I think this is why he likes the Andy Warhol piece. It is one Warhol did of Muhammed Ali. The greatest.'

After an hour's drive we reached our destination in the south west suburbs. It was a huge new mansion. But it lacked charm. I was thinking the owner would have been better to have spent his money and bought a house like that of the art dealer in the city. Then he could have lived in art. There were three cars parked out front and it had a four-car garage attached. The dealer rang the bell. A very tall fit looking African American man answered the door, obviously the basketball player.

'Aye man, aye man, come in, come in.' 'How are you today, sir?' the dealer asked. 'Sir?' The dealer was being very polite. Of course this African American had money. But maybe I was wrong maybe the dealer was genuinely not racist. But I had my doubts, my experience was the higher up the income scale the greater was the racism. Just on occasion better covered up, especially when there was money involved.

I brought in the paintings and my step ladder. Perching on the ladder I measured up the spot on the wall overlooking the front doorway where we came in. I drove in the hanging and the two of them handed me up the Warhol. Hanging there it transformed the entrance to the house. They both stood back and looked at it. I got down and looked too. After a few minutes the African American man turned to me and said: 'What do you think about it man?' I looked him in the eye. I respected that he had asked me. I could feel he was from a working background like myself and he thought my view was as valuable to him as that of anybody else, as that of the dealer.

'I think it is great. I never thought much of Warhol before. I thought he only painted cans of beans. But that was my loss. He has got Ali just right with his defiance and anger and aggression and power and humour. You made a great choice.' 'Aye it is a good one alright. He got Ali good, he got the man good.' And he chuckled to himself with satisfaction and pride.

We then brought in the much smaller Old Master. Warhol's Ali had impressed me but the Old Master was of a different world. We put it in the basketball player's small study hanging it on one of the side walls so when he was sitting at his desk he could swivel round and take it in, have a look at it when he wanted to take a break, have his soul nurtured. Its richness transformed his home in a different way from the Warhol. The Warhol dominated the entrance and open centre of his house. It stood out for you and it was right for where it was and what it did. It welcomed you and challenged you and filled you with excitement and energy and power. It demanded your attention.

The Old Master was different. It was there for you to chance upon. When you did it invited you to absorb it, to bring it into yourself. It created a soul for the house. It made the house rich and beautiful and mysterious and wondrous. This tiny piece of canvas covered in oil by a man long dead had this power. I could see what would happen. It would grow on its owner and nurture him and his house more every day. I admired this African American man from Chicago poverty who had fought his way on the basketball courts to be able to afford these pieces and who had kept his spirit sufficiently intact to be able to want and to appreciate this great art.

On the way home the dealer turned in the truck and said to me: 'Pull in at that steakhouse where we put in the pieces the last time. You remember the one. I want to see if they are still satisfied and also for the job you have done, especially what you said to my client, I will buy you lunch.' And that is what we did. The food was good. Wild caught salmon, backed up with mashed potatoes, vegetables and salad. Both of us tucked in. The dealer threw back a few more whiskies. So that is how he survives the drinking, I thought, he eats well. The owners of the restaurant were all over us, they still loved the art and the food was on the house.

He was only one of the clients I had that was rich and sold to the rich. I had another client, an elderly lady, on Lake Shore Drive who imported and sold and lived amongst antique Chinese and Japanese art and furniture. Her apartment was decorated with this Oriental art. It was a pleasure to look at and a pleasure to move it. This lady came to see this appreciation of mine and came to respect me. Her apartment looked out over the lake and with the Chinese and Japanese art was a very attractive place too. But she was always complaining as she had bought the apartment in the winter when the trees were bare of leaves and when she had a good view of the lake. It was only when the first spring came and the trees got their leaves back that she realised her view was only part time. Her continual complaining was accompanied by a bit of a humorous laugh at herself. I did not show it but when I would leave I would laugh also.

This lady had her very expensive apartment. She bought extremely expensive art. She had a Mexican cleaning lady who came in every day. She herself did not work. I wondered where she got all her money. What company, in what country, in what sweatshop, in what foundry did she have her shares? Maybe she only deserved to have a view of the lake for six months of the year.

I moved paintings and art work for a group of artists who occupied a large building on the south-west side of the Loop. I would park in the alley to the side and load up. One winter's day when there was snow and ice everywhere, I had loaded up and went to drive off. Then I noticed. I swore in rage. I had a flat tire. I got out the tools and started to jack up the truck to change the wheel. The problem was the ground under the truck was covered with ice. I had to get down under the truck and lie on my back to be able to situate the jack in the right place. I was soon wet and frozen. I also worried that the jack would slip in the icy ground and the truck would come down on top of me and that would be the end of me. I was lucky and things worked out. I never passed that alley again without remembering this.

The moving work let me get to know not only the brutally hot and humid summers but also the brutally cold and frigid winters. The moving work also let me get to know many areas of Chicago. I got to know the African American South side better than most European American Chicagoans. The work also took me into the top art galleries and antiques stores, into warehouses and family homes. I got to know a lot of Chicago.

In this moving work when I moved art from the School of the Arts Institute I was around some of the greatest art of the world. I also moved art for many young aspiring and experimental artists. My mind was opened up as I moved the different art works and met the different artists. Some of this I could not decide was it art or was it not. I thought more about what was art. I read some of Trotsky on art. This helped me to think that art was the ability to bring the unconscious on to the page or the canvas or the piece of stone or metal. But did this explain it all? What about the painting of a landscape? Was this bringing the unconscious onto the canvas? Maybe that was it. If it was just a copy of the landscape it was not art, it was just like a photograph. Maybe it was only art if the painter could bring something of his or her own unconscious onto the canvas. Maybe if they could not do this it was not art. It was just copying. I read what Van Gogh said about art. That it was: 'Nature. Reality. Truth. But with a conception the artist brings out in it which he disentangles and makes free and clears up.' I read also where he said that Millet's painting of a man sowing grain had 'more soul' than the actual sower himself. I struggled more to understand. Moving art was good for me and opened up my mind. I wished that I had got the chance to move a Van Gogh or a Millet.

I regretted having to give up the moving work as my health deteriorated. I had earned a living at it. I had met new people. I had got to know a lot of Chicago. I felt good being able to do the physical work. It seemed like it reaffirmed me in my confidence that I was still alive and able to function. It was therapeutic. It worked out my frustrations and angers and homesickness.

Throughout my moving career I never gave up the political struggle. I involved myself in strikes and student struggles. I read the enemy's press every day. I followed events. I organised as best as I could a small group dedicated to revolutionary ideas. I tried, but without success, to bring some older former revolutionaries back into organised collective struggle with me but in the main they were unable to overcome the damage done to them by sectarianism and ultra-leftism. But politically this period, the period of my faction fight within the CWI, of my expulsion and my fight against my expulsion from that organisation, the period of my trying to build the LMV, the period when I was again immersed in blue collar work and with people from all racial backgrounds, this was one of the most fruitful periods of my life. I was able to better develop my critical thinking and my self-criticism and to understand why the revolutionary left had failed to put down roots in the working class. As I drove the Chicago streets, carried the loads of furniture, moved the precious and not so precious art, my mind never ceased struggling to understand the lessons of my own revolutionary experience. Every day the shackles were further removed from my mind. And along with that every day I saw the brutal racial segregation and the vicious class oppression and exploitation of the city's racial minorities and its working class, and with this my hatred of capitalism was strengthened. And so was my determination to carry on the struggle to contribute to building the revolutionary alternative. My moving career, far from making me give up my revolutionary work, instead strengthened my commitment to my revolutionary work, to my struggle to build the revolutionary socialist nucleus. It never occurred to me to give up.

CHAPTER 42

A NIGHT OUT IN CHICAGO

I TRIED TO DRAW CONCLUSIONS from the political events and my political experiences of the past years in a number of ways. One was by directly discussing with Richard and others who had gone through similar experiences. But another was by making sure I maintained some personal and social life and by observing more closely and carefully other peoples' personal and social lives, by more closely listening to and having a dialogue with people. By being more open to the reality that I could learn from everybody, well if not from everybody from every social interaction. Partly to this end, and also I have to say for the pleasure, I started to go out on Friday nights to a local Mexican American pub. I was always the only European American in this pub. I usually wore my black pants, black shoes and charcoal grey shirt. If I say it myself I did not look bad for a man in his fifties. In the Mexican American pub they had live music on Friday nights and people worked out their stress. When the music would play, phony steam would shoot out from under the stage every now and then. It was a madhouse. The noise would be terrible. There was a great raw buzz to it. It was a bit like an Irish pub in Camden Town in the old days with the emigrant Irish trying to get rid of their Catholic hierarchy created demons.

One night when I got to this pub, the effects of the day's work and the food and my bad health had left me half asleep. I laid down across the front seat of the truck to close my eyes for a few minutes and rest. I dozed off. When I awoke, I sat back up and got out and I found myself beside two young Latino American men. They thought I had been hiding in the truck to watch them. One of them started shouting at me and pulled a gun and pointed it at me. 'Mother fucker, mother fucker,' he shouted and worked himself up into a threatening frenzy. I drew on my few words of Spanish. 'Yo no tengo una problema con tigo.' This calmed him down a bit. 'Take it easy, take it easy,' his friend said to him. I pointed to the bar and myself and the bar again and things quieted down. It was a close thing.

There was usually a security man inside the door of the bar to search people for weapons as they entered. But tonight a short round lady was doing this job, searching the men as well as the women as if there was nothing unusual in it. I smiled and tried to catch her eye but she was all business. I took my seat at the bar and ordered my usual whiskey. I only ever drank whiskey as it was the only liquor that calmed me. Wine made me aggressive and beer I thought was just drinking a concoction of water that the beer industry came up with to take people's money. The owner of the pub was always very friendly to me. He probably hoped I was the first of a new wave of European Americans, maybe even yuppies, who would bring him more business.

I was sitting sipping my whiskey when I heard my name being called. 'Irelanda. Hey man. How is it going?' It was José, a Mexican American man who lived a few doors from me. He had told me he had been born in Texas and moved to Chicago where he had his own landscaping business. Some Mexican people had little landscaping businesses which did the gardens of people's homes. I could not understand why people would have gardens and not work them themselves. Or better still let them grow wild. But this was America and anyway, if a dollar could be edged into human life it was edged in, and to help the profit makers, governments passed laws to make gardens be trimmed and neat. What a country? I much preferred a wild garden. But anyway. My Mexican friend was tall and big for his race. I had seen him without his shirt once and he had two healed bullet hole scars in his upper shoulder. He was not stupid and he followed events.

'Irelanda. What about that country of yours? Are you ever going to stop that fighting? Bombings and killings. And what about those ones who won't let others worship their god or walk through their neighbourhoods. That is no good that. I could solve it for you. It would be no bother at all.' I would normally have been angry at somebody who told me they had some simple answer for the problems at home. But with the whiskey in me I was mellow enough and interested enough to hear his 'solution.'

'You know what the problem is with you Irish. I can tell you. You have too long of a memory. You have to forget. You have to let things go. Otherwise it will go on and on and destroy the lot of you. I was like that one time. I would not let things go. My memory was too long. But I had to stop it. I had to let things go, to forget about the revenge, otherwise it would have ruined me. If I hadn't I would not be here now.' I thought about the bullet hole scars. So that was it. He had to forget whoever gave him those scars.

He had to forgo his revenge in order to live. He knew what Confucius knew when he had written that those who set out on a journey of revenge should dig two graves. I just smiled and said: 'You might be right.' He said: 'You know I am right.'

Having received a civil response from me on Ireland he went on to talk about what was really on his mind, what he really wanted to share with me. 'You know what else. I will tell you this, life is a fucker. I split up with that woman of mine last week. She is gone now. Finished. She left and went back to her mother's. Took the young ones too. Well fuck her and fuck the lot of them.' I could hear the pain and anger in him. In spite of his macho talk he was hurting. 'Aye fuck that and fuck her and fuck the lot of them. I do not need them. I am going to get me another woman. But I won't make the same mistake this time. That one that just left me and took my kids was a city one, born and reared a city one. Them city ones, they are too much above themselves, anything they want they just ask for it and expect the man to get it for them. And I mean money, a house, whatever for the kids, and I mean pussy too. They just tell you do it this way, do it that way, do it their way. They have no respect for a man at all. That is how bad it is. That is not how a woman should act. Wanting to dictate the pussy business, sure everybody knows, that is for a man to decide. There will be no more of that. This time I am going to Mexico and get a woman there, a Mexican woman from a village. Them Mexican village women know their place. I will bring one back and train her. That is the best way.'

I looked at him with a smile, at this man who was trying to stand against the stream in his personal world as I was standing against the stream in my political world, standing against the tide in his family world as I was doing in my political world. 'I do not know José, my friend. I am not sure that will work. The Mexican village women are like all women, when they come to the city and get a job they learn fast. They start earning their own money, they have their own money, and then they are not so dependent on a man and so they feel they can speak out and stand up for themselves. Your new woman will get a job up here in the big city and start earning her own money. And as a Puerto Rican city woman told me recently, "I earn my own money now so I do not have to take shit from any man." You know you will need your Mexican woman to work. When you have kids in this country and are a working class family both parents have to work to make ends meet and when this happens the woman knows she not only has the right to speak out but that she has the economic base to speak out, and to make her own demands. I think your plan will not work my friend. I think it might be an idea from the past, I do not think it works anymore, especially in a big city in a big modern country like here. And anyway do you not think a woman who speaks out is better to be around? More life in her.'

I smiled as I said this to take the edge of our disagreement. But he was not going to retreat. He was determined. He had lost a lot in the last week or so and had to keep this plan in his head to try and maintain some sort of equilibrium. 'It will work. It will work. I will make it work.' But he was smart and I could see I had sown some doubts. Also at the centre of him was a kindness and he would not be immune to the needs and kindness of his new Mexican woman. 'I will be off here Irelanda. It was nice to see you.' 'You too my friend. Adios.' We shook hands, I felt his hard callused hand and liked him for it and for his sharing of his pain with me.

As far as I could see I was the only European American in the bar. The rest were Mexican Americans. I was only coming to understand that some Mexican people looked down on African American people, also on Puerto Rican people, saying they had 'black blood'. This was a bit of a shock to me. The black revolt had not had as much of an effect on Mexican and Central Americans as it had on African Americans and Puerto Ricans, and even to an extent on European Americans. Part of the reason was that many Latino Americans had only come to the US after the Black revolt and also partly because some Latino Americans saw the best way to get jobs was by working for less and in this way replacing African American people. This was an obstacle to unity and solidarity and empathy.

'Como esta?' I asked the barman and owner. I was showing my respect by using my few words of Spanish. I had gone down to Mexico a few times to discuss with people. I had gone to Zapata's state of Morelos to see where the revolutionary had come from. 'Bien, bien.' I held up my glass for another drink. He turned to get it. As he did so a small shot glass went flying through the air. This was a weapon that was occasionally used in this bar. If it got you on the face or head you would know you were hit.

I turned to see what was happening and saw that for the first time in my visits to that bar there was an African American man in the pub. The glass had been thrown at him. And after the glass came half a dozen customers who began to hit him with their fists. He threw himself up from his seat and plunged for the door dragging his assailants with him. He was half thrown out and half ran out of the bar. Like myself he had wanted a night out with the music and a good time and there he was, thrown out and beaten because of his race. I was not thrown out and beaten because of my race. The men who had attacked him gathered round in a clump talking excitedly to each other, obviously proud of what they had done. I felt enraged as I thought of the humiliation the African American man would be feeling. That was not right.

I turned to the owner to see his reaction. He was pleased. He didn't want African Americans in his pub. Just like with the owners of the Irish American pubs it was better for business to try and keep the pubs segregated, to keep the Irish Americans coming to the Irish American pubs, the Latino Americans coming to the Latino American pubs. The Irish American pub owners especially tried to keep out African Americans. Too many African American customers and they might lose their Irish American customers. In the case of the Mexican American pub owner too many African Americans and he might lose his Latino American customers and where would he be then? The owner waved away my money when I went to pay for the drink. He wanted to keep me, the European American, coming back. Not like the African American man they had just thrown out. But I was finished in that bar. I was not going to drink where they threw out African American people or for that matter anybody for their race. The stress that had been leaving me came back as I thought about this racist crap. Without another word I threw my drink back and headed for the door.

José caught me by the arm on my way out. 'What is up man? Why are you leaving?' I looked at him. 'José, did you not see that. It is as bad as my country. Northern Ireland. There the Protestants and Catholics fight. Here we just saw Mexican Americans attack that man because he is African American. That was not right. I am not going to drink in a bar that allows that to go on. What do you think José?' He answered: 'You are right. What can I say, you are right.' And he turned away ashamed and I moved on and left the bar. I never went back. I started going to a local Puerto Rican bar instead.

Climbing up into my truck I headed for home. There was a group of young African American men and women on the corner of Western and Division. They were dressed in jeans and T-shirts and shouting and playing and running around. I had to stop at the lights and some of them saw that I was what they thought European American. They also saw that I had a truck and so was not totally broke. 'Hey, man. Fuck you. What are you looking at?' I had my window open as the air conditioning did not work. As cautiously as possible, trying not to let them see, I pushed down the lock on the door with my elbow. It was a good job I did. One young man rushed off the side walk grabbed the door handle and tried to pull the door open. If it had been unlocked I would have been in trouble. At that point the lights changed and I moved off. 'Mother fucker you and your mother fucking truck,' he shouted after me.

His rage was justified but misdirected. He could not afford a truck. It was the centuries of slavery again and on top of that the racism of US capitalism. He was most likely unemployed. Over 40% of the young African American men in that area had no jobs. The majority of those who did have jobs were paid the lowest of wages, were not in a union and could be laid off any time the boss felt like it. I called them Greenspan's boys and girls after Alan Greenspan, the then head of the Federal Reserve, the US central Bank who always made sure there was never full employment. No matter how hard the youth studied, no matter how hard they tried for work, there would always be millions with no jobs. The system was set up to make sure this happened. It could not function in any other way. And to make this more possible politically, the racist regime made sure unemployment was concentrated more amongst African Americans and Latino Americans. This was the cause along with the lack of unemployment pay for men that there was the huge illegal drug business and the violence that flowed from it. Along with this US capitalism saw the illegal drug business as another way to keep people down and to allow them carry out their policy of mass incarceration.

I cursed America and its capitalist system as I passed corner after corner of Greenspan's youth. I took a drive over to California and 26th, where sat the huge square concentration camp prison of Cook County jail. The youth and workers who had not been able to endure the regime of Greenspan and his class on the streets were in the cells inside that nightmare of a building. It was full of the vicious repression of the guards and with drugs and inter-gang violence as the people in it were driven to madness. I thought again of the US having only 5% of the world's population and yet having 25% of the world's prisoners. This was a staggering reality that was hardly mentioned in the mass media of US capitalism. Aye, land of the free alright. I screwed down the window and spit out. What a system. US capitalism in all its glory, the street corners filled with Greenspan's boys and girls and the concentration camp of Cook County jail to lock them up. Only twenty miles from these corners and this jail there were scores of multi-millionaires and billionaires such as the Pritzkers and the war criminal Donald Rumsfeld, living in mansions overlooking the lake. I wished I could drag them and all their class by the neck and make them live here amongst the poverty and misery they made happen, lock them up in Cook County jail which they had got working people to build.

I had visited a prisoner in the jail on a few occasions. To get in you had to arrive around 5 am and get in line. The line was made up mostly of African American and Latino mothers and children. The prisoner I was visiting was as they all were brought to a seat inside a clear bullet-proof screen in which there were holes. You had to speak to each other and listen to each other through these holes. I tried to do so. In my first visit, I spoke, then turned my head and put my ear to the holes to hear the response. But the noise of all the other visitors and prisoners was so great I could not hear. Then a visitor beside me, a Puerto Rican man, took me by the arm. 'This your first time man?' he asked. I nodded. 'Look this way.' Then he showed me how to do it. It was solidarity between prison visitors.

Standing up he shouted through the holes at the prisoner he was visiting. He made sure he and the prisoner could see each other's mouths and to better help they made exaggerated mouth movements so they could lip read what each other said. At the same time he and the prisoner gestured and jumped around to make their meaning even more clear. I could see that some children were at ease with this, but others were frightened, some weeping and calling as they could not escape the noise and theatrics of the waiting room. And it was theatre, and a theatre created by the needs of the prisoners and their visitors. I was never able to really manage to do this theatre but I went some way to being on the stage at Cook County jail.

After I drove past the jail I felt dehydrated so I pulled into a store and bought some juice. I was unlocking the pick-up truck again to drive on home when I heard a woman's voice at my back. 'Hey man,' I turned and saw a short, slim, attractive, Puerto Rican woman looking up at me. 'Hey man, where are you going? Will you give me a ride up to Fullerton? I have nothing for the bus.' This did not sound right. If she wanted to take the bus she would have been more likely to ask me for money for the fare. I thought she had a different plan. But it was on my way and I felt like talking to somebody.

As she climbed up into the truck, a European American stoutly built woman came running over. She was with a Latino American man who was much shorter and who walked behind her with his head down. He looked like he was ashamed of being with her. 'Hey Maria, where are you going? Are you alright?' The Puerto Rican woman answered impatiently: 'Sure. I am just getting a ride up home. I will see you tomorrow.' And she closed the door on her friend. I started the truck, backed up and moved off. 'Is your friend okay?' I asked. 'Sure, she is alright. Just stupid that is all. She hangs with that loser and gives him pussy and he gives her nothing. That's not for me. If somebody wants pussy from me they have to give me something. I have nothing else to sell.'

I was taken aback by the woman's words. She was making no bones about her sex being a commodity. Here was capitalist ideology in its most unadorned form. But the woman did not stop there. 'What about yourself. Do you want a date?' I looked at her and smiled. 'No thanks. You look very good but I do not pay for sex.'

'Come on man, everybody pays for sex one way or another. Man or woman we all pay for it. That is how it is. Come on. We can go to my place. You will have a good time. I will take care of you. It will be a load of your mind. You look like you know your way around a pussy.' I had never before in such a short time heard the full hypocrisy stripped off sex under capitalism.

I laughed out loud. What an avalanche of powerful expressions. It would be a load of my mind. She had nothing else to sell. Knowing my way around a pussy. I thought this woman should be a writer. She was able to express her feelings, observations and insights with extreme sharpness, precision, clarity, power and originality. I could never have thought up these expressions in this context. How many men, with all the sexual pressures, felt just the way she said after having sex, felt that a load had been taken of their mind? I felt this way myself sometimes. I turned in the seat and looked at her as we stopped at a red light. What experiences this woman must have had, what strength she must have to survive these experiences with this clarity of thought, this sharpness of insight and phrase. I admired her.

Feeling guilty for turning down her offer of sex I felt I had to explain myself. 'If I paid for sex I would feel bad afterwards, feel that I had treated you badly and feel that I had treated myself badly. It would take me days to get over it. I would be damaged by it. I am sorry. I feel we are very vulnerable when we have sex and if we do not have trust with our partner then we have to harden and brutalise ourselves, have to put up protective walls, to try and not get hurt. This is not good. I used to think I could just switch off my mind and have the pleasure but I learned that I could not.'

Coming right back at me she said: 'I do not know what you are talking about. But anyway just give me twenty bucks then to help me out. We do not have to have sex. Or if you do not want to have sex I could just put these soft lips on you. I know you would like that. That is not really having sex as you call it, just a common or garden blow job that is all.' I laughed and said: 'You are a tough woman alright.' And with that she gave me a look and said we had reached her corner. I pulled over, reached in my pocket and gave her $10.00. She said thanks and off she went. I wished I could have got her to put her life down on paper. It would have been a best seller and it would have helped many people to better understand their worlds.

I thought about my personal life, such as it was at that time. I was exhausted with my moving work. My head and thoughts were taken up with trying to get a new revolutionary nucleus off the ground. But even with this, being the very social person I was I had a few personal relationships over this period. But as usual I did not let them come to anything as I was focused on my political work and also I had my moving work to do.

That night after the pub I got home and poured myself a Powers. I mourned I was not in Ireland. I was in Chicago. But Ireland was pulling at me. If I lived one hundred years in the US I would still miss Ireland. But the Powers helped. I sang to myself. If I ever go across the sea to Ireland, be it even at the closing of my day ... Aye Galway Bay ... I wish I was in Carrickfergus ... I would swim over the ... aye anything to get home. I will arise and go now and go to Innisfree ... In spite of his later politics that Yeats was a poet alright. He was the man. Well no, Joyce was the man, but so far ahead, so much higher on the cliff face than anybody else it was hard to remember bits of him to recite to myself. I thought again of home and sat in my chair with my head down in loneliness.

CHAPTER 43

AN ALTERNATIVE IRISH NIGHT

INEVER SHIFTED FROM THE STRUGGLE to build the revolutionary nucleus. This involved discussions with anybody who was interested, and writing articles and documents and flyers and getting them distributed. The Internet had entered my world and I was able to circulate my ideas more than ever before. From selling 400 copies of the paper a month back in Ireland at one time, I was able with Richard's help to get our ideas out to tens of thousands every month. I continued my revolutionary work, seeking to change the consciousness of workers and youth I would meet or with whom I would be in contact and convince them to help build a revolutionary nucleus.

I had not fought to find my place in the world as a revolutionary, not invested all I had in building the CWI and learnt all I had from this, to give it up just because the CWI turned out to have a corrupt leadership which had expelled and fired me and lied about me and slandered me. Building the revolutionary nucleus was my life. I used everything to this end, including my Irish background. But I had a problem, I detested the majority of the people who ran the very large Irish American world that existed.

This Irish American world was dominated by Irish American racist politicians, business people and the hierarchy of the Catholic Church. The class these formed sought to claw its way up in US capitalist society by ingratiating itself with the US capitalist class as a whole. To do so it threw out the revolutionary tradition of Irish history and its people. It was alright to sing songs of glorious defeats in pubs as long as this singing filled the pockets of the Irish American pub owners, to go beyond that was unacceptable. This Irish American elite would not have been welcome within the US capitalist class if it spoke positively of James Connolly, the Irish revolutionary socialist, or James Larkin, the Irish trade union leader, both of whom had organised as revolutionaries in the US as well as in Ireland. The Irish American elite's substitute for Ireland's revolutionary heritage was to dye the river green on 17th March. This Irish American elite nauseated me.

This Irish American elite had its vast network of churches, schools, hospitals and full-time organisers from the Cardinals down to the priests and the nuns. The majority of the US Supreme Court at the time were members of this Catholic organisation, this Catholic apparatus, this male-dominated, this anti-women organisation. The Irish American Catholic elite above all wanted to keep their snout in the US capitalist trough and hold onto their power. So it worked together to suppress any knowledge of Ireland's revolutionary heritage. Never mentioned was how the Catholic Church came to Ireland, destroyed the country's culture, smashed its Brehon laws which were much more equitable and which had much greater rights for women than the then new Catholic laws that it imposed.

I came to see a significant difference between myself and most Irish American people, not just myself and the Irish American elite. Born in the US, most Irish Americans bought into 'the US is the best country in the world' propaganda. Racism tended to be strong amongst them. They dominated the building trades unions which had right wing policies and which sought to exclude African Americans from these organisations and jobs in this sector. The trade union bureaucracy in those unions, with a large Irish American membership, played a major part in pushing this racism and in destroying Irish revolutionary traditions.

And of course all these forces were linked to the Chicago cops with their large Irish American component and whom I never forgot had murdered Black Panther leader and socialist Fred Hampton. I did not frequent the Irish American world.

Myself and most Irish who had been born and lived in Ireland were the product of centuries of oppression. We had developed a way to deal with that oppression. We sought to prevent the ruling British colonial and imperialist class from understanding us and so easily repressing us. This took the form of regular uprisings and struggle. But not only that. It also permeated every aspect of peoples' lives. People born in Ireland tended to speak indirectly, rarely answered a question directly, tended to create their own new words or used existing words differently. On first coming to the US I thought I was always being insulted because people spoke so directly and bluntly. Coming out of the Irish-born culture, I understood from my historical experience that the less the rulers could understand what was being said the better. The less they could prove the oppressed were rebellious the more difficult it was to justify repressing them. This was why Irish speech and culture was indirect and subtle. It was summed up in the expression: 'Whatever you say, say nothing.' For this reason it was amongst the African American population not the Irish American population I felt most at home. It was there I felt that my pattern of speech and thought were most similar. They too had suffered centuries of oppression, much worse oppresion.

While my health allowed I organised my own activities around 17th March. I called them Alternative Irish Nights. I knew Jimmy Lee Robinson, an African American man and a world class Blues musician. I asked him to play at one of these. The theme was to thank the Black revolt, the US civil rights movement, the African American people for inspiring the civil rights movement in Ireland and in doing so sparking off a new interest in Irish culture. An Irish American man offered an art gallery as a venue. It was run by his African American girlfriend. When we arrived the gallery was closed. I went to his house. He whined that he had been drunk and smoking dope the night before and had fallen asleep. I could see he was lying. He had just been hoping I would not be able to find his house.

I knew why he had not opened the gallery. He and his African American girlfriend feared for their careers if they hung out with Jimmy Lee and I. His girlfriend worked for the Mayor Daly political machine, one of the African Americans it hired to try and hide its racism. I told the two of them this home truth. 'You won't let us in because you work for that racist Daly in City Hall. You do not want to be seen with Jimmy Lee and me. Jimmy Lee does not kiss Daly's boots and I am a socialist. That is why you have not opened the gallery.' I turned to the man: 'You are just a wimp who talks about being against racism, has a black partner but when push comes to shove you back down.' His girlfriend called me a white honky and to go back to where I came from and they went into their house and slammed the door.

With the gallery closed we went to Chicago's biggest Irish pub and asked could Jimmy Lee join in on the music session that was going on. There were about a dozen musicians sitting in a circle playing. It was like I had taken a grenade, pulled the pin, and thrown it in amongst them. They huddled and whispered and huddled and looked over their shoulders. Then one of them came over to tell us that Jimmy could not sit in because the Blues was different from the Irish music. A different beat and rhythm you see. Their racism made me ashamed to be Irish, and I was utterly humiliated for Jimmy Lee.

I turned. 'Jimmy Lee I apologise. I got you into this. Those are a bunch of racists. Come on. Let us go.' Jimmy said nothing. His face was impassive. He had no doubt experienced this many times before. We turned to leave together. I thought of the woman in Australia who had curled up her lip at me and called me a dirty Irish.

As we left a man and woman separated themselves from the group that was playing the music and hurried after us. 'Wait, wait. I know a place we could have a bit of a session.' The man had a pronounced Cork accent. I was sceptical. I did not want to put Jimmy in another humiliating situation. 'Are you sure? I will not put Jimmy through that racist crap again. Because that is what it was.' 'I know, I know, you are right. But this will be okay.'

Jimmy and I got into my truck and followed the two Cork people to another pub. Before we went in we exchanged introductions. 'Neiley and Mary, pleased to meet you.' We went into the pub. There was Patricia behind the bar and two other customers. It was not going to be a wild night going by the numbers. But Patricia gave a big smile shouted a welcome to Neiley and Mary and to Jimmy and myself. She was genuinely pleased to see us. 'Set up there in the corner.' Jimmy plugged in his guitar and Neiley got out his bodhrán.

Jimmy wore a long coat with shoulder pieces and a cowboy hat. He wore high top boots and spurs which he tapped as an accompaniment when he played his guitar and sang. He had his guitar, his percussion spurs and his voice. All in all he was his own ensemble. He began to play the Blues.

Neiley sat and joined in. Jimmy sang a line and then gestured to Neiley to sing a line in response. Neiley was used to knowing the words to the song in advance. But gradually and with help from Jimmy, Neiley got into it. And in no time at all we had this wonderful sight and sound, Jimmy and his Blues guitar and spurs and singing, and Neiley with his very good voice and bodhrán producing a synthesis of the two traditions, the Blues and the Irish music. I thought of the racists in the other pub and their lies and how their lives were made worse by their racism. I felt no sympathy for them.

Some years later Jimmy Lee developed cancer in his sinuses. He knew the pain and indignity that lay ahead. He drove out to a forest preserve and surrounded by the trees and grass and the beauty of the natural world he shot himself in the head. What courage. What a sensitve man. Choosing to die amongst the beauty, the nature of the forest reserve.When I heard I thought about my Aunt Lizzie. They both ended their lives. He in a wooded park, she in a small water-filled dam, both back to nature, both were part of nature. I wished I could sit and talk to Jimmy Lee and my aunt and hear their wisdom and hear Jimmie Lee's music. My aunt had never had the chance to learn to play a musical instrument. The owners of the big houses to whom she worked all had pianos but they never allowed her to learn on them. What different life experiences Jimmy Lee and my Aunt Lizzie had to both end up taking their own lives and both in nature. I tried to find Jimmy Lee's grave but could find no trace of it. I grieved. Jimmy Lee was a good, strong, cultured and heroic African American man. I thought of the racists in the pub who would not let him play. It was no wonder I stayed away from the racist Irish American world.

I thought of Billy Holliday singing *Strange Fruit*. The strange fruit were the bodies of lynched African American men hanging by the neck by ropes from trees after being hanged by the Ku Klux Klan. The KKK was a racist terrorist movement organised by the white ruling class and made up of European American mobs. The KKK brought their whole families along to brutalise them to the barbarity of hanging African American men and burning their bodies. They brought their children along to wean them onto this monstrous crime. After the African American men were lynched and their bodies burnt they were left hanging on the trees as a warning. Hence the 'strange fruit'. This whole barbaric slaughter and the KKK itself was organised by the former slave-owning class who were transforming themselves into the new capitalist class in the South and were making sure the power and wealth did not slip from their hands in the process of this transition.

I thought of Jimmy when he was told he had cancer. He would have weighed things up, taken into account the centuries of oppression and suffering of his African American people. When he did so, putting an end to things probably did not seem so terrible. After all, his and his people's lives were close to terrible a lot of the time anyway. He had probably never expected much of a life in the first place. Like so many African American people, Jimmy would have thought he was 'blessed' just to have survived the nightmare of racist America as long as he had and to have become the musician he had. So to Jimmy Lee, ending his life with his own hand had probably drifted in and out of his mind before.

If your life was so hard, bitter, brutal and humiliating that it could end at any time with a lynching or a cop's bullet, that the odds were always stacked against you, then ending your life by your own hand was not such a big deal. My aunt ending her own life was directly related to her suffering and the difficulty of her life. Balancing and judging and weighing up what should be done is different for different people. African American people, given their historical experience do not expect to, nor do they, live as long as long as European American people. European Americans and especially the European American upper classes expect to live much longer and in better circumstances and so in general were less likely to take their own life. The irony was that the world would have been a better place if more of the European American upper class had taken their own lives. The tendency of European American working class people to take their own lives would increase in the future as the crisis of US capitalism would develop and as their living standards would come under greater attack.

One night I was out for a meal with Neiley and Mary. He asked me: 'John I want your opinion on something. I am always getting into arguments and falling out with the different musical groups I am with. Is there something wrong with me? I am not sure. What do you think? ' 'What are the issues you get into disagreement on Neiley? I would need to know this to have an opinion.' 'Well the last one was we were having a session and the man that was introducing the songs talked about the 'k........s' back home. I took offense to this and said so. As you know this is a bad term for the travelling people, like the N-word is for African American people here. I said that the word 'k.......s' should not be used. The result was I got thrown out of the group. I am worried there is something wrong with the way I go on, that I am always getting into these fights.'

'Neiley you must not think there is anything wrong with you. It is exactly the opposite. Think about the example you just gave me. You were right and the other crowd was wrong. What would happen if you kept quiet? You would lose respect for yourself, go along thinking it was wrong and saying nothing. You would end up a bootlicker. Or a voiceless man. Naw, you were right to speak out. So it costs you an easy life with some groups. It would cost you far more if you kept quiet. It could cost you your soul, that is, it would cost you your principles and self-respect, your essence. And who knows if your soul went maybe your music might not be far behind? I do not mean soul like the religious organisations mean it. Like they say it separates us from all other species, like they use the idea of the soul to try and intimidate us by saying if we do not do what they tell us our soul will burn in hell for ever. When I use the word soul I mean the rich complex fighting centre of us that is formed by our experiences and our struggle to endure these experiences. I mean soul like the African American culture means it, soul music, the soul in this way, the soul as Van Gogh used it when he spoke of the painting by Millet of The Sower. Naw, Neiley, you are right, keep speaking up whether it costs you your membership in some group or not. Sure we would not have met if you had not stood up against the racists in that bar when they would not let Jimmy Lee play. Neiley, I always meant to say to you how much I admired you and Mary for standing up that night and walking out with Jimmy Lee and I. It took courage and principle. Thank you.'

Neiley went on: 'Sean, I have never heard anybody talk as much about racism as you, why is this?' 'It is not hard to answer that Neiley. African American people, the African American revolt in America, African American culture, saved my life, saved me from a life of rural backwardness, gave me a way to live my life that has been rewarding and positive. That has allowed me to live my life to my fullest potential. My life would have been a catastrophe without the struggle and inspiration of the African American people. Seeing them marching, refusing to be beaten or hosed off the streets by US regimes and their racist police, reading Malcolm X, Martin Luther King, the Black Panthers, Huey Newton, George Jackson, this changed my life. It let me see that the rural backwardness that was my Donegal in the 1950s and 1960s was not all that existed. Allowed me to see that I could find another life, that I could live another way.

'Neiley I would never want to be like that boy O'Keefe. Let me tell you his story. A relative got him over here on a green card and into one of the skilled trade unions and into a job with good wages and benefits. There were only two or three African Americans in the whole union local and only one on the job O'Keefe was on. He told me this African American man did not like him was not friendly to him. O'Keefe said, and I believe him, that he tried his best to build a friendship but no good. O'Keefe was a good enough man in himself but that is not enough in this country. You have to take a stand. He complained, he had never done nothing to the African American man. Well I let him have it.'

'"O'Keefe," I said. "You are only off the plane. Flew over in a soft seat, meal service served by a flight attendant, even a drink of two if you wanted. Coffee, a warm face towel, the lot. No middle passage for you where if things went wrong you would be thrown over the side to the sharks. You travelled over in comfort and then straight into this well paid union job with benefits. Now compare that to the experience of that African American man you work with. His ancestors brought here against their will centuries ago. Paid no wages for three centuries. Paid no wages for three centuries!!! Can you imagine that? Whipped or hanged and burnt if they objected. His ancestors' families stolen and sold from under them. Then only after the big battles of the 1930s and 1960s was he even able to get into a union and a half decent job. But you were able to fly over from Kerry and straight in. O'Keefe, you are an artist, a singer and poet. You must use imagination? That man has many relatives and neighbours who could fill your job and your union position. But no they are not there, you are there, because you have an Irish relative and along with that you have white skin. That is why that man has no time for you. One of his relatives could be in your job and if there was any justice would be. Then from what you tell me, they give the task of training you in the job to this African American man. This is just to humiliate him further, it is to rub it in further. He has to train the very person whose job one of his family members could have."'

'I told O'Keefe what to do. Fight against the racism in the union and on the job. If he did this then he might begin to get some respect and friendship from the African American man. You know what he said to me? "Oh, I could not do that. It would embarrass my uncle who got me the job and if I lost my job my wife would leave me." Neiley. What the ... ?! I spit upon this excuse. I broke with my whole family to fight religious sectarianism, loyalism, religion of all kinds, the Irish equivalents of racism. O'Keefe made the mistake of coming over here and entering into the Irish American racist world, of marrying into that world, of going into debt and having a family that accepted that world. He could not take a stand against racism without disrupting that world. I know it is hard for him. But my sympathy is limited. I broke from my background. He should break from his. Life is tough.'

I did not have Neiley's company for long. One winter evening his truck would not start in the parking lot at Walmart. He asked the man in the car in the next space for a jump start. The man said: 'If you were my own brother, I would not give you a jump start.' Neiley made up his mind there and then. He came to see me that night. He was enraged. 'I am not going to bring my son up in this country. I am going home.' And this is what he did, left me some of his pieces of sculpture and pieces of furniture he had made, some of his art, which I still treasure, packed up the rest of his things and he and his family went home to Cork. Neiley did not think the US was the 'best country in the world'. Neither did I and with Neiley and Mary gone I was even more isolated in that country.

CHAPTER 44

MOTHER'S AND AUNTS' DEATHS

IT WAS 1997. I got the call: 'Mother is dying, come home.' My mother had been suffering from Alzheimer's. When I would go to see her previous to her illness developing, we would always have our struggles. These were painful. But after she was stricken with the Alzheimer's she would sit there and look at me with empty eyes, eyes which had once been so full of intelligence and life and fight. In these end years she would not know who I was. This was terrible. Much worse than when we had our disagreements and struggles. In those times it was my heart that was breaking.

My mother spent these last years of her life in the home of my sister Mary and her husband Ernie and their children. I was travelling somewhere or back and forward to and within the USA and Canada. Mary and her husband Ernie did more for my mother and looked after her better than I did. I can still see them with their arms around her helping her up their stairs to bed. They were kindness itself. I am ashamed by the little help I gave. Mary and Ernie had very different political views from me. They were Unionist. I was revolutionary socialist. But they had very good hearts. Their care for my mother taught me not to be so rigid and harsh and one-sided in my view of the world and life and people. Taught me to be more dialectical.

Along with my sister Mary and all her family, I stood by my mother's deathbed. She breathed in and out, each breath coming further apart and weaker. Then there were no more. This woman, who had gone through so much in her life, who had struggled and worked until she could no longer do so was now gone. I looked down at that small woman, at that lady, at my mother, at that lady who had given birth to me, who had fed and clothed me, who had guided me, who had fought with me to prepare me as she saw it to have the best in the world she inhabited. Oh what a life of pain. Oh what pain. Oh how regretted that my way of looking at life was so different from her way and from this conflict came the hurt, the breaking of her heart. All that she had worked and fought to give me I rejected for a life which she could not understand. And now she was gone, there was no way I could make up for the hurt I caused her. Life is very harsh.

I had been at my father's bedside when he had died. I had watched his last breath. Now I had been at my mother's bedside when she had died and I had watched her last breath. As I had when my father died, I went outside and breathed the air and grieved alone. Then it had been the air of the wood in Donegal. Now it was the air of the Waterside of Derry and I was sitting on the step outside my sister's home.

I thought about my mother dying there in my sister's house in Derry. She was ninety-seven years old. She had worked in Derry as a domestic servant when she was young. Her employers were liberal capitalists. One of their grandsons would later join the international revolutionary organisation of which I was then part and we became friends. I thought about my mother and how if she had been alive she would have been proud that her daughter had become deputy mayor of the city in which she herself had been a servant.

My father's sister was on her deathbed at the same time my mother was dying. She was in Altnagelvin Hospital just up the road from my sister's house. After my mother died we went up to see her. She had been on strong pain-killing medicine. But the Catholic doctors who were in charge had taken her off it because they said to continue to use it would kill her. They wanted her to die a 'natural death' in 'natural' pain. They wanted to be able, in their stupid conscience, to say the medicine did not kill her, they wanted to be able to tell themselves that some god had killed her. That it was god's will. Whether it was their Catholic god or my aunt's Protestant god I did not know. But my aunt was about to die anyway and the real reason they had taken her off was their backward religious beliefs. They did not want it to be said their treatment had killed her. Their religious beliefs dictated that my aunt died without painkillers, twitching and writhing in suffering in the bed. I hated and detested them and their cruel religious garbage.

I challenged the nurse and doctor to give my aunt the pain-killing medicine. They refused. 'Do you want us to kill her?' they demanded again and again. I was not intimidated by their sneaky religious semantics. 'I want you to stop her pain.' They just kept repeating their stupid mantra until the doctor ran from the room and abandoned the nurse on her own. 'Do you know who that is?' the nurse asked me, referring to the doctor. 'I do not care who he is. I want my aunt put out of pain.' 'That doctor is married to Gerry Adams' sister.' She said this as if identifying this doctor as having links to this right wing, petit bourgeois, Catholic nationalist would have some intimidating effect on me. 'I do not care who he is married to. I want my aunt to get pain-killing medicine.' I did not know if she was telling me the truth about who the doctor was married to or not but to whom he was married made no difference to me.

My aunt's body was brought to my sister's house and my mother and aunt were buried together from there. Carried side by side from the house, my aunt to be buried in Strabane graveyard and my mother to be buried in the old Lifford graveyard where my father and uncle were buried. With my sister Mary's help I arranged for a piper to play at both funerals. My mother's favourite hymn was Amazing Grace. This was played.

A mixture of people attended my mother's funeral. There were family members, relatives, family friends and neighbours, there were some Marxists and Trotskyists. Even some Republicans. The piper played and the preacher preached. But I did not let him speak for me. After he was finished I took my place at the head of the grave and gave my eulogy.

'My mother was born in the Eastern Foothills of the Donegal Mountains. She worked hard all her life. She brought my sisters and I into the world and clothed and fed us. Her life was made much harder by the early death of my father. My mother and I had many struggles over our different ideas. She being who she was and I being who I was, these differences and struggles were substantial. But she taught me many things.'

'She taught me to work hard. For that I am grateful. But most of all she taught me to stand up for what I believed in. She did this by example, as we had different beliefs. The intermingling of our lives was dominated by the reality that we did not believe in the same things and that we were strong people who fought for our different beliefs. I deeply regret the pain I caused my mother in these struggles. I wish with all my being this could have been different. I owe my mother a lot.'

'In recognition of all that she gave me, I would like to read two poems in her honour and out of respect and to try and express what she has meant to me. They are by James Joyce the greatest writer and fighter for intellectual and artistic integrity ever to come out of Ireland. My mother, like Joyce, fought for what she saw as true things. They were both as she might have said, 'sticklers' for the truth.'

'This first poem is by Joyce on giving a flower to his daughter. I think it is appropriate for my mother.'

'A Flower Given To My Daughter

Frail the white rose and frail are
Her hands that gave

Whose soul is sere and paler
Than time's wan wave.

Rosefrail and fair – yet frailest
A wonder wild
In gentle eyes thou veilest,
My blue veiled child.'

'And this is also by Joyce. I would like to read it for my mother and also my father and my uncle both of whom have been dead for many years.

'Tilly

He travels after a winter sun,
Urging the cattle along a cold red road,
Calling to them, a voice they know,
He drives his beasts above Cabra.

The voice tells them home is warm.
They moo and make brute music with their hoofs.
He drives them with a flowering branch before him,
Smoke pluming their foreheads.

Boor, bond of the herd,
Tonight stretch full by the fire!
I bleed by the black stream
For my torn bough!'

With that I stepped back from the head of my mother's grave. I was in pain and sad but there was also in a way some peace. At last my mother's struggle was over. I listened to the silence of those who stood there amongst the old grave stones. They were held by their thoughts and memories of my mother. They did not want to leave her there alone. Between them they knew many secrets of her life and the many struggles she had gone through. They respected her for her strength, her endurance and her integrity. A man approached me and told me I had done my mother proud. An elderly woman approached me and thanked me for what I had said about my mother. 'Women never get their due, they are never spoken about like the way you spoke about your mother. Thank you.'

I thought about another side of what had just happened. The words of Joyce, banned for decades, had been spoken and listened to in that small village graveyard in Donegal. When ideas correspond to reality, when there is genius, or as Joyce said when people were able to let their world lift them into a state of 'exaltation', their ideas force their way to the surface. My mother did not know Joyce but he would have recognised her. That is why I read his words at my mother's funeral. I was proud to have him speak there.

The following year, 1998, my Aunt Martha, my uncle's wife, my second mother who had lived with us in our house in Portinure, died. I had just returned from where I was visiting a man in the South side of Chicago. I had been trying to convince him he should help me organise for socialism. I got the call. My aunt, my second mother, was dead. I thought of her, a very good and kind person, I thought about my home in Ireland, about my uncle and mother and father and what was I doing here on a cold night in South Chicago. I felt alone.

My aunt was buried in Lifford, in the same grave as her husband, my uncle, my mother and my father. I went home and with the help of the local grave digger dug the grave like I had done for my uncle and my mother. The grave was covered with a giant flat stone with names and dates which were so old they were not legible. Down at the lowest depths of the grave were the remains of my father and his coffin, then on top of that the remains of my uncle and his coffin, then on top of that the remains of my mother and her still intact coffin. There was barely enough room for a few inches of soil and the flat stone to be slid over to cover my aunt's coffin. I was glad that my aunt was buried in the same grave as the rest of my family's older generation but I wept as I thought that as in life, so it was in her death and in her grave, my aunt was not getting the space she deserved.

Like at my mother's funeral, we had a piper play. I made a speech for her too, explaining that she had been our second mother and spoke of her kindness. My second oldest sister, like she had done at my mother's funeral, kept muttering and trying to disrupt and bring disrespect on the ceremony. She detested that I would have the effrontery to speak at the funeral. But neither she nor her husband had the courage to try and stop me. Her husband would later take revenge by banning me from my sister's, his wife's funeral.

My sister Mary had looked after both my mother and aunt much more than I had. She would have been much more entitled to give the eulogy for both of them than I. But the idea of a woman playing a leading role at events such as funerals was not accepted in the Protestant culture of the time. When I suggested that some of my sister's daughters' could help carry the coffin of my mother if they wished this was very firmly rejected as women carrying coffins was seen in the Protestant culture as something that was done only at republican funerals.

As my mother's Alzheimer's had worsened, it had become more difficult for my sister Mary to keep both my mother and my aunt in her home. My aunt had also been developing Alzheimer's. We had to put my aunt in a home. I had gone back to do this as it was very painful for my sister. On the way to the home my aunt said: 'Will none of the rest of them take me?' She was referring to my other sisters, not Mary, who was keeping my mother. Her question broke my heart. But then I was not taking her either. I was in Chicago. I had the privileges of the male. My other sisters could have taken her except they were so mean-spirited. They were jealous that my mother chose to stay with my sister Mary even though they themselves were not prepared to take my mother or my aunt. If they could not get my mother to lord it over Mary they would not take my aunt. They looked at my aunt as lesser than my mother. Their actions were despicable.

At my aunt's funeral and after her coffin was lowered into the grave I was approached by an older, obviously a country man, whom I did not know. He explained that he had lived in the next townland to that of my aunt when she was young. Apparently in later years there was a dispute over a field of his with another person claiming to own it. The dispute went to court. The man who was at the funeral and who had ownership of the field for decades was a Catholic. The man who had recently come forward to claim ownership of the field was a Protestant. This Catholic man asked my aunt would she go to court as a witness as she knew from playing in the field in her youth that he owned the field. My aunt did so and she, a Protestant, went to court and gave evidence that this man, a Catholic, owned the piece of land, not the other man the Protestant. My aunt acted in a principled manner.

This man obviously never forgot this and had been thinking of my aunt with respect and gratitude all these years. And also in spite of living some distance away making sure he knew how she was and knowing when she died. I wondered who he had told to keep their ears open and let him know when my aunt died. He approached me and told me of these events. I was impressed as I thought of my aunt's principled stand. And also thought about my uncle. He too had acted in a principled manner. He would have been involved in my aunt's decision and approved of it. It was another occasion when he and other members of my family put aside sectarianism, to do what was right.

At the funerals of my uncle, my mother and my aunt I refused to go along with the new corporate, profit-driven burial methods where graves were dug by mechanical diggers and the coffin lowered in and the hole in the ground covered with phony grass and then everybody goes home, leaving their family member lying alone in the cold earth with strangers with machines to fill in the grave. At the three funerals, my mother's, my aunt's, my uncle's, along with the man who looked after the graveyard we dug the graves with shovels. The clay was piled up by the graves. When digging the grave for my mother I had found my uncle's skull and one shinbone in the grave. I looked at the skull and thought how much it and I had been through.

As soon as my aunt's coffin was lowered in, I and other men stepped forward and took hold of the shovels and filled the graves. Like at my father's and uncle's and mother's and now aunt's funerals we had the traditional closing of the grave and the solidarity and ritual of the old ways. The closing of my aunt's grave was an end to another chapter in my life. The old generation was all gone.

CHAPTER 45

BONNIE

T HE NEW CENTURY was unfolding, I maintained my revolutionary work to the extent my health allowed. I continued to participate in various struggles. I wrote and distributed my writings on the Blog and the Internet. I carried on my fight for my own revolutionary conscious-ncss and I struggled to influence the consciousness of the workers and youth I could reach. I understood that the struggle against capitalism was the struggle for the consciousness of the working class. So I played my part in fighting the capitalist class for the consciousness of the working class. If the international working class consciousness was such that it believed that it could build an alternative to capitalism then capitalism would be in trouble. The development of the Internet allowed me to fight to influence the consciousness of the working class to a much greater extent than would have been the case in the past. However my health was getting worse, illness was piling on illness, crisis upon crisis. As my primary care doctor told me, there were not many people of my age with all my diseases still walking around. I had a good laugh at that. However it was not all one way. I was about to enter the richest period of my personal life.

James Joyce said that a man without a woman was an incomplete man. In these times, when different sexual orientations have become more understood and recognised and respected it would be more correct to say a person without a person is an incomplete person. When Joyce spoke he was not talking about a weak woman, not about a subservient woman, not about a woman to look after him, to wash his socks, to do the dishes, to cook. He was talking about a tough, fighting, independent woman. One who would not be hesitant now and then to give the world's greatest writer a good kick in the backside. He was talking about a woman like his partner Nora who got so mad with him one night she threw the manuscript of Ulysses in the fire. Joyce had to claw it out, burning his hands and then get bits and pieces back from people to whom he had sent them for their opinions. He also had to rewrite parts of it, no doubt improving it along the way. By throwing the manuscript in the fire, Nora made her own contribution to the editing of Ulysses. I wonder did Joyce think about this in that way. I was sure that if he had he would have had a good laugh and been proud of and thankful to Nora.

Nora gave Joyce little praise and this was good for him. He gave himself enough. Nora referred to Ulysses as that 'chop suey of a book'. Did not even read it. Gave away the first edition copy he gave her. Nora was sexually powerful, energetic, strong and demanding, to a much greater extent than most women could have been expected to have been in her circumstances coming from the small Irish city of Galway in Ireland in that day and age. She was a fighter. With all these qualities and capacities she made Joyce a more complete man.

The woman who moved me in this direction was Bonnie. Like Nora, she was a tough and smart and independent-minded woman. She had the advantage over Nora in that she lived in the more modern world and in the age of the Internet. But like Nora she was not up for any messing. She would rear up on me every now and then. We met pretty much by accident but we recognised each other not by accident.

It was 1999 and I was still doing small moving jobs. I had one at a high-end antique mall on Michigan Avenue, Chicago's most expensive and upscale shopping street. I maintained my work in the antique and art world as I was known as careful and reliable. That day I was moving items out of a booth in the Michigan Mall, which was closing, to a mall out in the North West suburb of Elk Grove. The owner of the booth was a Greek American male chauvinist and nationalist. An arrogant man who thought he knew everything. He was not hesitant to share his views. I had to put him in his place a few times. When I did so he did not know how to respond. After all I was only one of the bog Irish while he was from Greece, the 'cradle of civilisation'.

Anyway, I set off with my load of antiques. Elk Grove was a gritty industrial centre and transport hub north-west of the city close to O'Hare Airport. I travelled out the 90 expressway, got off at the Elmhurst exit going North and turned west on Oakton Street. The antique mall was called the Oakton Street Antique Centre. I had no idea how important it and its owner were to become in my life.

I knew nothing of the antique world. I thought it was confined to extremely expensive items like Chippendale furniture and thousand year-old furnishings of one kind or another. I had no idea about the whole collectible sub-culture that existed. Along with the tens of thousands of people who collected the high end antiques were the tens and tens of thousands of people who dealt in these collectibles. These could be and were just about anything. Salt and pepper shakers, old toy trains, hats, old magazines, postcards, old tools, shoes, army hats and belts and boots and uniforms, dolls, just about anything, there was practically nothing that was not a collectible to somebody. I was astounded by it all.

All my life I had lived with the objective of having as few things around me as possible. I saw success in life as dying with nothing. But this deliberately collecting things, this was something entirely new and foreign to me. I mean, what was the point? I later concluded that it was to some extent an American thing, partly fuelled by the emptiness of life under US capitalism, partly by the fact that the country had not been invaded in mass destructive wars by foreign armies, partly by the vacuum that existed in people's lives, partly by the surplus of goods that had developed through the post-War boom in the US, and along with these factors the strength of the capitalist idea that if you could buy something and keep it, its value would inevitably go up. I shook my head. There would be a lot of people in for a rude awakening in the future.

The antique mall in Elk Grove was divided into fifty booths rented by different dealers. The overall mall was owned by one lady who kept six of these booths to herself to sell her own items and rented out the rest to dealers who paid rent for their space and commission on their sales. The owner's daughter also worked full-time in the mall. The dealers brought in their own merchandise and sold it in their booths.

I arrived to make my delivery. While I was doing so I noticed that people came in from the street and sold items to the dealers and staff. I thought about this as sometimes I would get things that people did not want.

A few days later I got a job moving items from a lady's basement. She wanted no money for any of it. One item was a barber's chair. It was downstairs in the basement. I was alone and the chair was very heavy. I set it on my thighs and stepped it up one step at a time to the ground floor where I put it on my two-wheel dolly and loaded it on my van. I also loaded up the other items the lady did not want. From what I had seen at the Elk Grove Mall I thought maybe I could sell some of them there.

It was a lovely spring day. The sun was shining and there was a nice cool breeze. I had a load of antiques in my van to sell and for which I anticipated getting a few dollars. I was planning afterwards on going for dinner and a whiskey or two with the proceeds. Life was good. I did not know it was about to get better.

I pulled into the mall, went inside and asked could I bring in some things to sell. Right away I could feel there was a different atmosphere about the place. Everybody seemed to be more on their toes, more alert and welcoming. There was also a different lady there. She was very attractive with blond hair, about five foot nine, slim and sexy. She was obviously in charge, setting the tone and seeing what was going on. Hhmmm, I thought, I would have to keep an eye on this one. She called people up one by one to see if they wanted to buy anything. I pretended I was not checking her out while of course making sure she knew I was checking her out. I was sneaky in my Irish way. Or as my friend Richard's dad said, you had to watch them Irish boys they were cute, meaning crafty.

One by one dealers bought my items. Knowing a bit about buying and selling from my young days with my father in the fairs and even though I hated it then, I was not an idiot so I bargained back and forward. One elderly lady was nasty to me as she looked at my pieces and turned up her lip in mock contempt but did not go away. She was not fooling me with that. It was like my uncle pretending he did not like the white cow. This older lady eventually bought some pieces. I said nothing about her rudeness. Eventually I sold everything including the barber's chair. The blond lady, whom I by then assumed was the owner, bought this and I moved it to a spot inside the door where she said she was going to keep it for weary shoppers.

I did not find the bargaining back and forward off-putting as I had when I was in my uncle's field when I was young. The reason was not difficult to understand. Back then it threatened to be my future. Now there was no chance of that. My past and future were well mapped out by then and there was no chance I would end up in a life of buying and selling and 'lying' about the price of some animal or the price of any other item or good. So I was able to use what I had learned from the days on my uncle's farm without any danger of this becoming my way of life.

I prepared to leave. I could see the attractive blond lady had been watching the exchanges between myself and the dealers. She came over to me and said quietly about the older nasty lady: 'Do not mind her. She still thinks the '6o's was a bad thing.' My thoughts went into overdrive. An attractive lady who described another woman as nasty because she thought the '6os was a bad thing. Hhmmm again. I was definitely interested in this lady. Sounded like on some things we thought the same way. I would have to find an excuse to come back. One of her assistants was watching the goings on.

I got my dolly and moving pads and left the store. The owner's assistant followed me outside. 'Hey. I have this for you. This is Bonnie's phone number. Give her a call sometime.' 'Who is Bonnie?' 'She is that blond woman in there you were looking at. Don't try and tell me you were not.'

And with that and a mischievous grin, the lady went to go back into the mall. I looked at the number written on the piece of paper and asked: 'Does she know you are giving me this?' 'Yes, sure she does.' Things were definitely looking up.

I drove back towards the city. Not wanting to get stuck in traffic as it was by then close to 6.00 pm I went over into Des Plaines and sat and had a whiskey in a bar which I called in my own mind 'The Dive'. And it was a dive. The owner was a scruffy man about fifty. On a couple of occasions I had seen attractive women in very sexy sophisticated outfits come into the bar and he would take them into a backroom. They would emerge an hour or so later. It was not hard to see what was going on. They were not doing his books. But the dive had a good juke box. I played some of my favourites. Old sentimental ones which along with the whiskies softened my edges and made me think of old times and people no longer of my life. *Maggie* by an Irish tenor whose name I could not remember. My mother was called Maggie. *I Can't Stop Loving You*, by Ray Charles, *Old Man River*, by Louis Armstrong, *Funny How Time Just Slips Away*, by Willie Nelson, *Crazy*, by Patsy Cline, *Pardon Me If I'm Sentimental*, by Bob Dylan, *It Ain't Me Babe*, also by Bob Dylan. They did not have Sam Cooke on the juke box. Hard to escape the racism in America.

I sat at the bar with my head bent over my whiskey and let the memories and emotions flow in me, let the whiskey soften me. How did I end up here in 'The Dive' in this ugly suburb of Des Plaines? I shook my head and smiled to myself. I thought of the twists and turns of my life. Those people in that old, corrupt, revolutionary organisation had not broken me. The capitalists had not broken me nor bought me. I smiled into my whiskey. I cursed them all. Then the lady behind the bar put another whiskey in front of me. 'What is that? I did not order one?' 'It is from those two over there,' and she pointed across the bar at two men. They raised their glasses. And one of them shouted: 'For the good music,' I raised my glass back. This was America too. It had its good points.

I finished the men's whiskey, waved to them in thanks, and left to go and get some food up at a small Italian place in Mount Prospect. The food was good. I had one of my favourites, home-made pasta with pesto. The other thing about this place was that the bread was good. I had another whiskey. I was getting more mellow by the minute. As I waited for my pasta in between bites of bread dipped in olive oil and grated cheese I sang softly under my breath to myself, Patrick Kavanagh's, *On Raglan Road on an Autumn Day*. I missed Dublin. The food came, I ate it paid, and left. I was thinking about the blond woman at the mall.

Not being stupid I did not call the lady the next day. Better to take it easy. Hopefully let her think about it a bit. These good looking, smart ones, if you appeared too eager they could go off you. I called the following day. Bonnie answered. 'Hello. I hope you do not mind me calling you. I was at your store the day before yesterday selling some items. Remember I had a barber's chair. And you mentioned to me about a lady thinking the '60s was a bad thing.' 'Yes, I remember.' 'I am sorry I do not know your name. My name is Sean. Can I know your name please?' I was being very polite. 'Yes. I am Bonnie.' 'Pleased to meet you Bonnie. I am calling to see if you would consider going out with me some day and we could take a drive and have something to eat? Maybe tomorrow or the next day, or whatever day suits you.' No beating about the bush, we were both adults, polite and direct. I was very happy with her answer. 'Yes that would be fine. It would probably have to be the day after tomorrow as I would have to organise for somebody to work for me and a few other things.' 'That is fine,' I replied, 'whenever suits you.'

We arranged for me to collect her at her house in Des Plaines in two days' time at 1.00 pm. I wrote down the directions. I was looking forward to it. I sang to myself as I drove home. Life was good. I was still alive and I had a date with a very good looking and smart and strong woman. And she was as crafty as myself. After me not calling her right away she made me wait a day for a date. I would have to watch her. I smiled again to myself.

The day came and I drove up to Des Plaines. A terrible drab place altogether. Some people called it Dead Plaines. It had a river but even that could not rescue it. It was more like a channel of liquid mud. There was some kind of a malaise in the downtown of the suburb. It felt like some old European American dead head business people had their equally dead hand running the place and keeping all life and spirit at bay. They had theirs and that was enough and do not rock the boat or who knows what might turn up. Maybe there could develop some competition for a piece of the pie. And God forbid, even worse, maybe even some African American or Latino American or Asian American people might move in. I could have told them it was already too late. I shook myself to get rid of the feel of it. But its atmosphere and the look of the place did not subdue my enthusiasm for my date with Bonnie.

I arrived at Bonnie's house and knocked at the door. A terrible howling of dogs went up. I had no problem with that. In fact all the better, I got on with dogs. Bonnie opened the door. She was looking good. She was dressed in a tan trouser suit which set off her blond hair and natural skin colours. She had on her eye shadow, make up and nail polish, and she had her blue eyes and her shape. It was 'Hhhmmmmmm ...' again! I wanted to take a grip of her there and then. But instead I played it cool. Showing only friendship and mild interest. Again I reminded myself, you had to be careful with these smart, good looking ladies. They could go off you if they thought you were too interested. I was not an idiot.

'Hello Bonnie. How are you doing?' 'Fine. I am well.' I could see that Bonnie had the dogs locked out on the back deck. One was a Rottweiler and one a three-legged Manchester terrier. 'I am alright with dogs. Can I see them?' 'Okay but the big one is big.' 'That is okay.' Bonnie opened the door slowly and let the dogs in the house. They rushed at me and sniffed and sniffed and barked. I stood motionless and they gradually quieted down. Then I moved a hand slowly and they came round to me and very soon I was sitting on the couch with them all over me. Good I thought. I had passed the dog test.

'Bonnie I was thinking, if you would like, seeing it is a nice day, we could take a drive up to the Botanical Gardens and take a walk. I like the Japanese Gardens there especially. They are peaceful and beautiful. It is not too far away.' 'That is good. Okay.'

Bonnie was still sizing me up. Seeing what kind of a person I was. That was okay with me. I was not lacking in confidence and if people did not like me they did not like me. That was the way it was. I thought if people did not like me then it was something wrong with them or there were some wider social, economic, political or class reasons for it. I did not give too much thought to it being anything to do with me. What was the point at that stage in my life, I was pretty much fixed as who I was. That was the way I thought. It was a useful way to think.

We headed off in my big moving van. It was only a couple of years old, had a good stereo and went well. I had a big 'No Smoking' sign in front of the passenger's seat. I did not know that Bonnie smoked. She must have been having a hard time of it not lighting up. Later I would think it meant something that she stayed with me after seeing the sign. Of course it also meant something that I stayed with her after I came to know that she smoked.

The botanical gardens were about a half hour's drive away, north-east in the Ravinia Highland Park area. They were beautiful. The Japanese Garden with its little house and zigzag paths combined into a work of art. The spring blossoms were out. Bonnie and I walked and talked and examined trees and plants and bugs and flowers and creatures of all kinds. We drifted along in nature. We marvelled at the prairie grass. We spoke of how the invasion from the East had changed the American landscape, the cultivated US farmlands had wiped out the wild prairies to the extent small patches had to be preserved in gardens like this so we would know what had been. I spoke with sorrow and anger at the genocide of the Native Americans.

I talked to Bonnie about my being a socialist and an atheist. It did not seem to put her off in any way. I spoke about being brought up in rural Ireland and about being a revolutionary socialist organiser. I also spoke about all my health problems. Bonnie spoke to me about her Mall but was not so open about her life and world as I was. She told me about her five children and that she had formerly been married but that her ex-husband had died. I did not ask many questions. I found that in general it was better to get to know people by letting them tell you what they wanted to tell you rather than asking them questions.

An hour or two into our walk, things began to change. I took Bonnie's hand. 'Am I embarrassing you by holding your hand?' I asked. 'No not at all.' 'That is good. Would you like to go and have some food? We could go to a good Jewish deli I know up here or we could buy some food and take it back to my place? I also have some food there which we could eat. Or we could go to a place you know of and like?' 'Why do we not go back to your place? I can see where you live.' 'Are you sure?' I asked. Bonnie reassured me. I asked her again as I did not want to spoil things by trying to move things along too fast. But Bonnie said: 'No, let us go to your place.' So we set off back toward the city.

I lived in a very tough neighbourhood at the time on the top of a house in an attic. Gang wars were the norm. Killings regular. Both my old van and even this new one had a bullet hole in the door panels. To get to the attic we had to walk up a narrow spiral staircase inside the house. I was impressed by Bonnie's courage and audacity in venturing down from her quiet suburb to this tough neighbourhood and into this strange house with this strange man.

The attic was very bright and looked out over the city's downtown skyline. It had large skylights. Bonnie went over and stood looking out through the largest from which you could see towards the lake and the city's sky line. I put on, what else, Sam Cooke on the CD player and he filled the apartment. *Change is Gonna Come.* Just about my favourite song. I went back to Bonnie and put my arm around her waist and we looked out the skylight together. Our hours of walking and talking and getting to know each other were with us. And then the beautiful tide broke. We were washed away in that which was powerful and passionate and good for us. When we had reached our heights a few times we rested and we smiled at each other and laughed and held each other. At one stage Bonnie had to insist on a special break to go out onto the back porch of the attic and have a smoke. This was the first time I knew she smoked. She probably thought she could risk letting me know by that time seeing the pleasure we had just given each other. The big dog, the half Chow and half German Shepherd from downstairs came up to see us and give us its blessing. It was a wonderful day.

Bonnie and I went out regularly from then on. But we had a problem. We could never see a movie or a show without the tide coming in and washing all else away. Then we would have to leave and get together in privacy. We were in our youth again. It was great but my Irish peasant background would get annoyed at us paying to go to movies and shows and then having to leave half way through to enjoy each other and not getting the full value for our money. I wondered if I could ask for a special passionate half-price ticket rate or were there places you could watch a show and take a break and then come back and watch the rest of the show.

I was in the process of being evicted from the apartment where I lived and moving into a vegan cooperative. In that I had one small room and Bonnie and I personalised there. It was more than pleasant. I went home one night with Bonnie and about fifteen of the other co-op residents were sitting on the front porch. They were all about twenty years old. Bonnie was twelve years younger than me but kept herself in a way that made her look even younger. I said: 'Bonnie. These are my friends. My friends, I would like you to meet Bonnie.' Politely they said 'hello'. I knew what they were thinking. He is one old dude to have a good looking woman like that.

Gradually Bonnie told me more about her family and five children. She was a great mother to them. None of them were racist, none of them were in jail, none of them were violent to their partners, this was an achievement in the US at that time. Her children did not know what to make of me. Except that I treated their Mom okay. Her siblings did not like me. Even to the point of almost never coming to see me nor inviting me to see them. I found this attitude very different from the welcoming hospitable culture of Ireland. To Bonnie's siblings, as an Irish person and an emigrant I was suspect. And as a leftie and atheist, I was worse than suspect. And on top of that I was not interested in US sports, another US god I did not worship. I mean what kind of a freak and dangerous character was I anyway?

Bonnie's in-laws never met me but they were extremely hostile to me. They would have been hostile to anybody who would have got together with Bonnie unless that person did what they told them. Bonnie's previous husband had died and she was supposed to remain the isolated, broken, grieving widow, a weeping broken monument to her dead husband's memory. This was the in-laws' plan. These were the same in-laws who swindled Bonnie and her children out of most of their share of her husband's estate. It took eight years going to court to get only a tiny fraction of what was theirs. American capitalism!

When Bonnie's husband died he had left her with five children and a business that was deep in debt due to the bad practices of himself and her in-laws. But Bonnie took the reins and with the help of some friends she dragged it out of debt and built it into a successful business. She achieved wonders. She achieved this against all the efforts and previous bad practices of her ex-husband and ex-in laws and also against the male chauvinist world of business in which she had to operate.

When her previous husband died she had to decide what to do. He had left her and the business in debt. He had made no will. Her family members told her to walk away from the bankrupt business and get a job. But Bonnie was tough and stubborn. One day an elderly lady who was a dealer in the store was talking to her about what she should do. This lady said, in the direct US way: 'Keep the store. Make it work. Otherwise you will be working for some man who will be wanting you to take him in your mouth every day.' What kind of a life experience had that elderly lady had? Bonnie kept the store and made it a great success. Bonnie did not take enough credit for her success.

After a few months going out together, Bonnie and I went on holiday to Half Moon Bay and Monterey in California. It is my favourite part of America. We stayed in a high-rise motel looking out over the ocean. We looked at the spectacular sea life, especially the sea otters, one of my favourite creatures, and walked in the wonderful pathways. We visited Salinas, Steinbeck country.

We went to Muir Woods, redwood country. To walk amongst these giant trees, the tallest life form on the planet, to see their colours and smell their smells, to look up from the small brook that flowed through them down to the Pacific to their tops high in the sky. I was in awe. We lay down on our backs in reverence and looked at their tops swaying high above us in the wind. We closed our eyes and lay and hugged. It was a time and a place to be alive.

I thought about my own life. Of my family, my mother, aunt, father and uncle. I thought about the struggles I had been through, the struggle to break from my old rural right wing world, the struggle to find my place as a revolutionary, the struggle to survive after being expelled and lied about and slandered by the revolutionary organisation to which I had given most of my life. I thought about people who I had known who were no longer alive. I thought about my many illnesses and the many close scrapes with death that I had experienced. I thought about all this as I lay there in the redwoods with Bonnie. I had done okay. Life was okay. And it was better now that I was with Bonnie.

I also thought how it was possible now for me to commit myself to a permanent, exclusive relationship. It was partly Bonnie's qualities. But it was also that I had come to see that my old way of working to build the revolutionary nucleus, that is, brutally sacrifice all to that end, had been damaging. There were other factors involved. I could not build the revolutionary nucleus just by pure will. I had to relate to and take into account the world in which I lived, was the revolutionary tide going out or coming in, was the task to risk all in a revolutionary act or rather to work patiently to try and put together a revolutionary nucleus? I concluded it was the latter.

Bonnie never on any occasion sought to impede my revolutionary work.

Just as I supported and encouraged Bonnie in her work in building her Mall she, while not being an actual part of it, supported me in my revolutionary work. And over a period did more than this. She gave her opinion increasingly on events in society which helped me see things in a more rounded way. I was content in my permanent relationship with Bonnie. My world had changed and I had met Bonnie with her very good qualities and these two factors had come together to allow us to have our relationship.

I had no problem being together with Bonnie because of the way she made a living. She was not a capitalist who lived on capital. She was a very hard-working woman who had her own business which survived and prospered not because she had capital but because she put her own resources, knowledge, personality, energy into it. She was also a very kind person. Her being the owner of the mall never brutalised her, never took away her humanity, her human qualities, her kindness. Her mall was more like a family and she was the mother. Definitely in charge but caring. The only problem I had was I thought she worked too hard. She expended her own personal capital too much. She endangered her health. We both accepted the division of labour in our worlds. Bonnie ran her store. She would share her experiences there with me and we would laugh or be indignant or be angry about things that would happen there. I was still carrying on some few moving jobs while at the same time doing my revolutionary work and I would share my experiences in these areas of my life and she would give her views and opinions.

In between times, Bonnie and I played indoors and out. We added more laughter to our passion. This was good. There was nothing I found more unattractive than sex of grinding and pounding, of gritted teeth, like the participants were in pain or at war. Bonnie and I never had that. We had passion and laughter and gentleness and tenderness. We played and I was able to tickle Bonnie as we were sexually together and at times she would go into peals of laughter and passion in our beds.

Bonnie was a liberated and sexual woman. She was not repressed by backward ideas. She had confidence and sexuality and laughter and was not constrained by the ways of European American upper class hypocrisy. She was into rock 'n' roll, not swing.

Our good life together did not mean that Bonnie and I never had a cross word. On occasion we would. But this is what I understood to be what Joyce meant when he said that a man without a woman is an incomplete man. He meant to have a testing, struggling, mutually life-asserting relationship. Bonnie and I would, as was only right and inevitable, have disagreements. These would, on occasion, be exhausting and wearing and at times would make me angry but these made myself and our relationship more rich. I could have had a subservient woman, who did everything for me, and 'agreed' with all I said. But then I would have been further away from being complete. The same could also be said had the situation been the other way around. I could have been subservient to Bonnie. But this would have made her less complete. This would not have helped her in her life no more than if she had been subservient to me would have helped me in my life.

We understood that our relationship, that all relationships are journeys. I thought of my journeys when I was a child to my father's uncle's house at Aughadoey up deep into the mountains south of Donegal town. The last part of this journey was on a narrow un-surfaced road through the heather and lakes, the grey rocks, the beauty of it. But also the twist and turn of it, the rocky surface of it, the sharp edged protruding rock jolts of it. This was our relationship. We recognized that we had to make the turns, ride out the bumps, take the jolts, on the road on which our journey took us, that was our relationship. We recognized that there would be days when there would be tensions. Days when mistakes would be made, when incautious words would be spoken. But we also recognized what we meant to each other. And we recognized that we had to allow for mistakes, for incautious words. Allow each other on occasion to make these and allow each other to withdraw these and apologize for these. This was our relationship. Honest, respectful, caring, genuine, rich. It was good. It was complete as it could be.

The day after I was diagnosed with cancer I spoke to Bonnie. I said: 'Bonnie. You did not sign on for this. It is no problem if you feel we should separate.' Bonnie got very angry at me. Who did I think I was, what kind of a person did I think she was, and on. I was shocked. I thought my suggestion to her was reasonable, that I was not trying to tie her to me now that I was ill. I was no longer the person she had got together with. But Bonnie angrily rejected any suggestion of this and any further discussion of the idea of her separating from me. I did not know what I thought of this. Probably it just showed I was still and inevitably incomplete.

As the Internet reached further into our world Bonnie got herself an iPad. She downloaded books like there was no tomorrow. She lay awake at night after I was long asleep reading these and following world events. She was increasingly critical of the way society was organised. She helped me to have a more balanced revolutionary view.

Bonnie and I travelled overseas and as we did we grew even more together. We travelled to Dublin and Ireland. Connemara. We walked amongst the rocks and heather and lakes. We petted the Connemara ponies which came to the stone hedges seeking attention. Bonnie threw her head back in laughter and delight as they touched her face and neck with their soft lips. We walked down a path by a rushing, brown, bog water stream. I took a photo of her with a camera we had bought. I did not know it recorded sound. Just as I clicked it to take the photograph of Bonnie as she stood by the rushing stream a big dog ran out and barked welcome and jumped on Bonnie's legs. Bonnie, the Connemara landscape, the rushing bog-coloured brown stream, the bark of the dog, all was captured on the camera. It was a wonderful day.

We went to see my sister Mary and her family in Derry. We also visited friends. My sister Mary and her husband Ernie travelled to Chicago to visit us. I was very ill at the time and in and out of hospital. They were treated to numerous trips to Cook County Hospital when I had to go for treatment. We were both very grateful for their visit to our home. I moved in with Bonnie in her home in the working class suburb of Des Plaines. I did not like suburbs. I liked the life of cities. But you could not have everything.

Some of my Comrades and friends treated us to a trip to Monterey in California. It was a sort of an informal wedding from my friends on the west coast. We had a formal wedding in a Hungarian pub in Chicago with a lady judge from the Children's Courts doing the ceremony. We had another informal wedding party in Derry. This involved some negotiating to see whose house, in which religious area it would be held. It was eventually held in the home of my friends Dolores and Billy, both agnostics, but from a Catholic background. My sister and her husband and friends came. My friend Neiley and his companion Mary came from Cork and as was his wont, set up to sing. Then he thought what would he sing in this mixed religious company? He whispered to me: 'What will I sing?' I said: 'Sing the Woody Guthrie songs, *Pretty Boy Floyd the Outlaw* and those. *Pretty Boy Floyd* is about a US farmer, nobody should take offense!' So Neiley started up and brought the place to silence. He could sing. But after a few songs he 'lost it' and next thing he was into James Connolly the Irish rebel. Eileen Webster rescued the situation by singing the song of women workers *Bread and Roses*.

When I was young at school I was able to sing and always picked for the choir. But as soon as I became aware of myself as an individual I could no longer sing. I still had the physical capacity but I could not project. It was a psychological and social question. But getting together with Bonnie helped me. I still could not sing to audiences but I could sing to Bonnie. *You are the Sunshine of my Life, Down by the Sally Gardens*. It was all part of being a more complete man with Bonnie.

We have been together now for over twenty years. I have been in one health crisis after another. I have almost died at least five times. I have had numerous adrenal crashes and repetitive seizures and high fevers. I have had cancer a number of times. I have had syringes stuck in the arteries in my neck to pump in hormones to keep me alive, I have been in a coma for days with a tube stuck down my throat. I have had weeks and days when I could not walk and did not know who I was. I have been in intensive care, in quarantine, on gurneys and beds in long packed hospital corridors, strapped down to beds in hospital rooms, strapped down to stretchers in ambulances, fighting to get free from leather straps and catheters, yes the health crises of the last years of my life have been a challenging adventure. My life has not been boring.

Bonnie was there for me through all of this, through all of these health crises. They have been worse for her than me. She has had to see me in my seizures, in my bouts of unconsciousness, in my comas, in my traumas. Bonnie is a powerful, strong heroine. On numerous occasions she saved me from death. She is a great, wonderful companion.

Two women have had the most powerful impact in my life. One was my mother with whom I struggled for decades over ideas and how we related to each other and society. Neither of us ever recovered from how much my struggle for my ideas hurt her. I apologise to her. I thank her. I weep for all the pain I caused her. I remember the many disagreements between us which caused her pain. If only I could take them back. But I cannot. And anyway even if I could go back in time my mother and I would still disagree and we would still have our pain.

The other woman who has been most important in my life and who has had the greatest impact in my life is Bonnie. I am ashamed to say this but I have to tell the truth. It is part of my responsibility to my mother and her teaching me to be a 'stickler' for the truth. When my mother died I was deeply sad. I had brought so much unhappiness into her life. But even as she died, while thinking about and mourning her death, I was also thinking about how this would affect me. I thought about myself too. I was and am ashamed of this.

When I later wrote the book *The Donegal Woman*, I took the first proceeds and bought six Connemara ponies and put them in some fields my uncle had owned in Donegal. One of the ponies was called Big Dan. He was very big for his breed. Bonnie had rode horses in competition when she was younger. Bonnie got up on Big Dan's back in a mucky trotting yard in Stranorlar. She rode him round and round. Then he lost his footing in the slippery surface and Bonnie was thrown flying through the air landing on her shoulder.

I went running shouting: 'Bonnie, Bonnie, are you alright, are you alright?' She got up smiling and reassured me that she was. It was then I realised that as Bonnie went flying through the air from Big Dan's back and I thought she might be killed I ran to her and called her name and when I did so I had not thought of myself in any way. I was only thinking of her. This was the first time in my adult life I had thought only and totally exclusively of another person. This is what Bonnie means to me.

CHAPTER 46

COOK COUNTY HOSPITAL:
"ALL ARE WELCOME HERE. WE TREAT ALL IRRESPECTIVE OF THEIR ABILITY TO PAY".

BUT TO GO BACK A LITTLE ... as I have mentioned, my health crisis had continued to worsen. I was literally struggling to stay alive. Even after I had been diagnosed with hypothyroidism in London in the early 1980s things were far from right. I was still exhausted when I should not have been. I was still having small strokes. I fell unconscious on a regular basis. On numerous occasions I came round in some hospital emergency room not knowing where I was or how I got there. In the 1990s things reached a head.

It was a spring day and I realised I was hearing a screaming ambulance siren. It took me a while to figure out what was going on. I was in Chicago and I was strapped down in the ambulance that was screaming. There were two paramedics bending over me. 'He's coming round.' Then the other one said to me. 'Can you hear me? What happened? You were lying on the side walk up at Armitage and Clarke. What happened?'

I answered: 'I don't know. I have been occasionally passing out over the past few years. I was hoping it would stop. How did you get me?' 'We took a 911 call. We are on the way to Cook County hospital to see what is what.' 'We will get you checked out and see.' 'I have hypothyroidism,' I said.

I did not know as I lay there in that rushing, screaming ambulance that it would be the first of many such rides and that I was entering a whole new period in my life. And at the centre of that would be health crisis after health crisis and a relationship with the African American people of the South Side of Chicago where Cook County hospital was located. I did not know that

Cook County hospital was to become my second home. I was entering one of the most challenging, yet also most rewarding and enriching periods of my life. All this good stuff lay ahead and I was already in my fifties.

When we reached Cook County or County as it was known and as I came to call it, I heard siren after siren as more emergency cases rushed in. Running nurses lifted me onto a wheeled gurney. The emergency room was wall to wall with patients, almost all African American or Latino American. I was rushed ahead of them because as an older person who had just fallen unconscious the worry was of a heart attack and death. I felt bad that other patients would think I was being taken ahead of them because I was European American.

The emergency room was set up around a huge, lined board. My name was written on the left side along with other names. As I was checked and tested the results were written across it. I assumed it would eventually be written whether I was to be admitted or discharged what was wrong with me or whether I died. I could not see any sign of the word 'died' opposite any of the other names. Maybe they were diplomatic and just wrote goodbye, or *Danny Boy*, I thought with a grim smile to myself. After a while I drifted in and out of consciousness and dreamed of Ireland.

I came round to hear a young African American woman screaming at the doctor and nurses. 'Let me out. I do not want your fucking hospital. There is nothing wrong with me. Do not touch me. I pay your fucking wages.' The doctors and nurses kept calm. 'Please, we do not want to let you go until we find out what is wrong with you. Please cooperate.' 'No I want out. I am leaving,' and with that she dragged herself off her gurney and with her panties and bra showing through the slit in the back of her hospital gown, pulled her bag of clothes from under the gurney dressed and ran from the hospital.

The doctor and nurses moved on to me. 'So what is the matter with you sir?' I looked up and said nothing. The nurse said: 'He was unconscious on the street and the medics brought him in. He has a medic alert chain for hypothyroidism.' 'So you are hypothyroid sir?' 'Yes and I think I have Addison's. I have been reading and my symptoms seem to point to that. My skin has got dark. I suggested this to one of the hospitals where I was taken recently after I had a previous black-out but as I have no insurance they took no notice of my opinion and put me out.' The doctor answered: 'Well we will not do that here.'

In a couple of hours from being rushed into the emergency room I was diagnosed with Addison's disease. County did what none of the profit hospitals were prepared to do. I did not have insurance so the profit hospitals did not want to find out what was wrong with me because then they would then have had to spend money on treating me rather than just getting me on my feet again so they could put me out without me dying on their doorstep. County saw its role as to treat me until I was as good as they could get me whether I had insurance or money or not. And this is what they did.

When I was diagnosed with Addison's I had to take another medicine along with that which I had been taking for my hypothyroidism. When I did so this partially increased my energy and returned my skin to its original colour. It also partially reduced the number of small strokes I had been having. These affected me in different ways. I would pass out. When I would come round again for a time I would not remember my own name or those around me. I would not know where I was or what I had been doing. Each one of these small strokes did damage. They were similar to when I had concussions when I was playing sports in my youth.

I knew from my reading that Addison's was where the cortex in the adrenal glands no longer worked and so the glands no longer produced corticoids. As a result I had difficulty handling stress, either physical or mental. This was why I had been regularly passing out with the small strokes. I had once passed out at a tense political meeting where I was fighting against my expulsion. The Addison's also meant that I could not tolerate too much heat or cold or traumas such as broken limbs. A person with properly functioning adrenal glands could adjust their corticoid production upwards to deal with stress, mental and physical. But unless I got massive shots of adrenaline when I was in severe stress I would just sink down into death. Addison's also meant if my medicine was not properly regulated, my blood pressure could crash and this too could be fatal. This was known as an Addisonian crash.

I had a number of these and was rushed to County hospital. On one of these occasions Bonnie was with me at the hospital. The doctors put Bonnie out of the room. 'You will not want to be here for this Mam,' they said. They had to act immediately as my blood pressure was so low I was in danger of dying. They stuck a syringe, or was it two, I am not sure as I was not on top of things at that moment, full of adrenaline hormone, into my jugular vein to bring my blood pressure up and keep me alive. This was done without anaesthetic and I howled in pain. Bonnie thought they were killing me.

Some months later, I developed fevers. These sweated my medicines out of my body and as a result were life-threatening. I was put in quarantine for a time at County to see if I had an infectious disease which was causing these fevers. None could be found. I almost died from Addisonian crashes on five different occasions.

My friend, a nurse at the Veteran's Administration, came up with what appeared to be the solution for my fevers. He said he had been at the bus stop coming home from work and met an endocrinologist whom he knew from the Veterans' Administration. This doctor said I should increase my hydrocortisone medicine six times and the fevers would go away and then when they did, I should reduce the medicine gradually down again to its original dosage. I did so and sure enough the fevers went away.

My friend was an excellent nurse. He would come to see me when I had my health crises. He would tell me of his shenanigans. He was very intelligent, had a very good sense of humour and was audacious. His patients were mainly older men, over-weight and unhealthy and depressed. They had the usual urology problems, prostate cancer, urine problems, impotence. My friend had a great way with them. He would start off: 'I know what is wrong with you. I do not even have to examine you. I will anyway but I know already.' These patients would look at him sceptically. Then my friend would go on: 'What is wrong with you is too much sex. That is what is going on. Too much sex that is what it is.' These old men who had most likely never touched or been touched sexually for many years would get all brightened up and feel great again just to be accused of too much sex. My friend was a very good nurse as well as a very good friend. Being ill had its benefits also.

I had many interesting and amusing experiences at this time at County. I was put in quarantine, in a sealed room while they checked me for infectious diseases, seeking for a cause for my fevers. I laughed to myself as I felt important in my sealed room with the 'Keep Out' sign on the door and the masked nurses and doctors. The doctor in charge was a small Irish American woman. She took a look at me with her head cocked to one side. Then she said: 'I hate fucking endocrine patients. You never can find out what is wrong with them there are so many various combinations each working on and interacting with each other.' We laughed together. And she was right, sure enough she never could find out what was causing my fevers.

My epilepsy was getting worse at this time. My first seizure had been so violent that it broke my scapula, the large flat bone at the back of my shoulder. I was given very strong anti-seizure medication. This dulled my brain to such an extent that I would continually fall asleep. Along with the hypothyroidism and Addison's, which both went untreated for a long time, the TIAs, the seizures, the many concussions when I was young I was not in great shape.

I also had surgery for a number of cancers over this period. During my life overall I had ten surgeries, the most serious of these were one for cancer, one for a broken and partially crushed skull and another for the broken scapula. I was a seriously and chronically ill person. I would remain so for the rest of my life. But I never thought of myself in this way. I remained upbeat and optimistic and believing in the future and that I still had things to do and would get at least some of them done. My fighting spirit remained intact. Of course I had to keep taking the fifteen tablets every day. If I had not I would have died in a couple of weeks. I hoped that society would not break down to where I could no longer get these medicines. I would curse in impatience as I loaded my pill containers every week. I had no time for this. I had to help build the revolutionary nucleus. Goddamn pills and pill containers. Our two dogs, the Jack Russell and the Chihuahua would always sit with me when I was filling the pills. Making sure I did it right no doubt.

Bonnie helped me very much with my health. She was always there for me. Bonnie's five children also helped me with my health. On one occasion I had a rolling seizure which would not stop. I had to be immediately rushed to the nearest hospital. Bonnie and her daughter Jackie dropped everything and raced to the hospital in time to give permission to the hospital authorities to induce a coma to stop my brain surging, spinning out of it altogether and killing me. Bonnie and Jackie saved my life that day. While in the hospital Bonnie and her children came to visit regularly, talking to me and telling me what had happened when I had the rolling seizure.

I had been at home. I slumped in a chair, unconscious and involuntarily shaking. Bonnie called the ambulance. I was in such a serious condition I had to be taken to the nearest hospital. It was a profit hospital. I had no insurance. So they stabilised me, that is brought me back from the verge of death, what they had to do to stay within the law, then they 'dumped' me, that is threw me out. One doctor when treating me actually told me to my face as I lay close to death that he expected to be paid. I went to County where I wanted to be anyway. County was a publically funded, non-profit hospital. The admissions nurse at County took one look at Bonnie and myself and on hearing that I had been dumped said: 'Do not worry Mam, we will look after your husband.' County was a humane hospital. The other hospital, in fact all the previous hospitals I had been in were profit hospitals. That was the difference, humane versus profit.

I was in one particular profit hospital on one occasion. I did not have insurance. The nurse had no interest in me but had to at least go through the motions. She thought it was my inactive thyroid rather than my non-functioning adrenal cortex which caused my addisons disease. I had to correct her. The doctor could not get away from my bed quickly enough. She gave me options. Stay in the hospital and they would give me the medicine and monitor me or go home and take the medicine myself. Of course the doctor added quickly: 'You would not want to stay in the hospital, you would want to go home'. So after giving me the option of staying in and covering the hospital against any claim she then said of course I would not want to stay in. When the doctor went over this with me she had an ashamed look on her face. The whole culture of that profit hospital as with all profit hospitals was that the staff were organized against the patients. We were the source of the profit and we had to be treated as such, as objects. Not a decision was made that was not influenced by these hospitals' drive for profit. This not only resulted in improper treatment for the patients but created an uncaring attitude amongst the staff. Both patients and staff were brutalized by the profit motive of these hospitals.

I had strange dreams as I came out of my days long induced coma. In one I drove back to my mother's old farm house in Donegal. Going in I saw it was completely empty. There was not a stick of furniture. Like my former workmate Perry's had been that time. I could hear my mother's disembodied voice. She was calling: 'John is back, John is back.' This evoked a terrible sadness in me as I could hear her voice but try as I could, no matter how many times I searched the house, I could not find her.

When I was brought out of my coma I was not clear on what was what. I asked Bonnie was my mother dead. Bonnie did not want to tell me so she turned her head away. I lay silent in the bed for a time. Then I said, referring to my mother, my father, my uncle, my aunt, 'they are all dead aren't they?' This time Bonnie felt she had to answer and she said yes. I lay and wept. I saw them all walking and working there at Portinure, at the home place, I saw the fields, the farm house, the stables and byres, the farm animals, my mother's butter pats, my aunts little garden, all were there in my mind for a few minutes, but it was not real, it was all gone, they were all long gone, long gone before I ever was in my coma. And there I was lying having just escaped death in a Chicago hospital.

Cook County hospital saved my life on many occasions. As a public hospital it was entirely different from the profit hospitals where I had been on previous occasions when I had fallen unconscious. It was based on the needs of the patients while the others were based on the needs of the bottom line. Many of these 'bottom line', that is profit, hospitals were named after Christian so-called 'saints'. But their saint was in reality the dollar. And the patients were the source of the dollar. In those hospitals I was treated as a possible source of profit, of dollars. At County, which was not a profit hospital, I was treated as a human being. County became my second home.

County had its mission statement printed on its wall. It read: 'To provide a comprehensive programme of quality health care, with respect and dignity, to the residents of Cook County, regardless of their ability to pay. We treat all irrespective of their ability to pay.' This was County's mission and they lived up to it. If the profit hospitals had put up an honest mission statement it would have had read: 'To make as much profit as possible for our investors regardless of our patient's health and our staff's sense of humanity and decency.' I was in County for an appointment the day I wanted to write down this mission statement for this book. I wanted to get it right. I asked a clerk lady where it was as I could not remember given the after affects of a recent seizure. She rose from her desk and with determination and pride took me to it and stood while I wrote it down. It was obvious she was very proud of County and what it stood for, and proud to work there.

The culture at County was different. It existed to help people get well, not to make profit for the investors in the sickness industrial complex. While its resources were stretched to the limit, it was the heart of African American South Chicago, County was where so many from the area were born, treated, healed, had their children, were nursed and died. I cannot say enough good about County except to repeat again: it became my second home. And I was and always will be proud as well as extremely grateful to have it as my second home.

County had the first blood bank in the world, it had the first trauma unit in the Chicago area, it led the field in preventive medicine programmes, care for patients with AIDS and addictions, breast cancer screening and women and children's programmes. The right wing *Chicago Tribune*, no friend of County, reported in an article that of 100 hospitals surveyed, County had the second lowest mortality rate and this while drawing its patients mainly from African American Chicago with its much greater unemployment and poverty and consequently greater health problems. The health differential between African American Chicago and European American Chicago was so great that it was estimated that it killed over 3,000 African American people a year. This was never mentioned when the ruling class and its mass media spoke of violence and terrorism.

The overwhelming majority of the patients at County were African American. But as the Latino American population of the city increased so too did the Latino American proportion of County's patients. Smaller in stature, dressed more colourfully, speaking Spanish, they stood out. They were also less confident in fighting for their rights. They tended to try and get what they needed with softly spoken patience. They added to the diversity of County's population.

There were many reasons I liked going to County. I had come to realise that the corporations were more dominant in the US and in US culture than in any country in which I had ever been. This was reflected in every phase of life, from how hard people worked, the long hours they worked, in the popular culture and on and on. The mega more expensive stores which sold clothing were also a factor in this. They produced and sold clothes which were very similar, almost uniform. The result was that those who could afford to shop in the more expensive stores tended to look somewhat the same. But this was not the case at County. The patients were mainly less well off. Their clothes reflected this. The variation was enormous. People wore clothes handed down from generation to generation, passed from sibling to sibling. People wore clothes where the top half did not go along with the bottom half. People wore clothes bought in thrift stores or donated to them by charity. I was entranced by it all, by the variety. Sometimes I would bow my head so as not to be seen and laugh in pleasure at how the people were not slaves to the fashions of corporate America. I rejoiced that as well as all the other things I liked at County I liked that the corporations' influence was not so dominant there.

As the years went by, a small trickle of European American patients began to come to County. The economic times were getting worse and forcing more European Americans to get over the racist prejudices and the capitalist propaganda which was used to keep European American working class people from using County and instead keep them paying their every penny and more to the vicious greedy profit-addicted insurance companies and hospitals. Some of these European American patients did not act too well at first.

Some of them thought they were too good to be there amongst the African American and Latino American people and the poor. Some of them initially would try to tell the clerks how to do their job. It was a pleasure to see the clerks put them in their place. The mostly lady clerks took no nonsense. They were in charge.

Anytime I was in danger of getting impatient waiting in lines at County I thought of its achievements and how the country's resources were being spent on wars and tax cuts for the rich rather than on health care and public hospitals like County. The military spending alone could have transformed County, and at the same time built and staffed hundreds of new hospitals like County. The fault of the long lines at County were the corporate gangsters and war criminals who ran the country, not the over-worked and under-paid workers in County.

County could not have operated without the mainly African American and Latina American clerks who ran the check-in and registration and kept the records. These, mainly ladies, were the front line of the hospital in terms of where and when patients were checked in and directed to where they should go and given appointments for the future. These ladies had to be strong as the hospital did not have enough resources to help all the patients who came through its doors. It was non-stop stress. On top of this some patients, especially some of the European American patients, would try to intimidate these clerks and tell them how to do their jobs.

But these ladies were strong and confident. One day I was up in the dermatology clinic waiting for word on whether I had cancer or not. There was a Puerto Rican couple sitting a few rows of seats away from me. The man started to abuse his partner, shout at her and push her. Women patients, mainly African American and Puerto Rican, sitting on each side jumped up and shouted at him and made him back off. I was proud of them.

But this was not enough for the clerk in charge. A tall, physically strong good-looking African American woman, came out from behind her counter and went for the man. 'What do you think you are doing in my clinic? At this sister? Get your ass out of here.' She raised her two fists and advanced on him. Other ladies jumped up and down shouting encouragement and support. The man was astounded. Women had never treated him like this before. He slunk out with his beaten tail between his legs. The clerk threw back her head and strode back up to her desk. She was proud. I was proud. She was a good one. She reminded me of the care giver lady who looked after my sister's husband back in Ireland. I told the African American lady clerk I was putting her in my next book. Here she is. We have been friends since. County could not have functioned without the lady clerks.

These lady clerks had many tricks up their sleeves. One of these was the way they came to work every morning, all dressed up in their finery and with their great hairstyles. These mainly African American ladies had hair styles of all shapes and colours. Red, blond, pink, blue, even on one occasion I saw green. Sticking up spikes, corn rows, tightly pulled back, the lot. It made me smile to just look at them.

Then there was the African American lady clerk in general medicine. I would be sitting there in an uncomfortable plastic chair early in the morning feeling not too wonderful. This lady clerk would come sailing round the corner dressed to the nines. She was a good dresser. Then she would say in a loud voice. 'Good morning.' A few pathetic grumbled good mornings would come from us patients in response. This was not acceptable to her. She would stop and repeat again this time in a louder voice: 'Good Morning.' The response would be slightly better but she would not be content, she would not stop shouting 'good morning', until she got us to shout out at the top of our voices 'Good Morning!'. She was a happy woman. Her repeated greeting wakened and roused us all. She made us feel too guilty to be anything but upbeat. Sure were we not still alive? She made us patients happy. But she was not finished there. As she exited the waiting room to her office she would sometimes give a mischievous sexy wiggle to her bum. This made the day better too, all part of the County therapy. I gave this lady a copy of the book I had written, *The Donegal Woman* and she read it, as did many other African American lady clerks and nurses and doctors in County. They liked it and told me so.

Then there were the nurses. They were mainly African American but also some were Latina American, European American and some were Asian American. I was to spend many times in the hospital and was never treated with anything but the greatest respect and care by the all the nurses and all the staff. The nurses were strong and confident. Once I was in intensive care, close to death. A young, arrogant, European American male doctor ordered the African American nurse to give me a shot of something. She said yes and he left. She then examined the prescription he gave her and took a little book from her coat pocket. It was a drug dictionary. Looking up the drug the doctor had told her to give me she said half to herself and half to me: 'I am not giving ten CCs of that shit to anybody.' Then she said directly to me: 'Always question your medicine. Will it interact negatively with what you are already on?'

On one of my admissions I had the same African American nurse every early morning shift. She appeared to be close to sixty years old. She would wake me up to take my vitals at about 6.30 am. 'You must leave home awful early every morning nurse.' 'Yes I do. I leave at 4.15 am. I made a deal with my grandson. As long as he stays at school and gets good grades I will work this shift and pay for his schooling. If he quits, that day I quit too. I have enough for myself with social security.'

I thought of all the racist people I had met over the years who said African American people were lazy. They should meet this woman. I wished I could introduce her to the white woman from South Carolina who was taking care of the mixed race children to whom Perry and I had delivered the furniture. I knew they could recognise themselves in each other, I knew they could become friends.

Then there were the doctors at County. Most of those who were there long-term were dedicated to their skill and their patients and to County. They were not so dedicated to the dollar as were many doctors. They were essential to keeping the place going as were the nurses and the clerks, the medical technicians, the janitors, the cleaning staff, all the workers. It was this collective workforce at County which saved my life.

In spite of their central role, the doctors as a group did not leave the same powerful overall imprint on the hospital. With very important and notable exceptions they came and went too frequently. Most of them were not committed to working long-term at County. The younger ones doing their training there tended to be more superficial and just saw County as a stopping off point to a high paid job at a profit hospital. The powerful imprint was left by the clerks, the nurses, the doctors who were there long-term, the general workers and the patients. This is not to say the doctors did not play their part. To keep County open in the late 1970s they waged the longest doctors' strike in US history. Due to my regular attendance at the hospital I came to know some of the doctors.

There was Doctor La Questa, head of endocrine. We duelled regularly as I wanted her to give me organic medicine for my thyroid. She smiled and said 'no'. She was Chinese Philippino American. She shuffled into work in old runners. She was immovable in her refusal to give me the organic hormone. I was not happy with that but I admired her strength and determination in sticking to her guns. She was a tough one. By the way she dressed she looked more like a patient than a doctor. She was the brains in the endocrine clinic. Some of the male doctors who were being trained by her did not like having to take her orders but they had to do what she told them if they wanted their qualifications. I enjoyed watching her run the clinic and putting them in their place. She must have had to fight hard and be strong to get where she was. I tortured her by going on the Internet and researching my illnesses and in particular why she should give me the organic thyroid hormone. I brought her articles from *The New England Journal of Medicine*. She would not budge. Frustrated I said: 'Doctor, I thought doctors were in favour of patients researching their illnesses and exchanging ideas with their doctors?' She replied with a crafty smile, 'Only if they agree with us.' Good one I thought. I could only laugh. Dr. La Questa was a character.

Then there was Doctor Videl, my urologist. She was originally from Peru. She did the surgery on me for my prostate cancer. She was very skilled. She also had a good sense of humour. As she worked at my intimate parts I would occasionally tell her jokes. I told her about the dream I had that I was on one of her gurneys in the middle of O'Connell Street in Dublin and I had a huge erection. As anybody who was ever there knows O'Connell Street is very busy. People from both sides of the street saw what was going on and rushed towards me shouting: 'Get Bonnie, get Bonnie.'

On another occasion Doctor Videl was examining my scrotum after she had done surgery on me for a hydrocele. There were over a half dozen young student doctors there who were being taught by Doctor Videl. They were in awe of her as she was the top surgeon, extremely skilled, extremely respected. I said to her: 'Doctor, I have a question for you.' She laughed in anticipation as she knew by my tone I was going to make a joke. 'Doctor,' I said, 'Tell me, when will my scrotum be beautiful again?' Doctor Videl laughed and laughed. Her students stood totally silent. They could not figure out how somebody, like me just an ordinary patient, would have the audacity to talk to Doctor Videl, the top surgeon in urology and their teacher, in such a way. I thought I was just helping them to be relaxed in their field and to develop a good bedside manner.

After one of Doctor Videl's surgeries on me Bonnie was helping to push me along back to the ward. I sat up on the gurney and said: 'Bonnie.' Bonnie looked round. Then I sang: 'You are the sunshine of my life.' Doctor Videl was impressed. The nurse helping to push me said, 'We have a lively one here.' I felt better.

And then there was my neurologist Doctor Bardt. He was pure upper class WASP, or so I thought. A very good doctor but unable to do more than keep me alive given my epilepsy and all my other problems. He kept me on a very high dose of anti-seizure medicine, worried I would have another rolling seizure like the last one and this time I could very possibly die. He liked to hear my stories and would keep me in his office for half an hour or more so I could keep him entertained. Then one day he had an African American student with him. I asked this student did he like the Blues. He did not know what to say. I asked him did he know of Lead Belly the blues singer. He had never heard of him. Then I got a surprise. I regularly did at County.

Dr Bardt asked me. 'Do you know what my oldest daughter is called?' I looked at him. 'I call her Ellen, after Ella Fitzgerald.' So he was not as WASP as I had thought, calling his daughter after the great African American singer Ella Fitzgerald. Not bad. My respect for the upper class European American Doctor Bardt increased. It taught me once again not to be too general in my assessment of people.

There were also the skilled blue collar workers, the electricians, the painters, the carpenters at County. They were overwhelmingly European American. This made them stick out like sore thumbs at County. I felt alienated from them, almost hostile to them as they mainly kept control of their unions and their well-paid, good benefit jobs through racism and nepotism. Their unions and jobs in County were mainly European American. This was particularly offensive at County where the patients were mainly African American and Hispanic. I hated this discrimination and racism. One of these workers heard me talk on the elevator and recognised my Irish accent. He spoke to me and said he was from Donegal. He tried to establish something in common with me because of this. But I had none of it. Establishing something in common with me in the context of him being a skilled worker in County I knew this meant establishing that he saw himself having nothing in common with the mainly African American and Latino American patients.

Then there was the unskilled blue collar workforce. They also illustrated the nature of the unions and racism at that time. These workers, the ones who mopped the floor, worked in the canteens, delivered the food trays, were overwhelmingly African American or Latino American. These were low paid jobs in spite of the fact that they were unionised and also essential to the running of the hospital.

The hospital being unionised provided some protection for these workers. It also created somewhat of a positive atmosphere between the workers themselves. There was not as much competition between the workers as there were in the profit hospitals which were mainly non-union. Wages and conditions tended to be negotiated collectively, at least amongst the various sections of the workforce. There were posters for union activities regularly on the notice boards and many times some of the workers wore union badges. From the union base in the hospital came somewhat of a sense of solidarity and friendship. This atmosphere also made me feel more at home at County than at the profit hospitals which were mainly non union.

One night I was sitting on a bench waiting for my ride home from the hospital. A lady on crutches came hobbling along heading for the exit. Before she got there she threw up on the floor. In a couple of seconds a worker arrived with a bucket, a pan and a brush and some plastic bags. He wrapped the brush in a plastic bag. He wrapped the pan in a plastic bag. He placed a plastic bag inside his bucket. Then he meticulously worked his brush and pan around and around the vomit and brushed it with his plastic bag covered brush into his plastic bag covered pan, and emptied it into his plastic bag lined bucket. He repeated this a few times, each time putting a clean plastic bag on his pan and brush. When he was finished the floor was immaculately clean and when he peeled the plastic bags of his pan and brush it was as if they had never been used. I had been sitting watching him all this time. He had been unaware of this until he was finished and straightened up to move off. I said to him: 'Sir, I have been watching you. That was a work of art.' He looked at me and said nothing just nodded his head. And so it was a work of art. He was a skilled worker, an artist. I thought two things. Why was he not on a skilled workers' wage. And also I thought of my days on the boats when I used to clean the toilets.

Then there were the Mexican ladies who worked in the small coffee shop. It had a limited menu. I was always looking for a vegetarian sandwich or bagel. Initially the ladies, usually Latina ladies, were frustrated and annoyed with me as they usually did not have vegetarian sandwiches or the ones they had contained egg. I did not eat eggs as I was horrified at the egg capitalists who cut the nibs of the day old chicks with small circular saws and without any anaesthetic. Eventually these ladies and I came to be friends and they would search desperately for a vegetarian sandwich with no eggs. I could see they knew they did not have such a sandwich but they wanted to make sure I could see they wanted to help me and would if they could have. Good people.

When I first started my sojourn at County there was only the old Fantus building. There were many occasions when the wait was long. This building had a façade of a kind of art deco type. I liked it. The Fantus clinic was overwhelmed with patients. An estimated 400,000 patients came through its doors every year. The hospital pharmacy at County dispensed more medicine than any other pharmacy in the world. The TV series ER was based on life in the hospital's emergency room. Not that it could ever capture the drama and richness of life in the real ER of County where I had been treated so many times. County was no ordinary hospital. It was a whole world and culture of it own.

County fought to survive and it succeeded. In fact in spite of being under attack by the profit hospitals and the Chicago capitalist developers, it more than survived. Until the 1990s, very few of the profit hospitals in the city would take African American patients. When this racism was made illegal, after that came the 'dumping'. This was where the profit hospitals dumped patients who had no insurance and from whom they could make no profit. They dumped these on County. In many cases, the administrators and doctors in these profit hospitals lied to their patients about why they were being sent to County. The term 'wallet biopsy' was used as a cruel cynical term to describe why the patients were being dumped, that is because they had no insurance, because their wallet was empty. Some patients died through being dumped. There were murderers amongst the profit hospital administrators and system. I was dumped a few times myself but thanks to County survived.

In the early 1980s, 600 patients a month were being dumped on County by the profit hospitals which were run by the greedy capitalists and clerics and nuns. This dumping was only ended when, amongst other things, doctors and nurses with the cooperation of patients organised wheelchair rallies and marches and demonstrations and took patients back to the profit hospitals from which they had originally been dumped.

My understanding of Chicago was increased in another way by my times at County. The prisoners from Cook County jail were brought there when they needed treatment. Looking at them with their wrists and ankles shackled I lay enraged thinking how it should be the capitalist bankers and developers and military tops and war criminals and top cops who should be there. The prisoners would be chained to their beds and their guards would sit beside them. This included women prisoners, some of whom were pregnant. I would learn that when women prisoners were giving birth they were still chained, at least by one hand to the bed. What a society. US capitalism. The rattle of the prisoners' handcuffs and chains would keep me awake. I tried to imagine their lives, so young and so many of them African American and Latino American. I also tried to imagine the lives of their guards, many of whom were also African American. What a country. The youth and workers they could not employ and who were forced to starve or turn to crime they jailed. Then many mostly African American people, as far as Chicago was concerned, who did not have training in other skills were employed to jail them. Cook County jail, the concentration camp just a few blocks from the hospital, was built for 5,000 prisoners, but it often held 10,000. Its ill prisoners were treated at County.

I learnt so much, tragic and semi-tragic and funny and heroic, in County. One night I was in the emergency room yet again. On that occasion I was very nauseous. The nurse gave me Phenergan to counter this. We did not know at that time that I was allergic to this medicine. My face swelled up and I became disorientated. The nurse knew that I was not in danger and also that there was no alternative but to let it wear off. She and an assistant wheeled my bed into an alcove between two curtains and left me. I was in a state of panic. Meanwhile nurses, doctors and all sorts of people were walking up and down the corridors going as I saw it merrily about their business. I on the other hand was not at all merry and began to call out for help.

For hours I called. I got annoyed and stepped up the volume of my cries. Then I got poetic. 'In the name of humanity will somebody help me? Have I to lie here like a dying dog and be ignored. In the name of all that is kind and beautiful in this good earth will somebody not help me?' In between times images of the fields and rivers at home would flit through my head. Through the mist in my eyes and my swollen face and my disorientation I could see that the nurses were unconcerned, there was nothing they could do and they knew I was not in danger. They even seemed a bit amused at what I was coming up with to try and get their attention. After a few hours the affects of the medicine wore off. The nurses came back to check and we laughed together about what I had been saying.

One other night I needed to go to the toilet. Holding on to my IV stand for support I shuffled down to the bathroom. Opening the door I was hit by a gale of cigarette smoke. There were about a dozen men in the bathroom. They were all smoking. So, I thought, this was the way it worked, this was their way of getting round the 'No Smoking' ban. They had their own smoking club.

I hung out for a while for a chat. The men were all African American. I stood out like a sore thumb. Not only was I the only European American but I was the only non smoker. The smoking club members were very surprised to see me there but they were very friendly and welcoming. It was clear they saw it as their place, and as the hosts they wanted to be hospitable. In spite of the smoke I appreciated being welcomed into their club.

One of the smokers present was leaning on a crutch. He came over to me. 'Hey man what are you doing here? You must be dying or something. A white dude in County.' We all laughed in response. 'I hope not. What about yourself?' 'Aw man I have got it made. Look at that foot.' And he pointed to his bandaged foot. 'I just had half of it cut off. Gangrene. Now I will be able to get the disability. Set for life. It could not be better.'

I laughed with him for his 'good fortune'. But I was thinking what kind of a country was it when it was a good thing to get half your foot cut off? I put my hand on his shoulder, said good night to him and all his friends and went back to the ward and lay down.

On one of the occasions when I was kept overnight in County I was put in a small two bed ward. There was a curtain between my bed and the other bed which was empty. I fell asleep. Later I awoke to the sound of voices on the other side of the curtain. It was a lady taking information from the new patient. I heard her asking him his religion. Atheist he said. My ears pricked up. He went on to explain that religion only caused wars. When the lady was on the way out I congratulated her on having a ward where all the patients were atheist. Okay so there were only two patients but still it was a start. The man in the other bed was an African American working class man in his late fifties. We talked during our stay there and I gave him a card for the Blog I helped run. County was always an adventure.

On another night I was lying on a gurney in a corridor as the ER and the wards were full. There were other patients in gurneys all around me. I heard a voice whispering. 'Hey, hey man. Help me with these.' I looked. It was an elderly African American man on a gurney with his hands tied to the rails on the sides of the gurney. 'Here help me out of these.' I replied: 'I will not. The nurse would go after me.' I assumed he had been trying to pull out his IV and escape.

At that point a young Latino man came along with food trays. He went to give one to the man whose hands were tied to the gurney. The man said he could not eat with his hands tied. The young man, temporarily confused, seeing no alternative and intimidated by the patient undid one of the man's hands, gave him the tray and moved on. As soon as he did so the man on the bed used his free hand to untie his other hand, swung his legs over the side of the gurney reached for his clothes under the gurney and went to leave.

But then he realised he had a problem. His catheter. He had not thought about this. I could see his mind working. Then he reached for the plastic jagged-edged knife on the food tray, reached for the tube to his catheter, sawed it through, and freed, rushed for the door with his bag of clothes under his arm. The last I saw was his back sticking out through the slit of his hospital gown as he ran for it. I often wondered how he got on with the catheter. I knew about catheters. I had tried to pull one out of myself when I was half out of it in another hospital on a previous admission but all I achieved was to leave myself and the bed covered in blood, the catheter still in and two nurses giving me a severe talking to.

Then there was the time I had to have a procedure where I had to bring somebody along to take me home. As was often the case I forgot. 'Mr Throne, you have to have somebody to go with you.' 'But I have nobody. Please Nurse?' I always called the clerks 'nurse'. 'Please nurse I will be okay.'

But the clerk would not yield. She had her rules and I would have to obey. I was stuck. Then I saw a tall Eastern European lady in the waiting room of the clinic next door. I went in and explained the situation to her and asked her would she pretend to be with me so I could get out. Initially she looked at me suspiciously then a glint of mischief came into her eye and she agreed.

We went back into my clinic. I introduced the lady as my niece and she was there to take me home. I could see the clerk lady no more believed this than she believed there was a man or a woman on the moon. But she was covered and so she let me leave. The Eastern European lady, she was Polish American, and I shook hands and smiled at each other sharing a moment of mischief and laughter. That County!

On another occasion I was registering at the Orthopaedic clinic. As I was doing so I saw a very thin African American woman sitting in the waiting area weeping. Then I noticed that the clerk who was registering me was getting a few dollars from her bag and some from the other clerk and they were talking together under their breath about the thin lady. I said: 'What is wrong with that lady?' 'Her son was shot and killed a few months ago and she cannot get over it. She comes in most mornings and we give her a few dollars.'

I gathered in my pocket and gave the nurses two dollars. You would not see such humanity in the profit hospitals. They would be taking the money out of the thin African American lady's pockets. No matter if her son had been murdered.

On another occasion after Wall Street's government had begun to force us to pay something towards our medicines I was there and did not have the money. But I had run out of one particular medicine which was essential to keep me alive. I kept insisting I needed the medicine. After a while the lady who was in charge of dispensing the medicine began to look in her bag. I asked her what she was doing. She said she was seeing if she had enough money to give me for my medicine. I said under no conditions. I then went to the cashier and explained my situation that I had no money and he said: 'I will handle that.' And without another word he stamped the piece of paper and I was able to go back to the lady and she gave me my medicine. County was a humane hospital, and the people who worked in it also. What a difference from the profit hospitals.

On yet another occasion I was lying in County trying to sleep. It was around 10.00 pm. A nurse came into the ward and asked if anybody could speak Spanish as she had a patient who only spoke Spanish and she needed an interpreter. There was no one. I had a few smatterings of Spanish and I explained this to her. She said that was better than what she had and so come on. We went into another ward where a small thin Latino American man was sitting in a gown on the side of the bed. The nurse asked me to ask him how he felt. She explained to me that he had been restrained by the police when trying to scale a wall but could offer no explanation as to why he was doing this. He was not trying to steal anything just scale the wall. And he put up no resistance to the police. Even seemed to be enthusiastic to go along with them. The nurse also explained that he was bursting with nervous energy.

I thought maybe he was paranoid and running from some imaginary pursuer. I asked the man in Spanish how he was. With the most innocent enthusiastic broad smile he answered; 'Sí. Sí. Sí.' I asked him a few other questions which the nurse suggested but no matter what I asked him in my broken Spanish he would always respond the same way. With a most innocent and broad and enthusiastic smile he would say; 'Sí. Sí. Sí.' Nodding his head forward again and again. From his repetition of 'Sí', from his enthusiastic smiling seemingly very happy expression, from his head nodding, from his overall posture he seemed really eager to help me but all he would do was smile and repeatedly say 'Sí'. The nurse pulled me by the gown and said to leave it and thanked me. She walked me back down to my ward.

On the way I asked her what was the problem with the patient. She said that he seemed to be one of those cases where he had times when he had great bursts of energy and then times when it was the opposite. I said like up days and down days. She replied yes, that was it like up and down days. She said they were considering was he bi-polar. I had heard of this bi-polar and was struggling to understand it. Thinking about the nurse's comment about the patient having up and down days I remembered my own past.

In my teens and into my twenties I had my up and down days. Days when I would feel there was no point to anything, I thought of these as 'down days'. Then there would be days when something would go well in my work or personal life and I would feel good, I thought of these as 'up days'. This was a time when I did not know to which class I belonged, a time when I was being declassed. A time also when I did not know my role in the world, how to relate positively to the world. Then when I came to understand my place and role in the world, that is to fight as part of the working class to end the rotten system of capitalism, my up and down days ended completely. They ended completely and definitively. I lay there in my bed in County and thought of this.

Could this bi-polar, maybe more than just bi-polar, maybe many mental illnesses perhaps have as their cause the inability of people who suffered from such illnesses to find their proper place in the world? I thought about it this way. Every day we get the information through our senses that society is rotten, that the capitalist system is rotten. This information tells us that the system should be changed, tells us that we ourselves should try to change the system. If we try to do so then we are acting in a positive manner with the information we receive. Responding to the information we receive in this way points us in the direction in which lies the best chance of mental health.

If, on the other hand, we do not act to change the system, or can find no way to change the system, or have tried to change the system and had a bad experience in this effort and become demoralised, then we have to deny this information that continually comes into our brain that the system is rotten and should be changed. That is we have to fight against this information that we continually receive. Does this not involve trying to twist and turn mentally to fit into a system that is rotten and should be changed? Does this not involve deforming ourselves mentally to fit into a rotten system, into a system into which we should not try to fit, and does this not damage our mental and thought process? I concluded that this is the direction in which lies the least chance of mental health.

I would continually look at mental illness in this way, at psychological problems in this way. When I found my way to becoming part of, and to embrace being part of the working class, and to becoming a revolutionary, that is a way to fight to change the system, my up and down days ended completely and permanently. I had found my way to relate to the rotten system of capitalism. That is to work to overthrow it. That is to accept and act on the information that I was receiving continually, the information that the system was rotten and I should try to overthrow that system and act in the manner indicated by this information. This may sound simplistic. But as I thought about this, I used my imagination to consider the following.

Look at the massive propaganda machine of capitalism that every minute of our every day seeks to tell us that capitalism is the only system. The mass media, the capitalist and pro-capitalist political parties, capitalist state apparatus, the churches, all attack us with their propaganda that capitalism is the only system and that the choice is simple, that is, fit in. But this is a gigantic lie hammered daily into the heads of people. And when this mass lying and indoctrination, this attempt to make us deny reality, results in mental crises then here take some drugs, legal or illegal. Go to a therapist. The therapist will help us fit in. And of course there is plenty of money in it for the mental so-called health industry capitalists as they sell their drugs and charge hundreds of dollars an hour for therapy sessions.

This massive propaganda and indoctrination of capitalism does damage on another front. It discourages all that is best and healthy in our nature. It discourages kindness, collective action, solidarity. Just think about when there is a major crisis such as an earthquake or a major fire how people rush to help. Their best qualities come out. But capitalism brain washes that it is best if everybody acts for themselves and the devil take the hindmost. Encourages these backward features. Kindness, collective action, solidarity, these are dangerous to capitalism. They lead to people thinking about each other, thinking about taking collective action to build a different world based on kindness, collective action and solidarity. This is the last thing that capitalism wants. This indoctrination of capitalism does damage to people's mental health. It does so because it is a lie. It does not correspond to reality.

I once recruited a woman to socialism. She later moved away from the area where we had both lived. I received a letter from her. These were her words. 'Thank you for your socialism. Thank you for explaining that the capitalist system is rotten and should be overthrown. Before I understood this I used to think that there was something wrong with me. Now I see that I am alright and that it is the system that is wrong.' Exactly. This woman hit the nail on the head. The best chance of mental health is to be involved in the struggle to end capitalism. It is of course not an easy road. It is a road filled with conflict and wounds and damage. But it is the road that gives the best possibility of mental health. And not only mental health. But gives the best possibility of realising our potential to the fullest possible extent. I concluded this as I lay there in County.

I also thought about something else there that night in County. In my political work I argued that it was part of parental responsibility to organise and fight to end capitalism. Climate change, nuclear war, pollution, drought, starvation, rising sea levels would, if capitalism continued, end life on earth as we know it. There would be no future for our children. But was there perhaps something else. If we did not fight capitalism and sought instead to fit in to capitalism this would result in our thinking being damaged and deformed. This damage, this deforming had to be registered in our physical brain, in the electrical impulses, the chemical balances in our brain. We were dealing with a material world. Therefore was it not possible that the damage to our thinking and our brain that would result from not fighting the system could be passed on to our children. We could pass on our freckles, our physical features, our skin colour, and so on, so could we not pass on the damage that was done, the deforming that was done to our brain and the thought process which was rooted in our material brain to our children? I was not sure. I concluded I would have to think about this some more. There were many prices to pay for not fighting capitalism. Maybe there was more than first appeared in the old saying about the sins of the fathers and mothers etc.

There were serious economic and racist pressures on County. The capitalist developers could not look at it without grinding their teeth with greed thinking how much money they could make by tearing it down and developing new buildings on the site. After all it was near downtown and just off the 290 expressway. The right wing *Chicago Tribune* campaigned for it to be torn down. Their owners and editors and investors did not need it. But staff and patients and former patients and family members of these patients and former patients of County marched behind banners declaring: 'Keep County open. Health care for people not profit.' Hospital workers went on strike and marched. The powers that be tried to starve County of funds and in this way break this movement. This meant that for a time there were no sprinklers, and there were serious electrical wiring problems. There was no back-up generator. The starving of the hospital of funds and especially the effects on the health of mainly African American people was described by Dr Linda Rae Murray, the House Staff President at the time, in an interview with the BBC in this way: 'I call it murder.'

The fact that it served mainly African American and Latino American Chicago was a major issue. The mainly European American, racist, capitalist criminals who sat on the ruling bodies of the Chicago Stock Market, the Board of Trade, the city's big banks, etc., and who controlled the city government could not bear the thought of African American people, Latino American people, and poor people in general, having a hospital in which they could get help for nothing. This was unacceptable to these racist capitalists. But these creatures were defeated. They were never able to tear County down. In fact the opposite was the case. They not only had to keep the old Fantus building with its art deco façade going and in use, but they had to build a new one beside it. They were too afraid of the movement of patients and former patients and staff and the residents of South Chicago. This was a victory for all working people.

I thought about what all this meant for me. Not only did the African American people and their struggles give me a way forward in my life politically and psychologically, but in keeping County open they also saved my life. County was where I went and was diagnosed, was treated and where my life had on many occasions been saved. I am forever grateful to the African American people of Chicago and of County and to all the people who fought and successfully waged the struggles which kept County open. They saved me. I salute these heroines and heroes. County is a symbol of a victorious struggle against economic and racist and class exploitation in Chicago. I was and am proud and privileged to have spent so much time there and to have it become my second home. Going to County was also the closest I came in my life in Chicago to feeling that I was in Ireland. The working class atmosphere and culture reminded me of home.

I am also proud that during all this time of sickness and my being treated at County, it never once occurred to me to give up the revolutionary struggle. In fact it was the very opposite. What I experienced in all my times in County, my illnesses, my treatment, my getting to know the patients and staff, my getting to know South Chicago, all of these experiences strengthened my hatred of capitalism and strengthened my belief in the humanity and goodness of people if they got half a chance. My immersion in the working class life of County and South Chicago strengthened my commitment to my socialist struggle. This is another thing for which I have to thank Cook County hospital staff, Cook County hospital patients and the working people of South Chicago.

CHAPTER 47

THE DONEGAL WOMAN

IN SPITE OF BEING EXPELLED and fired from the CWI, in spite of the collapse of LMV, and in spite of my serious health problems, I carried on my revolutionary duties, reading, discussing, organising. For a while before my health got really bad, and even though I was not supposed to be driving, I took a chance and took small jobs to pay my bills. I would on occasion have breaks between these jobs when I would sit and think. Most of this thinking involved my revolutionary work, the lessons I had drawn and was drawing and what I was trying to do differently from the past. However, that was not all I was thinking about. As I sat in coffee shops and libraries between jobs, drove small loads of furniture, antiques and art from one place to another, I increasingly found myself thinking about my mother and her mother and their lives.

I would especially find memories of what my mother told me about her own mother, my grandmother, come and go in my head. I found myself more and more thinking about their world. Unconsciously at first, and then more consciously, I wanted to give them a voice, to share their experiences as widely as possible so people could learn from their lives. So people could be strengthened, could have their own consciousness raised by the experiences of my grandmother and mother. I wanted the lives of my mother and aunt to help more people than they had already helped. I also wanted to do this as I was increasingly conscious of the special oppression of women under capitalism and also the increasing struggles of women for a better life. So I thought about writing a book based on the life of my grandmother. I knew the basic facts of her life from a conversation I had had with my mother some years before.

I had been visiting my mother in her small farm house in Lifford on one of my trips back from Derry to Dublin. It was a Sunday night in the early 1980s. As usual I was having some food while my mother and aunt were packing up bread and cakes and duck eggs for me to take with me. No matter our disagreements my mother and aunt would always feed me and pack food for me to take with me. They were good people. In spite of all I had done which had hurt them and made their lives more difficult and unhappy my mother and aunt would always send me off with food to eat. When I would call to see my mother and aunt my mother would usually have been going on at me about the problems in her life and how if I would only come back I could help her out. I usually tuned her out. But that particular night I realised that something different was happening. My mother was talking very seriously about something else and wanted me to listen. I did so.

'John you know about your Aunt Lizzie, and her taking her own life. There was more to it than I told you at the time. Our mother was hired out to that Taylor crowd over near Castlefinn. They were a monied lot. The man of the house was bad to mother. She ended up with his wean. The wean was your Aunt Lizzie. The minister at Convoy church arranged for mother to be married to your grandfather. To my father.'

I looked up at my mother. Her eyes were searching my face for my reaction. I could see she was very anxious to hear what I would say. She went on: 'So there you see. That is the kind of people we are.' I could see that my mother, aware she was coming to the end of her life, could not live with herself any longer unless she told me the truth about our family's life.

I was enraged on behalf of my mother. She was speaking as if she was ashamed at what had happened to her mother. I knew she was struggling not to be, but at the same time the churches taught her she should be ashamed. I hated the churches and organised religion more by the minute. They had poured the guilt on my mother's mother and my mother to keep them under control. I knew from the expression on my mother's face that she desperately wanted support and reassurance from me. With all my power I gave her this reassurance and support. I spoke extremely strongly. 'Mother. You must not say this. You know me I do not believe in sin. But I say this because I know you do. If there was any sin it was not any sin of your mother or your family, it was that rapist farmer who abused your mother, who raped your mother. It is he you always have to keep in mind is the sinner. But not only that, there was more than enough sin to go around. There is the sin of the male-dominated churches that taught you to think this way.'

'Mother, I hear from you and your sisters and brother how well you speak of your mother, my grandmother. I never knew her directly. But I know her through what you say about her, how you speak of her, the tone of your voice, the reverence in your words, these tell me your mother, my grandmother, was a very good person. I remember also how well all the people who came to Aunt Lizzie's funeral spoke of Aunt Lizzie. Aunt Lizzie was also a very good person. I wish I had known your mother, my grandmother, I wish I had known Aunt Lizzie better. I wish Aunt Lizzie had felt secure enough to speak to me about her life, to share with me the secrets of her life. Both of them were heroines. In spite of all your mother and Aunt Lizzie came through, they survived as great persons. They were heroines. Please you must not think of your mother and Aunt Lizzie in anything but the best of light. Anyway I do not have to say this to you. I know you think of them only in the best of light.'

I hated the churches and religion more and more as I sat there and saw the sorrow and pain in my mother's face. But I also saw something else. I saw that she was very relieved that I had responded the way I did, that I had stood up for and praised and spoke so strongly and well of her mother and Aunt Lizzie. She was very thankful to me for that. And she was very relieved. She did not believe her mother and Aunt Lizzie were 'sinners'. But the churches tried to tell her that. She had wanted to be reassured by me, by her only son. This was one of the occasions when my beliefs and my being her son, my holding the beliefs I did, helped and comforted my mother and make her feel better about life. I was very glad I could do this for her. For one of the only times I felt I could stand with my mother without any qualification or difference. It was the closest I ever felt to my mother.

Of course it was not without its contradiction. I was able to speak as strongly as I did and support my mother as honestly and strongly as I did because of my revolutionary socialist and atheist ideas. I was able to speak in the most strong and convincing manner because of my genuinely held atheist and anti-religious beliefs, because I did not believe in the garbage of the churches, their so-called 'sin' and all their crap and hypocrisy. It was the dialectical contradiction again. Because I was an atheist and revolutionary I was able to reassure and comfort my mother so strongly, my mother, who was herself so strongly opposed to atheism and revolution.

My mother only told of her mother's experience to those whom she trusted. The shame that had been fed to her by the churches made her keep her mother's rape and having a child and not being married a secret. She dreaded this getting out. Instead of speaking of the injustice experienced by my grandmother she sought to keep this quiet. She thought that loyalty to her mother meant keeping what happened to her a secret. But then entered my two oldest sisters, Kathleen and Margaret, and our other sister, Angela. My mother did not trust these sisters and so did not tell them about what happened to her mother. In their resentment of our mother, for what they saw as favouritism to my other sister Mary, they wanted to hurt our mother. In some way they found out about my grandmother and Aunt Lizzie. When they did they had to tell my mother they knew, they had to tell my mother to hurt her, they had to attack my mother for not telling them. And they had to tell her in the way that would hurt her most. My mother asked them how they knew. They said a man they met on the street in Raphoe, they did not know his name, that is a stranger, had told them. This was a lie. The truth was they wanted to hurt my mother as much as possible by saying what had happened to her mother was being talked about by strangers in the street. This was a crushing blow to my mother. What nasty people. Hearing this about these three sisters I was glad that blood was not thicker than water.

The more I thought of these developments in my family, the more I became convinced that I had to speak out and let the world know what was what. So in the early years of the new century, I began to write a book about my grandmother's life. This was not a simple decision. My mother and her siblings has spent their lives hiding what had happened which they saw as their duty to their mother. And here now I was about to write a book about it. Let the whole world know. I thought a lot about this. When I would have doubts I would remember the expression on my mother's face when I spoke so strongly and supported her mother. She was so relieved and uplifted. I was determined my book would do the same for a much wider layer of people. And it would do so especially for women who suffered sexual oppression.

I did not hold back in this book. It was based on the basic information that I had received from my mother about my grandmother. But I also drew on my own experiences in life. I discussed with Bonnie who had five children, about childbirth and her experiences. From this evolved the book which I called The Donegal Woman. I had help in the editing and production of this book from two close friends back in Ireland, Dolores Meenan and Bridget O'Toole. Both were mothers and socialists. I also had help in the formatting and distribution of the book from two other friends Liam O Caomhanaigh and Denise Diver. The book was a great success receiving overwhelming praise from women and especially women in the Donegal area, who came from a similar small farmer background to my mother and grandmother. It had all this success without a publisher or an agent. It reached number two on the best sellers list in the North. It would have been number one only we ran out of copies at the height of sales. It has now sold 30,000 copies. Selling all across the English speaking world.

My mother was dead by the time I wrote The Donegal Woman. I am not sure what would have happened if she had been alive. I know I would have still written it and published it. As in other areas of my life, I would not have been silenced by the right wing capitalist and religious opinion which influenced my mother. But I am not sure what would have happened in relation to my mother. She had been keeping a secret about her mother and sister her whole life and there I would have gone and written a book about it. All my family, except my sister Mary, hated the book. They did not want to admit that we had been poor, that our grandmother had been hired out, that she had been raped, they wanted to keep the façade of their slightly better-off, small farmer, 'respectable' existence, and pretend that this was always the way it had been.

I spoke at a launch of this book in the court house in my home village of Lifford. There were over 100 people present. A neighbour who had been very good friends with my mother, and to whom my mother had taught many household skills, also spoke on my book. Diplomatically, but, and this I respected and thought was not unconnected to this lady's friendship with my mother, this lady said she very much appreciated the book, but she was not sure what my mother would have thought about it. She said she thought my mother would have probably thought it 'was a bit too close to the bone'. I think she was probably right in what my mother would have thought. But I also think that when alone, and if she had been alive and able to read The Donegal Woman, the expression that came on her face when I supported her and her mother when she told me about her mother having a child would have briefly, like the sun's rays briefly breaking through a cloudy sky, drifted temporarily across her face.

As I have written before my mother had an expression. She said she was a 'stickler for the truth'. The Donegal Woman was written adhering to this approach. My grandmother had been hired out in the hiring fair system in Ireland when she was very young. This system was where better off farmers, mostly, but not exclusively Protestant, from the better land in the east of Donegal and into the other counties of what is now Northern Ireland, would hire the children and workers, mostly Catholic, but not exclusively Catholic, from the poorer land in the west of Donegal, where the land could not feed a whole family, especially the big families of holy, no family planning, Catholic Ireland. These children and workers would work for six-month periods, would live in the farmers' barns or homes and would only get paid at the end of the six-month period. This gave the farmer great power over these workers. I always remember my uncle, to his credit, criticising this system and criticising a Catholic neighbour who exploited to the extreme the workers he hired through this system.

My uncle hired a farm labourer, but not on the hiring system. He paid him the legal wage set by the government and paid him his insurance stamp. My uncle was meticulous in keeping up with any raises the government made. This farm labourer lived in his own room in our house, ate at the same table with the family, ate the same food as the rest of the family, sat with the family round the fire in the evening. He was as part of the family. After he left and went back to live on his own small farm he would, every few months or so, come to visit and have his dinner with and sit and talk to my mother.

My uncle was particularly opposed to the hiring fair system because of what he observed in the case of another farmer who lived close by. This farmer was one of the few Catholic farmers who had enough land to hire workers though the hiring fair system. He had a number of these young workers. Some were male and some were female. This farmer encouraged the young male workers to have sex with, to rape the young female workers. This was part of keeping the young males under his control, in 'male solidarity with him' and working hard and doing what they were told. He was 'sharing' the young females' bodies with them in return for which he got more work out of the young males and more control over them. It was one of the 'perks' of their jobs. Not only were the young female workers being exploited in their work, but they were being raped by the other male workers as part of the perks of the young male workers and also the employer. As I saw on other occasions, when it came to employers, the Catholic employers were just as bad as the Protestant employers. I was told about this after my uncle died by another farmer who lived close by. He was a Catholic farmer, who like my uncle, a Protestant farmer, was disgusted by the actions of this farmer. There was no definitive line between the degenerate actions of employers, Protestant or Catholic, when it came to how they treated their workers.

My grandmother had been hired as an outside worker, that is, working on the land and with the animals and living and sleeping in the barn. Her employer was a Protestant. She was raped repeatedly and made pregnant by this Protestant farmer, one of 'her own'. To 'avoid the shame', to keep up the phony image that Protestants were superior to Catholics and therefore deserved to rule, the Protestant church of which she was part and of which the farmer was part, stepped in and had her married off to a man much older than her. He was my grandfather. He also raped her. This was not seen as rape because he had the blessing of the church in this as she was 'his wife', his property. So after all how could you 'rape' what you 'owned'? She had the child of the rapist farmer and four more children by my grandfather before she would die young of the flu.

I wrote the book *The Donegal Woman* as a tribute to my grandmother, my Aunt Lizzie, my mother and all women. I wrote the book as a contribution to allowing my grandmother and all women to speak, to have a voice. I wrote it to allow my grandmother, my Aunt Lizzie and my mother to have their voices heard after all these years. I saw writing it as part of my revolutionary duty and also part of my duty to my mother and my family. My grandmother would never have imagined it; that her life would have been written down in the coffee shops and libraries of Chicago by a man like me, a revolutionary socialist, an atheist, with a thing called a laptop. I was positively surprised at how my book helped to weaken sectarianism. It did so by exposing that it was not only Catholic people who were hired out and exploited, but sections of the Protestant poor also. My book did just about as much to weaken the sectarian divide as my day-to-day political work for working class unity.

With my three friends Dolores, Bridget and Liam back in Ireland, we set up our own 'publishing house'. This amounted to no more than ourselves, and a bank account. We called it Drumkeen Press after Drumkeen, the townland where my grandmother had been born. Bonnie also helped me with this book, helped me to understand life from a mother's point of view and helped me understand about childbirth and motherhood, helped me to understand what physically it felt like to give birth, what it felt like to have the pain of birth followed by the great pleasure of the new-born, living child on her breast. Something which neither I nor any man could ever experience. Thinking about this, about giving birth, about the harsh struggle to bring up a child, bring up children, about the great nurturing this demanded of the mother, about how this also enriched the mother, I came to conclude that women were stronger than men.

I thought of the act of procreation. What had the man to do? To provide his sperm. What had the woman to do? To nurture that sperm, to go through the enormous changes in her body as the foetus grew and the baby formed in her womb. Then to go through the trauma and pain of childbirth. Then to have the pleasure of the new born child. Then to breastfeed the child. The man's role in keeping the species going was much less than the woman's. Did this not mean that the women were stronger? I began to think that this was so. That men only ran things because of the class nature of society and through the development of the class nature of society during which a vicious assault had been carried out against women. There were some small groupings of people still extant in the world where the role of the sexes was much more equal, even where the woman was the central dominant figure in society. Writing The Donegal Woman raised my consciousness about the relationship between men and women. And made me think more about the advantages of being male and how these had been with me all my life. I concluded that a civilised society, if we could ever build one, would have women playing a central role in that society. In fact that would determine if the society was civilised or not.

We had over a dozen launches of the book in Ireland. These were mostly in small towns and villages, but also in Dublin and Derry. We had launches in London, the Bay Area of California and Chicago. We had no agent. But because of the content of the book, sexual oppression in the hiring fair system which had not been dealt with to any great extent before, and the related fact that women were increasingly conscious that their oppression should be talked about openly and opposed, and those and the organizations responsible held to account, the book was a great success.

These launches, especially in the small towns and villages, were extremely enriching and educational for me. The attendance was overwhelmingly middle aged and elderly women. Many spoke out and gave their experiences, some saying this was the first time they had done so. One meeting was held in a community hall in the small village of St Johnston in Donegal. As usual I did a short introduction and then there was a discussion. In the middle of the discussion a woman, short of stature, with her head bent over and eyes downcast and who had not spoken previously, burst out. 'I hate worms you know!' Everybody went quiet and looked at her. Nobody had been talking about worms or anything that could be seen to be related to worms. But in this lady's head there was obviously something about worms which related to the issue of the special oppression of women. She repeated, 'I hate worms you know. I was working in one of them big houses in Derry. One night the wife was out. I was in the house with himself on me own. He tackled me to the floor. Nothing happened you know, nothing happened.' She added quickly. She appeared to feel she had exposed herself too much and wanted to take back what she was saying. She looked up and around, seemingly shocked at what she was telling. 'Nothing happened. I never told anybody this before. I left that place the next day.' Obviously something had happened. Unfortunately this lady left hurriedly before the end of the meeting and before anybody could get to speak with her. I was guilty with all the rest of that meeting in letting that lady go without trying to help her, without trying to get her to speak more and without speaking to her more. Why had that lady come to that meeting? On that topic? There was a powerful story, a powerful experience there. I hoped that maybe by just coming to that meeting and hearing that topic discussed and being able to speak of her own experience, however briefly, had helped her. I hoped so. So many secrets, so much pain. The Donegal Woman had an impact.

My sister Mary promoted The Donegal Woman with the greatest energy and enthusiasm. She took it to book shops and told all she could about it and that I was her brother. She explained away the parts in it which were not so in line with her thinking or were in some people's eyes too explicit, as being the truth and you had to tell the truth. The other members of my family, it would not be too much to say, hated the book with a passion. They did not want to acknowledge that we had once been very poor, that our grandmother had been raped, that as I explained in the book my grandmother menstruated, that our grandmother had a child when she was not married. They, all in their backwardness, complained that I had made our grandfather look bad. They never mentioned that I had made our grandmother a heroine. Made her The Donegal Woman, a widely known heroine. Such pettiness and backwardness. Such male chauvinist thinking even by the females. Only worried about how their and my grandfather was portrayed.

I was thanked many times by women for writing The Donegal Woman. They would say that this should have been talked about before. In a grocery store in Donegal one day where my book was being sold, a lady approached me and asked was I the author. When I said 'yes' she said: 'Thank you. That was every women's story back then.'

The Donegal Woman was sold in bookshops, in grocery stores, garages, post offices, every kind of retail outlet. My friend and Comrade Anton had given me the idea to have the launches in the small villages and towns and to put the books in every kind of shop that would take it. The selling of the book was based on an orientation to the working class. It was politically the correct thing to do and also partially made for the great success the book would have. Many hundreds of copies were bought by two of the biggest trade unions in Ireland and distributed free to their members. This was one of the most satisfying experiences of my life.

However my old organisation, the CWI, once again outdid themselves in their sectarianism and pettiness. In spite of the book reaching number two on the best sellers list in Northern Ireland, my old comrades in the CWI had to have their whining say. They announced that the book was a 'flop'. Joe Higgins, in spite of being invited to speak at the launch in Liberty Hall in Dublin did not even respond to his invite. Only four or five members of the CWI from which I had been expelled attended. The sectarianism of this organisation even extended to the book about my grandmother. I mean what else is there to say about this organisation? Its guilt about how it had treated me would not allow it to say anything the slightest bit positive about me and this extended to my book. Other people who reviewed The Donegal Woman compared it positively to O'Donnell, McGill and other well-known writers from the north of Ireland. One reviewer also compared it positively to Steinbeck.

Writing this book was not an interruption from my revolutionary work. It deepened my understanding of the special oppression of women. It also humanised me further and allowed people, especially women, with whom I discussed, to see that I, and revolutionary socialism, were not some sort of dead and separate and male entity. In my ignorance and drive to write the book and keep building the revolutionary nucleus, I did not fully appreciate the amount of work and help Dolores, Bridget, Liam and Bonnie had contributed to the book. I take this opportunity to more fully thank them and to apologise.

After the book was published, a local community group in Drumkeen townland where my grandmother was born came together and erected a stone seat in remembrance of my grandmother's family. My grandmother would have been proud of this. My mother would have been proud of this. I regret that neither my grandmother or my mother or my aunt were alive to see this. I thank the people of Drumkeen. When I visit Ireland I go to Drumkeen and sit on this seat and look down over the valley and think of my grandmother and mother and their family. Life is not easy. But it is rich. And at times it is like the valley stretching down below my mother's family's stone seat, it is beautiful.

THE STRUGGLE AGAINST CAPITALISM IS THE STRUGGLE FOR THE CONSCIOUSNESS OF THE WORKING CLASS

— A LIFE UNENGAGED IN THIS STRUGGLE IS AN INCOMPLETE LIFE

I HAVE ENTERED my seventh decade. My beliefs remain the same: Capitalism is rotten. If it continues it will destroy life on earth as we know it. The working class can defeat capitalism and build a new society. My role in life is to fight to help build a mass revolutionary international of tens and hundreds of millions which can end capitalism and build an international, democratic, socialist, sustainable, planned economy and society. These are still my beliefs for which I still fight.

I continue to do so in spite of my age and having an armful of serious diseases, a number of which, if left untreated, would kill me in months. Some of these diseases I inherited and some are from life's wear and tear in the struggle to survive under capitalism. A doctor told me recently there are not many people my age and with all my diseases still walking around. I laughed in celebration and triumph when he told me this. The ability to continue to laugh has been part of what has kept me alive.

I am more optimistic and upbeat about life every day that goes past. I have to get up at 5.00 am every morning I am so excited to meet my day and not to miss any time which I can use to carry on my fight against capitalism, my fight to help weaken the hold that capitalism has over the consciousness of the working class. Given my age and my health, my fight today mainly takes the form of combating the ideas of capitalism within the consciousness of the working class through writing and discussing and reading. I can now do this more successfully and extensively than ever before given the existence of the Internet.

My determination to live for as long as possible and to combat capitalism's struggle for the consciousness of the working class, and to fight for a better and a socialist world, cultivates my spirit, my laughter, my will, ensures that these remain intact and gain in strength. I look forward to every day and to my remaining time on earth with enthusiasm, excitement and joy. I am never low in spirit, I am never depressed, I am never bored. I have a great life. There is a simple reason for this. I am fighting as part of the working class to end the capitalist system and replace it with a democratic socialist sustainable system that can give a better life to everybody and which can prevent the destruction of the planet.

I am part of the progressive class in the world at this time in history. The importance of being on the right side of history cannot be overestimated. Being on the wrong side is like trying to climb a cliff with only one arm and with a rock tied to your back. A fall is inevitable. I am on the right side of history. This is why I continue to have a great life and this is why my spirit remains combative and intact. That is why I can still laugh when I should laugh. That is why I can still cry when I should cry.

I am inspired by the struggles that are taking place around me. On one day in 2003, millions of people in 600 cities throughout the world marched against US imperialism's invasion of Iraq. This was the biggest coordinated movement of the world's working class and youth in history. The catastrophe that has followed the invasion proved that these millions of working class people and youth were right and the war criminals of capitalism who launched that invasion were wrong. It has proved that these war criminal capitalists were and are on the wrong side of history.

In the spring of 2015, there were major actions in over 200 US cities for a $15.00 an hour minimum wage and the right to join a union. Similar demonstrations took place on that day on similar issues in over thirty other countries. Mass movements and general strikes have swept many European countries against the attacks on living standards. Mass anti-racist and anti-police violence movements have taken place in the US. The giant working class of China is in the first stage of rising to its feet with its strikes and demonstrations. Women the world over are rising to their feet. There were the millions of women in the women's marches against Trump. The Arab Spring of 2010 brought down four dictatorial regimes and saw mass movements in six other countries. Radical left governments have come to power in a number of countries in Latin America. Millions of working people and youth who have never before moved into action are now doing so. In my home country of Ireland, tens of thousands of people are also on the march. It is because I am part of these struggles, that I am intact and full of life and laughter and joy.

Being on the right side of history also means that I am not intimidated by the rise of the new technology, the social media, the staggering advances in communication, and the spreading of knowledge. These do not frighten me. In fact they motivate and inspire me as I can use them to better conduct my struggle against capitalism and its attempt to dominate the consciousness of the working class. In the old days I could sell 400 copies of my socialist paper a month. Now I can spread articles and ideas to tens of thousands of people with the click of a key. I contribute to the struggle of the working class at this time by using the resources of my existing and remaining years to assist this struggle of the working class for knowledge and consciousness and information. I do so by developing the Blog - weknowwhatsup.blogspot.com - and other Internet outlets that I run with other revolutionaries.

I play my role in the cyber war that is going on. This cyber war is a class war. Capitalism has to use the new technology but as it does so it fights to try and ensure that this new technology is used solely for its benefit. It does so in vain. It seeks to impose its technological imperialism in vain. The various capitalist powers hack into their rivals' economies and political and military systems. As they do they disrupt each other's control and workings. This cyber war is not just a war between the various capitalist powers, it is also a war between the working class and the capitalist class. However, as in every other field, this class war is not being waged by the leaders of the working class. They are not mobilising the working class as a class to fight capitalism in this cyber war. This is particularly to be condemned given that it is working class people who are working the computers and have access to all the data and the technology and who could be mobilised in this fight.

The opposition to technological imperialism is being waged at the moment mainly by the youth, hackers, leakers, acting as small groups or as individuals and widely diffuse forces internationally. The role of these leakers and hackers will increasingly come to be seen as positive. But in the meantime Chelsea Manning spent years in solitary confinement and others are on the run, some driven to suicide, others hiding in fear of their lives. Capitalism seeks to prevent more leaks. But this will be in vain. As their system goes deeper into crisis and alienates more people, the working class leakers and hackers will become a veritable tide. It is working class people and youth who are at the computer hard drives and screens and in the offices and have access to the information.

The theme of my work is simple. The working class can build a new world. I base myself on what that worker in a rubber factory in Finglas, Dublin, said to me many years ago. He said: 'There is enough brain power on the floor [that is the factory floor] to run the industry more efficiently and more responsibly than existing management.' I agree with this. I thank this worker for his confidence and his statement and for strengthening my own confidence. And I fight to spread this opinion far and wide. Unlike the labour and trade union leaders and bureaucrats, this worker believed that the working class can run industry.

I carry on my fight for this idea with optimism for a few reasons. Along with the increasing dislocation, divisions and crisis of capitalism, there is the increase in the size and reach of the global working class. It is now three billion strong. This is the largest working class in the history of the world. I make no apology for repeating again here that half the factory workers in the world are now women. More than ever before women are not isolated in their homes instead they are part of the paid workforce. With this comes increased power for women workers, increased consciousness of that power and increased power for the entire working class and unity of the working class. And as capitalism's economic centre of gravity moves from the previously economically more advanced capitalist countries, hundreds of millions of more workers, male and female, have entered the working class in China, Asia, Latin America and Africa. This too means a strengthening of the international working class.

Two hundred million workers in one hundred and sixty three countries are organised in trade unions of one kind or another in the International Trade Union Confederation. Huge corporations in industry and transport and retail control, employ and organise hundreds of millions of workers. The Fortune Global 500 companies employ and bring together and seek to dominate the consciousness of forty-seven million people. But the other side of this is that these corporations also bring together in common experience these forty-seven million people. At the same time hundreds of millions are employed in the financial companies, the industrial and transport industries, the utility sectors, the health industry, the fast food outlets. And many of these are pushing on similar screens, operating similar machines and in many cases wearing the same uniforms. A new and larger and objectively more unified and diverse working class is being created.

These are not the only reasons I am optimistic about the future. While the working class is stronger than ever before capitalism as a system is increasingly in crisis. As it continues its downward plunge it will again and again show its real nature to the working class and to humanity. While this will bring increased suffering and risk to the working class it will also educate the working class. The more it exposes its real nature the more capitalism will drive the working class to its feet and force it to think and to act. As Marx said, sometimes the revolution needs the whip of the counter-revolution.

As capitalism experiences more and more crises and as the working class moves into action this will cause earthquakes under the feet of the trade union leadership and bureaucracy. This leadership, which controls the two hundred million trade union members in the world's trade unions, is the main obstacle to human society moving forward. It is so because it uses its position in the leadership of the organised working class, which is the progressive class at this time in history, to support capitalism, the system that is dying and that is threatening to destroy life on earth as we know it. This working class leadership does not believe that the working class can build a new society. As a result this leadership sees any independent movement of the working class leading only to chaos and a threat to its own positions of power and privilege. So inevitably because of this it seeks to, at all times, hold down and undermine the movement of the working class, the movement of its own members, against capitalism. The trade union and labour leadership is a counter-revolutionary force.

The working class is faced with no small problem. It is this: How can it, the working class, the progressive class in history at this time, remove its pro-capitalist leadership, remove this utterly reactionary leadership, a leadership with no historical knowledge or imagination from off its back? And replace this leadership with an organised revolutionary leadership of tens and hundreds of millions committed to building a new world?

Having said this is not to say that the working class is champing at the bit to overthrow capitalism. The working class is a sober class. It also has different views and layers within it. While in the main it sees that capitalism is rotten, it also sees that ending capitalism is not an easy task. So it is cautious. But having said this there have been and are times too numerous to count when the working class and/or sections of the working class have risen up to challenge capitalism. One of the most dramatic and powerful and more recent of these was the 1968 ten million-strong movement of the French working class. They struck and occupied their workplaces and elected workplace committees through which they carried out their action. The French capitalist class thought the game was up. This action of the French working class was only ended with capitalism being left in power because of the betrayals of the mass French communist party and socialist party.

The last century was dominated by the crisis of capitalism with its economic crises and its military conflicts, but also by attempts by the working class to carry through its revolutions. The reason these attempts were unsuccessful was not because the working class did not have the power to achieve their ends. But they were unsuccessful because the leaderships of the working class were not up to the task and were in fact, on just about every occasion opposed to the revolutionary efforts of the working class. The task is to build a new international revolutionary leadership for the working class.

The world historical situation remains as I stated in the foreword to this book. Capitalism is in a deepening crisis and threatens life on earth as we know it. At the same time the working class, the progressive class in history at this time is like a huge chisel. It has weight, strength and heft. But it is blunt. It has no cutting edge. Therefore it cannot do its job. Putting a cutting edge on this chisel is the task of tasks of this time in history. Forging in struggle, beating in the blazing white heat of the class battles, turning and shaping and hammering on the anvil of history, a cutting edge has to be put on the chisel that is the working class. This is the priority of priorities for the working class, for society, for all working people and youth, and for revolutionaries. Nothing else is more important. It is the reason for my living. It also is a reason, if necessary, for dying.

Any new leadership will face an enormous challenge. It will be confronted by all the ferocity and power and savagery of capitalism. The system which brought us the non-stop wars of the past century and today, which brought us Hiroshima and Nagasaki, which brought us Nazism, which brings us the terrorism and wars of US imperialism and all the imperialisms, which today brings us the non-stop wars and the developing destruction of the planet. What we see taking place in the area of the Middle East around Syria where society is being blown to pieces will threaten the world if capitalism is not overthrown.

The new leadership of the working class will have to learn the lessons of class struggle and history and learn them quickly. The main lesson that it will have to learn, is that it itself is the only progressive class in history, that to take society forward it will have to lead and act independently, and clearly see its task to be to destroy capitalism and change the world. No other force is going to do its job for it. It must stop any impulse to look for other forces to end capitalism. Human society stands at a fork in the road. Either the working class takes power and builds an international democratic socialist world, or capitalism will destroy life on earth as we know it. We all must be, the working class must be, as a collective class, all individuals as part of that class, must be prepared to sacrifice all to ensure that human society makes the correct choice at this fork in the road.

Consciousness determines discipline. The consciousness that capitalism will destroy life on earth, the consciousness that the working class can build a new world, this is the consciousness that can allow the working class to step forward and sacrifice all, to have the discipline to risk all to change the world. When the working class becomes conscious that capitalism will destroy life on earth as we know it, when it becomes conscious that it itself can build a new world, then it will be prepared to risk all, and to take the most ruthless and merciless action to end capitalism.

Of course building a new leadership of the working class will not be easy. Nor will it develop in a straight line. There will be victories but also there will be defeats, and serious defeats. And more: it might not happen. The struggle to overthrow capitalism could be defeated. Capitalism will not give up its rule without the most ferocious struggle. This has been shown over the past century. It has slaughtered tens of millions to put down revolutionary and radical movements. At the same time there are many extreme right wing movements that will offer themselves as so-called alternatives as capitalism goes deeper into crisis. This is already taking place here and there, such as the right wing movements in Europe. The impulses we can see around Trump. There are also events such as the catastrophic wars and civil wars which have followed the invasion of Iraq and the Arab Spring.

There are also the approximate 19,000 nuclear warheads. Capitalism is a system of war. It presently conducts its wars by proxy or conventional weaponry. But it showed what it is prepared to do in Hiroshima and Nagasaki. If capitalism is not overthrown, nuclear war will be inevitable. In the struggle against capitalism the sections of the working class who have their fingers on the buttons and who can unleash or leash the rockets in the silos will be vital. They have to be won to the side of the socialist revolution and the revolutionary socialist international. Human society is on a knife edge.

If a new democratic socialist world is built, a life of unimaginable plenty and wonder can be opened up. Life on earth can not only be preserved but can develop as never before. But if a new democratic socialist sustainable world is not built, there is an alternative. This alternative has to be considered. The planet is currently experiencing the worst destruction of species since the loss of the dinosaurs 65,000,000 years ago. Unless change is brought about, up to 50% of all species, animal and plant, are headed for extinction by 2050 and 99% of this destruction is by human action, that is by capitalism. One billion people in the world today are starving. 60% of those hungry are women. Every twenty seconds a child dies from water-related illnesses that are caused by capitalism. And it is only going to get worse if capitalism continues.

The poisonous methods of capitalist agriculture, the lack of access to clean water and food, drought which is related to climate change and which reduces crop production all combine to create the starvation and the poisoned foodstuffs which stalks the world. Along with this imperialism loots the wealth and the food of the super exploited countries and leaves the people in these countries starving. It is as when British colonialism, British imperialism, at the time of the Irish starvation, used its military power to seize the grain and meat from Ireland when the potato crop failed. There was plenty to feed the Irish population but it was looted and taken out of the country by force and the people were left to starve to death. Capitalism, imperialism, insists today through its propaganda and violence to the working people of the world that they have to give the capitalists their rent interest and profits. Even if this means, as it does for the majority of the world's population, that they do not have enough to eat. Capitalism and its allies preach to the working people of the world that they have to choose starvation, they have to choose destruction of life on earth as we know it, over revolution. All the religious organisations and the mass capitalist media and political forces internationally advocate this alternative, that is mass starvation and the destruction of life on earth as we know it over international socialist revolution. The system cannot be changed they insist. The majority of the people of the world must starve to allow the system to continue, they insist. Just like the years of the Irish starvation, only the faces and the names of the elite organisations have changed. Now the role that was played by British imperialism and the Church hierarchies in Ireland is played by world imperialism and the mass propaganda organisations, including its religious organisations world-wide. The people of the world are told that they must starve rather than rise up and change the system. They are told that if they are meek, that is subservient, that is not revolutionary, they will get their reward in heaven.

The super-exploited countries in the world today have sufficient resources to feed themselves many times over, as Ireland had in the time of starvation. But these resources are either being looted by the imperialist powers or not allowed to be developed by these imperialist powers. Tens of millions of people in the advanced capitalist countries are also starving and or killing themselves with drugs of one kind or another. There are enough resources in the world to feed the world's population many times over. If capitalism is ended, if the working class builds a new international, democratic, socialist system based on a democratic, socialist, sustainable plan, the human species can have a wonderful future. But if it does not there is another alternative. It is not so bright.

The National Aeronautical and Space Agency of the USA, the Pentagon, the United Nations, over 90% of the world's scientists, the Vatican, none of these are anti-capitalist voices, yet they all agree: climate change is on the way to destroying life on earth as we know it. And along with this there is the threat of nuclear war, the silos with the approximate 19,000 nuclear war heads. These have not been built for nothing and capitalism, while temporarily held back by the threat of all-out destruction in a new world war with nuclear weapons, is a system of war and will enter into a new world war, or partial world war at some stage if it continues to exist. The leopard has not changed its spots, cannot change its spots. Capitalism, imperialism, these systems mean war and partial or all-out nuclear war. Life on earth as we know it will be destroyed unless the present existing system, that is capitalism, is ended. This threat is at most only decades away.

That polar bear, that black rhino, that elephant, that eagle, that great whale, that dolphin, that silverback, that Connemara pony, that Chihuahua, that sparrow, that fat breasted robin, that great redwood, that cherry blossom tree, that daffodil, that brilliantly coloured parrot, and not to mention that human being, all will be things of the past. Gone, to be replaced by a planet of near lifelessness, or of hideously deformed creatures. It is almost beyond our imagination, the nightmare that capitalism will produce if it is left to rule.

If capitalism continues, the human species will be wiped out. At best it will be reduced to a few clumps of gibbering, hideously deformed, dying creatures. The child in every mother's womb, the baby that has just been born, the child that is just entering adulthood, the adult, none of them will see life on earth as it is today unless capitalism is ended. It is the first time in human experience that it is those of us around my age, the generation in our sixties and seventies and eighties who have lived in the economically advanced capitalist countries, who are the lucky ones. This is the threatening reality. But that is to look on the bleak side, the defeatist side. Yes life on earth as we know it can be destroyed. But it can also not only survive, but survive and be transformed to great and new and near unimaginable heights.

If we can organise a new mass international revolutionary leadership, put a cutting edge on the chisel which is the working class, then a new wonderful world is possible. In this new world, with the knowledge that now exists, all would be able to eat and drink and have good health and education, a good roof over our heads, clothes on our backs, and healthy social relations with our fellow human beings. And even have healthy social relations with some of our fellow species also. As a struggling vegetarian I hope this would be possible. I look forward if I live long enough to tickling a gorilla, to grieving with an elephant, to not being spat upon by a Llama. Or maybe spitting back a welcome at a Llama. A lot would be possible in the new international socialist world. But we have to get there.

I have explained earlier in this book how such a new international socialist sustainable world would work. The dominant sectors of the world economy would be taken out of private ownership, out of the hands of the profit addicted capitalist classes and put into collective ownership. The world economy would be organized on the basis of need and potential and sustainability not profit. This new socialist world economy would be based on democratically elected workers and peasants councils. These would be linked together in regular international gatherings but even more so on a daily basis through the use of the new world of technology and communications. Through this the working class and peasantry would be able to bring together their knowledge of what resources were available and what needs existed. Who else would know better what is available and what is needed? This democratic process would be able to draw up an international, sustainable, democratic, socialist plan of production and distribution. From this plan decisions would be taken democratically about how long we would work every day, what priorities of production would be best. This would be broken down industry by industry, economic sector by economic sector, workplace by workplace, worker by worker. Continual interaction and discussion throughout the working class internationally both directly and through the use of the new communications and media would allow for the continual adjustment, the continual fine tuning, of the plan and of priorities, would allow for the adjustment of the hours of the working day and the allocation of hours of work, of leisure and of rest.

The great collective brain of the working class would become the great collective, determining, decision making factor in the world. The result would be that the alienation that exists under capitalism would be ended. Rather than as under capitalism, where decisions are taken by the tiny minority crazed criminal capitalist class, where the product of our labour is taken from us by this class, we the working class and peasantry collectively would make the decisions, and we the working class and peasantry would receive the fruits of our labour. Alienation would be ended. We would see the direct connection between the decisions we would make, the work we would do, and the distribution of the products of our work. A new world would be born.

In this new socialist world there will also be the other great potential treats. The possibility of the cerebral, the artistic breakthroughs would be shared by all. It would not be as Marx said was the case that under capitalism that the spark of genius is killed in the working class. The sudden flash of the coming together of the synapses as they clash in creative energy and a new idea is born, or a new painting is born, or a new piece of sculpture is born, or a new symphony is born, or a new piece of jazz or a new blues song is created, or a new music or dance explodes out of the villages and cities of the world, or an entirely new form of art explodes into being or comes about by the merging or partial merging of existing art forms. Or we all become one with the exaltation of Beethoven, of Van Gogh, of Joyce when we express ourselves and communicate and the entire world becomes a world of art and the human species, and who knows what other species, combines to put new flowers on the stems of life.

I have had my ups and downs as I have fought for revolutionary ideas and to build a revolutionary organisation over the years. I have made mistakes which I try to explain in this book. I have had to watch others make mistakes and refuse to explain or learn from these and so go on to repeat these mistakes and weaken the struggle against capitalism. But no matter what way I look at it I have not wasted my life. My struggles, successful and unsuccessful, have increased my knowledge that capitalism is rotten and that there is a socialist alternative, and they have helped educate me and inform others.

I have argued and organised against capitalism and for international democratic socialism. I continue to do so. I have helped sow the seeds of international democratic socialism. This has helped negate the capitalist propaganda amongst many people, has helped negate the capitalist propaganda that nothing can be done, has helped negate the struggle of capitalism to dominate the consciousness of the working class. I recognise that the climate for these seeds to grow has not been so great in the last decades. But times are rapidly changing and these seeds I have helped sow will increasingly take root and flourish, are increasingly taking root and flourishing.

I regret that I have not succeeded in helping to build a mass revolutionary international which was capable of taking power. The reason for this failure was mainly the time that has been in it, the ebb tide that has been flowing against achieving this task, the catastrophe of Stalinism and the false policies of the leaderships of the existing mass workers' organisations. But there are also the mistakes made by myself and by others who consider themselves revolutionary socialists. I have tried, in this book and increasingly in recent years in my daily work, to openly and honestly face up to these mistakes, admit these mistakes, draw lessons from these mistakes, so they will not have been made for nothing, so they can contribute to helping to inform the emerging new movement. So they can be, to paraphrase Joyce, 'portals of discovery'.

I have one other regret as well as not being able to help build the revolutionary international of hundreds of millions. This one is more intimate and directly personal. I have never had the time or the opportunity to have had any significant success in accessing the world of art, literature, music and dance. To what Trotsky called the flower on the stem of our world. I do not have the time left now to catch up with this. I wish I did, I wish I had the years left to read Joyce line by line and study his every word and the order of his every word, to study his writings and his sentences line by line, to learn the extra languages and let loose my unconscious to the extent that would allow me to get more than just a glimmering into the pages of *Finnegans Wake*. I wish I had the time to absorb Van Gogh and his magnificent coloured and political and defiant creations, what is what in his magnificent self-portrait. And to absorb Millet and to understand more thoroughly what he understood when he said that: 'The art it is war.' I wish I had the time and ability to let the great classical and blues and jazz musicians into my head and to be able to perform them with my own hands and mouth.

Perhaps most of all in this category of personal regret I wish that I had had the opportunity to learn to play a musical instrument, especially to learn to play the violin, or the piano, or the harpsichord or the trumpet. Especially perhaps the violin. I occasionally wonder could I yet learn to play the theremin. But perhaps that instrument while on the surface appearing more easy to learn would in fact be the most difficult. I would have liked to have been able to hear the sounds, to make the sounds, to let these sounds enter into and emanate out from my brain and body and spirit. It seems to me that a person who does not play a musical instrument is an incomplete person. I wish I had been able to feel the way of it, the up and down of it, the precision and the mystery of the art of it turn my head, twist my neck, curl and un-curl my hands and feet, and most of all make me feel the great powerful stretch and reach in me for new feelings and knowledge which flows from all the great art and the great creation. I wish I could have, for just once, lost myself in a great wondrous floating away of searching, exploring, defiant creation.

Only once I came close to this. It was not in an artistic setting. I was speaking at a large Labour conference. I was confronting the leader and the leadership of that organisation. I stepped to the podium. My notes at the ready. But something happened. The atmosphere of the working class audience, the conflict between the views, the opposition of the right wing leaders of that conference, these combined to lift me out of myself. The ideas I had prepared to explain, the examples I had prepared to use to demonstrate these ideas, all dissolved into the air. New arguments, new ideas, new analogies, ones I had never thought of before, forced their way out of my sub-consciousness and into my consciousness and out of my mouth. For a brief time I was transformed. I think that is the only time that my unconscious forced its way decisively to the surface and transformed me, pushed me close to what Joyce called exaltation, that is, to being lifted out of myself, but in fact to being more deeply rooted in myself than ever before.

I wish I could have had the time and ability to learn to conduct a great orchestra. To walk to the podium, to be confident of all the musicians and their instruments, to lift the baton and stand still, sternly central while all were silent, while the audience waited, while all brought together their beings, our beings, and readied ourselves to collectively create one great sound. Would this not be like the world's working class setting in motion its collective brain, creating a new sustainable world in which the potential of all would be realised? Would this not be like the collective brain of the working class building a new world? I wish I had had the time and the opportunity and the ability to have done these things, to have learned how to conduct the great orchestra.

I have had only the tiniest glimpse here and there of the world of art and fine culture. It is too late now to have more. I regret this. But I got my priorities right. In this period working to help build the mass revolutionary international takes precedence over all. If this is not done there will be no orchestras left for anybody to conduct. Scraps of broken violins, torn covers of great books, destroyed paintings and sculptures, all wrecked apart by war and climate change and pollution and the destruction of the environment – this is what capitalism holds out for the future. There will be no art, no literature, no music, no dance, none of these will be left to envelop and enrich the people of the world. I have had my priorities right.

I hope that all future generations will not only be able to have good food and water to put in their mouths, a roof to go over their heads, clothes to wear and shoes for their feet, but will also have the opportunity of having access to these finer things in life. I hope that the working class can end capitalism and build a new world and the human species and all species can have a better and greater and more wonderful life on the planet.

As I head towards the last years of my life I am more and more aware of history. Lenin said that a revolutionary needed a sense of history, a sense of proportion and a sense of humour. I agree. I have explained earlier that history is the tale of one class overthrowing another, one system being replaced by another. Primitive communism being overthrown by slavery, slavery being overthrown by feudalism, feudalism being overthrown by capitalism. The movement from one system to another was ferocious and extremely violent and drawn out over centuries. It took capitalism and the capitalist class over 500 years to establish itself as the dominant system worldwide. It did so with the most extreme ferocity and mass slaughter. Hundreds of millions of people were slaughtered as capitalism clawed its way to power, as Marx described it, with blood dripping from every tooth and claw and fang. The peoples of the colonial world, the working class of the more advanced countries, the millions of women who died as they were driven into second place in society, all were sacrificed on the altar of capitalism's brutal drive for profit and power and world domination.

The blind madness shown in the history of the ruling capitalist class means that if it is a choice between its continued existence and rule, and the destruction of the human species capitalism, unless it is stopped, will take the latter road. Hiroshima, Nagasaki, the first and second World Wars, the non-stop wars of the last century and today, the mass destruction of the societies and the people's lives in the Middle East at present, mass rape as an instrument of war, mass starvation and poverty, climate change, pollution, worldwide starvation for working people, these are the names and the futures which will be synonymous with capitalism as it hurtles towards its end, these are the signposts on the road it is travelling. Capitalism is a mad, deranged system led by mad deranged monsters and war criminals such as the Bushes, the Cheneys, the Kissingers, the Trumps, the Obamas, the Thatchers, the Putins, the Mays, the Macrons, the Clintons, the Merkels, the XI Jinpings, the Abes, the Saudi so-called princes. These creatures in one way or another represent or seek to preserve the 147 super connected corporations (figure from the Swiss Federal Institute of Technology) that are at the core of, and dominate, the world economy, and control the military tops that work for them and which so far dominate the consciousness of the world working class. This class, and its system will destroy life on earth as we know it if it is allowed to continue to rule.

The greatest waste in the world today is the brain of the working class. It is not organised collectively and internationally, it is not conscious of itself as the brain of the progressive and the potentially collective class, and it is not democratically and collectively in charge of and in ownership of the world economy and society. This is what has to be changed if society is to take a step forward, if history is to take the next step forward.

While exposing and opposing the leadership of the workers' mass organisations for suppressing the struggle against capitalism we must not let other forces off the hook. There are millions of workers and youth who have struggled and came up against the opposition of capitalism and the obstacle of the working class leadership and have given up. There are many others who, while they see capitalism is rotten, stick their heads in the sand and do not fight. There are small groups who see themselves as revolutionaries who sit in arrogant smug isolation refusing to face up to their failures and mistakes and change their ways. All these forces also own a share of the blame for the inability of the working class to end capitalism. These layers and groupings also have a responsibility to organise and fight capitalism. They must end their self-indulgence and cynicism and pessimism, break from their inertia, openly recognise their mistakes, learn the lessons from the past, especially their own past, they must dedicate and re-dedicate themselves to building an alternative leadership which will be able to successfully fight capitalism.

Refusal to study and learn the lessons of history, inactivity, cynicism, racism, sexism, inertia, lack of belief that another world is possible, refusal to be self-critical and look at past mistakes, drowning in the bottle, turning to drugs and crime, turning to the illusions of religion, these approaches have to be rejected, they allow capitalism to continue and allow the pro-capitalist leaders of the working class organisations to suppress the movement for change. There is no excuse for taking any of these roads. They are unacceptable and self-indulgent and, sorry to put it harshly, they are cowardly.

The task is clear: Organise to build an international, revolutionary, socialist leadership for the working class. Put a cutting edge on the chisel. To take any other path is to refuse to accept our responsibility, it is to waste our life, it is to stand by while the human species and life on earth as we know it comes to an end. This is not acceptable. If capitalism continues to exist the destruction of life on earth as we know it is only decades away. Unless we, that is the working class, face up to our responsibility, it will soon be too late. Time is not on our side. We cannot afford to waste time and our lives. But while recognising this reality, there is no place for pessimism. The force, the international working class that can change the world and take society forward already exists and is objectively stronger than ever before. What is necessary is the most urgent action to build a new revolutionary mass leadership of this working class that can allow it to change the world.

This is my view of the world today. It is the big picture as far as I can see it. It is very different from what I was taught in rural Donegal. It is the foundation on which I presently stand and live. It is the basis of my life and my life's work. Because it is the most important task in the world in this period, this work of organising the revolutionary mass international is the most satisfying and enriching way in which I and all of us can spend our lives. Like no other activity it ensures that we reach our greatest potential. It ensures that we hate those forces and systems and individuals who should be hated. It ensures that we stoke and fan the class hatred and aim it at the class to whom it should be aimed, the war criminal, capitalist gangs that rule the world. Marx said that the basis of wisdom was class hatred. This is especially true in this period of history. But it is not the only truth. The work of building the alternative force that can end capitalism while demanding we hate what has to be hated, also demands that we embrace that which should be embraced. It demands that we see ourselves as part of a great world collective movement for progress, demands that we see our task as to bring about a world which is organised by the collective brain of the working class in the interests of all and of the planet. This is the way to live.

To help in this work of building an alternative to capitalism, to work to save life on earth as we know it, to give a future to our children and to the generations to come, to realise our own full potential, please contact myself and or the publishers of this book. Together, collectively, we can help build a new world and have the best possible life for ourselves, for our children, for all future generations and for life on earth.

Loughfinn@aol.com   Facts For Working people   aactivist@igc.org

Blog   weknowwhatsup.blogspot.com

Photograph of John Throne visiting with the whales, Monterey Bay
on the coast of California, is by RICHARD MELLOR

The author John Throne – born in Lifford, County Donegal, Ireland, in 1944 –
first became involved in politics in Derry in the tumultuous events of 1968/1969.
He has spent all his life since then as an activist in the labour movement and in
the struggle against capitalism in Ireland and abroad. He is also the author of
the best selling book – *The Donegal Woman* – www://thedonegalwoman.com This
book is based on the life of his grandmother.